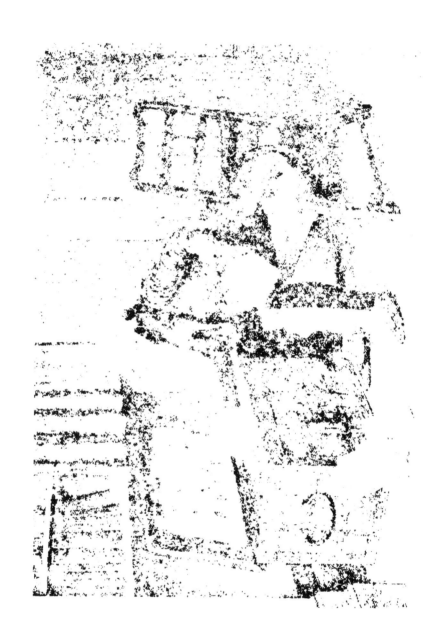

The Thomas Book

giving the Genealogies of Sir Rhys ap Thomas, .K.G., the Thomas Family descended from him, and of some Allied Families

By

Lawrence Buckley Thomas, D.D.

Imprinted at New York City by The Henry T. Thomas Company mdcccxcvi

SIC VOLO

SIC JUBEO

Copyright 1896 by
Lawrence Buckley Thomas

Trow Print New York

INTRODUCTORY

EDWARD GIBBON somewhere wrote: "A lively desire of know-
ing and recording our ancestors so generally prevails, that it must
depend on the influence of some common principle in the minds of
men."

Doubtless in many cases the feeling is similar to that which led
Darius the Great to inscribe upon the rock of Behistun his proud
boast: "From ancient time our family have been kings. I am the
ninth king by lineal descent." But family pride is not the only reason for these records; historians quite generally elucidate their
annals by genealogical tables, and scientists like Dr. Francis Galton
testify to their utility in the study of heredity and of social science.
A recent writer wisely declares that "the day has gone by when self-
respecting men may boast of ignorance of those who bore their name
before them."

On the other hand there is profound truth in the remark of a
speaker at a recent banquet of the Society of Colonial Wars in New
York City, that "the man who does not respect his ancestors is un-
likely to do deeds for which posterity will respect him." It is therefore well that this society and others organized in late years to
honour the memory of the men who fought the battles of the Revolution, or of their descendants who by their swords in the field or in
other ways defended the supremacy of the Government then established, have greatly increased the interest in the whole subject
of genealogy and family history, and given a stimulus to the compiling and printing of pedigrees. There is in this neither arrogance nor
pride unfitting to the citizens of a republic. For, despite the sonorous

v

periods of the Declaration of Independence, we do not need the teachings of modern science to convince us that men are *not* " born equal."

The inheritance of a good name and the memory of the noble deeds of our forefathers, or merely of their simple honesty and their self-respecting labour for daily bread, must have its influence on our lives. *Noblesse oblige,* if not misapplied, is a true principle, and one of special value to our American civilization, which is too apt to measure every thing by the yardstick of commerce, and to value a man by his present possession of material wealth, quite irrespective of his antecedents. These cannot be known unless they have been recorded in some permanent shape. Left to be handed down by tradition or popular report, they will soon be forgotten.

" Time," says Sir Thomas Browne in his *Hydriotaphia,* "which · antiquates the erections of man's hands, hath yet an art to make dust of all things, and oblivion blindly scatters her poppy, and deals with the memory of men without any distinction to the merit of perpetuity. There is no antidote against the opium of Time ! Our fathers find their graves in our short·memories, and sadly tell us how we may be buried in those of our survivors. Even our gravestones tell truth scarcely forty years—generations pass while some trees stand, and old families last not three hardy oaks." How much then does it become us to guard against this "eating tooth of time," by recording in permanent form that which we know of the history and fortunes of our own families ; each one, in the language of the Book of Nehemiah, " doing the work over against his own house."

The process is not so difficult as it seems at first sight, and there are few families but can trace their ancestry back to the emigrant progenitor if they set about it in the right way. One important preliminary, in most cases, is to put out of consideration the accepted family tradition ; for, as the historian Freeman wrote in his entertaining essay on " Pedigrees and Pedigree-Making " : " The family tree, the family tradition, the roll of Battle Abbey, are simply so many forms of sheer falsehood." Descents may be proven, but it must be by something very different from all these.

Public records and documents, wills which give the names of the testator's family and state their relationship, deeds which convey particular estates in land, church and court records, the entries in the family Bible so far as they state facts within the writer's personal knowledge, the names of parents, the births of children, etc., all are of value in compiling a genealogy.

The first step is to set down, as far as possible, all the known facts, with exact dates of births, marriages, deaths, and other noteworthy events, and then to follow out the traces pointing in one direction or another, until the evidence of records either confirms them and gives the investigator clues to a further extension of the genealogy, or directs attention to a fresh line of research. It would also be well to write to other members of the family and enlist as many as possible in the subject, that all branches may receive due attention and the genealogy be complete. If the ancestors of one individual merely are to be recorded, Mr. William H. Whitmore's ancestral tablets furnish a most convenient method and place of registration. A last recommendation, and one of great importance, is to print, in however inexpensive form, the result of your investigations, so that copies may be multiplied sufficiently to secure its permanent preservation ; and also to deposit it in more than one library, thereby giving students an opportunity to make use of your labours, for of all men the genealogist, who works for others, should be most generous in contributing his knowledge to the common stock. The history of few families of fair social position can be written without touching others at many points and often casting unexpected light upon the dark places in their pedigrees.

Each compiler of a genealogy must confess his deep obligation to those who have gone over the field before him, as well as to those who have responded to his direct requests for information. It would be impossible to name all to whom the author of this volume is indebted for assistance, but he would mention as deserving of especial gratitude, the late Messrs. Samuel Chew, of Germantown, Pennsylvania ; William G. Thomas, of Yonkers, New York, and his father,

Philip E. Thomas, of Baltimore, the compiler of the first Thomas Tree ; Messrs. Beverly Chew and John C. Chew, of New York ; Dr. Francis Thomas, of Sandy Spring, Maryland, and others of his family ; Mr. Charles P. Keith, of Philadelphia, author of the "Provincial Councillors of Pennsylvania ;" Dr. A. R. Thomas, of the same city, author of "The Thomas Family of Hardwick, Massachusetts ;" Messrs. Charles W. Evans, of Buffalo, author of a "History of the Fox, Ellicott and Evans Families ;" John D. Crosfield, of Forest Hey, near Northwich, England ; Nicholas Brewer, genealogist, Annapolis, Maryland ; and notably the Librarians of the Historical Societies of Pennsylvania and Long Island, and Mr. John G. Gatchell, Assistant Librarian of the Maryland Historical Society.

LAWRENCE BUCKLEY THOMAS

S. Thomas's Day, 1895

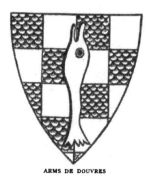

ARMS DE DOUVRES

EXPLANATORY NOTE

IN this book the attempt has been made to give the records of as many branches of the Thomas family as are accessible, and to furnish in the Appendix a brief biographical sketch of every notable person of the name not found in the genealogies. A number of allied families have also been included.

The genealogies, excepting those that give the book its title and are placed first, appear in alphabetical order. References to principal authorities are somewhat liberally made, and an adequate Index is added. Where exact dates confirm a statement, accuracy may be assumed ; in all other cases the effort has been made so to word the language that the weight of authority may be determined by the reader, and the author must not be held responsible for anything more than he distinctly says.

The genealogies are written, as far as possible, in historical form, proceeding directly down the line of descent. Where, however, the record of the issue of any one child would occupy so large a space as to confuse the reader, it is transferred below, and a new series begun. In all cases these are placed in the order of their dates, the record of the eldest son immediately following that of his parents, and each new line is completed before another is taken up. Surnames of children are not given, except in cases where they differ from the main line.

The generations upon a page are usually distinguished by different styles of type, according to a system easily understood.*

Everything has been done with a view to making the subject matter of the book clear to others besides professional genealogists, rather than technically and scientifically correct in form.

All dates before A.D. 1752 are Old Style, the year beginning on March 25 ; therefore dates between that day and the previous December are written as of both years, *e.g.*, February 7, 1701, New Style, would appear as February 7, 1700-1. (It should be remembered that in Quaker phraseology March was known as First Month.) Great care has been taken in reducing such dates to a uniform system.

* In each paragraph the first generation is in this type: **THOMAS** *m.* **MARTHA.**
The second in this: **JOSEPH** *m.* **GRACE DESHON.**
The third in this: **FRANCES** *m.* **GABRIEL SISTARE.**
The fourth in this: Joseph *m.* Mary Christophers.
The fifth in this: Charles *m.* —— Bassett.

ix

ABBREVIATIONS

ap.	= son of, or descendant, a Welsh term.
b.	= born.
bapt.	= baptized.
bu.	= buried.
Co.	= County.
co-h.	= co-heiress.
d.	= died.
dau.	= daughter.
d. s. p.	= died *sine prole* (without issue).
d. u.	= died unmarried.
d. i.	= died in infancy.
d. y.	= died in youth.
inq. p. m.	= *inquisitio post mortem.*
l.	= living at the following date.
m.	= married.
p., pp.	= page, pages.
q. v.	= *quem vide*, a reference to the Index, which will show on what page a further account may be found.
s. p. d.	= State papers, domestic series, published by the English Government.
s. p. m.	= without male issue.

HERALDIC

ar.	= *argent*, or white.
az.	= *azure*, or blue.
erm.	= *erminois*, or furry.
gu.	= *gules*, or red.
or	= gold, or yellow.
sa.	= sable, or black.
ppr.	= proper or natural colour.

CONTENTS

PAGE

CONTENTS

CONTENTS

APPENDIXES

For genealogies of the following-named families, see the pages indicated :

ILLUSTRATIONS

PLATES

TEXT ILLUSTRATIONS

COATS OF ARMS

CAREW CASTLE, PEMBROKESHIRE

SEAT OF SIR RHYS AP THOMAS

SECRET ET HARDI

SIR RHYS AP THOMAS, K.G.

SIR RHYS AP THOMAS, K.G., in the reigns of Henry the Seventh and Henry the Eighth of England, according to the Welsh antiquaries and historians, had an extant pedigree[1] going back to Adam ; but the historical part probably begins with Urien Rheged, a British prince, living, according to the best authorities,[2] in the sixth century after Christ. Possibly the links that connect him with Sir Rhys may not all be of equal certainty, but that the latter was descended from Urien is the uniform judgment of all writers upon Welsh history and genealogy. Urien is called the son of Cynvarch Oer ap Meirchion Gul, a prince of the North Britons in Cumbria, on the borders of the kingdom of Strath Clyde. Driven out by the invading Saxons in the sixth century of our era, Cynvarch took refuge in Wales and entered the ranks of the clergy, founding the church of Llangynvarch or S. Kinemark's, Maelor in Flintshire.[3] His name is on the pillar of Eliseg near Llangollen. He *m.* Nevyn, daughter of Brychan, who likewise entered religion and founded the church of

---

[1] Manuscript copy in the possession of the author.

[2] See Professor Rhys : Celtic Britain, *pp.* 142-251 ; Grant Allen : Anglo-Saxon Britain, *p.* 52 ; Babcock : Two Lost Centuries of Britain, *p.* 176 ; Iolo Morganwg's Welsh MSS., 457, 520, 653 ; Lappenberg's England, by Thorpe, *p.* xxvi ; Price's *Hanes Cymri* (1842), *p.* 284 ; and S. H. Gurteen, the Arthurian Epic (1895), *p.* 94.

[3] Smith and Wace : Dictionary of Christian Biography, i., 737.

S. Nevyn, Caernarvonshire. By her he had issue :[1] Urien ; Eurddyl, his twin sister, who *m.* Elider of the numerous clan ; Aron, who was one of Arthur's " knights of counsel, so wise and prudent that no one could at any time defeat him ; " and Llew or Llewellyn, who *m.*, according to the Romances, Anna, sister of King Arthur, and had two sons, Gwalchmai and Medrawd or Mordred, the traitor, one of the three royal knights, "whom neither king nor emperor could vanquish ; if they could not succeed by fair means, they would by foul and disgraceful ones." Gwalchmai, Walweyn, or Gawain, the other son, is by some authorities described as the son of Anna and a second husband, Gwyar. He is celebrated as one of the three golden-tongued knights, and such was their eloquence " that no one could refuse whatever they asked." Other Triads call him " one of the three most courteous men of Britain," and one of the " three scientific ones of the Isle, to whom there was nothing of which the elements were not known." William of Malmesbury states that in the year 1086 his tomb was discovered on the seashore of Rhos on Pembrokeshire, where there is a district called Walwen's castle.

Urien, the eldest son of Cynvarch, was a great patron of the bards, by whom he is called " brave as a lion and gentle as a maid." The Welsh Triads name him as one of " the three Bulls of Conflict " and " the three pillars of battle." In the Arthurian romances he appears as Sir Urience. All the authorities agree in representing Urien and his sons as strenuously opposing the Saxon advance, and fighting, Taliesin declares, as many as ten battles against Ida and Deoric of Northumbria.[2] His greatest exploit was the expulsion of the Goidels, Gwyddelians, or Irish Scots, from the territory lying between the Tawe and Tavy rivers, and comprising Gowerland, Cydweli, Iscenen, Carnwallon, and Cantrev Bychan, to which was given the name of his father's northern principality, Rheged. About 567 he was treacherously slain by Llovan Llawdivo, while besieging Ida's son Deoric in the island of " Medcant," possibly Lindisfarne. Llywarch Hen, one of the greatest of the bards and the son of his father's younger brother, Elider Lydanwyn, in a long elegy celebrates his prowess and bewails his death.[3] The Welsh pedigrees marry

[1] Myvyrian Archaiology. ii., 49 ; Owen's Heroic Elegies of Llywarch Hen., *p.* vii.

[2] Palgrave's Anglo-Saxons, *pp.* 47, 48 ; Babcock : Lost Centuries, *pp.* 206–211 ; Iolo Morganwg's Welsh MSS., *p.* 457. Recently Professor Rhys, in The Arthurian Legend, *pp.* 238 to 272, adopting the theory of Sir G. W. Cox, calls Urien Rheged a mythical divinity—lord of the evening and the dusk, the twilight realm of illusion and glamour—and identifies him with Bran the Blessed.

[3] Owen's Llywarch Hen, *pp.* 23–43.

URIEN RHEGED
PRINCE OF THE NORTH BRITONS

him to Modron, *dau.* of Avallech, but the family history and other authorities[1] say he *m.* Morgaine Le Faye, of Castle " La Belle Regard," *dau.* of Gorlois, Duke or Lord of Cornwall, and Igerne, who bore King Arthur to Uther Pendragon through the device of Merlin. His children were Pasgen, *of whom presently ;* Elwri, who *m.* Morgan Morganwdd ; Rhun, or Rum,[2] who is said to have preached Christianity in Northumbria before the mission of Paulinus ; Rhiwallon, Elphin, Garth, and Cadell, who died fighting against the Saxons ; Morvydd, a *dau.*, and Owaine or Ewaine, Knight of the Round Table,[3] called by the Triads one of the "three blessed princes of Britain," also with Lancelot du Lac and Cadwr of Cornwall the "three knights of battle of Arthur's Court," because they would not retreat either for spear, for arrow, or for sword, and the King never had shame in battle the day he saw their faces there. He is said to have slain Ida of Northumbria, and himself been killed in battle by Ida's son Deoric, Flamdwyn or flame-bearer, as the bards call him. Taliesin the Bard laments his death in the following lines : [4]

> " The soul of Owain the son of Urien ; may the Lord consider its need,
> The Chief of Reged the heavy sward conceals him ;
> His knowledge was not shallow.
> A low cell contains the renowned protector of bards.
> The wings of dawn were the flowing of his lances,
> For there will not be found a match for the chief of the glittering West ;
> The reaper of tenacious foes ;
> The offspring of his father and grandfather
> When Flamdwyn killed Owain there was not one greater than he sleeping.
> A wide number of Lloegr went to sleep with the light in their eyes."

Owain *m.* Dwynwen, *dau.* of Llewddyn Lueddag, of Dinas Eidyn (Edinburgh), and was the father of Cyndeyrn [5] (S. Kentigern or Mungo), who is said to have been *b.* at Culross, in Perthshire, and arriving at manhood went to Cathures, now Glasgow, founded a monastery and was made Bishop there. The increasing

---

[1] All the Peerages, Morte d'Arthur, etc.

[2] Hinde's History of Northumberland, *p.* 77, suggests that Rhun, after the fall of Urien, went to Rome, and changing his name at ordination (which was not uncommon), became Paulinus. See also Smith and Wace's Dictionary, iv., 248.

[3] Clark's Orders of Knighthood, i., 160.

[4] Babcock, as above, *p.* 199 ; Skene's Ancient Books of Wales, ii., *pp.* 189, 199 ; Lady Guest's Mabinogion, i., 88 ; Williams's Enwogion Cymru. 366.

[5] Rees : Welsh Saints ; Smith and Wace : Dictionary, iii., *pp.* 603, 604 ; Rhys : Celtic Britain, *p.* 143 ; Bishop Forbes : Vita Kentegerni, *pp.* 29-119, etc.

power of the pagans caused him to go into Wales, where he settled in Flintshire and built a church on the site of what is now S. Asaph's, named from his disciple, whom he left in charge when he returned to the North. After the battle of Ardderyd, in 573, when Rhydderch Hael defeated the heathen party under Guendolen, Cyndeyrn was recalled to Strathclyde and *d.* there in A.D. 603.

Some authorities derive Sir Rhys ap Thomas from Owain through S. Kentigern, but the family history and the Welsh annalists usually make Pasgen the eldest son of Urien, his ancestor. He succeeded his father in the principality of Rheged, but was deposed for his cruelty, his sister's husband, Morgan Morganwdd, being put in his place. The Triads called Pasgen one of the "three haughty chiefs of Britain." He had issue : Mor,[1] who became a saint, *i.e.*, a Celtic monk, and is *bu.* at Enlli or Bardsey Island ; Nidiaw,[1] also an anchorite ; and Gwrvyn,[1] who founded a church in Anglesey and had a son, Nidan,[2] Confessor to the monastic community of Pennion, in Anglesey. Mor was the lineal ancestor of Rhys ap Goronwy, ap Einion, ap Lloarch, ap Kymbathwye, ap Gurwared, ap Syssylt, ap Rhyne, ap Llarch, ap Mor, ap Pasgen, of whom nothing more than their names[1] has descended to posterity. Rhys ap Goronwy *m.* Margaret, *dau.* and *heir.* of Griffin ap Kiddy, Lord of Gwynvey, and had a son, Elider ap Rhys, *m.* Gladwys, *dau.* of Philip ap Bah ap Gwathvoed. Gwathvoed was possibly the Gwathvoed Vawr who *m.* Morfyd, *dau.* and *heir.* of Ynys Ddu, King of Gwent, and refused to be one of the subject princes who rowed King Edgar, the Saxon, in his boat upon the River Dee, in 973, bidding the King in reply to his threats, rather "*ofner na ofni angau*"—"fear him who fears not death." Another Gwathvoed lived a century later and was Prince of Ceredigion and Lord of Cilwyr. Some say Gladwys who *m.* Elider ap Rhys was his descendant ; Philip ap Bah, Lord of Esginbrath, being his grandson. Elider and Gladwys had a son, Sir Elidur Ddu, Knight of the Holy Sepulchre, who *m.* Cecily, *dau.* of Syssilt ap Llewelyn, Lord of Cantrescliffe, and had issue : Katherine, *m.* David Morthye, Lord of Odyn Castle and Fountain Gate ; and Philip, *m.* Gladys, *dau.* of David Vras, and was the father of Philip, who had issue : Crisley, *m.* Richard Aubrey ; Gwylliam (ancestor of Captain John Vonderhorst Rees, of Killymaenllwyd, J. P., in 1872) ; and Nicholas his eldest son, who *m.* Janet, *dau.* and *heir.* of Gruffyd ap Llewelyn Voethes, descended from Elystan Gloddryd, Prince of

---

[1] See Williams's Enwogion Cymru, under their various names.
[2] Smith and Wace : Dictionary, iv., 43.

Ferlys, sometimes called Ethelystan. He was a godson of King
Athelstane, of England, and son of Cuhelyn ap Ivor, Lord of Builth,
descended in the seventh generation from Teon, Bishop of Gloucester, who had Cassibelaunus as his ancestor. Elystan was Lord of
Caermarthen and Prince of Ferlys between the Wye and Severn
rivers, *m.* Gladys, *dau.* of Rhun ap Ednowen, or Gwenllian, *dau.* of
Einion ap Howel Dda, and *d.* about the year 1000, founding one of
the Royal tribes of Wales.

Nicholas ap Philip and Janet ap Gruffyd had an only son and heir,
Gruffyd ap Nicholas, who was a remarkable and most ingenious gentleman. The possessor of an ample fortune and allied by marriage
with some of the principal families both in North and South Wales,
his power and influence in Caermarthenshire were very great. He
appears to have had property in Caermarthen town, for his mother
d. there, and was *bu.* at Whitland.

His hasty spirit and violence of temper often involved him in
complications with his neighbours, from which it required the exercise of all his ingenuity to extricate himself. He even incurred
the enmity of no less a personage than Richard, Duke of York, by
withholding from him a piece of land in Herefordshire, and he inso-
lently and peremptorily refused to obey the summons of the Sheriff
to answer for his conduct. At the head of a numerous and war-
like clan, which was strongly attached to him, he gave shelter
and encouragement to innumerable Welsh thieves, who were in the
constant habit of plundering and ravaging the English border. The
frequency and severity of these predatory incursions raised against
him a host of enemies, the most powerful of whom, Humphrey, Duke
of Buckingham, Richard of York, Jasper Tudor, Earl of Pembroke, and
the Earl of Warwick, made such representations to the King, Henry
VI., accusing him of being an encourager and harbourer of thieves,
that he was deprived of the Commission of the Peace and Captaincy
of Kilgarran Castle, which that sovereign had granted him. It is alleged that his hatred of the English was Gruffyd's reason for harbouring those who ravaged their territory. A Commission was finally
appointed by the King in 1441 to arrest the accused and investigate
the charges against him, at the head of which was placed Lord Whitney.[1] Gruffyd, who had heard of the Commission, but was not informed of its precise object, laid his plans with the craftiness and exe-

---

[1] Probably Sir Eustace Whitney, Knt., " Lord " of the Manor of Whitney. See Cooke's Visit of Herefordshire, *p.* 75.

cuted them with the boldness peculiar to his character. He met the Commissioners on their entry into Caermarthenshire, himself meanly dressed, and accompanied only by four or five attendants raggedly attired, and as miserably mounted. Right glad was Lord Whitney to find the truculent Welshman apparently in his power, and he was not a little astonished also to hear him offer his services to guide him to Caermarthen, the place of his destination. Their road followed the windings of the Bran to where that river unites with the Gwydderig in its confluence with the Towey. On the western bank, on a rocky eminence, was Gruffyd's Castle of Abermarlais, hidden from the Commissioners by the thick woods which lined the shores of the river. A graceful curve of the road, however, brought them to the foot of the gentle eminence on which the castle stood, and then Gruffyd, turning to the surprised Commissioners and pointing to the open postern, invited them, with a smile, to enter and refresh themselves. They were received with demonstrations of extreme respect by Gruffyd's son Thomas, at the head of one hundred horsemen handsomely dressed and gallantly mounted, and began to open their eyes to the real power and consequence of their companion. After having well refreshed themselves, the whole party, including Thomas ap Gruffyd and his armed retinue, left the castle. A little farther on their way they came to the ancient fortress of Dinevawr, not far from the town of Llandeilo Fawr, then the stronghold of Owen, Gruffyd's son. He received them at the head of a chosen body of two hundred armed horsemen, and played the part of host with such address that he contrived to draw from his guests the secret of their commission. The whole party then proceeded on their way, leaving the mountains for the plain where the Towey meets the Gwili, at the little village of Abergwili. Here they were met by a splendid body of five hundred " tall men " on foot, well armed and accoutred, and led by Gruffyd's eldest son. Thus magnificently attended the Commissioners entered Caermarthen, then the capital of South Wales. Gruffyd now excused himself from attendance on the Commissioners and committed to his sons the care of entertaining them at the banquet prepared in their honour at the Guild Hall. Lord Whitney privately sent for the Mayor, Stephen Griffith, and the Sheriff, and showing his commission, demanded their assistance to arrest Gruffyd, which it was determined should be done on the following morning.

The banquet was now prepared, and the Commissioners were escorted to it with much pomp by the sons of Gruffyd. The tables had been arranged along the centre of the floor, and according to the architecture of the time a row of pillars separated the upper end of the room, which was slightly elevated, from that part which was assigned to the less distinguished members of the assembly. Lord Whitney was conducted to a seat on the dais, splendidly hung with cloth of gold, and Owen placed himself upon his right hand. On either side of this elevated dais galleries had been raised, in which were placed the bards of that land of minstrelsy. The guests betook themselves with right good-will to the noble cheer provided, and Owen in particular plied them with Ypocras, Garhiofilac, and other delicate and precious drinks, which soon produced the desired effect upon the Commissioners. Lord Whitney after his conference with the authorities, and exhibiting to them his commission, carelessly placed it in his sleeve, which was made very wide after the fashion of the time, and often used for such purposes. During the revel, Owen abstracted it from its hiding-place, while Lord Whitney was in such a state of mental obscuration from the strong potations that had been pressed upon him, that he not only did not notice its loss at the time but retired to bed without doing so. Owen communicated to his father the success of their plans, but Gruffyd abated nothing of his formal courtesy to the Commissioners, and the next morning presented himself before them in the Guild Hall, splendidly dressed and attended by his sons and armed retainers. He was immediately arrested by the officers of the Court, to whom he made no resistance, but with an air of great humility requested that the proceedings against him might be conducted according to law, and asked to see their commission. Lord Whitney readily assented to his request, but upon putting his hand into his sleeve and finding the warrant gone, his consternation may be easily imagined. "Methinks Lord Whitney," said Gruffyd, "if he comes here, as he says, by the King's grace, must have valued his commission too highly to have committed it to the safe-keeping of that ruffle or carelessly to have lost it." Then dropping his assumed deference, clapping his hat upon his head, and turning to his friends and followers, he exclaimed : "What ! have we cozeners and cheaters come hither to abuse the King's Majesty's power and to disquiet his true-hearted subjects ?" Then looking on the Commissioners with a bitter frown, he said, "By the mass, before the next day come to an end, I will hang up all your bodies for traitors and impostors." The Commissioners were panic-stricken, and entreated for their lives ; which Gruffyd at last granted on condition that Lord Whitney should put on his livery coat of blue and wear his cognizance, and be bound by an oath to go to the King so arrayed, acknowledge his own offences, and justify the Welshman's proceedings.

In 1451 a great eistedfodd was held at Caermarthen under the patronage of Gruffyd ap Nicholas, at which the rules of the Welsh metres *Dosbarth Caerfyrrdin* were determined. Gruffyd continuing his depredations upon the Lords Marchers was at length found guilty of felony on an indictment preferred against him in the Co. of Salop. This decision at once illumined his mind as to the rival claims of the Houses of York and Lancaster. A Lancastrian King had adjudged him a felon, the Duke of York was therefore of necessity the champion of a good cause and him he would support. He joined Edward of March, the Duke's son, at Gloucester, with eight hundred men well armed and provisioned, and marched with him to Mortimer's Cross, in Herefordshire. Here on February 2, 1461, a battle was fought between the Yorkists and the Lancastrians under Jasper, Earl of Pembroke, in which Gruffyd was mortally wounded, surviving only long enough to know that his friends were victorious.

GRUFFYD AP NICHOLAS, *m.* 1st, Mabel, *dau.* of Meredith ap Henry Donne, of Kidwelly Castle, by whom he had a son and heir, Thomas; he *m.* 2d, a *dau.* of Sir John Perrott of Pembroke, by whom he had a *dau.* Maud, *m.* Sir John Scudamore, of Kentchurch, *q. v.*, and 3d, Joan, *dau.* and *co-h.* of Jenken ap Rees ap David of Gilvach Wen, by whom he had Mabel, *m.* Philip Mansel. He also had younger sons Owen, *m.* Olive, heiress of Henry Maliphant of Upton Castle, Pembroke, whose line ended in heiresses in 1760, and Thomas, junior. He was succeeded by his son Thomas ap Gruffyd, who is described as a man of a character very different from his turbulent father, and one of the most accomplished gentlemen of the age, with a mildness of disposition and elegance of manners rarely found in those cruel times of civil warfare. To avoid taking part in the contests of the rival houses of York and Lancaster he withdrew to the accomplished Court of Burgundy, then ruled over by Philip the Good, in whose service he enrolled himself. There he became famous for his boldness and skill in the tilt and tourney, and in single combat. After the death of his first wife, Elizabeth Griffith, his gallantry and gracious disposition are said to have won the affections of a near relative of the Duke, and Thomas, having probably offended by his presumption the Duke's heir, the Count of Charolois (afterward so well known as Charles the Bold) was compelled to return to Wales. There he had constant encounters with his neighbours, particularly Henry ap Gwilym of Court Henry in the Vale of Towey, between whose family and his there seems to have existed an ancient feud. His last duel took place some time toward the end of Henry the Sixth's reign, or the beginning of that of Edward the Fourth, when he fought with David Gough somewhere in Merionethshire and killed him. Having laid aside his armour and thrown himself upon the ground to rest after the combat, he was treacherously run through the body and killed by one of Gough's retainers. He was buried in the Abbey of Bardsey, Caernarvonshire.

He was *m.* to Elizabeth, *dau.* and heiress of Sir John Griffith of Abermarlais, and possibly[1] to another Elizabeth, *dau.* of James de Burgoigne, natural son of Philip, Duke of Burgundy, or herself a natural *dau.* of the Duke ; from her descended the great clan of Johnes of Abermarlais, Dolau Cothy, Llanbadarnfawr, and Hafod. It has given ten high sheriffs to Cardigan, Caermarthen, and Pembroke ; numbered among its members Thomas Johnes, the translator of Froissart, and was represented by John Johnes, Esq., of Dolau Cothy, J. P. and D. L. for Caermarthen in 1872. By his first wife Thomas ap Gruffyd had issue :

i. **MORGAN**, killed in the Civil Wars.
ii. **DAVID**, killed in the Civil Wars.
iii. A *dau.*, *m.* **GRIFFITH AP HOWELL**, issue.
  JAMES AP GRIFFITH (*q. v.*).
iv. **MARGARET**, *m.* **SIR RICHARD HERBERT**, of Coldbrook (*q. v.*).
v. **RHYS** or **REES**, his heir, *of whom presently.*
vi. Another *dau.*, *m.* **JOHN**, 4th son of **WILLIAM HERBERT, Earl of Pembroke** (*q. v.*).
vii. **DAVID** 2d.
viii. **JOHN.**
ix. Possibly a second **MARGARET**, *m.* **JOHN HERLE**, of Brecknock.

Thomas ap Gruffydd's two elder sons, Morgan and David, became, immediately on their father's decease, warm partizans, on opposite sides, of the houses of York and Lancaster. When Jasper, Earl of Pembroke, after the overthrow of Queen Margaret at Tewkesbury, retired to Pembroke, accompanied by his nephew, Henry, Earl of Richmond, Morgan ap Thomas invested the castle, in order to prevent their escaping out of the country. Upon this David ap Thomas hastily collected together about two thousand men, armed any way,

---

[1] Reusnenes says: "One such daughter married *apud Britones.*"

fell on the besiegers by surprise, obliged them to retire, and gave the Earl and his young charge an opportunity to escape to Tenby, whence they immediately sailed to Brittany. This is nearly all that is recorded of these two brothers. But both are said to have lost their lives in the Wars of the Roses.

RHYS AP THOMAS, his favorite son and eventual heir, was *b.* in 1449, and was educated at the Court of Burgundy, where he held a post of honour in the Duke's household. This he relinquished to accompany his father on his banishment to Wales. His bravery was so noted that after his death one of the Welsh bards lamented that a "drum had not been covered with his skin; the sound of which alone," he assures us, "would have always ensured the victory to the British." He seems to have been as wise and politic as brave. He put an end to the long-established feud between his own family and that of Court Henry by marrying Eva, the only *dau.* and heiress of Henry ap Gwilym, the head of that house. By this marriage he added to his possessions a property not much inferior to his original patrimony, and became one of the most opulent subjects of the realm.

The anonymous author of his life, exalting the family of his hero, quotes Mr. Camden, the Herald, as saying "that they were the best born gentlemen in Wales, and furthest spread in their branches of any family in England, being allied with the Houses of Northfolk, Worcester, Pembroke, Bullinbrooke, and Barkley."

His establishment and hospitality were in every respect suitable to his immense wealth, and indeed displayed the magnificence of a prince, rather than of a private gentleman. He acquired unbounded popularity, and by degrees very formidable power, by re-establishing the games of his country on his estates, and by training the young men to the use of arms, under the guise of sham fights and spectacles. It is stated that he had nineteen hundred tenants bound by their leases to attend him at the shortest call, and that brief warning having been given, he could bring into the field five thousand disciplined men, mounted and armed. He was a great builder and enlarger of castles, built New Castle Emlyn, and greatly added to Carew Castle, which came into his possession by a forfeited mortgage from Sir Edmund Carew, erecting the magnificent state apartments there and making it his favourite residence. He was proprietor of the Lordships of Dinefawr, Carew, Llansadyrn, Cilsane, Emlyn, Cilcenin, Aberayron, Llanrystyd, Narberth, Llangybi, and several others, as records an old list of his possessions. Fuller writes of him, "though never more than a knight, he was little less than a prince in his native country." Ocland called him " Flos Cambro Britannicum," and a poet of those days wrote :

> " Y Brenin bia'r Ynys
> Ond sy o ran i Syr Rhys."

"The King owns the island except what pertains to Sir Rhys." Every effort was made to interest him in the cause of Henry of Richmond, with whom he was connected in blood by their common descent from Rhys ap Tewdwr of the Royal House of South Wales.[1]

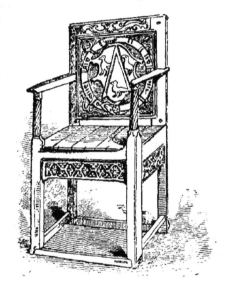

By the Earl of Richmond, Rhys ap Thomas's assistance was regarded as of great consequence ; especially as Milford Haven was the safest, if not the only place at which the Earl could land, and here Rhys was completely master ; his friendship was therefore most essential, and consequently a reconciliation was effected between him and the Duke of Buckingham. Enmity having existed between the families since the time of Gruffydd ap Nicholas, at

CHAIR OF SIR RHYS AP THOMAS, K.G.

about this period Buckingham had sent Rhys a message to say that unless he gave him satisfaction for a certain injury he would come shortly and cudgel him out of his castle of Caermarthen. Rhys coolly answered that the roads being hilly and rough, his highness might spare himself the trouble of the journey, for he intended waiting upon him shortly at Brecknock, to receive his commands.

[1] Thomas Thomas: Memoirs of Owen Glendower, 1822, *p.* 187, and the tabular pedigree of Sir Rhys.

The mission from the Lancastrians to Rhys was entrusted to Dr. Lewis, a former tutor of Rhys and now physician to the Countess of Richmond. Dr. Lewis found Rhys at Abermarlais, preparing for the expedition to Breconshire, and succeeded in obtaining Rhys's consent to make up his difference with Buckingham. Rhys and Buckingham, soon after this, met at Trecastle, where they agreed to bury all past animosities in oblivion; but Rhys's views on the main question — Red or White Rose — were not then ascertained. Richard being apprised that a plot was hatching, demanded distinct assurances and hostages from those whose fidelity he doubted. Among others, Commissioners were sent to Rhys ap Thomas at Caermarthen, to administer to him the oaths of fidelity and to require his only son, Gruffydd, five years of age, as an hostage. Rhys took the oath without hesitation, but wrote a letter to the King, praying to be excused from parting with his son, on account of his tender age. He expressed indignation at the suspicion of his loyalty, observing that such suspicion might read to some of fickle minds and unstable thoughts, evil lessons against themselves. He made, however, the following voluntary protestation: "Whoever, ill-affected to the State, shall dare to land in those ports of Wales where I have anie employments under your Majestie, must resolve with himself to make his entrance and irruption over my bellie." The general opinion is that Rhys was perfectly sincere in his declarations in this celebrated letter, "which is a very able composition," drawn up by the Abbot of Talley, a zealous—though, to Rhys, concealed—Lancastrian. It is filled with such expressions of loyalty as were likely to satisfy Richard, but, at the same time, couched in such equivocal terms as might leave Rhys (under the guidance of his spiritual counsellors, the Abbot of Talley and the Bishop of S. David's) at liberty to break with the King, with what he might deem a safe conscience, should he afterward see cause to do so. Finally, becoming offended at the King's suspicions and moved by a letter from Richmond, in which it was stated that all his fortunes hung on Rhys ap Thomas's decision, the chieftain called a council of his most trusty friends to consider the question. At this were present the Abbot of Talley, the Bishop of S. David's, several of the more influential gentry, and two of his father's veteran officers in whom he had great confidence. They advised his aiding Henry, and when he spoke of his oath, the Churchmen silenced his scruples and one of them proposed a method by which he might keep its letter while evading its spirit. Still he hesitated, and it was not until he had consulted his soothsayer or prophet that he sent a messenger to Henry assuring him of his assistance. This prophet, by name Robert of the Dale, answered his first inquiry as to the success of the enterprise quite plainly :

> " Full well I wend
> That is the end ;
> Richmond, sprung from British race,
> From out this land the Boar shall chase."

But Sir Rhys was not satisfied. Richmond might indeed win the crown and dispossess the Boar of Gloucester, but unless he did this by the help of the Knight of Carew and entered Britain over his territory, what opportunity would there be for his action and what hope of reward ? So by the threat of death he forced the prophet, after a day's delay, in order to learn the will of Heaven, to declare the future more exactly, which he did in the following verse :

> " Hie thee to the dale. I'll to the vale
> To drink gude ale and soe I pre have a care of us all,"

which was understood to mean that Richmond would land at Dale in Milford Haven, and being successful, the lives and fortunes of the people were to be the care of Sir Rhys.

This being deemed sufficient encouragement, the knight consented to join the conspiracy on condition that he be made Justiciary of Wales. Henry immediately set sail for England and directed his course for Milford Haven, where he was met upon landing by Rhys ap Thomas at the head of two thousand picked men. It is said that he carried out the suggestion of the Bishop of S. David's by crouching under one of the arches of a bridge over which the Earl rode, thus " passing over his bellie." Henry appointed Shrewsbury as the place of rendezvous for his friends and divided his army into two bodies, one of which he led himself by way of Cardiganshire and the other he committed to Rhys ap Thomas. On the march the chieftain's army was augmented by vast numbers of the Welsh, from whom he made a selection of two thousand horse, the flower of his attendants, and five hundred foot, dismissing the rest to their homes. The infantry he placed under the command of his younger brothers, David and John, and left in the principality to secure it for Henry. The horse he led himself to Long Mountain, on the borders of Shropshire, and there joined the Earl.

King Richard, though taken by surprise, rose to the occasion, and hastily gathering an army, marched to meet them. The hostile forces came in sight of each other on the field of Bosworth, near Leicester, August 22, 1485. The events of the battle are familiar and need not be described here.

Richard, toward its end, made a desperate plunge at the Earl of Richmond ; he killed with his own hands the Earl's standard-bearer, Sir William Brandon, and dismounted Sir John Cheyney and many a high-born gentleman who attempted to stay him in his career. He had nearly reached the spot where Henry stood, when Rhys ap Thomas perceived the Earl's danger, and mounting his favourite charger, " Llwyd y Bacse," or Grey Fetterlocks, with Sir William Stanley bore down between. The Welsh tradition asserts that it was Rhys who slew King Richard, fighting with him hand to hand. Whatever may be the foundation for this story, his conduct on that day was so distinguished that Richmond ascribed to it the issue of the battle and in gratitude ever after applied to him the title of " Father Rhys." He also knighted him on the field after the victory. The spoils of King Richard's tent were shared by Rhys and Sir William Stanley. Other honours were subsequently heaped upon him by the grateful monarch when established on the throne. He was appointed a member of the King's Council, and it is said that he declined the Earldom of Pembroke or Essex, alleging that knighthood was the greatest honour that could be conferred on a soldier. November 3, 1485, he received a grant for life of the offices of Constable, Lieutenant, and Steward of Brecknock. November 6th, of the same year, he was appointed Chamberlain of Caermarthen and Cardigan and Steward of the Lordship of Builth. February 26, 1485-1486, he was appointed one of the Commissioners of the King's Mines. Loaded with these marks of the King's gratitude and friendship, Sir Rhys was sent to South Wales to heal the disorders which had arisen from the distracted state of the supreme government, and to restore the authority of the laws, a task which he appears to have executed with great judgment and success. Sir Rhys's next appearance on the public theatre was during the attempt of Lambert Simnel to impose himself on the country as the young Duke of York. Simnel brought to the field a considerable force of Irish recruits, and encamped at Stoke. Henry, wishing to crush the plot in its infancy, marched against him with the utmost expedition. As Sir Rhys had not time to collect his Welsh followers, the King gave him a troop of

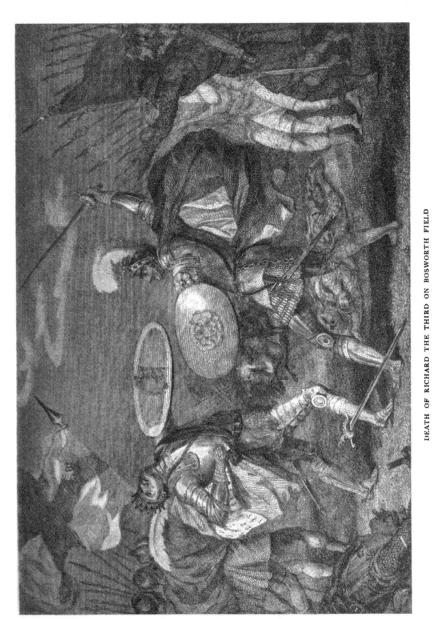

DEATH OF RICHARD THE THIRD ON BOSWORTH FIELD

From an English History published in the Eighteenth Century

English horse. The eager valour of our hero had nearly cost him his life in this engagement, June 16, 1487 ; for, being imperceptibly drawn forward from his men, in an encounter with one of the Irish commanders he was suddenly beset by several of the enemy, and only escaped destruction by the timely succour of the Earl of Shrewsbury. Henry, hearing of his narrow escape, addressed him jocularly, "How now, Father Rhys ? how likest thou of the enter-tainment here ? Whether is better, eating leeks in Wales or sham-rock among the Irish ?" "Both certainly, but coarse fare," replied Rhys ; "yet either would seem a feast with such a companion," point-ing to the Earl who had rescued him.

In 1492 he accompanied Henry in his French expedition, and the military appearance and handsome equipment of the soldiers of "Richard Thomas," as he calls him, is spoken of by Bacon in his "History of the Reign of Henry VII."

August 6, 1494, "Res ap Thom's Knyghte" executes a deed to his (step) son, Edward Stradlyng, on the latter's coming of age, and seals it with a square seal bearing ·a raven between two flowering plants, over the Raven the letter R.[1]

June 22, 1497, with fifteen hundred horse, he was at the battle of Blackheath, fought between the King's forces and the revolted Cor-nishmen under Lord Audley, and after a fierce conflict took the latter prisoner, and totally defeated his followers. The leaders in the revolt were immediately executed, but the bulk of the insurgents returned home and shortly afterward joined Perkin Warbeck, when he landed on their coast at the head of an Irish army. Failing to take Exeter at the first attack his courage left him, and taking sanctuary at Beaulieu Abbey he finally surrendered himself to Henry, and, it is said, afterward attempting to escape from confinement, was ex-ecuted. April 22, 1505, Sir Rhys was elected a Knight Companion of the most noble Order of the Garter, and occupied the twelfth stall of the sovereign's side in S. George's Chapel, Windsor, where his Garter plate still remains.[2] The motto, "*Secret et Hardi*," and his badge of a raven, is a boss in the vaulting of the choir.[3] He was

---

[1] Topographer and Genealogist, 1846, vol. i., *p.* 562.

[2] Quarterly of 4. 1. Paternal. *Ar.* a chevron sable between 3 ravens *ppr.* 2. Llewellyn ap Vo-ethes. *Ar.* on a cross sable, 5 crescents *or.* 3. Einon clud (?) *Gu.* a lion rampant *ar.* 4. A rose seeded, between 3 bears' or wolves' heads. Crest : A raven *ppr.* between 2 spears' shafts *or*, blades *ar.*, points imbrued *gu.* Supporters : 2 Griffins per fesse *or* and *ar.*

[3] Anstis's Memorials of the Garter, vol. i., *pp.* 237, 247, 279, 369, etc. Notes and Queries, 4th Series, xi., 245. See also Ashmole's Institution, etc., of the Order of the Garter, folio 713, for his arms.

frequently employed by King Henry in negotiations on the Continent, and the records of the Garter show that he was excused from
attendance at several Chapters of the Order " as being absent on the
King's business." In 1507 he gave a tournament at Carew Castle in
honour of his admission to the Order, which " The Beauties of England
and Wales," 1812, describes as " the most magnificent spectacle that
was ever perhaps exhibited by a private individual at his own charge."

Sir Rhys having announced his intention of holding this solemn
joust and tournament, with other martial exercises, the gentry of the
different counties of the Principality, to the number of five or six
hundred, exclusive of their attendants, assembled.[1] Every necessary
accommodation was made for their entertainment. "Tentes and
pavilions were pitched in the parke, near to the castle, wheare they
quartered all the time, everie man according to his qualitie, the place
being furnished aforehand with all sortes of provisions for that purpose. This festival and time of jollitie continued the space of five
days," beginning on the day before S. George's Eve (April 21st),
when Sir Rhys viewed the company and selected five hundred of
"the properest and tallest men of their hands from amongst them."
These he divided into five bands under captains. The second day was
spent in exercising these chosen troops in all points, as if they were
to go on service. The third day the drums beat, the trumpets
sounded, and the martial host, armed at all points, as in battle array,
proceeded to Lanphey, the palace of the Bishop of S. David's, about a
mile from Carew Castle. At their coming thither they bade good
morrow to the Bishop, in the language of soldiers, with arquebuses,
muskets, and calivers, and then dividing themselves made a lane for
Sir Rhys to pass to the gate. After a parley with the Bishop's officer, in which the Knight assured him that although in arms on S.
George's Day in honour of the Martial Saint, his errand was peaceful,
to pray for the rest and peace of S. George's soul, in which he would ·
have the Bishop's assistance. Sir Rhys then arrayed himself in " S.
George his livery," and the Bishop coming forth with the Abbot of
Talley and the Prior of Caermarthen, all vested in rich copes, they
proceeded to the chapel and the Bishop sang a mass ; whereupon the
whole party returned to Carew. After a dumb show of serving the
(absent) King at a high table with all due ceremony, a rich feast
was served to all present, Sir Griffith Rhys, as having more courtly
accomplishments than the other youth, acting as Server. Before

---

[1] Rees: South Wales, ii., 791, etc., from which this account is abridged.

separating for the night, Sir William Herbert stepped forth before the company and challenged all comers, four to four, at jousts and tournament the next morning. This was instantly accepted and Sir Rhys appointed judge. Arrayed in fair gilt armour, two pages on horseback before him, a herald and two trumpeters and four footmen in attendance, while two hundred tall men in blue coats went before and after, he presided at the lists. After gallant deeds performed, and sundry tilts run and the tourney fought, supper was served, and so ended the fourth day of the festival; Sir Griffith ap Rhys having made challenge to Sir William Herbert to tilt with him, four to four, in the ring next morning, the losers to pay for a supper at Caermarthen "for theyre farewell at parting." The next morning they ran their six courses, and as had been agreed between them, "Sir Rhys gave sentence against his son, that he might show his friends what entertainment the place was able to afford." After a dinner, as formal as before, Sir Rhys gave a hunting party in his park, where they killed divers bucks, bestowed upon them for their supper at night. That feast over, a comedy was acted by some of Sir Rhys's own servants, with which, says the annalist, " these majesticall sights and triumphs were concluded." He thinks it noteworthy, that for the space of five days, among not less than one thousand people, " there was not one quarrel, cross word, or unkind look that happened among them."

November 7, 1509, Sir Rhys was appointed Justiciary for South Wales. May 12, 1510, he was made Chamberlain of the same District. In a list of the Vanguard retinue of Henry in his French expedition, dated May 15, 1513, appears Sir Ryce ap Thomas with captains and petty captains, foot-soldiers, demi-lances, in all 2,993. The MSS. diary of John Taylor, Clerk of Parliament, under June 25th, of the same year, says : " The French fled before Sir Rice ap Thomas ; " June 29th, " Sir Rice recaptured one of the King's great guns which had been taken by the French." At the battle of Guinegate or Spurs he took four French standards, and was instrumental in the capture of the Duke of Longueville. August 22d, he was present at the siege of Therouenne, and September 9th at that of Tournay. June 4, 1515, there is recorded a confirmation and quit-claim from the King to " Sir Rhesus ap Thomas son and heir of Thomas and heir of Griffin Nicholas, of the Castle and Lordship of Trayne March, and third part of the Ville of St. Clair in Caermarthen." May 16, 1517, he was granted the offices of Steward and Chancellor, in survivorship with his son, Sir Griffith, of Haverford West and Rowse in the Marches

of Wales.   July 5th, of the same year, he was one of the witnesses
to a treaty executed between Henry, Maximilian, and Charles.   In a
list of the persons who should accompany the King to the Field of the
Cloth of Gold, drawn up March 12, 1518–19, Sir Rhys was one of the
four Knights of the Order, *i.e.*, the Garter, who were to go, each having 22 servants, 2 to be chaplains, and 2 gentlemen, with 48 horses.
In 1520, Henry, writing to Thomas, Earl of Surrey, Lord Lieutenant
of Ireland, says that he has " writen to our trusty and right welbi-
loved Sir Rice ap Thomas to putt the nomber of fifte horsemen of
Walys in arredinesse for the Irish wars."   May 27, 1522, he was appointed to attend the King at the visit of Charles the Fifth,[1] the first
Knight on the list.   He was Mayor of Caermarthen in 1488, 1494,
and 1500.   The exact date of his death I have not been able to ascertain, but it is on record that February 2, 1524–5, he made his will,
and died that year, the will being probated July 5, 1525.   (Appendix
II.)   He was buried in the Church of the Grey Friars at Caermarthen ; but his body was afterwards removed to the eastern aisle of S.
Peter's Church, in the same town, where his monument, a sculptured
marble block, surmounted by recumbent figures of Sir Rhys and his
wife, Elizabeth Herbert, is the most remarkable which the church
contains.[2]   After remaining for three hundred years, unskillfully put
together in the northeast corner of the chancel, this monument was,
in September and October, 1865, restored to its original form and removed to a position under the arch between the chancel and the
consistory court, by the fourth Lord Dynevor.   The effigy of Sir
Rhys and the slab on which it lies consists of one piece of the stone
called *clunch*, 10 feet long by about 3 feet wide and 2 feet thick.
The Knight is lying in the attitude of prayer, clothed in mail and
chain armour, armorial bearings on the breast, with the cloak and
collar of the Garter, head resting on a pillow, shield, helmet, and
lambrequin ; his hair is flowing in ringlets over his shoulders ; the
crest is broken off just above the wreath.   The pillow, etc., is curi-
ously supported by the Dragon of Wales, lying on its back clasping
the shield, its head issuing out of the wreath.   At each top corner of
the slab the arms are repeated.   The feet rest against a couchant
lion with his head twisted back.   The figure of Lady Rhys is of small
size, in the act of prayer, cap almost square, a necklace, a tucker
above her gown, which is short, showing the petticoat beneath ;

[1] See a full account of the proceedings in Rutland Papers, *pp.* 59–100.
[2] Topographer and Genealogist for 1846, *p.* 562.

around the waist a gold cord ending in tassels ; over all, a flowing robe with large sleeves, no animal at her feet. Sir Rhys was married more than once, and it is difficult to state with absolute certainty his marriage relations. His first wife would appear to have been Eva,[1] *dau.* of Henry ap Gwilym of Court Henry, derived from Elystan Gloddryd, by whom he had a son, Sir Griffith ap Rhys, K.B., *b.* 1478, (*of whom presently*). There seems to be no question that he also married Elizabeth,[2] sister of William Herbert, first Earl of Pembroke of

TOMB OF SIR RHYS AP THOMAS, K.G.

that family, and *dau.* of Sir William ap Thomas, Knight of Ragland Castle by Gwladys, *dau.* of Sir Davy Gam. She was the widow of Sir Harry Stradling, Knight, of St. Donat's Castle, Glamorganshire, *d.* at Picton in Pembrokeshire, February 5, 1535, and is *bu.* with Sir Rhys at Caermarthen. Although the union was apparently unblessed by the sacrament of the Church, and she was not recognized as such by the English law, there would seem little doubt that in his active middle life, Gwenllian, sister of his intimate friend and counsel-

<hr />

[1] Cambrian Register, vol. i., *pp.* 49-145 ; MS. history of the family, about 1600 ; Brydges : Collins Peerage, vol. vii., 504 ; Ralph Brooke's pedigree of 1600 ; Rees : South Wales, 298, etc.

[2] Collins's Peerage, Pedigree of Herbert and Dinevor ; several pedigrees of Herbert in G. T. Clark's Genealogies of Morgan and Glamorgan ; the numerous books upon the Antiquities of South Wales, and the inscription upon the tomb of her first husband.

!or Robert ap Gwylim Harry ap Jevan Gwyn, of Mydhifinych, Abbot
of Talley, was his real wife;[1] Eva ap Gwilym probably dying young,
and Elizabeth Herbert being the wife of his old age, as she certainly
survived him. By Gwenllian he had issue :

i.   **MARGARET**, *m.* 1st, **HARRY JOHN**; *m.* 2d, **ROBERT GRIF-
FITH**; *m.* 3d, **PHILIP MORGAN**, of Cydwelly.
ii.   **ELLEN**, the elder, *m.* 1st, **RHYDDERCH AP JEVAN LLWYD** of
Builth ; *m.* 2d, **JENKIN LLWYD**, of Llanstephan.
iii.   **ELLEN**, the younger.
iv.   **MARGARET**, the younger.
v.   **WILLIAM AP RICE**, of Sandy Haven, Sheriff of Pembrokeshire 1557.
vi.   **DAVID**, the elder, *m.* **ALSON**, heiress of Arnold Martin, of Richardston
or Richeston, Pembrokeshire, and had a son.
       JOHN, Sheriff in 1582 and 1593, *m.* **CATHARINE**, heiress of Sir John Perrott, of
       Scotsborough, near Tenby,[2] Sheriff in 1550.
vii.   **DAVID**, the younger, *m. dau.* and *co-h.* of John ap Rhys David Thomas
of Blaentrèn, and founded the house of Gwynn, of Taliaris, in Caermarthenshire, extinct about 1650, in the seventh generation.
viii.   **THOMAS AP RHYS**, ancestor of THOMAS FAMILY OF WEST RIVER (*q.v.*).
ix.   **PHILIP**, Mayor of Caermarthen in 1522.

Sir Rhys is also said to have married Jenet, *dau.* of Thomas Matthews, whose rights are reserved in the attainder of Rice Griffith,[3]
and the *dau.* and heiress of Sir John Ellis descended from Sir Henry
Elys, of Yorkshire, *temp.* Richard I.[4] He had illegitimate issue : by
Elizabeth, *dau.* of John Mortimer, Lord of Coedmor, near Cardigan,
a *dau.* Jane ; by Alice Kyffin, of Montgomeryshire, he had a *dau.*
d. y.; and by a *dau.* of Howell ap Jenkin of Ynys y Maen-Gwyn, he
had his favourite *dau.*, Anne or Catherine, *m.* Henry Wirrion, Esq., of
Orielton, High Sheriff of Pembrokeshire, 1547, whose heiress *m.* Sir
Hugh Owen, of Bedowen, in Anglesea, ancestor of the Owens of Orielton, whose line ended in Sir Hugh Owen, Bart., Sheriff 1804, *d. u.*, 1809.

In the eye of the English law, Sir Rhys would appear to have had
only one legitimate son, Sir Griffith ap Rhys, whose son was his heir,
but in Wales it must have been otherwise, judging from the position
and marriages of his other children.

---

[1] Cambrian Register, vol. i., *pp.* 49 to 145 ; the MS. history of the family written about 1600.
Reprinted in abstract, Retrospective Review, vol. xi., quoted and endorsed as authentic history in
James Gairdner's Life of Richard III.

[2] Cliffe's Book of South Wales, 1848, *p.* 266, notices the tomb of Thomas ap Rhys, of Scotsbor-
ough, his wife and family, in the massive style of James the First's era, as standing in Tenby Church.
He was son of John ap David Rhys Thomas, and was Sheriff 1610.

[3] Statutes of the Realm, vol. iii., *p.* 415.

[4] Nichols's Herald and Genealogist, vol. iv., *p.* 526, article by W. S. Ellis.

As Mr. G. T. Clark, in his "Genealogies of Morgan and Glamorgan," notes : "The Welsh squires of the fifteenth and sixteenth centuries paid but little attention to the sacrament of marriage, and even after the Reformation continued to form unions of a patriarchal character, which though regularly recognized and recorded, had not the sanction of the Church."[1] In a case occurring at Builth, 27th, Edward I. (1299) the jurors report " that they say in these parts both legitimate and illegitimate succeed to the heritage of their ancestors, and that such has always been the custom."

A noteworthy instance of this is the noble family of Herbert. The proud Earls of Pembroke and Montgomery descend illegitimately from its founder, a contemporary of Sir Rhys ap Thomas. Indeed, Henry VII., the king whom Sir Rhys seated on the throne of England, apart from the fact that there is no *evidence* existing to prove a marriage between Katherine of France and his grandfather Owen Tudor,[2] derived his royal Lancastrian blood illegitimately. His mother, Margaret of Richmond, being a granddaughter of John Beaufort, eldest *natural* son of John of Gaunt, by Catharine Roet or Swinford (sister-in-law to the poet Chaucer), who afterward became his third wife.

GRIFFITH AP RHYS, the only son of Sir Rhys ap Thomas by his first wife Eva, of Court Henry, *b.* 1478, was once nominated as a candidate for the Garter, but failed to secure an election. When Henry VII. revived the Order of the Bath, November 17, 1501, on the marriage of his son, Prince Arthur, to Katherine of Aragon, Griffith ap Rhys was created a knight of that ancient order. He was a favourite companion of the Prince, and as such gave some curious testimony at the proceedings in reference to the divorce of Queen Katherine. In April, 1502, at the funeral of Prince Arthur, a contemporary account (printed in Grose's Antiquarian Repertory, ii., 327–330) says " Sir Griffith Vap Sr. Ris rode before the corpse in mornyng Abitt on a courser trapped with black, bearing banner of Prince's arms." And at the interment in Worcester Cathedral, April 27th, "Sir Griffith Vap Rise Thomas offered at the Gospel the rich embroidered banner of my Lord's Armes." The standard of Sir Griffith ap Rhys, K.B., was: per fess murrey and blue ; device repeated twice, a trefoil slipped and barbed *ar.* charged with a raven *ppr.* Motto, Psalm cxlvii. 9, "*Puluis* (sic.) *corvorum invocantibus eum.*"

---

[1] This irregularity was largely owing to the canonical restrictions enacted by the mediæval authorities, one suspects for venal reasons, dispensations being readily furnished for a money payment.

[2] Rev. C. E. Moberly : Early Tudors, *p.* 14.

At his father's tournament at Carew, 1507, he was one of the principal challengers. He was Mayor of Caermarthen, 1504–5–11–13.

The Rutland list of those at the Field of the Cloth of Gold notes Sir Griffith Rice, with two other knights, as in command of a body of one hundred light horsemen "for scurrers." Lady Rice was also in attendance on the Queen. He *m.* about 1504, Katherine, *dau.* of Sir John St. John, and aunt of the first Lord St. John of Bletshoe, from whom descended Pope's friend, Lord Boling-

TOMB OF SIR GRIFFITH AP RHYS, K.B.

broke. After Sir Griffith's death she *m.* Sir Piers Edgecombe, ancestor of the present Earl of Mount Edgecombe. She made her will at Cothele, in Cornwall, December 4, 1553, *d.* that month and is *bu.* with her first husband in Worcester Cathedral.[1] Sir Griffith ap Rhys *d.* September 29, 1521. Issue :

i.   **RICE**, his heir (*of whom presently*).
ii   **AGNES**, *m.* 1st, **WILLIAM**, 6th **LORD STOURTON**, and 2d, **SIR EDWARD BAYNTON, KNT.**, of Rowden, in Hertfordshire. She *d.* August 19, 1574, and is *bu.* with her 2d husband in Bromham Church, Wilts.[2] Their quaint epitaph runs thus :

---

[1] Notices of Sir Griffith ap Rhys will be found in Calendar of State Papers, reign of Henry VIII., vol. ii., *pp.* 69, 193, 235, 1489, etc. A view of the tomb of Sir Griffith ap Rhys may be seen in Thomas's Worcester, opposite *p.* 71, which quotes the inscription ; and also in Wild's Worcester, plate viii., and Dingley, ii., plate cclxxxv.

[2] Dingley's History from Marble, part i., plate xxxiii., gives drawings and epitaph from the tomb.

Here lieth Syr Edwarde Baynton Knyght within this marble clad,
By Agnes Ryce his firste trew wyfe Yt thyrtyne chyldrene had
Whearof she left alyve withe him at hir departure thre
Henery, Anne and Elyzabeth whose pictures here you see.
The XIX daye of Auguste she decesed of Christe the yere
These little figures standing bie present ye number here.   1574.

iii.   **MARY,** *m.* **SIR JOHN LUTTERELL, KNT.,** before 1553, when she is mentioned as his wife in her mother's will.

iv.   **ELIZABETH,** the only sister of **RICE AP GRIFFITH** named in his grandfather's will.

RICE AP GRIFFITH, the only son of Sir Griffith ap Rhys and Lady Katherine St. John, was the heir of his grandfather, Sir Rhys ap Thomas, K.G., and as such succeeded to a position of high rank and large possessions. A true Celt, he was a gallant youth, fond of splendour and display. Brought up with a knowledge of his great wealth and position, and *m.* to a *dau.* of the proud Duke of Norfolk, he seems to have shown an arrogant disposition, which made him dangerous enemies. With a numerous and devoted tenantry he felt secure and able to defy them ; but in the end, by obtaining the ear of the jealous King, they effected his ruin. The history of his fall is brief, though tragic. In July, 1528, we find him at the height of his power, and in his loyalty writing from Caermarthen to Cardinal Wolsey to complain of the numbers of Irish rebels from Desmond's country, who came into Pembrokeshire, and that the Mayor and Council of Tenby encourage them. March 3, 1528–9, he writes to Wolsey, complaining that his tenants are disturbed by persons under Lord Ferrars, the King's Justiciary for South Wales ; and reminding the Cardinal that he encouraged him to declare any grievance of himself or tenants, asks to be Lord Ferrars's Deputy. "Would be content to give my Lord such sum as Wolsey thought convenient for it."

The eleventh of the same month he notifies Wolsey that he has taken a pirate vessel, and thanks the Cardinal for his continued goodness. July 8th, he writes again, giving an account of the trial of the master of the pirate vessel, one William Hughes. Whether this is the same person afterward concerned in Rice ap Griffith's treason, I do not know. Between these two dates occurred an event which was probably the cause of Rice ap Griffith's conspiracy. June 16th of this year, Walter Devereux, Lord Ferrars, writes from " Kermarthen " to Wolsey, " that during his sessions in that town, Rece Griffith, Esq., encouraged the malefactors by causing proclamation to be made in divers churches to induce the people to attend upon him, instead of the Justiciary, and by making quarrels in Kermarden. On Tuesday, June 15th, he came to the Castle with his armed servants, where I was with other gentlemen, and picked a quarrel with me about Thomas ap Howen,[1] his kinsman, who was in ward for various misdemeanours, and hurting the people when they came to complain of him. Rece drew his dagger on me, and I took it from him and put him in ward. His friends stir up the people to rebellion, but he shall not be let out until he find security." The next day Lady Katherine Ryx writes Wolsey, reminding him of his friendship for her family, and telling him that " his servant, master Ryx Griffith, is in Caermarthen Castle on false surmise of desiring Thomas ap Owen, servant to the King, then in ward, to take out of the constable's hands one Jankyn, servant to Ryx, upon which Ferrers drew his dagger, and Ryx his also in self-defence. No harm was done except that Ryx was hurt in his arm and arrested, at which the county is greatly discontented. Great dissatisfaction has prevailed ever since Ferrers' coming to Caermarthen. Ryx would have written, but is kept from pen and ink." In conclusion she begs that Wolsey "will not allow them to have shame and rebuke."

The arrest seems to have caused a great disturbance among the people ; and Lady Ryx and her friends seem to have tried to release her husband by force without waiting for Wolsey's action, as we find Ferrars writing, June 18th, to Wolsey, about " the great insurrection in these parts at the instigation of Rece Griffith and Lady Haward. There has not been such in Wales in anyone's memory. Everything is now quiet, and the captains and ringleaders have returned home."

From the fact of his presiding at the trial of William Hughes, master of the pirate vessel, Rice ap Griffith appears to have given the necessary security and been released by the Justiciary. The insult, however, no doubt rankled in his memory ; and two years after, when he went up to London, predisposed him to listen to the proposals of some of the papal emissaries.

" The history of his conspiracy is a very mysterious one," says the historian Froude, and my investigations have enabled me to throw very little additional light on the subject. William Hughes, called

---

[1] Thomas ap Owen, Sewer of the Chamber, who was appointed Constable of Builth Castle, vice Sir Rhys ap Thomas, September 10, 1525, and was Mayor of Caermarthen the same year.

TOWER OF LONDON IN 1530

After an Old Engraving

in the act of attainder, "gentleman of London," who was his partner in the plot, was actively engaged in behalf of Queen Katherine of Aragon at the time of the proceedings in regard to her divorce. From a conversation between two friars after the execution of Rice ap Griffith, reported in Froude's second volume, from the testimony of one who overheard them, it would appear that the unfortunate youth was in reality innocent of the crime charged against him. It is doubtful if he committed any fault other than offending the jealous susceptibilities of the King by adding "Fitz Uryan" to his name, which is complained of in the plea against him,[1] as implying an intention of making himself an independent Prince of Wales. The case of his wife's nephew, the chivalrous Earl of Surrey, was not dissimilar. The conspiracy itself was probably part of the great Papal movement against England which was carried on all through the sixteenth century. The intention seems to have been to assassinate the King, and in the uncertainty with regard to the succession, Rice ap Griffith may have been persuaded to think that his claim as a descendant of the British and Welsh princes might be sufficient to give him the throne of Wales at least. An old prophecy that "James of Scotland, with the bloody hand, and the Raven" (Rice's crest), should conquer England, was also brought to mind to encourage him. Probably Rice was not guilty of doing more than listening to their treasonable propositions, but that was sufficient to ruin him. Some time in the autumn of 1531, probably October 2d, he was arrested. His friends in Wales broke out in open insurrection, and we find that a warrant was addressed to Lord Ferrars, dated October 7, 1531, directing the arrest of James ap Griffith ap Howell, sister's son to Sir Rhys ap Thomas, who had fortified himself in the Castle of Emlyn. He seems to have directed the revolt, and probably was the last of Rice's adherents to surrender. At its session of January 15, 1531-2, Parliament passed an act[2] forfeiting "Rychard ap Gruffyth late of London Esquire, otherwise Rice ap Griffith of Carewe and William Hughes late of London gentleman, as indicted and convicted in the Court of the King's Bench

---

[1] Mich. 23, Henry VIII., Rot. 6, *Inter Placita Regis:* "Quod præfatus Ricæus ap Griffith novum nomen. Videat Rice ap Griffith Fitz Urian in se præditorie assumpsit hac intentione videat quod in se statum et honorem dictæ principalitatis Walliæ—dignius et sub pretenso tituli colore prædiorie obtinere poterat et habere."

[2] Statutes of the Realm, vol. iii., *p.* 415. Spurrell's Caermarthen, 2d edition, *p.* 113, says, "Besides his large estates, £30,000 worth of jewels and plate were confiscated to the crown," which must greatly exaggerate the value of his personal property, although the statement is confirmed by the Life of Sir Rhys ap Thomas, *p.* 56.

of having at Iseldon (or Islington) in Middlesex, on August 28, 1531, and elsewhere compassed, &c. the death of our Lord the King."

January 4, 1531-2, Carlo Capello, their English Agent, writes as follows to the Signory of Venice: "The heretic friar was burnt alive; and, three days ago, they sentenced to death Master Ris, who had been put in the Tower before October 3, 1531, and this morning, on Tower Hill, he was beheaded in public, and one of his servants (presumably William Hughes) was hanged and quartered."[1]

In the act of forfeiture the rights of Lady Katherine Rice were scrupulously reserved, but uselessly; for in the Parliamentary Session of 1541-2 we find her name, Katherine, Countess of Bridgewater (she had m. 2d Sir Henry Daubeney, Earl of Bridgewater), among others, as attainted of misprision of treason, along with Queen Katherine Howard.

March 26th, of uncertain year, but apparently after the attainder, William Brabazon and Hugh Whalley write from Carew that they are there, preparing for the safe conducting of the King's stuff. "A chaplain of my Lady Howard's (Rice's wife) came with the King's command about her jointure, and asked leave to lie in the castle, that he might have the rooms cleaned. Suspected and searched his room, and found four boxes of evidences belonging to Narberth, Carew, and Kidwelly. Among other things a silver raven worth £40."

Rice ap Griffith m. Lady Katherine Howard, the sixth dau. of Thomas, second Duke of Norfolk, of that family, by his second wife, Agnes, dau. of Hugh Tilney, and sister and heiress of Sir Philip Tilney, Knight, of Boston (Doyle's Baronage calls her dau. of Sir Philip Tilney), by whom he left issue: Griffith, his heir, and Agnes.

Griffith Rice (q. v.) was restored in blood, though not to the estates of his father, in the reign of Queen Mary, is said to have m. Eleanor, dau. of Sir Thomas Jones, Knight, and is the lineal ancestor of the present Lord Dynevor, of Dynevor Castle, Caermarthenshire.

[1] State Papers, Foreign, Venetian under the year; Wriothesley's Chronicle. 17; Calendar of State Papers, Henry VIII., vol. iv., 2342. Other notices of Rice ap Griffith may be found at 1962, 4481, 4501, 4504, 4511, 4513, 4574, 5041, 5044.

THOMAS, OF WEST RIVER, MARYLAND

PHILIP THOMAS, of the mercantile house of Thomas &
Devonshire, at Bristol, England, son of Evan Thomas of Swansea,
Glamorganshire, Wales, who died in 1650, is the earliest ancestor of
this family of whom we have legal and documentary proof, although
I have little doubt that the descent given in this genealogy is accu-
rately taken from Sir Rhys ap Thomas, K.G., and will be confirmed
by further investigations. A curious old tradition in the family derived them from Thomas de Douvre[1] (*d.* November 18, 1100), the first
Norman Archbishop of York, whose nephew, Thomas, son of Sampson, Bishop of Worcester, was Archbishop from 1109 to 1114, but it
is utterly without foundation. The coat of arms[2] (*ar.*, a chevron
checquy of *or* and *sa.*, between three ravens, close, of the last) borne
by Philip Thomas upon his gold-headed cane and service of silver,[3]
served to point out the true affiliation when I came across the arms
of Sir Rhys ap Thomas of Carew, in an old copy of Guillim's "Display of Heraldry" (viz., *Ar.* a chevron *sa.* between three ravens, close,
of the last). The connection with the Knight of Carew I first·at-
tempted to trace through a supposed younger son of his unfortunate
grandson, Rice ap Griffith, by the name of Thomas; but the docu-

[1] See his biography in the Appendix.

[2] These arms were authenticated for the late Philip E. Thomas, of Baltimore, by Sir Charles
George Young, Garter King at Arms.

[3] George Lynn-Lachlan Davis: Daystar of American Freedom, *pp.* 82, 288. The cane is still in
the possession of his descendants. The silver was last owned by William Thomas, of Sandy Spring,
Md., but has disappeared. It is reported to have been exchanged at a silversmith's in Baltimore by
Mrs. Thomas for plated ware of newer pattern, and been melted by the purchaser not long before the
Civil War.

ment at the Record Office in London which I understood to state that such a person was at the Court of Scotland with James ap Griffith (*q. v.*) instead, declares "that ap Griffith called himself Rice."

Further research satisfied me that the descent was to be taken directly from Sir Rhys through one of his sons by Gwenllian (*q. v.*), sister of his friend and counsellor, Robert ap Gwylim Harry ap Jevan Gwyn of Mydhifinych, Abbot of Talley.[1] Referring then to the genealogy of Sir Rhys ap Thomas for its earlier history, we begin the present family with this **THOMAS AP RHYS**, *b.* after 1478, whose son Philip ap Thomas *m.* Sybell, *dau.* of Philip and Joan (Warnecombe) Scudamore, and dying before 1585 left a son and heir, John Philip Thomas, who appears to have inherited from his mother the demesne lands of Grosmount Manor, Monmouthshire, and a grist-mill near by, before 1585, when he held them "in right of Philip Skidamore,"[2] and in 1591 was Queen's lessee of mills at Kentchurch in the same shire.[2] He *m.* Gwenllian, fourth *dau.* of Walter Herbert, Esq. (*q. v.*), of Skenfrith, Sheriff of Monmouthshire in 1552, and had issue: Evan Thomas, *b.* 1580, whose name begins the pedigree compiled by the late Philip E. Thomas, Esq., of Baltimore. I find notices,[3] of Evan Thomas ap Evan, Under Sheriff of Glamorganshire in 1615; Evan Thomas, who was one of the Awennydion, or College of Bards, of Glamorgan in 1620; Major Evan Thomas, killed on the part of the King, at the battle of St. Fagans, near Cardiff, May 8, 1648; Evan ap Thomas of Eglwysilan, Wales, *b.* 1581, *d.* 1666; E. (probably Edward) Thomas, printer of Deacon's "History of James Naylor," at "his house in Green Arbor, London, 1657;" and Evan Thomas, of Pembrokeshire, who was fined for absence from church as a Quaker, but whether any of these are Evan of Swansea I cannot say. His wife's name is unknown. Philip, his son, was *b.* about 1600, and may have been the Philip Thomas in the East India Company's service who petitioned for unpaid wages in 1621, but his behaviour was complained of and he was discharged their service on December 17th. Another Philip Thomas, with Thomas Lawrence and Martin Saunders, gives information about a Romish plot April 1, 1628; and there was a Philip Thomas called to account for saying at the Castle Tavern in St. Clement's parish, London, January 20, 1638, that "the punishment of Prynne, Bastwick and Burton, the Puritans, by ear-cropping, etc., was not more

---

[1] The probability of this descent has recently been confirmed by the well-known Welsh antiquary, Alcwyn C. Evans, Esq., of Caermarthen.

[2] *Proceedings in Chancery*, Queen Elizabeth, II., 2-8.

[3] These notices are mostly from the calendars of the English Record Office. See their indexes.

than they deserved." Before 1638 a Philip Thomas was messenger of the Chamber for charitable uses, and August 13, 1638, he suggested a new commission. Philip Thomas, the emigrant, before 1650, formed a business partnership with one Devonshire at Bristol, and some time in the year 1651, only seventeen years after Leonard Calvert and Lord Baltimore's first colonists landed at St. Mary's, removed to the province of Maryland. The earliest land patent in his name, dated February 19, 1651–2, conveys to him 500 acres of land called " Beakely " or " Beck-ley " on the west side of Chesapeake Bay, " in consideration that he hath in the year 1651 transported himself, Sarah, his wife, Philip, Sarah, and Elizabeth his children, into this our province."

CANE OF PHILIP THOMAS

He would appear to have come direct-ly from Bristol to Maryland. An exami-nation of the land records of the colony of Virginia, made by the well-known genealogist, R. A. Brock, Esq., of Rich-mond, fails to show any grant to a Philip Thomas in the seventeenth century, and there would seem to be no reason to sup-pose that he was in America before coming to Maryland, or, as some have thought, was a member of the Puritan Colony in Virginia and removed thence along with them, when in 1649 and 1650 about seventy families of Puritans from Colonel Richard Bennett's plantation at Nansemond, Va., emigrated to Maryland and settled first on Greenbury's Point, at the mouth of the Severn River, principally on 250 acres sur-veyed in 15-acre lots, and called the " Town lands of Severn." The first meeting-house was erected on land adjoining that of Elder Durand, their minister. Mr. Philip Thomas is said to have lived on the premises and guarded the sanctuary. About five years later the settlers transferred their lands to Bennett, and moved away. Between 1658 and 1661 Philip Thomas had patented to him 100 acres called " Thomas Towne ; " in 1665 a patent of 120 acres called

"Fuller's Poynt;" in 1668, of 300 acres called "The Planes;" in 1672, of 200 acres called "Phillip's Addicion," and numerous other patents[1] of unnamed tracts. This land lay mostly in Anne Arundel County, near what is now known as West River. "Fuller's Poynt," between the Severn and South Rivers, is now called Thomas Point, and is the site of a light-house. A man of character and resolution, the emigrant soon acquired influence amongst his neighbours, and, affiliating himself with the Puritan party, he became one of its leaders in the conflict with Lord Baltimore, the Proprietary, and his representatives in the province. When Cromwell and the Parliamentary party were supreme in England, their sympathizers in Maryland broke out in open rebellion under Colonel Richard Bennett, and Philip Thomas, holding a military commission as lieutenant, was of their muster in Anne Arundel County, Md. Governor Stone immediately summoned the militia of the province, and with a little army of 250 men, after seizing a magazine of arms collected by the Puritans, set out for Providence on the Severn, the head-quarters of Bennett's partisans. Part of his men were transported in small vessels, and part marched along the Bay shore. As they drew near Providence, Stone sent forward a messenger to the enemy, summoning them to surrender; but the messenger did not return; and on the evening of the same day, March 24, 1654-5, the Governor's little fleet, with all his army now on board, made its appearance in the Severn.

Captain Fuller, the commander at Providence, put some men on board a ship lying in the harbour, who fired on Stone's boats as he landed his forces, but did no damage. On the next morning, which was Sunday, Governor Stone and his force came marching up to the attack, under the black and yellow flag of the colony, while over Fuller's men, 107 in number, drawn up in order of battle, floated the blue cross on a crimson field, the standard of the Commonwealth of England. The battle was short, but sharp; about fifty of the Governor's men were killed or wounded, and Stone himself, with nearly all his force, compelled to surrender, under a promise that their lives should be spared.

The Puritan annalist writes: "After the battle our men were so tired with watching and anxiety (before the attack) that the guards set over the prisoners fell asleep at their posts; yet the Catholics were so disheartened by their defeat, that no one of them

[1] Land Office: Liber 2, *p.* 430; Liber 4, *pp.* 60, 111, 204; Liber 5. *pp.* 416, 537; Liber 7, *pp.* 7, 85, 429; Liber 10, *p.* 433; Liber 11, *pp.* 96, 97; Liber 15, *p.* 446; Liber 16, *p.* 377.

attempted to escape." "Hammond against Heamans," a contemporary pamphlet[1] by one of the Governor's party, notes that "three days after the battle Captain Fuller, Wm. Burgees, Richard Evans, Leo Strong, Wm. Durand, Roger Heamans, John Brown, John Cuts, Richard Smith, one Thomas (Philip Thomas), one Bestone, Sampson Warren, Thomas Meares, and one Crouch, sat as a Council of War, condemned a number of the prisoners to die, and executed four of them."

March 20, 1656–7, Lieutenant Philip Thomas was appointed one of the six High Commissioners of the Provincial Court, the father of his son - in - law, John Mears, being another.[2] When Oliver Cromwell ordered the revolutionists to return the province to the Proprietary he was one of the commissioners to make the surrender, which was effected on March 24, 1658–9, when the articles of surrender were signed, sealed, and delivered.[3] After this he does not seem to have taken an active part in the political affairs of the province, the notices of his name upon the colonial records having to do with

CAECILIUS, SECOND LORD BALTIMORE

transfers of land, etc., the number of which were considerable.

From a petition to the Colonial Assembly, dated April 16, 1666, we learn that he had returned from a voyage to England in the preceding month. Tuesday, October 17, 1671, the Upper House of As-

---

[1] MS. copy at Maryland Historical Society Library, *p.* 23.
[2] Maryland Archives, original Liber B, folio 343, and Liber B, No. 3, folio 260.
[3] Council Record Book, Liber Hh, folios, 12–16 and 17.

sembly consents to a bill for ferries, among them being one "over Potapsco River, from Philip Thomas point in Anne Arundel Co. to Kent Co."

In April, 1672, George Fox, the founder of the Society of Friends or Quakers, arrived in Maryland, landing at the Patuxent just in time to reach a "general meeting for all the Friends in the Province of Maryland," which had been appointed by John Burnyeat to be held at West River. He describes it [1] as a "very large meeting," and held four days, "to which, besides Friends, came many other people, divers of whom were of considerable quality in the world's account." Immediately after this meeting Fox appears to have continued his labours by preaching his doctrines and establishing meetings for discipline at various places in the province. He remained in America until after the "general meeting" at West River, which commenced on the 17th of 3d month (May), 1673, and lasted four days. The next day, being the 21st, he set sail for England. In describing this meeting he says, "divers of considerable account in the government and many others were present, who were generally satisfied, and many of them reached, for it was a wonderful glorious meeting." It is possible, from the language of his will, that Philip Thomas himself was one of those "reached" by George Fox, and there can be no doubt that during his missionary tour his preaching brought a number of the family under the influence of Quakerism, as we find their names enrolled upon the early records of the Society immediately afterward. In point of fact, an examination of those records shows that, for the generation then living and their children, in Maryland at least, George Fox, John Burnyeat, Samuel Bownas, and the other preachers of Quakerism, did very much the same work as was done a century later by John Wesley and the Methodists. Such religion as they had was formal and lifeless ; many, indeed, had cast off all restraint, and were living in utter neglect of the ordinances of religion and common morality. The Quaker missionaries coming amongst them with their fervid zeal, and speaking, as they thought, messages direct from heaven, aroused the slumbering souls of their hearers, and reaped a large harvest of converts to what was in fact the first presentation of a spiritual religion they had known.

As a result of this, the Quaker Registers of the end of the seven-

[1] Journal of George Fox, *pp.* 123, 144 ; J. Saurin Norris: Early Friends in Maryland, 12 ; and Life and Travels of Samuel Bownas and John Burnyeat.

A QUAKER MEETING IN THE SEVENTEENTH CENTURY

After a Dutch Print by Tanje

teenth century are a veritable *Libro d'oro* in Maryland, containing as they do the names of so many of the leading families of the province. Whether Philip Thomas became a Quaker or not, his widow certainly was one, and probably a preacher of the sect. September 9, 1674, he made his will, which was proved August 10, 1675. A copy, apparently made by one of his sons-in-law, is still preserved at the family seat, "Lebanon," West River, Md. From this he appears to have disposed of much of the land granted him, only mentioning "Beckley," "Fuller's Poynt," and the "Playns," and his two houses in Bristol, England. The clause in the will making "the body of Quakers" a final Court of Appeal in the event of any dispute arising under its provisions, was a common one amongst the Society of Friends, and in this case recourse was had to it. After the death of his widow, Sarah Thomas, his son Samuel claimed all her estates by virtue of a verbal will which he alleged she had made in his favour. This claim was resisted by his brother-in-law, Edward Talbot, and the West River Meeting of Friends was appealed to, to decide the question. The Meeting decided that although she had expressed a wish that Samuel Thomas should be her sole heir, she had not given legal effect to it, and that the estate should be equally divided between her several heirs. The two houses in Bristol were sold before September 13, 1690, when John Talbot claimed an interest in the proceeds of the sale in right of his wife, the granddaughter of Philip Thomas, to the extent of £10, and £50, as her share of the whole landed estate.

PHILIP THOMAS, the Emigrant, *m.* in England, **SARAH HARRISON,**[1] who survived him, dying early in 1687.[2] Issue :
Born in England before 1651 :

i.   **PHILIP,** probably *d. s. p.* before 1688, as his name does not appear among Sarah Thomas's heirs at that date, though it is to be noted that his father is spoken of as Philip Thomas, *Senior.*

ii.   **SARAH,** *m.,* in 1672, **JOHN,** son of **Thomas** and **Elizabeth Mears,** who *d.* in 1675.[3] His wife *d.* in the same year. Issue (surname MEARS) :

         An only *dau.,* SARAH, *b.* August 4, 1673 ; *m.,* before 1690, JOHN TALBOT (*q.v.*).

---

[1] Possibly *dau.* of Edmund Harrison, Embrotherer to King Charles the First, and Jane his wife, *dau.* of Thomas Godfrey, and *granddau.* of Christopher Harrison, merchant tailor, of London, who *m.* E'iza, *dau.* of Thomas Cooke, of Wakefield. Visitation of London, 1634, *p.* 353.

[2] Herring Creek Meeting, November 25, 1687, "Sarah Thomas is taken away by death."

[3] Will proved May 25th, Liber 2, *p.* 72. "Bequeathed to Samuel Thomas my silver tobacco-box and soite of cloathes made me lately by Richard Arnold."

iii.   **ELIZABETH**, *m.*, as his 3d wife, **WILLIAM COALE** (*q. v.*); he *d.* October 30, 1678, and his widow *m.* 2dly, before 1683, **EDWARD**, 2d son of **Richard and Elizabeth Talbot** (*q.v.*), who *d.* in January, 1692–3, his wife in 1726.

Born in Maryland after 1651 :

iv.   **MARTHA**, *m.* after 1672, **RICHARD ARNELL** or **ARNOLD**, who *d.* in 1684 ; [1] his wife died before 1688.   Issue :

    i.   **SAMUEL**, *d. i.*
    ii.   **SARAH.**
    iii. **ELIZABETH**, *b.* December 24, 1682 ; *m.* 1st, January 8, 1702, **JACOB GILES**, and had issue Sarah, and *m.* 2d, July 30, 1704, **THOMAS HAWKINS.**

v.   **SAMUEL**, *b.* about 1655, *of whom presently.*

SAMUEL, son of **Philip** and **Sarah (Harrison) Thomas**, *b.* about 1655, was probably a minister of the Society of Friends as early as August 4, 1686, when Herring Creek quarterly meeting approved of his proposal to attend the yearly meeting at Philadelphia.   April 13, 1688, he was appointed a Committee on "drowsiness" by the West River meeting.   He held 72 acres of Talbot's Ridge, north side of West River, surveyed in 1674, and after 1698, at a rental of 6*s.* 8*d.*, 200 acres of his Lordship's manor on the Ridge.   He *m.*[2] May 15, 1688, at his own house in Anne Arundel Co., **MARY**, *dau.* of **Francis Hutchins**, of Calvert Co., who had previously been engaged to Thomas Smith.   At the second time of their "passing meeting" he appeared and "discharged her of any ingagement whatsoever," so the meeting gave its consent to their marriage.   She *d.* in July, 1751,[3] and her husband before February 10, 1743, when she made her will [3] as "Mary Thomas, widdow."   Issue :[4]

i.   **SARAH**, *b.* March 31, 1689 ; *m.* October 25, 1705, **JOSEPH RICHARDSON** (*q. v.*).
ii.   **SAMUEL**, *b.* February 1, 1691, *d. i.*
iii.   **SAMUEL**, the 2d, *b.* March 11, 1693, *d. i.*
iv.   **PHILIP**, *b.* March 1, 1694, *of whom presently.*
v.   **JOHN**, *b.* April 15, 1697 (*q. v.*).
vi.   **ELIZABETH**, *b.* December 28, 1698 ; *m.* December 19, 1717, **RICHARD SNOWDEN** (*q. v.*).
vii.   **MARY**, *b.* November 6, 1700 ; *m.* July 31, 1718, **JOHN GALLOWAY** (*q. v.*).
viii.   **SAMUEL**, the 3d, *b.* November 12, 1702 (*q. v.*).

[1] Will proved June 16, 1684, Liber G., 123.
[2] West River Book of Marriages, *p.* 19.
[3] Will-book, Liber D. D. No. 7, folio 109.   Proof July 25, 1751.
[4] W. R. Register of Births, etc., *p.* 15.

ix.   **ANN,** *m.* October 8, 1730, **EDWARD FELL,** of Over Kittel, Lancashire, England, who *d.* in March, 1743. Issue : **Anne.**

x.   **MARGARET,** *b.* 1710; *m.* after 1735, **WILLIAM HARRIS** (*q. v.*).

PHILIP, eldest son of **Samuel** and **Mary (Hutchins) Thomas,**
b. March 1, 1694, is spoken of by Governor Sharpe in his correspondence[1] as a man of ability, whose understanding and capacity were
never questioned, well affected to the proprietary, though something
in his conduct appeared at one time to have given a different impres-
sion about his feelings. He would seem to have been somewhat like
William Penn in position and character, evidently, from the Governor's account, a courtier, and interested to advance himself, but at the
same time he and his wife were both recorded ministers of the Society of Friends.[2] November 24, 1732, he was a member of a Committee on the part of West River meeting to prepare an address of welcome to Lord Baltimore. At least as early as May 20, 1742, he was
a member of the Governor's Council.[3]

March 13, 1743-4, the Honourable Philip Thomas, Esq., was commissioned Judge and Register of the Land Office.[4] In 1744, with
Edmund Jennings, R. King, and Thomas Colvill, he represented
Maryland in a treaty with the Indians at Lancaster, Penn., to settle
the western bounds of the province.[5] On the journey he is spoken of
as having "a great disputation with one Gatchell, a Quaker of Nottingham, concerning carnal weapons," which would imply that he was
hardly of Quaker principles at that time. Governor Sharpe writes of
him as generally well esteemed. He had, at least in the latter part
of his life, a very bad constitution, was a little melancholy, and frequently indisposed for a long time together and unable to go up to
Annapolis from his plantation, some twelve miles away, near Arundel Manour. In 1755 the Governor writes of him as a member of his
Council, and as "not averse to writing to the Lower House as the
other members were." Another letter of the Governor puts the
matter even more strongly : "Scarcely any of the Council except
Mr. Thomas have ever taken upon themselves to pen a common message, yet all of them except Mr. Thomas enjoy lucrative offices."

---

[1] Maryland Archives, Correspondence of Governor Sharpe, 2 vols. ; ix., 181, 209, 382, 450 ; x., 233, 412, 416, 426, etc.

[2] Records of Meeting for Ministers and Elders held at Herring Creek, November 22, 1756.

[3] Archives original Liber C, B. Council proceedings, folio 144.

[4] Liber I, R. Commissions, etc.

[5] Griffith's Sketches of the Early History of Maryland, 51 ; Journal of Witham Marshe, Secretary of the Maryland Commissioners, edited by Dr. W. H. Egle, 1884, *pp.* 6, 7, 9.

This was a matter of concern to his Excellency, and comes up a number of times in his letters, various suggestions being made, among them that he should be joint commissary with Colonel Tasker, "which," he writes, "I hope he will accept, there being no gentleman else in the Council at all acquainted with law except two on the Eastern Shore." This failed, Mr. Tasker refusing to have a co-partner in the office. Another proposition was to appoint him Deputy to the non-resident Secretary, Calvert, as on being sounded he was found not averse to making the Secretary a "more reasonable and handsome consideration" than Colonel Tasker offered for the office. But this also fell through ; and the appointment of his eldest son as rent-roll keeper seems to have been the only favour actually shown him. In 1758 he is spoken of as a suitable person to be of the commission on the Maryland and Pennsylvania boundary, if his health would "permit him to undergo the fatigue."

May 23, 1760, the Governor speaks of him "as such an invalid that he hardly ever goes from home, nor is it expected that he will again enjoy a better state of health." Secretary Calvert about this time proposed that Philip Thomas, then the third member in age, should resign his seat in the Council to his eldest son ; but the Governor objected strongly to it ; writing May 26, 1760, "that in the office he enjoys (rent-roll keeper), I believe the son may serve his Lordship very well, but I hope you will not think of recommending him to a seat in the Council, since such a promotion would disoblige numbers here and oblige nobody that I know except possibly the Messrs. Hanbury [Baltimore's business agents] ; not even his father, to my knowledge, would wish to see it." January 28, 1761, the Governor notes that Philip Thomas could not be present at the proclamation of King George III., "being confined by sickness." He *m.* 1st, in March, 1721,[1] **FRANCES**, *dau.* of —— **Holland**, and had issue by her : **WILLIAM**, *b.* about 1722, *of whom presently.* He *m.*[2] 2d, August 11, 1724, **ANN**, *dau.* of **Samuel** and **Mary** (——) **Chew** (*q. v.*), who *d.* May 20, 1777, and was *bu.* at West River graveyard.[3] Philip Thomas made his will November 29, 1760,[4] in which he divides Perry Point on the Susquehanna in Cecil Co., between his sons Richard and Samuel, and gives his son John the home plantation ("Lebanon,"

[1] Herring Creek Monthly Meeting gave its consent March 3, 1720-1.
[2] Original Certificate at "Lebanon," West River, recorded at West River meeting.
[3] West River Register, etc., *p.* 45.
[4] Liber D. D. No. 1760, etc., folio 1007.

LEBANON, WEST RIVER, MARYLAND, IN 1889

RESIDENCE OF PHILIP THOMAS BEFORE 1724

at West River, the house having been built before 1724), besides providing for his other children by name. He *d.* November 23, 1762, leaving further issue :[1]

i.   **SAMUEL**, *b.* June 12, 1725 (*q. v.*).
ii.   **PHILIP**, *b.* July 3, 1727 (*q. v.*).
iii.   **MARY**, *b.* January 1, 1730–1 ; *m.* 1st, May 12, 1748, **HENRY HILL.** Issue :

> **HENRIETTA MARGARET**, *m.*, September 13, 1770, **BENJAMIN OGLE**, of Annapolis, who *d.* in July, 1809, his wife in August, 1815. Issue :
> Ann, *b.* January 4, 1773 ; *m.* John Tayloe ; **Mary**, and **Benjamin**.

> **MRS. HILL**, *m.* 2dly, February 7, 1760, **ROBERT**, son of John Pleasants, of Virginia. Issue :

> **ANN THOMAS.**

iv.   **ELIZABETH**, *b.* March 8, 1732–3 ; *m.* **SAMUEL SNOWDEN** (*q.v.*).
v.   **RICHARD**, *b.* July 17, 1736 ; *m.*, April 29, 1760, **DEBORAH**, *dau.* of **THOMAS** (dec.) and **ELIZABETH HUGHES**, of Charlestown, Cecil Co., Md. Issue :

> **PHILIP**, *m.* — **MYERS** ; and **ELIZABETH**, *m.*, before November 23, 1777, **STEPHEN**, son of Stephen and Elizabeth (Ward) **STEWART**, who was active in the Revolution, and devised an armour-plated vessel, which, however was not built.

vi.   **JOHN**, *b.* August 26, 1743 (*q. v.*).

WILLIAM, only son of **Philip Thomas,** by his first wife **Frances Holland,** was *b.* about 1722. Governor Sharpe writes in February, 1755, " that he could not, as his father wished, propose him for a seat in the Council, but would serve him the first opportunity offered." This promise he made good in 1756 by appointing him keeper of the Eastern Shore rent-rolls, and October 16th of that year he notifies Secretary Calvert of the appointment, saying : " He is a gentleman that has endeavoured to deserve well of the government, the son of Mr. Thomas of the Council, and one that I persuade myself will not spare any pains to give his Lordship the satisfaction he expects and requires." The Secretary at first objected to the appointment on the ground of his residence on the opposite shore of the Bay ; and suggested his being put in another office. There is quite a correspondence on the subject, which resulted in leaving him rent-roll keeper. Some years later the Governor, as we have seen, refused to put him in his father's seat in the Council. April 29, 1773, he was reappointed roll-keeper by Governor Eden.[2] June 27, 1776, he returned

---

[1] West River Register, etc., *p.* 32.
[2] Liber I, R. Commissions, etc., *p.* 311.

this by carrying provisions from his plantation to the Governor's vessel, when the latter was leaving the province at the bidding of the Revolutionists, and was called to account and reprimanded for doing so by the committee of safety.[1] This would make it improbable that he was the William Thomas appointed adjutant of the Twenty-fifth Battalion of Maryland militia, commanded by Colonel Joseph Beall, March 6, 1776; the family, it would seem, remaining true to their allegiance in the Revolution. He *m.* **MARY WYAN,** and *d.* in 1783, his will being proved December 16, 1783.[2] Issue:

i.   **PHILIP WILLIAM,** *b.* May 12, 1759, *of whom presently.*
ii.   **MARY ANN,** *m.* **CAPTAIN JOSEPH LEONARD.**

PHILIP WILLIAM, only son of **William** and **Mary (Wyan) Thomas,** *b.* at "Hill's Delight," near Annapolis, May 12, 1759, was educated in England, but returned to Maryland and held some political office there. A few years later he went to England and engaged in business in London, founding the Banking House of P. W. Thomas, Sons & Co., at No. 50 Threadneedle Street, in that city, somewhere about 1784.[3] He *m.* second, between 1784 and 1787, **SARAH,** *dau.* of **Graves Aikin,** of Newry, Ireland, and *d.* January 31, 1840. Issue:

i.   **HENRY,** *b.* January 4, 1788; *m.* **HARRIET ELWES,** and *d.* April 4, 1882. Issue:

    EMMA, HARRIET, and **MARY ANNA.**

ii.   **ANNE,** *b.* September 26, 1789; *d. u.* April 15, 1833.
iii. **HARRIET,** *b.* July 4, 1791; *m.* **JAMES FERN,** and *d.* April 12, 1846. Issue:

    EMILY VIRGINIA.

iv.   **EMILY,** *b.* March 3, 1792; *d.* April 2, 1806.
v.   **ELIZA,** *b.* September 6, 1794; *d. u.* June 2, 1830.
vi.   **SARAH,** *b.* August 22, 1796; *m.* **JOHN BLAKEWAY** (*q. v.*).
vii. **JOHN,** *b.* May 23, 1798; *m.* **MARY ANN FORSTER,** of Manuden House, Bishop Stortford, Essex, who was patroness of Manuden Vicarage, value £130. He *d. s. p.* February 18, 1869, and his widow in July, 1892.
viii. **CHARLES,** *b.* October 5, 1799; *d. u.* January 6, 1841.
ix.   **MARY ANN,** *b.* December 5, 1801; *d. u.* May 19, 1868.

---

[1] Correspondence of Committee, printed by Peter Force.   [2] Liber T., G. No. 1, folio 146.
[3] Through extensive stock transactions engaged in by W. E. Blakeway, then managing partner, the firm failed in January, 1884, for upward of £800,000 stg.

1. **WILLIAM ALEXANDER**, *b*. August 26, 1803 ; *m*. **ANNA**, *dau*. of **Thomas Bush**, and *d*. December 30, 1879. His widow *d*. February 7, 1889. Issue :

    i.   **PERCY WILLIAMS**, *b*. September 15, 1854, a stock-broker at London, residing in Kensington Gardens Terrace, and for some time Church Warden of S. Paul's Church, Kensington. He *m*., January 27, 1881, **AMY**, *dau*. of L. W. **Sedgwick, M.D.**, of Gloucester Terrace, Hyde Park, London, formerly of Boroughbridge, Yorkshire, and *d*. September 18, 1894, from exhaustion after a severe burning received three days previously. Issue : **Muriel Amy**, *b*. August 20, 1882, and **Geoffrey Alexander Percy**, *b*. August 26, 1884, the present head of the THOMAS FAMILY.

    ii.   **PHILIP ALEXANDER**, *b*. November 5, 1856, residing in Park Lane, London ; a civil engineer.

    iii.   **JOHN WYAN**, *b*. March 11, 1860, was matriculated at Trinity College, Oxford, as 3d son of William Alexander Thomas, armiger, of London, May 31, 1879, B.A. 1883.

SAMUEL, eldest son of **Philip Thomas** by his second wife, **Ann Chew**, *b*. June 12, 1725, resided at Perry Point on the Susquehanna River near Havre-de-Grace and was proprietor of ferry rights on both sides of the river. He seems to have led a retired life, the only notice of him in the Maryland State papers being in connection with the lease of 100 acres of Talbot Manor and a lawsuit resulting from it in 1752,[1] in which he defended the title of Lord Baltimore to the manor, which had been disputed ; and seems to have put himself to considerable expense by his loyalty and been thought by Secretary Calvert to have had some "pretence to satisfaction in connection with the affair.[2] It is doubtful, however, if he received any, and he does not appear to have held any office under the provincial government. He *m*., October 23, 1750, his cousin **MARY**, *dau*. of **Samuel** and **Mary (Snowden) Thomas** (*q. v.*). For this he was disowned by the Meeting, and February 23, 1759, they acknowledge their error in marriage and ask lines to Nottingham meeting, Cecil Co., from the meeting at West River. The certificate of transfer was given them April 27, 1759. Mrs. Thomas *d*. March 4, 1770, and her husband *d*. July 17, 1784. Issue :[3]

i.   **ANN**, *b*. October 2, 1751 ; *m*. **THOMAS RUSSELL** (*q. v.*).

ii.   **PHILIP**, *b*. August 12, 1753 ; *d. s. p.*

iii.   **SAMUEL**, *b*. June 20, 1757 ; *d*. May 20, 1759.

iv.   **RICHARD SNOWDEN**, *b*. February 25, 1762, *of whom presently*.

v.   **JOHN CHEW**, *b*. October 15, 1764 (*q. v.*).

[1] Harris & Johnson's Maryland Reports.
[2] Maryland Archives, ix., *pp*. 179–206 ; x., 171, 452.
[3] Nottingham Record of Births, etc., folio 94, and other registers of that meeting and of Indian Spring and Herring Creek.

vi. **SAMUEL**, *b.* February 2, 1766 ; was a Minister of the Society of Friends ;
     m. **ANNA**, *dau.* of **Dr. Charles Alexander Warfield**, who *d.*
     May 19th, and her husband *d.* October 1, 1820.   Issue :

    i.   ELIZABETH WARFIELD, *b.* November 5, 1790 ; *m.*, October 7, 1806, NICHO-
          LAS SNOWDEN (*q. v.*).
    ii. HARRIET ANN.
    iii. JULIANNA MARIA, *b.* January 16, 1795 ; *m.*, September 24, 1811, ISAAC
          KNIGHT (*q. v.*).

vii. **EVAN WILLIAM**, *b.* February 6, 1769 (*q. v.*).

RICHARD SNOWDEN THOMAS, eldest surviving son of
Samuel and **Mary (Thomas) Thomas**, *b.* February 25, 1762,
resided at Perry Point, near Havre-de-Grace. He *m.*, December
13, 1784, **MARY**, only *dau.* of **Sutherland Mifflin**, and *d.* July
29, 1814.   Issue :

i.   **SAMUEL**, *b.* September 1, 1785 ; *d. s. p.*
ii.   **RICHARD SNOWDEN**, *b.* January 11, 1787 ; *d. s. p.* April 23, 1871.
iii. **MARY**, *b.* June 25, 1788 ; *m.* **DAVID JONES** (*q. v.*).
iv.   **ANN**, *b.* November 4, 1789 ; *d.* February 7, 1793.
v.   **JOHANNAH**, *b.* November 16, 1790 ; *d.* October 13, 1792.
vi.   **DEBORAH**, *b.* March 17, 1792 ; *m.* **GUSTAVUS WRIGHT**.   Issue :
          GUSTAVUS.
vii. **WILLIAM**, *b.* August 8, 1793 ; *d. s. p.*
viii. **ELIZABETH**, *b.* January 25, 1795 ; *d. s. p.*
ix.   **MIFFLIN**, *b.* April 11, 1796 ; *d. s. p.* October 9, 1821.
x.   **HENRY**, *b.* September 15, 1797 ; *d.* August 28, 1798.
xi.   **JOHN**, *b.* March 7, 1799, *of whom presently.*
xii. **HENRY EDWARD**, *b.* January 1, 1802 ; *d.* September 11, 1803.

JOHN, eleventh child of **Richard Snowden** and **Mary Thomas**,
b. March 7, 1799, *m.*, in May or June, 1826, **HARRIET
MARIA STRONG** ; he *d.* August 18, 1837, and his wife
January 7, 1866.   Issue :

i. **MARY SUSANNA**, *b.* in May, 1829 ; *d.* in September, 1829.
ii. **HENRY MIFFLIN**, *b.* April 1, 1831 ; *m.*, November 27, 1860, **SARAH
    LOUISA CHAMBERLAIN**, and *d.* April 15, 1889.   Issue :

    i.   MIFFLIN WILBER, *b.* September 12, 1861.
    ii.   ELLA CHAMBERLAIN, *b.* May 7, 1864 ; *m.*, January 21, 1892, JAMES AL-
          FRED PERKINS, JR., of Philadelphia.
    iii. RICHARD SNOWDEN, *b.* January 23, 1866.
    iv.   LAURA REBECCA, *b.* September 16, 1867.
    v.   JOHN ALEXANDER, *b.* June 8, 1874.
    vi.   LOUISE HENRY, *b.* March 3, 1877 ; *d.* October 21, 1881.

iii. **JOHN EVAN**, *b.* January 28, 1834 ; *m.*, February 22, 1865, **LAURA
     CORNELIA TILDEN**, who *d.* September 4, 1893.   Issue :

JOHN CHEW THOMAS
From a Portrait by St. Memin

i.   **GEORGE HINES**, *b.* February 23, 1866; *m.*, January 15, 1889, **KATHERINE ESTELLA BRICE**. Issue: Robert Earle, *b.* July 29, 1890, and **William Harvey**, *b.* April 11, 1893.

ii. **JOHN EVAN** and **HARRIET MAUD**, twins, *b.* November 7, 1867; the former *d.* August 23, 1868; the latter *d. u.* February 9, 1887.

iii. **MARY MIFFLIN**, *b.* December 12, 1870.

iv. **LAWRENCE ALEXANDER**, *b.* March 6, 1837.

JOHN CHEW, fourth son of **Samuel** and **Mary (Thomas) Thomas**, *b.* October 15, 1764, entered the University of Pennsylvania 1780, graduated in 1783, A.M.; resided after his marriage at "Fairland" in Anne Arundel Co. (now site of a post town), which place he afterward sold for $50,000. He was a man of high character, and an active member of the Society of Friends. He was a lawyer by profession, admitted to the Bar at Philadelphia, Pa., December 15, 1787, and in early life took an interest in politics and was elected by the Federal party in Maryland one of their representatives in the Congress of 1799–1801. As a member of that House he took part in the celebrated election of President in the last-named year, which, after three days of intense excitement, and thirty-five ballots, resulted in the election of Thomas Jefferson, and the transfer of the government to the Republican party. After this he declined a re-election. At Indian Spring Monthly Meeting, held at Sandy Spring June 21, 1811, Mary S. Thomas and her five children, Henrietta, John C., Richard Henry, Samuel E., and Julia request that "they be received as members of Society." Committee appointed to visit the family July 19, and her husband's consent being given, they were admitted September 20, 1811. Mr. Thomas appears to have been a Friend, and lost his membership, probably because of marrying out of meeting and to a slaveholder. February 12, 1812, he manumitted his slaves to the number of over one hundred, and, April 11, 1812, applied to be re-instated, and before August 7th of that year was received again into membership with the Society. February 21, 1817, he was appointed clerk of Indian Spring Meeting. He *m.*, September 18, 1788,[1] **MARY**, only *dau.* and heiress of **Richard** and **Eliza (Rutland) Snowden** (*q. v.*) of "Fairland," Anne Arundel Co., Maryland, and *d.* at his residence in Ridley, Pa., May 10, 1836. His wife *d.* November 13, 1844, at the residence of her son, Dr. Richard H. Thomas. Issue:[1]

[1] Family Bible of Hon. J. C. Thomas, now in the possession of his grandson, Dr. Richard H. Thomas, of Baltimore.

i.   **MARY ANN,** *b.* January 23, 1789 ; *d.* April 4, 1790.
ii.   **ANN SNOWDEN,** *b.* March 13, 1791 ; *d.* October 2, 1791.
iii.   **ELIZA SNOWDEN,** *b.* August 8, 1792 ; *m.,* May 3, 1810, **GEORGE GRAY LEIPER,** of " Lapidea " (*q. v.*).
iv.   **SAMUEL,** *b.* March 28, 1794 ; *d.* September 14, 1804.
v.   **THOMAS SNOWDEN,** *b.* February 19, 1796, *of whom presently.*
vi.   **JOHN CHEW,** *b.* August 21, 1797 ; *d.* March 15, 1799.
vii.   **HENRIETTA MARIA,** *b.* July 30, 1799 ; *d. u.* January 17, 1874, at the residence of the family of her brother, Dr. Richard H. Thomas, over which she had exercised a mother's care from the time of their own mother's death.
viii.   **MARY SNOWDEN,** *b.* September 22, 1801 ; *d.* August 13, 1802.
ix.   **Dr. JOHN CHEW,** *b.* September 22, 1803 (*q. v.*).
x.   **Dr. RICHARD HENRY,** *b.* June 20, 1805 (*q. v.*).
xi.   **SAMUEL EVAN,** *b.* March 12, 1807 (*q. v.*).
xii.   **JULIA,** *b.* August 16, 1808, a Minister of the Society of Friends ; *m.,* April 20, 1845, **BOND VALENTINE,** of Bellefonte, Centre Co., Pa., a Minister of the Society of Friends, and *d. s. p.* April 14, 1892.
xiii.   **HARRIET,** *b.* March 20 and *d.* March 27, 1811.
xiv.   **MARIA RUSSELL,** *b.* August 29, 1812 ; *d.* in November, 1816.
xv.   **CHARLES,** *b.* August 18, 1816 ; *d.* in 1817.

THOMAS SNOWDEN, eldest son of **John Chew** and **Mary (Snowden) Thomas,** *b.* February 19, 1796, was at one time a member of the Legislature of Maryland, *m.,* December 21, 1819, by Reverend William Duke, Protestant Episcopal Minister of Elkton, Md., to **ANN,** *dau.* of **William** and **Frances (Russell) Sewall,** who *d.* October, 1882. He resided at North East, Cecil Co., Md., where he *d.* May 31, 1857. Issue :

i.   **JOHN CHEW,** *b.* November 9, 1820, a minister of the Methodist Episcopal Church, to which denomination his parents belonged. He *m.,* March 16, 1847, **ANNIE HEATH WILLIAMS,** of Newton, Bucks Co., Pa., and *d.* at Stroudsburg, in the same State, January 18, 1860. Issue :

    i.   **ANN,** *b.* July 19, 1848 ; *m.* **WILLIAM HARMAR THOMAS** (*q. v.*).
    ii.   **THOMAS SNOWDEN,** *b.* October 15, 1849 ; *d. y.*
    iii.   **GRIFFITH WILLIAMS,** *b.* February 10, 1853 ; *m.* February 10, 1874, **LIZZIE,** *dau.* of Peter B. Melick, of Philadelphia, and *d.* April, 1892. Issue : **Marion,** Peter Brittan, and Harrington.
    iv.   **FANNY BOSWELL,** *m.,* October 18, 1876, **HUBERT LYON SMITH,** of New Jersey.

ii.   **RUSSELL,** *b.* August 7, 1822 , *m.,* January 15, 1852, **ELIZABETH A. MITCHELL,** of Elkton, Md., and *d.* April 22, 1876. Issue :
    MARY ALICIA.

iii.   **ANN,** *b.* September 30, 1824 ; *d. u.* August 8, 1873.

iv. **FRANCES LOUISA**, *b.* August 26, 1826; *m.*, March 16, 1851, Reverend **WILLIAM LAWS BOSWELL**, a minister of the Methodist Episcopal Church, and at one time Professor at Dickinson College, Pa. She *d.* after a short illness, April 17, 1876. Issue (surname BOSWELL) :

  i. **JAMES IVERSON**, *b.* January 9, 1852. For some time a minister of the Methodist Episcopal Church ; *m.* **ELIZABETH HOOPER**, *dau.* of John and Mary Alicia (Mitchell) Stump.
  ii. **THOMAS SNOWDEN**, *b.* November 6, 1856; *d.* January 17, 1891.
  iii. **WILLIAM LAWS, JR.**, *b.* July 18, 1859.
  iv. **RUSSELL THOMAS**, *b.* November 27, 1863, attorney-at-law ; *m.* January 22, 1895, **MARTHA WEST**, *dau.* of Adam S. Bare, of Philadelphia.

  Professor **BOSWELL** *m.* 2d, March 16, 1882, **MARY ROWLAND**, *dau.* of Robert and Elizabeth (Rowland) Ervien. Issue :

  MARY ERVIEN, ETHEL, and **EDGAR ROWLAND.**

v. **THOMAS SNOWDEN**, *b.* July 28, 1828, a minister of the Methodist Episcopal Church, Chief Clerk of the Maryland House of Delegates 1860–61, U. S. Hospital Chaplain, 1862–65, and now editor of the *Peninsular Methodist ; m.*, April 20, 1854, **ANNA M. MILLER**, since *d.* Issue :

  i. **JOSEPH MILLER**, *b.* February 4, 1855 ; *m.* February 16, 1893, **SALLIE ALEXA**, *dau.* of Mrs. Mary A. Tyler. Issue : Anna Mary, *b.* December 5, 1893.
  ii. **MARY RUSSELL**, *d.* January 3, 1890.
  iii **ANN ELIZABETH.**
  iv. **FRANCES LOUISA.**
  v. **HENRIETTA MARIA.**
  vi. **MARTHA SNOWDEN**, *m.* October 17, 1894, **ALFRED KNIGHT CHAPMAN,** of Philadelphia.

vi. **EVAN W.**, *b.* September 13, 1829, was a Lieutenant in the Maryland Volunteers, United States Army, during the Civil War ; *m.*, June 7, 1866, **MARTHA GRAY**, *dau.* of Dr. **Samuel Thomas,** of Whitby Hall (*q. v.*). Issue :

  i. **SAMUEL**, *d. y.*
  ii. **EVAN W., JR.**
  iii. **ANNA.**
  iv. **RICHARD H.**, *d. i.*
  v. **MARTHA G.**, *d.* September 18, 1891.
  vi. **MARY M.**
  vii. **EMMA W.**

vii. **JAMES SEWALL**, *b.* December 21, 1831, a minister of the Methodist Episcopal Church ; *m.*, June 6, 1863, **EUNICE D. DRAKE.** Issue :

  i. **EVAN WALDEN**, *b.* February 26, 1864.
  ii. **ANNIE HEATH**, *b.* May 3, 1865 ; *d.* July, 1885.
  iii. **HELEN LOUISA**, *b.* February 4, 1867.
  iv. **THOMAS SNOWDEN**, *b.* March 17, 1869.
  v. **CARRIE RUSSELL**, *b.* September 20, 1871.

vi.   **GRACE WILBUR**, *b.* January 24, 1874.
vii.   **EDITH.**
viii. **EUNICE.**

viii.   **MARY RUSSELL**, *b.* May 24, 1835 ; *d.* January 11, 1849.
ix.   **ELIZA SNOWDEN.**

JOHN CHEW, JR., second surviving son of Hon. **John Chew** and **Mary (Snowden) Thomas**, *b.* at " Fairland," September 22, 1803, entered the University of Pennsylvania in 1818, was a member of the Philomathean Society, graduated 1821, A.M., and April 8, 1824, M.D., of its medical school, studying under Dr. N. Chapman, Dr. Physick, and others. He was for some time in the United States Government Service as Clerk of Works at the building of the Newcastle Breakwater, and was baptized in November, 1839, and confirmed by Bishop Onderdonk, in November, 1840, at Immanuel Church, Newcastle.[1] He finally settled in Baltimore, Md., practising his profession there very successfully, and residing first on Lombard Street and afterward at 55 Sharp Street, in a house which he built. He was a man of great social gifts, considerable inventive genius, and some artistic talent, painting quite well in oils. He was *m.*, March 2, 1848, at No. 89 East Broadway, New York City, by the Hon. William V. Brady, Mayor of the City, to **JANE LAWRENCE**, *dau.* of **Thomas** and **Anna (Lawrence) Buckley** (*q. v.*), a member of the Society of Friends, who afterward was baptized and confirmed in the Protestant Episcopal Church. Dr. Thomas *d.* August 29, 1862, at No. 54 McCulloh Street, Baltimore. Issue :[2]

i.   **LAWRENCE BUCKLEY**, *b.* December 6, 1848, *of whom presently.*
ii.   **JULIA**, *b.* March 9, 1850 ; *m.*, October 14, 1879, **JAMES VALENTINE WAGNER**, now Cashier of the National Marine Bank, Baltimore, and Consul of Nicaragua. Issue (surname WAGNER) :

    i.   **EFFINGHAM BUCKLEY**, *b.* October 22, 1883.
    ii. **EDGAR**, *b.* March 25, 1887.
   iii. **JULIAN T.**, *b.* April 9, 1894.

iii. **WALTER WOOD**, *b.* June 11, 1852 ; *m.* **MARY**, *dau.* of **Samuel**, dec'd, and **Sarah (Duck) Ellicott** (*q. v.*), who *d. s. p.* Whitsunday, June 9, 1889, at Brooke Meadow, Montgomery Co., Md.

LAWRENCE BUCKLEY,[3] eldest son of **Dr. John Chew** and **Jane Lawrence (Buckley) Thomas**, *b.* on Lombard Street, Baltimore, Wednesday, December 6, 1848 ; baptized June 8, 1851, by

---

[1] Parish Register.
[2] See his family Bible.
[3] The dates in this sketch are from records made at the time.

LAWRENCE BUCKLEY THOMAS, D.D.

Rev. H. V. D. Johns, D.D.; educated at Topping and Carey's Academy and the public schools of Baltimore ; Clerk, Librarian (Assistant at the Mercantile Library) ; Antiquarian Bookseller ; January 15, 1876, elected Secretary and Treasurer of the Baltimore Book Trade Association ; Librarian, Bishop Whittingham's Library, 1878–79 ; active lay worker in Emmanuel P. E. Church ; September, 1879, entered the General Theological Seminary, New York, and was graduated from it May 31, 1882 ; ordered Deacon by Bishop Horatio Potter, of New York, at S. John's Church in that city, Trinity Sunday, June 4, 1882 ; and Priest by Bishop Thomas M. Clark, of Rhode Island, at Grace Church, Providence, May 19, 1883 ; the following day received the degree of B.D. from the General Seminary, New York ; and June 20, 1894, that of D.D. from S. John's College, Annapolis, Md. Was minister at Eltingville, Staten Island, 1882 ; Rector, Pontiac, R. I., September 1882 ; established a Public Library there, 1884, and began a building fund for a church ; Assistant Minister Church of the Redeemer Bryn Mawr, Pa. ; April 10, 1885, organized the parish, gathered the congregation, and built the Church of S. Mary, at Ardmore, Pa., becoming its first Rector, May 1, 1887. In temporary charge of Christ Church, Pottstown, Pa., during the summer of 1888, in which time a fund was started under his auspices which has resulted in the erection of a town hospital there.

September 1, 1888, he accepted a call to the Rectorship of S. Stephen's Church, Beverly, N. J. ; while there paid off its debt, and began an endowment and a Parish building fund. In summer of 1892 in charge of S. Andrew's, West Philadelphia ; December 1,. 1892, Rector of Trinity Church, Antrim, Pa. ; October 1, 1893, Senior Curate of S. Peter's, Philadelphia ; and in November 1894, returned to Antrim, taking charge also of S. Andrew's, Tioga. Is author of "Genealogical Notes of Thomas and Other Families," Baltimore, 1877 ; supplement, 1878 ; "Dream of Arcadia," and other verses, 1879 ; "Pedigrees and Notes," 1883, and the present work. He is a member of the Society of Colonial Wars in the State of New York, of the New York Shakespeare Society, of the Conservative Club, Philadelphia, the Elmira Theological and Literary Society, and a corresponding member of the Wisconsin Historical Society, elected in 1879, the only official recognition accorded his genealogical labours. Dr. Thomas was *m.* October 11, 1882, at the Church of the Reformation, Brooklyn, N. Y., by the Rev. D. V. M. Johnson, D.D., assisted by the Rev. John G. Bacchus, to **MARY BERRY**, youngest *dau.* of **Thomas Farrell** and the late **Marion L. (Berry) McCobb** (*q. v.*), originally of Baltimore, Md., who *d. s. p.* Sunday, November 16, 1884, and is *bu.* in S. John's Churchyard, Waverly, Md.

DR. RICHARD HENRY, tenth child of **John Chew** and **Mary (Snowden) Thomas,** *b.* June 20, 1805, was educated at the University of Pennsylvania, graduated in 1822, sharing the first honours and having the English salutatory ; was graduated in its Medical School in 1827 ; afterward he settled in Baltimore, where he had one of the largest practices ; was a Professor in the Medical School of the University of Maryland, and an eminent Minister of the Society of Friends, in which capacity he travelled extensively in Europe and America. He *m.* 1st, May 13, 1830, **MARTHA,** *dau.* of **James** and **Hannah (Ellicott) Carey** (*q. v.*). Issue :

i.   **JAMES CAREY,** *b.* March 5, 1832 ; *d. i.*
ii.   **JAMES CAREY,** *b.* July 3, 1833, *of whom presently.*
iii.   **JOHN CHEW,** *b.* January 3, 1833 ; *d. i.*

DR. R. H. THOMAS, *m.* 2d, February 9, 1840, **PHEBE,** *dau.* of **John** and **Phebe (Hicks) Clapp,** of New York. Issue :

i   **JOHN CLAPP,** *b.* December 11, 1842 ; *m.*, June 11, 1873, **EUGENIA,** *dau.* of **Richard Cromwell,** of Baltimore.
ii   **HENRY,** *d. y.*
iii.   **ALLEN CLAPP,** *b.* December 26, 1846, Librarian and Professor of History at Haverford College, Pennsylvania, appointed, in 1878 ; author of a school history of the United States, and joint author with his brother Richard of a History of Friends, 1894 ; *m.*, August 20, 1872, **REBECCA H.,** *dau.* of **Russell** and **Phebe A. Marble,** of Woonsocket, R. I. Issue :

    i.   **EDWARD,** *b.* June 21, 1877.
    ii. **MIRIAM,** *b.* September 14, 1880.

iv.   **MARY SNOWDEN,** *m.*, October 14, 1890, **ISAAC,** son of **Charles Lloyd** and **Susannah (Wilson) Braithwaite** (*q. v.*).
v.   **CHARLES YARNALL,** *b.* October 16, 1851 ; *m.*, August 16, 1877, **REBECCA S.,** *dau.* of **Joseph** and **Mary Edge,** of Deer Creek, Md. Issue :

    i.   **RICHARD HENRY,** *b.* February 18, 1881.
    ii.   **ELIZABETH S.,** *b.* October 6, 1882.
    iii. **JOSEPH E.,** *b.* September 3, 1884.
    iv. **CHARLES EDGAR,** *b.* January 13, 1888.

vi.   **DR. RICHARD HENRY,** *b.* January 26, 1854 ; *m.*, March, 1878, at London, England, **ANNA LLOYD,** *dau.* of **Joseph Bevan Braithwaite,** Barrister, of that city. Issue :

    HENRIETTA MARTHA, *b.* May 24, 1879.

DR. R. H. THOMAS, *m.* 3d, February 9, 1859, **DEBORAH C. HINSDALE,** of New York City, a Minister of the Society of Friends, and *d. s. p.*, January 15, 1860 ; his widow *d.* July 2, 1889.

DR. JAMES CAREY, surviving son of **Dr. Richard H.** and **Martha (Carey) Thomas,** *b.* July 13, 1833, a practising physician, a trustee of the Johns Hopkins University of the City of Baltimore, and a prominent minister of the Society of Friends, President of the Young Men's Christian Association and actively engaged in religious and charitable work.

He *m.*, October 31, 1855, **Mary,** *dau.* of **John M. Whitall,** of the firm of Whitall, Tatum & Co., manufacturers of glass, Philadelphia and New Jersey. She became deeply interested in religious and phil-anthropic work, especially amongst women ; was an eminent minister of the Society of Friends ; one of the founders of the Young Women's Christian Association and the Women's Christian Temperance Union in Baltimore ; was State President of the latter from 1879 ; was for many years President of the Young Women's Christian Association, and of the Baltimore McAll Mission ; Vice-President of the Baltimore Orphan Asylum, and led a weekly Bible Class at Friends' Meeting House. July 2, 1888, she *d.* Issue :

i.   **MARTHA CAREY,** *b.* January 2, 1857, studied at Howland College, and Cornell University, New York ; went abroad and studied for some years at Leipsic and Zurich, receiving, in 1883, after a severe exam-ination and a learned thesis on "Sir Gawayne and the green knight," the degree of Ph.D., "*summa cum laude*," from the latter University. Returning home she was elected the first Dean of the Faculty of the new Taylor College for Women, established at Bryn Mawr, Pa., and, November, 1893, President of the college.

ii.   **JOHN M. WHITALL,** *b.* April 11, 1859 ; *m.*, October 24, 1883, at Twelfth Street Meeting, Philadelphia, **MARY CLARK,** *dau.* of **Richard L. Nicholson.** Issue :

    i.   **JAMES CAREY, JR.,** *b.* May 5, 1885.
    ii.   **RICHARD LINDSAY,** *b.* July 5, 1886 ; *d.* May 16, 1890.
    iii.   **MARJORIE NICHOLSON,** *b.* February 17, 1888.
    iv.   **LEONARD VON HOESEN,** *b.* September 27, 1893.

iii.   **DR. HENRY M.,** *b.* May 26, 1861 ; *m.*, October 10, 1889, **JOSEPHINE GIBSON,** *dau.* of **George G.** and **Josephine (Poe) Carey** (*q. v.*). Issue :

    i.   **GEORGE CAREY,** *d. i.*
    ii.   **HENRY MALCOLM,** *b.* December 30, 1891.

iv.   **BOND VALENTINE**, *b.* March 23, 1863; *m.*, October 13, 1886, **EDITH**, *dau.* of **Judge A. P.** and **Julia (Goodall) Carpenter**, of Concord, N. H., and is manager of Whitall, Tatum & Co.'s flint glass works, Millville, N. J.

v.   **JAMES W.**, *b.* March 4, 1865; *d. y.*

vi.   **MARY GRACE**, *b.* August 27, 1866; *m.*, May 24, 1887, **THOMAS KIMBER WORTHINGTON**. Issue (surname WORTHINGTON):

> **BOND VALENTINE, MARY DOROTHY,** and **HAROLD,** *b.* November, 1890.

vii. **MARGARET CHESTON**, *b.* March 13, 1869; *m.* **ANTHONY MORRIS CAREY** (*q. v.*) Issue (surname CAREY):

> **GALLOWAY CHESTON,** *b.* February 14, 1894.

viii. **HELEN W.**, *b.* August 14, 1871.

ix.   **FRANK SMITH**, *b.* February 15, 1873.

x.   **DORA C.**, *b.* June 12, 1877; *d. i.*

SAMUEL EVAN, youngest surviving son of **John Chew** and **Mary (Snowden) Thomas,** *b.* March 12, 1807; *m.* **ELLEN BROWN,** and was lost at sea in 1851; his widow *d.* in 1883. Issue :

i.   **ANNIE JULIA**, *m.* in 1859 **BENJAMIN C. WRIGHT**, druggist, who *d.* in 1879. Issue (surname WRIGHT):

> **ELLEN ELIZA.**

ii.   **JOHN CHEW**, *m.* **MARY ETHERIDGE**. Issue:

> **FRANK SMITH,** *b.* 1874.

iii. **MARY ELLEN**, *m.* **EDWARD H. GRANT** and *d.* 1874; her husband *d.* 1875. Issue (surname GRANT):

> i.   **ELIZABETH VIRGINIA.**
> ii. **EVELINA.**

EVAN WILLIAM, youngest son of **Samuel** and **Mary (Thomas) Thomas,** *b.* February 6, 1769; *m.* January 5, 1792, **MARTHA,** *dau.* of **George** and **Martha Gray,** of Whitby Hall, near Philadelphia, who *d.* February 9, 1868; he *d.* August 27, 1840. Issue :

i.   **MARY**, *b.* March 15, 1793; *m.* October 27, 1810, **DR. GUSTAVUS WARFIELD** (*q. v.*).

ii.   **GEORGE GRAY**, *b.* December 28, 1794; *d.* July 17, 1795.

iii. **EVAN WILLIAM**, *b.* May 22, 1796; *m.*, May 18, 1826, **ELIZA**, *dau.* of **Gen. Josiah Harmar,** of Philadelphia, and *d. s. p.* at Greenwood, near Whitby, September 17, 1838.

iv.   **GEORGE GRAY,** *b.* October 5, 1798 ; *m.,* 1st, September 29, 1834, **JANE H. GRAFF** ; 2d, **ANN GRAY,** *dau.* of **Thomas** and **Elizabeth Leiper** (*q. v.*), of Philadelphia, who *d.* April 18, 1881 ; he *d.* March 9, 1854. Issue by his 1st wife :

      EVAN WILLIAM, *b.* July 19, 1835 ; *d. n.* September 10, 1860.

v.   **SAMUEL,** *b.* July 20, 1802, *of whom presently.*

SAMUEL, youngest son of **Evan W.** and **Martha (Gray) Thomas,** *b.* July 20, 1802 ; entered the University of Pennsylvania, 1818 ; graduated, 1821, A.M.; member of the Philomathean Society ; M.D., 1825 ; resided at Whitby Hall, which he inherited under the will of his aunt, Ann Gray. The Hall was originally built by Colonel James Coultas in 1741, who made an addition in 1754. Dr. Thomas added another wing in 1849. He *m.,* April 11, 1832, **HENRIETTA GRAFF,** and *d.* February 17, 1864 ; his widow *d.* November 10, 1876. Issue :

i.   **GEORGE,** *d.* aged twelve.
ii.   **MARY,** *d. i.*
iii. **ANN,** *d. i.*
iv. **MARTHA GRAY,** *b.* January 26, 1841 ; *m.* **EVAN W.,** son of **Thomas S. Thomas** (*q. v.*).

v.   **HENRIETTA GRAFF,** *b.* May 30, 1843 ; *m.,* June 7, 1866, **CHARLES JAMES,** son of **Andrew Eastwick,** of Bartram Hall, Philadelphia, and *d.* February 9, 1883. Issue (surname EASTWICK) :

    i.   HENRIETTA THOMAS, *b.* May 21, 1868.
    ii.   CHARLES HENRY, *b.* August 22, 1870.
    iii. GEORGE GRAY THOMAS, *d. y.*
    iv. EMMA, *b.* December 29, 1874.
    v.   ROBERT, *b.* July 18, 1879.
    vi. RALPH, *b.* April 11, 1882 ; *d.* April 24, 1885.

vi. **WILLIAM HARMAR,** *b.* March 22, 1845 ; a real estate broker, Girard Building, Philadelphia ; inherited Whitby Hall and resides there ; *m.,* June 2, 1870, his cousin **NANNIE,** *dau.* of **Rev. John C.** and **Annie H. (Williams) Thomas** (*q. v.*). Issue :

    i.   ANNIE HEATH.
    ii.   JULIA V.
    iii   MABEL GRAY, *b.* September 12, 1880.

vii. **EMMA WARFIELD,** *b.* February 1, 1847 ; *m.,* June 2, 1870, **WILLIAM,** son of **Andrew Eastwick,** who *d.* Issue (surname EASTWICK) :

    i.   LYDIA (LILLIE), *b.* March 14, 1871.
    ii.   HENRIETTA THOMAS, *b.* July 14, 1872 ; *d. y.*
    iii. WILLIAM, *b.* November 19, 1874.
    iv. HENRY THOMAS, *b.* April 3, 1877.
    v.   MARY EMMA, *b.* August 5, 1879.
    vi. HARMAR THOMAS, *b.* January 20, 1882.
    vii. GEORGE KLEMM, *b.* November 19, 1885.

PHILIP, second son of **Philip** and **Anne (Chew) Thomas**, *b.* July 3, 1727, inherited from his father one-half of his estate at Susquehannah Ferry, including Mount Ararat, and extending from Perryville to Port Deposit, in all about two thousand acres. He resided at West River, where he *d.* February 22, 1784. He *m.*, April 30, 1754, **ANNE (Harris)**, widow of **Joseph Galloway**. Issue:

An only son, **PHILIP**.

This Philip Thomas, Jun., son of Philip and Anne (Harris) Thomas, lived at Rockland, Cecil Co., Md. He owned large quantities of land, embracing Mount Ararat and Yorkshire, and others near the ferry at Port Deposit. After his death this property, not being susceptible of division, was taken by his eldest son, he agreeing to pay the other heirs for their portions of the estate, and October 21, 1812, he caused the lower part of the town of Port Deposit to be laid out in streets and lots, by Hugh Beard, surveyor.[1] It is of him the family legend is told, which relates that one evening he and two of his cronies, Thomas Rutland the 4th, and Thomas Snowden, of Summerville, were together waiting for the fourth member of their party to engage in playing cards, as was their custom, for high stakes. A furious storm was raging, and he failed to come. A dummy was tried, but to little satisfaction. Excited by frequent potations Snowden finally expressed a wish for another partner "if it were the Devil himself." The words were hardly spoken before a terrible clap of thunder sounded, and in the lull that followed a rap was heard at the door. On its opening a gentleman dressed in sombre black appeared, who was uproariously greeted by the party, and by all pressed to take a hand in the game. "Nay," he is reported to have answered, "but ye will all take a hand with me ere the year is ended." The story goes on to relate that within the fatal year all three died suddenly.

He *m.*, March 7, 1782, at her father's residence, **SARAH MARGA-RET**, *dau.* of **William** and **Catherine (Compton) Weems**, of Weems Forest, Calvert Co. She *d.* July 22, 1784, and her husband April 3, 1809. Issue:

i.   **PHILIP**, *b.* October 22, 1783, *of whom presently.*
ii. **CATHERINE**, *b.* October 2, 1785; *m.* May 1, 1804, at Rockland, **GEORGE DAVIDSON**, of the Eastern Shore, and *d.* Issue (surname DAVIDSON):

[1] Johnston's Cecil County, *p.* 394.

  i. **DR. JAMES P.**, *m.* **ANN**, *dau.* of Governor William Paca, of Maryland. Issue: **Philemon.**
  ii. **PHILIP**, *m.* **MARY**, *dau.* of —— **Earle**, and *d. s. p.*
  iii. **SARAH**, *d. u.*
  iv. **ELIZABETH**, *m.* **BENJAMIN T. OWEN**, and had one son, **George**, *m.* Hannah Mercier, and had a *dau.*
  v. **FANNIE**, *d. u.*
  vi. **WILLIAM.**

iii. **ANN WEEMS**, *b.* July 18, 1787; after her sister's death *m.* **GEORGE DAVIDSON** as his second wife, June 2, 1825, and *d.* Issue (surname DAVIDSON):

  i. **CHARLES HENRY WHARTON**, *d. u.*
  ii. **JOHN MERRYMAN**, *m.* —— and has issue.

iv. **JOHN WEEMS**, *b.* January 27, 1789, educated at S. John's College, Annapolis, Md. ; *m.* January 7, 1813, **ANN WEBSTER**, of Baltimore. He resided near Port Deposit, Cecil Co., Md. ; was manager of the Canal there, at one time member of the State Legislature, and *d.* about 1834. Issue :

  i. **PHILIP**, *m.* and had issue.
  ii. **ELIZABETH WEEMS**, *m.* **REV. OWEN PATTEN THACKARA**, of Florida, in 1860 Rector of S. Peter's Church, Fernandina ; *d.* August 2, 1885. Issue (surname THACKARA): Juan Serrano, John Weems, Elizabeth James, *m.* June 11, 1874, Arthur W. Palmer, of Baltimore, and had one child, Emma Louise ; Samuel, and Philip Thomas.

v. **JAMES**, *b.* December 20, 1792 ; *d. u.* November 27, 1826.
vi. **MARY**, *b.* April 15, 1795 ; *d. i.*
vii. **WILLIAM**, *b.* December 3, 1796 ; *d. i.*
viii. **WILLIAM THORNTON**, *b.* November 3, 1797 ; *d. i.*
ix. **MARY FRANCES CAROLINE**, *b.* April 1, 1798 ; *m.* February 28, 1828, **JEREMIAH S. H. BOIES**, of Boston, Mass., and *d.* May 30, 1858. Issue (surname BOIES) :

  i. **JEREMIAH S.**, *b.* September 11, 1831 ; *d. u.* October 4, 1858.
  ii. **JAMES THOMAS**, *b.* December 26, 1832 ; *d. u.* April 2, 1859.
  iii. **SARAH H.**, *b.* March 31, 1834 ; *m.*, September 28, 1858, **RICHARD A. F. PENROSE, M.D., LL.D.** (*q. v.*).
  iv. **WILLIAM HUBBARD**, *b.* April 9, 1836.

x. **CHARLES HENRY**, *b.* July 10, 1799, *d. i.*
xi. **BENJAMIN OGLE**, *b.* November 5, 1800, *d. i.*
xii. **ELIZABETH ALICE**, *b.* September 20, 1802, *d. i.*
xiii. **CAROLINE LOUISA**, *b.* January 3, 1804, *d. i.*
xiv. **GEORGE ARCHER**, *b.* October 31, 1805, *m.* **HENRIETTA MARIA**, *dau.* of Samuel Chamberlain, of Talbot Co., Md., and *d.* Issue :

  NANNIE.

PHILIP, eldest son of **Philip** and **Sarah Margaret (Weems) Thomas**, *b.* October 22, 1783 ; *m.*, October 29, 1807, **FRANCES MARY**, *dau.* of **James** and **Elizabeth (Harrison) Ludlow**, of New York City, and *d.* about 1848. Issue :

i. **ELIZABETH FRANCES**, *d. u.* December 30, 1884.

ii. **SARAH MARGARET**, *m.* **SAMUEL TONKIN JONES**, of Philadelphia, and *d.* Issue (surname JONES) :

    i. **FRANCES MARY**, *m.*, 1st. **RICHARD MONTGOMERY PELL**, and 2d, June 11, 1894, **LOUIS T. HOYT.**

iii. **CATHERINE ANN**, *m.* **WILLIAM BRADFORD BEND**, of New York, since *d.*, and *d.* August 1, 1884. Issue (surname BEND) :

    i. **WILLIAM BRADFORD**, *m.* **ISABELLA TOMES**. Issue : i. Isabella Hadden *m.* George Edward Ward. ii. Edith Ludlow. iii. Harold F. iv. Meredith.

    ii. **FRANCES LUDLOW**, *d. y.*

    iii. **GEORGE HOFFMAN**, stock broker, *m.* **ELIZABETH TOWNSEND**. Issue : 1. Amy. ii. Beatrice.

    iv. **KATHARINE ANN**, *m.* **JAMES KENNEDY WHITAKER**. Issue (surname WHITAKER) : i. Ogden Hoffman, *d.* April 24, 1885. ii. Marion L.

    v. **ELIZABETH PELHAM**, *m.* **HENRY A. ROBBINS**. Issue (surname ROBBINS) : i. Maud. ii. Henry Pelham.

    vi. **MARY LUDLOW.**

    vii. **FANNY**, *d. y.*

iv. **PHILIP WILLIAM**, *m.* **Mrs. ANNA (ELLIARD) RAYMOND.** Issue :

    FRANCES MARY LUDLOW.

v. **MARTHA MARY**, *m.*, as his second wife, **SAMUEL TONKIN JONES.** Issue (surname JONES) :

    i. **SARAH MARGARET**, *m.* **HENRY BEADEL**. Issue : i. Henry Ludlow. ii. Gerald Woodward.

    ii. **SAMUEL TONKIN**, Jr., *d. y.*

    iii. **SHIPLEY.**

    iv. **ELIZABETH LUDLOW**, *m.* **JOHN DASH VAN BUREN**, Jr. Issue (surname VAN BUREN) : i. John Dash, Jr., *b.* April 28, 1884. ii. Maurice Pelham.

vi. **LUDLOW**, educated at Columbia College ; began business with William B. Bond & Co. ; afterward joined the firm of S. T. Jones & Co. ; then entered the Stock Exchange in 1853 ; was for more than twenty-five years active as a vestryman of Christ Church, Brooklyn ; *m.*, in 1854, **MARY SMART**, *dau.* of **Samuel Thompson**, of Brooklyn, owner of the Black Star Liverpool Packets, and *d.* at Glengariff, Ireland, August 11, 1894. Issue :

    MARY LUDLOW.

JOHN, youngest son of **Philip** and **Ann (Chew) Thomas**, *b.* August 26, 1743 ; resided at Lebanon, West River, Anne Arundel Co., Md.; he was one of the original visitors and governors of S. John's College, Annapolis, 1784 ; President of the Senate of Maryland ; wrote a number of occasional verses printed in a collection at Annapolis, 1808 ; *m.*, August 23, 1777, **SARAH**, third child of **Dr. William Murray**, and *d.* February 3, 1805. Issue :

i.   **ANNE,** *b.* July 6, 1788 ; *d. u.* April, 1848.
ii.   **PHILIP JOHN,** *b.* July 29, 1782, *of whom presently.*
iii. **SARAH,** *b.* October 28, 1784 ; *d. u.* October 12, 1860.
iv. **JOHN,** *b.* April 27, 1788 (*q. v.*).

PHILIP JOHN, eldest son of **John** and **Sarah (Murray)**
Thomas, *b.* July 29, 1782 ; resided at Mt. Lothian, West River,
Md.; educated at S. John's College, Annapolis ; was author of
" Tales of an American Landlord," in 2 vols., 12mo ; *m.,* No-
vember 8, 1804, **CORNELIA,** *dau.* of **Thomas Lancaster**
Lansdale, and *d.* June 15, 1859. Issue :

i.   **MARY** and ii. **CORNELIA,** both *m.* **DR. JAMES CHESTON** (*q. v.*).
iii. **JOHN MOYLAN,** *of whom presently.*

JOHN MOYLAN, only son of **Philip John** and **Cornelia (Lans-**
dale) Thomas, *b.* September 26, 1805 ; practised medicine in
Washington, D. C.; *m.,* July 25, 1829, **SARAH BROOKE**
LEE, *dau.* of **Tench Ringgold,** and *d.* October 15, 1853. Issue :

i.   **MARY,** *b.* May 11, 1830.
ii.   **ELIZA LEE,** *b.* August 8, 1831 ; *d. u.* October, 1865.
iii. **JOHN MOYLAN,** *b.* March 2, 1833, an attorney-at-law, of Philadelphia,
      Pa. ; *m.,* October 24, 1860, **ADELE,** *dau.* of **Charles Ingersoll** (*q.*
      v.), of that city. Issue :

    i.   **HELEN RINGGOLD,** *b.* January 12, 1862.
    ii.   **CHARLES INGERSOLL,** *b.* November 27, 1865.
    iii. **MARY GEORGINA LEE,** *b.* September 9, 1870 ; *m.,* January 22, 1890, **FRANK**
        WALTER, of Yew Lodge, Felcourt, Surrey, England.

iv. **CORNELIA LANSDALE,** *b.* September 5, 1834.
v.   **LAWRENCE RINGGOLD,** *b.* September, 1836.
vi. **SAMUEL SPRIGG,** *b.* March 31, 1838.
vii. **SARAH BROOKE LEE,** *b.* April 6, 1840.
viii. **ANNA MARIA,** *b.* January 19, 1842.
ix. **WILLIAM LANSDALE,** *b.* June 26, 1844 ; *d. i.*
x.   **CATHARINE LOUISA,** *b.* June 29, 1845 ; *d. i.*

JOHN, youngest son of **John** and **Sarah (Murray) Thomas,** *b.*
April 27, 1788 ; educated at S. John's College, Annapolis, Md.;
Member of the House of Delegates ; *m.,* December 31, 1817,
ELIZABETH, fourth *dau.* of **Commodore Alexander**
Murray, of Philadelphia, and *d.* December 27, 1858 ; his wife
also *d.* Issue :

i.   **SALLY.**
ii.   **JULIA MURRAY.**

iii. **ALEXANDER MURRAY**, educated at S. John's College, Annapolis, Md.; *d. u.* July 11, 1882.

iv. **DANIEL MURRAY**, graduated at S. John's College, Annapolis, Md., 1846 ; Visitor and Governor of the College, 1859 ; an attorney-at-law of Baltimore, and a prominent member of the Protestant Episcopal Church.

v. **MARY**, *m.* **A. HAMILTON HALL**, of West River, who *d.* June 2, 1885. Issue, an only son (surname HALL) :

> JOHN THOMAS, *m.*, January 21, 1886, ELLA, *dau.* of Colonel Frank M. Hall, of Prince George Co., Md. Issue (surname HALL) : i. Eugenia, *b.* May 4, 1887. ii. Daniel Thomas, *b.* October 20, 1888. iii. Elizabeth Snowden, *b.* October 18, 1890. iv. John Thomas, *b.* September 6, 1892.

vi. **CORNELIA**, *d. u.* March 5, 1887.

JOHN, the second son of **Samuel** and **Mary (Hutchins) Thomas**, *m.*, in April, 1727, **ELIZABETH**, *dau.* of **Richard** and **Mary Snowden** (*q. v.*), and *d.* in February, 1749-50. Issue by his wife, who pre-deceased him :

i. **RICHARD**, *of whom presently.*

ii. **SAMUEL**, *d. s. p.*

iii. **ELIZABETH**, *m.* **RICHARD RICHARDSON** (*q. v.*).

iv **JOHN**, *b.* in 1734 ; *m.* **MARGARET HOPKINS**, who *d.* March 16, 1806, aged seventy-five years, and her husband February 15, 1826, without issue surviving.

RICHARD, eldest son of **John** and **Elizabeth (Snowden) Thomas**, *b.* about 1728 ; *m.* **SARAH**, *dau.* of **Skipwith** and **Margaret (Holland) Coale** (*q. v.*) ; was disowned by the meeting, and December 25, 1766, they acknowledged their error in marriage and with their children were received into membership of West River Meeting. Issue :

i. **SAMUEL** 3d, *b.* December 2, 1753, *of whom presently.*

ii. **ELIZABETH**, *b.* October 28, 1755 ; *m.* **ROGER JOHNSON** (*q. v.*), and was disowned by Sandy Spring meeting, February 16, 1781.

iii. **RICHARD**, *b.* February 21, 1758 (*q. v.*).

iv. **JOHN**, *b.* September 27, 1760 ; *d. s. p.*

v. **MARY**, *b.* March 12, 1762 ; *m.* **WILLIAM ROBERTSON**. Issue (surname ROBERTSON) :

> i. SARAH, *m.* JOSEPH HOWARD (*q. v.*).
> ii. THOMAS, *m.* JANE RITTENHOUSE.

vi. **SARAH**, *b.* November 26, 1764 ; *m.* **BERNARD GILPIN** (*q. v.*).

vii. **HENRIETTA**, *b.* February 17, 1767 ; *d. i.*

viii. **MARGARET**, *b.* June 11, 1769 ; *m.* **GERARD BROOKE** (*q. v.*).

ix.   **WILLIAM,** *b.* December 11, 1771 (*q. v.*).
x.   **ANN,** *b.* May 25, 1774 ; *d. s. p.*
xi.   **HENRIETTA** 2d, *b.* March 7, 1777 ; *d. s. p.*

SAMUEL, eldest son of **Richard** and **Sarah (Coale) Thomas,**
b. December 2, 1753, settled in Montgomery Co., Md., and *m.*,
October 31, 1775, **MARY,** *dau.* of **John Cowman,** at her
father's residence, who *d.* before 1808.   Issue :

i.   **SAMUEL,** *b.* November 13, 1776, *of whom presently.*
ii.   **JOHN** 3d, *b.* January 30, 1778 (*q. v.*).
iii. **SARAH,** *b.* January 25, 1781 ; *m.* September 21, 1808, **WILLIAM
      CANBY.** Issue (surname CANBY) :

      SAMUEL, *m.* JULIET COCUS, and had a son : William T.

iv.   **HENRIETTA,** *b.* December 9, 1782 ; *m.* **CALEB BENTLEY** (*q. v.*).
v.   **ELIZABETH,** *b.* April 28, 1784 ; *m.*, October 13, 1825, **JAZER GAR-
      RETTSON,** and *d. s. p.*
vi.   **MARY,** *b.* November 16, 1785 ; *m.* **JOSEPH HOWARD** (*q. v.*), and was
      testified against by Sandy Spring Meeting, February 3, 1803, for doing
      so.

SAMUEL, eldest son of **Samuel** and **Mary (Cowman) Thomas,** *b.* November 13, 1776 ; *m.* **MARY,** *dau.* of **Joshua** and
Rebecca (Owings) Howard (*q. v.*).   Issue :

i.   **REBECCA OWINGS,** *b.* December 15, 1797 ; *d. s. p.*
ii.   **MATILDA BEALL,** *b.* February 10, 1800 ; *d. s. p.*
iii. **MARY ANN,** *b.* December 27, 1801 ; *m.* 1st, **CHARLES WORTH-
      INGTON,** and had a son, **Joseph Wilson;** and after his death *m.*
      2d, **JACOB SCHLEICH.**
iv.   **JOSHUA HOWARD,** *b.* March 10, 1804 ; *m.* 1st, **LUCY COL-
      STON.** Issue :

      i.   MARY ELIZABETH, *m.* Dr. SAMUEL WATKINS.
      ii.   SUSAN MATILDA, 2d wife of Dr. SAMUEL WATKINS.
      iii. LUCY HOWARD, *m.* WILLIAM EDSON.
      iv.   ANN REBECCA, *m.* her cousin, SAMUEL WALLACE THOMAS (*q. v.*).
      v.   VIRGINIA YOUNG, *m.* —— NALL.
      vi.   ALICE HENRIETTA, *m.* JOHN G. CLOYD, of Decatur, Ill.

      JOSHUA H. THOMAS, *m.* 2d, **FANNY OWINGS.** Further issue :

      vii. FANNY ZORAYDA, *m.* SAMUEL ROBERTSON, of Elizabethtown, Ky.
      viii. SAMUEL HOWARD.

v.   **JAMES BAYARD,** *b.* February 4, 1806 ; resided in Jefferson City, Mo. ;
      m. **ELIZABETH J. A. GOODWIN,** of Boston, Mass.
vi.   **HENRIETTA ELIZA,** *b.* July 3, 1809 ; *m.* **WILLIAM HENRY
      BRIGGS,** of Brookeville, Md. (*q. v.*).

vii.   **SAMUEL BEALL,** *b.* August 4, 1811, *of whom presently.*

viii.   **SALLY CATHERINE,** *b.* February 5, 1814; *m.* **THOMAS B. MUNFORD.** Issue (surname MUNFORD):

    i.   **THOMAS SAMUEL,** *b.* in May, 1840; *m.* **ETTA GUNTER.**
    ii.   **SARAH ELIZA,** *b.* in 1841; *m.* **W. H. BRENTZ.**
    iii.   **ZORAYDA OWINGS,** *m.* **J. W. MATTHIS.**
    iv.   **ANN AMELIA,** *m.* **GEORGE BROWNFIELD.**
    v.   **ELLEN BAYARD,** *m.* **JOHN Q. WYMAN.**
    vi.   **WILLIAM HENRY.**

ix.   **JOSEPH HENRY,** *b.* February 18, 1817; *m.* **AMANDA LA RUE.** Issue:

    i.   **WARREN LA RUE,** *b.* January 25, 1845; *m.* **MARY H. WARDROPER.**
    ii.   **MARY HELEN,** *b.* August 16, 1847; *m.* **A. C. HODGES.**
    iii.   **ELIZA HOWARD,** *b.* November 14, 1849; *m.* **CHARLES W. SWANSON.**
    iv.   **VIRGINIA BEAL,** *b.* September 15, 1851; *m.* **SAMUEL V. LEIDOM.**
    v.   **ANNA BROOKS,** *b.* June 27, 1853.
    vi.   **ELLA OWINGS,** *b.* September 26, 1856.
    vii.   **WILLIAM BAYARD,** *b.* February 14, 1861.

x.   **SUSAN AMELIA,** *b.* December 10, 1820; *m.* **JAMES COX.** Issue (surname COX):

    i.   **DAVID YOUNG.**
    ii.   **MAY THOMAS,** *m.* —— **AYRE.**
    iii.   **ROLAND HUGHS.**
    iv.   **MEHETABLE.**
    v.   **JAMES HENRY.**
    vi.   **BOYD.**
    vii.   **SAMUEL HENRY.**
    viii.   **ELI.**
    ix.   **NANNIE.**

SAMUEL BEALL, third son of **Samuel** and **Mary (Howard) Thomas,** *b.* August 4, 1811, at the age of twenty removed to Kentucky, and went into the employ of Colonel Edward P. Johnson, of Scott Co., then the largest stage contractor in that State. Assisted by that gentleman, after a few years he went into the same business on his own account and soon became very successful, controlling a number of lines. He was among the first who suggested the Louisville & Nashville Railroad and afterwards was one of its most efficient directors. Some time since he originated the project of building a road at right angles with the Nashville line, and after years of labor and the liberal use of his money and influence in its favor, the Elizabethtown & Paducah Railroad was built. Naturally he was made its first president, and after the election of Mr. Dulaney he remained a director, which position he held up to the time of his death.

Colonel Thomas amassed a large fortune during these busy

years of his life. Much of his property was in the city of Louisville, and the splendid "Thomas Building," on Fourth Street near Walnut, will long remind the citizens of him. After the disastrous fire of 1869, which laid waste one half of the city, he procured money for the sufferers with which to rebuild, he himself going security without asking a guarantee in his favor, and to him is owing in a great measure the beautiful row of buildings, of which Main-Cross Street boasts to-day. He *m.* **ZORAYDA YOUNG**, who *d.* in January, 1873, and her husband *d.* December 3, 1874. Issue :

i. **JAMES HOWARD,** *b.* in 1836 ; *d.* in 1856.
ii. **SAMUEL WALLACE,** *b.* in 1838 ; *m.* **ANNA REBECCA,** *dau.* of Joshua H. and Lucy (Colston) Thomas, and *d. s. p.*
iii. **MARY LIZZIE,** *b.* in 1840, *m.* Colonel **JAMES B. PAYNE,** of Elizabethtown, Ky. Issue (surname PAYNE) :

    i.   **SAMUEL THOMAS.**
    ii.   **LIZZIE ROBINSON.**
    iii.   **ELLA THOMAS.**
    iv.   **ZORAYDA YOUNG.**
    v.   **EDWARD CHURCHILL,** *d.*
    vi.   **SUSAN CHURCHILL.**
    vii.   **MARY,** *d.*
    viii. **JAMES B.,** *d.*
    ix.   **ELIZA C.**
    x.   **JULIA BLACKBURNE.**

iv. **ANN ZORAYDA,** *b.* in 1844.
v. **ELLEN MATILDA,** *b.* in 1846 ; *m.* **GEORGE W. WELCH,** Jr., Cashier First National Bank, Danville, Ky. Issue (surname WELCH) :

    i.   **ZORAYDA YOUNG.**
    ii.   **MARY BREATH.**
    iii.   **THOMAS SAMUEL,** *d.*

JOHN, second son of **Samuel** and **Mary (Cowman) Thomas,** *b.* January 30, 1778 ; *m.* ——— **BERRY.** Issue :

i. **CHARLOTTE,** *m.* **WALTER GODEY** (*q. v.*).
ii. **NICHOLAS,** living in Georgia in 1845, removed probably to California ; [1] *m.* ——— **HIGGINS.** Issue :

    i.   **JOHN.**
    ii.   **MARY.**
    iii.   **NICHOLAS.**
    iv.   **WILLIAM.**

iii. **MARY.**
iv. **CAROLINE,** *d. s. p.*

---

[1] The author would be very glad to be put on the track of this branch of the family, the only one of which he has not a full record.

RICHARD, Jr., second son of **Richard** and **Sarah (Coale) Thomas,** *b.* February 21, 1758, resided at Brookeville, Montgomery Co., Md. He *m.* **DEBORAH,** *dau.* of **Roger** and **Mary** (——) **Brooke** (*q. v.*), who was disowned for her marriage, by Sandy Spring Meeting, April 18, 1783, and *d.* November 12, 1814, and her husband November 6, 1821. Issue :

i.   **ELIZA P.,** *b.* August 1, 1784 ; *d. u.* in 1854.
ii.   **FREDERICK AUGUSTUS,** *b.* September 27, 1788 ; *d.* August 16, 1794.
iii. **MARY,** *b.* October 18, 1791 ; *d.* August 21, 1794.
iv.   **SARAH BROOKE,** *b.* April 26, 1794 ; *d.* September 25, 1826.
v.   **DEBORAH,** *b.* March 2, 1796 ; *d.* May 27, 1797.
vi.   **MARGARET E.,** *b.* March 3, 1798 ; *m.,* May 22, 1816, **ROBERT H.,** son of **William** and **Hannah Garrigues,** of Philadelphia.
vii. **ROGER BROOKE,** *b.* April 9, 1803.

WILLIAM, fourth son of **Richard** and **Sarah (Coale) Thomas,** *b.* December 11, 1771. Sandy Spring Meeting states, was *m.* before December 20, 1799, " by a hireling teacher," to **MARTHA PATRICK,** who is reported to have exchanged the Emigrant Philip Thomas's silver service about 1860, somewhat battered probably by this date, for shining new plated ware. Issue :

i.   **ANNE POULTNEY,** *b.* April 14, 1801 ; *d. u.* March 5, 1830.
ii.   **ELIZA,** *b.* April 10, 1803 ; *m.* **WILLIAM HENRY STABLER** (*q. v.*).
iii. **MARIA R.,** *b.* November 23, 1804.
iv.   **HENRIETTA,** *b.* February 21, 1807 ; *d.* October 14, 1821.
v.   **RICHARD,** *b.* April 19, 1809 ; *d.* October 15, 1820.
vi.   **EDWARD,** *b.* June 22, 1811, *of whom presently.*
vii. **WILLIAM JOHN,** *b.* September 15, 1813 (*q. v.*).
viii. **SAMUEL PATRICK,** *b.* January 23, 1816 ; *m.* **ELIZA G. PORTER.**
ix.   **JANE,** *b.* May 20, 1818 ; *m.* **CHARLES G. PORTER.**
x.   **MARTHA,** *b.* February 3, 1822 ; *m.* **THOMAS P. HARVEY,** and *d.* July 9, 1881. Issue (surname HARVEY) :

    i.   **GRACE.**
    ii.   **WILLIAM.**
    iii. **JAMES CLARENCE,** *m.* ——, and had issue : James Clarence, *b.* June 10, 1890.
    iv.   **EDWARD EUGENE,** *m.* **MARTHA CARSON,** who *d.* November 6, 1891. Issue : Grace Swann, *b.* December 25, 1885.
    v.   **SWANN.**

EDWARD, eldest surviving son of **William** and **Martha (Patrick) Thomas,** *b.* June 22, 1811 ; resides at Ashland Farm, in Montgomery Co., Md. He *m.,* April 25, 1833, **LYDIA S.,** *dau.* of **Joseph** and **Sarah Gilpin.** Issue :

i. **MARCELLA,** *b.* February 13, 1834 ; *m.*, in May, 1853, **ROBERT SUL-LIVAN,** and *d.* 1893, leaving a son, **Joseph,** who resides at Moorestown, N. J.

ii. **RICHARD PIERCE,** b. January 6, 1836, removed to Baltimore and engaged in mercantile life ; *m.*, September 29, 1857, **HARRIET,** *dau.* of **John** and **Mary E. Cowman,** of Alexandria, Va., who was *b.* December 17, 1836. Issue :

   i. **HERBERT,** *b.* November 6, 1859 ; *m.*, October 18, 1883, **CARRIE A. MUNDER.** Issue : i. **Helen M.,** *b.* September 6, 1885. ii. **Charles F.,** *b.* January 16, 1888. iii. **Edith,** *b.* October 2, 1891.
   ii. **MARGARET,** *b.* October 25, 1860 ; *d.* October 7, 1861.
   iii. **MABEL,** *b.* June 24, 1862 ; *d.* February 27, 1865.
   iv. **HARVEY,** b. August 5, 1864 ; *m.* April 26, 1892, **ANNIE E. HORNER.**
   v. **LOUISA,** *b.* February 1, 1867.
   vi. **RICHARD HENRY,** *b.* March 12, 1876.

iii. **JOSEPH GILPIN,** *b.* December 28, 1837 ; *d.* July 7, 1854.

iv. **SAMUEL,** *b.* January 21, 1840 ; *d.* November 22, 1875.

v. **ALBAN GILPIN,** *b.* April 29, 1843 ; *m.*, September 12, 1871, **SUSAN-NAH HAYDOCK,** *dau.* of **Thomas** and **Patience Leggett,** of New York. Issue :

   i. **ANNA LEGGETT,** *b.* December 3, 1872.
   ii. **HELEN LEGGETT,** *b.* June 2, 1874.

vi. **LOUISA,** *b.* August 17, 1845 ; *m.*, September 14, 1871, **ROGER BROOKE** (*q. v.*).

vii. **MARY PHILLIPS,** *b.* December 8, 1847 ; *m.* **FREDERIC JACK-SON,** and has a *dau.* **Ellen.**

viii. **EMILIE,** *b.* September 6, 1852 ; *m.*, September 8, 1872, **J. LLEWEL-LYN,** son of **John E.** and **Margaret A. Massey,** of Virginia. Issue (surname MASSEY) :

   i. **MARY GERTRUDE,** *b.* December 7, 1873.
   ii. **MARGARET,** *b.* August 10, 1875.

WILLIAM JOHN, third son of **William** and **Martha (Patrick) Thomas,** *b.* September 15, 1813, resided at Clifton, Montgomery Co., Md.; *m.* **REBECCA M. PORTER,** and *d.* 1884. She *d.* 1889. Issue :

i. **MARY ELIZABETH,** *b.* October 24, 1838 ; *m.* **WILLIAM W. MOORE,** of Sandy Spring. Issue (surname MOORE) :

   i. **CLARA PAINTER,** *b.* June 16, 1860 ; *d.* August 8, 1863.
   ii. **ROBERT ROWLAND,** *b.* April 15, 1863 ; *m.*, July 20, 1886, **MARGARET G.,** *dau.* of **Henry** and **Mary (Gillingham) Tyson** (*q. v.*). Issue : Henry Tyson, *b.* July 4, 1887. William W., Jr., *b.* December 12, 1888. Hadassah J., *b.* January 24, 1890. Mary Elizabeth, *b.* February 3, 1894.
   iii. **SARAH THOMAS,** *b.* October 17, 1865.
   iv. **REBECCA THOMAS,** *b.* July 9, 1872 ; *m.* **TARLTON B. STABLER** (*q. v.*).

ii. Dr. **FRANCIS,** *b.* January 30, 1840 ; resides at Lucknow Farm ; *m.* **BEULAH L. HAINES.** Issue :

i.   WILLIAM FRANCIS, *b.* June 21, 1871 ; *m.* PERLE SHEPHERD COOKE.
ii.   ELLEN HAINES, *b.* March 5, 1875.

iii.   SARAH T., *b.* April 12, 1841 ; *m.*, September 18, 1862, BENJAMIN H.
        MILLER.   Issue (surname MILLER) :

    i.   REBECCA T., *b.* February 1, 1864.
    ii.   ELIZABETH T., *b.* August 13, 1867 ; *m.* WILLIAM TAYLOR THOM. Issue
            (surname THOM) : i. Julia D. ii. William Taylor. iii. Benjamin Miller.
    iii.   MARTHA T., *b.* July 2, 1870 ; *d.* 1894.

iv.   EDWARD PORTER, *b.* January 16, 1844 ; resides at Belmont ; *m.*,
        November 30, 1865, MARY HENRIETTA, *dau.* of Richard
        T. and Edith (Needles) Bentley (*q. v.*).   Issue :

    i.   EDITH BENTLEY, *b.* October 30, 1866 ; *m.* GEORGE BROOKE FAR-
            QUHAR (*q.v.*)
    ii.   MARY E., *b.* February 28, 1870.
    iii.   RICHARD BENTLEY, *b.* October 19, 1873.
    iv.   EDWARD CLIFTON, *b.* June 17, 1875.
    v.   AUGUSTA NEEDLES, *b.* June 12, 1877.

v.   JOHN, *b.* April 20, 1846 ; resides at Glencoe Farm ; *m.*, in November,
        1876, CATHERINE D. VICKERS, of Baltimore, Md.   Issue :

    i.   EDNA V., *b.* August 28, 1877.
    ii.   MARY M.
    iii.   WILLIAM J.
    iv.   KATHERINE D.

vi.   WILLIAM, *b.* August 20, 1848 ; *d.* May 30, 1871.
vii.   CHARLES, *b.* August 3, 1850.
viii.   MARTHA, *b.* July 18, 1852.

SAMUEL, third son of **Samuel** and **Mary (Hutchins) Thomas,**
b. November 12, 1702 ; was a minister of the Society of Friends,
present as such at a meeting at Herring Creek, January 26, 1758.
With Roger Brooke was an overseer of Herring Creek Meeting,
October 29, 1762. He *m.* August 11, 1730, **MARY,** *dau.* of **Richard** and **Eliza (Coale) Snowden** (*q. v.*), who *d.* August 15, 1755,
in her forty-third year ; her husband *d.* February 3, 1780.   Issue :

i.   MARY, *b.* November 3, 1731 ; *m.* her cousin, SAMUEL THOMAS (*q.v.*).
ii.   SAMUEL, *b.* September 23, 1733 ; *d. s. p.*
iii.   PHILIP, *b.* April 18, 1735 ; *d. s. p.* in November, 1754.
iv.   ELIZABETH, *b.* March 10, 1736–37 ; *m.* JOHNS HOPKINS (*q. v.*).
v.   EVAN, *b.* January 21, 1738–39, *of whom presently.*

EVAN, only surviving son of **Samuel** and **Mary (Snowden)
Thomas,** *b.* January 21, 1738–39 ; resided at Mount Radnor, Montgomery Co., Md. ; was a minister of the Society of Friends, as was
also his wife.   In his Memorial [1] it is said that he was a delegate to
the first Convention of Maryland, but refused to serve in the second.

[1] West River MS. Book of Memorials, folio 75.

after being elected, having returned to Friendly principles. Possibly, like Joseph Galloway and others, his loyalty allowed him to take part in peaceful protests against oppression, but kept him from joining in acts of rebellion. After the Revolution a Meeting for Sufferings held at Pipe Creek, May 23, 1795, notes that from Evan Thomas there were taken 118¾ acres of land, valued at £30 5s. 7½d., by distraint, for taxes for the purpose of sinking debts incurred in the war. Before his death he freed his slaves, over two hundred in number, and gave them small allotments of land to cultivate.

EVAN THOMAS, *m.*, December 26, 1766, at Indian Spring Meeting House, **RACHEL**, *dau.* of **Gerard** and **Mary (Hall) Hopkins** (*q. v.*), who *d.* December 3, 1825, and her husband *d.* November 10, 1826. Issue :

i.   **MARY**, *b.* August 14, 1768 ; *m.* **ELIAS ELLICOTT** (*q. v.*).

ii.   **ANN**, *b.* August 6, 1771 ; *m.* **THOMAS POULTNEY** (*q. v.*).

iii. and iv. **PHILIP** and **SAMUEL**, twins, *b.* January 12, 1774 ; both *d.* in 1775.

v.   **PHILIP EVAN**, *b.* November 11, 1776, *of whom presently.*

vi.   **ELIZABETH**, *b.* March 26, 1779 ; *m.* **ISAAC TYSON** (*q. v.*).

vii.   **EVAN, Jr.**, *b.* March 8, 1781 ; was in business with his brother at Baltimore. He·is described by a contemporary[1] as "a man who forgot nothing. Of an active, nervous temperament, of great fluency of speech, of active intellect, full of all sorts of information, and universally respected for sterling qualities of head and heart, he talked railroad wherever he could find, or, perhaps often the case, force a listener." This was after his return from England, where he had seen the first railway, that from Stockton to Darlington. No doubt he was of great use in bringing the question before the public, for though not a man to lead in any undertaking he was the man of all men to urge others to be leaders. His invention, the Aeolus, a car moved by sails, was rather a curious toy than a practical machine, though Baron Krudener, the Russian ambassador, sent a model of it to the Czar ; for it required a good gale to drive it, head winds being fatal, and a strong side wind not to be trusted, lest it should be upset. Evan Thomas remained a bachelor, and *d. s. p.*

viii.   **MARGARET**, *b.* September 26, 1783 ; *d.* October 5, 1783.

PHILIP EVAN, third son of **Evan** and **Rachel (Hopkins) Thomas**, *b.* at Mount Radnor, Montgomery Co., Md., November 11, 1776 ; was educated at the District School under a Mr. Knox,[2] at Bladensburg. Arriving at manhood he went to Baltimore, then a town of only 15,000 inhabitants, and was received into the store of

[1] J. H. B. Latrobe, Personal Recollections of the B. & O. Railroad, 1868.
[2] Rev. Samuel Knox, v. Steiner's Education in Maryland, p. 46.

his brother-in-law, Thomas Poultney. In 1800 he commenced business on his own account as a hardware merchant, at 106 W. Baltimore Street, afterwards taking into partnership his wife's brother, William E. George, and finally his brother Evan. He early took an interest in municipal affairs and public charities, and in 1802 was a manager of the Baltimore General Dispensary and Humane Society, in 1807 its Treasurer, and was the first President of the Maryland Bible Society, and of the Mechanical Fire Company, one of the founders of the Baltimore Library Company, for many years President of the Mechanics' Bank, and advanced the first $25,000 to enable the State to begin building the Washington Monument.

During the fall of 1826 Philip E. Thomas held frequent conferences with George Brown, then a Director of the Mechanics' Bank, of Baltimore, in reference to the loss which Baltimore had sustained by the diversion of a large part of its Western trade to Philadelphia and New York through the Erie Canal, and similar facilities for internal navigation and traffic in the States of New York and Pennsylvania. General Barnard's report, showing the cost of completing the Chesapeake and Ohio Canal, and the difficulties that lay in its way, convinced them it would not accomplish the desired end in directing the trade to Baltimore. At this time Evan Thomas was in Europe, and wrote from England to his brother, giving him an account of the railroad just built from Stockton to Darlington, in Durham, by the enterprise of Edward Pease of the latter place.

Philip E. Thomas at once saw the utility of railroads as a means of communication and carriers of passengers and freight, and resigning his position as a State Director of the Canal Company turned his whole attention to the projection of a railroad connecting Baltimore with the West. One who knew him well, said, " he was remarkable for his self-possession, clearness of perception, and admirable judgment. His persuasiveness was remarkable. Never thrown off his balance, quiet in his speech, laborious in his search for facts, and eminently successful in his own affairs, people listened to him with conviction, and he had great influence in the community."

If one examines the list of contemporary Baltimore business men, it will also be seen how large and influential was his connection. By blood or marriage, the Poultneys, Ellicotts, Tysons, Wethereds, Georges, and Hopkins, were all of his near kindred, and from 1825 to 1830 among the leading commercial, banking, and manufacturing firms of the city.

February 12, 1827, twenty-five of the most influential merchants of Baltimore met at the residence of Mr. Brown, pursuant to a call issued by Messrs. Thomas and Brown. At this meeting Philip E. Thomas ably presented the various advantages the railroad system had over the canal and the old-fashioned turnpike in efficiency, rapidity of carriage, and ultimate economy, and a committee was appointed to further examine the subject, and report to a public meeting. This committee consisted of Philip E. Thomas, Chairman, Benjamin C. Howard, George Brown, Talbot Jones, Joseph W. Patterson, Evan Thomas and John V. L. McMahon. The following Monday the committee presented their report, written by their chairman, which was unanimously adopted and fifteen hundred copies ordered printed and distributed.

A recent historian of Baltimore [1] remarks, "it almost seems as if the author [of the report] was touched with the spirit of prophecy when he unfolded the possibilities of the great scheme in the prosecution of which he was destined to play so conspicuous a part." Yet far-reaching as was his vision and comprehensive as was his intellect, he did not dream all that the new force which they were calling into existence would accomplish. It is at this day impossible to estimate the effect which that report produced upon the public. Its clear reasoning and ample statistics carried conviction to every reader's mind, and it gave an immediate impulse to railroad building throughout the whole country. That pamphlet, entitled "Proceedings of Sundry Citizens of Baltimore, Convened for the Purpose of Devising the Most Efficient Means of Improving the Intercourse between that City and the Western States," printed by William Wooddy, 1827, containing thirty-eight octavo pages of small type on gray paper, a copy of which lies before me as I write, is the most memorable document in the annals of American Railways, the very first of the long series of reports which have since been issued. Immediately after the meeting a charter drawn by John V. L. McMahon, the eminent lawyer, was submitted to the Legislature, then in session, and an act of incorporation passed February 27, 1827. As one has written of that time, "then came a scene which almost beggars description. By this time public excitement had gone far beyond fever heat, and reached the boiling-point. Everybody wanted stock. Parents subscribed in the names of their children, and paid the dollar on each share that the rules prescribed. Before a survey had been made—before common-sense

[1] Scharf's History of Baltimore City and County, *pp.* 315-327.

had been consulted, even, the possession of stock in any quantity, was regarded as a provision for old age and great was the scramble to obtain it. The excitement in Baltimore roused public attention elsewhere, and a railroad mania began to pervade the land. But Baltimore led all the rest." In eleven days the subscriptions to the stock amounted to $4,178,000. April 24th of that year the Baltimore & Ohio Railroad Company was duly organized, being the first constructed for general purposes in America ; the short tram-roads at Leiperville and Mauch Chunk, Pa., and Quincy, Mass., being only for local carriage of private freight.

The first Directors were : Philip E. Thomas, President ; George Brown, Treasurer ; Charles Carroll of Carrollton, William Patterson, Robert Oliver, Alexander Brown, Isaac McKim, William Lorman, George Hoffman, Thomas Ellicott, John B. Morris, Talbot Jones, and William Steuart.

Space cannot be given for a detailed history of the railway, but the main facts may be recounted so far as they fall within the scope of Mr. Thomas's presidency.

A Committee of Engineers was appointed, consisting of Lieutenant-Colonel Stephen H. Long and Jonathan Knight, on the part of the Company, assisted by a number from the U. S. Topographical Corps ; Philip E. Thomas being its chairman. April 5, 1828, Messrs. Long and Knight reported the completion of their surveys, and the choice of a route along the Valley of the Patapsco, and thence in the direction of Linganore Creek to Point of Rocks.

July 4th, of the same year, the "first stone" was laid by Charles Carroll of Carrollton, with great ceremony and a magnificent procession of associations, trades, and professions. Before the road passed four miles from the city, it encountered a high dividing ridge, which had to be cut down fifty-four feet through a hard clay, involving an expense far beyond the estimates, and the funds prepared to meet them. The President and nine of the Directors immediately advanced $20,000 apiece, which met the difficulty.

By January 7, 1830, the section of the road nearest the city being completed, the company established a station at the end of Pratt Street, and ran cars, drawn by a single horse, out to the Carrollton Viaduct, about a mile and a half distant. It is said that travellers passing through the city would stay an extra day in order to enjoy the pleasure of a "ride upon the railway." May 22, 1830, the road was formally opened to Ellicott's Mills, horse and mule power being used to propel the cars. The average number of passengers during June exceeded four hundred per day, and the railroad was proven a success. After trying various expedients and setting the inventive genius of Peter Cooper, Jonathan Knight, and, especially, Ross Winans to work upon the problem of the steam engine, January 4, 1831, the President published an advertisement offering a premium for two locomotives, which is remarkable for the thorough knowledge it exhibits of what a railroad engine should be. One made by Davis & Gartner, of York, Pa., tried on July 12th of that year, won the prize offered, making a mile in three minutes on its first trip, drawing a car carrying forty persons, and the company adopted locomotives as their motive power. A long litigation took place about the right of way, in which the Chesapeake & Ohio Canal Company opposed the railroad, blockading the latter company for five years at Point of Rocks, Va., and it was only by a compromise that they were at last able to surmount that barrier, and by 1835 to open the line to Harper's Ferry. August 25, 1835, the Washington branch was also completed. The bridge on that line across the Patapsco at the Relay House was, at the time it was built, the finest structure of the kind in the United States. It was designed by the late Benjamin H. Latrobe, and, by its unfamiliar name of the Thomas Viaduct, is the only monument in Baltimore or its vicinity to the projector and builder of the railroad, to which, more than any other agency, the commercial prosperity of the city is due. His true monument we might well claim to be the railroad system of the United States. A recent writer has said "that no one can read the reports and memorials which he prepared when the construction of an extended line of railway was yet an untried experiment, without being impressed with his broad comprehension of commercial affairs and his acute perception of the relations between trade and transportation. His style in writing was clear, forcible, and even elegant, and the words and phrases which he used seem to have been handed down as part of the railroad system which he founded." June 30, 1836, impelled by the state of his health, he resigned the presidency of the Company, "to the great regret of the directors, the stockholders, and the people of the State at large."

In one of the resolutions passed by the Board of Directors on this occasion, they say : "On the commencement of this work, of which he has been, in fact, the father and projector, everything connected with its construction was new, crude, and doubtful, with little to guide the way, and that derived from distant and uncertain sources ; now, such has been the increase of information and experience acquired under his auspices and direction, as to insure the completion and success of the undertaking, if prosecuted with the same zeal, assiduity, and integrity which have ever marked his course."

Philip E. Thomas was a prominent member of the Society of Friends, of which his father had been an eminent Minister. He was much interested in the cause of the Indians ; several of their young men were educated at the same school with his sons, and it was owing to his exertions that the remnants of the Six Nations, residing in Western New York, were not driven from their reservation by the intrigues of the Ogden Land Company with their chiefs ; the chiefs were deposed, and a republican form of government established. He was afterwards made a chief of the Swan tribe of Seneca Indians, by the name of "Sagouan," or bountiful giver, and represented them in their intercourse with the Government at Washington. In the summer of 1861, he went, as was his usual custom, to his daughter's, in Westchester Co., N. Y., and died there September 1, 1861.

He *m.*, April 20, 1801, **ELIZABETH**, *dau.* of **Robert** and **Ann (Edmundson) George**, (*q.v.*) of Kent Co., Md.   Issue :

i.   **ANN**, *b.* February 17, 1803 ; *m.* **THOMAS E. WALKER** (*q.v.*).

ii.   **RACHEL**, *b.* February 1, 1805 ; *m.* **J. J. WALKER** (*q.v.*).

iii. **EVAN PHILIP**, *b.* November 19, 1806 ; *m.*, November 17, 1835, **ELIZABETH**, *dau.* of **Joseph** and **Eliza (Onion) Todhunter**, (*q.v.*) and *d.*   Issue :

    i.   **PHILIP WILLIAM**, *b.* March 21, 1842 ; *d.* July 14, 1861.

    ii. **KATE TODHUNTER**, *m.*, December 24, 1866, **EDWARD GOODWIN DYKE**, of Boston.

    iii. **JOSEPHINE**.

iv.   **WILLIAM GEORGE**, *b.* February 9, 1809, *of whom presently.*

v.   **MARY**, *b.* October 11, 1813 ; *m.* **JOHN WETHERED** (*q.v.*).

vi.   **ELIZABETH**, *b.* January 22, 1817.

vii. **HARRIET**, *b.* October 25, 1820 ; *m.*, April 10, 1845, **JAMES CHRISTY BELL**.   Issue (surname BELL) :

    i.   **PHILIP THOMAS**, *b.* February 28, 1846 ; *unm.*

    ii. **JOHN WETHERED**, *b.* February 8, 1848 ; *unm.*

    iii. **JAMES CHRISTY**, *b.* January 12, 1850 ; *m.*, February 5, 1885, **MARY ELIZA DENNIS**, *dau.* of **Alfred L.** and **Eliza Shepard Dennis**, of Newark, N. J.   Issue :

        i.   Alfred Dennis, *b.* August 7, 1886.

        ii. James Christy, Jr., *b.* February 4, 1889.

        iii. Samuel Dennis, *b.* January 19, 1892.

iv. LIZZIE, *b.* August 22, 1851 ; *unm.*
v. JACOB HARVEY, *b.* October 11, 1853 ; *m.*, November 9, 1882, LILLIE COCK, *dau.* of William and Mary Cock, of Flushing, N. Y. Issue :

    i. Harriet Thomas, *b.* October 28, 1883.
    ii. Mary Elizabeth, *b.* October 21, 1886.
    iii. Harvey William, *b.* April 7, 1889.

WILLIAM GEORGE, second son of **Philip E.** and **Elizabeth (George) Thomas,** *b.* February 9, 1809 ; was a prominent merchant of Baltimore, succeeding his father in the hardware business on Baltimore Street. To him the city of Baltimore is indebted for her first improved public square, Franklin Square, in the northwestern section of the city ; her first charitable institution erected by private subscription, the Widow's Home, and her first line of omnibuses. He *m.*, May 16, 1832, **MARY LEWIN,** *dau.* of **Lewin** and **Elizabeth (Ellicott) Wethered** (*q. v.*). Issue :

i. ELIZABETH E., *b.* in April, 1833 ; *d. i.*
ii. PHILIP EVAN, *b.* April 28, 1834, *of whom presently.*
iii. ANN P., *b.* November 7, 1835 ; *m.*, 1st, December 8, 1853, **WILLIAM BELL,** of New York City. Issue (surname BELL) :

    i. MARY LEWIN, *b.* March 11, 1855 ; *m.* CHARLES SETON LINDSAY. Issue : Lewin Seton, *b.* June 1, 1879, and Harvey, *b.* August 31, 1880.
    ii. REBECCA, *b.* August 20, 1858 ; *d.* in 1866.
    iii. ANN, *b.* June 10, 1861 ; *m.* June 3, 1885, ALEXANDER SPENCER LE DUC, who *d.* November 12, 1891. Issue (surname LE DUC) : Jack Clinton, *b.* March 8, 1886, and Lewin Bell, *b.* December 12, 1887.
    iv. ELIZABETH, *b.* March 6, 1862.
    v. TACY, *b.* October 23, 1871 ; *d.* August 13, 1872.

iv. **LEWIN WETHERED,** *b.* March 6, 1837 ; *d. u.* December 8, 1877.
v. EVAN, *b.* October 28, 1838 ; has been for twenty-five years conspicuous in New York business circles. Studied law under John H. B. Latrobe, of Baltimore, and was admitted to the Bar but never practised. Came to New York and operated on the street five years before entering the Produce Exchange. During his connection with it he has been almost continuously one of the Board of Managers, and no committee of importance has been without his name. He is for the third time its president, the only one who has for so many consecutive times occupied the chair. He is President of the Business Men's Democratic Association, a Presidential Elector and Secretary of the last Electoral College. Was Commissioner for the City on the North River Bridge, and President of the Commission on the Storage of Water for the Erie Canal. He *m.*, April 24, 1880, **ZAYDEE A. BARKER.** Issue :

i. EVAN BARKER, *b.* May 5, 1881.

vi.   **MARY LEWIN,** *b.* November 14, 1841 ; *m.,* October 3, 1876, **ALEX-ANDER SMITH,** of Yonkers, N. Y., who *d. s. p.* by her.

vii.   **ELIZABETH,** *b.* December 13, 1845 ; *m.,* April 27, 1871, **CHARLES S. LINDSAY,** and *d.* November 21, 1874.

viii. **MATILDA,** and ix. **HARRIET GEORGE,** *b.* December 5, 1849 ; the former *d. i.,* and her sister *d.* June 19, 1866.

x.   **WETHERED BROTHERS,** *b.* June 11, 1853 ; *m.,* February 4, 1880, **ADELAIDE M. MELICK.** Issue :

> EVANINA WETHERED, *b.* October 28, 1880 ; *d.* May 9, 1881.
> BRYANT ELLICOTT, *b.* January, 1883, *d.* in 1885.
> GLADYS EVELINE, *b.* July 11, 1885.

PHILIP EVAN, eldest son of **William G.** and **Mary (Wethered) Thomas,** *b.* April 28, 1834, was a merchant of New York City. He *m.,* April 30, 1859, **MARIE SUZETTE,** *dau.* of **Mandeville de Marigny,** whose father, Bernard de Marigny, of New Orleans, was a veteran of the war of 1812, and by birth a Duke and Marquis of France ; Miss de Marigny was also a granddaughter of William C. C. Claiborne, the first American Governor of Louisiana, and a great granddaughter of Don Juan Ventura Morales, the last Spanish Governor of the Colony. Philip Evan Thomas *d.* January 2, 1882. Issue :

i.   **WILLIAMINE,** *b.* in 1860.

ii.   **MARIE SUZETTE,** *b.* March 13, 1861 ; *m.,* September 8, 1880, **WILLIAM C. HALL.** Issue (surname HALL) :

> i.   WILLIAM C., *b.* July 10, 1881.
> ii.   MANDEVILLE, *b.* November, 1882.
> iii.   MARIE SUZETTE, *b.* September, 1884.
> iv.   AGNES, *b.* 1886.

iii.   **PHILIP EVAN,** *b.* May 5, 1862.

iv.   **MARY LEWIN,** *b.* August 28, 1863 ; *m.,* December 12, 1893, **MAX EMIL DE JÖNGE.**

v.   **MANDEVILLE DE MARIGNY,** *b.* March 25, 1865.

vi.   **CLAIBORNE,** *b.* December 7, 1867.

vii.   **SOPHRONIE COALE,** *b.* September 28, 1869 ; *m.,* June 25, 1890, **JOHN RANDOLPH GRYMES.** Issue (surname GRYMES) :

> MARIE ATHENAIS, *b.* July, 1891.

HERBERT

THOMAS, OF ABERGLASNEY, WALES

SIR WILLIAM THOMAS, Knt., of Aberglasney, was High Sheriff of Caermarthenshire, Wales, in 1540 ; *m.* **JANE,** *dau.* of **Sir William Herbert, Knt.,** of Coldbrook, and *d.* leaving issue.

REES THOMAS, of Aberglasney, sheriff in 1565, was probably his son. **WILLIAM,** son of Rees Thomas, was of Aberglasney, and sheriff in 1576 and 1582. After this date the family disappears from the records. Sir Rice Rudd, Bart., sheriff in 1619, being styled of Aberglasney. He may have married a *dau.* and *heir* of **William Thomas.**

Authority : Nicholas's Annals of Wales, i., 265, 274.

THOMAS, OF ALBEMARLE COUNTY, VA.

JOHN THOMAS, of North Garden, Albemarle Co., Va. Issue :

    JOHN, who had four sons :

i.   **WARNER.**
ii.   **NORBORNE.**
iii.   **JAMES WILTON,** *m.* and removed to Missouri with three children in 1826 ; his son, John Lilburn, *b.* 1833, was Assistant Attorney-General of United States Post Office in 1895.
iv.   **JOHN LILBURN,** *d. u.*

    CORNELIUS, removed to Pennsylvania ; *m.* a **MISS MOORE,** of Lebanon, and *d.* in Baltimore, Md., during the Civil War. Issue :

i.   **NORBOURN,** was *d.* in 1895.
ii.   **WILTON.**
iii.   **CORNELIUS,** *m.* a Roman Catholic lady of Baltimore and has a son, **Rev. Charles F.,** rector of the Roman Catholic Cathedral of Baltimore.
iv.   **WARNER,** was *d.* in 1895.
v.   **MARIA.**
vi.   **HARRIET.**
vii.   **VIRGINIA.**
viii.   **FANNY,** was *d.* in 1895.

        Authorities : Rev. C. F. and Hon. John L. Thomas.

THOMAS, OF BAYEUX

THERE was an ancient family in that city, several members of which held high office in England after the conquest. The first one of note was Thomas, son of Osbert and Muriel, *b*. in Bayeux, who sought learning beyond the bounds of Gaul, and even beyond those of Christendom. Like his Metropolitan, Mauritius, he studied in the schools of Saxony and other German lands. His love of learning carried him into the South as well as the North ; he crossed the Pyrenees, and returned to Bayeux full of all the learning of the Spanish Saracens. He became a Canon of its cathedral, and Odo, the Bishop, who made up somewhat for his own misdeeds by generous promotion of merit in others, placed him in the treasurer's stall. This was an office for which one who had studied in the land of the goldsmith's craft might be supposed especially fit. He is said to have been a chaplain of William of Normandy, and after his conquest of England the King nominated him at Whitsuntide, 1070, as the first Norman Archbishop of York. A French memoir speaks of him as worthy by his virtues and his learning, and Dr. Freeman says " that he stood high in every way, and has left a special name behind him in the history of his own church as the restorer alike of its fabric and its discipline. Godwin [1] describes him as of fine stature, with ruddy complexion, courteous, and affable ; hair white as swan's down, skilful in music, an accomplished vocalist, and expert performer on the organ. In 1070 Thomas came to Canterbury and sought consecration at the hands of Lanfranc. Before the actual performance of the rite the archbishop demanded a profession of canonical obedience from Thomas. He refused the demand, claiming the independence of the Northern See, and the writers on the rival side confess that the refusal was not prompted by pride or perverseness. Thomas went away unconsecrated and appealed to the King. William decreed a temporary compromise. Thomas was to make a written profession

---

[1] De Præsul. Pt. II., *p*. 23 ; Joyce : Convocation of the Church of England, *p*. 123.

to Lanfranc, *personally*, pledging himself to full canonical obedience ; but he should not be bound to do the like to any successor of Lanfranc until the dispute was settled by a competent tribunal. Thus far Thomas was content to yield, though with some unwillingness, and he was consecrated Archbishop of York by Lanfranc.

The next year both went to Rome, and Alexander the Pope was minded to deprive Thomas of his see ; not because he stood charged with any offence of simony or plurality, but because he was the son of a priest, his father having been a canon of Bayeux. This, by the way, was nothing wonderful either in English or Norman eyes, and when the matter was referred to Lanfranc for decision his judgment was that Thomas should remain archbishop. While in Rome Thomas craved the Pope's decision of his controversy with Canterbury. Alexander referred it to an English council of bishops, which met the next year and decided in favour of Canterbury. In the metropolitan see of York Thomas sat with all honour for nearly thirty years. He instructed his people by his discourse and by his example, and composed some Books upon the Ecclesiastical Chant. The old dispute between the two metropolitan sees was not fully healed, and when it fell to the lot of Thomas to consecrate Lanfranc's successor Anselm on December 4, 1093, it would seem that Canterbury yielded so far, that he was consecrated not as Primate of all Britain, but vaguely as Metropolitan. The claim of independence came to nothing under the strong hand of William I., and Thomas found better scope for his energies in the reform of his own church. He became the fifth founder of the Cathedral by rebuilding, or rather it would seem repairing it, on a scale of greater magnificence than ever before. He recalled its Canons who had fled at the conquest and increased their number. At first he introduced the Lotharingian discipline, but wiser counsels led him afterwards to adopt the system generally prevalent in the English Cathedrals of secular foundation. His work still lives ; the constitution of the Church of York, as laid down by him, is nearly unaltered ; and in no cathedral in England have the rights of the whole capitular body been so little encroached on by the growth of a residential oligarchy. He *d.* November 18, 1100. Malmesbury says he crowned King Henry I., but this is doubtful.

Samson, brother of Thomas, was Canon of Bayeux and afterwards Bishop of Worcester in England. He was elected in the year 1096, but not having received full orders was ordained priest on Saturday, and the day following, Sunday, June 8, 1096, by Anselm, Archbishop of Canterbury, his brother Thomas, of York and three other Bishops, was consecrated at S. Paul's, London, Bishop of Worcester.

In 1100, with two other Bishops, he dedicated the great church of Gloucester, which Abbot Serlo had built, and took an active part in the affairs of the Church during his episcopate. He was in great favour with King Henry I. The Monkish writers, though opposed to him, give him the character of a man of great learning and no contemptible eloquence, keeping a handsome table, and very bountiful to others. Before becoming canon he was *m.*, and *d.* on Sunday, May 5, 1112, and lies buried before the rood-loft of his cathedral, at the bottom of the steps going up into the choir. He left issue Richard, who was Bishop of Bayeux, and Thomas, who was chaplain to Henry I., Provost of Beverly Abbey, in 1108 nominated to the see of London, and June 27, 1109, consecrated at S. Paul's, London, by Richard de Beames, Bishop of London and five other Bishops, Archbishop of York. He revived the claim of independence of Canterbury made by his uncle, and had great debate with S. Anselm about it, during which the latter died. The Bishops of the province being summoned by the king to decide the matter, Samson, the archbishop's father, gave his opinion downright against his own son that he should not receive the pall sent him from Rome until he made his profession of canonical obedience to the See of Canterbury, and so the matter was settled. It is reported that on one occasion, being ill of a grievous malady, and the physicians having indicated to him a remedy opposed to purity, he declared " that he loved better to expose himself to death, than to rescue his life at such a price." The pious narrator adds, " God blessed his constancy and faith by restoring him to his former health." He *d.* February 24, 1114. An old French historical dictionary calls the archbishop " Thomas de Douvre," and speaks of an Isabelle de Douvre of their family who was mistress of Robert of Gloucester, natural son of King Henry I., and had by him a son Richard, Bishop of Bayeux, in 1133. She *d.* in 1166 at a very advanced age.

Authorities : Freeman's Norman Conquest, iv., 352 and 372 *et seq.* ; Dictionnaire Historique, vi. 344 ; Rapin's England, ii., 255 ; Winkle's Cathedrals, i., 41 ; Hook's Archbishops, vol. ii. ; Thomas's Worcester Cathedral, 103, 105 ; Ormsby's History of York, 109 *et seq.* ; Drake's Eboracum, etc.

THOMAS, OF BOSTON, MASS.

GEORGE THOMAS, of Boston, is said to have been a son of **Evan,** who came from Wales in 1640, bringing his wife **Jane** and four children. Was a wine dealer; joined the Artillery Company 1653; *d.* August 25, 1661. **GEORGE** *m.* **REBECCA** ——. Issue:

i.   **PETER,** *b.* February 5, 1683, *of whom presently.*
ii.   **GEORGE,** *b.* March 16, 1685.
iii.   **MAVERICK,** *b.* March 19, 1694.

PETER, eldest son of **George** and **Rebecca Thomas,** *b.* February 5, 1683, was a successful merchant; *m.* **ELIZABETH,** *dau.* of **Rev. George Burroughs** (executed for witchcraft, August 19, 1692). Issue:

i.   **GEORGE.**
ii.   **ELIAS.**
iii.   **PETER.**
iv.   **WILLIAM.**
v.   **MOSES.**

MOSES, the youngest son, *b.* 1712, was at various times a soldier, sailor, trader, farmer, and school-teacher. Finally, leaving his family in Boston, he emigrated to North Carolina, and *d.* there in 1752, leaving by his wife, Fidelity Trant, of Hempstead, L. I., five children.

ISAIAH, the youngest, *b.* at Boston, January 19, 1749, was a printer, and had a book-store in Boston; in 1770 began to publish the *Massachusetts Spy ;* removed to Worcester a few days before the Battle of Lexington, where the *Spy* is still published. He formed the Worcester Antiquarian Society, published the *Massachusetts Magazine,* and *New England Almanac ;* was the author of a valuable "History of Printing," in two volumes; *d.* in Worcester, April 4, 1831. His grandson, Benjamin Franklin, *b.* at Boston, February 12, 1813, studied law. Was a member of the Legislature, 1842, Presidential Elector, 1848,

Justice of the Supreme Court of Massachusetts, 1853–1859, member of Congress, 1861 ; *d.* at Salem, Mass., September 27, 1878.

EBENEZER SMITH THOMAS, nephew of **Isaiah Thomas,** *b.* at Lancaster, Mass., January, 1780, removed to Charleston, S. C., in 1795 ; edited the *City Gazette,* 1810–1816 ; removed to Baltimore ; Member of the Legislature, 1818 ; moved to Cincinnati, O., in 1829 ; edited *Daily Advertiser* until 1835, the *Evening Post* till 1839 ; *d.* in Cincinnati, August, 1844. Author of "Reminiscences of the Last Sixty Years," published 1840, and " Reminiscences of South Carolina." Issue :

i.   **FREDERICK WILLIAM,** *b.* 1811 ; admitted to the bar, 1828 ; Methodist minister, 1850. Professor of Rhetoric, University of Alabama. In 1860, literary editor of the *Richmond Inquirer.* A successful lecturer ; author of several novels and other books ; *d.* in Washington, September, 1866.

ii.   **LEWIS FOULKE,** *b.* 1815, studied law, edited the *Daily Herald,* Louisville, Ky.; author of " Osceola," and " Cortez," tragedies, and " Inda and Other Poems ; " *d.* in Washington, September, 1868.

iii.   **MARTHA McCANNON,** *b.* November, 1823. Author of " Life's Lessons," 1846, and " Captain Phil," 1882.

iv.   **MARY VON EDEN,** *b.* December, 1825 ; author of " Winning the Battle," a novel ; a computer in the United States Coast Survey since 1854.

Authority : Savage's Dictionary ; and Thomas Family of Hardwick.

THOMAS, OF BUCKS COUNTY, PA.

DANIEL THOMAS, possibly the sheriff of the County in 1783, had a son **MORDECAI**, manufactured flour at the Billet Mill, now Hatboro', Pa.

JONATHAN, son of **Mordecai Thomas,** *b.* 1768, removed to Torresdale, and rented the Poquessing Mills there. He *m.* **SARAH SPENCER** and *d.* 1842. Issue :

i.   **SAMUEL,** *of whom presently.*
ii.   **SPENCER,** whose grandson is **Howard M. Jenkins,** of Philadelphia.
iii.   **MORDECAI** (*q. v.*).
iv.   **SARAH,** *d. y.*
v.   **ELIZABETH,** *m.* **NATHAN T. KNIGHT.**

SAMUEL, son of **Jonathan** and **Sarah (Spencer) Thomas** ; *m.* **MARTHA** ———, and had a son, **SAMUEL,** *b.* March 9, 1836 ; who *m.*, April 24, 1860, **Frances,** *dau.* of **Mordecai** and **Grace (Wilson) Thomas.** Issue :

i.   **EMMA,** *m.* **REV. WILLIAM HARRISON DECKER** and had a *dau.* **Ruth.**
ii.   **GRACE W.,** *m.* **WILLIAM G. BUCKMAN.**
iii.   **HERBERT LLOYD.**
iv.   **CLARENCE WILSON.**

MORDECAI, third son of **Jonathan** and **Sarah (Spencer) Thomas,** *b.* October 16, 1797, with his brother **Spencer** was a miller in 1826. He relinquished the business to his sons in 1852. He *m.* **GRACE WILSON,** *b.* August 16, 1802. Issue :

i.   **WILSON,** *b.* May 28, 1828, *m.* **ELIZABETH EGBERT.** Issue :
     W. EGBERT, carrying on the mills at Milford, N. J., with his father, in 1893.

ii.   **EDWARD,** *b.* December 13, 1830 ; milling with his brother from 1852 to 1893, when he retired from the firm. He *m.* **VIRGINIA VAN SYCKEL** and has one son and three daughters.

iii.   **FRANCES,** *b.* December 20, 1836 ; *m.* her cousin, **SAMUEL THOMAS** (*q. v.*).

Authority : Family papers, through Messrs. Edward and Clarence W. Thomas.

ARMS OF BISHOP THOMAS

THOMAS, OF CAERMARTHEN, WALES

JENKIN or John ap Adam, time of Edward III. and Richard II., was father of **GWILIM**, Lord of Kevendyglwydd, who *m.* **GWENLLIAN**, *dau.* of Howel Vychan ap Howel ap Jorwerth; *b.* about 1377, and had a third son, HOWELL; *m.* 1st, MATILDA ap Jevan ap Rhys, widow of Walter Sais; *d.* before 1384; *m.* 2d, ANN, *dau.* of Sir Robert Wallis, and had an eldest son, Jenkin, *of whom presently.*

JENKIN, son of **Howell** and **Matilda,** *m.* **CONSTANCE,** *dau.* of Roger Vaughan. Issue:

> **DAVID,** *m.* **MARGARET,** *dau.* and *co-heir* of Thomas Huntley, of Tredwen, and was killed at Banbury battle in 1469. Issue:
>
> i.   THOMAS, *m.* MARGARET, *dau.* of Morgan Kemys, of Began; or ANN, *dau.* of David Kemys, of Ceffn-Mably.
> ii.   GWILIM, had a son Thomas ap Gwilim, *of whom presently.*

THOMAS AP GWILIM was of Caermarthen; *m.* **JENET,** *dau.* of **Hugh Parry.** Issue:

> **WILLIAM THOMAS,** *m.* **CATHERINE,** *dau.* and *heir* of **Lewis Higgon,** of a family that furnished many officials to the borough. Issue:
>
> WILLIAM, Recorder of Caermarthen; *m.* 1st, —— WYLT, of Westerton; and 2d, ELIZABETH, *dau.* of Humphrey and Elizabeth (Veel) Smart, and had a son John, *of whom presently.*

JOHN, son of **William** and **Elizabeth (Smart) Thomas,** removed to Bristol, was a linen-draper there, and lived in his own house

77

on the Bridge. He *m.* **ELIZABETH,** *dau.* of **Thomas Blunt,** of Bristol, of a Worcestershire family. Issue :

i. **WILLIAM,** *b.* 1613, *of whom presently.*
ii. **ANN,** *m.* —— **ATWILL,** a tailor.
iii. **SARAH,** *m.* **THOMAS BEYNON.**

WILLIAM, only son of **John** and **Elizabeth (Blunt) Thomas,** *b.* 1613, at Bristol, was chaplain to the Duke of York, afterwards King James II., and preceptor to Princess Anne. Was driven from his vicarage of Langhorn, Northumberland, and suffered many hardships from the Puritans ; became Bishop of S. David's January 27, 1678, translated to Worcester in 1683 ; was about to resign from scruples about the oaths when he died. He *m.* **BLANCHE,** *dau.* of **Peter Semine,** of Bristol, and *d.* June 25, 1689. Issue :

i. **JOHN,** *of whom presently.*
ii. **WILLIAM,** a merchant of London.
iii. **SARAH,** *m.* **DR. GEORGE OWEN.**
iv. **ELIZABETH,** *m.* **JONATHAN ANDREWS,** of the Hill, Worcester.
v. **BRIDGET,** *b.* —— ; buried at Llaugharne, 1651.

JOHN, eldest son of **Bishop William Thomas,** *m.* **MARY,** *dau.* of **William Bagnall,** of Worcester, and had a son **WILLIAM,** *b.* 1670 ; was Rector of S. Nicholas in Worcester, in 1723 ; published a survey of Worcester Cathedral with numerous copper-plates, and was author of other works, and *d.* 1728.

Authorities : Clark's Morgan and Glamorgan, etc., and Thomas's Worcester.

THOMAS, OF CALDICOT, MONMOUTHSHIRE

REV. JOHN THOMAS, Parson of Coity, Monmouth, Wales, about 1630 ; *m.* **SARAH,** youngest *dau.* of **John** and **Martha (Lougher) Gamage,** of the Coity Castle family.   Issue :

i.   **JOHN,** incumbent of South Petherton and Ilminster, Somerset Co. ; *m.* the widow of ——— Prouse, Barrister-at-Law, and *d. s. p.*

ii.   **EDWARD,** rector of S. Bride's Minor, Glamorganshire, and Vicar of Caldicot ; *m.* **ANN LLOYD.**   Issue :

    i.   **THERESA.**
    ii.   **EDWARD,** Vicar of Llangwm.
    iii. **JAMES,** of Mount St. Albans.
    iv. **SAMUEL,** a lawyer.
    v.   **JOHN,** *d. y.*
    vi. **ANN.**
    vii. **WILLIAM.**

Authority : Nicholas's Wales, ii., 568.

ARMS OF HUGHES

THOMAS, OF CARNARVONSHIRE, WALES

RICE THOMAS, of Aber in Carnarvonshire, was High Sheriff of Anglesea in 1564. **WILLIAM,** of Aber, probably his son, was sheriff in 1579, and **WILLIAM,** styled "of Carnarvon," presumably the same, was High Sheriff of Carnarvonshire in 1581, and **SIR WILLIAM THOMAS, KNT.,** of Carnarvon, in 1608. William of Aber, his son or grandson, was Sheriff of Carnarvonshire in 1638. John, called of Carnarvon, probably a grandson, was the High Sheriff of Anglesea in 1693, and as "of Aber," in 1695. In 1710 John Griffith was of Aber and the Thomas family disappears from the records of the county under that title. At about the same date there begin notices of a family seated at Coed Helen, near Carnarvon, of which Rice Thomas was High Sheriff of Anglesea in 1720. William was High Sheriff of the county in 1746; another Rice sheriff in 1771. This family is now represented by Rice William Thomas, of Coed Helen (paternal name Hughes), High Sheriff in 1869, who succeeded in the estate Rice Thomas (*d.* 1853), High Sheriff of Carnarvon in 1831. Rice Thomas, of Cemmaes, High Sheriff of Anglesea in 1777, and another Rice Thomas of the same place, High Sheriff in 1817, may be of this family.

Authorities: Nicholas's Annals of Wales and Lists of Sheriffs.

THOMAS, OF CARROLL'S MANOR, MD.

GEORGE THOMAS, *b.* November, 1778, bought in 1821 part of
"West work," one hundred and sixty-eight acres on the east side
of Monocacy River, granted to John Alington, last called part of
"New Bremen;" he also owned a manor farm in Frederick
Co., Md. In 1807 he *m.* **CHARLOTTE THOMAS,**[1] *b.*
September, 1787, of German descent, and *d.* July 12, 1845. His
wife *d.* March 4, 1878. Issue:

i. **ELI,** *b.* August 14, 1808 ; *m.* **CHRISTIANA HUGH,** and *d.* April 25, 1864. His widow resides in Baltimore.

ii. **CHRISTIAN,** *b.* July 29, 1810; *m.* **MARY E. KEMP,** and *d.* December 8, 1891. Issue:

    i. **EDWARD NEWTON.**
    ii. **CATHERINE.**
    iii. **EMA.**

iii. **WILLIAM HENRY,** *b.* October 24, 1811 ; *m.* **MARY A. HARDING,** and *d.* September 7, 1865.

iv. **SAMUEL,** *b.* December 23, 1813 ; *m.* **MARIA HARGETT,** and *d.* March 4, 1888.

v. **DAVID,** *b.* November 4, 1816 ; *m.* **ELIZABETH HILDEBRAND,** and *d.* June 6, 1873.

vi. **SOPHIA,** *b.* May 22, 1818 ; *m.* **EZRA MICHEL,** and *d.* August 9, 1840.

vii. **JOHN,** *b.* September 21, 1819 ; *m.* **ANN E. MYERS,** and *d.* July 8, 1865.

viii. **MARY,** *b.* September 2, 1821, *d.* October 30, 1894.

ix. **CHARLOTTE,** *b.* March 29, 1823 ; *m.*, September 3, 1865, **JOHN W. COOK,** of Buckeystown, Md.

x. **GEORGE P.,** *b.* April 1, 1825, *of whom presently.*

xi. **ANN M.,** *b.* February 21, 1828 ; *m.* **GEORGE W. MYERS,** of Frederick, Md.

xii. **EDWARD J.,** *b.* February 9, 1830 ; *d.* August 27, 1831.

---

[1] Almost certainly *dau.* of Gabriel and Anna Maria (Hoffman) Thomas (*q. v.*).

GEORGE P., tenth child of **George** and **Charlotte (Thomas) Thomas,** *b.* April 1, 1825. About 1845 went to Winchester, Va., and entered the store of an elder brother. Not being satisfied with a subordinate position, and Winchester not affording scope for his enterprising spirit, he went to Baltimore in 1848, without letters of introduction, or influential friends there, depending only on his own efforts.

In 1849, he associated in the management of the Globe Inn, corner of Baltimore and Howard Streets, with a former resident of Frederick Co. In this he continued about a year and a half, when he engaged as clerk in a wholesale dry-goods house, which was more congenial to his tastes.

Though not yet having accumulated any funds, he made acquaintances in the commercial community, and demonstrated his business qualities, so that he began to seek opportunities for establishing himself in business.

In August, 1852, he formed a partnership in the wholesale wine and liquor trade. The business was successful for fourteen years, when in 1866 Mr. Thomas retired, to establish a house in the same branch, under his own name, at No. 385 West Baltimore Street, and in 1874 he purchased the valuable warehouse of Drakely & Fenton, southeast corner of Baltimore and Paca Streets.

Continued success always gives a man a prominent position in the mind of his community, and an influence which he may wield either for himself or general interests. In addition to his success, Colonel Thomas possessed such a genial spirit and courteous bearing toward all, that he became universally popular, and though by nature retiring, was compelled by his fellow-citizens to occupy many public positions. In 1852, they elected him as an *independent* candidate to the City Council from the Fourteenth Ward, over a popular competitor who had served several terms. His success was due not so much to the political issue of the canvass as to his personal popularity.

His importance in the Council was at once recognized by the President of the First Branch, the late John S. Brown, who appointed him chairman of the Committee on Internal Improvements.

As such he urged and secured the passage of the ordinance giving the city's endorsement of a million dollars to the Pittsburg and Connellsville Railroad Bonds, believing that this road would become greatly profitable to Baltimore, a belief that has been abundantly verified since its completion. He perceived not only its importance as forming a short line to the West, but connecting Baltimore with Pittsburg and the mining and manufacturing portion of Pennsylvania, thereby developing a new trade.

Governor E. Louis Lowe about this time appointed him one of his staff, with the rank of colonel, in recognition of his popularity as well as from personal regard for him.

GEORGE P. THOMAS afterwards became President of the Maryland Life Insurance Company. He *m.*, November 28, 1854, **MARIA LOUISE KEMP**, and *d.* November 17, 1887. Issue :

i.   **FRANCIS WORTHINGTON**, *b.* December 22, 1855 ; *m.*, January 2, 1884, **LOUISE E.**, *dau.* of **James W. Singleton**, of Quincy, Ill.
ii.   **CORA ELDER**, *b.* June 22, 1858.
iii.   **GEORGE P., Jr.**, *b.* July 28, 1862 ; represents in Baltimore the Goodyear Rubber Co. ; *m.*, June 6, 1888, **IDA M.**, *dau.* of **William H. Stran**, of Baltimore.
iv.   **WILLIAM CHRISTIAN**, *b.* March 27, 1874 ; *d.* June 12, 1877.

Authorities : Frederick Co. Records, etc., and family papers through Mrs. George P. Thomas and Mrs. John W. Cook.

THOMAS, OF CATASAUQUA, PA.

DAVID THOMAS, *b.* in South Wales, November 3, 1794, was the founder of this family, as also of the anthracite iron manufacture in America. Applications to the family have received no answer, and the following sketch is derived from newspaper sources. He began work as an iron-founder in 1812; in 1817 going to the Yniscedwin furnaces, Brecknockshire. In 1820, with George Crane, one-third owner of the works, he began to experiment in the use of anthracite as fuel, the works being located on the southern edge of an anthracite coal-basin. Their first efforts were unsuccessful. In 1834, one Neilson, of the Glasgow Gas Works, discovered the use of the hot blast, and Thomas, reading his pamphlet, saw its importance, and in 1836 applied it to use at Yniscedwin. This new method was so applicable to the needs of Pennsylvania that shortly afterwards, on the recommendation of Mr. Crane, David Thomas was asked to come over and superintend the erection of furnaces for the Lehigh Crane Iron Company. He finally accepted the offers made him, and in May, 1839, sailed with his family from Liverpool in the clipper ship Roscius, reaching New York June 5th. Furnaces were immediately built at Craneville, now Catasauqua, Pa., and the first run of iron made July 4, 1840. David Thomas acted as superintendent until 1855, when his sons succeeded him. In 1854 the Thomas Iron Company was formed and the works at Hokendauqua, Pa., begun. Mr. Thomas was a ruling elder in the Presbyterian Society at Catasauqua for over forty-two years, and largely instrumental in the erection of their house of worship. He *m.* Elizabeth Hopkins (*b.* in 1796, *d.* in July, 1890); and *d.* June 20, 1882, leaving, with other issue, three sons, John, Samuel, and Thomas, and a *dau.* who *m.* Joshua Hunt. Samuel R., son of John Thomas, *m.,* October 4, 1894, Bessie May, *dau.* of Alexander P. A. Laury. Another grandson is Edwin Thomas of Catasauqua, whose wife is a prominent member of the Pennsylvania Daughters of the American Revolution.

THOMAS, OF CHARLES COUNTY, MD.

THOMAS THOMAS was one of the early settlers on the Patuxent River, in Maryland, there being a surveyor's warrant to lay out for him the Broad Neck there, say fifty acres, July 15, 1651. He was probably the Thomas Thomas who first came over with Thomas Passmore, in the latter part of 1635. (See Land Records, Liber I., folio 73.) June 1, 1652, he demanded a warrant for six hundred acres for "transporting himself, his wife **ELIZABETH,**[1] son James Thomas, and Robert and Elioner Paterson and Matthew Smith his servants to the province in 1651," and received one to lay out for him with Will Batten one thousand acres north side of Patuxent River over against or near Buzzard's Island. (Liber A. B. H., folio 202.) November 22, 1652, there was laid out for "Thomas Thomas and Wm. Batten, planters of Putuxent River, 1,100 acres north side of Putapsco River.' March 31, 1656, he was, with Captain Philip Morgan, Mr. William Ewens, Lieutenant Philip Thomas, Mr. Samuel Vethers, and Lieutenant Richard Woolman, a High Commissioner of the Provincial Court held at Patuxent. December 28, 1670, he made his will.[2] Proved, February 2, 1670–71. (Liber I., folio 411.) It makes no mention of his son **JAMES** (*of whom presently*), but names

i.   **WILLIAM,** to whom was left the home plantation and one hundred acres in the woods ; he *m.* **ELIZABETH** ——, remained in S. Mary's Co., and *d.* in 1685, leaving to his son **THOMAS,** "Newinton ;" *dau.* **SARAH,** "Batchell's Rest ;" and to "child his wife is pregnant with," one hundred and thirty acres.

ii.   **MARY,** left one-third of four hundred acres of land and "two pewter dishes, one pewter Bason, three poringers, six spoons, one Dutch Pott and pott hookes and one dish."

iii.   **GRACE,** left one-third of four hundred acres, "one pewter dish, one plate, two Poringers, six spoons and one Iron Kettle ;" she *m.* —— **BREWER.**

iv.   **ELIZABETH,** left one-third of four hundred acres, "one Iron Kettle and one small Dutch Pott, one pewter dish and two Poringers, half a dozen of spoons and one plate." She *m.*, about 1672, **WILLIAM,** son of Dr. Peter Sharpe.

[1] *Dau.* of William Barton, Senior. See Maryland Archives, x., 568.
[2] No residence is stated, but the witnesses show him to have been of S. Mary's Co.

JAMES, eldest son of **Thomas** and **Elizabeth (Barton) Thomas**, *b.* before 1651, in which year he came over to Maryland with them ; *m.* **TERATIA** ——, and made his will as of " Charles County," June 7, 1701. Proved November 29, 1701. (Liber T. B., folio 215.) He left three hundred acres in that county on the west side of Patuxent River, called " Ware," to his three children,

i.   **JOHN,** *of whom presently.*
ii.   **THOMAS** (*q. v.*).
iii.   **ANNA MARY.**

JOHN, eldest son of **James** and **Teratia Thomas,** was of Charles Co., made his will April 30, 1756, proved July 7, 1757, from which it appears that he was of advanced age, and his wife deceased. He named his children as follows :

i.   **JOHN,** the eldest, left tract called " Ware," and made executor, *of whom presently.*
ii.   **LEONARD,** left " Bowling Green," two hundred acres.
iii.   **JAMES,** left negroes, sheep, and tobacco.
iv.   **WILLIAM,** left rest of lands and ' two negroes in compliance with a letter sent to Thomas Reeves, his wife's father, at the time of their marriage." (See Thomas, of S. Mary's Co.)
v.   **JANE,** *m.* **EDWARD SWANN,** and *d.* before 1756, leaving a *dau.*, **ELIZABETH,** who *m.* **THOMAS ADAMS.**
vi.   **ELIZABETH,** *m.* **BENJAMIN WOOD,** and *d.* before 1756, leaving a *dau.*, **ELIZABETH.**

JOHN, eldest son of **John Thomas,** of Charles Co., *m.* **MARY** ——, who made her will, in 1763, as of Dorchester Co., and as the widow of John Thomas, naming her brother-in-law, Captain William Thomas, and son **JOHN,** probably the **JOHN THOMAS,** of S. Inigoes, S. Mary's Co., Md., who *m.* **SARAH** —— (who *d.* in 1774), and made his will March 29, 1768 ; proved April 11, 1770. Issue (order uncertain) :

i.   **PHILIP.**
ii.   **JOHN.**
iii.   **WILLIAM.**
iv.   **ANN,** wife of **STEPHEN MILBURN.**
v.   **MARY,** possibly *m.* **DR. WILLIAM LANSDALE,** and had a *dau.*, **Elizabeth,** *m.* Dr. William Thomas (*q. v.*).
vi.   **SARAH.**
vii.   **ELIZABETH.**

THOMAS, younger son of **James** and **Teratia Thomas,** *d.* before February 20, 1723-24, when **SUSANNAH,** his widow, being " very weak and sick," made her will, proved August 31, 1724 (Liber W. B. No. 1, folio 335), in which she names the following children :

i.   **THOMAS,** her executor, *of whom presently.*
ii.   **GEORGE** (*q. v.*).
iii.   **WILLIAM,** bequeathed the reversion of her personal estate.
iv.   **ELIZABETH,** *m.* —— **ADAMS.**

THOMAS, probably eldest son of **Thomas** and **Susannah Thomas,** *m.* **ELIZABETH** ——, was of Charles Co., and March 6, 1733-34, being " sick and weak," made his will, proved October 22, 1734 (Liber T. & D., folio 216), naming the following children :

i.   **JAMES,** the eldest, to whom is left " part of my dividend of tract called ' Ware ; ' his mother is to have the rest."
ii.   **THOMAS,** *of whom presently.*
iii.   **WILLIAM,** of Charles Co., *m.* **ANN** ——, and *d.* before August 30, 1776. Issue :

       THOMAS, JAMES, ALLEN, WILLIAM, NEHEMIAH, ISAAC, JOSIAH, ZACHEY, ARCHIBALD, SARAH, TERESA, and **ELIZABETH,** named in his will.

iv.   **ELIZABETH.**
v.   **SOPHIA.**
vi.   **TERESA.**
vii.   **SOPHANIA.**
viii.   " The child my wife is now big with," mentioned in his father's will, and possibly the " Jesse Thomas," of his brother Thomas Thomas, Senior's, will, 1772.

THOMAS, second son of **Thomas** and **Elizabeth Thomas,** is called " Thomas Thomas, Senior," and was left by his father " Thomas's Fancy." He *m.* **ELEANOR** ——, and *d.* in Prince Georges Co., Md., having made his will in October, 1772 (Liber W. F. No. 1, folio 111), in which he left to his son **THOMAS,** " After Stamp," Prince Georges Co.; to his son **WILLIAM** (see Thomas of Wilmington, Del.), a negro boy, etc.; to his son **JAMES,** a negro girl, etc.; and declared : ' It is my will my daughters Jane Siscle (or Sivele), Elizabeth Siscle, Mary Siscle, and Sophania Maenuse, and likewise Jesse Thomas, shall have an equal part of all and singular my goods and chattels." The puzzle here is to determine the relationship of the last five persons to the testator. The first three—Jane Siscle, Elizabeth Siscle, and Mary Siscle—may have been his step-daughters ; but what about Sophania Maenuse and Jesse Thomas? The Christian name of the latter (Jesse) is unique among the Thomas wills in Maryland prior to 1775. It is believed, but without absolute proof thus far, that Sophania Maenuse was the testator's youngest sister, married to a Mr. Maenuse, and that Jesse Thomas was his youngest brother.

GEORGE, second son of **Thomas** and **Susannah Thomas,** resided in Charles Co., made his will November 21, 1738, proved December 22d (Liber D. D. No. 1, folio 20). His wife appears to have been deceased, and is unnamed ; his children mentioned are :

i. **JAMES,** to whom he left " Godfrey's Chace," two hundred acres.

ii. **GEORGE,** left " S. George's," one hundred and twenty acres, where Matthew Martin now lives ; *m.* **ANN** ——, and *d.* in April, 1752. Issue :

  TYER, JOHN, left sixty acres at Cedar Point, known as " Button ; " MARY, and PHILIP, all under age in 1752.

iii. **WILLIAM,** to whom he left " Bowen's Dispute," ninety-four acres.

iv. A *dau., m.* —— **BROOKS,** left " Thomas's Port," two hundred acres.

v. **SUSANNA,** *m.* —— **FARR.**

vi. **ELIZABETH,** *m.* —— **TOMPKINS.**

vii. A *dau., m.* —— **COMPTON,** and had a son,

  BENJAMIN,

viii. **BENJAMIN,** is left the residue of the estate, and he is to be executor of the will, though " also to be under the care of Capt. Benjamin Douglass, and my son, George Thomas, 'till he is 20."

Authorities : Land Records and Wills at Annapolis, Md., with some assistance from Judge Goldsborough, of Baltimore.

THOMAS, OF CHELTENHAM, PA.

JOHN THOMAS, of Pembrokeshire, Wales, *b.* in October, 1673 ; *m.*, June 27, 1706, **JENNET** ———, *b.* in June, 1683, and, September, 1713, came with her and his two eldest children to America, settling in the vicinity of what is now Cheltenham, on a farm of one hundred and ten acres purchased of John Ashman. He *d.* December 25, 1747, and his widow, January 22, 1755. Issue :

i.   **ANN,** *b.* in Wales, December 12, 1708 ; *m.*, May 13, 1729, **BENJAMIN MORRIS.**
ii.   **ELIZABETH,** *b.* in Wales, November 6, 1711.
iii. **MARY,** *b.* November 13, 1713 ; *m.*, May 21, 1731, **WILLIAM BRITTIN.**
iv.   **JOHN,** *b.* January 19, 1716 ; *m.*, March 5, 1752, **LUCRETIA,** *dau.* of John Hart.
v.   **SARAH,** *b.* June 24, 1717 ; *m.* **JOHN WHITE.**
vi.   **ISAAC,** *b.* February 7, 1719 ; *d. u.* 1760.
vii. **NATHAN,** *b.* January 26, 1721, *of whom presently.*
viii. **MARGARET,** *b.* February 20, 1723 ; *m.*, November 23, 1752, **MATTHIAS KEEN.**
ix.   **HANNAH,** *b.* March 30, 1725 ; *m.*, December 24, 1747, **ELIAS KEEN.**
x.   **JACOB,** *b.* September 11, 1727.

NATHAN, seventh child but third son of **John** and **Jennet Thomas,** *b.* January 26, 1721, near Cheltenham, Pa. ; *m.*, April 11, 1756, **ELIZABETH,** *dau.* of **Richard** and **Sarah (Penrose) Mather,** granddaughter of **Bartholomew** and **Hester (Leech) Penrose,** and great-granddaughter of **Toby** and **Hester Leech,** of Cheltenham, England. He *d.* in December, 1776. Issue :

i.   **RACHEL,** *b.* July 21, 1757 ; *d. u.*
ii. **SARAH,** *b.* February 5, 1759 ; *d. u.*
iii. **ISAAC,** *b.* May 29, 1762 ; *m.*, October 19, 1786, **ANN,** *dau.* of John and Ann Nanna Roberts.
iv. **JOSEPH,** *b.* June 20, 1765 ; *m.*, May 20, 1790, **REBECCA,** *dau.* of Benjamin Cottman.

v.   JACOB, *b.* January 20, 1768, *of whom presently.*
vi.   NATHAN, *b.* October 30, 1770 ; went to sea and never returned.
vii.   JOHN, *b.* March 22, 1774 ; *m.,* March 29, 1810, ELIZABETH, *dau.* of
        Joseph Hart.
viii.   ELIZABETH, *b.* May 20, 1778 ; *m.,* December 12, 1799, SAMUEL
        RUTH ; *d.* January 21, 1863.

JACOB, third son of **Nathan** and **Elizabeth (Mather) Thomas,**
b. January 20, 1768 ; *m.,* April 28, 1793, ANN, *dau.* of Jonathan
Johnson.   Issue :

i.   MARGARETTA, *b.* August 17, 1794 ; *d.* April 16, 1795.
ii.   JAMES CONNELLY, *b.* February 9, 1796 ; *d. u.,* April 24, 1830.
iii.   ELIZABETH, *b.* February 13, 1798 ; *m.,* November 18, 1819, ISAAC
        ELLIOTT ; *d.* September 12, 1871.
iv.   MARY ANN, *b.* January 19, 1800 ; *m.,* May 4, 1826, JOHN B.
        JEWELL, and *d.* August 22, 1881.
v.   JOHNSON, *b.* May 3, 1802 ; *d.* 1803.
vi.   CHARLES JOHNSON, *b.* August 13, 1803 ; *m.,* November 12, 1829,
        ANN, *dau.* of James Molony ; *d.* August 20, 1871.
vii.   JOSEPH MATHER, *b.* August 14, 1805, *of whom presently.*
viii.   JOHN BURTIS, *b.* April 21, 1808 ; *d. u.* at sea.
ix.   LUCRETIA ELEANOR, *b.* October 9, 1811 ; *m.* first, July 1, 1829,
        WILLIAM J. KIRK ; *m.* second, October 20, 1836, WILLIAM
        HART CARR.

JOSEPH MATHER, fourth son of **Jacob** and **Ann (Johnson)**
Thomas, *b.* August 14, 1805 ; *m.,* February 20, 1834, LYDIA,
dau. of **Anthony** and **Mary (Ogden) Cuthbert,** and *d.* December 16, 1861.   Issue :

i.   MARY CUTHBERT, *d. u.* July 14, 1860.
ii.   ANTHONY CUTHBERT, *m.,* December 5, 1861, MARIA, *dau.* of J.
        M. Crossman, who *d.* July 4, 1872.   Issue :

        WALTER CUTHBERT.

iii.   JOSEPH H., *d. y.*
iv.   ANNIE JOHNSON.
v.   ELIZABETH ROBERTS.
vi.   ALLENA.
vii.   THEODORE, *m.,* April 25, 1876, CORDELIA, *dau.* of Edwin Lle-
        wellyn and Cassandra Berry (Lansdale) Parker, of Baltimore,
        Md. ; no issue.
viii.   JOHN McCAWLEY, *d. i.*
ix.   GEORGE CUTHBERT, *m.,* June 17, 1875, ADA, *dau.* of Joseph C.
        Canning, Esq., of Stockbridge, Mass.   Issue :

        DOROTHY CUTHBERT.

x.   **HENRY B.,** *m.*, April 5, 1880, **FRANCES,** *dau.* of **Herman** and **Elizabeth (Shaw) Melville.** Issue:

      i.   **ELEANOR MELVILLE.**
      ii.   **FRANCES CUTHBERT.**
      iii. **KATHERINE GANSEVOORT.**
      iv. **JEANNETTE OGDEN.**

Authorities : Family papers through Mr. A. Cuthbert Thomas ; General W. H. H. Davis's Hart Family, and Gregory B. Keen's History of the Kyn or Keen Family.

ARMS OF WOLCOTT

THOMAS, OF CULPEPER COUNTY, VA.

MAHLON, or **MELLEN THOMAS,** of this county, emigrated about 1812 to the West ; volunteered in the war with Great Britain ; served creditably under General William Henry Harrison, and was detailed by him to serve on Commodore Perry's flotilla, in the battle of Lake Erie.   He *m.* a **WOLCOTT,** of Connecticut descent, and had a son, **GEORGE W.,** at college with Judge Dent, brother-in-law of President Grant.   Of the same family no doubt was —— Thomas, of Culpeper Co., *m.* Mildred Taylor, and had a son James, *m.* Elizabeth Pendleton, and after all his children were grown, removed to Kentucky.   Their son Pendleton *m.* Sarah S. Dunklin, and had a *dau.* Martha Ann, who *m.* Dr. D. C. Case.   Issue : a son Charles T., of Nashville, Tenn., *m.* Roberta L. Staples.

Authority : Family papers, through Mr. Charles T. Case.

THOMAS, OF DANYGRAIG, GLAMORGAN-SHIRE, WALES

THIS family claims descent from Einion ap Collwyn, through Owen Philip, Portreeve of Swansea, 1600 ; son of Philip John ap Rhys, of Glyn-Nedd. In the fifth generation was buried **WILLIAM THOMAS,** in the south aisle of S. Mary's Church, Swansea. Issue : **WALTER,** High Sheriff of Glamorganshire, in 1648 ; and **WILLIAM,** High Sheriff in 1644 ; both *d. s. p.* The latter gave his estate to his uncle, Bussy Mansel, of Briton Ferry. Edmund Thomas, of Orchard, High Sheriff of Glamorganshire in 1670, may have been of the family.

Authority : T. Nicholas's Annals of Wales.

93

THOMAS, OF DUFFRYN FFRWD, WALES

GWILIM AP RALPH had a son **MEURICE**, and grandson **EVAN**, *of whom presently.*

EVAN ap MEURIC *m.* **GWENLLIAN**, *dau.* of **Gwilim ap Evan ap Howel**; *d.* 1572. Issue :

i.   **THOMAS**, *of whom presently.*
ii.   **EVAN**. Issue :

    i.   **DAVID EVAN.**
    ii.   **EVAN.**
    iii.   **THOMAS.**
    iv.   **CATHERINE**, *m.* **WILLIAM BASSETT**, clerk.
    v.   **MORGAN.**
    vi.   **THOMAS**, who had two sons, Richard and Francis.

THOMAS, eldest son of **Evan ap Meuric** and **Gwenllian ap Gwilim**, was of Eglwysilan, and *m.* **JANET**, *dau.* of **Howel Cadwgan**, of Abergorkey, who *d.* in 1590. He *d.* in 1612. Issue :

i.   **EVAN**, *b.* 1581, *of whom presently.*
ii.   **GWENLLIAN.**
iii.   **MARGARET**, *m.* **THOMAS DAVID**, of Eglwysilan.

EVAN, son of **Thomas ap Evan** and **Janet ap Howel**, *b.* 1581 ; *m.* **CATHERINE**, *dau.* of **Edward Lewis**, of Llanishen, and *d.* 1666. Issue :

i.   **BARBARA**, *b.* 1610, *m.* **EDWARD WATKIN**, of Kellygaer. Issue :

    i.   **THOMAS**, *b.* 1632.
    ii.   **CATHERINE**, *b.* 1634.
    iii.   **RICHARD**, *b.* 1636.
    iv.   **MARY**, *b.* 1639.
    v.   **SARAH**, *b.* 1643.
    vi.   **EVAN**, *b.* 1645.
    vii.   **RACHEL**, *b.* 1647.
    viii.   **REBECCA**, *b.* 1650.

ii.   **MARGARET,** *b.* 1613 ; *m.* **THOMAS MORGAN,** of Llanedern.
iii.   **THOMAS EVAN,** *b.* 1615, *of whom presently.*
iv.   **EVAN,** whence descended **Evan Thomas,** *d.* 1797.
v.   **EDMUND,** *b.* 1628 ; *m.* **MARGARET,** *dau.* of **Llewellyn Morgan.**
       Issue :
       i.   **THOMAS.**
       ii. **CATHERINE.**
       iii. **JANET.**

THOMAS EVAN, eldest son of **Evan ap Thomas** and **Catherine Lewis,** *b.* 1615 ; *m.* **ELEANOR,** *dau.* of **Rev. Morgan Jones, D.D.,** of Frampton in Llantwit Major. Issue :

i.   **THOMAS,** *b.* 1636, *of whom presently.*
ii.   **EVAN,** *b.* 1634 ; *m.* **SARAH,** *dau.* and *heir* of —— **Gilbert,** of Longtown, Herefordshire, *b.* 1640.

THOMAS THOMAS, son of **Thomas** and **Eleanor (Jones) Evan,** *b.* 1636 ; *m.* **CATHERINE,** eldest *dau.* of **Edward Watkin.** Issue :

i.   **THOMAS,** *b.* June 21, 1668.
ii.   **EVAN,** *of whom presently.*
iii. **ELEANOR,** *m.* —— **WATKIN,** of Vaendra Vawr.
iv. **BARBARA,** *m.* **MORGAN ap THOMAS MORGAN,** of Ruperra.

EVAN, second son of **Thomas** and **Catherine (Watkin) Thomas ;** *m.* **JANE,** *dau.* of **Philip,** son of **Edward Herbert.** Issue :

i.   **EVAN,** *m.* **ANN,** *dau.* of **William Gibbon.** Issue :
      MARY, *m.* **MORGAN WILLIAMS.**
ii.   **THOMAS,** *d. u.*
iii. **JANE,** *m.* **JOHN,** son of **Joshua Ward.**
iv. **ELEANOR,** *d. y.*

Authority : Clark's Genealogies of Morgan and Glamorgan, p. 519.

THOMAS, OF EDEN, MAINE

JOHN THOMAS came from Wales to Boston and *m.* there, March 30, 1666–67, **ELIZABETH** ———. Issue:

> **JOHN**, an "Inn Holder," *m.*, at Providence, 1696, **ELIZABETH VIALL**. Issue:
>
> i. **JOHN**, *of whom presently.*
> ii. **JAMES.**
> iii. **NICHOLAS.**

JOHN, eldest son of **John** and **Elizabeth (Viall) Thomas** was a cooper by trade; *m.* **ELIZABETH BOZARD** and *d.* at Providence in 1790. Issue:

i. **JOHN**, *of whom presently.*
ii. **MORRIS.**
iii. **LEWIS.**
iv. **MARY**, *m.*, October 7, 1750, **JOHN STEWART.**
v. **SARAH**, *m.*, November 26, 1761, **JONATHAN VIALL.**
vi. a *dau.*, *m.* ——— **MASON.**
vii. a *dau.*, *m.* ——— **CHAFFEE.**
viii. a *dau.*, *m.* ——— **PECK.**

JOHN, son of **John** and **Elizabeth (Bozard) Thomas**, resided at Eden, Me., was a cooper and sea captain, *m.*, at Providence, R. I., October 18, 1744, **ELIZABETH PECK.** Issue:

i. **ELIZABETH P.**, *b.* July 29, 1745; *m.* **JAPHET OLVERSON.**
ii. **ZENA**, *b.* December 29, 1747; *d.* July 28, 1836.
iii. **JOHN**, *of whom presently.*
iv. **NICHOLAS**, *b.* March 22, 1753 (*q. v.*).
v. **HANNAH**, *b.* January 16, 1756; *d.* March 1, 1840.
vi. **PEGGY**, *b.* December 18, 1759; *d.* June 28, 1817.
vii. **HULDAH**, *b.* May 10, 1762; *d.* January 9, 1811.
viii. **AMOS**, *b.* July 17, 1764.

JOHN, son of **John** and **Elizabeth (Peck) Thomas,** *b.* February 9, 1750 ; *m.* first **ELIZABETH COUSINS,** who *d.* May 23, 1802. Issue :

i.   **JOHN,** *b.* November 6, 1777, *of whom presently.*

ii.   **BENJAMIN,** *b.* May 5, 1780 (*q. v.*).

iii.   **HANNAH,** *b.* October 31, 1782 ; *m.,* January 1, 1807, **JOEL EMERY,** house carpenter, and *d.* September 12, 1825.

iv.   **OLIVER,** *b.* March 21, 1785, was a master mariner and *m.,* June 30, 1808, **SARAH RODICKS.** Issue :

> ELMENIA, *b.* 1808 ; *m.,* February 13, 1834, **EDWARD HAMOR,** master mariner, of Eden ; *d.* March 30, 1839.

v.   **BETSEY,** *b.* April 2, 1787 ; *m.* **SOLOMON STEVENS,** millwright, of Trenton, and *d.* April 8, 1828.

vi.   **COMFORT,** *b.* September 6, 1789 (*q. v.*).

vii.   **CYLINDA,** *b.* May 13, 1794 ; *m.,* November 2, 1818, **SAMUEL BEAN,** farmer, of Sullivan, Me.

viii.   **SARAH,** *b.* April 14, 1797 ; *m.,* November 6, 1814, **CORNELIUS THOMPSON,** farmer, of Eden.

ix.   **EBENEZER C.,** b. April 27, 1801.

JOHN THOMAS, *m.,* second, June 4, 1803, **MRS. ELIZABETH PARKER,** and *d.* April 13, 1841. Further issue :

x.   **CAROLINE,** *b.* May 4, 1804 ; *m.,* November 28, 1822, **SAMUEL S. INGALLS,** housewright, of Sullivan, Me.

xi.   **MARGARET,** *b.* February 13, 1807 ; *m.,* February 25, 1831, **PERLEY HAYNES,** farmer, of Dedham, Me.

xii.   **J. PARKER,** *b.* July 10, 1810, was a blacksmith, resided at Bluehill, Me.; *m.,* October 8, 1834, **MELINDA HOLT.** Issue :

> i.   **MARY E.,** *b.* October 14, 1835.
> ii.   **MELINDA A.,** *b.* September 23, 1838.
> iii.   **EDWARD P.,** *b.* April 17, 1840.
> iv.   **GEORGE W.,** *b.* November 8, 1842.
> v.   **DELIA A.,** *b.* November 25, 1845.
> vi.   **SARAH J.,** *b.* October 23, 1850.

xiii.   **SUSANNA,** *b.* July 10, 1810 ; *m.,* December 8, 1833, **SYLVESTER OSGOOD,** blacksmith, of Ellsworth, Me.

xiv.   **SOPHRONIA,** *b.* August 28, 1812 ; *m.,* November 29, 1833, **BENJAMIN FRANKLIN INGALLS,** shipwright, of Sullivan, Me.

JOHN, eldest son of **John** and **Elizabeth (Cousins) Thomas,** *b.* November 6, 1777 ; was a ship carpenter and farmer ; *m.,* June 1, 1801, **JUDITH THOMPSON,** and *d.* January 29, 1829. Issue :

i.   **JUDITH B.,** *b.* July 12, 1802 ; *m.,* December 18, 1828, **THOMAS KNOWLES,** ship carpenter, of Eden.

ii.   **JOHN**, *b.* February 10, 1804, was a sea captain ; *m.*, October 23, 1828, **JEDIDAH EMERY**, and *d.* July 17, 1843. Issue :

      i.   **JOEL OSCAR**, *b.* July 20, 1830.
      ii.   **MELETIAH O.**, *b.* April 4, 1832 ; *d.* October 27, 1837.
      iii. **AMORET J.**, *b.* May 27, 1834.
      iv. **GEORGE GAY**, *b.* July 2, 1841.

iii.   **LUCINDA**, *b.* September 26, 1805 ; *m.*, October 5, 1834, **ANDREW ULMER**, lime-dealer, of Rockland, Me.
iv.   **C. THOMPSON**, *b.* April 24, 1807 ; *d.* December 13, 1828.
v.   **MARY H.**, *b.* April 21, 1809 ; *d.* July 5, 1811.
vi.   **MELETIAH L.**, *b.* February 25, 1811.
vii.   **MARY E. H.**, *b.* April 8, 1813 ; *m.*, October 26, 1848, **ALONZO D. AMES**, tin-plate worker, of Bangor.
viii. **WILLIAM T.**, *b.* April 10th ; *d.* April 15, 1815.
ix.   **WILLIAM T.**, *b.* May 6, 1816 ; was a trader ; *m.*, December 22, 1841, **CLARINDA HIGGINS**. Issue :

      i.   **ELEANOR H.**, *b.* October 12, 1842.
      ii.   **JOHN W.**, *b.* April 18th ; *d.* November 4, 1845.
      iii. **EMMA F.**, *b.* November 6, 1849.

x.   **SAMUEL T.**, *b.* August 3, 1819 ; was a blacksmith ; *m.*, August 31, 1845, **HENRIETTA S. LINDSAY**. Issue :

      i.   **EDWIN H.**, *b.* January 17, 1847.
      ii.   **CLARA LOUISA**, *b.* April 14, 1849.

BENJAMIN, second son of **John** and **Elizabeth (Cousins) Thomas**, *b.* May 5, 1780 ; was a master mariner ; *m.*, September 2, 1806, **POLLY THOMPSON**, and *d.* Issue :

i.   **BETSEY C.**, *b.* December, 1806 ; *d.* August 18, 1823.
ii.   **LEWIS**, *b.* March 22, 1809 ; *d.* August 9, 1834.
iii.   **CORNELIUS T.**, *b.* January 1, 1812 ; was a mariner ; *m.*, September 10, 1840, **MARY ANN RICHARDS**. Issue :

      i.   **TULLIA A.**, *b.* July 29, 1846.
      ii.   **SELENA B.**, *b.* August 15, 1848 ; *d.* April 9, 1850.
      iii. **SELENA B.**, *b.* May 20, 1850.

iv.   **EMELINE**, *b.* March 1, 1815 ; *d.* January 10, 1829.
v.   **SPOFFORD P.**, *b.* December 8, 1816 ; lived at Ellsworth ; was a blacksmith ; *m.*, July 23, 1843, **MIRANDA MORRISON**. Issue :

      i.   **JOHN L.**, *b.* December 20, 1843 ; *d.* August 17, 1846.
      ii.   **CAROLINE E.**, *b.* July 8, 1847.
      iii. **JOHN L.**, *b.* October 11, 1848 ; *d.* January 4, 1849.

vi.   **OLIVER**, *b.* July 28, 1819 ; *d.* August 25, 1825.
vii.   **BENJAMIN F.**, *b.* June 8, 1822 ; lived at Eden ; was a house carpenter ; *m.*, January 22, 1846, **SOPHIA SMITH**. Issue :

      i.   **ORRIN L.**, *b.* December 8, 1846.
      ii.   **CHARLOTTE E.**, *b.* December 25, 1848.

viii.   OLIVER P., *b*. December 31, 1825 ; lived at Eden ; was a blacksmith ; *m*., November 10, 1850, MARTHA HOPKINS.
ix.   EMELINE, *b*. August 4, 1830.

NICHOLAS, second son of John and Elizabeth (Peck) Thomas, *b*. March 22, 1753 ; was the first person baptized by immersion at Mount Desert ; was for thirty years a deacon of the Baptist Congregation at Eden, Me., and a soldier in the Revolutionary War, under Colonel John Allen. He *m*., first, February 22, 1779, LUCY, *dau*. of Captain Abraham Somes, of Gloucester, Mass. Issue :

i.   NICHOLAS, *b*. May 18, 1780, *of whom presently*.
ii.   LUCY, *b*. July 2, 1782 ; *d*. September 29, 1793.
iii.   BETSEY, *b*. February 13, 1784 ; *d*. September 30, 1793.
iv.   ABRAHAM, *b*. November 14, 1785 (*q. v.*).
v.   ISAAC, *b*. November 20, 1787 (*q. v.*).
vi.   JACOB, *b*. November 2, 1789 ; *d*. October 5, 1793.

NICHOLAS THOMAS, *m*., second, October 18, 1792, JANE RICHARDSON, of Mount Desert. Further issue :

vii.   LUCY, *b*. June 20, 1793 ; *m*., November 8, 1822, PETER STEPHENSON, merchant tailor, of Boston, and *d*. April 26, 1836.
viii.   BETSEY, *b*. August 24, 1794 ; *m*., January 1, 1817, WILLIAM LELAND, tanner, of Eden, and *d*. March 31, 1826.
ix.   JACOB S., *b*. March 17, 1796 ; was a shipwright and member of Maine Legislature ; *m*., July 16, 1817, NANCY P. TOWNSEND. Issue :

   i.   OZIAS BUDDINGTON, *b*. March 15, 1818 ; *d*. March 18, 1822.
   ii.   ELIHU, *b*. March 22, 1820 ; *d*. May 25, 1844.
   iii.   JOHN MILTON, *b*. September 12, 1823, a mariner ; *m*. October 15, 1846, HANNAH C. MOORE, and *d*. September 24, 1848, leaving a daughter.
   iv.   AMELIA S., *b*. May 1, 1837.

x.   AMOS, *b*. June 13, 1798 ; *d*. September 7, 1803.
xi.   JAMES, *b*. January 9, 1800 ; *d*. February 24, 1804.
xii.   DAVID, *b*. November 3, 1802 ; *d*. in September, 1832.

NICHOLAS THOMAS, *m*., third, December 21, 1820, LYDIA HADLEY, of Eden, and *d*. January 20, 1838, without further issue.

NICHOLAS second, the eldest son of Nicholas and Lucy (Somes) Thomas, *b*. May 18, 1780, was a farmer, member of the Convention which formed the Constitution of Maine, a mem-

ber of the Legislature, and justice of the peace ; resided at Eden ;
m., February 22, 1803, **HANNAH WASGATT.** Issue :

i.   **ROXOLANA,** *b.* September 12 ; *d.* December 23, 1803.
ii.   **LEONARD J.,** *b.* March 30, 1805, Collector of Customs, Member of Legislature ; *m.*, December 15, 1830, **AMELIA F. TOWNSEND.** Issue :

      FRANCES A., *b.* April 14, 1839.

iii. **ROXOLANA,** *b.* November 11, 1807 ; *m.*, December 15, 1830, **WILLIAM HAYNES,** of Trenton, farmer and justice of the peace.
iv.   **LUCY S.,** *b.* July 30, 1810 ; *m.*, January 24, 1840, **HENRY HODGEKINS,** of Trenton, house- and ship-joiner.
v.   **NANCY W.,** *b.* March 24, 1813 ; *m.*, December 5, 1832, **ASA EDWARDS,** of Ellsworth, Me., housewright.
vi.   **NICHOLAS J.,** *b.* September 11, 1815, farmer, shoemaker, and justice of the peace ; resided at Eden ; *m.*, February 22, 1837, **NANCY T. TREWORGY.** Issue :

    i.   **COLUMBIA L.,** *b.* January 11, 1839.
    ii.   **MORTON,** *b.* October 21, 1840; *d.* January 27, 1842.
    iii. **ZARESSA A.,** *b.* February 20, 1843.
    iv.   **LAFAYETTE,** *b.* September 16, 1845 ; *d.* April 4, 1846.
    v.   **ELBA H.,** *b.* December 24, 1848.

vii. **HANNAH W.,** *b.* July 1, 1817 ; *m.*, April 20, 1837, **DANIEL F. TREWORGY,** farmer, of Blue Hill, Me.
viii. **BANCROFT W.,** *b.* August 12, 1820, a housewright ; lived at Ellsworth, Me.; *m.*, December 18, 1848, **NANCY CROSS.**
ix.   **LEONORA,** *b.* May 29th ; *d.* October 28, 1823.
x.   **GEORGE W. L.,** *b.* September 8, 1824 ; a carriage-maker ; lived at Ellsworth ; *m.*, January 6, 1848, **HENRIETTA CROSS.** Issue :

    i.   **SITTARA A.,** *b.* November 30, 1848.
    ii.   **NICHOLAS O.**
    iii. **MELANIE Z.,** *b.* September 3, 1851.

xi.   **LEONORA E.,** *b.* February 10, 1828 ; *d.* May 28, 1830.

ABRAHAM, second son of **Nicholas** and **Lucy (Somes) Thomas,** *b.* November 14, 1785 ; was a farmer and member of the Maine Legislature ; lived at Eden ; *m.*, February 18, 1811, **JANE BERRY,** and *d.* November 15, 1838. Issue :

i.   **AMOS B.,** *b.* March 3, 1812 ; a housewright ; lived at Farmington, Ill.; *m.*, November 26, 1838, **MARY HART.** Issue :

    i.   **ELIZABETH J.,** *b.* February 20, 1842.
    ii.   **HENRIETTA H.,** *b.* July 21, 1843.
    iii. **FREDERICK,** *b.* February 5th ; *d.* July 16, 1847.

ii.   **MATILDA J.,** *b.* March 22, 1814 ; *m.*, January 9, 1840, **BENJAMIN PEACH,** of Eden, seaman.

iii. **ISAAC H.,** *b.* June 20, 1817 ; a farmer, at Eden ; *m.*, July 20, 1839, **COR-DELIA HAMOR.** Issue :

    i.   **ARVILLA O.,** *b.* March 29, 1840.
    ii.   **M. MORTON,** *b.* October 30, 1842.
    iii.   **MATILDA J.,** *b.* February 22, 1845.
    iv.   **MARY ANN,** *b.* January 12, 1847.

iv. **BLOOMFIELD,** *b.* August 11, 1819.

ISAAC, third son of **Nicholas** and **Lucy (Somes) Thomas,** *b.* November 20, 1787, a farmer of Presque Isle, Me.; *m.*, July 7, 1821, **SARAH A. PARKS.** Issue :

i. **LEONARD J.,** *b.* February 28, 1822 ; a farmer, of Presque Isle ; *m.*, December 18, 1847, **DEBORAH BROWN.** Issue :

    OSCAR E., *b.* May 29, 1849.

ii. **HARRIET,** *b.* October 22, 1823 ; *m.*, October 20, 1847, **ARCHIBALD SCOTT,** farmer, of Mattamawamkeag, Me.

iii. **ALMIRA,** *b.* July 16, 1825.

iv. **NATHANIEL,** *b.* July 25, 1827.

v. **DAVID,** *b.* December 23, 1829.

vi. **IRENE E.,** *b.* February 10, 1831.

vii. **GEORGE G.,** *b.* August 23, 1834.

viii. **MOSES T.,** *b.* June 16, 1837.

ix. **ISAAC R.,** *b.* December 16, 1840; *d.* November 19, 1850.

x. **AUGUSTUS G.,** *b.* December 13, 1842.

xi. **CHARLES A.,** *b.* December 20, 1848.

COMFORT, fourth son of **John** and **Elizabeth (Cousins) Thomas,** *b.* September 6, 1789 ; was a farmer ; *m.*, October 19, 1808, **MELINDA PARKER.** Issue :

i. **MARIA,** *b.* December 12, 1808 ; *m.*, August 3, 1830, **WILLIAM SOM-ERBY,** merchant tailor and justice of the peace, of Ellsworth, Me.

ii. **JOSEPH P.,** *b.* November 11, 1811 ; lived at Franklin, Me., was a ship master ; *m.*, December 29, 1839, **MARY SCAMMONS.** Issue ·

    i.   **LEWIS A.,** *b.* November 11, 1840 ; *d.* July 12, 1841.
    ii.   **HARRIET A.,** *b.* January 22, 1842.
    iii.   **ELLEN F.,** *b.* April 6, 1843.
    iv.   **CALVIN C.,** *b.* June 17, 1844.
    v.   **EDWARD J.,** *b.* November 29, 1845.

iii. **CHARLOTTE G.,** *b.* July 30, 1814 ; *m.*, May 3, 1838, **DANIEL S. BEAL,** butcher, of Ellsworth, Me.

iv. **JULIA ANN,** *b.* March 5, 1818 ; *d.* May 22, 1818.

v. **JULIA ANN,** *b.* November 1, 1820.

vi. **BENJAMIN C.,** *b.* May 11, 1823.

vii. **BETSEY M.,** *b.* October 10th ; *d.* October 25, 1825.

viii. **RUFUS R.,** *b.* May 25, 1827 ; manufacturer of sash and door frames, etc., at Philadelphia, Pa.

    Authority : The rare tabular pedigree of the family.

THOMAS, OF ESSEX, ENGLAND

GEOFFREY LE SCROPE, ninth and last Baron Scrope of Masham and Upsale, *d.* 1517, leaving three sisters and coheirs, one of whom, **ALICE,** *m.* Sir **JAMES STRANGWAYS,** and was grandmother of Robert Roos, of Igmanthorpe, Yorkshire.

ROBERT ROOS had a *dau.* **BRIDGET,** *m.* **PETER ROOS,** of Laxton, Nottinghamshire, and had a son, ɢɪʟʙᴇʀᴛ, whose only surviving child, ᴇʟɪᴢᴀʙᴇᴛʜ ʀᴏᴏs, *m.*, before 1635, ᴡɪʟʟɪᴀᴍ ᴛʜᴏᴍᴀs, of Essex, and was party to a suit, October 13, 1638, to determine whether she or Rose Roos, wife of Richard Brest, was next heir to the aforesaid Robert Roos.

Authority: Nichols's Collectanea Topographica, etc., viii., 163.

THOMAS, OF ESSEX COUNTY, VA.

Two brothers, **ROBERT** and **WILLIAM THOMAS**, emigrated from Wales to Virginia in the seventeenth century, and received large grants of land in the Province. One tradition makes them of the family seated at "Pwllyrach," in Glamorganshire; another brings them from Caermarthen.

WILLIAM THOMAS had a patent of land in Lancaster Co., July 13, 1653.[1]

ROBERT THOMAS had a grant, November 20, 1654; probably[2] *m.* —— **MASSIE**, and had a son, **EDWARD**, *b.* 1643. High Sheriff of Essex Co., Va., June 10, 1696; received patents for 8,880 acres in Essex, Middlesex, and Rappahannock Counties; resided at Thomas Neck on the Rappahannock River, and had a son, WILLIAM, *b.* about 1683, who was a large contributor in 1730 to the building of S. Anne's Parish Church (called Vawters), in Essex Co. The bricks were stamped with the contributors' names, and "**Thomas**" may still be read on some of them. He sold 1,000 acres of "Thomas Neck" to —— Layton. He *m.* **ELIZABETH** ——. Issue:

William, *of whom presently.*

WILLIAM, Jr., son of **William** and **Elizabeth Thomas**, *b.* about 1716; *m.* **SUSANNAH**,[3] *dau.* of **John Boulware**, and heiress in 1739, at death of her brother **John** and sisters **Mary**

[1] See Appendix X., for this and other patents.

[2] See a land patent to him under that date, in Appendix X.

[3] Her prayer-book, containing a list of their slaves, is in possession of her great-granddaughter, Mrs. Annie Hert, of Detroit, Mich.

and **Elizabeth,** of her father's estate, six hundred acres, in Essex Co. Issue :

i.   **LEWIS,** *b.* 1759 ; *m.* **MARGERY NOËL.** Issue :

    i.   **WILLIAM** (**Captain Billy Thomas**), sold " Thomas Neck," in 1818, to R. Payne Waring, for $17,300, and moved north. He *m.* **SALLIE** ——, and *d.* at Fall River, Mass. ; a son, James, went West. " Thomas Neck " was bought in 1890 for $5,000 by George Ellis.

    ii.   **MARGERY NOËL.**

ii.   **EDWARD,** *b.* 1760 ; *d. y.*

iii. **SUSAN,** *b.* 1761 ; *m.* —— **CROSS,** of Stafford Co., Va.

iv.   **CATHERINE,** *b.* 1763 ; *m.* **CAPTAIN WILLIAM WHITE,** of Hanover Co., Va., now in Kentucky. Her descendants have the Thomas Family Bible.

v.   **JAMES,** *b.* March 2, 1765, *of whom presently.*

vi.   **ELIZABETH,** *b.* 1766 ; *m.* **JOSEPH BIRNIE** or **BROEM,** of Caroline Co., Va.

JAMES, third son of **William** and **Susannah (Boulware) Thomas,** *b.* March 2, 1765 ; *m.,* January 9, 1793, **ELIZABETH,** *dau.* of **Joshua** and **Joicie (Garnette) Andrews,** of Caroline Co., Va. (*b.* November 28, 1768). Issue :

i.   **NANCY,** *b.* November 3, 1793 ; *d.* July 30, 1795.

ii.   **ARCHER** or **ARCHIBALD,** *b.* March 28, 1796 ; *m.* **CATHERINE PULLER.** Issue :

    i.   **JULIA,** *m.* **ALBERT WORTHAM.** Issue (surname WORTHAM):
        Alberta, Kate, and Julia Dean.

    ii.   **WILSON,** *m.* **REBECCA TEMPLE.** Issue :
        Lewis and Temple.

    iii. **CALLIE,** *m.* **JOSIAH RYLAND.** Issue : a *dau.,* Callie.

iii. **SUSANNAH,** *b.* August 12, 1798 ; *m.* **JOSEPH PATTERSON.** Issue (surname PATTERSON) :
    EMILY, ARCHIE, and **JOSEPHINE.**

iv.   **JAMES,** *b.* January 1, 1800, *d. i.*

v., vi. **IRA** (*m.* —— **MORGAN**) and **EMMELINE,** *b.* May 13, 1803, twins.

vii., viii. **JAMES,** *of whom presently,* and **WILLIAM,** twins, *b.* February 8, 1806, the latter *d.* 1827.

ix.   **ELIZABETH G.,** *b.* November 11, 1811.

JAMES, Jr., son of **James** and **Elizabeth (Andrews) Thomas,** *b.* February 8, 1806, settled early in life at Richmond, Va. ; *m.,* first, **MARY CARMICK PULLER.** Issue :

i.   **WILLIAM DANDRIDGE,** *of whom presently.*

ii.   **MARY ELLA,** *m.,* 1862, **DR. WILLIAM D. QUESENBERRY,** and had a *dau.,* **MARY ELLA,** *d. y.*

JAMES THOMAS, *m.,* second, **MARY WOOLFOLK WORTHAM,** of Richmond, and *d.* 1882. Issue :

iii.　MARY WORTHAM, *m.*, 1867, DR. J. L. M. CURRY, of Alabama,
late United States Minister to Spain ; member of Congress ; General
Manager and Trustee of the Peabody Education Fund, and of the John
F. Slater Fund.

iv.　ALICE COLEMAN, *m.*, 1865, JOHN KERR CONNALLY, of
Asheville, N. C.　Issue (surname CONNALLY) :

   i.　MARY WORTHAM THOMAS, *m.* OTIS COXE.　Issue : a son, Francis
Tench.
   ii.　ALYS KERR.
   iii.　LILY MOREHEAD, *d. y.*
   iv.　MARY CURRY.

v.　LAURA WAYLAND, *m.* THOMAS MELDRUM RUTHER-
FOORD, of Richmond, Va.　Issue (surname RUTHERFOORD) :

   i.　JAMES THOMAS.
   ii.　THOMAS MELDRUM, Jr., *d. y.*
   iii.　LAURA THOMAS.
   iv.　GWENDOLYN MELDRUM.

vi.　BETTIE LINCOLN, *m.* JAMES WATERS ALLISON, and *d.*
leaving a son, JAMES THOMAS, *d. y.*
vii.　SALLIE A., *d. y.*
viii.　JAMES R., *d. y.*
ix.　KATE CORNICK, *m.* CALDERON CARLISLE, of Washington,
D. C.　Issue (surname CARLISLE) :

   i.　JAMES MANDEVILLE.
   ii.　MARY WORTHAM.
   iii.　KATE THOMAS, *d. y.*

x.　GABRIELLE, *m.* RICHMOND PEARSON.　Issue (surname PEAR-
SON) :

   i.　RICHMOND MOUNTFORD, *d. i.*
   ii.　RICHMOND, Jr.
   iii.　MARJORIE NOEL WORTHAM.
   iv.　JAMES THOMAS.

REV. WILLIAM DANDRIDGE, only son of James and Mary Carmick (Puller) Thomas, *m.*, first, ELLA HORACE, *dau.* of Colonel John R. and Gilley (Marshall) Jones, of Charlottesville, Va.　Issue :

i.　JAMES CARMICK.
ii., iii.　ELLA MARSHALL and WILLIAM RUSSELL, twins.
iv.　MARY WORTHAM.

REV. WILLIAM D. THOMAS *m.*, second, MARIA LE-VENA, *dau.* of Colonel Leven and Maria Louise (Grady) Powell, of Loudon Co., Va.　Issue :

v.　MARIA LEVENA.

Authority : Family papers, through Miss Ella M. Thomas, of Richmond, Va., and Mrs. J. L. M.
Curry, of Washington, D. C.

THOMAS, OF FAYETTE COUNTY, IND.

MINOR, third son of **Recompense Thomas,** was *b.* in the New York Colony, July 8, 1770, and became the pioneer Baptist preacher in Ohio and Indiana about 1820; settling first in the Miami Valley near the present site of the city of Cincinnati. A few years later he bought a tract of land in Fayette Co., Ind. He was a powerful preacher and wore himself out in frontier work, organizing many Baptist congregations in Ohio and Eastern Indiana. He *m.* first, in New York, April 1, 1792, **ELLEN FAIRCHILD,** who *d.* September 20, 1794. Issue:

i.   **DAVID FAIRCHILD,** *b.* September 12, 1794; *m.* **PHEBE ———,** and *d.* October 6, 1881. Issue:
     i.   **MINOR,** *d.* leaving three children.
     ii. **HARRIET** *m.* ——— **KING.**
     iii. **ERASTHMUS D.**

MINOR THOMAS, *m.* second, September 7, 1795, **NANCY WINANS,** of Seneca Co., N. Y., who *d.* November 1, 1818. Issue (born in Seneca Co., N. Y.):

ii. **LAWRENCE,** *b.* April 27, 1796; *d.* May 10, 1796.
iii. **ELLEN,** *b.* May 28, 1797; *m.* **MINOR BUCK,** of New York State; *d.* September 28, 1863. Issue (surname BUCK):
     i.   **DUDLEY.**
     ii. **ADELINE.**

iv. **RACHAEL,** *b.* April 21, 1799; *m.* **MINOR MEEKIE,** in New York State, *d.* March 7, 1881. Issue (surname MEEKIE):
     i.   **MARCELLA,** *d.*
     ii. **CHESTER,** living at Muncie, Ind.

v.   **WILLIAM W.,** *b.* June 24, 1800, *of whom presently.*
vi. **HEWITT L.,** *b.* April 27, 1805. Settled at Galveston, Ind.; *m.* and *d.* October 23, 1895. He had issue, with other children, a son (**Edward L.** ?) who was a general in the C. S. A.
vii. **SAMANTHA,** *b.* December 3, 1812; *m.* ——— **ELLIS;** *d.* June 18 1887.

MINOR THOMAS, *m.* third, in New York State, January 15, 1820, **LYDIA HALL** ; and *d.* at Harrisburg, Ind., June 26, 1830 ; his widow *d.* at the same place, August 1, 1863. Issue, *b.* in Fayette Co., Ind. :

viii.   **WILSON T.,** *b.* August 10, 1822 ; *d.* September 17, 1825.

ix.   **NANCY,** *b.* July 22, 1826 ; *d.* September 17, 1829.

x.   **ANGELINE WOODWORTH,** *b.* July 6, 1830; *m.* **JOHN BATES,** and had with other issue (surname BATES) :

> WILLIAM OSCAR, *b.* at Harrisburg, Ind., September 19, 1852 ; graduated Ph.B. at Cornell University in 1875 ; a journalist by profession ; *m.*, October 23, 1893, CLARA ADELAIDE, eldest *dau.* of George Nixon, of Ballyshannon, Ireland (she was *b.* at Chaffpool, Co. Sligo, Ireland, October 2, 1868). Issue : John Nixon, *b.* at Brooklyn, September 13, 1894.

WILLIAM WINANS, fifth child of **Minor Thomas** and his second wife, **Nancy Winans,** *b.* June 24, 1800 ; removed with his father to Indiana and was employed as a surveyor, afterwards as a teacher in the log school-houses of the early settlers, and finally engaged in farming and storekeeping. He was an active Baptist, and clerk of the local society for over fifty years. He was well known in the State and highly esteemed, and was a member of the First Constitutional Convention of Indiana. He *m.*, August 23, 1827, **POLLY TROWBRIDGE** ; *d.* August, 1883. Issue :

i.   **NANCY T.,** *b.* May 12, 1830 ; *m.*, November 18, 1852, **JAMES CALDWELL.** Issue (surname CALDWELL) :

> i.   **ELBERT C.** *b.* 1854; *m.* **MARTHA SHIPLY.** Issue: i. **Edna**, ii. **Paul**, iii. **Carl**, iv. **Mary**, v. **Harry**.
> ii.   **LAWRENCE,** *b.* 1864, lives near Topeka, Kan.

ii.   **HUBBARD T.,** *b.* June 9, 1833 ; in the Civil War enlisted as Lieutenant of the Third Indiana Artillery, July, 1861. Was promoted to the captaincy of the Wilder Battery, February, 1862. He enlisted his Battery January, 1864. Was at the siege of Knoxville, Tenn., under General Ambrose E. Burnside. At the close of the war he settled in Philadelphia, Pa ; *m.*, September, 1867, **MINNIE A. SWENSON.** Issue :

> i.   WILLIAM W., *b.* in Philadelphia, 1869 ; *d.* 1871.
> ii.   CORA I., *b.* in Philadelphia, 1871.
> iii.   HERBERT TROWBRIDGE, *b.* in Indiana, 1876.
> iv.   CLARK GAPEN, *b.* 1880 ; *d.* 1881.

iii.   **BUEL J.,** *b.* September 21, 1835 ; occupation, farmer and stock-grower ; *m.*, May 27, 1857, **MARTHA CALDWELL.** Issue :

> i.   ELINER, *b.* 1858 ; *d.* 1864.
> ii.   CHARLES I., *b.* 1860.
> iii.   HUBBARD T., *b.* 1861.
> iv.   HARRY H., *b.* 1864 ; *d.* 1892.

iv.   **FRANKLIN Y.**, *b.* November 10, 1837 ; is County Commissioner of Fay-
            ette Co., Ind. ; *m.*, December 31, 1861, **BARBARA BEESON.**
            Issue :

   FLORA I., *b.* 1865 ; *m.*, 1890, **CHARLES D. FLOREA.**

   Authority : Family papers, through Messrs. Hewitt L. and Hubbard T. Thomas, and W. O. Bates.

THOMAS, OF FREDERICK COUNTY, MD.

THIS family is of German origin, and descends from ancestors who settled in the first half of the eighteenth century in or near what is now the city of Frederick, Md. There would appear to have been four brothers (order of birth uncertain) named Thomas or Thomassin. The name is at first written both ways on the records :

i. CHRISTIAN, *of whom presently.*
ii. GABRIEL (*q. v.*).
iii. JOHN (*q. v.*).
iv. VALENTINE (*q. v.*).

CHRISTIAN THOMAS lived at Beaver Hole plantation, 209 acres ; *m.* MARIA BARBARA, *dau.* of Philip Jacob and Anna Elizabeth Weber, who was *b.* at Wernfeld, Austria, July 15, 1725, and *d.* May 11, 1777 ; her husband was church-warden 1772-3-4 ; made his will May 14, 1777, and it was proved December 24, 1777. Issue :

i. CHRISTIAN, *of whom presently.*
ii. HENRY, left Maryland about 1768.
iii. BARBARA, *m.* BENJAMIN STONER.

iv. MARY, *unm.* in 1777.
v. Another *dau. m.* ANTHONY TERRICK in 1777. Issue (surname TER-
RICK) :

i. DANIEL.
ii. JACOB.
iii. JOHN.
iv. JOSEPH.
v. BARBARA.
vi. MARY.

CHRISTIAN THOMAS, apparently eldest son of Christian and Maria Barbara (Weber) Thomas, lived at " Beaver Den," a farm of 509¼ acres ; *m.* SUSANNA BEHR, who *d.* in 1820. He made his will July 9, 1798 ; proved August 16, 1798 (signature in German). Issue :

i. **MICHAEL,** *b.* March 15, 1774 ; *m.* **ELIZABETH,** *dau.* of **Benjamin** and **Rebecca (Stilley) Ogle** (*b.* October 16, 1785; her will proved in 1828). Issue :

    i.   **SYBILLA REBECCA.**
    ii.   **MARY SUSAN.**
    iii. **CHRISTIAN.**
    iv. **JOSEPH.**
    v.   **DAVID OGLE.**
    vi. **MARGARET.**

ii. **MARIA** or **MARY,** *b.* February 19, 1776.

iii. **CATHERINE,** *b.* November 11, 1777 ; *m.,* April 18, 1802, **GEORGE FREDERICK MEYER** or **MYERS.** Issue :

    i.   **VALENTINE.**
    ii.   **LEWIS W.**
    iii. **MARIA.**

iv. **WILLIAM,** *b.* December 19, 1778 ; *m.* **CATHERINE ——.** Issue :

    i.   **WILLIAM R.**
    ii.   **CAROLINE ELIZABETH,** *b.* August 5, 1813.
    iii. **CATHERINE.**

v. **ELIZABETH,** *b.* October 23, 1780.
vi. **GABRIEL,** *b.* April 29, 1782.
vii. **SOPHIA,** *b.* October 10, 1787.
viii. **HENRY,** *b.* February 5, 1790.
ix. **SUSANNA,** *b.* February 6, 1792.
x. **JOHANNES,** *b.* January 1, 1794.
xi. **VALENTINE,** *b.* November 19, 1796.

GABRIEL THOMAS, the second emigrant, *m.,* about 1745, **ANNA MARGARET ——,** and made his will October 30, 1788, proved February 5, 1794. In this he leaves to his son John, "The plantation where I now live," viz. : part of Poplar Thicket, 109 acres, part of Longhope, 43 acres, and 25 acres bought of Abraham Haff. He is to pay himself and his brothers and sisters £550, share and share alike, "only Catherine has had £34, Betsey £16 17*s.* 6*d,* and George £120." To his youngest daughter Peggy he leaves all his household goods, and to his son Jacob the land over the mountain, part of a tract called Piles Hall. The residue to be divided amongst all his children equally. He had issue :

i. **JACOB,** of Piles Hall, apparently the eldest, who *m.* **SUSANNA ——** ; made his will January 6, 1817 ; proved October 5, 1824. Issue :

    i.   **HENRY,** *b.* January 2, 1775.
    ii.   **MAGDALEN,** *b.* in August, 1778.
    iii. **ELIZABETH,** *b.* January 23, 1780.

iv.   **GEORGE**, *b.* March 12, 1782.
v.   **ANNA BARBARA**, *b.* December 22, 1786.
vi.   **CHARLOTTE**, *m.* **JOHN STOCKMAN.**
vii.   **MARGARET.**
viii.   **JACOB.**

ii.   **CATHERINE**, *b.* July 22, 1748.
iii.   **BARBARA**, *b.* May 7, 1749.
iv.   **GABRIEL**, *b.* March 8, 1753 ; *m.* **ANNA MARIA**, probably a *dau.* of
     Franz and **Barbara Hoffman.**   Issue :

     i.   **GABRIEL**, *b.* August 4, 1784.
     ii.   **GEORGE**, *b.* November 8, 1785.
     iii.   **CHARLOTTE**, *b.* August 20, 1787, probably *m.* **GEORGE THOMAS** (*q. v.*),
        of Carroll's Manor.
     iv.   **ANNA MARGARETH**, *b.* November 16, 1791.
     v.   **PETER**, *b.* October 17, 1793.
     vi.   **ANNA MARIA**, *b.* June 8, 1796.
     vii.   **ELIAS**, *b.* September 17, 1798.

v.   **ELIZABETH**, *b.* March 23, 1755 ; *m.*, June 20, 1790, **CONRAD
     JUNG** (afterwards called " Young ") ; he was *b.* May 1, 1759, and
     made his will August 28, 1813 ; proved October 5, 1813 ; had two
     sons (surname YOUNG) :

     i.   **JOHN.**
     ii.   **DANIEL.**

vi.   **JOHN**, *b.* September 25, 1757, *of whom presently.*
vii.   **GEORGE**, *b.* September 22, 1759 ; *m.* **ROSINA** ———.   Issue :

     ANNA MARGRETH, *b.* April 8, 1786.

viii.   **MARGARET**, *b.* June 5, 1763.
ix.   **HENRY**, who *m.*, November 23, 1790, **ANNA MARIA**, or **MARY
     REMSPERGER** (afterwards written Ramsburgh).   Issue :

     i.   **ANNA MARIA**, *b.* October 25, 1791.
     ii.   **MICHAEL**, *b.* August 25, 1793.

x.   **PETER**, mentioned in his father's will.
xi.   **ADAM**, mentioned in his father's will.

JOHN, third son of **Gabriel** and **Anna Margaret Thomas,**
b. September 25, 1757, lived at Poplar Thicket, near Jefferson, Frederick Co., *m.*, March 18, 1787, **MRS. CATH-
ERINE THOMAS,** widow of his cousin John, son of John
Thomas, and *dau.* of **Peter Wirtz,** of Lovettsville, Va. He
made his will August 17, 1804 ; proved March 5, 1805. In it he
leaves to his eldest son, Joseph, land northeast of the lane between my land and William Johnson's containing part of Burgesses lot, 11 acres, Delashmuth's Folly, 60 acres, part of Longhope, 15 acres, and " that tract called mountain conveyed to my

father by Thomas Duckett," also a man-slave named John, and a boy-slave named Isaac. To his son Jacob is left the residue of his real estate, one female slave called Susanna and her son Stephen. He is to pay Joseph £200 on account of his land being unimproved. He had issue :

i. PHILIP HENRICH, *b.* December 23, 1787 ; probably *d. y.*
ii. JOHN PETER, *b.* March 12, 1791 ; probably *d. y.*
iii. JOSEPH, *b.* June 16, 1795.
iv. JACOB, *b.* December 24, 1797, brought up by his uncle Conrad Young, near Burkettsville, Md., and lived near Middletown, Frederick Co., Md., until 1851, when he removed to Clark Co., O., where he *d.* in 1877. He had *m.*, December 20, 1825, SOPHIA, *dau.* of Henry Bowlus. Issue, all born in Maryland :

    i. JOHN HENRY, *b.* October 4, 1826, *of whom presently.*
    ii. RICHARD P., *d.* in Colorado, in 1893.
    iii. HARMON, *d. i.*
    iv. EDWARD, *d. i.*
    v. ELIZABETH, *m.* A. RAFFENSPERGER.
    vi. MARGARET, *d.*
    vii. JOSEPHINE.
    viii. AMADA, *d.* 1892.
    ix. JOSEPH WERTZ, lives at San Diego, Cal.
    x. CHARLES E.
    xi. ALDA.
    xii. ANNIE.

JOHN HENRY, eldest son of Jacob and Sophia (Bowlus) Thomas, *b.* October 4, 1826, moved to Clarke Co., O., in 1851, and engaged in the manufacture of agricultural implements, founding in 1857 what is now the Thomas Manufacturing Company, of Springfield, O., makers of Thomas rakes, tedders, lawnmowers, and iron pumps. In this he was very successful, and has been prominent for many years in commercial, banking, political, and social circles of Ohio. He *m.*, at Chillicothe, O., in 1854, MARY BONSER. Issue :

i. WILLIAM S., *b.* 1857, graduate of Wooster University, 1875 ; is Secretary and Treasurer of the Thomas Company ; *m.*, December 8, 1877, FANNY M. SENTENY, of Louisville, Ky. Issue :

    i. JOHN HENRY, Jr., *b.* 1888.
    ii. LUCRETIA, *b.* 1892.
    iii. WALLACE SENTENY, *b.* 1893.

ii. FINDLAY B., *b.* 1859.
iii. NELLIE, *b.* 1862 ; *m.*, 1887, A. N. SUMMERS.
iv. MABEL, *b.* 1877.

JOHANNES THOMASSIN or THOMAS, the third brother of the emigrants, *m.* **CATHERINE** ——, and made his will (signed in German), March 8, 1800, proved February 24, 1801. He leaves to his son, Henry, " all my part of Poplar Thickett, 90 acres, part of Johnson's Folly and Johnson's Neglect, 50 acres, part of Victory, 12 acres, he paying Catherine £100, Barbara, £200, and my grandson, John Thomas, £200." He had issue :

i.   **HENRY,** probably the eldest, and father of the **John** named in the will. .
ii.   **ANNA MARIA,** *b.* March 7, 1755.
iii.   **CATHERINE,** *b.* March 13, 1757 ; *m.,* January 26, 1783, **CHRISTOPH WETTEKIN, WEDAKIN, or WEDEKIND.**
iv.   **JOHN,** *b.* April 29, 1859 ; *m.,* April 13, 1783, **CATHERINE,** *dau.* of Peter Wirtz, and *d.* before 1787. Issue :

         JOHN, *of whom presently.*

v.   **GABRIEL,** *b.* April 30, 1762.
vi.   **BARBARA.**
vii.   **ELIZABETH,** possibly, though uncertain.

JOHN, only son of **John** and **Catherine (Wirtz) Thomas,** *m.* **MARGARET DAILY** and had two sons :

i.   **HENRY WIRTZ,** *b.* October 20, 1812, removed to Virginia, represented his county in the Legislature many years, during the Civil War was Auditor of the State, at its conclusion was Judge of the Court of Conciliation, in 1866 appointed Judge of the 9th Circuit, in 1870 elected Lieutenant-Governor of Virginia. His family reside at Fairfax Court House. He *m.,* February 20, 1839, **JULIA JACKSON,** of the family of President Andrew Jackson, and *d.* June 20, 1890. Issue :

     i.   **JOHN HENRY,** in the C. S. A., now *d.*
     ii.   **ANNIE,** *m.* **BENJAMIN EGLIN,** of England, and *d.* leaving a son, **Henry Wirt Thomas,** and three *dau.*
     iii.   **WILLIAM EARLY.**
     iv.   **ROSALIE.**
     v.   **MAGGIE.**
     vi.   **MRS. PINCKNEY (THOMAS) JANNEY.**

ii.   **JOHN DESKIN,** *b.* January 15, 1815.

VALENTINE THOMAS, fourth of the emigrants, appears to have *m.* first, **ELIZABETH** ——. Issue :

i.   **ANNA BARBARA,** *b.* April 25, 1753.
ii.   **ANNA MARIA,** *b.* April 30, 1754 (*d. y. ?*).

8

He *m.*, second, **MARGARET** ——, and made his will October 17, 1794, proved September 16, 1795, leaving to his son Valentine, part of Poplar Thicket, 109 acres, part of Rubby (?) Hollow, 35 acres, and 19 acres called Folly's Neglect. To his son Leonhard, his house and lot in the town called Newtown, and to his other children £100 apiece. Issue by second wife:

iii.   **GABRIEL**, *b.* September 24, 1752 ; *m.* **ANNA MARGARET** ——, will proved March 13, 1795. Issue:

    i.   **GEORGE.**
    ii.   **MARGARET.**
    iii.   **ELIZABETH BARBARA**, *b.* October 26, 1786.

iv.   **VALENTINE**, *b.* April 8, 1757 ; *m.*, March 17, 1799, **ELIZABETH KELLER.** Issue:

    i.   **GEORGE**, *b.* June 15, 1800.
    ii.   **MARGARET**, *b.* January 3, 1802.
    iii.   **MARY ANN**, *b.* March 22, 1807.
    iv.   **SOPHIA**, *b.* April 11, 1810.

v.   **PHILIP HENRY**, *b.* May 7, 1761.
vi.   **ANNA MARIA**, *b.* February 17, 1765.
vii.   **JOHN VALENTINE**, *b.* October 31, 1771.
viii. **MARIA MAGDALENA**, *b.* February 28, 1774.
ix.   **SUSANNA MARGARET.**
x.   **BARBARA.**
xi.   **CATHERINE.**
xii.   **LEONHARDT**, *m.* **BARBARA.** Issue:

    i.   **BARBARA**, *b.* June 15, 1792.
    ii.   **LEONHARDT**, *b.* December 19, 1794; *m.*, June 3, 1824, **CATHERINE TABLER.**

Possibly of this family was **EDWARD THOMAS**, of Frederick Co., made his will August 17, 1817, proved February 17, 1819 (Liber H. S. No. 2, folio 250), leaving his *dau.* **Ann Hebb**, "Pile's Delight," about 305 acres ; *dau.* **Eleanor**, wife of **William R. King**, "Dayspring," "Hobson's Choice," etc., about 314 acres ; his *dau.*, **Cassandra Johnson**, $300, and names his grandchildren : Edward T. Hebb, Sarah Hebb, Mary Hebb, Ann Hebb, Mariatta Hebb, Mary S. Good and Thomas R. King.

Authorities: Registers of the Lutheran and Reformed Churches of Frederick, Wills at Annapolis and Frederick, Md., and family papers through Miss Rose Thomas and William S. Thomas.

THOMAS, OF GLAMORGAN, WALES

JOHN J. THOMAS, of Gyngelly, Wales, son of **John** and **Sarah Thomas,** *m.* **ELIZABETH,** *dau.* of **Henry Jeffries** (*b.* at Llanbaie), and his wife, a Landor, of Gower in Glamorgan, and had a son, **HENRY JEFFRIES,** who was *b.* at Creig Trewfa, Glamorganshire, and emigrated to America in 1848, landing first at Baltimore, Md. He *m.* **ELEANOR,** *dau.* of **Rowland** and **Jane (Jones) Lloyd,** Welsh emigrants settled at Ebensburg, Cambria Co., Pa. Issue :

i.   **JENNIE ELEANOR,** *b.* at Pittsburg, Pa. ; *m.* **WALTER T. DAVIS.**
ii. **JOHN JEFFRIES.**
iii. **ARTHUR LLOYD,** *b.* August 22, 1851, at Chicago, Ill. Republican Governor of the Territory of Utah, afterward secretary and treasurer of the Utah Title and Trust Company of Salt Lake City.

ROWLAND LLOYD, *b.* at Llangadken, was a son of **Griffith Lloyd,** *b.* at Machynlleth, and his wife, **Mrs. Jane (Morris) Evans,** *b.* at Abarhosan, Montgomeryshire.

Authority : Family papers through Governor Arthur L. Thomas.

THOMAS OF HALIFAX, ENGLAND, AND BAY RIDGE, LONG ISLAND

WILLIAM THOMAS, *b.* January, 1726, and *d.* February 26, 1806, at Halifax, England. Issue :

i. **WILLIAM,** *b.* March 20, 1750, *of whom presently.*
ii. **GRACE,** *b.* March 18, 1757.
iii. **SUSY,** *b.* 1761.

WILLIAM THOMAS, JR., *b.* March 20, 1750 ; *m.,* November 11, 1781, **ANN HAMPTON,** and *d.* October 20, 1810, at " Poplar Hill," the family seat, back of the site of the old New York Hotel. Issue :

i. **WILLIAM HENRY,** *b.* August 20, 1782 ; *d.* August 14, 1814.
ii. **THOMAS HAMPTON,** *b.* February 23, 1784, *of whom presently.*
iii. **ANN,** *b.* January 27, 1786 ; *d.* November 21, 1810.
iv. **JAMES,** *b.* March 27, 1788 ; *d.* November 15, 1791.
v. **MARIA,** *b.* May 2, 1790 ; *d.* June 27, 1791.
vi. **ROBERT,** *b.* February 1, 1792 ; *d.* December 25, 1836.
vii. **MARY,** *b.* December 6, 1794 ; *d.* August 20, 1863.
viii. **SARAH,** *b.* March 6, 1797 ; *d.* October 10, 1831.
ix. **ALFRED,** *b.* January 22, 1799, was the first child baptized in S. Mark's Church in the Bowery, New York.
x. **HENRY,** *m.* **ANN WAGSTAFFE,** and *d.* September 3, 1833.

THOMAS HAMPTON, second son of **William** and **Ann (Hampton) Thomas,** *b.* February 23, 1784 ; *m.,* April 24, 1815, by the Rev. William Harris, to **MARY JOSEPHINE WINTER** ; *d.* November 20, 1851. Issue :

i. **WILLIAM HENRY,** *b.* January 22, 1816, *of whom presently.*
ii. **JOSEPH WINTER,** *b.* September 5, 1817 ; *m.* **ANNA LOCKHART,** of Columbus, Ga. ; *d.* February, 1859. Issue :

    i. WILLIAM HENRY.
    ii. MARY JOSEPHINE.
    iii. HENRY.
    iv. ROBERT BEALL.
    v. NANNIE.

iii. **ROBERT HAMPTON,** *b.* January 30th ; *d.* August 16, 1819.

iv. **ROBERT HAMPTON,** 2d, *b.* June 26, 1820 ; *m.* **ELIZA M. DIS-BROW,** of New York City ; *d.* June 6, 1881. Issue :

    i. **CLARA HAMPTON.**
    ii. **MARY JOSEPHINE.**
    iii. **EDWARD WALTON,** *d. y.*

v. **SARAH ELIZABETH,** *b.* July 6, 1822 ; *m.* **MARSHALL BRYAN,** and *d.* January, 1895. Issue (surname BRYAN) :

    i. **MARSHALL THOMAS,** *m.* **ALLISON WEATHERHEAD.** Issue :
       i. Helen. ii. Agnes Hampton. iii. Effie, *d. y.*
    ii. **AGNES HAMPTON.**
    iii. **WILLIAM HENRY.**

vi. **AGNES HAMPTON,** *b.* April 19, 1824 ; *d.* October 26, 1846.

vii. **MARY WINTER,** *b.* February 16th ; *d.* May 2, 1826.

viii. **SAMUEL WINTER,** *b.* February 21, 1827 (*q. v.*).

ix. **THOMAS FREDERIC,** *b.* September 9, 1828 ; *m.* **MARY CHICHESTER,** of New York. Issue :
    FREDERIC CHICHESTER.

WILLIAM HENRY, eldest son of **Thomas Hampton** and **Mary Josephine (Winter) Thomas,** *b* January 22, 1816 ; *m.* **FRANCES AMANDA BAILEY,** of Portsmouth, N. H. Issue :

i **WILLIAM HENRY,** *m.* **CHARLOTTE TOWNSEND,** of Bay Ridge, L. I.

ii. **FANNIE LOUISE,** *m.* **HARMON B. VANDERHOEF.** Issue (surname VANDERHOEF) :

    i. **FRANCIS BAILEY.**
    ii. **FANNIE LOUISE.**
    iii. **NATHALIE WYCKOFF.**
    iv. **HARMON BLAUVELT,** Jr.

iii. **THOMAS HAMPTON,** *m.* **MARGARET WILKINS.** Issue :
    ELLA MAY.

SAMUEL WINTER, fifth son of **Thomas Hampton** and **Mary Josephine (Winter) Thomas,** *b.* February 21, 1827, resides at Bay Ridge, L. I. ; *m.* **JANE SALTER,** of New York. Issue :

i. **FRANK SALTER,** president of the Montgomery Auction Company, *m.* **ESTELLA DERBYSHIRE,** of New York.

ii. **AGNES HAMPTON,** *m.* **WILMOT TOWNSEND,** of Bay Ridge, L. I. Issue (surname TOWNSEND) :

    i. **SUSANNAH BELL.**
    ii. **JANET SALTER.**

iii. **ROBERT HAMPTON.**

Authority : Family papers, through Mrs. Robert H. Thomas.

THOMAS, OF HARDWICK, MASS.

WILLIAM THOMAS, of Hardwick, Mass., believed to have been a son of **William,** of Newton, Mass., and grandson of **Evan,** who came from Wales to Boston in 1639 or 1640, was *b.* in Newton (?) August 31, 1687. Was the first white settler in Hardwick; *m.,* first, **PATIENCE** ———, second, **SUSANNA STOW,** April, 1747; *d.* May 22, 1747. Issue :

> i. **AMOS,** *of whom presently.* ii. **ZERVIAH.** iii. **TEMPERANCE.** iv. **HANNAH.** v. **ELIZABETH.** vi. **DANIEL.** vii. **NATHAN.** viii. **AARON.** ix. **MARY.** x. **ISRAEL.**

AMOS, eldest son of **William Thomas,** of Hardwick, *b.* in 1707; *m.* **ABIGAIL** ———, in 1732. Lived in Hardwick and *d.* there July 31, 1754. Issue :

> i. **ELIZABETH.** ii. **WILLIAM** (*d. y.*). iii. **ABIGAIL.** iv. **OLIVE.** v. **WILLIAM,** a physician. vi. **AMOS,** *of whom presently.* vii. **JOSEPH.** viii. **DANIEL.** ix. **MERCY.** x. **ISAAC.**

AMOS, third son of **Amos** and **Abigail** (———) **Thomas,** *b.* in Hardwick, April 6, 1746; *m.* **EUNICE BANGS,** December 20, 1770, *d.* April 29, 1831. Issue :

> i. **ISAAC.** ii. **NATHANIEL.** iii. **AMOS.** iv. **ABIGAIL.** v. **EUNICE.** vi. **DAVID.** vii. **BEALS.** viii. **AZARIAH,** *of whom presently.* ix. **HEMAN.** x. **MARY.** xi. **RHODA,** 1st. xii. **RHODA,** 2d. xiii. **ARDON.** xiv. **RHOBA.** xv. **ALPHEUS.**

COLONEL AZARIAH, sixth son of **Amos** and **Eunice (Bangs) Thomas,** *b.* in New Salem, Mass., December 15, 1782; *m.* **SARAH AVERY,** January 18, 1812; *d.* in Watertown, N. Y., September 14, 1831. Issue :

i.   **LOUISA,** *d. y.*
ii.   **AVERY.**
iii.   **HARRIET.**
iv.   **MELINDA.**

v. **CHARLES,** *d. y.*
vi. **AMOS RUSSELL,** *of whom presently.*
vii. **JAMES M.**
viii. **CHARLES A.**

AMOS RUSSELL, physician, author, professor, second son of **Azariah** and **Sarah (Avery) Thomas,** was *b.* in Watertown, N. Y., October 3, 1826. A.M. Ursinus College ; M.D. Syracuse Medical College, 1854 ; Professor of Anatomy in Hahnemann Medical College of Philadelphia from 1867 ; and Dean of Faculty from 1874 to present time (1895); *m.*, September 26, 1847, **ELIZABETH M. BACON.** Issue :

i. **CHARLES MONROE,** *of whom presently.*
ii. **FLORENCE L.,** *m.* **J. N. MITCHELL,** and *d.* May 17, 1880, leaving one son, **CHARLES T. MITCHELL.**

CHARLES MONROE, physician and professor, only son of **Dr. Amos R.** and **Elizabeth (Bacon) Thomas,** *b.* in Watertown, N. Y., May 3, 1849. A.B. Philadelphia High School, 1869 ; M.D. Hahnemann Medical College, 1871 ; Professor of Surgery and Ophthalmology in above from 1877 to date (1895) ; *m.* **MARION E. TURNBULL,** April 18, 1876. Issue :

i. **RUSSELL E.**
ii. **FLORENCE P.**
iii. **CHRISTINE L.**
iv. **ALICE L.**
v. **LAWRENCE.**
vi. **AVERY,** *d. y.*
vii. **CARL BACON.**
viii. **FRANK M.**

Authority : Dr. A. R. Thomas, Records and Sketches of the Descendants of William Thomas, of Hardwick, Mass. Philadelphia, 1891.

THOMAS, OF HIGHGATE, LONDON

DAVID THOMAS, Gent., of Mighell Church, Hereford, aged twenty-two, had a license to marry **DIANA**, *dau.* of **Henry Campion**, of Great S. Mary, Cambridgeshire, poulterer, at S. Clements', Eastcheap, London, March 21, 1624. **GEOFFREY THOMAS**[1] was possibly of the same family, who *m.* **MARY SHETTERDEN**, and *d.* in 1681, aged seventy-five ; his wife *d.* 1693 aged sixty. They had a son **DANIEL**, *m.* **DEBORAH DASHWOOD** and *d.* 1703, aged fifty-five ; his wife *d.* in 1686, aged twenty-seven. **GEOFFREY** and **MARY THOMAS** had seven other sons and several daughters. **GEOFFREY**, his fourth son, *d.* 1695, having an only son, **ROBERT**, *m.* first, **SUSANNA CAMPION**, who *d. s. p.* 1722 ; he *m.* second, **SUSANNA ——**, *d.* 1749, aged forty-four, and he *d.* 1776, aged eighty-five. His youngest daughter, **Elizabeth**, *m.* **David Orme, M.D.**, and *d.* 1777. **SHETTERDEN**, fourth son of **Daniel Thomas**, *d.* 1700, aged twenty-six. All were buried at Highgate Burial Ground, London, from which records this pedigree is compiled.

[1] See Thomas, of Islington.

120

THOMAS, OF HILLTOWN, PA.

This family descends from **WILLIAM THOMAS**, *b.* at Llanwenarth, Monmouthshire, Wales, in 1678 ; *m.* **ANN**——— (possibly
GRIFFITH), and emigrated to America, February 14, 1712, by way
of Bristol.   In 1713 was at Radnor, now in Delaware Co.,
Pa.; February 12, 1718, bought 440 acres at Hilltown, Bucks
Co., and settled there ; September 28, 1723, he bought 300
acres more, near the sources of the Neshaminy River.   He˙
was a Baptist preacher, and gave the land and built at his own
expense the first Baptist Meeting-house at Hilltown, in 1737.
He *d.* October 6, 1757 ; his wife *d.* November 5, 1752.   Issue :

i.   THOMAS, *b.* in Wales about 1711.
ii.   JOHN, *b.* December, 1713, a Baptist preacher ; *m.*, in 1738, **SARAH
JAMES**, and *d.* October 31, 1790, leaving descendants.
iii.   GWENTLY, *b.* 1716 ; *m.*, 1736, **MORRIS**, son of **Cadwalader Morris**,
and *d.* April, 1785.
iv.   EPHRAIM, *b.* about 1719 ; *m.*, 1740, **ELEANOR BATES**, and *d.* July
31, 1776, leaving descendants.
v.   ANNA, *b.* 1719–20 ; *m.*, August, 1757, **STEPHEN**, son of **Owen** and
Joan Rowland, who emigrated from Wales in 1725.   Issue (surname
ROWLAND) :

      i.   OWEN.
      ii.   JOHN.
      iii.   WILLIAM.
      iv.   STEPHEN.
      v.   MARGARET.
      vi.   MARY.
      vii.   THOMAS, whose son, Albert G. was father of George L. Rowland, of the Cornelius
            & Rowland Co., of Philadelphia. He *m.*, 1872, Sarah Petty. Issue : William
            P., *b.* 1872 ; Albert L., *b.* 1882.

vi.   MANASSEH, *b.* 1721 ; *m.* **ELIZABETH EVANS**, and *d.* February 7.
1802, leaving descendants.
vii.   WILLIAM, *b.* about 1723 ; *m.* **ABIGAIL DAY**, and *d.* July, 1764, leaving descendants.

THOMAS, eldest son of Elder **William** and **Anna Thomas,** *b.* about 1711 ; *m.*, first, **MARGARET BATES.** Issue :

i.   **MORGAN,** *d. u.*
ii.   **ANN.**
iii.   **ALICE.**

He *m.*, second, **MARY WILLIAMS,** and *d.* January, 1780.   Issue :

iv.   **ELIZABETH,** *m.* **HENRY GODSHALK.**
v.   **ESTHER,** *m.* **WILLIAM WILLIAMS.**
vi.   **JOB,** *b.* 1751, *m.* **REBECCA BATES,** and *d.* June, 1798, leaving descendants.
vii.   **AMOS,** *b.* 1752 or 1753 ; *m.* **RUTH BATES.**   Was a captain in the Revolution ; *d.* in Maryland, leaving descendants.
viii.   **JONAH,** *b.* about 1754 ; *m.* **SARAH FREEMAN,** and *d. y.*, leaving descendants.
·ix.   **CATHERINE,** *b.* 1756 ; *m.* **CHARLES MILLER.**
x.   **ASA,** *of whom presently.*
xi.   **SARAH,** *b.* 1760 ; *m.* **PATRICK MAITLAND.**
xii.   **ABEL,** *b.* 1762 ; *m.* **MARY,** *dau.* of Abel James, and left descendants, most of whom removed to the West.
xiii.   **ANNA,** *b.* 1762 (twin of Abel) ; *m.* **JOHN MATTHIAS.**

ASA, fourth son of **Thomas** and **Mary (Williams) Thomas,** *b.* February, 1758, served in the Revolution ; *m.*, about 1783, **MARTHA,** *dau.* of **Abel** and **Mary (Howell) James,** and *d.* May 8, 1839. His wife *d.* April 14, 1854, having had twelve children, among them a son, **ABEL,** *b.* July 3, 1799. Held various commissions in the State militia, becoming finally, April 27, 1839, Colonel of the 92d Militia Regiment of Bucks and Montgomery Counties.   He *m.* **MARY CRAIG,** and *d.* July 8, 1883.   Issue :

i.   **ALBERT,** *b.* March 25, 1824 ; *d.* November 24, 1877.
ii.   **ALLEN,** *b.* January 20, 1827, in the hardwood business at West Point, Pa., *m.*, December 25, 1848, **ANNA REBECCA GOUCHER,** and had ten children, of whom Arthur K., printer and publisher since 1872, now owner and editor of the *Gazette,* Ambler, Pa., since 1885 ; published a History of the Family (compiled by Edward Matthews), in 1884.
iii.   **ASHER,** *b.* April 25, 1829 ; *d.* August 7, 1830.
iv.   **ANN ELIZABETH,** *b.* June 8, 1831.
v.   **ASHBEL C.,** *b.* January 9, 1834.
vi.   **CHARLES B.,** *b.* April 17, 1836 ; *d.* October 14, 1863.
vii.   **ABEL,** *b.* August 7, 1839.

Authority : Matthews' Thomas family, of Hilltown.

JESSE BURGESS THOMAS
THE AUTHOR OF THE MISSOURI COMPROMISE

THOMAS, OF ILLINOIS

JESSE THOMAS, believed to have descended in a direct line from **Thomas Thomas,** who came from England in 1651, settled in S. Mary's Co., Md., on the Patuxent River, and *d.* in 1671 (*q. v.*), and to have been the youngest son of **Thomas** (*d.* 1734) and **Elizabeth** (——) **Thomas,** of Charles Co., Md., (*q. v.*), was *b.* 1734; *m.* **SABINA,** *dau.* of **Richard** and **Mary (Brooke) Symmes;** settled at Frederick, Md., and *d.* before 1774. Issue:

i.   **RICHARD SYMMES,** *b.* May 22, 1773, *of whom presently.*
ii.   **JESSE BURGESS,** *b.* 1777 (*q. v.*).

RICHARD SYMMES, elder son of **Jesse** and **Sabina (Symmes) Thomas,** descended on his mother's side from the family of Lord Baltimore, *b.* at Frederick, Md., May 22, 1773; removed with his mother, about 1775, to Redstone, Fayette Co., Pa., and thence about 1792, to Washington, Mason Co., Ky., where he read law with Governor Chambers. He removed about 1803 to Lebanon, O., where he practised law. Was a member of the first Ohio State Constitutional Convention and a prominent candidate for the United States Senate. In 1811 he removed to Ste. Genevieve, Mo., and about 1814 to Jackson, Cape Girardeau Co., Mo. December 6, 1820, he was appointed Judge of the Fourth Judicial Circuit of the State of Missouri, and held this position until his death, which occurred near Jackson in 1828. While riding from one court to another, accompanied by several members of the bar, he was thrown from his horse and killed. He was a man of commanding presence, fine intellect, and high character. He *m.*, June 4, 1795, in Bracken Co., Ky., **FRANCES,** *dau.* of **John** and **Ann (Saunders) Pattie,** *b.* in Culpeper Co., Va., March 16, 1772, who had removed thither the same year from Culpeper Co., and settled there. She removed with her family, in 1836, from

123

Missouri to Spring Creek, Sangamon Co., Ill., near Springfield, and *d.* there September 20, 1855.   Issue:

i.   **SABINA SYMMES,** *b.* March 28, 1796 ; *d. u.* 1836.

ii.   **NANCY,** *b.* May 8, 1797 ; *m.*, November, 1814, **GEORGE BULLITT,** who *d. s. p.* She *m.*, second, 1837, **JAMES BRUCE,** and *d. s. p.* February 10, 1853.

iii. **SALLY,** *d. i.*

iv.   **MARY,** *b.* November 16, 1799 ; *m.*, first, March 14, 1821, **SAMUEL CUPPLES,** who *d.* April, 1828.   Issue (surname CUPPLES) :

    i.   **MARY,** *d. u.*
    ii. **FANNY,** *m.* —— **ROOT** ; *d.* in Iowa.
    iii. **ROSETTA C.,** *m.* **JESSE M. SHEPARD.** Issue (surname SHEPARD):
      i.   **Frances Lelia.**
      ii. **Ella Rosetta,** *b.* October 24, 1854.

    MARY (THOMAS) CUPPLES, *m.*, second, March 22, 1834, **JOHN TAYLOR,** who *d.* April, 1853.   She *d.* June, 1881. Issue (surname TAYLOR) :

    i.   **ELIZA,** *b.* November 25, 1834 ; *d. u.* February 6, 1850.
    ii. **RICHARD SYMMES,** *b.* May 25, 1838 ; *m.* December 27, 1867 ; *d.* October 6, 1892.
    iii. **ADELINE,** *b.* August 8, 1836 ; *m.* March, 1854, **JOHN P. ATTIX.**
    iv. **MARGARET AMELIA,** *b.* June 18, 1840.
    v.   **JOHN WILLIAM,** *b.* August 10, 1842 ; *m.* February 25, 1864, **MARGARET L. STEPHENSON.**

v.   **LOUISA,** *d.* when nineteen months old.

vi   **CLAIBORNE SYMMES,** *b.* November 14, 1803 ; *m.*, 1828, **ANN BRAWLEY ;** *d.* 1838.   Issue : **JOHN.**

vii. **JESSE BURGESS,** *b.* July 31, 1806, *of whom presently.*

viii. **ELIZA ANN,** *b.* March 11, 1809 ; *m.* May 4, 1830, **JONATHAN NASH BURR,** of Mount Vernon, O., *b.* November 15, 1800, at Bridgeport, Conn. ; *d.* March 27, 1887.   He *d.* October 2, 1889.   Issue (surname BURR) :

    i.   **JESSE THOMAS,** *b.* August 22, 1841 ; *m.* March 21, 1893, **ELIZABETH L. POYNTER,** of Glasgow, Ky.
    ii. **JESSIE REBECCA,** *b.* May 16, 1843 ; *m.*, October 6, 1862, **FRANCIS CUNNINGHAM CRAWFORD,** of Terre Haute, Ind.; *b.* October 9, 1838.

ix.   **CATHARINE CRAIG,** *b.* July 20, 1811 ; *m.*, July 1, 1830, **BENJAMIN SMITH BROWN,** of Mount Vernon, O., who *d.* November 26, 1838.   Issue (surname BROWN) :

    i.   **FRANCES ANN,** *b.* July 8, 1831 ; *d.* February 1, 1834.
    ii. **BENJAMIN JAY,** *b.* July 8, 1833 ; *m.*, August 12, 1862, **ELIZA JANE HART,** of Oconto, Wis.   Issue :
      i.   **De Witt,** *b.* June 9, 1863 ; *m.* **Margaret Woessner,** September 15, 1886. Issue :

        Benjamin Jay, *b.* April 26, 1887.
        Edwina, *b.* February 1, 1889.
        Frederick Crawford, *b.* February 14, 1891.
        Charlotte, *b.* March 16, 1894.
        Merrill Woessner, *b.* February 1, 1896.

  ii. Franklin Hart, *b.* December 5, 1865; *m.,* August 9, 1886, **Charlotte Ault**, of Oshkosh, Wis. Issue:

     Jessie, *b.* March 8, 1887.
     Jennie, *b.* September 18, 1888.
     Alexander, *b.* November 24, 1889.
     Kathryn, *b.* August 30, 1891.

  iii. Catharine, *b.* August 9, 1867; *m.,* May 5, 1891, **Arthur L. Lewis**, of Manistee, Mich. Issue (surname LEWIS):

     Adelaide, *b.* November 22, 1895.

  iv. **Mary**, *b.* January 3, 1872; *d.* September 7, 1873.
  v. **Adelaide**, *b.* March 28, 1874; *d.* November 14, 1895.
  vi. **Bessie**, *b.* April 28, 1876.
  vii. **Edwin Hart**, *b.* June 9, 1879; *d.* January 12, 1888.

 iii. **RICHARD THOMAS**, *b.* January 22, 1835; *m.,* September 15, 1859, **MARY JANE KEELY**, of Indianapolis, Ind.; *d.* September, 1867. Issue:

  i. **William**, *b.* August 1, 1860.
  ii. **Jessie**, *b.* September 8, 1861.
  iii. **Kate E.**, *b.* October 6, 1862.
  iv. **Richard Harry**, *b.* May 31, 1866.

 iv. **JESSE BURGESS**, *b.* July 18, 1836; *m.,* May 11, 1857, **LEAH McCURDY**, of Mount Vernon, O. Issue:

  i. **Elizabeth Ann**, *b.* June 20, 1858; *m.,* September 13, 1876, **Adolf Schleicher**, of Stuttgart, Germany. Issue (surname SCHLEICHER):

     Adolf Burgess, *b.* June 3, 1877.
     Gertrude Ann, *b.* September 7, 1880.
     Benjamin Fredrick, *b.* April 22, 1885.
     Fredrick, *b.* August 28, 1894.

  ii. **Benjamin Smith**, *b.* July 31, 1860.
  iii. **Ada Ellen**, *b.* April 30, 1865; *m.,* March 15, 1887, **James A. Dodson**, of Terre Haute, Ind. Issue (surname DODSON):

     Albert Burgess, *b.* January 27, 1888.
     Ray Richard, *b.* December 25, 1891.
     Leah Angeline, *b.* August 14, 1894.

  iv. **Jesse Burgess**, *b.* October 18, 1868.
  v. **Richard Thomas**, *b.* November 6, 1871.

 v. **CATHARINE ELIZA**, *b.* June 18, 1838; *m.,* August 20, 1862, **THOMAS MEEKER JAMES**, of Cincinnati, O. Issue (surname JAMES):

  i. Catharine, *b.* August 20, 1863; *m.,* February 25, 1891, Franklin Wellington Warner, of Lockport, N. Y. Issue (surname WARNER):

     Catharine Emily, *b.* April 14, 1892.

  ii. **Benjamin Stanbery**, *b.* May 18, 1865.
  iii. **Sarah Potter**, *b.* May 27, 1872.

x. **FRANCES AMELIA**, *b.* March 27, 1814; *m.,* November 8, 1838, **WILLIAM S. BURCH**; *d.* December 25, 1855. Issue (surname BURCH):

 i. **RICHARD SYMMES**, *b.* 1849; *m.,* 1869, **ISABELLE JONES**. Issue:

  i. **Harry S.**
  ii. **William S.**
  iii. **Anna.**
  iv. **May.**
  v. **Frank Russell.**

ii.   FRANCES AMELIA, *b.* July 8, 1847; *m.* June 13, 1877, WILLIAM GRIMS-
LEY. Issue (surname GRIMSLEY) :
Fannie Burch, *b.* April 25, 1878.

xi.   **RICHARD SYMMES**, *b.* June 3, 1817 (*q. v.*).

JESSE BURGESS, second son of **Richard Symmes** and **Frances (Pattie) Thomas**, *b.* at Lebanon, O., July 31, 1806. He was educated at Transylvania University and practised law for a number of years at Springfield, Ill., removing in 1845 to Chicago, where he afterward resided.   He was Attorney-General of Illinois ; also Judge of one of the Circuit Courts and presided at the trial of Joseph Smith, founder of Mormonism, at the time of Smith's assassination.   He was twice elected Associate Justice of the Supreme Court of Illinois and served with distinction. He *m.*, February 18, 1830, at Edwardsville, Ill., **ADELINE CLARISSA**, *dau.* of **Theophilus W.** and **Clarissa (Rathbone) Smith**.   She was *b.* in New York City, May 13, 1812, and *d.* at Chicago, Ill., December 14, 1866.   He *d.* at Chicago, February 21, 1850.   Issue :

i.   **RICHARD THEOPHILUS,** *b.* December 28, 1830 ; *m.*, first, January
17, 1858, **HELEN BENTLEY** ; second, March 15, 1884, **JOSIE
M. RYAN** ; *d. s. p.*, at Chicago, August 9, 1890.

ii.   **JESSE BURGESS,** *b.* at Edwardsville, Ill., July 29, 1832. He was
educated at Kenyon College, Gambier, O., graduating in 1850. He
was admitted to the bar in 1855.   Prior to that time he had entered the
Rochester Theological Seminary, with a view to preparing for the ministry, but was compelled by ill-health to leave that institution.   He began the practice of law at Chicago in 1857 and continued until 1862,
when he resolved to devote his life to the ministry, and accepted a call
to the Baptist Church at Waukegan, Ill.   In 1864 he became pastor of
the Pierrepont Street Baptist Church, of Brooklyn, N. Y., which he
left to accept a call from the First Baptist Church at San Francisco.
Thence he went to the Michigan Avenue Baptist Church, Chicago. In
1873, on the union of the Pierrepont Street Church and the First
Baptist Church, of Brooklyn, he accepted the pastorate of the united
churches, and held it until January 1, 1888, when he accepted the Chair
of Church History at the Newton Theological Institution, Newton,
Mass., which he still occupies. He *m.*, May 30, 1855, **ABBIE**, *dau.*
of **Timothy** and **Mary Jane Eastman**, of Eastmanville, Mich. Issue :

i.   JESSE BURGESS, *b.* March 6, 1856 ; *d.* October 20, 1862.
ii.   WILLIS EASTMAN, *b.* December 10, 1857 ; *d.* August 7, 1858.
iii.   ADA VIRGINIA, *b.* June 4, 1860 ; *d.* October 16, 1862.
iv.   JESSIE EMMA, *b.* October 19, 1862 ; *m.*, June 8, 1887, MERWIN E., son of
Charles G. Leslie. Issue (surname LESLIE) :

  i. **Edwin Thomas**, *b.* June 1, 1888.
  ii. **Harold David**, *b.* August 26, 1889.
  iii. **Jesse Burgess**, *b.* September 9, 1891.

  v. **CHARLES HUNTINGTON**, *b.* August 19, 1864; *d.* June 13, 1875.
  vi. **LEO**, *b.* August 25, 1869; *m.*, July 15, 1895, **EVELYN G. DUDLEY.**
  vii. **MEDORA CARLOTA**, *b.* November 15, 1870.
  viii. **RAPHAEL CLARKE**, *b.* October 3, 1873.

iii. **CHARLES CARROLL**, *b.* October 27, 1834; *d.* December 26, 1837.
iv. **CLARA FRANCES**, *b.* December 2, 1836; *m.*, October 4, 1859,
  LYNDE C. HUNTINGTON, of Chicago, who *d.* May 22, 1887.
  Issue (surname HUNTINGTON) :

    CHARLES O., *b.* October 16, 1860; *m.*, June 21, 1889, **HARRIET IGO.**

v. **FRANCES RATHBONE**, *b.* August 2, 1839; *d.* October 6, 1841.
vi. **GEORGE WASHINGTON**, *b.* May 17, 1841; A.B., University of
  Chicago, 1862; A.M., 1865; *m.*, December 22, 1874, **LAURA
  KATHARINE**, *dau.* of **Henry W.** and **Lucy Ann Camp.**
  Issue :

    i. **EDITH MABEL**, *b.* October 19, 1875.
    ii. **GERTRUDE MARION**, *b.* June 23, 1880; *d.* June 12, 1881.
    iii. **MIRIAM BEATRICE**, *b.* April 3, 1882.

vii. **MARY ADELINE**, *b.* August 17, 1843; *m.*, January 22, 1880,
  GEORGE WILLARD, son of **Hezekiah** and **Eunice (Rathbone) Goddard**, of New London, Conn. Issue (surname GODDARD) :

    i. **EUNICE RATHBONE**, *b.* September 22, 1881.
    ii. **WILLARD THOMAS**, *b.* January 1, 1883; *d.* January 6, 1883.
    iii. **GLADYS ADELINE**, *b.* January 29, 1884.

viii. **LUCY EUDORA**, *b.* June 20, 1846; *m.*, first, October 22, 1868, **JO-
  SEPH FRANCIS BONFIELD**, of Chicago, Ill., who *d. s. p.*
  February 18, 1881; *m.*, second, February 25, 1885, **JESSE B.
  BARTON.** Issue (surname BARTON) :

    i. **JESSE B.**, *b.* November 21, 1885.
    ii. **WALTER I.**, *b.* June 9, 1888.
    iii. **LUCY A.**, *b.* September 26, 1891.

ix. **CATHARINE LOUISA**, *b.* March 2, 1848; *d.* September 2, 1848.
x. **ELLA AUGUSTA**, *b.* November 13, 1849; *m.*, September 30, 1875,
  JOHN M. TUDOR, of Cincinnati, who *d.* January 19, 1877. Issue
  (surname TUDOR) :

    WILLIAM B., *b.* November 1, 1876.

RICHARD SYMMES, youngest son of **Richard Symmes** and
Frances (Pattie) Thomas, *b.* at Jackson, Mo., June 3, 1817.
He removed to Illinois in 1836, and read law for two years with
his brother, Jesse Burgess Thomas, of Springfield. He entered

Illinois College, at Jacksonville, but shortly thereafter it was broken up by the slavery agitation, and he returned to Springfield. About 1839 he went to Mount Vernon, O., and read law with Henry B. Curtis, brother of General Samuel R. Curtis. Returning to Springfield, he was admitted to the bar of Illinois, June 29, 1840, and shortly afterward settled at Virginia, Cass Co., Ill., where he began the practice of law. August 2, 1841, he was elected School Commissioner of the Co. July 9, 1843, he was appointed Adjutant, Twenty-first Regiment Illinois Militia. He removed to Beardstown, Ill., in November, 1845, but in June, 1846, returned to Virginia. August, 1848, he was elected to the Legislature for Cass and Menard Counties. He followed his profession at Virginia until 1854, when he removed to Chicago, but returned a year later to Virginia, and established a newspaper to advocate the building of the Illinois River Railway. On the organization of the Company, September, 1856, he was elected President, and retained the position for seven years and until the completion of the road. During the presidential campaign of 1860 he edited the *Independent*, published at Virginia, and took an active part in the canvass for Mr. Lincoln's election. In November, 1862, he returned to Chicago and resumed the practice of law in that city, residing at Waukegan after May, 1864. He was appointed by Governor Yates one of the Commissioners to audit the State War Claims, and performed the duties without compensation, waiving the salary to which he was entitled. He was for many years a member of the Board of Trustees and of the Executive Committee of the University of Chicago, and also of the Board of the Baptist Theological Union. He was an able lawyer, of courteous bearing, sound judgment, and unimpeachable integrity. He *m.*, March 4, 1843, at Virginia, Ill., **HELEN MALVINA**, *dau.* of **William** and **Lucy (Clark) Naylor**, who was *b.* at Edmonton, Ky., December 4, 1825. She removed with her family, April, 1880, to Boonton, N. J. He *d.* December 14, 1865. Issue (all born at Virginia, Ill., excepting Richard Symmes) :

i.   **HENRY THEODORE**, *b.* June 27, 1844 ; President of the Henry T. Thomas Company, of New York, Publishers of " The Thomas Book," " The Works of Alfred Lord Tennyson," " Venice of To-Day," and other works ; *m.*, June 18, 1868, at Yonkers, N. Y., in the First Presbyterian Church, by Rev. Dr. Seward, **JULIETTE RATHBONE**, *dau.* of James Edward and Catherine Fredrika (Jennings) Goddard, who was *b.* in New York City, September 8, 1845. Issue :

RICHARD SYMMES THOMAS
BORN 1817, DIED 1865

i.   Theodora, *b.* January 18, 1870, in Chicago.
ii.   Juliette Rathbone, *b.* August 30, 1874, in Chicago; *m.*, November 27, 1895, at the Archiepiscopal Residence, New York City, by Archbishop Corrigan, **Captain Giulio Martini**, of Naples, Italy.
iii. Richard Symmes, *b.* July, 1879, in New York City; *d. i.*

ii.   **FRANCES LUCY,** *b.* August 29, 1846; *d.* August 28, 1847.
iii. **REBECCA CATHARINE,** *b.* September 12, 1848; *d.* February 8, 1853.
iv.   **JESSE BURGESS,** *b.* June 13, 1851.
v.   **WILLIAM NASH,** *b.* April 3, 1854; *d.* September 10, 1854.
vi.   **MARY,** *b.* April 29, 1856.
vii. **HELEN,** *b.* March 24, 1859.
viii. **ELIZA,** *b.* August 24, 1862; *m.*, April 15, 1884, in New York City, by Rev. W. S. Rainsford, **SAMUEL SHEPARD,** son of Alfred Lewis and Eliza (Shepard) Dennis, of Newark, N. J., who was *b.* September 11, 1854. Issue (surname DENNIS):

i.   Helen Eliza, *b.* June 27, 1885.
ii.   James Shepard, *b.* October 27, 1887.
iii. Dorothy, *b.* September 8, 1891.

ix.   **RICHARD SYMMES,** *b.* February 19, 1866, at Waukegan, Ill. A.B., Yale College, 1887; LL.B., Columbia College, 1889. Admitted to the bar, March, 1890.

JESSE BURGESS, younger son of **Jesse** and **Sabina (Symmes) Thomas,** was born at Shepardstown, Va., in 1777. He removed to the West in 1799, and studied law with his brother, Richard Symmes Thomas, at Washington, Mason Co., Ky. Here he served as Clerk of the County Court until March, 1803, when he removed to Lawrenceburg, Indiana Territory, and engaged in the practice of law.

In January, 1805, he was elected a Delegate to the first Assembly of Indiana Territory, at Vincennes. He was chosen Speaker of that body, and presided from 1805 to 1808. He was commissioned in 1805, by William Henry Harrison, Captain in the Dearborn Co. Militia.

In 1808 he was chosen Delegate to Congress from Indiana Territory, and secured the organization of Illinois Territory. At the close of his term in 1809 he removed to Kaskaskia, afterward to Cahokia, and later to Edwardsville. March 7, 1809, he was appointed, by President Madison, Judge of the United States Court for Illinois Territory. He served in this position until 1818, when he was elected, August 3d, a delegate from St. Clair Co. to the Convention which framed the Constitution of the State of Illinois. He was unanimously chosen President of that body.

At the first session of the State Legislature, at Kaskaskia, he was elected United States Senator, and was re-elected January 9,

1823, at Vandalia, serving continuously from 1818 until March 3, 1829.

In 1820, he introduced the Missouri Compromise, of which he was the author, and was Chairman of the Committee of Conference on that measure. February 9, 1826, he reported in the Senate the Illinois and Michigan Canal Bill, and secured its adoption.

Shortly before the close of his Senatorial career he removed to Mount Vernon, O., where he lived up to the time of his death. In 1840 he was a Delegate to the National Whig Convention at Columbus, and was active in securing the nomination of William Henry Harrison for the Presidency.

He was a man of broad and generous nature, talented, dignified, and refined, an upright judge and an able statesman. He *m.*, at Vincennes, Ind., December 2, 1806, **REBECCA HAMTRAMCK,** widow of Colonel John F. Hamtramck, U. S. A., who *d.* June 1, 1851. He *d. s. p.* at Mount Vernon, O., May 3, 1853.

Authorities : Family Bibles of Jesse Burgess Thomas and Richard Symmes Thomas, and family papers. through Miss Helen Thomas and Henry T. Thomas.

THOMAS, OF ISLINGTON, LONDON

THIS family claims as arms : Argent, a fesse dancette between three
birds sable, quartered with lozengy, argent and sable, on a fesse
gules, three lions passant argent. Crest: A Cornish chough,
rising proper between two spears erect, all proper. Descends
from **RICHARD THOMAS,** of Brittens, in Sevenoaks, Kent,
who *m.* **ELIZABETH,** *dau.* of one of the heirs of **Thomas
Tottenhurst,** of Chevening, Kent, and had a son, **RICHARD,** of
Sevenoaks, Gent., who *m.* **MARY,** *dau.* of **Christopher Clarke,** of
Chevening, Gent. Issue :

i. **CHRISTOPHER,** of Sevenoke, Gent.
ii. **JEOFFRY,** *of whom presently.*

JEOFFRY,[1] younger son of **Richard** and **Mary (Clarke)
Thomas,** was of Islington, Esquire, fined for alderman, Sheriff
of London and Middlesex, eleventh year of King Charles II.;
m. **ELIZABETH,** *dau.* of **Daniel Shatterden,** Esquire, of
Elsham, Kent. Issue, in 1664 :

i.   **DANIEL,** aged fourteen.
ii. **ELIZABETH,** aged four.
iii. **GEOFFRY,** aged one year.

R. PROCKLER THOMAS, living 1742, whose book-plate bears the
same paternal arms, was evidently of this family, which may descend
from Sir Rhys ap Thomas.

Authority: Ryley and Dethick's Visitation of Middlesex in 1620, published 1820, *p.* 44.

[1] See Thomas, of Highgate.

THOMAS, OF KENTUCKY

REES THOMAS, *b.* June 4, 1690, in Pembroke, Wales, emigrated with his family to Rockingham Co., Va. He *m.*, first, **Katharine** ——. Issue :

i.   **MARY,** *b.* August 25, 1719 ; *d. i.*
ii.   **JAMES,** *b.* October 5, 1720 ; *d.*, February 5, 1747, in Bourbon Co., Ky.
iii.   **MARGARET,** *b.* May 16, 1723.
iv.   **JOHN,** *b.* April 16, 1725, *of whom presently.*

He *m.*, second, **ELLEN** ——. Issue :

v.   **GRACE,** *b.* September 21, 1730.
vi.   **KATHARINE,** *b.* November 19, 1732.
vii.   **MARY,** *b.* November 3, 1734.
viii.   **JANE,** *b.* May 13, 1737.

He *m.*, third, **JANE** ——. Issue :

ix.   **EVAN,** *b.* February 10, 1743.
x.   **DAVID,** *b.* June 22, 1745.
xi.   **REES,** *b.* October 1, 1747.

JOHN, youngest son of **Rees** and **Katharine Thomas,** removed to Paris, Bourbon Co., Ky.; *m.* —— **MILLER.** Issue :

i.   **SILAS.**
ii.   **HENRY.**
iii.   **ABRAHAM,** *of whom presently.*
iv.   **EVAN.**

ABRAHAM, third son of **John** and —— **(Miller) Thomas,** *b.* December 20, 1774, in Virginia, removed with his father to Kentucky, and from thence to Adams Co., O. ; *m.*, August 8, 1799, **MARGARET BARKER,** and *d.* 1856. Issue :

i.   **JOHN,** *b.* May 20, 1801 ; *d. s. p.* November 1, 1826.
ii.   **ABRAHAM,** *b.* September 5, 1805 ; *d. s. p.* July 13, 1827.
iii.   **JAMES B.,** *b.* May 16, 1811, *of whom presently.*

iv.   **SILAS,** *b.* March 10, 1814 ; *d. s. p.* June 22, 1856.
v.   **WILSON B.,** *b.* April 19, 1820.

JAMES B., third son of **Abraham** and **Margaret (Barker) Thomas,** *b.* May 16, 1811 ; *m.,* December 29, 1836, **ESTHER A. MOORE,** and *d.* March 17, 1892.   Issue :

i.   **FRANCIS M.,** *b.* July 9, 1838.   Physician, residing at Samantha, O. ; *m.* March 15, 1871, **ANNETTE HOLMES.**
ii.   **W. C.,** *b.* October 30, 1843 ; *d.* September 8, 1860.
iii.   **SILAS N.,** *b.* August 7, 1845 ; *d.* August 13, 1864, in the Union Army.
iv.   **ALBERT L.,** *b.* April 25, 1848.
v.   **JOHN W.,** *b.* September 16, 1850 ; a physician of Aumsville, Ore.; *m.,* May 8, 1895, **ROBERTA BUTLER.**

Authority : Family Bible of Rees Thomas, the Emigrant, printed in Welsh, London, 1717, through Dr. F. M. Thomas

THOMAS OF CHESTER

THOMAS, OF KESGRAVE, ENGLAND

GEORGE THOMAS, of Kesgrave and Brockley, Suffolk, Eng-
land, *m.* **SARAH**, *dau.* of **Thomas Jones**, of Swansea,
Wales, who *d.* December 4, 1766, and is buried at Kesgrave.
He *d.* May 10, 1770 ; is buried at Ipswich, Suffolk.   Issue :

i.   **GEORGE**, *of whom presently.*
ii.   **PHILIP.**
iii.   **MICHAEL.**
iv.   **SARAH,** *m.* **JOHN WHYMPER.**

    GEORGE, eldest son of **George** and **Sarah (Jones) Thomas,**
m. **ANNE**, *dau.* and *co-h.* of **George Cochrane** ; *d.* April 4, 1806,
and is buried at Kesgrave. His widow *d.* June 3, 1812. They had
a son, **GEORGE**, of Woodbridge, Co. Suffolk, Sheriff in 1820.
    Arms : A chevron sable between three Cornish choughs. Crest :
A Cornish chough rising proper between two spears erect or. Motto :
Virtute et labore.

Authority : Clark's Genealogies of Morgan and Glamorgan.

THOMAS, OF LELANT, CORNWALL

This family descends from **Sir William ap Thomas,** of Wales, whose arms were allowed to its head at the Heralds' Visitation of 1620. They settled in Lelant about the end of the fourteenth century, by the marriage of RICHARD THOMAS, a Welsh merchant, with the *dau.* and *heir.* of John Hickes, of Lelant. **JOHN THOMAS,** his great-grandson, *m.* the *dau.* and heiress of —— **Rosmell,** of Bodmin, and their grandson, WILLIAM THOMAS, of Cury, registered his pedigree at the Visitation of 1620. He was recently represented by **Edward Thomas,** of Helston and Callington, descended through **John Thomas,** of Tremayne, Gent., February 9, 1709, and **Edward Thomas,** of Lelant, *d.* 1790. A pedigree of this family will be found in Maclean's " History of Trigg Minor, Cornwall," *pp.* 304, 305.

ARMS OF CAREW

THOMAS, OF LLANBRADACH, GLAMORGAN, AND LLYN MADOC, BRECON, WALES

THOMAS BEVAN AP LLEWELLYN DAVID, of Llanbradach, *m.* **ANN,** *dau.* of **Lewis Richard Gwyn,** of Morlais Castle, and *d.* about 1500. Their son, **RHYS THOMAS,** *m.* **ELIZABETH,** *dau.* of **Richard Carne,** of Nash, and had a son, WILLIAM THOMAS, *m.* a *dau.* of Thomas Carew, Esq., of Crocombe, Somerset, and had Thomas, *m.* Dorothy, *dau.* of Sir John Carew, Knt., Sheriff of Pembroke, 1622, and had a son, Rowland, and another, William, *of whom presently.*

WILLIAM, son of **Thomas** and **Dorothy (Carew) Thomas,** was High Sheriff of Glamorgan in 1674 ; *m.* a *dau.* of **Thomas Morgan,** of Machen. His son, **THOMAS,** was Sheriff in 1705 ; his great grandson, **James,** was Sheriff in 1728, and *d. s. p. ;* his uncle, William, of Tredomnan, inherited, and his great grandson, **Thomas,** *d.* leaving a *dau.,* **Clara ;** *m.* **Henry Thomas,** of Llyn Madoc, Brecon.

Authorities : Nicholas's County Families of Wales, and Somersetshire Wills.

136

THOMAS, OF LLANFIHANGEL AND BRI-GAN, WALES

THIS family, said to be of the lineage of Jestin ap Gwrgant, descends from **THOMAS AP GRONW**, called **THOMAS DDU**, the "black," because of his hair, living about 1500. His son, or grandson, **JAMES THOMAS**, was High Sheriff of Glamorganshire, 1551 ; JAMES, his son, being Under-Sheriff. John, son of the second James, was sheriff in 1579. **EDWARD**, probably grandson of **John Thomas**, by **WILLIAM**, Gent., who was M.P. for Cardiff, in 1614, was sheriff of Glamorgan in 1633, and created a Baronet, March 3, 1641–42 ; he *m.* **SUSAN**, *dau.* of Sir Thomas Morgan, of Ruperra, Knt., and *d.* at Windsor in 1673. Issue :

> SIR ROBERT, his heir, M.P. for Cardiff, 1678–80 (some say SIR ED-WARD, of whose heirs nothing is known). SIR ROBERT is said to have *m.* MARY, *dau.* of David Jenkens, of Hensol, and his only *dau.*, Susannah, *m.*, but *d. s. p.* in her father's lifetime.

Another branch of the family, descended maternally from **STE-PHEN BASSON**, or **BAUSON**, who commanded the English army against Prince Llewellyn ap Gruffyd in the battle near Llandeilofawr, 1257, and was repulsed with great loss by the Welsh. He became Lord of Brigan that same year. His *granddau.*, BEATRICE, *m.* AARON ap HOWEL VYCHAN ap CADWGAN ap BLEDDYN ap MAENARCH. About 1450 the heiress *m.* Thomas, brother of Gronw, above mentioned,

137

and fifth son of Ivan ap Leyson, Lord of Baglan, near Aberavon. The male line of their descendants became extinct when ANTHONY THOMAS, who *m.* ELINOR, *dau.* of William Bassett, Clerk of Newton Nottage, *d. s. p.* about 1800.

Another **Thomas** family, styled of Llanvihangel, used the arms of Herbert, and descended from **Jevan ap Gwilim,** of Perthir (see Bishop William Thomas's family), and had among its members **James Thomas,** Bluemantle Pursuivant, April 24, 1587, Chester Herald, March 26, 1592. **William Thomas,** last direct male of the older line, was living about 1675. **Thomas,** of Tregroes, junior branch of this family, ends in **Edward Thomas,** living in 1702. **Thomas,** of Garth, another line, took name of **Deere** in the eighteenth century.

Authorities: Clark's Morgan and Glamorgan, *p.* 272, and Nicholas's Annals of Wales, ii., 583.

THOMAS OF LLANON

THOMAS, OF LLETTYMAWR AND LLANON, . CAERMARTHENSHIRE, WALES

THIS family descends from **Sir HUGH TREHERNE, or TRA-HERNE, KNT.**, who fought in the battle of Poictiers. The name became Thomas in the reign of Henry VIII. **REES THOMAS** *d.* 1759, leaving three sons, **REES**, *d. s. p.* 1777 ; **DAVID**, of Llewdeved ; whose *granddau.* and heiress, Anne David Thomas, *m.* Thomas Lloyd, and **MORGAN**, of Llanon, *m.*, 1768, **FRANCES**, only *dau.* and heiress of **Henry** and **Sarah (Gilbert) Goring**, of Frodley Hall, Staffordshire. Their grandson was Rees Goring Thomas, of Llanon and Tooting Lodge, Surrey, High Sheriff of Caermarthenshire, 1830. Rev. John Montagu Traherne, the antiquary, was of this family, resuming the original surname, and there are branches named Treheron, or Traherne, in Cornwall.

Authorities : Burke's Landed Gentry, and Nicholas's Annals of Wales.

139

THOMAS, OF MARSHFIELD, MASS.

JOHN THOMAS emigrated September 11, 1635, in the Hopewell, from London, and settled at Marshfield, in 1635; he *m.*, December 21, 1648, **SARAH**, *dau.* of **James Pitney**, who *d.* 1682; he *d.* in 1676. Issue :

i. **JOHN**, *b.* 1649, *m.* **SARAH** —— and *d. s. p.* 1699.
ii. **ELIZABETH**, *b.* September 12, 1652.
iii. **SAMUEL**, *b.* November 6, 1655, *of whom presently.*
iv. **DANIEL**, *b.* November 20, 1659, *m.*, 1698, **EXPERIENCE**, *dau.* of Thomas Tilden.
v. **SARAH**, *b.* September 20, 1661, *m.*, 1681, **BENJAMIN PHILLIPS.**
vi. **JAMES**, *b.* November 30, 1663, *m.* **MARY**, *dau.* of **Stephen Tilden.**
vii. **EPHRAIM**, *b.* 1667-68, removed to Little Compton.
viii. **ISRAEL**, *b.* 1670, *m.* **BETHIAH SHERMAN.**

SAMUEL, 2d son of **John** and **Sarah (Pitney) Thomas**, *b.* November 6, 1656, *m.*, May 27, 1680, **MERCY**, *dau.* of Deacon **William Ford.** Issue :

i. **BETHIAH**, *b.* January 25, 1681.
ii. **JOHN**, *b.* November 8, 1683, *of whom presently.*
iii. **SAMUEL**, *b.* December 7, 1685, *q. v.*
iv. **NATHAN**, *b.* November 21, 1688.
v. **JOSEPH**, *b.* 1690.
vi. **GIDEON**, *b.* 1692.
vii. **JOSIAH**, *b.* 1694 (?).

JOHN, eldest son of **Samuel** and **Mercy (Ford) Thomas**, *b.* November 8, 1683, *m.*, 1714, **LYDIA WATERMAN**, and *d.* April 14, 1773; his wife *d.* January 17, 1750. Issue :

i. **ZENIAH**, *b.* 1714, *m.* **JAMES BRADFORD** and removed to Plainfield, Conn.
ii. **ANN**, *b.* 1716, *d.* December 7, 1723.
iii. **ANTHONY**, *b.* 1719, *of whom presently.*
iv. **JOHN**, *b.* 1724, lived at Kingston. He commanded the army at Roxbury at the beginning of the Revolutionary War. He was an officer in the expedition against Canada, and his diary has been printed. After the

GENERAL JOHN THOMAS

*From Irving's "Life of Washington," by Permission
of G. P. Putnam's Sons*

death of General Richard Montgomery he succeeded him in the command, and *d.*, of small-pox, June 2, 1776. He *m.* **HANNAH**, *dau.* of **Nathaniel Thomas**, of Plymouth, who *d.* in 1819. Their grandson was **John Thomas**, of Irvington, N. Y., in 1850. Thomaston, Me., is named after General Thomas.

v.   **SARAH**, *b.* 1726, *m.* **JEREMIAH KINSMAN**, and removed to Connecticut.

vi.   **KEZIAH**, *b.* November 7, 1730, *d. u.* December 11, 1751.

ANTHONY, eldest son of **John** and **Lydia (Waterman) Thomas**, *b.* April 20, 1719, commissioned Colonel in the Militia ; *m.* **ABIGAIL TILDEN**, and *d.* July 14, 1781, leaving a son, **BRIGGS**, *m.* **ABIGAIL**, *dau.* of Deacon **Nehemiah** and **Abiah (Winslow) Thomas**, and had a son, **WINSLOW**, *b.* 1763, *m.* **ABIGAIL DELANO**. Issue :

    i.   **Nehemiah.**
    ii.   **Abigail**, *b.* May 10, 1800.
    iii.   **Abraham.** *m.* **Sybil Gregory. Issue :** i. Manly. ii. Ezra. iii. Nehemiah. iv. John. v. Hannah. vi. Sally. vii. Abigail, *m.* Abraham Polmanteer.

SAMUEL, younger son of **Samuel** and **Mercy (Ford) Thomas,** *b.* December 7, 1685, settled with his wife, **JEANNETTE** (who *d.* August 18, 1756, aged fifty-six), at Worcester, Mass. He *d.* May 20, 1755, leaving a son, **DAVID**, removed to Pelham, Mass., and *m.*, second, November 18, 1755, ——, at Lancaster, Mass., and had a son, **DAVID**, *b.* June 11, 1762, who served as volunteer in 1777. Joined the 5th Massachusetts Regiment in 1781 as a Corporal, became Sergeant of the 3d Massachusetts Regiment. In 1784 removed to Salem, Washington Co., N. Y., and the same year *m.* his cousin, **JEANNETTE**, *dau.* of **James Turner**, and for some nine years kept a tavern there. In 1793 gave up the tavern and began merchandizing, in partnership with a Mr. Hawley. His wife *d.* February 14, 1795, leaving an only surviving child, **Jane**. In 1793 he was elected a Member of the Assembly, and again in 1798–99. He *m.*, second, January 15, 1800, **MARY**, *dau.* of **Stephen Hogeboom**. In 1800 elected to Congress, and twice thereafter. February 18, 1808, appointed Treasurer of the State, holding the office two years. In 1813 his wife went to live with a married sister, he broke up housekeeping, and fitted up his house for a tavern, and it has ever since been occupied for that purpose. Soon after coming to New York State he was commissioned Captain in the State Militia, June 23, 1786, and rose to the rank of Major-General of the Northern Division of the Mi-

THOMAS, OF MICHIGAN

STEVEN THOMAS, *b.* in Connecticut about 1778 ; *m.*, about 1802, in the same State, —— **PECK,** who *d.* in Illinois in 1863 ; her husband *d.* at Lapeer, Mich., about 1867. Issue :

i.   **CALVIN PECK,** *b.* September 2, 1805, *of whom presently.*

ii.   **HARVEY,** *b.* about 1808, at Pompey, N. Y. ; *m.*, about 1828, **BETSY HIGHBEE,** and *d.* about 1881, leaving five children.

iii.   **MARIA L.,** *b.* 1810 (?), at Pompey ; *m.*, 1830 (?), **LYMAN MORGAN,** and resides at Marengo, Ill.

iv.   **JOHN,** *b.*, 1812 (?), at Pompey, N. Y. ; *m.*, 1838, at Pontiac, Mich., **MARY E. WETMORE ;** *d.*, 1892, at Oxford, Mich.

v.   **CAROLINE,** *b.* 1814 (?) ; *d.*, 1843 (?), at Marengo, Ill.

vi.   **ALONZO,** *b.*, 1816 (?), at Pompey, N. Y. ; *m.*, 1850 (?), **CLARISSA SPENCER,** at Marengo, Ill., and *d.* about 1854, at Oxford, Mich.

vii.   **DANIEL,** *b.* about 1818, at Pompey, N. Y., resides in Grand Traverse Co., Mich.

viii.   **LOUISA,** *b.* at Pompey, N. Y. ; *m.*, 1850 (?), —— **SPENCER,** and resides in Kansas.

CALVIN PECK, eldest son of **Steven** and —— **(Peck) Thomas,** *b.* September 2, 1805, at Pompey, Onondago Co., N. Y. ; *m.*, October 22, 1826, at the same place, **HANNAH G. GRIMES** (*b.* October 4, 1808 ; *d.*, March 10, 1885, at Lapeer, Mich.), and *d.*, October 11, 1848, at Lapeer, Mich. Issue :

i.   **HOMER A.,** *b.*, April 8, 1828, at Pompey ; *m.*, July 4, 1850, **BETSEY ROSSMAN,** and *d.*, February 23, 1883, in Kansas, leaving five children.

ii.   **STEPHEN VAN RENNSELAER** (*sic*), *b.* November 2, 1830, *of whom presently.*

iii.   **JOHN W.,** *b.*, August 8, 1832, at Pompey ; *m.*, 1867, at New Orleans, **HATTIE LEWIS ;** *d.* there, March 9, 1881, leaving three children.

iv.   **CALVIN P.,** *b.*, September 29, 1834, at Pompey ; *m.*, December 10, 1857, at Lapeer, Mich., **ADELINE E. SHUE,** and resides at Grand Rapids, Mich., having five children.

144

v.   **CHARLOTTE E.,** *b.* January 19, 1837, at Pompey ; *m.,* 1853, **JOHN E. DEMING ;** *d.* May 7, 1875, at Lapeer, Mich., leaving seven children.

vi.   **HANNAH AMELIA,** *b.* June 25, 1839, at Pompey ; *m.,* March, 1858, at Lapeer, Mich., **GEORGE CLARK,** and *d.* September 21, 1876, leaving two children.

vii. **QUINCY A.,** *b.* May 12, 1842, at Pompey ; *m.,* 1863, **MARY MILLER ;** has three children, and resides at Duluth, Minn.

STEPHEN VAN RENNSELAER, second son of **Calvin P.** and **Hannah (Grimes) Thomas,** *b.* November 2, 1830, in the Township of Pompey, N. Y. ; resides at West Branch, Mich., and is Judge of Probate of Ogeman County in that State. He *m.,* 1850, **CAROLINE LOUISA LORD.** Issue :

i.   **CHARLES SHERMAN,** *b.* 1852, *d. i.*

ii.   **CALVIN,** *b.* October 28, 1854, Professor of Germanic Languages and Literature, University of Michigan.

iii. **BLANCHE,** *b.* January 5, 1860 ; *d.* February 24, 1881.

Authority : Family papers, through Professor Calvin Thomas, A.M.

THOMAS, OF MIDDLEBORO', MASS.

WILLIAM THOMAS had a son, **BENJAMIN**, a Deacon of the first Congregational Church in Middleboro', who *m.* **ELIZABETH CHURCHILL**, and had a son, EZRA, *m.* LUCY STURTEVANT, of Carver, Mass. Issue :

i.   EZRA, *b.* at Middleboro', May 15, 1786, *of whom presently.*

EZRA, son of **Ezra** and **Lucy (Sturtevant) Thomas**, *b.* May 15, 1786 ; was *m.*, February 19, 1812, at Carver, Mass., by Rev. John Shaw, to **HANNAH COLE**, *b.* January 4, 1786 ; he *d.* July 13, 1825, at Middleboro'. Issue :

i.   EZRA, *b.* May 17, 1814, at Middleboro', *of whom presently.*
ii.   ISAAC, *d.* some years ago.
iii.   CHARLOTTE, *m.* —— BURGESS, of Carver, Mass., since *d.*
iv.   LUCY.

EZRA, son of **Ezra** and **Hannah (Cole) Thomas**, *b.* May 17, 1814, was *m.*, October 25, 1837, at Middleboro', by Rev. Mr. Barrows, to **MARY NELSON**, *dau.* of **Rev. Ebenezer Briggs**[1] (*b.* 1768) and **Hannah Nelson**, his wife (*b.* 1771). **EZRA THOMAS**, *d.* September 28, 1891, at Cleveland, O. Issue :

i.   EBEN BRIGGS, *b.* December 22, 1838, at Chatham, Canada, elected, in 1894, 1st Vice-President of the New York, Lake Erie & Western Railway ; resides in New York City ; *m.*, October 7, 1868, by Rev. H. P. Bailey, at Cleveland, O., to **HELEN GERTRUDE**, *dau.* of **Dr. Worthy Stevens** (*b.* October 16, 1816) and **Sarah Wakely (Sterling) Streator** (*b.* December 9, 1819), and descended from **Dr. John Streator**, through **Isaac H.**, *b.* 1758, and **Isaac H., Jr.,** *b.* October 18, 1786. Issue :
       GERTRUDE STREATOR, HELEN STERLING.
ii.   MARY NELSON, *b.* 1842, *d. u.* 1862.
iii.   ANNA, *d.* aged two.
iv.   ANNA NELSON, *b.* May 5, 1845.
v.   EUNICE, *b.* May 22, 1847.
       Authority : Family papers, through Mrs. Eben B. Thomas, of New York City.

[1] Rev. Ebenezer Briggs was son of Ebenezer (*b.* 1731) and Elizabeth (Smith) Briggs, and grandson of Nathaniel Briggs and Sarah Whitaker, of Rehoboth, Mass., who were *m.* in 1719.

FRANCIS THOMAS
BORN 1743, DIED 1835

THOMAS, OF MONTEVUE, MD.

HUGH THOMAS, according to family tradition of the same stock as Bishop William Thomas, of Caermarthen (*q. v.*), is said to have emigrated from Wales to Pennsylvania between 1702 and 1714, removing shortly afterward to Maryland. He *m.* **ELIZABETH** or **BETTIE**, *dau.* of **Francis Edwards**, said to have been a maid-of-honour to Queen Anne, and *d.* Issue: a son **WILLIAM**, *of whom presently*.

WILLIAM, son of **Hugh** and **Bettie (Edwards) Thomas**, emigrated at or about the same time with his parents, first to Shepherdstown, Va., afterward was in Frederick Co., Md. Issue :

i.   **WILLIAM**,[1] said to have *m.* a lady of Hagerstown, Md., and had two daughters.
ii.   **FRANCIS**, *b.* April 8, 1743, *of whom presently.*
iii. **KITTY**, *d. y.* or *m.* —— **EVANS**, of Kentucky.

FRANCIS, second son of **William Thomas**, *b.* April 8, 1743, resided at Montevue, near Frederick, Md. ; *m.* **GRACE MET-CALFE** (*b.* March 11, 1741 ; *d.* November, 1829), supposed to have been widow of —— **CATLETT**, or —— **SHEPHERD**, and *d.* June 27, 1835. Issue :

i.   **ELIZABETH**, *m.* **LLOYD BELT**, of a family early prominent in Maryland. Tradition says some of their seven children removed to Indiana and a granddaughter, Sarah Belt, *m.* at St. Louis, Charles Carroll.

[1] At Frederick, Md., on the Lutheran Church register, there is record of the baptism of Francis William, *b.* August 3, 1779, and John Coslett, or Catlett, *b.* August 3, 1783, both children of William and Æmilia Thomas. Witnesses: Francis Thomas and his *dau.* Elizabeth.

ii. ANN, *m.* COLONEL WILLIAM ANDERSON (*q. v.*), from whom are descended the families of ANDERSON, BRUCE, JUNKIN, POIN-DEXTER, HOBSON, and GLASGOW (*q. v.*).

iii. ELEANOR METCALFE, *m.* REV. SAMUEL MITCHELL,[1] *b.* in Orange Co., Va., March 23, 1764. Issue (surname MITCHELL):

   i. MARY GRACE, *m.* JOHN H. ROUNTREE, *b.* in Kentucky, settled afterward at Plattsville, Wis., and *d.*, aged eighty-five. Issue (surname ROUNTREE):

      i. Samuel H., *m.* Sophie A. Aspinwall.
      ii. Ellen R., is Regent of the Chicago Chapter of the Daughters of the American Revolution and President of "the Antiquarians" since 1882; *m.* John N. Jewett, a prominent lawyer of Chicago. Issue (surname JEWETT):

         i. Edward R., *m.*, 1885, Frances Campbell, of Maine.
         ii. Samuel R., *m.*, 1889, Lucy McCormick, of Chicago.

      iii. John Mitchell, *m.* Mary Bancroft.

iv. CATHERINE, *m.* DR. SEYMES, SEMMES, or SIMS.

v. MARY, *m.*, May 3, 1787, RALPH CRABB (*q. v.*).

vi. LILEY, *b.* March 11, 1778; *bapt.* by the Lutheran pastor, at Frederick; *m* REV. JOSEPH REID. Issue:

   JANE, *m.* ROBERT NAPOLEON WEIR, M.D., and removed to Mississippi.

vii. JOHN, *b.* July 5, 1767, *of whom presently.*

JOHN, only son of **Francis** and **Grace (Metcalfe) Thomas**, *b.* July 5, 1767; *m.*, June 11, 1789, **ELEANOR McGILL** (*b.* August 17, 1768; *d.* May 17, 1822), and *d.* August 13, 1849. Issue:

i. KITTY, *b.* March 13, 1790; *d.* 1791.

ii. LLOYD, *b.* April 13, 1791; *m.*, April 8, 1823, **MARY RUTHER-FORD BROWN**, and *d.* January 4, 1867. Issue:

   i. FRANCIS JOHN, *b.* January 10, 1824.
   ii. MARY ELEANOR RUTHERFORD, *b.* September 9, 1825.
   iii. SARAH ELIZA, *b.* August 7, 1827.
   iv. CATHERINE GRACE, *b.* September 29, 1829.
   v. VIRGINIA SUSAN, *b.* February 3, 1832.
   vi. MARGARET, *b.* August 10, 1834.
   vii. JAMES H. B., *b.* February 10, 1837.

iii. ELIZA (twin sister of LLOYD), *b.* April 13, 1791, *d. u.* September 26, 1867.

iv. JOHN, *b.* May 13, 1793; *d.* 1796.

v. GRACE METCALFE, *b.* February 24, 1795; *m.*, May 30, 1825, COL-ONEL THOMAS SHANKS (*q. v.*).

vi. MARY CRABB, *b.* December 25, 1796; *m.*, April 29, 1823, DR. LEWIS SHANKS, and *d.* July 7, 1833. Issue (surname SHANKS):

   i. ELLEN HANNAH, *b.* June 24, 1824; *m.* THOMAS HAMPTON ALLEN.
   ii. CHARLES LEWIS, *b.* February 18, 1827.
   iii. LEWIS, *b.* August 3, 1829.
   iv. McGILL.

---

[1] In 1780 enlisted under General Daniel Morgan, in his campaign against Colonel Tarleton, in North Carolina, afterward served in Washington's army at the siege of Yorktown. Morgan made him a bearer of important despatches. He refused a pension, saying "he had exposed his life not for money but for the honour and independence of his country, and he was better able to do without the pension than the Government was to pay it."

FRANCIS THOMAS
GOVERNOR OF MARYLAND, 1841–1844

v. FRANCIS THOMAS, *b.* March, 1830.
vi. CASSANDRA PATTON, *b.* November, 1832.

vii. FRANCIS, *b.* February 3, 1799; educated at St. John's College,
Annapolis; admitted to the Maryland Bar, 1820; member of the
House of Delegates, 1822, 1827, and 1829; Speaker during his last
term; Representative in Congress 1831–41; in 1839 President of
the Chesapeake & Ohio Canal Co.; from 1841 to 1844 Governor of
Maryland; a member of the State Constitutional Convention, 1851;
and of Congress again, 1861–69; Internal Revenue Collector, 1870;
United States Minister to Peru, 1872–75; was a recognized leader in
Congress and one of the most popular political orators of Maryland.
A Democrat in early life, during the Civil War a pronounced Un-
ionist, raising a brigade of three thousand volunteers, but declining a commission for himself. He *m.* SALLIE CAMPBELL
PRESTON, *dau.* of Governor James McDowell, of Virginia,
and was accidentally killed January 22, 1876, crossing the Baltimore &
Ohio Railroad track, near his residence. He resided at " Montevue,"
d. s. p.

viii. DR. JOHN McGILL, *b.* December 9, 1801; *m.*, first, May 12, 1823,
CATHARINE CONTEE TURNER, who *d.* September 22,
1831; *m.*, second, November 25, 1832, MARGARET H. DUN-
LOP, and *d.* December 23, 1834. Issue by first wife:

i.   CHARLES COATSWORTH, *b.* September 5, 1827.
ii. THOMAS TURNER, *b.* March 19, 1829.
iii. JOHN THOMAS, *b.* June 25, 1830.
iv. FRANCIS CONTEE, *b.* July 8, 1831.

Issue by second wife:

v.   JAMES DUNLOP, *b.* December 13, 1833.
vi. ELIZA McGILL, *b.* December 12, 1834.

ix. CHARLES COATSWORTH, *b.* June 24, 1803; *d.* August 15, 1822.

x.   CATHERINE L. A., *b.* December 1, 1806; *m.*, July 31, 1834, COL-
ONEL HENRY DUNLOP, and *d.* December 13, 1872. Issue
(surname DUNLOP):

i.   HENRY, *b.* July 25, 1835.
ii.   ELIZABETH, *b.* March 2, 1837.
iii. ELLEN, *b.* January 31, 1839.
iv.   MARGARET GRACE, *b.* June 25, 1840, *d. i.*
v.   JOHN THOMAS, *b.* January 25, 1842.
vi.   HELEN, *b.* September 8, 1843.
vii. GEORGE THOMAS, *b.* March 25, 1845.
viii. CATHERINE ELIZA, *b.* January 7, 1847.

xi. LEVIN, *b.* October 7, 1809; *d.* 1811.

xii. SARAH ANN ELEANOR, *b.* July 31, 1811; *m.* DR. RICHARD
SCOTT BLACKBURN, of Jefferson Co., Va. (*q. v.*).

Authorities: Records of Lutheran Church, Frederick, Md., and family papers, through Mrs. R.
T. Ely, Mrs. John N. Jewett, and Francis T. A. Junkin, Esq.

THOMAS, OF NEW HAVEN, CONN.

JOHN THOMAS, of New Haven, Conn., was a freeman, 1669 ; proprietor later ; *m.* **TABITHA** ——— ; *d.* December 15, 1671. Issue :

i.   **DANIEL,** *of whom presently.*
ii.   **JOHN,** *q. v.*
iii.   **SARAH,** *m.,* October 14, 1658, **WILLIAM WILMOT.**
iv.   **ELIZABETH,** *b.* March 15, 1649 ; *m.,* January, 1674, **JOHN HOLT.**
v.   **SAMUEL,** *b.* September 5, 1651.
vi.   **TABITHA,** *b.* December 18, 1653.
vii.   **JOSEPH,** *b.* November 10, 1661.

DANIEL, eldest son of **John** and **Tabitha Thomas** ; freeman, 1670 ; *m.,* February 3, 1670, **REBECCA THOMPSON,** who survived him and *m.* ——— **PERKINS.** He *d.* February, 1694. Issue :

i.   **DOROTHY,** *b.* 1672.
ii.   **JOHN,** *b.* 1674.
iii.   **DANIEL,** *b.* February 14, 1677.
iv.   **DINAH,** *b.* December 26, 1678.
v.   **SAMUEL,** *b.* January, 1681 ; *d. y.*
vi.   **RECOMPENSE,** *b.* March 27, 1683.
vii.   **ISRAEL,** *b.* 1689.

JOHN, second son of **John** and **Tabitha Thomas** ; *m.,* 1671, **LYDIA,** *dau.* of **Edward Parker,** of New Haven. Issue :

i.   **SARAH,** *b.* December 13, 1672.
ii.   **ABIGAIL,** *b.* November 21, 1674.
iii.   **JOHN,** *b.* March 4, 1676.
iv.   **HANNAH,** *b.* April 26, 1678.
v.   **ISAIAH,** *b.* January 15, 1680.
vi.   **REBECCA,** *b.* September 20, 1681 or 82.
vii.   **JEREMIAH,** *b.* February 16, 1685.
     And possibly others.

Authority : Savage's Dictionary of New England Settlers.

THOMAS, OF NEW PLYMOUTH COLONY, MASS.

WILLIAM THOMAS, said to be of Welsh descent, and a merchant, was at Green Harbour, afterward known as Marshfield, about 1641, and became a permanent settler there in 1645. Was one of the eleven founders of the New Plymouth Colony ; Assistant Deputy-Governor, 1642–50; Member of the Council of War, 1643. The alarm beacon was placed on his estate. He *d.* August, 1651, aged seventy-eight. Issue :

> **NATHANIEL,** *b.* 1606 ; commanded one of the watches against the Indians in 1643. One of the volunteers of the Pequod Expedition, 1643 ; commissioned Ensign of the Marshfield Company of the Colonial troops commanded by Captain Miles Standish ; Lieutenant of the same, August 29, 1648, and Captain, March 5, 1654, succeeding Miles Standish. He served in the expedition against the Pequods, 1645, and that prepared against the Dutch of New Amsterdam, 1653 ; *d.* February 13, 1674–75, leaving issue :

i. **WILLIAM,** *b.* 1638 ; *d. u.* March 30, 1718.
ii. **NATHANIEL,** *b.* 1643, *of whom presently.*
iii. **MARY,** *m.* **CAPTAIN SYMON RAY,** of New Shoreham, R. I.; their *dau.*, Sybil, *m.* **Captain John Sands,** and had the Hon. John Sands, *m.* Catharine Guthrie, and had issue: John, *m.* Eliza Cornell. Their son, Hon. Joshua Sands, *m.* Ann Ayscough, and had a *dau.*, Eliza, *m.* Captain E. Trenchard, U. S. N., whose son, Admiral S. D. Trenchard, *m.* Ann Barclay, and was father of Edward Trenchard, of New York City, Deputy Secretary General of the Society of Colonial Wars.
iv. **ELIZABETH,** *b.* 1646.
v. **DOROTHY.**
vi. **JEREMIAH.** Issue:

    i. **Nathaniel,** *b.* January 2, 1686.
    ii. **Sarah,** *b.* December 25, 1687.
    iii. **Jeremiah,** *b.* February 14, 1689.
    iv. **Eliza,** *b.* November 19, 1690.
    v. **Mary,** *b.* June 5, 1692.
    vi. **Lydia,** *b.* March 26, 1694.
    vii. **Thankful,** *b.* June 30, 1695.
    viii. **Jedediah,** *b.* August 19, 1698.
    ix. **Bethiah,** *b.* March 27, 1701.
    x. **Ebenezer,** *b.* November 1, 1703.
    xi. **Priscilla,** *b.* October 13, 1705.
    xii. **Sophia,** *b.* 1707.

NATHANIEL, second son of **Captain Nathaniel Thomas,** *b.* 1643; was Captain of Light Horse; served in King Philip's War; was Representative in 1687–88; *m.,* first, January 19, 1663–64, **DEBORAH,** youngest *dau.* of **Nicholas Jacobs,** of Hingham, Mass., who *d.* June 17, 1696; and he was *m.,* second, November 3, 1696, by Rev. Cotton Mather, to **ELIZA,** widow of **Captain William Condy,** who *d. s. p.* October 11, 1713. Issue by his first wife :

i.   **NATHANIEL,** *of whom presently.*
ii.   **JOSEPH.**
iii.   **DEBORAH.**
iv.   **DOROTHY,** *b.* November 6, 1670.
v.   **WILLIAM.**
vi.   **ELISHA.**
vii.   **JOSHUA.**
viii.   **CALEB.**
ix.   **ISAAC.**
x.   **MARY.**

NATHANIEL, eldest son of **Captain Nathaniel and Deborah (Jacobs) Thomas,** *m.,* 1694, **MARY APPLETON,** who *d.* October 7, 1727, and her husband *d.* 1738.   Issue :

> **JOSEPH, NATHANIEL,** and **JOHN,** his eldest son, who *m.,* 1724, **MARY,** *dau.* of **Simon** and **Judith (Mainwaring) Ray,** of New London, Conn.   Issue :
>
>> **NATHANIEL RAY,** a Loyalist, who held a commission in the British Army. The family removed to Nova Scotia after the Revolution. He *m.* **SARAH,** *dau.* of **Henry** and **Eliza (Packer) Deering,** of Boston, and *d.* 1810, aged seventy-six.

Another branch of the descendants of William Thomas, of New Plymouth, is represented by **Chauncey Thomas,** of Chauncey Thomas & Co., of Boston, Mass., son of **Prince,** and grandson of **Prince Thomas,** twin brother of a **Consider Thomas,** in about the seventh generation from the emigrant.

WILLIAM THOMAS, *b.* in Boston, in 1718, was a descendant, in the sixth generation, of **William** the emigrant. He was on the medical staff of the expedition against Louisbourg in 1745, and at Crown Point in 1758. With his four sons he joined the Revolutionary army immediately after the battle of Lexington, in 1775. He was thrice married, and *d.* in 1802. By his second wife, —— **BRIDGHAM**, he had issue :

i. **JOSHUA**, *b.* 1751, Aide-de-Camp to General John Thomas, in Canada ; for many years President of the Bar in Plymouth Co. ; *m.* **ISABELLA STEVENSON**, and *d.* January 10, 1821. Issue :

  JOHN BOISE, WILLIAM, and **JOSHUA BARKER.**

ii. **JOSEPH**, Captain of Artillery in the Revolution.

iii. **JOHN**, *of whom presently.*

iv. **NATHANIEL**, had a son, **ROBERT**, a physician at Poughkeepsie, N. Y.

v. A *dau., m.* —— **BRECK**, and settled in Charlestown, N. H.

JOHN, third son of **Dr. William Thomas**, established himself after the Revolution at Poughkeepsie, N. Y. During the war he had served as surgeon, and he practised medicine, becoming one of the leading physicians of Poughkeepsie. Having no issue by his first wife, he *m.*, second, **GERTRUDE FONDA**, of a Dutch family on the Hudson River, and *d.* 1818. Issue :

i. **JOSEPH**, *d. i.*

ii. **WILLIAM BARBER**, *of whom presently.*

iii. **MARY CAROLINE**, *m.* **CHRISTOPHER Y. LANSING, Esq.**, of Albany, N. Y.

WILLIAM BARBER, only surviving son of **Dr. John** and **Gertrude (Fonda) Thomas**, became a clergyman of the Protestant Episcopal Church, ordained October 21, 1821 ; was Rector of Christ Church, Duanesburgh, N. Y., for fourteen years. He *m.* **JANE P.**, *dau.* of **Henry Livingston**, of Poughkeepsie, N. Y. Both are *d.* Issue :

i. **HENRY LIVINGSTON**, became a linguist of ability, and has been for many years the translator of the United States Department of State at Washington ; *m.* **MRS. ALICE JAMES**, of Poughkeepsie. Issue :

  DR. WILLIAM S., a physician of New York City.

ii. **JOHN**, early entered into railroad service, and rose from the position of telegraph operator to that of General Superintendent. During the Civil War he was connected with the United States Military Telegraph Corps, and later with the military railroads in Virginia. He has withdrawn from railroad service, and is engaged in other business at Cleveland, O. He holds the honorable position of Treasurer of the Diocese of Ohio. In 1865 he *m.* **ELIZABETH BEAN**, of Ohio. Issue :

i. **JOHN**, *d. i.*

ii. **HUGH LIVINGSTON**, residing at Seattle, Wash., *m.* **LUCIE ROBINSON**, and has a son, John.

JOHN THOMAS, *m.*, second, **MARGARET H. BOUTON**, of Brooklyn, N. Y. Issue :

iii.   **MARGUERITE LIVINGSTON.**
iv.   **HELEN ELECTA.**

iii.   **WILLIAM REED**, after spending some time in railroad service, entered the ministry of the Episcopal Church. Deacon, June 30, 1872 ; Priest, November 14, 1872. He has been for more than twenty years Rector of Holy Innocents' Church, Highland Falls, N. Y., and since 1887 Archdeacon of Orange. Has received the degree of D.D. from S. Stephen's College, Annándale, N. Y. He declined an election as Missionary Bishop of Northern Michigan, in 1889. He *m.* **LOU-ISA,** only *dau.* of **Judge E. Q. Eldridge,** of Poughkeepsie, N. Y. Issue :

GERTRUDE, ELDRIDGE, and HAROLD.

iv.   **JANE LIVINGSTON,** *m.* **MARK A. KING,** Attorney-at-law, who *d.* Issue (surname KING) :

ALICE MURIEL, and MABEL, *d. i.*

v.   **GERTRUDE FONDA.**
vi.   **CAROLINE MARY,** *d.*, aged nineteen.

Authorities : Marcia Thomas's History of Marshfield, 53–60 ; Savage's Dictionary ; Massachusetts Colonial Civil Lists ; Thatcher's History of Plymouth ; Diary of General John Thomas ; Edward Trenchard, Esq., of New York City, and John Thomas, Esq., of Cleveland, O.

THOMAS, OF PORTLAND, MAINE

THERE is a family of this name of great respectability in Portland, one of whose most prominent members is the **HON. WILL-IAM W. THOMAS**; he was of a family of ten children, of whom four others, **EDWARD, GEORGE, CHARLOTTE**, and **MRS. VARNUM,** are still living. **WILLIAM W.,** *b.* November 7, 1802; engaged in business before 1823 in the retail dry-goods trade; afterward became a wholesale merchant and an importer and shipper, accumulating a large fortune and becoming one of the largest owners of real estate in the city. He was Mayor of Portland during the first two years of the Civil War, and a strong Union man. His son, **HENRY GODDARD,** *b.* April, 1837, enlisted as a private at the opening of the Civil War; rose to a colonelcy, organized and commanded the first regiment of colored troops enlisted by the United States, brevetted Brigadier- and Major-General of Volunteers. **WILLIAM WIDGERY,** *b.* August, 1839; another son studied law, was in the consular service at Galatz, Moldavia, and Gothenburg, Sweden; Member of Legislature of Maine; United States Minister to Sweden and Norway, 1883 and 1889; author of a "History of Sweden."

Authority: The Biographical Encyclopædias.

THOMAS, OF PROVENCE, FRANCE

Louis Morèri, in his "Grand Dictionnaire Historique," etc., vol. x., 157, gives a pedigree of the house of **Thomas,** which he calls one of the most noble in Provence, beginning in 1096. Arms : *Ecartelé de gueules et d'asur à la croix pommetteè ou fleuroneè, au pied fiché d'or brochant, sur le tout.* Le Père Anselme, in his "Histoire Genealogique," etc., of the Royal House of France, Paris, 1726, notes that in 1552 **HONORE DE THOMAS** *m.* **ANNE DE VINTIMILLE,** *dau.* of **Melchior, Compte de Marseilles,** and notices of the family may be found in vols. ii., iv., v., vi., and vii. The family still flourished at the end of the last century, two members proving their nobility, and sitting in the Estates of Provence, assembled at Aix in 1787 and 1789, **FRANCOIS-LOUIS CLAIR DE THOMAS DE LA VALETTE,** " *Lieutenant-Général pour le roi en la Province de Bourgoyne, Gouverneur de la Garde-les-Toulon, ancien Capitaine de dragons, Chevalier, Seigneur de la Garde, Sainte Marguerite, Pierrefeu, et autres places,*" and **JEAN-BAPTISTE-HENRY-BRUNO DE THOMAS,** Seigneur de Gignac, Roquefuze et autres places."

THOMAS, OF PROVO CITY, UTAH

DANIEL THOMAS, said to have descended from a Welsh Quaker in Maryland, served in the Revolution ; *m.* **SARAH COVINGTON,** and *d.* in Richmond Co., N. C., about 1825. Issue :

i. **ELIJAH,** *b.* in Richmond Co., N. C. ; *m.* **MRS. RACHEL (ROE),** widow of **William Thomas,** probably his father's cousin. Issue :

    i. **HENRY,** *m.* **NANCY LOVE.**
    ii. **HOLCOMBE,** and a *daughter.*

ii. **DANIEL,** *b.* 1776 ; *m.* **NANCY M. MOREHEAD ;** *d.* in 1830. Issue :

    i. **JOSEPH M.,** *b.* January 11, 1811 ; *m.* **MARY A. THOMAS.**
    ii. **ELIZABETH,** *b.* July 31, 1812 ; *m.* **JAMES M. MOREHEAD.**
    iii. **PRESTON,** *b.* February 14, 1814 ; *m.* ── **MOREHEAD ;** *d.* 1877.
    iv. **DANIEL CLAIBORNE.**

iii. **HENRY,** *b.* 1778 ; *m.* **ESTER,** *dau.* of **William** and **Rachel (Roe) Thomas.** Issue :

    i. **DANIEL M.**
    ii. **WILLIAM.**
    iii. **HENRY.**
    iv. **ELIJAH.**
    v. **JOSEPH.**
    vi. **ROBERT T.,** *m.* **ANNIE CATHERINE EARLKSON.** Issue :
        William, of Provo City, Utah.
    vii. **JOHN.**
    viii. **RACHEL.**
    ix. **AMANDA.**
    x. **HARRIET N.**
    xi. **CATHERINE N.**

iv. **JOHN,** *d. u.*

v. **WILLIAM,** *m.* ── **WILLIAMS.** Issue :
    ABNER, CALHOON, and **JAMES.**

vi. **ROBERT,** *m.* ── **POUNCEY.**

vii. **BENJAMIN,** *d. u.*

viii. **SUSAN,** *m.* **STEPHEN PANKANY.**

ix. **PRISSY.**

x. **SARAH,** *m.* ── **SIMON.** Issue :
    DANIEL, NATHAN, ANN, SUSAN, ELIZABETH, and **JOHN.**

Authority : Family papers, through Mr. William Thomas, of Provo City.

THOMAS, OF QUEEN ANNE'S COUNTY, MD.

THOMAS, eldest son of **Trustram** and **Anne Thomas** (*q. v.*), resided in Talbot Co., Md.; *m.* **ELIZABETH** ——, and *d.* in 1706. Issue :

i.   **EDMOND,** left three hundred acres and over ; resided in Queen Anne's Co. ; *m.* **ANNE (TILDEN),** and *d.* in 1731. Issue :

         EDMOND, JAMES, TILDEN, MARY ANN, and **MARTHA.**

ii.   **TRUSTRAM,** left three hundred acres and more, *of whom presently.*

iii.   **THOMAS,** left eight hundred and fifty acres.

TRUSTRAM, second son of **Thomas** and **Elizabeth Thomas,** was of Tully's Neck, Queen Anne's Co. ; *m.* **JANE** ——, and his will was proved as Trustram, Senior, March 4, 1745–46. Issue :

i.   **STEPHEN,** *m.* **MARY** ——. Issue :

         ROBERT (left Hawkins' Pharsalia).

ii.   **PHILEMON,** left land in Tuckahoe Creek, whose son probably was **CHRISTOPHER THOMAS,** of Tuckahoe Creek. Will, November 29, 1750, naming wife, **MARY,** and children, **William, Risdem, Ann,** and son-in-law, **Andrew Cox.**

iii.   **BENJAMIN.**

iv.   **TRUSTRAM,** *of whom presently.*

v.   **SIMON.**

vi.   **PENELOPE.**

vii.   **ANN,** probably *m.* —— **JARMAN.**

viii.   **NANCY,** *m.* —— **LANDMAN** ; deceased in 1745.

TRUSTRAM, third son of **Trustram** and **Jane Thomas,** resided on Land called " Trustram," Queen Anne's Co. ; *m.* **ANN** ——, and *d.* in May, 1746. Issue :

i.   **CHRISTOPHER,** *m.* **JULIANY** ——, and *d.* 1777. Issue :

     i.   **TRUSTRAM.**

     ii.   **EDWARD.**

iii. . ANN.
iv. MARY, *m.* —— KENT.
v. JULIANY.

ii.   TRUSTRAM, of Queen Anne's Co.; *m.* MARY, and *d.* in October, 1761. Issue:

      SAMUEL, had a son, Joshua; JOSHUA removed to Caroline Co., and *d.* in 1775, leaving a son, Samuel; ELIZABETH, and SARAH MEREDITH, probably a step-daughter.

iii.   JOSEPH.
iv.   EDMUND, inherited " Trustrum," and *d.* in 1768. Issue:

    i.   SAMUEL WRIGHT, *of whom presently.*
    ii.   MARY.
    iii.   ANN.
    iv.   FRANCES.
    v.   SUSANNAH.

v.   THOMAS, resided in Queen Anne's Co. His will was proved November 29, 1770, in which he names his sons, JAMES, who had issue, James and Ann; THOMAS had a *dau.*, Susanna Clother; and his *dau.* SOPHIA, deceased, and her son, Thomas Roberts, and his children (each left one shilling), ELIZABETH BAKER, SUSANNA RATCLIFFE, ANN CHAIRES, JANE WATKINS, SARAH CHAIRES, and MARY FARR.

vi.   JOHN.
vii.   RACHEL.
viii.   ELIZABETH, *m.* PRYER.

SAMUEL WRIGHT,[1] eldest son of **Edmund Thomas**, resided at Springfield, Wye Neck, Queen Anne's Co., and was active in the Revolutionary War, attaining the rank of colonel in the Maryland troops. He *m.* four times: a **MISS CLAYTON**, two **MISSES WRIGHT,** and a sister of **Vernon Emory**. **RICHARD**, his son, *m.* first, —— WEBB, and second, SARAH, *dau.* of Rev. **Robert Sparks**, and had a son, RICHARD, resides at Easton, Md.

    Authorities: Wills at Annapolis, Md., and Hon. H. H. Goldsborough, of Baltimore, Md.

    [1] Repeated requests have failed to secure further details of this family.

THOMAS, OF RHOS AND TYGLYN, WALES

The **REV. ALBAN THOMAS,** of Rhos, descended from the ancient lords of Towyn, had a grandson, DR. ALBAN THOMAS, whose son, the Rev. Alban Thomas, of Newcastle Emlyn, assumed the name Jones on marrying his cousin, Susanna Maria, *dau.* of John Jones, Esq., of Tyglyn, Sheriff of Cardigan, 1728. By a former wife he had a son and heir, Alban Thomas Jones, *of whom presently.*

This **ALBAN THOMAS JONES** added the name of **GWYNNE** on inheriting his cousin's estate of Monachty. He *m.* **ANNE VEVERS,** of Herefordshire, and had, with other issue, a son and heir :

    CAPTAIN ALBAN LEWIS THOMAS JONES GWYNNE, *m.* **JANE CRAWSHAY,** *dau.* of **Crawshay Bailey,** of Llanfoist House, Abergavenny, and *d.* Issue :

     i.   ALBAN THOMAS JONES, *b.* February 4, 1852.
     ii.   GERTRUDE.
     iii.   JANE.
     iv.   AGNES.
     v.   EDITH.

        Authorities : Nicholas's Wales, i., 195 ; Rees's South Wales, 521.

THOMAS, OF S. MARY'S COUNTY, MD.

WILLIAM, youngest son of **John Thomas,** of Charles Co., who made his will in 1757 (*q. v.*), was *b.* in 1714, removed in early life to S. Mary's Co., and resided there until his death. He represented the county in the House of Delegates in 1761 ; was commissioned Captain before 1761, Major afterward ; was a delegate to the Revolutionary Convention of 1775, and a member of the Committee of Safety for S. Mary's Co, January 5, 1775. Re-elected from that county to the General Assembly of 1777, and again in 1779 and 1781. He *m.* **ELIZABETH,** *dau.* of **Thomas Reeves,** and *d.* at his residence, Deep Falls, S. Mary's Co., in March, 1795. Issue :

i.   **JOHN,** resided in Charles Co., which he represented for many years in the Legislature ; *m.* and had a son, **PERCY,** *d. s. p.*, and *dau.*, *m.* —— **HANSON,** and had a son, *d. s. p.*

ii.   **WILLIAM,** *of whom presently.*

iii.   **GEORGE,** killed in the Revolution.

iv.   **JAMES,** killed in the Revolution.

v.   **ELIZABETH,** *m.* **MAJOR WILLIAM COATES,** of the Maryland Line, and had a *dau.*, **ELIZA,** *m.* **DR. JAMES THOMAS** (*q. v.*).

WILLIAM, second son of **Major William** and **Elizabeth (Reeves) Thomas,** was *b.* at " Deep Falls," near Chaptico, S.

Mary's Co., held the commission of Major in the Maryland Line ; was a member of the House of Delegates, and for twelve years previous to his death was President of the State Senate. He was a prominent Freemason, first Master of the lodge at Leonardtown, and elected in June, 1799, Grand Master of Maryland, and re-elected the next year. Resolutions of thanks for his ability and impartiality in the chair were voted him, by the lodge in 1799, and by the Senate in January, 1808. He *m.*, in 1782, **CATHERINE**, *dau.* of —— and **Mary (Brooke) Boarman** (through whose brother the estate of De la Brooke came into the family, and *d.* at his estate of De la Brooke, on the Patuxent, August 1, 1813. Issue :

i.　　**JAMES**, who resided at Deep Falls, educated at S. John's College, Annapolis, Md., was a physician, member of the Lower House, President of the Senate, and Governor of Maryland in 1833 ; *m.* his cousin, **ELIZA**, *dau.* of **Major William** and **Elizabeth (Thomas) Coates.**

ii.　　**GEORGE**, inherited De la Brooke, and *m.* **MARY TUBMAN.**

iii.　　**RICHARD**, was a member and also Speaker of the House of Delegates, President of the Senate, and President of the Maryland Colonization Society ; *m.* **JANE WALLACE ARMSTRONG.** Issue :

　　　　CAPTAIN GEORGE, of Mattapany.

iv.　　**WILLIAM**, *b.* at " De La Brooke," March 8, 1793, *of whom presently.*

v.　　**MATILDA**, *m.* **GEORGE BRENT**, of Charles Co.

vi.　　**ANNA**, *m.* **THOMPSON MASON**, of Loudoun Co., Va.

vii.　　**CATHERINE**, *m.* **WILLIAM D. MERRICK**, of Charles Co., U. S. Senator from Maryland, who gave the casting vote for declaring war against Mexico. Reproached for sending others to the war while he stayed at home, his son, **RICHARD THOMAS**, volunteered and served in Mexico. This son was at the time of his death the leader of the Washington bar.

WILLIAM, youngest son of **Major William** and **Catharine (Boarman) Thomas**, *b.* March 8, 1793, was a physician, studied under Dr. Physick, in Philadelphia ; graduated in 1814, and resided at Cremona, S. Mary's Co. He *m.*, first, August 6, 1816, **ELIZA**, *dau.* of **Henry** [1] and **Mary (Sothoron) Tubman** (*b.* September 16, 1793) and granddaughter of **Henry Greenfield**

---

[1] He was a judge of election for S. Mary's Co., November 25, 1777, under the new Constitution. Kilty's Laws of Maryland, vol. i. (1799).

Sothoron and **Mary Bond,** of Chaptico Manor. The former represented S. Mary's Co. in the Convention of June 22, 1774. Issue :

i.   **PERCY,** *d. i.*

ii.   **JANE,** *m.* **DR. HENRY FORD.** Issue (surname FORD)

    i.   **ELIZABETH LANSDALE.**
    ii.   **ROSA H.**
    iii. **LEWIS,** *d. u.* in October, 1893.
    iv. **WILLIAM T.,** *d. u.* in August, 1893.
    v.   **ANN,** *m.* —— **GREENWELL.**
    vi. **MARIA LOUISA,** *m.* **WALTER BRISCOE,** and has a son, John H. Thomas.

iii. **ANN,** *m.* **JAMES T. BLAKISTONE.** Issue (surname BLAKI-
         STONE) :

    i.   **BETTIE.**
    ii.   **TEACKLE WALLIS.**
    iii. **WALTER,** *m.* **SARAH SINCLAIR,** and *d.* Issue :
            Ann, Walter, and Clare.
    iv. **JANE T.,** *m.* **JOSEPH R. FOARD.** Issue (surname FOARD) :
            Addison K., Wallis, and Elizabeth.
    v.   **NANNIE T.,** *m.* **WILLIAM M. CONWAY,** and has a *dau.,* Ella.
    vi. **ELLA,** *d. u.*
    vii. **GEORGE,** *m.* **MAUD PRICE.**
    viii. **JAMES T.**
    ix. **ANDREW,** *m.,* and has two daughters.

iv. **JOHN HENRY,** *of whom presently.*

DR. THOMAS, *m.,* second, April 8, 1828, **ELIZABETH,** *dau.* of **Dr. William** and **Mary (Reeder) Lansdale,** and *d.* at Cremona, September 30, 1849, having had further issue :

v.   **WILLIAM LANSDALE.**
vi.   **MARIA.**
vii. **SUSAN,** *m.* **REV. WALTER MITCHELL.** Issue (surname MIT-
        CHELL) :

    ELIZABETH LANSDALE, MARY THOMAS, EDWIN, and **KATE L.**

viii. **KATE.**
ix. **EDWIN,** an officer of the C. S. A., *d. u.*
x.   **SOPHIA,** *m.* **REV. WILLIAM CHRISTIAN,** who *d. s. p.*

JOHN HENRY, only surviving son of **Dr. William** and **Eliza (Tubman) Thomas,** removed to Baltimore and practised law there, becoming one of the leading members of the bar. He received, by devise of his maternal cousin, John Truman Hawkins, "Trent Hall," which came to him through ancestors whose tombstones still exist upon the plantation ; among them may be noted those of **James Truman, Gent.**, *d.* August 7, 1672, aged fifty; **Nathaniel Truman, Gent.**, *d.* March 4, 1678; **Thomas Truman, Esq.**, *d.* December 6, 1685, aged sixty; **Mary,** his wife, *d.* July 6, 1686; and **Thomas Truman Greenfield**, *d.* December 10, 1733, aged fifty-one. **MR. THOMAS**, *m.*, November 12, 1851, **MARY THOMAS**, *dau.* of **George Gray** and **Eliza (Thomas) Leiper** (*q. v.*), who *d.* June 15, 1893. Issue :

i. **GEORGE LEIPER**, Attorney-at-Law.
ii. **WILLIAM,** *d.* April 7, 1857.
iii. **ELIZA SNOWDEN.**

Authorities : Wills at Annapolis, Md., and family papers, through Miss Eliza Snowden Thomas and G. Leiper Thomas, Esq., of Baltimore.

THOMAS, OF SARATOGA COUNTY, NEW YORK

DANIEL THOMAS, a Revolutionary soldier, was born November 21, 1754, in Berkshire Co., Mass. Tradition says that his forefathers came from Wales in the early history of New England. He was an old-time Democrat, and moved about 1786 from Lenox with his wife and young family, to the township of Milton, Saratoga Co., N. Y. (then a part of Albany Co., which extended to the Canada line), and probably after the death of his father. It is related that he returned to Massachusetts within a few years to bring his widowed mother to Saratoga Co., where at least two of her daughters had also settled. One of these daughters married Jacob Weed, and the other married Stephen Jackson, and with these daughters the old lady spent her last years.

The children, it is said, had urged the old lady to come from Massachusetts and live with them; but she, learning that it implied crossing the "great Hudson River," said she would never make the long journey until a bridge should be built across the river. Finally, one winter, Daniel and one or more of her other children drove over to Lenox and informed her that the bridge was built and that they had crossed it in coming for her. With this assurance she packed up, and protected against the cold by many wrappings, started in a sleigh for their homes in Saratoga, N. Y. After crossing the Hudson they asked her to look out of her wrappings and see what a fine bridge had been built. When she saw that their "bridge" was the ice she felt hurt and frightened that she had been deceived by her children and led into what she thought was such a danger, and declared if she could get safely back to Lenox they could never again tempt her to leave it.

Saratoga Co. was then new, and Daniel Thomas, soon after his first arrival, purchased a tract of forest at $4.00 per acre and commenced clearing it to make a home for himself and family. Privation and trouble came during the first year or two. The forest must first

165

be cleared away before crops could be raised. A gunshot wound received in the Revolution broke out afresh in Daniel's hand, to prevent him for a long time from doing the hard pioneer work of felling trees or of planting. Then their cow sickened and died, adding to their trouble, so that for a long time they were badly off. Some of their relatives in Maryland and Virginia learned of their suffering and sent them corn by sloop to Albany—about forty miles away through the woods—to help them along until Daniel should again be able to resume his hard work and provide for his family. During the years that he was disabled he was obliged to search the forests and dig ginseng root to earn what he could. This root was then plentiful there, and was in demand for export to China. That he might not lose his bearings in the woods while searching for ginseng, a birch log was laid up free from the ground near the cabin door, and his little son, Moses, would frequently beat it with the head of an axe, sending the ringing sound out as a signal to his father.

He never fully recovered from his wound, and it was only after his sons grew large enough to take up farm work that they were able to make much progress. From the timber cut they finally realized some money, and afterward utilized a part of the lumber in building a large house, which for many years was used as a hotel.

On a Sunday morning, early in April, 1825, this house took fire while the family were at church. Daniel's exertion to save some of the personal property resulted in aggravating old physical troubles to such an extent that he had to be removed to the home of a neighbor, and afterward to the house of his son Freeman, where he died within a few days in great agony.

DANIEL THOMAS, *m.,* October 30, 1777, at Becket, Berkshire Co., Mass., **EUNICE FOSTER** (*b.* October 20, 1756; *d.,* at Ballston Spa, N. Y., August 9, 1846), and *d.* April 23, 1825. Issue :

i.　　**MOSES,** *b.* May 22, 1779, *of whom presently.*

ii.　　**DANIEL,** *b.* February 28, 1781, removed to Herkimer Co., and spent his life there as farmer and woollen manufacturer, near Frankfort and Ilion ; *m.,* September 19, 1805, **ABIGAIL MARVIN,** of Charlton, Saratoga Co., N. Y., who *d.* July 10, 1842, at Frankfort, and *d.* May 2, 1864, at his daughter's residence, Lanesboro', Mass. Issue :

　　i.　　HANFORD, *b.* May 21, 1806 ; *d. u.,* September 26, 1838.
　　ii.　　HANNAH, *b.* October 26, 1808 ; *d. u.,* March 27, 1889, in Philadelphia, Pa.
　　iii.　　MARY, *b.* May 16, 1812 ; *m.* REV. J. V. AMBLER, and *d.,* September 18, 1840.
　　iv.　　ABIGAIL, *b.* August 3, 1818 ; *m.,* as his second wife, REV. J. V. AMBLER, since deceased.

iii.   **EUNICE**, *b*. August 26, 1783 ; *m*. **WILLIAM W. ELLIOTT**, and *d*. June 24, 1854.

iv.   **ABRAHAM**, *b*. October 2, 1785 ; *d*. April 9, 1788.

v.   **LYMAN**, *b*. November 2, 1787, removed to Fayette Co., Ind., and *d*. 1851, leaving descendants.

vi.   **JAMES**, *b*. June 2, 1790 ; removed to Indiana.

vii.   **FREEMAN**, *b*. June 24, 1792 (*q. v.*).

viii.   **ABIGAIL**, *b*. September 8, 1794 ; *m*. **JOSEPH TAYLOR**, and removed to Indiana.

ix.   **HANNAH**, *b*. January 11, 1797 ; *m*. **JOHN GREEN**, of Galway, N. Y.

x.   **SIDNEY**, *b*. June 1, 1799 ; *d*. February 23, 1815.

MOSES, eldest son of **Daniel** and **Eunice (Foster) Thomas**, *b*. May 22, 1779, lived upon a farm near Milton, Saratoga Co., N. Y. ; was colonel in the New York State Militia before 1814 ; a deacon and leading member of the Baptist congregation at Milton ; prominent in county affairs, but never accepting political office. He *m*., December 29, 1803, **LAURA**, *dau*. of **Silas Adams**, of Milton, N. Y. (*b*. March 24, 1784 ; *d*. October 11, 1846), and *d*. May 19, 1855. Issue :

i.   **PHEBE**, *b*. December 10, 1804 ; *m*., first, February 24, 1825, **JOSEPH WARING** ; *m*., second, **JOHN TERHUNE**, both of Saratoga Co.

ii.   **HERMON**, *b*. March 24, 1807, *of whom presently*.

iii.   **ALMIA**, *b*. June 25, 1809 ; *d. u.* June 23, 1879.

HERMON, only son of **Moses** and **Laura (Adams) Thomas**, *b*. March 24, 1807, was in business for some years at Ballston Spa, afterward removed to the homestead of his grandfather Silas Adams, in the same township, where he remained as farmer and vinegar manufacturer until 1869, when he sold the homestead and took up his residence with his then unbroken family in Philadelphia, where several of his sons had located. He was very active in public enterprises of his county, but never allowed his name to be put forward politically. He, like his parents and grandparents, was much attached to the old Stone Church (Baptist) in Milton, and for many years was its strongest supporter. He was never active in business after removing to Philadelphia, but spent much of his time in reading and study, of which he was very fond. He was *m*., March 2, 1836, by Rev. Thomas Powell, to **HARRIET**, *dau*. of Deacon **Hezekiah Middlebrook**, at her father's residence, Ballston Spa, and *d*. September 12, 1893, at Bryn Mawr, Pa., where he had been spending the summer. Issue :

i. **EMMA LYDIA**, *b.* December 19, 1836.
ii. **CHARLES HERMON**, *b.* December 4, 1839, a prominent physician of Philadelphia ; *m.* there, March 18, 1873, **E. MARCELLA KIRK.** Issue :

> **PAUL K. M.**, *b.* January 31, 1875.

iii. **AUGUSTUS**, *b.* June 8, 1842, dealer in military goods at Philadelphia, Pa. ; *m.*, March 28, 1878, **CARRIE M. KINSEY**, of Philadelphia.
iv. **FREDERICK**, *b.* July 1, 1846 ; *m.*, October 30, 1879, **GERTRUDE STODDART**, of Philadelphia, and *d. s. p.* February 14, 1881.
v. **HORACE GAY**, *b.* October 29, 1848.

FREEMAN, sixth son of **Daniel** and **Eunice (Foster) Thomas**, *b.* June 24, 1792 ; *m.* **SALLY BRIDGES**, at Ballston Spa, N. Y., where she *d.* He *d.* there August 10, 1866. Issue :

i. **GEORGE.**
ii. **JOHN B.**, *b.* November 14, 1823, *of whom presently.*

JOHN B., second son of **Freeman** and **Sally (Bridges) Thomas**, *b.* November 14, 1823 ; *m.*, first, in 1850, **PHEBE GILDERSLEEVE** (*d.* July 1, 1862) ; *m.*, second, in 1864, **REBECCA DAVIS**, who *d. s. p.* September 17, 1883. Issue by first wife :

i. **FRANK B.**, *b.* January 24, 1852 ; *m.*, 1880, **DELIA QUADE**, at Ballston Spa. Issue :

> i. **JOSEPH ALBERT.**, *b.* December 8, 1881.
> ii. **MAY VIOLET**, *b.* February 10, 1884.

ii. **JOHN L.**, *b.* March 1, 1854 ; *m.*, July 4, 1877, **JULIA A. BATEMAN**, of Ballston Spa. Issue :

> i.   **FREEMAN THEODORE**, *b.* June 24, 1881.
> ii. **MARY PHŒBE**, *b.* May 25, 1883.
> iii. **WALTER BATEMAN**, *b.* March 22, 1886.
> iv. **JOHN ROY**, *b.* July 23, 1891.

iii. **SARAH**, *b.* February 28, 1857 ; *m.*, November 25, 1880, **WILLIAM MOONEY** ; has a *dau.*, **NELLIE**, *b.* September 25, 1883.

Authority : Family papers, through Mr. Horace Gay Thomas, of Philadelphia, Pa.

THOMAS, OF SOUTH CAROLINA

In June, 1702, **REV. SAMUEL THOMAS** was appointed by the Venerable Society for Propagating the Gospel in Foreign Parts,[1] as its first missionary to South Carolina. His testimonials show that he was from Bally-don near Sudbury, a town on the borders of Essex and Suffolk, England. They speak of him as "a person of eminent piety." He arrived at Charleston on Christmas Day, 1702, and took up his residence in a section afterward known as S. James Parish, Grove Creek. Sir N. Johnson, Knt., Governor of the Carolinas, and the members of his Council, in a testimonial sent to the Venerable Society, speak of him "as leading a religious and virtuous life, and by his diligent and constant preaching he hath done much good in the province." He *d.* December 16, 1706, in South Carolina, aged about thirty-four years, and leaving in England a widow **ELIZABETH**, and five children. The Governor and Council speak of his death as "a very great loss to the Province, he being a person of great piety and virtue, and by his exemplary life and diligent preaching, and obliging carriage he had the good-will of all men."

EDWARD, son of **Rev. Samuel Thomas**, resided at "the Forest," a plantation in S. Stephen's Parish, and was wounded in a fight with the Indians at a place called Barker's Savannah, in 1715. He is described in Ramsay's "History of South Carolina" as somewhat whimsical, living for fifteen years in complete solitude on his plantation—walking so constantly up and down his piazza for exercise that he wore a path in the boards. Suddenly his ideas changed, he visited all his friends, went over to England, and figured there as a beau and man of society. Being about to return to America he was seized with gout in the stomach, and *d.*, aged ninety. His son, **SAMUEL**, was settled by his father at Betaw Plantation, S. Stephen's Parish, and *m.*,

[1] Digest of S. P. G. Records, London, 1893, *pp.* 12-15, 18, and 850.

first, **MARY** *dau.* of **James Child,** of Childburg, now Strawberry, S. C. Issue :

EDWARD, *of whom presently.*

He *m.,* second, **ANNA,** either sister or *dau.* of **Rev. Thomas Has-ell,** a missionary of the Venerable Society, arrived in South Carolina in 1705 ; *m.* **Eliza,** *dau.* of **Thomas** and **Elizabeth (Le Jean) Ashby,** and was *bu.* October 10, 1744. **Samuel Thomas** was poisoned by some of his negroes, and *d.* Issue (by his second wife) :

THOMAS HASELL (*q. v.*)

EDWARD, only son of **Samuel** and **Mary (Child) Thomas,** was an officer of the South Carolina Militia, 1775–1783, and Lieuten-ant in Captain Benjamin Marion's Company of Colonel Single-ton's regiment, appointed December 22, 1775 ; [1] *m.* **ANNA,** *dau.* of **William** and **Elizabeth (Hasell) Gibbes** (who were *m.* Feb-ruary 18, 1747) ; *b.* January 4, 1752 ; *d.* February 15, 1781. Issue :

i.   **DR. SAMUEL,** *m.* and left descendants.
ii. **DR. EDWARD,** *m.* and left descendants.
iii. **ELIZABETH,** *m.* —— **WITHERS.**
iv. **MARY,** *m.,* May 10, 1792, **WILLIAM HERIOT.**

EDWARD THOMAS, *m.,* second, —— **BURRINGTON.** Is-sue :

THOMAS BURRINGTON, *d. u.,* 1829.

THOMAS HASELL, only son of **Samuel** and **Anna (Hasell) Thomas** lived at Betaw Plantation on the Santee River, Craven Co. ; *m.,* May 29, 1794, **ANNE,** *dau.* of **Thomas** and **Anne (Peyre) Walter.** **Thomas Walter,** her father, was an Englishman. First resided as a merchant at Dorchester, afterward at the mouth of the Santee River, where he had a celebrated garden. He was a botanist of distinction, and author of " Flora Caroliniana," London, 1789, in Latin. His wife was a *dau.* of **Sam-uel,** son of **David** and **Judith Peyre,** French Huguenot emi-grants, and **Sarah Cantey,** his wife, *dau.* of **John Cantey,** the third white male *b.* in South Carolina. **THOMAS HAS-ELL THOMAS,** *d.* November 10, 1804, and his wife *d.* April 25, 1818. Issue :

---

[1] See Journal of Council of Safety : De Saussure's Officers of the Revolution.

i.   **ANNA HASELL**, *b.* 1795 ; *d. u.*, January 17, 1833.
ii.   **JOHN PEYRE**, *b.* December 23, 1796, *of whom presently.*
iii.   **THOMAS WALTER**, *b.* 1798 ; *m.*, 1831, **ELIZABETH KIRK**, and *d.*, 1855, at Abbeville, S. C. Issue :

> i.   **DR. JAMES W.**, *b.* October, 1832 ; *m.*, February, 1858, **MARY CHEATHAM.** Issue :
>
>> i.   Leunnie Walter, *b.* February, 1862 ; *m.* Dr. —— Brooks.
>> ii.   Charles B., *b.* July, 1867 ; *m.* —— Penny.
>> iii.   Sara Catherine, *b.* September, 1869.
>> iv.   Elizabeth Hamilton, *b.* August, 1874 ; *m.* F. Wilson.
>> v.   Grace, *b.* April, 1878.
>> vi.   Jane, *b.* 1880.
>> vii.   Walter.
>> viii.   William.
>
> ii.   **THOMAS WALTER.**
> iii.   **ELIZA ANN**, *b.* 1841.
> iv.   **HENRY WALTER.**
> v.   **MARY WALTER**, *b.* May, 1846 ; *m.*, April, 1874, **WILLIAM PARKER.**
> vi.   **DAVID WALTER**, *b.* August, 1849.

iv.   **EDWARD**, *b.* 1800 (*q. v.*).
v.   **THOMAS HASELL**, *b.* 1802.
vi.   **SAMUEL PEYRE**, *b.* 1804 ; *m.*, 1833 or 1834, **JANE ROSBOR-OUGH** ; *d.* in Fairfield Co., S. C., 1854. Issue :

> i.   **ANNE WALTER.**
> ii.   **JOHN ROSBOROUGH**, *b.* 1836.
> iii.   **FRANCIS PEYRE.**
> iv.   **ANN**, *b.* December 31, 1840 ; *m.* her cousin, **CHARLES EDWARD THOMAS** (*q. v.*).
> v.   **EDWARD**, *b.* 1843 ; settled in Missouri ; *m.* **SUSAN DYER.** Issue :
>> Jane, Samuel Peyre, and Alfred.
> vi.   **PEYRE**, *b.* September, 1846 ; settled in Texas ; *m.* **ELOISE FOSCUE.** Issue :
>> i.   Edward Peyre, *b.* 1875.
>> ii.   Virginia, *b.* 1879 ; *d.* 1887.
> vii.   **WILLIAM ROSBOROUGH**, *b.* December, 1848 ; settled in New York City.

JOHN PEYRE, eldest son of **Thomas Hasell** and **Anne (Walter) Thomas**, *b.* December 23, 1796 ; was a physician ; graduated at the College of South Carolina in 1816, and resided at Mount Hope Plantation, Fairfield Co., S. C. ; *m.*, first, 1826, **HARRIET**, *dau.* of **Elias Couturier** (*b.* 1810 ; *d.* 1835). Issue :

i.   **ANNA HASELL**, *b.* July, 1827 : *d.* September, 1830.
ii.   **HENRIETTA ELEANOR**, *b.* February, 1829.
iii.   **EMILY WALTER**, *b.* April, 1831.
iv.   **JOHN PEYRE**, *b.* March 17, 1833, *of whom presently.*
v.   **ELIAS COUTURIER**, *b.* June, 1834 ; *d.* August, 1834.
vi.   **HARRIET COUTURIER**, *b.* July 19, 1835 ; *m.*, July 11, 1877, **ROBERT H. McKELVEY.**

DR. JOHN P. THOMAS, *m.*, second, 1836, **CHARLOTTE COUTURIER** (*b.* 1817 ; *d.* April 7, 1892), and *d.* January 1, 1859. Issue :

vii.　**WILLIAM SINKLER,** *b.* May, 1837 ; *d.* June, 1848.
viii.　**ROBERT KIRK,** *b.* February, 1839 ; *d.* April, 1860.
ix.　**PETER COUTURIER,** *b.* May, 1840.
x.　**THOMAS HASELL,** *b.* September, 1841 ; *d.* January, 1842.
xi.　**FRANCIS MARION,** *b.* January, 1843 ; *m.*, first, November 1, 1874, **ELIZABETH WATSON.** Issue :

  i.　FRANCIS MARION, *b.* February, 1876.
  ii.　SEABORN, *b.* September, 1877 ; *d.* August 3, 1894.
  iii.　ANNA REBECCA, *b.* May, 1879.
  iv.　HASELL COUTURIER, *b.* 1880.
  v.　CHARLOTTE ELIZABETH, *b.* 1882.
  vi.　WILLIAM LAWRENCE, *b.* January, 1885.

    FRANCIS MARION THOMAS, *m.*, second, **MARY MEYNARDIE.** Issue :

    ISAAC STONEY, *b.* March 8, 1895.

xii.　**CHARLES EDWARD,** *b.* November 14, 1844 ; *m.*, October 20, 1870, **ANN C.,** *dau.* of **Samuel Peyre** and **Jane (Rosborough) Thomas,** and *d.* February 1, 1887. Issue :

  i.　CHARLES EDWARD, *b.* August, 1871.
  ii.　SAMUEL PEYRE, *b.* March, 1873.
  iii.　ANNIE LEE, *b.* October 25, 1875.
  iv.　ROBERT CHARLTON, *b.* February, 1877.
  v.　JANE COUTURIER, *b.* November 7, 1879.
  vi.　MARY ANNA, *b.* May 31, 1883.
  vii.　WILLIE ROSA, *b.* August, 1885.

xiii.　**MARY ANNE,** *b.* November 16, 1846.
xiv.　**ANNA REBECCA,** *b.* February 13, 1849 ; *m.*, December 8, 1869, **ROBERT H. EDMUNDS.**
xv.　**JOSIAH OBEAR,** *b.* March 29, 1851 ; *m.*, December 13, 1882, **MARY PARKS.** Issue :

  i.　MARY HASELINE, *b.* June 2, 1885.
  ii.　LOUISE COUTURIER, *b.* November 13, 1890.

xvi.　**ISAAC COUTURIER,** *b.* February 7, 1853.
xvii.　**GABRIELLA MARION,** *b.* September 23, 1853.
xviii.　**CHARLOTTE HENRIETTA COUTURIER,** *b.* February 2, 1858.

JOHN PEYRE, eldest son of **Dr. John P.** and **Harriet (Couturier) Thomas,** *b.* March 17, 1833 ; Colonel C. S. A. ; *m.*, November 20, 1855, **MARY CAROLINE,** *dau.* of **Dr. Robert Wilson Gibbes** (*b.* April 1, 1835 ; *d.* September 7, 1890). Issue :

i.   MARY GIBBES, *b.* August 22, 1856 ; *d.* November 21, 1894.
ii.   JOHN PEYRE, Jr., *b.* December 9, 1857, counsellor and attorney-at-law
        of the firm of Abney & Thomas, Columbia, S. C.; *m.*, January 29,
        1879, MARY SUMTER, *dau.* of Captain John and Frances
        Colhoun (Parker) Waties (*b.* January 29, 1859). Issue :

        i.   JOHN WATIES, *b.* December 27, 1879.
        ii.   MARY SUMTER, *b.* March 7, 1885.
        iii.   CAROLINE GIBBES, *b.* March 12, 1887.

iii.   ROBERT GIBBES, *b.* July 22, 1859.
iv.   HASELL, *b.* February 22, 1861 ; *m.*, May 22, 1889, EMMA IRENE
        WOLFE. Issue :

        i.   THOMAS HASELL, *b.* March 20, 1890.
        ii.   MARY GIBBES, *b.* December 11, 1891 ; *d.* May 19, 1892.
        iii.   CORNELIA LEE, *b.* February 19, 1893.
        iv.   A *dau., b.* April 11, 1895.

v.   JULIET ELLIOT, *b.* January 9, 1863 ; *d.* April 20, 1865.
vi.   BENJAMIN GIBBES, *b.* December 16, 1864.
vii.   CAROLINE ELIZABETH, *b.* November 3, 1866.
viii.   WALTER COUTURIER, *b.* May 8, 1868.
ix.   HARRIET COUTURIER, *b.* March 19, 1870 ; *m.*, October 1, 1889,
        REV. ALEXANDER R. MITCHELL. Issue (surname
        MITCHELL) :

        i.   ALEXANDER ROBERT, Jr., *b.* September 8, 1890.
        ii.   MARY GIBBES, *b.* June 22, 1891.
        iii.   HARRIET COUTURIER, *b.* July 28, 1894.

x.   ALBERT SIDNEY, *b.* February 6, 1873.
xi.   DWIGHT, *b.* August 15, 1875 ; *d.* the same month.
xii.   HAROLD, *b* September 14, 1876.
xiii.   ELEANOR WALTER, *b.* September 10, 1880.
xiv.   WASHINGTON ALLSTON, *b.* March 4, 1882.

EDWARD, third son of **Thomas Hasell** and **Anne (Walter)
Thomas**, *b.* 1800, was ordered Deacon by Bishop Bowen, of
South Carolina, February 6, 1825, became Rector of the church
in Edisto Island, and afterward of S. John's, Berkeley Parish,
S. C. ; *m.*, 1825 or 1826, **JANE MARSHALL**, *dau.* of **Judge
Theodore** and **Cornelia (Marshall) Gaillard**, and *d.*, July 11,
1846, at Whiteville, S. C. Issue :

i.   ANNA HASELL, *b.* October, 1828.
ii.   EDWARD WHITTINGHAM, *b.* 1830 ; resides in Nebraska ; *m.*
        KATE ALLISON. Issue :
        i.   ANNA, *b.* 1866.
        ii.   CORNELIA, *b.* 1869.
        iii.   EDWARD, *b.* 1871.

    iv.   **GAILLARD,** *b.* 1873.
    v.   **WALTER,** *b.* 1877.
    vi.   **KATE,** *b.* 1879.

iii.   **THEODORE GAILLARD,** *b.* November 21, 1831, *of whom presently.*
iv.   **CORNELIA M.,** *b.* March, 1833; *d.* 1864.
v.   **JANE MARSHALL,** *b.* 1835; *m.,* 1856 or 1857, **DR. E. GAILLARD,**
        and *d.* 1860.

THEODORE GAILLARD, second son of **Rev. Edward** and **Jane Marshall (Gaillard) Thomas,** *b.* November 21, 1831, on the island of Edisto, S. C.; graduated first honor man in Medicine at Charleston College, 1852; became Resident Physician, Bellevue Hospital, New York; went to Europe, was Resident Physician at the Rotunda Hospital, Dublin; returned to New York City, and has been Professor of Obstetrics and Diseases of Women at the College of Physicians and Surgeons, and Surgeon of numerous hospitals. Is author of "Diseases of Women," 1868, and one of the authors of the "Centenary of American Medicine," 1876; an honorary member of the Gynæcological and Obstetrical Societies of London, Edinburgh, and Berlin, etc. He *m.,* first, a **MISS GAILLARD;** *m.,* second, in 1862, **MARY THEODOSIA WILLARD,** *granddau.* of **Mrs. Emma Willard,** of Troy Female Seminary. Issue:

i.   **JOHN METCALFE,** *m.* —— **JACKSON.**
ii.   **SARAH WILLARD.**
iii.   **EDWARD.**
iv.   **HOWARD L.**
v.   **T. GAILLARD.**

Authorities: MS. Tabular Pedigree compiled by John Peyre Thomas, Jr., Esq., of Columbia, S. C.; Samuel Dubose's Reminiscences of Craven County, S. C., and F. A. Porcher's Historical and Social Sketch of Craven County, both reprinted by Dr. T. G. Thomas in 1887; Dalcho's Church History. *pp.* 51, 52, 73, and 245; Ramsay's History of South Carolina, *p.* 292, etc.; Digest Records of S. P. G., London, 1893.

THOMAS, OF SPRINGFIELD, MASS.

ROWLAND THOMAS, emigrated in 1646; was of Hadley, 1669; Westfield, 1670; took oath of allegiance at Springfield, December 31, 1678; *m.*, April 14, 1647, **SARAH**, *dau.* of **Samuel Chapin**. She *d.* August 5, 1684, and he *d.* February 21, 1698, at Springfield. Issue:

i.   **JOSEPH**, *b.* January 6, 1647-48; *d.* 1648.
ii.   **SAMUEL**, *b.* March 2, 1648-49; *d. i.*
iii. **MARY**, *b.* March 25, 1650; *d. i.*
iv. **JOSEPH**, *b.* March 25, 1651; swore allegiance February 8, 1679; admitted Freeman, 1690; resided first at Hatfield, afterward probably at Springfield and Lebanon; *m.* **MARY ——**. Issue:

    i.   **MARY**, *b.* 1674; *d. y.*
    ii.   **SAMUEL**, *b.* 1677.
    iii.   **MARY**, *b.* December 29, 1679.
    iv.   **JOSEPH**, *b.* June 14, 1682.
    v.   **ROWLAND**, *b.* March 29, 1685.
    vi.   **SARAH**, *b.* February 5, 1686-87.
    vii.   **EBENEZER**, *b.* November 24, 1688.
    viii. **JOSIAH**, *b.* October 7, 1690.
    ix.   **MERCY**, *b.* December 12, 1692; and two *d. y.*

v.   **BENJAMIN**, *b.* May 23, 1653; *m.*, 1688, **ANN BELDING**, of Hartford. Issue:

    i.   **SARAH**, *b.* September 2, 1690.
    ii.   **MARY**, b. December 26, 1692.
    iii.   A son, *b.* December 20, 1694.
    iv.   **ANN**, *b.* November 2, 1696.
    v.   **SAMUEL**, *b.* January 7, 1699.

vi.   **JOSIAH**, *b.* April 4, 1655; *d. i.*
vii. **JOSIAH**, *b.* October 28, 1657; *d. i.*
viii. **SAMUEL**, *b.* May 6, 1662; *d. u.*, aged thirty-nine.
ix.   A *dau.*, *b.* September 14, 1666; *m.*, 1692, **JAMES WARRINER**.
x.   **MARY**, *b.* January 9, 1668-69; *d. i.*
xi.   **MERCY**, *b.* May 15, 1671; *m.*, March 30, 1689, **JOHN BAGG**.
xii., xiii. Two *d.* unnamed.

Authority: Savage's Dictionary of New England Settlers

THOMAS, OF SUSSEX, ENGLAND

JOHN THOMAS, of an old Monmouthshire family, commanded, as Colonel, the Barbadoes regiment, and distinguished himself greatly at the taking of the island of S.
Christopher's in 1690. His grandson, GEORGE THOMAS, *b.* 1705,
was a wealthy planter of Antigua, and member of the Council of that colony. In 1737 he was appointed Lieutenant-
Governor of Pennsylvania; at first was very unpopular, but
afterward yielding to the Quaker element in the colony gained
their favor, and was much regretted at his departure, in 1747.
He was Captain-General and Governor-in-Chief of the Leeward
and Caribbee Islands, 1752 to 1766, and, September 6, 1766,
was created a Baronet, as of Yapton Place, Sussex. He *m.*
LYDIA, *dau.* of John King, and *d.* December 31, 1774. Issue :

i.   William, *of whom presently.*
ii.   Eliza, *d. u.*
iii. Margaret, *m.* Arthur Freeman, of Antigua, and *d.* 1797 ; issue, with others,
      a son, Inigo, assumed the surname of Thomas.

WILLIAM, only son and heir of **Sir George Thomas, Bart.,**
succeeded his father as second Baronet, was High Sheriff of Sussex, in 1767, *m.* **MARGARET,** *dau.* and *heir* of **Walter Syd-
serffe,** of Soho, and had one son and six daughters. **SIR GEORGE,**

their only son, was an M.P.; *m.*, first, **MADEMOISELLE SALES**, of Pregny-la-Tour. Issue :

WILLIAM LEWIS GEORGE, *of whom presently.*

He *m.*, second, **SOPHIA**, *dau.* of **Admiral Montagu**, who *d. s. p.*, and **SIR GEORGE** *d.* May 6, 1815.

SIR WILLIAM LEWIS GEORGE, fourth Baronet, *m.* **ELIZABETH**, *dau.* of **Richard Welsh** (who *d.* January 1, 1848), and *d.* August 24, 1850. Issue :

Two sons and four daughters.

SIR WILLIAM SIDNEY, the eldest, *b.* 1807, succeeded as fifth Baronet ; was a Captain, R.N.; *m.*, first, 1843, **THOMA-SINE**, *dau.* of **Captain Henry Haynes**, R.N. (who *d.* March 6, 1863). He *m.*, second, August 14, 1856, **FANNY LAURA**, *dau.* of **John Coulson**, of Clifton Wood (who *d.* November 9, 1870). He *d.* April 27, 1867, and was succeeded by his eldest son, **SIR GEORGE SIDNEY MEADE**, *b.* February 12, 1847, as sixth Baronet. He *m.*, May 9, 1874, **EDITH MARGARET**, *dau.* of **Morgan Hugh Foster, Esq., C. B.**, of Birchhill, Bedfordshire. Issue :

i.   **MONTAGU SIDNEY**, *b.* February 23 ; *d.* April 22, 1880.
ii.   **GEORGE ALAN**, *b.* June 14, 1881.
iii. **ISABEL EDITH THOMASINE**.
iv. **RUBY GRACE**.

Authority : Cyclopædia of American Biography, and Burke's Peerage, 1886.

ARMS OF SIR PHILIP FRANCIS

THOMAS, OF TALBOT COUNTY, MD.

CHRISTOPHER THOMAS, the emigrant ancestor, would appear to have first explored the land at another's expense before settling in it, as in Liber i., folio 87, of the Maryland Land Records, under date of September 7, 1640, Thomas Butler, of the Isle of Kent, planter, claims land for having transported to the province Christopher Thomas and two other men-servants at some time previous. In 1638 he was one of two Burgesses in the Lower House of Assembly from Kent Co., showing his estimation among his neighbors, as this was the first Assembly called by the Governor, and Kent then included all the Eastern Shore of Maryland. October 27, 1664, he demands land for transporting to the province in that year himself, Elizabeth, his wife, Susan Higgins and Catherine Higgins, his children, John Edge, and William Ladds and Jane, his wife, and received a warrant for three hundred and fifty acres (Liber vii., folio 471). He *d.* March 25, 1670, but his will is not found on record. It would appear from the above entry he *m.* a widow, **ELIZA-BETH HIGGINS,** who after his death, and before 1679, *m.* **CAPTAIN MATTHEW SMITH,** and made her will as widow, March 11, 1697, proved March 26th, making bequests to Mary Martin, wife of John Martin Smith ; Blanche, wife of Cleborne Lomax, and Mrs. Elizabeth, wife of John Hawkins. By her second husband, **CHRISTOPHER THOMAS,** she

seems to have had issue, a son, **TRUSTRAM THOMAS.**[1] This
TRUSTRAM THOMAS was an early emigrant, as appears
from a land record referring to his son Christopher in 1664–65
as " son of Trustram who settled early on the Wye River." He
was Commissioner to improve trade in Talbot Co. in 1685.
Probably *m.* a sister of **William Coursey,**[2] who deeds to him, as
his brother-in-law, November 10, 1670, "Trustram," four hundred
acres near the head of the northeast branch of the Wye River.
He made his will apparently without date, but proved May 22,
1686, in which he names his wife, **ANNE** (living in 1701) and
issue :

i.   **THOMAS,** *of whom presently.*
ii.   **CHRISTOPHER,** living in 1664–65, *d. s. p.*
iii.   **TRUSTRAM** (*q. v.*).
iv.   **WILLIAM,** *b.* October 18, 1669, was commissioned High Sheriff of Talbot Co., October 15, 1735. He *m.* **JEAN** ——, and made his will
as Yeoman, of Talbot Co., March 20, 1739–40, proved December 10,
1740 (Liber D.D., No. 1, folio 284), naming his sons :

    i.   TRUSTRAM, left "my part of our servant-man called William Moores," and the
       reversion of the plantation left to his mother during her life.
    ii.   WILLIAM, left " tables, scrutore, and two negroes ; " he probably had a son named
       William.

    WILLIAM THOMAS had also daughters.

    iii.   ANN, *m.* WILLIAM MARTIN, and had a son Thomas. To her is forgiven
       "all the debts she oweth me on account of her former husband and herself
       during widowhood."
    iv.   JANE, lately deceased leaving heirs: Elizabeth and Juliana.

v.   **JULY,** *b.* October 15, 1671, probably *m.* **JOHN KING.**
vi.   **STEPHEN,** *b.* January 15, 1673–74, left by his father two hundred and
thirty-three acres, lying by John Glandwing's (Glendinning) on the
Bar, " he to serve his mother until twenty-one."
vii.   There were other daughters, as four are enumerated in the will.

THOMAS, eldest son of **Trustram** and **Anne (Coursey ?).**
Thomas inherited from his father the reversion of the home

---

[1] See Deed, dated November 19, 1679. from Elizabeth Smith, conveying to her son " Trustram,"
by her former husband, Christopher Thomas, " Barbadoes Hall," three hundred and fifty acres on the
south side of the Wye River.

[2] Land Records, Liber ix., 327, William Coursey enters these rights following : Trustam Thomas,
Ann Thomas, his wife ; Thomas Thomas, Christopher Thomas, Trustram Thomas, his children ;
Francis Birkettson, Jane Richardson, Derrink Peterson, Neckey Peterson, Peter Peterson, which
said rights are to complete his conditional warrant and an assignment of warrant for two thousand
and fifty acres from Symon Carpenter, dated April 23, 1665.

plantation after his mother's decease, and "all his father's right in the land and plantation att Chester." He *m.* **ELIZABETH** ———, and made his will as of Talbot Co., August 11, 1701, proved May 8, 1706 (Liber J. C. and W. H., No. 2, folio 24), mentions his "brother and kinsman, John King and William Coursey." Issue :

i. **EDMOND**, *see Queen Anne's County family.*
ii. **TRUSTRAM**, *see ditto.*
iii. **THOMAS,** left by his father three hundred acres in the forks of Tuckahoe, purchased of Robert Smith, "but if he does not convey it then three hundred and fifty acres, called Barbados Hall, lying in Corsica Creek, and also two hundred acres lying on Tuckahoe Creek, which I bought of John Hawkins and William Coursey."

TRUSTRAM, third son of **Trustram** and **Anne (Coursey ?). Thomas,** seems to have left no record. He inherited two hundred and thirty-three acres on the back of Madbury's Branch and was under age in 1686. He had issue :

TRISTRAM, *b.* January 17, 1701 ; one of the Commissioners of Talbot Co., February 1, 1745–46 ; Justice of the Peace, 1751–54 ; *m.* **ELIZABETH MARTIN,** and *d.* July 17, 1769. Will made July 13, 1769, proved December 5, 1769 (Liber W. D., No. 2, 443). Issue :

i. **WILLIAM,** a minor to whom was left " my dwelling plantation called ' Double Ridge,' also ' Rudley' (Roadley), ' Sutton,' the addition, and my part of ' Thief Keep Out.' "
ii. **ELIZABETH,** left part of " Studd's Point," " Killingworth," " Hill's Neck," and " Aire's Venture."
iii. **TRISTRAM,** *b.* December 25, 1769, *of whom presently.*

TRISTRAM, second son of **Trustram** and **Elizabeth (Martin) Thomas,** *b.,* posthumously, December 25, 1769, on Reedy Creek, Bolingbroke Neck, Trappe District, Talbot Co.; removed to Easton, Talbot Co., and practised medicine there. He *m.,* first, December 30, 1792, **SUSAN GEDDES,** of Wilmington, Del., who *d.* leaving two sons and three daughters. **DR. THOMAS,** *m.,* second, March 4, 1804, **MARY ANN,** *dau.* of **Howes** and **Rebecca Goldsborough,** who *d.,* leaving a son and daughter ; and **DR. THOMAS** *m.,* third, November 23, 1809, **MARIA,** *dau.* of **Philip** and **Henrietta Maria (Goldsborough) Francis,** *granddau.* of **Tench Francis,** Attorney-General of Pennsylvania, 1744, descended from **Philip Francis,**

PHILIP FRANCIS THOMAS
GOVERNOR OF MARYLAND, 1847–1850

Mayor of Plymouth in 1644, and father of **Sir Philip Francis**, reputed author of the "Letters of Junius." By his third wife, **DR. THOMAS** had issue :

i.   **PHILIP FRANCIS**, *b.* September 24, 1810, *of whom presently.*
ii.   **CHARLES**, *b.* November 30, 1812.
iii. **HENRIETTA MARIA**, *b.* July 18, 1815.
iv.   **ELLEN FRANCIS**, *b.* May 25, 1819.
v.   **MARY**, *b.* May 15, 1820, *d. y.*

PHILIP FRANCIS, eldest son of **Dr. Tristram** and **Maria (Francis) Thomas**, *b.* at Easton, September 24, 1810 ; admitted to the bar in 1831 ; member of the Maryland Legislature, 1838 ; and several times afterward ; member of Congress, 1839–41 ; Comptroller of Maryland ; Governor, 1848–51 ; Collector of the Port of Baltimore under President Pierce ; Commissioner of Patents, and in 1860 Secretary of the United States Treasury under President Buchanan.   March, 1867, he was elected Senator from Maryland, but was refused a seat ; afterward elected a Representative in the Forty-fourth Congress.   He *m.* **SARAH MARIA KERR**, and *d.,* October 4, 1890.   Issue :

i.   **MARIA PERRY**, *m.* **FRANK MARKOE** (*q. v.*).
ii.   **NANNIE B.**, *m.* July, 1878, **TILTON**, son of **William** and **Annie (Wright) Hemsley**.   Issue :

   MARIA KERR and **MARY STERRET.**

Authority : Wills at Annapolis, and documents and family papers through Messrs. H. H. Goldsborough and Frank Markoe, Baltimore, Md.

THOMAS, OF "THOMAS PROFIT," FREDER-ICK COUNTY, MD.

ELIZABETH THOMAS, of Frederick Co., made her will December 10, 1772, proved October 6, 1779 (Liber G. M., No. 1, folio 154), naming her sons, **DANIEL, WILLIAM, JOSEPH, JONATHAN,** and **NOTLEY,** and *dau.,* **ELIZABETH** and **ANN.** Other sons probably were **ANTHONY THOMAS,** *m.* **LOUSY** ——, and had a son **NODLEY,** *b.* November 26, 1784, and **SAMUEL SKINNER THOMAS,** who occupied "Thomas Profit," seven hundred acres of land three miles north of the Potomac River. His father is said to have come originally from S. Mary's Co.

SAMUEL S. THOMAS, *m.* —— **PALMER,** of Philadelphia, and had thirteen children, the order of whose birth is uncertain.

i.   **RICHARD W.** (Will February 5, 1826.)
ii.   **ARCHIBALD,** *d. s. p.* (Will proved March 21, 1825.)
iii. **BENJAMIN.**
iv. **LEVIN.**
v.   **OTHO.**
vi. **NOTLEY.**
vii. **THOMAS.**
viii. **SAMUEL S.,** *of whom presently.*
ix. **SARAH,** *m.* —— **RENENBERGER.**
x.   **REBECCA.**
xi. **ELIZABETH,** *m.* **EDWARD THOMAS.**
xii. **MARY** and **PHEBE,** *d.* 1872 ; one of whom *m.* —— **DAVIS,** and had a son, **WILLIAM THOMAS DAVIS.**

SAMUEL S., youngest son of **Samuel Skinner** and —— **(Palmer) Thomas,** *m.* —— and *d.* ——. Issue :

    BRUCE, a physician, has a son, **SAMUEL B. ; NOTLEY W. ;** and another son, whose son, **SAMUEL SKINNER,** resides near Berryville, Va., and has a son, **Samuel B.**

Authorities : Wills at Frederick, Md., and Dr. Bruce Thomas, of Washington, D. C.

THOMAS, OF THOMASTON, CONN.

SETH, son of **James** and **Martha Thomas,** *b.* at Wolcott, Conn., August 19, 1785, founded this family. His advantages of education consisted of a very short attendance upon a distant public school. He served an apprenticeship to the trade of carpenter and joiner, and worked for some time on the construction of Long Wharf, in New Haven. Leaving at his majority with a small kit of tools and a very small sum of money, he began the manufacture of clocks in the southeastern part of the town of Plymouth, now Hancock Station, on the New York and New England Railroad, with Eli Terry and Silas Hoadley, under the firm name of Terry, Thomas & Hoadley. In 1810 Mr. Terry sold his interest to his partners, and the firm continued two years as Thomas & Hoadley. Then Mr. Thomas sold his interest and removed to the western part of the town, then known as Plymouth Hollow, and purchased the ground where the case-shop is now located. Here he continued the manufacture of clocks, on his own account, becoming very successful and building up a very large business from small beginnings. He also erected a cotton-mill and a brass-rolling and wire-mill. Politically he was a Whig, and by religious affiliation a Congregationalist, contributing largely to the building of their meeting-house in Plymouth Hollow. In 1853, feeling the infirmities of age approaching, and in order to avoid the stoppage of his works at his death, he organized the Seth Thomas Clock Company, under the laws of Connecticut. After his death the town of Plymouth was divided by act of Legislature, and the western part named Thomaston in his honor. He *m.*, first, April 20, 1808, **PHILENA TUTTLE,** who *d.* March 12, 1810 ; *m.*, second, April 14, 1811, **LAURA,** *dau.* of **William** and **Submit Andrews,** who *d.* July 12, 1871. He *d.* January 29, 1859, having had nine children. His three eldest *d.* in September, 1815 ; those who survived him were : **SETH, Jr.,** *b.* December, 1816 ; *d.* April, 1888 ; **MARTHA,** *m.* **DR. WILLIAM WOODRUFF** ; **AMANDA,** *m.* **THOMAS J. BRADSTREET**; **EDWARD** ; **ELIZABETH,** *m.* **GEORGE W. GILBERT** ; and **AARON.** All *d.* before November, 1894, except Elizabeth and Aaron.

Authority : Mr. Seth E. Thomas, New York City.

THOMAS, OF WENVOE CASTLE, WALES

CATHERINE, the heiress of **Thomas ap Thomas,** of Wenvoe Castle, about 1500 *m.* **JEVAN HARPWAY,** of Tre Simon, who assumed her surname. A descendant, **EDMUND THOMAS,** of Wenvoe Castle, was Sheriff of Glamorgan in 1627 ; his grandson, EDMUND, was Sheriff in 1664, and his son, John, was created a Baronet, December 24, 1694, with remainder to the male issue of his father. He was Sheriff in 1700 ; *d. s. p.* in 1703. His brother, Edmund, was his heir, who *m.* Mary, *dau.* of John Howe, of Stowell, Gloucester, and *d.* 1723. Issue :

> i. Edmund, *of whom presently.* ii. John. iii. William, *b.* 1718.

EDMUND, eldest son of **Sir Edmund** and **Mary (Howe) Thomas,** succeeded as third Baronet in 1723 ; *m.,* 1740, **ABIGAIL** (*b.* 1777), *dau.* of **Sir Thomas Webster,** Bart., of Battle Abbey, Sussex, and widow of **William Northey,** and *d.* 1767, having previously sold the Wenvoe Castle estates. Issue :

i.   **EDMUND,** fourth Baronet, *d. u.* 1789.

ii.   **JOHN,** succeeded his brother in the title; *m.* **MARY,** *dau.* of John Parker, of Hasfield Court, Gloucester, and is now represented in the direct line by **SIR GODFREY VIGNOLLES THOMAS,** ninth Baronet, *b.* March 27, 1856, Captain R. A., fourth class Medjidie, succeeded his father in the title, July 13, 1861 ; resides at "The Plâs," Chingford, Essex.

Authority : Nicholas's Wales, and Baronetages.

JONATHAN THOMAS, of Philadelphia, Pa., claiming descent from the Wenvoe Castle family (*q. v.*), *m.* **RUTH CAM-**

ERON, of Lochiel, Scotland, and had a son **COLONEL NATHAN THOMAS,** who emigrated to Virginia ; *m.* **MARY APPLER,** of a Holland family.   They had a son MAJOR WILLIAM ALLAYNE THOMAS, removed to Illinois ; *m.* CAROLINE, *dau.* of General John J. Neely, of Indiana, and had a son, John R. Thomas, five times Member of Congress from Illinois ; *m.* Charlotte Culver.   Issue :

     John R., Jr., Caroline, Mary Logan.

       Authority : Family papers, through Hon. John R. Thomas.

THOMAS, OF WEYMOUTH, MASS.

CAPTAIN JOHN THOMAS came to Boston prior to 1700 and
settled at Braintree, Mass. He claimed to have carried the
pacquet of letters which invited William of Orange to England
in 1688, and to have commanded the yacht that carried him over
in October of that year. He removed to North Weymouth, *m.*
LYDIA, *dau.* of Deacon **Abiah Whitwon,** before August 8,
1704, and *d.* October 4, 1714; his widow *d.* 1757. Issue:

i.   **ANDREW,** *b.* January 15, 1702, *d. y.*
ii.   **LYDIA,** *b.* July 17, ——; *m.* **WILLIAM SALISBURY,** of Braintree.
iii.   **JOHN,** *b.* February 27, 1710, *of whom presently.*
iv.   **MARY,** *b.* November 28, 1714; *d.* September 4, 1734.

JOHN, surviving son of **Captain John** and **Lydia (Whitman)**
Thomas, *b.* February 27, 1710; *m.,* January 30, 1750, **SI-**
LENCE, *dau.* of **Benjamin** and **Elizabeth (Randall) Orcutt**
(who *d.* 1799), and *d.* 1782–83. Issue:

i.   **JOHN,** *b.* June 16, 1751; *m.,* December 4, 1774, **LYDIA,** *dau.* of Deacon **Nathaniel** and **Tamar (White) Bayley;** *d.* July 10, 1834;
his widow *d.* 1838, aged eighty-three. His grandson, **John W. Thomas,**
was Sheriff of Norfolk Co., and had a son, Henry A., Private Secretary to Governor Greenhalge, of Massachusetts.
ii.   **MARY,** *b.* September 21, 1753; *m.,* April 1, 1776, **CALEB HUNT,**
and *d.* 1781.
iii. **SARAH,** *b.* May 12, 1755 or 1775, and *d. u.,* July 28, 1828.

Authority: Hon. Joseph W. Porter, in New England Historical and Genealogical Register, xlix.,
p. 172.

THOMAS, OF WICKFORD, R. I.

THE first of this family known was **JOHN THOMAS,** *b.* in Pembrokeshire, Wales, in 1640 ; sailed for Rhode Island with John Neyles,
Baptist minister of Swansea, Nicholas Tanner, Obadiah Brown,
and other Baptists, about 1662. He lived for a time at Portsmouth,
then at Jamestown, Conanicut Island, being of the Grand Jury
there in 1688 ; Freeman of North Kingston, April 30, 1700 ; on
March 26, 1701, he bought of Benoni and Mary Gardiner eighty
acres in Pettaquamscott Purchase for £48, and another tract
of Nicholas and Hannah Gardiner for the same price. Part of
this land the family still owns. January 28, 1707, he purchased
of John, Sr., and Rebecca Watson, of Kingston, eighty acres for
£30. March 6, 1713, he deeded one hundred and eighty acres
to his son George, and a year later other tracts of land, he to
allow his parents sufficient maintenance. August 23, 1715, he
testified as to land in Jamestown he had known about thirty-six
years before. October 8, 1728, his will was proved. Issue :

i.   **GEORGE,** *b.* August 20, 1681, *of whom presently.*
ii.   **JOHN,** *b.* 169– ; *m.* **ABIGAIL** ——, before July 12, 1718.
iii.   **EBENEZER,** living March 29, 1721, when he makes a deposition concern-
        ing some land.

GEORGE, eldest son of **John Thomas,** *b.* August 20, 1681, was
Freeman in 1703. Bought thirty-six acres in Kingstown, December 20, 1706, Deputy in 1733, a Colonel at the time of his death.
Will proved January 26, 1740 ; *m.,* first, January 20, 1804, **ALICE,**
dau. of **Benjamin** and **Sarah (Carder) Gorton,** and second,
MRS. ELIZABETH, widow of **John Phillips,** who *d.* in
1748. By his first wife had issue :

i.   **SARAH.**
ii.   **MARY.**
iii.   **GEORGE,** *b.* February 7, 1708 ; *m.* **ELIZABETH** —— ; *d.* 1735.

iv.   **JOHN.**
v.   **BENJAMIN.**
vi.   **PETER.**
vii.   **SAMUEL,** *b.* 1720, *of whom presently*
viii.   **A DAUGHTER.**
ix.   **ALICE,** *m.* —— TILLINGHAST, before 1740.
x.   **ELIZABETH,** *m.* —— FREE, before 1740.

   SAMUEL, fifth son of **Colonel George Thomas,** *b.* 1720, was his father's executor and residuary legatee in 1740 ; a farmer, and had a son, **CAPTAIN SAMUEL,** *b.* 1748, served in the Revolutionary War, and was father of RICHARD THOMAS, merchant, whose son, Allen Mason Thomas, merchant, was for fifty years Warden and Vestryman of S. Paul's Church, Wickford, R. I., and father of the Rev. Elisha Smith Thomas, *b.* March 1, 1834, clergyman of the Protestant Episcopal Church, consecrated Assistant Bishop of Kansas in 1887, became Bishop 1889 ; *d.* March 9, 1895, leaving a son, Rev. Nathaniel Seymour Thomas.

Authority : Austin's Rhode Island Genealogies and Bishop Thomas.

THOMAS, OF WILMINGTON, DEL.

WILLIAM THOMAS, of Cecil Co., Md., supposed to have been originally of Charles Co., *b.* 1723 ; *m.* **HANNAH BUCKING-HAM,** and *d.* March 25, 1798 ; his widow *d.* November 9, 1800, aged sixty-three. Issue : Eleven children, of whom survived :

i.   **MARY,** *b.* in 1760 ; *d.* ——.
ii.   **JANE,** *b.* in 1762 ; *d.* ——.
iii.   **LEWIS,** *b.* in 1767 ; was in the Maryland Legislature ; *m.* four times, and *d.* ——. Issue :

     i.   HENDERSON, *d.* ——.
     ii.   LEWIS CAMPBELL, *d.* ——.
     iii.   SUSAN, *d.* ——.
     iv.   JANE, *d.* ——.
     v.   DAVID, living in 1891.

iv.   **THEODORE,** *b.* in 1772 ; *m.* **MARY MOORE,** and *d.* ——. Issue :

     i.   HANNAH, *d.* ——.
     ii.   ANN, *m.* —— BOULDEN, and *d.* ——. Issue (surname BOULDEN) : Charles, Hattie, and William.
     iii.   ELIZA, *m.* —— TAYLOR, who was living at Elkton, Md., in 1894.
     iv.   WILLIAM, *d.* ——.
     v.   MARY, *d.* ——.

v.   **ASENTAH,** *b.* 1775.
vi.   **JOHN BUCKINGHAM,** *b.* 1777, *of whom presently.*
vii.   **HANNAH,** *b.* in 1782 ; *d.* ——

JOHN BUCKINGHAM, youngest son of **William** and **Hannah (Buckingham) Thomas,** *b.* in 1777 ; *m.*, June 19, 1806, **ELIZABETH,** *dau.* of **Judge John Way,** and *d.* April 24, 1824. Issue :

i.   **ANNE JANET,** *b.* June 10, 1807 ; *m.* **BENJAMIN PHISTER,** of Philadelphia.
ii.   **ALLAN,** *b.* March 17, 1809 ; *d.* December 30, 1810.
iii.   **WILLIAM WAY,** *b.* July 9, 1811, *of whom presently.*
iv.   **JAMES BAYARD,** *b.* September 24, 1815 ; *d. s. p.* April, 1894.

WILLIAM WAY, second son of **John B.** and **Elizabeth** (Way) Thomas, *b.* July 9, 1811 ; *m.*, first, June 30, 1836, **HANNAH PRESTON,** of Chester Co., Pa. Issue :

i. **AMY ANNA,** *b.* July 19, 1837 ; *m.*, December 27, 1855, **H. L. GUY.**
   Issue (surname GUY) :

   WILLIAM, EMMA, HELEN, and CHARLES.

ii. **JAMES BAYARD,** *b.* December 22, 1838 ; *m.*, May 8, 1866, **SARAH E. POOLE.** Issue :

   i. WALTER LINCOLN, *b.* February 14, 1867 ; *d.* February 4, 1874.
   ii. JESSIE B., *b.* February 10, 1869 ; *m.*, October 2, 1894, DR. HORACE BETTS.
   iii. OSCAR GERALD, *b.* August 3, 1873 ; *d.* February 4, 1874.

iii. **EMMA LUCRETIA,** *b.* June 23, 1841 ; *m.* **JOHN W. WISE,** and *d.* August 6, 1887. Issue (surname WISE) :

   i. MABEL P., *b.* August 25, 1869.
   ii. HERBERT, *b.* June 12, 1873.

iv. **CHARLES FOLLEN,** *b.* May 24, 1843 ; *m.*, October 15, 1868, **RUTH A. BYE.** Issue :

   i. VICTOR SUMNER, *b.* March 10, 1874.
   ii. EDNA VINETA, *b.* October 12, 1879.
   iii. LEON, *b.* January 11, 1883.

v. **WILLIAM LLOYD GARRISON,** *b.* August 22, 1845 ; *m.*, December 9, 1867, **MARY E. HIBBERD.** Issue :

   i. STIRLING HIBBERD, *b.* November 19, 1868 ; *m.*, October 10, 1894, EDITH NEEDLES TRUMP.
   ii. MARY, *b.* November 25, 1872.

WILLIAM WAY THOMAS, *m.*, second, April 24, 1850, **BEU-LAH PRESTON,** sister of his first wife, and *d.* March 3, 1890. Further issue :

vi. **SEYMOUR PRESTON,** *b.* December 20, 1851 ; *m.*, November 8, 1884, **SUSAN W. RICHARDSON.** Issue :

   i. GEORGE, *b.* April 3, 1886 ; *d.* May 3, 1887.
   ii. ANNA CRAIGE, *b.* July 21, 1887 ; *d. i.*

vii. **EDGAR GOSEWISCH,** *b.* August 11, 1853 ; *m.*, May 2, 1878, **ELLA C. REEVES,** of Philadelphia. Issue :

   CHARLOTTE REEVES, *b.* March 14, 1885.

viii. **FRANK HOWARD,** *b.* September 4, 1859 ; *m.*, October 6, 1880, **PHŒBE T. CHAMBERS.** Issue :

   i. MABEL, *b.* July 8, 1882.
   ii. JEANNETTE KENT, *b.* September 17, 1894.

Authority : Family papers, principally through Mr. James Bayard Thomas.

THOMAS, OF WORNY-BORNY, WALES

JOHN THOMAS, *b.* at Worny-Borny, in Wales, March 1, 1775; emigrated to America, and *m.* at Philadelphia, May 6, 1802, **MARTHA TAYLOR,** *b.* April 26, 1781, in Delaware; *d.* January 1, 1832, and her husband *d.* March 15, 1850. Issue, two sons:

i.   **JOHN WILLIAM,** *b.* November 11, 1814, *of whom presently.*
ii.   **GEORGE CLIFFORD,** *b.* November 1, 1817, residing in Germantown.

And four daughters:

i.   **JULIA A.,** *m.* **CHARLES H. ROGERS,** for many years President of the Tradesmen's National Bank of Philadelphia, since deceased.
ii.   **LOUISA,** *m.* **JAMES P. WARWICK,** both *d.*
iii   **MARY ANN.**
iv.   And a fourth, *d. y.*

JOHN WILLIAM, eldest son of **John** and **Martha (Taylor) Thomas,** *b.* November 11, 1814; *m.,* March 2, 1837, **KEZIAH S.** (*b.* 1818, *d.* July 5, 1895), *dau.* of **John Atkinson,** of Mount Holly, N. J., and *d.* March 18, 1882. Issue:

i.   **JOHN WILLIAM,** *d. i.*
ii.   **GEORGE CLIFFORD,** *b.* October 28, 1839, a partner in the banking house of Drexel & Co., Philadelphia; *m.* **ADA ELIZABETH,** *dau.* of **Joel Barlow** and **Elizabeth (Hirons) Moorehead.** Issue:
      i.   **GEORGE CLIFFORD, Jr.,** *b.* 1873.
      ii.   **SOPHIE,** *b.* 1876.
      iii. **LEONARD M.,** *b.* 1878.
iii.   **ELLA MARY,** *b.* October 15, 1841; *m.* **GEORGE H. LEONARD,** of Boston, Mass. Issue (surname LEONARD):
      i.   **JOHN W. T.,** *d.* aged twenty-one.
      ii.   **GEORGE H., Jr.,** *b.* about 1870; studying art in Paris.
      iii. **EDITH GWENDOLIN.**
iv.   **RICHARD NEWTON,** *b.* September 9, 1844, a clergyman of the Protestant Episcopal Church, last Rectorship that of S. Philip's, West Philadelphia, which by his exertions he left without debt and provided with an endowment of $16,000. He *m.,* December 30, 1869, **CLARA LOUISA HORSTMANN.** Issue:

  i. **EMMA SOPHIA**, *b.* April 3, 1871 ; *m.,* October 27, 1892, **NORMAN ELLISON.**
  ii **WALTER HORSTMANN**, *b.* December 29, 1876.

 v. **IDA MARTHA**, *b.* January 25, 1847 ; *m.* **CHARLES B. NEWCOMB,**
    of St. Paul, and *d.* January 17, 1882. Issue (surname NEWCOMB) :
    EDGAR CLIFFORD, VIRGINIA THOMAS, and MARIAN.

 vi. **VIRGINIA LETITIA**, *b.* November 1, 1849 ; *m.* **JAMES DAY**
    ROWLAND, of Ogontz, Pa. Issue (surname ROWLAND) :
    BENJAMIN, IDA, and VIRGINIA.

 vii. **JOHN WOOLSTON**, *b.* August 26, 1852, *d. y.*
 viii. **LAURA COOKE,** *b.* February 14, 1854 ; *d.* in January, 1870.

    Authorities : Family papers through Messrs. R. N. and George C. Thomas.

TOMMASI, OF NAPLES, ITALY

This ancient and noble family was originally established at Cortona, in Tuscany, having also branches at Siena and Capua. It had given a Grand Master to the Order of Malta, **GIOVANNI BATISTA TOMMASI,** and Alphonso V. of Aragon made them Barons. In 1584 **MARIO TOMMASI,** going to Palermo with Marc Antonio Colonna, the Spanish Viceroy, *m.* the only *dau.* and *heir.* of **Ferdinando Caro,** and received the fief of Monte Chiaro. They had issue :

FERDINANDO and MARIO.

FERDINANDO had two sons. **CARLO** built a castle on his fief called Palma, was decorated in 1638 with the title of Duke by Philip IV., of Spain. Shortly afterward he resigned the fief and title to his younger brother and became a Theatine monk. This brother, **GIULIO,** second Duca di Palma, Principe de Lampadosa, Barone de Monte Chiaro, Cavaliere de S. Giacomo, *m.* **ROSALIA TRAINA,** his brother's intended bride, and was father of GIUSEPPE MARIA, *b.* September 12, 1649, at Alicata, Sicily ; a younger son, FERDINAND, and four daughters who became Benedictine nuns, at Palma, in a convent erected by their father. The eldest son also became a monk, in 1666, of the same order with his uncle. Devoting himself to study he published some thirteen volumes, among them a valuable Sacramentary in 1680. May 18, 1712, Pope Clement XI. created him Cardinal Priest of S. Silvestro, to which he added S. Martino a Monte. January 1, 1713, he died, having made the College di Propaganda Fide his heir. June 5, 1803, Pope Pius VII. decreed his beatification. His life was published at Rome the same year, with a portrait, by N. A. Oddi, in quarto, 188 pages.

Authority : The Anonymous Italian Life of 1803.

ANDREWS

COLONEL TIMOTHY PATRICK ANDREWS, of the
U. S. Army, *b.* in 1794, in Ireland ; served as aide to Commodore
Barney in the War of 1812, was distinguished for bravery at the
battle of El Molino, in Mexico, in 1847, and brevetted Brigadier-
General for gallantry at Chapultepec. Appointed Paymaster-
General of the Army, September 6, 1862. He *m.* **EMILY
ROSEVILLE,** fourth *dau.* of **Richard** and **Eliza (Warfield)
Snowden,** and *d.* March 11, 1868. Issue :

i.   **RICHARD SNOWDEN,** *b.* October 29, 1830, *of whom presently.*

ii.   **LOUISA,** *m.* **SAMUEL S. EARLY.** Issue (surname EARLY) :

         EMILY, JACOB, SAMUEL, and **CHARLES.**

iii.   **EMILY ROSALIE,** *m.* **CHARLES MARSHALL,** and *d.* Issue
       (surname MARSHALL) :

         EMILY ROSALIE SNOWDEN, *m.* **JUDGE S. PINKNEY TUCK**
         (q. v.).

       Colonel **MARSHALL** *m.,* second, **SARAH REBECCA,** *dau.* of
         Thomas and Ann Rebecca Snowden.

iv.   **CAROLINE.**

v.   **ALBERT S.,** *d.* in 1890.

RICHARD SNOWDEN, eldest son of **Colonel Timothy P.**
and **Emily Roseville (Snowden) Andrews,** *b.* October 29,
1830, is by profession an architect. In 1861 he was commissioned at Richmond Major of Virginia Cavalry, later Captain of
Mounted Artillery, and the same year promoted to be Major.
1863 Lieutenant-Colonel, commanding Andrews's Battalion of
Artillery of Stonewall Jackson's Division of the Army of Northern Virginia and on the staff. Having received severe wounds
in three battles was incapacitated for field service, and sent
abroad by General R. E. Lee to examine and report on the artillery of leading European armies. After the close of the war,

Topographical Engineer on the Imperial Mexican Railway. Returned to Baltimore in 1867, and appointed to positions on the staff of two Governors of Maryland, as Brigadier-General of Artillery. He *m.*, in 1855, **MARY C. LEE.** Issue :

i.   **LOUISA LEE,** *b.* November, 1856 ; *m.*, December, 1891, **HENRY BACON,** the American artist, residing in Paris.

ii.   **CHARLES LEE,** *b.* November, 1858 ; *m.*, June, 1884, **EDYTHE,** *dau.* of **Daniel T. Walden,** of Brooklyn, N. Y.

iii.   **EMILY ROSALIE,** *b.* February, 1860 ; *m.*, February, 1882, **TUNSTALL SMITH,** and *d.* October, 1889. Issue (surname SMITH) :

     i.   ROSALIE TUNSTALL, *b.* December, 1882.
     ii.   ANITA TUNSTALL, *b.* August, 1884.
     iii.   MARION TUNSTALL, *b.* March, 1889.

iv.   **CAROLYN SNOWDEN,** *b.* January, 1862 ; *m.*, June, 1884, **GIBSON FAHNESTOCK,** of New York City. Issue (surname FAHNESTOCK) :

     i.   SNOWDEN ANDREWS, *b.* March, 1886.
     ii.   GIBSON, Jr., *b.* March, 1888.

v.   **GEORGE SNOWDEN,** *b.* March, 1868.

Authority : Family papers, through General R. S. Andrews.

ANTROBUS OF CHESHIRE

ANTROBUS

WALTER ANTERBUS (ANTROBUS), of S. Albans, Herefordshire, England ; *m.*, first, February 16, 1579–80, **BARBARA LAWRENCE**. Issue :

i.   **WILLIAM,** *bapt.* November 20, 1582, probably *m.*, July 6, 1607, **ALICE DENT**, and *d.* November 24, 1617.

MRS. BARBARA (LAWRENCE) ANTROBUS *d.* June 27, 1585, and **WALTER ANTROBUS** *m.*, second, February 8, 1586–87, **JANE ARNOLDE**, and *d.* April 5, 1614. Further issue :

ii.   **WILLIAM,**   *bapt.* June 25, 1587.
iii.   **WALTER,** *bapt.* June 1, 1589.
iv.   **ROBERT,** *bapt.* February 21, 1590.
v.   **JOANE,** *bapt.* June 25, 1591–92 ; *m.* **THOMAS LAWRENCE** (*q. v.*).
vi.   **ELIZABETH,** *bapt.* August 6, 1598.
vii.   **HENRIE,** *bapt.* April 25, 1600 ; *d.* June 14, 1602.

A **Dorothy Antrobus** *m.* **Philip Gray**, a scrivener of London, and was the mother of **Thomas Gray**, the poet, who was indebted to two brothers of his mother for his education. They were Fellows of Cambridge and tutors at Eton where he was educated :

Authority : Registers of S. Albans.

TOUCHET, LORD AUDLEY

AUDLEY AND TOUCHET

HENRY DE ALDITHELY, or AUDLEY, inherited the castle from **Nicholas de Verdon,** 16th King Henry III., and *m.* **BERTRADE,** *dau.* of **Ralph de Meisnilwarin.** Issue:

i.   **EMMA,** *m.* **GRIFFITH AP MADOC,** of Bromfield (*q. v.*).
ii.   **JAMES,** *d.* 1272. Issue:

     i.   JAMES, *d. s. p.*, 1273.
     ii.   HENRY, *d. s. p.*, 1276.
     iii.   WILLIAM, killed, *s. p.*, in Wales, 1282.
     iv.   NICHOLAS, first Baron Audley, in 1296-97; *m.* CATHERINE, *dau.* of John and Maud (de Clifford) Gifford. Issue:
         Thomas, *d. s. p.*, and Nicholas, *of whom presently.*

NICHOLAS, second Baron Audley, *m.* **JOAN,** *dau.* and *co-h.* of **William, Lord Martin,** of Kemeys, and *d.* 1299. Issue:

     JAMES, the great Lord Audley, who distinguished himself greatly at Poictiers; *m.* **JOAN,** *dau.* and *co-h.* of **Roger Mortimer,** Earl of March (*q. v.*), and *d.* 1385-86. Issue:

     i.   NICHOLAS, *d. s. p.*, 15th King Richard II.
     ii.   JOAN, *of whom presently.*
     iii.   MARGARET.

JOAN, eldest *dau.* of **James Lord Audley,** *m.* **SIR JOHN TOUCHET.** Issue (surname TOUCHET):

     JOHN, had a son JOHN, eventual heir to his great-uncle, Lord Audley; *m.* **ISABEL ——,** and *d.* 1409. Issue:

     i.   James, from whom descended the later Lords Audley.
     ii.   Elizabeth, *m.* Sir John Baskerville, Knt. (*q. v.*).

Authority: T. C. Banks's Baronia Anglica Concentrata, etc.

BASKERVILLE

SIR ROBERT BASKERVILLE, KNT., of Erdisley in Herefordshire ; *m.* **AGNES**, *dau.* of **Galfrid Rees**, some say of **Nesta**, of Wales, and had a son, **SIR RALPH**, living *temp.* Henry II. From him lineally descended **SIR RICHARD, KNT.**, M. P. for the shire in 1300 ; High Sheriff of Hereford, 1315 ; *m.* **JOANNA**, *dau.* of **Sir Richard Poynings.** Issue :

> **SIR RICHARD**, whose son, Sir Richard, attained his majority 17th Richard II., and *d.* 1395 ; his son was Sir John, *of whom presently.*

SIR JOHN, son of **Sir Richard Baskerville**, living in 1403, *m.* **ELIZABETH**, widow of **Piers Mylbourne**, and *dau.* and heiress to **Sir John Eynsford**, by a *dau.* of **Gerard Furnival** (*q. v.*), second brother of the last lord of that family. Issue :

i. **SIR JOHN,** *of whom presently.*

ii. **RALPH**, *b.* 1410 ; *m.* **ANN**, *dau.* and *co-h.* to **Sir John Blakett.** Issue :

> **JANE**, *m.* **SIMON MYLBOURNE**, of Tillington, in Burghill. Issue :
>
> > **Sybell**, *m.* first, Richard Hakelute, *m.*, second, John, son of Thomas (ap William ap Roger) Breynton, by a *dau.* of Harper of Wellington, Herefordshire, and *d.* 1535. Her *dau.*, Elizabeth, *m.* Sir James Baskerville (*q. v.*).

SIR JOHN, eldest son of **Sir John** and **Elizabeth (Eynsford) Baskerville**, *b.* February 12, 1403 ; *m.* **ELIZABETH**, *dau.* of **John Touchet, Lord Audley** [1] (*q. v.*), and *d.* December 23, 1455. Issue :

---

[1] Through this marriage the family is of founder's kin to the Frankland fellowship, Brasenose College, Oxford.

SIR JAMES, Knt. Banneret, Knight of the Bath at the marriage of King Henry VII.; M.P., 1476; High Sheriff, 38 Henry VI., 4 Edward IV., and 14 Henry VII.; *m.* SYBELLA, *dau.* of Sir Walter Devereux, by Anne, *dau.* and heiress of William Lord Ferrars, of Chartley. Issue:

SIR WALTER, Sheriff, 9 Edward IV., Knight of the Bath at marriage of Arthur, Prince of Wales; *m.* ANNE, *dau.* of Morgan John ap Philip, of Pencoyd, in Glamorganshire, and *d.* September 4, 1505. Issue: i. Sir James, *of whom presently.* ii. Joane or Sibil, *m.* Sir James Scudamore (*q. v.*).

SIR JAMES, son and heir of Sir Walter and Anne Baskerville, was of Eardisley, Co. Hereford; *m.* ELIZABETH, *dau.* and *co-h.* of John Breynton (*q. v.*), and *d.* 1546. Issue: Five sons, whose male issue became extinct early in this century, and ELIZABETH, *m.* CHARLES VAUGHAN, son of Walter Vaughan,[1] of Hergest, and had a son, WALTER, Constable of Huntington Castle, Herefordshire, whose *dau.*, Sibill, *m.* John Scudamore (*q. v.*).

Authorities: R. Cooke's Visitation of Herefordshire, edited by Weaver, *pp.* 7, 36, 97; G. T. Clark, Genealogies of Morgan and Glamorgan, *pp.* 233, 238; C. J. Robinson's Herefordshire, *p.* 163; Burke's Landed Gentry, 1858.

[1] Roger Vaughan *m. dau.* and *heir* of —— Bredwardine, of Bredwarden, Herefordshire, and had a son, Sir Roger, *m.* as her first husband, Gladis, *dau.* of Sir David Gam ap Llewellyn ap Howell. Knt., of Peytin, Breconshire, their third son Thomas was father of Walter Vaughan.

BENTLEY

CALEB, son of **Joseph** and **Mary Bentley,** *m.,* first, April 20, 1791, **SARAH,** *dau.* of **Roger Brooke,** who *d.* September 9, 1805, and her husband *m.,* second, August 26, 1807, **HENRIETTA,** second *dau.* of **Samuel** and **Mary (Cowman) Thomas.**   Issue :

i.   **MARY THOMAS,** *b.* August 29, 1808, *of whom presently.*
ii.   **SARAH BROOKE,** *b.* November 16, 1814, *m.* **Dr. GEORGE WARFIELD.**   Issue (surname WARFIELD) :

> **LOUIS M.,** *b.* October 27, 1837, cotton manufacturer at Savannah, Ga.; *m.,* January 6, 1875, **PHEMIE D. WAYNE.**   Issue :
>
> > **Louis M.,** Jr., *b.* May 15, 1876; **Edith Wayne,** *b.* November 17, 1878; and **William Henry** and **James Wayne,** *b.* August 9, 1885, the former *d.* August 11, 1885.

iii.   **RICHARD THOMAS,** *b.* July 20, 1819, resided at Sandy Spring, Montgomery Co., Md.; *m.,* June 20, 1842, **EDITH D. NEEDLES** (who *d.* February 8, 1894).   Issue :

> i.   **ELIZA NEEDLES,** *b.* August 25, 1843; *m.,* 1887, **JOSEPH T. MOORE,** and *d.* October 29, 1889.
> ii.   **MARY H.,** *b.* December 14, 1845; *m.* **EDWARD P. THOMAS** (*q. v.*).
> iii.   **SARAH BROOKE,** *b.* February 26, 1848; *m.,* June 21, 1867, **LIEUTENANT WILLIAM LEA,** of the Delaware Battery.   Issue (surname LEA) :
>
> > **Jennie Lovett,** *b.* June 1, 1868; **Edithe Bentley,** *b.* April 7, 1872; and **Edward Tatnall,** *b.* November 12, 1873.
>
> iv.   **ANNA M.,** *b.* February 26, 1850; *m.,* November 12, 1872, **WILLIAM J. PARKER.**   Issue (surname PARKER) :
>
> > **Mary,** *b.* November 17, 1873; **Richard Bentley,** *b.* November 13, 1875; and **Henry Melville,** *b.* December 28, 1876.
>
> v.   **JOHN CALEB,** *b.* April 30, 1852; *m.* **CORNELIA M. HALLOWELL.**   Issue :
>
> > **Florence M.; Agnes,** *d. i.;* **Mildred H.; Edith D.; Eliza** and **John Needles.**
>
> vi.   **EDWARD NEEDLES,** *b.* September 16, 1854; *m.* **HARRIET J. CHANDLEE.**   Issue :
>
> > **Hubert** (*d. y.*); **Mary C.; Maurice L.,** and **Richard T.**

vii. **EDITH HELEN**, *b.* August 26, 1856; *m.*, June 4, 1878, **HENRY T. LEA.** Issue:

  Beulah ; John and Henry, twins ; Anna B.; Helen (*d. y.*) ; Robert Brooke, and Lucy R.

viii. **RICHARD LOUIS**, *b.* October 28, 1859; *m.* **ANNA VAN BUSKIRK.** Issue : Lilian H.

MARY THOMAS, eldest *dau.* of Caleb and Henrietta (Thomas) Bentley, *b.* August 29, 1808 ; *m.*, first, LAWRENCE MOORE. Issue (surname MOORE) :

i. **FREDERICK LAWRENCE**, *b.* June 4, 1835 ; *m.*, September 18, 1855, **C. VIRGINIA CAMPBELL.** Issue :

 i. **MARY ELLA**, *b.* June 27, 1856.
 ii. **JULIA BENTLEY**, *b.* November 2, 1857 ; *m.*, June 29, 1878, **ROBERT BARNARD TENNEY**, mill-owner of Washington, D. C. Issue (surname TENNEY) :

  Robert Barnard, *b.* November 16, 1879 ; Ellette Campbell, *b.* August 13, 1881.

 iii. **ELOISE C.** *d. i.*
 iv. **LAWRENCE C.**, *b.* October 23, 1860.
 v. **WILLIAM P.**, *b.* November 22, 1862.
 vi. **EDITH BENTLEY**, *d. i.*
 vii. **VIRGINIA**, *d. i.*
 viii. **LEON**, *d. i.*

MRS. MARY BENTLEY MOORE, *m.*, second, EBEN G. BROWN, and *d.* before 1895. Issue (surname BROWN) :

ii. **SARAH BENTLEY** *m.* **JOHN PARKES**, and *d.* before 1895. Issue (surname PARKES) :

 i. **LAWRENCE.**
 ii. **MABEL.**
 iii. **HOWARD.**
 iv. **HENRIETTA.**
 v. **ANNA A.**
 vi. **FRANK THOMAS.**
 vii. **EDITH E.**

iii. **HENRIETTA E.**, *m.* **DARIUS CLAGGETT.** Issue :

 MARY ETHELYND.

Authority : Friends' Records and Family Papers.

BIGOD, OF NORFOLK, ENGLAND

ROGER, son of **Hugh le Bigod**,[1] a Norman, at the time of the Domesday Survey, held twenty-three lordships in Suffolk and Essex, was Lord of the castle of Norwich, and founder of Thetford Abbey. He *m.* **ADELIZA** ——, and *d.* 1107. **WILLIAM**, his eldest son and heir, *d. s. p.*, on the ill-fated white ship, with the favourite son of King Henry I., and was succeeded by his brother **HUGH**, *b.* before 1100, Lord of Logis and Savernay, in Normandy, Lord of the Honours of Forncet and Framlingham, Hereditary Patron of Thetford and Felixstowe Priories. He was a witness to King Stephen's second charter of liberties, 1136, shortly afterward was created Earl of Norfolk, styled Earl of East Anglia, February 2, 1141 ; was Sheriff of Norfolk, 1156–57 ; a crusader, 1177 ; *m.*, first, **GUNDREDA** —— ; *m.*, second, **JULIANA**, *dau.* of **Alberic de Vere**,[2] afterward Earl of Oxford, and *d.* before March 9, 1177.

ROGER, his son, *b.* before 1150, *d.* 1221, succeeded to his titles and estates ; was restored as second Earl of Norfolk, and confirmed Hereditary Steward of the King's Household, November 25, 1189. He was frequently a judge in the King's Court, ambassador to France and Scotland, Chief Judge, April, 1197, one of the twenty-five barons, guardians of the Great Charter, June, 1215 ; *m.*, before 1195, **ISABEL DE WARRENNE**, *dau.* of **Hamelyn Plantagenet**, natural son of **Geoffrey of Anjou**. Her mother was **Isabel**, *dau.* of **William** (by **Ella**, *dau.* of **Robert de Belesme**), and granddaughter of **William de Warrenne**, who *m.*, as her second husband, **Isabel de Vermandois** (*q. v.*).

HUGH, son of **Roger** and **Isabel (de Warrenne) le Bigod**, *b.* before 1195, had seisin of his father's lands, August 2, 1221 ; was Earl of Norfolk, Hereditary Steward of the Household, Bearer of the Banner of S. Edmund, Warden of Ranford Forest,

---

[1] Arms ; *or*, a cross *gules*.
[2] Arms of De Vere, quarterly *gules* and *or*, in the first a mullet *argent*.

etc.; *m.*, in 1212, **MAUD**, *dau.* of **William Marshal**, Earl of Pembroke (*q. v.*), and *d.* February, 1225. Issue :

i.   **ROGER**, his heir, *b.* 1213.

ii.   **RALPH**, *m.* **BERTA**, *dau.* of **Thomas**, Lord **Furnival** (*q. v.*). Issue :

         ISABEL, *m.* **GILBERT**, son of **Walter de Lacy**,[1] by **Margaret de Braose** (*q. v.*). Issue :

             Margaret, *m.* John de Verdon (*q. v.*).

             Maud, *m.* Peter de Genevil, said to be a brother of de Joinville, the chronicler.

Authorities : Doyle's Official Baronage, ii., 574–77. Bouillet, Atlas d'Histoire, etc. (1865), 396–97. Sir T. C. Banks, Baronage of England, iii., 553–687. F. P. Barnard, Conquest of Ireland, *pp.* 62–111.

---

[1] He was son of **Hugh de Lacy**, of Webbely Castle, Lord of Meath, and Justice of Ireland, who *m.* a *dau.* of **Roderick**, King of Connaught, and was murdered by Malvo Miadach in 1186. He was third in descent from **Walter de Laci**, who founded S. Peter's Church, Hereford, and *d.* 1084. Arms, *or* a fesse *gules.*

BLAKEWAY, OF SHROPSHIRE, ENGLAND

THIS family is of standing in the neighbourhood of Shrewsbury, and its pedigree is traced to **Thomas Blakeway**, of Cronkhill, Salop, who *d.* in August, 1593.

JOHN BLAKEWAY, of Clapham Common, and latterly of Brighton, *b.* October 11, 1789 ; *m.*, May 19, 1818, **SARAH**, fifth *dau.* of **Philip William** and **Sarah (Aikin) Thomas** (*q. v.*), and *d.* January 10, 1877, and is buried at Brighton Cemetery ; his wife *d.* February 4, 1869, and is buried beside her husband.   Issue :

i.   **SARAH**, *b.* April 15, 1819 ; *m.*, first, May 8, 1845, **PHILIP HENRY ROUQUETTI**, of Walthamstow, Essex, who *d.* February 11, 1871. Issue (surname ROUQUETTI) :

    i.   PHILIP JOHN GRACCHUS.
    ii.   MARGARET ALMA CRISIS.
    iii. HENRY SEYMOUR, *m.* CATHERINE THURBURN.
    iv.   HERMANN EDWARD.
    v.   GEORGE ALFRED, *m.* SUSAN HUGHES.
    vi.   SARAH ELEANORA, *m.* GEORGE HUBBARD.
    vii. LOUIS PRESTWICH, *m.* LUCIE ST. AMAND.
    viii. WILLIAM FREDERICK BLAKEWAY.

    MRS. ROUQUETTI *m.*, second, October 14, 1886, **CHARLES ECCLES**, of Shackleford House, Surrey, and Shentwood, in Honiton, Co. Devon, who *d. s. p.* June 9, 1890.

ii.   **CATHERINE**, *b.* October 9, 1820 ; *m.*, June 28, 1842, **EDWARD I'ANSON**, of Clapham, President of the Institute of British Architects, and *d.* October 11, 1866.   Issue (surname I'ANSON) :

  i. EDWARD BLAKEWAY.
  ii. PHILIP, *d. u.*
  iii. CATHERINE BLAKEWAY.
  iv. LAVINIA, *d. y.*
  v. MARY, *m.* DAVID DE PURY, of Neuchatel.
  vi. HARRIET, *m.*—— HENSLOW.
  vii. EMMA.
  viii. ISABEL, *d. y.*

iii **ELLEN,** *b.* December 13, 1822 ; *m.,* June 20, 1850, **HENRY SAMUEL KING,** of Manor House, Chigwell, Essex, and *d.* February 17, 1860. Issue (surname KING) ·

  i. HENRY SEYMOUR, knighted K.C.I.E., now M.P. for Kingston-on-Hull ; *m.* JULIA JENKINS, of Canada.
  ii. HAROLD, *d. u.*
  iii. RICHARD.
  iv. ELLEN, *m.* DR. MURPHY.

iv. **HARRIET,** *b.* November 4, 1824 ; *d. u.,* June 21, 1888.

v. **PHILIP EDWARD,** *b.* December 4, 1826 ; *m.,* June 27, 1857, **MARIA ANN,** *dau.* of **Thomas Wootton,** of St. John's Wood Road, London, by **Maria Ann,** *dau.* of **John Cordy,** of Shenley, Co. Herts, and *d.* December 27, 1871, and is buried at Shenley. Issue :

  1. MABEL WOOTTON.
  ii. ELLEN MARIA, *m.,* January 10, 1882, ANDREW ARCHIBALD, third son of Sir Andrew Buchanan, Bart., of Craigend Castle, Stirling. Issue : Andrew Sinclair, *b.* 1882.
  iii. PHILIP JOHN THOMAS, *m.,* August, 1893, SYBIL, *dau.* of Francis Ricardo, Esq.
  iv. THOMAS WOOTTON.

vi. **MARY ANN,** *b.* October 27, 1828 ; *m.* February 12, 1852, **ROBERT MUSHET,** of the Royal Mint. Issue (surname MUSHET) :

  MARION, GRACE, ROBERT S., and PHILIP BLAKEWAY.

vii. **JOHN THOMAS,** *b.* February 28, 1830 ; *d. u.,* August 28, 1860, is buried at Southampton.

viii. **ELIZABETH,** *b.* August 2, 1831 ; *m.,* February 11, 1854, **GEORGE SMITH,** of Park Lane, Middlesex, and Brackley Lodge, Co. Surrey. A member of the great publishing house of Smith, Elder & Co., London. Publishers for Thackeray and the Brownings. Issue (surname SMITH) :

  i. ELIZABETH ALEXANDRINA, *m.* HENRY YATES THOMPSON, of Thingwall, Co. Lancaster.
  ii. ETHEL SARAH.
  iii. GEORGE MURRAY, *m.* Hon. ELLEN STRUTT, *dau.* of Edward, first Lord Belper.
  iv. ISABEL MARION, *m.* REGINALD JOHN SMITH, Queen's Counsel.
  v. ALEXANDER MURRAY, *m.* EMILY, *dau.* of the Very Rev. George Granville Bradley, D.D., Dean of Westminster.

ix. **ISABEL,** *b.* October 20, 1832 ; *m.,* July 13, 1854, **ISAAC HADWEN,** of Liverpool, who *d.* February 23, 1876. Issue (surname HADWEN) :

i.   ISABELLA DOROTHEA, *m.* JOHN DYMOND CROSFIELD, of Forest Hey, Sandiway, near Northwich, to whose courtesy the author is indebted for this Blakeway pedigree, and the revision of that of the Thomas family of Highbury Grove, England.
ii.   EDITH ELLEN.
iii. MARGARET ZOË.

WILLIAM EVAN, *b.* November 1, 1837, became the managing partner of the banking-house of Messrs. P. W. Thomas's Sons & Co. He *m.*, February 7, 1863, MARY ANN, *dau.* of Samuel Tomkins, of Lombard Street, by Jane Walker, only *dau.* of Captain James Urquhart Murray Leith, of Barrack, Co. Aberdeen, N. B. Issue :

i.   LILIAN MARY, *m.* SYLVAIN MAYER.
ii.   AMY JANE.
iii. JOHN PRESTWICH.
iv.   DENYS BROOKE.
v.   ISOBEL ALICIA.
vi.   EVAN ROYCROFT, *d. i.*

BORDLEY

REV. STEPHEN BORDLEY, Prebendary of S. Paul's Cathedral, London, England, had, with other issue : **STEPHEN,** who settled in Kent Co., Md. ; and **THOMAS,** *b.* in 1682, removed with his brother to Maryland in 1694, practised law at Annapolis, and became very celebrated in his profession. Was Attorney-General of Maryland from 1715 until his death. He *m.*, first, **RACHEL BEARD,** of Annapolis, and had issue by her : **STEPHEN,** *b.* in 1709, practised law at Annapolis, and *d. s. p.* December 6, 1764 ; **WILLIAM,** *b.* in 1716 ; *m.* —— **PEARCE,** and had a son and daughter, who both *d. i. ;* **ELIZABETH,** *b.* in 1717 ; *d. u.* November 28, 1789, at her brother Beale's residence ; and **JOHN,** *b.* in 1721, *m.* and settled near Chestertown, Md. ; *d. s. p.* in 1761.

THOMAS BORDLEY *m.*, second, September 1, 1723, **MRS. ARIANA (VANDERHEYDEN) FRISBY,** and *d.* October 11, 1726. Further issue : **THOMAS,** *b.* in 1724, practised law, and *d. s. p.* in England in 1747 ; **MATTHIAS,** *b.* in 1725, at Annapolis, *m.* **PEGGY BIGGER,** who *d.* in childbirth, in 1756, and her husband followed her in a few months, leaving no issue ; and **JOHN BEALE,** *of whom presently.*

JOHN BEALE, third son of **Thomas** and **Ariana (Vanderheyden) Bordley,** *b.* February 1, 1726–27 ; in 1753 appointed Clerk of Baltimore Co., which then included Harford, and removed to a farm near Joppa, where he resided some twelve years. In 1765 removed to Baltimore City, and practised law there ; in 1766 appointed one of the Judges of the Provincial Court ; in 1767 Judge of Admiralty. In 1770 removed to Wye Island, to an estate bequeathed his wife by her brother, Philemon Lloyd Chew, who *d. s. p.* that year. In 1774 he was a member of the Committee of Public Safety, and in 1777 appointed one of the Judges of the General Court. In 1791 he removed to Philadelphia, and resided there during the rest of his life. He published

"Sketches on Rotation of Crops," 1792 ; "Essays on Husbandry,"
1799 ; and "Courses of Crops in England and Maryland," 1804.
He *m.*, first, in 1751, **MARGARET**, *dau.* of **Samuel** and **Henrietta Maria (Lloyd) Chew**, and had issue by her :

i.   **THOMAS**, *b.* in 1755 ; *d.* in 1771.
ii. **MATTHIAS**, *b.* in 1757 ; *m.* **SUSAN GARDNER**, *dau.* of **Daniel**
       Charles and **Mary (Key) Heath.**
iii. **JOHN.**
iv. **HENRIETTA MARIA**, *m.* **MAJOR DAVID ROSS**, of Chambersburg, Pa.

J. BEALE BORDLEY was *m.*, second, October 8, 1776, at
Philadelphia, by Rev. William White, afterward Bishop of Pennsylvania, to **Mrs. SARAH MIFFLIN**, *dau.* of **William** and **Jane
(Roberts) Fishbourne**, and *d.* January 26, 1804. His widow *d.*
May 16, 1816, leaving a *dau.*, **ELIZABETH**, *b.* October 21, 1777 ; *m.*,
June 5, 1817, **DR. JAMES GIBSON**, and *d. s. p.* August 23, 1863.

Authority : Mrs. E. B. Gibson's Sketches of the Bordley Family, 1865, and Maryland Records.

BOWNE

THOMAS BOWNE, baptized May 25, 1595, at Matlock, in Derbyshire, England ; *d.* September 18, 1677, having had issue :

i. **JOHN,** *b.* March 9, 1626-27, *of whom presently.*
ii. **DOROTHY,** *b.* August 14, 1631, who left England for Boston in 1649.
iii. And another *dau.*, **TRUTH,** who remained at Matlock.

JOHN, only son of **Thomas Bowne,** *m.*, first, August 7, 1656, **HANNAH,** *dau.* of **Lieut. Robert Feake** (*q. v.*). She *d.*, February 2, 1677-78, at the house of John and Mary Edson, of London, England. Issue :

i. **JOHN,** *b.* March 13, 1656-57 ; *d.* August 30, 1673.
ii. **ELIZABETH,** *b.* October 8, 1658 ; *m.* **SAMUEL TITUS,** and *d.* February 14, 1721-22.
iii. **MARY,** *b.* January 6, 1660-61.
iv. **ABBIGALL,** *b.* February 5, 1662-63 ; *m.*, March 25, 1686, **RICHARD WILLETTS,** of " Jericoe, on Long Island, husbandman," and *d.* May 14, 1703.
v. **HANNAH,** *b.* April 10, 1665 ; *m.* **BENJAMIN,** "son of **Anthony Field Yeoman,** of Long Island, *dec'd*," and *d.* December 30, 1707.
vi. **SAMUEL,** *b.* September 21, 1667, *of whom presently.*
vii. **DOROTHY,** *b.* March 29, 1669 ; *m.*, May 27, 1689, **HENRY FRANCKLYN,** "of Flushing, bricklayer, son of **Matthew,** *dec'd*," and *d.* November 26, 1690.
viii. **MARTHA JOHANNAH,** *b.* August 17, 1673 ; *m.*, November 9, 1695, **JOSEPH,** son of **John Thorne,** who *d.* in May, 1727 ; his wife *d.* August 11, 1750.

JOHN BOWNE *m.*, second, February 2, 1679-80, **HANNAH BICKERSTAFFE,** who *d.* June 7, 1690. Issue :

ix **SARAH,** *b.* December 14, 1680 ; *d.* May 18, 1681.
x **SARAH,** *b.* February 17, 1681-82.
xi. **JOHN,** *b.* September 10, 1683 ; *d.* October 25, 1683.

xii.   **THOMAS,** *b.* November 26 ; *d.* December 17, 1684.
xiii.   **JOHN,** *b.* September 9, 1686 ; *m.* July 21, 1714, **ELIZABETH,** *dau.* of
          Joseph and **Mary (Townley) Lawrence** (*q. v.*).
xiv.   **ABIGAL,** *b.* July 5 ; *d.* July 13, 1688.

JOHN BOWNE, *m.,* third, June 26, 1693, **MARY,** *dau.* of **James**
and **Sarah Cock,** of Mattinecott, L. I., and *d.* December 20,
1695.   Further issue :

xv.   **AMY,** *b.* April 1, 1694.
xvi.   **RUTH,** *b.* January 30, 1695-96.

SAMUEL, second son of **John** and **Hannah (Feake) Bowne,** *b.*
September 21, 1667 ; was a minister of the Society of Friends.
October 4, 1691, Philadelphia meeting licensed his marriage to
MARY, *dau.* of **Captain Becket** (said to have been killed
fighting under Marlborough), and his wife, **Eleanor Percy,** of
Northumberland.   By her he had issue :

i.   **SAMUEL, JR.,** *b.* January 29, 1692-93, *of whom presently.*
ii.   **THOMAS,** *b.* April 7, 1694 (*q. v.*).
iii.   **ELLNER,** *b.* April 20, 1695 ; *m.,* October 9, 1718, **ISAAC HORNER,**
          of " Mansfield, Bourlington Co., Wast New Jursey."
iv.   **HANNAH,** *b.* March 31, 1697 ; *m.,* April 6, 1717, **RICHARD LAW-
          RENCE** (*q. v.*).
v.   **JOHN,** *b.* September 11, 1698 (*q. v.*).
vi.   **MARY,** *b.* October 21, 1699 ; *m.,* January 14, 1719-20, **JOHN KEESE.**
vii.   **ROABORD,** *b.* January 17, 1700-1 ; *m.,* November 16, 1724, **MAR-
          GARET,** *dau.* of **Joseph Latham,** of Cow Neck, Hempstead, L. I.,
          and *d.* before July 3, 1746, when his *dau.* **MARY** *m.* **HENERY,** son of
          Robert and **Rebeckah Haydock.**
viii.   **WILLIAM,** *b.* April 1, 1702 ; *d.* April 15, 1702.
ix.   **ELIZABETH,** *b.* October 11, 1704.
x.   **BENJAMIN,** *b.* March 13, 1707 ; *d.* May 13, 1707.

MARY, wife of **SAMUEL BOWNE,** *d.* August 21, 1707, and he
m., second, December 8, 1709, **HANNAH SMITH,** of Flushing, and had further issue :

xi.   **SARAH,** *b.* September 30, 1710 ; *m.,* March 12, 1729, **WILLIAM,** son
          of **William Burling** (*q. v.*).
xii.   **JOSEPH,** *b.* February 25, 1711-12 ; *m.,* first, November 13, 1735, **SA-
          RAH,** *dau.* of **Obadiah Lawrence,** who *d.* January 5, 1740, and
          second, June 13, 1745, **JUDITH,** *dau.* of **Jonathan Morrell,** *dec'd.*
xiii.   **ANNE,** *b.* October 17, 1715.
xiv.   **BENJAMIN,** *b.* August 1, 1717.
xv.   **ELISEBETH,** *b.* November 26, 1720.

October 11, 1733, **MRS. HANNAH (SMITH) BOWNE** *d.*, and her husband *m.*, third, November 14, 1735, **MRS. GRACE COWPERTHWAITE**, widow (who *d.* November 22, 1760), and *d.* May 30, 1745, at his own house. "A man serviceable in his day, bore a public testimony in meetings, and his house was always open to entertain Friends."

SAMUEL, eldest son of **Samuel** and **Mary (Becket) Bowne**, *b.* January 29, 1692–93; *m.*, September 20, 1716, **SARAH FRANKLIN, JR.**, and *d.* 1769. Issue :

i.   **WILLIAM**, *b.* March 6, 1719–20, *of whom presently.*
ii. **SAMUEL**, *b.* May 14, 1721 (*q. v.*).
iii. **MARY**, *b.* March 3, 1723–24 ; *m.* **JOSEPH FARRINGTON.**
iv. **AMY**, *b.* 1724 ; *m.* **GEORGE EMBREE.**
v.   **SARAH**, *b.* 1726 ; *m.* **WILLIAM TITUS.**
vi. **JAMES**, *b.* 1728 (*q. v.*).

WILLIAM, eldest son of **Samuel** and **Sarah (Franklin) Bowne**, *b.* March 6, 1719–20 ; *m.* **ELIZABETH WILLETT**, and *d.* October 18, 1747 ; his wife *d.* the same year. **WILLETT**, their son, *b.* August 8, 1745 ; *m.*, first, **DEBORAH ———**. Issue :

i.   **WILLIAM**, *b.* March 15, 1771 ; *m.* **MARY ———**. Issue :
       Isaac Willett, *b.* August 2, 1795.

WILLETT *m.*, second, **HANNAH ———** (*b.* March 26, 1755). Further issue :

ii.   **PHILIP**, *b.* August 5, 1785.
iii. **JAMES**, *b.* October 26, 1787.
iv.   **SAMUEL**, *b.* January 1, 1789.
v.   **JOHN**, *b.* October 17, 1790.
vi.   **HANNAH**, *b.* July 23, 1792.
vii. **BENJAMIN**, *b.* February 9, 1794.
viii. **SCOTT**, *b.* September 30, 1796.

SAMUEL, second son of **Samuel** and **Sarah (Franklin) Bowne**, *b.* May 14, 1721, *m.* **ABIGAIL BURLING** (*b.* February 25, 1723–24) and had issue :

i.   **EDWARD**, *b* September 3, 1742 ; *d.* the 22d.
ii.   **JAMES**, *b.* March 20, 1743–44.
iii. **SAMUEL**, *b.* August 4th ; *d.* August 21, 1746.
iv.   **ELIZABETH**, *b.* November 19, 1748 ; *d.* November 22, 1752.
v.   **SAMUEL**, *b.* June 25, 1750 ; *d.* July 23, 1752.
vi.   **MATTHEW**, *b.* July 19, 1752.
vii. **ABIGAIL**, *b.* October 21, 1754.

viii.   **SARAH**, *b.* January 14, 1757 ; *d.* May 22, 1760.
ix.   **MARY**, *b.* August 8th ; *d.* August 24, 1761.
x.   **WILLIAM**, *b.* March 9, 1763.
xi.   **SAMUEL**, *b.* April 5, 1767 ; *m.* **HANNAH** —— and had issue :

    i.   **ELIZA**, *b.* January 15, 1790.
    ii.   **THOMAS P.**, *b.* November 30, 1792.

JAMES, youngest son of **Samuel** and **Sarah (Franklin) Bowne**, *b.* 1728, *m.*, 1767, **CAROLINE RODMAN.** Issue :

i.   **CATHERINE**, *m.* **JOHN MURRAY.**
ii.   **WALTER**, *b.* September 26, 1770, *of whom presently.*
iii.   **ELIZABETH**, *b.* March 10, 1772 ; *m.* **GEORGE TOWNSEND.**
iv.   **JOHN R.**, *b.* May 27, 1774 ; *m.* **GRACE SANDS.**
v.   **CAROLINE**, *b.* March 25, 1779.

WALTER, eldest son of **James** and **Caroline (Rodman) Bowne**, *b.* September 26, 1770 ; was a prominent politician and business man of New York City, Mayor in 1828–33 ; *m.*, May 1, 1803, **ELIZA**, *dau.* of **Dr. Robert** and **Mary (King) Southgate**, and *d.* leaving issue :

i.   **WALTER**, *b.* 1806 ; *m.* **ELIZA RAPELYE.** Issue :

    i.   **ELIZA**, *m.* **SPENCER SMITH.**
    ii.   **WALTER**, *d. u.*
    iii.   **SIMON**, *m.* **EMMA SMITH.**
    iv.   **HELEN**, *m.* **SYLVANUS RIKER.**
    v.   **FREDERIC**, *m.* **MRS. HUNTINGTON.**
    vi.   **ROBERT**, *m.* **JESSIE DRAPER.**
    vii.   **MARY**, *m.* **JAMES MURRAY.**
    viii.   **CAROLINE.**

ii.   **MARY KING**, *b.* ——, 1808 ; *m.* **JOHN W. LAWRENCE** (*q. v.*).

THOMAS, second son of **Samuel** and **Mary (Becket) Bowne**, *b.* April 2, 1694, lived at Oyster Bay, L. I. ; *m.*, March 7, 1715–16, **HANNAH**, *dau.* of **John Underhill**, *dec.*, of Mattinecock.' Issue :

i.   **MARY**, *b.* July 4, 1717.
ii.   **THOMAS**, *b.* May 12, 1719.
iii.   **DANIEL**, *b.* February 6, 1722–23 ; *m.*, December 11, 1746, **SARAH**, *dau.* of **Samuel** and **Hannah Stringham.** Issue :

    i.   **THOMAS**, *b.* March 27, 1748 ; *d.* September 12, 1751.
    ii.   **ANN**, *b.* July 31, 1751.
    iii.   **MARY**, *b.* January 5, 1754.
    iv.   **SARAH**, *b.* February 19, 1763.

iv.   **JACOB**, *b.* October 6, 1724.

JOHN, third son of **Samuel** and **Mary (Becket) Bowne,** *b.* September 11, 1698; *m.*, 1738, **DINAH UNDERHILL,** and *d.* 1757. Issue:

i.   **THOMAS,** *b.* May 11, 1739.
ii.   **MARY,** *b.* April 14, 1741.
iii.   **JOHN,** *b.* January 31, 1742–43; *m.* **ANNE** ——. Issue:

     i.   **MARY,** *b.* January 7, 1784.
     ii.   **ANNE,** *b.* September 5, 1785.
     iii.   **ELIZABETH,** *b.* September 30, 1787.
     iv.   **CATHERINE,** *b.* September 20, 1789.

iv.   **ROBERT,** *b.* January 31, 1744–45; *m.* **ELIZABETH** ——. Issue:

     i.   **MARY,** *b.* September 7, 1774.
     ii.   **ROBERT H.,** *b.* October 27, 1776.
     iii.   **JOHN L.,** *b.* February 11, 1779.
     iv.   **SARAH,** *b.* September 7, 1781.
     v.   **HANNAH,** *b.* August 14, 1784.
     vi.   **ELIZABETH,** *b.* October 4, 1789.
     vii.   **JANE P.,** *b.* January 31, 1792.

Authorities: Friends' Records of Long Island and New York, A Girl's Life Eighty Years Ago, New York, 1887, and Family Papers through Mrs. W. B. Lawrence.

BRAITHWAITE, OF KENDAL AND LONDON

WILLIAM BRAITHWAITE, *m.* **AGNES SATTER-THWAITE,** and was *bu.* at Hawkeshead Church, October 10, 1641. Their son **GEORGE,** baptized at Hawkshead, April 30, 1644, *m.* **AGNES BENSON,** and d. 1708. Their son, GEORGE, of Kendal, *m.* SARAH —— (*d.* 1722); he *d.* 1735, leaving a son George, *of whom presently.*

This **GEORGE BRAITHWAITE,** *b.* 1714; *m.* at Darlington, in 1744, **ALICE,** youngest *dau.* of **Thomas** and **Sarah Forster,** of Hawthorne, Durham; and *d.* September 18, 1753, leaving an only surviving son, **GEORGE,** *b.* March 29, 1746; *m.,* May 13, 1767, **DEBORAH,** *dau.* of Isaac and Rachel Wilson; *d.* September 11, 1821. He *d.* January 5, 1812, leaving, besides GEORGE, his eldest son, and three daughters, a second son, ISAAC, *b.* January 3, 1781; *m.* March 16, 1808, ANNA, *dau.* of Charles Lloyd, Esq., of Birmingham; *d.* December 18, 1859; he *d.* December 27, 1861, leaving with other issue a third son, Charles Lloyd, of Gillclose, Kendal, *of whom presently;* and a sixth son, Joseph Bevan (*q. v.*).

CHARLES LLOYD, third son of **Isaac** and **Anna (Lloyd) Braithwaite,** *b.* December 10, 1811, *m.,* July 3, 1838, **SU-SANNA,** *dau.* of **Isaac** and **Mary Wilson,** of High Wray. Issue:

i.   **CHARLES LLOYD,** *b.* March 24, 1840.
ii.   **ISAAC,** *b.* August 9, 1844; *m.,* October 14, 1890, **MARY SNOWDEN,** *dau.* of **Dr. Richard Henry Thomas,** *q. v.,* and resides at "Elmhurst," near Kendal.
iii. **ANNA MARY.**

JOSEPH BEVAN, sixth son of **Isaac** and **Anna (Lloyd) Braithwaite,** *b.* June 21, 1818, is a Barrister-at-Law of London, and Minister of the Society of Friends ; he *m.*, at Banbury, August 27, 1851, **MARTHA,** *dau.* of **Joseph Ashby Gillett, Esq.,** who *d.* 1895. Issue :

i.   **JOSEPH BEVAN,** *b.* October 5, 1855.
ii. **GEORGE,** *b.* March 5, 1861.
iii. **WILLIAM CHARLES,** *b.* December 23, 1862.
iv. **MARTHA.**
v.   **ANNA LLOYD,** *m.* **DR. RICHARD HENRY THOMAS** (*q. v.*).
vi. **MARY CAROLINE.**
vii. **ELIZABETH.**
viii. **RACHEL BARCLAY.**
ix. **CATHERINE LYDIA.**

Authority : Foster's Pedigree of Braithwaite, of Kendal.

BRAOSE, OF BRAMBER, ENGLAND

WILLIAM DE BRAOSE, Lord of Bramber, in Sussex, in 1075 had a son, **PHILIP,** recorded as about to go to the Holy Land in 1095. His son, WILLIAM, *m.* BERTA, *dau.* and *co-h.* of Milo Fitz Walter, Earl of Hereford (who *d.* December 24, 1144), by Sibil, *dau.* and *heir.*

DE BRAOSE

of Bernard Newmarch, and Nesta ap Griffith, of Wales, with whom he received the lands of Brecknock, Overwent, and Gower. Their son, William, living in 1140, was Sheriff of Herefordshire 1192–99, and had an uncle, Philip De Wigornia, in Ireland, for the King, in 1175.

WILLIAM, Jr., son of the second **William de Braose,** was Lord of Bramber and Brecknock, probably Sheriff, 1206–07, and a great Baron, active in the Welsh marches. He *m.* **MAHAULT DE S. WALERIE,**[1] lady of Haye, a noble and high-spirited woman, who was captured in Ireland, with her eldest son, in 1210, and starved to death at Windsor by order of King John. Her husband rebelling against the King, she had fled there for safety. William de Braose escaping beyond sea, *d.* in 1211, in poverty, at Paris. Issue:

i.   **WILLIAM,** starved, with his mother, leaving issue:

    i.   JOHN, who founded the house of Braose of Gower.
    ii. ANNORA, *m.* HUGH MORTIMER (*q. v.*).

[1] Arms: Or two lions passant guardant gules.

216

ii.   **GILES**, consecrated Bishop of Hereford, September 24, 1200, who succeeded in regaining the confiscated estates of the family for his younger brother, Reginald, and *d.* 1215.

iii.   **REGINALD**, *of whom presently.*

iv.   **JOHN**, called "of Knyll."

v.   **JOANE**, according to Dugdale, *m.* **RICHARD**, Lord Percy.

vi.   **LORETTA**, *m.* **ROBERT FITZ PERNELL BEAUMONT**, Earl of Leicester.

vii.   **MARGARET**, *m.* **WALTER DE LACY** (*q. v.*).

viii.   **MAUD**, *m.* **GRIFFITH AP RHYS**, Prince of South Wales.

REGINALD, third son of **William** and **Mahault de Braose**, *m.*, first, **GLADYS**,[1] *dau.* of **Llewellyn ap Jorwerth**, *d. s. p.* ; *m.*, second, **GRACIA**, *dau.* and *co-h.* of **William**, son of **Henry Briwere**,[2] and *d.* 1222–28. Issue :

    WILLIAM, engaged in frequent warfare with his Welsh neighbours ; having been treacherously seized at a banquet by Prince Llewellyn ap Jorwerth, was hanged in April, 1229, on suspicion of alienating the affections of his wife. He *m.* **EVE**, *dau.* of **William Marshall** (*q.v.*). Issue :

i.   **ISABEL**, *m.* **DAVID**, son of Prince Llewellyn.

ii.   **MAUD**, *m.* **ROGER MORTIMER** (*q. v.*), and carried to him the lands of Radnor, the third part of the town of S. Clears, and the commotes of Amgoed and Pebidiog, the castle, manor, and forest of Narberth, in Pembrokeshire, etc.

iii.   **EVE**, *m.* **WILLIAM DE CANTILUPE**.

iv.   **ELEANOR**, *m.* **HUMPHREY DE BOHUN**, sixth of the name, who *d.*, October 27, 1265, a prisoner in Beeston Castle, Cheshire, after Evesham battle.

Authorities : Banks's Baronia, i., 42, Courthope and Nicolas's Peerage, 71. Bridgeman's Princes of South Wales, 40, 81, etc. Barnard's Conquest of Ireland, A. C. Evans's Royal Charters of Caermarthen, 1878, *pp.* 48, 49. Eyton's Itinerary, King Henry II., 53, 191, 215, etc. Thomas Nicholas's Annals of Wales, i., 66–70. Elwes and Robinson, Western Sussex, 1876, *pp.* 45-50.

[1] Banks's Baronage calls her second wife, *m.* afterward Ralph Mortimer.

[2] Arms : Gules two bends wavy or.

BROOKE

ROBERT BROOKE, *b.* June 3, 1602, at London ; *m.*, first, February 27, 1627, **MARY BAKER,** who was *b.* at Battel ; and second, May 11, 1635, **MARY,** *dau.* of **Roger Mainwaring, D.D.,** Dean of Worcester, and afterward Bishop of S. David's. June 29, 1650, **ROBERT BROOKE** arrived out of England in Maryland, bringing his family and twenty-eight servants with him, and his family record says " was the first that did seat Patuxent about twenty miles up the river at Della Brooke.   July 20, 1652, he took oath as a member of the Provincial Council, and was afterward its President.   In the year 1652 he removed to Brooke Place, being right against Della Brooke.   July 20, 1655, he departed this world, and lyeth buried at Brooke Place Manor, and his wife, **MARY,** departed this life November 29, 1663."   By his first wife he had issue :

i.   **BAKER,** *b.* November 16, 1628, at Battel.
ii.   **MARY,** *b.* February 19, 1630–31.
iii.   **THOMAS,** *b.* June 23, 1632.
iv.   **BARBARY,** *b.* at Wickham.

By his second wife he had further issue :

v.   **CHARLES,** *b.* April 3, 1636, at S. Giles's-in-the-Fields, Middlesex.
vi.   **ROGER,** *b.* September 20, 1637, *of whom presently.*
vii.   **ROBERT,** *b.* April 21, 1639, at London, in S. Bride's Parish.
viii. **JOHN,** *b.* September 20, 1640, at Battel.
ix.   **MARY,** *b.* April 14, 1642, at Battel.
x.   **ANN,** *b.* January 22, 1645–46, at Bretnoe (Brecknock).
xi.   **FRANCES,** *b.* May 30, 1648, at Worwell, in Hampshire.
xii.   **ELIZABETH** and **HENRY,** *b.* November 28, 1652, at Patuxent.
xiii. **BASIL,** *b.* in 1651, at Della Brooke, and *d.* same day.

Of **ROGER,** second son of **Robert** and **Mary (Mainwaring) Brooke,** *b.* September 20, 1637, at Bretonew (or Brecknock) College, the family record says, " Robert Brooke, Sr., son of Robert Brooke, died April 8, 1700, and lyes buried in the graveyard at his own Plantation on Battel Creek, between his two wives, Dorathy Neal, and second, Mary Wolsley. Where also lyes buried his two daughters by his second wife, Cassandra and Mary, and his grandson, Roger, son of Roger, Jr."

ROGER BROOKE, JR., eldest son of **Roger** and **Dorothy (Neale) Brooke,** *b.* April 12, 1673 ; *m.,* February 23, 1702, **ELIZA,** third *dau.* of **Francis** and **Elizabeth Hutchins** (*q. v.*). Issue :

i.   **ROGER,** *b.* December 3, 1703 ; *d.* May 28, 1705.
ii.   **JAMES,** *b.* February 21, 1705-06, *of whom presently.*
iii.   **ELIZA,** *b.* November 23, 1707.
iv.   **DOROTHY,** *b.* July 3, 1709.
v.   **MARY,** *b.* December 29, 1710.
vi.   **ANN,** *b.* March 29, 1712.
vii.   **ROGER,** *b.* June 10, 1714.
viii.   **CASSANDRA,** *b.* April 3, 1716.
ix.   **PRISCILLA** and **BASIL,** twins, *b.* November 16, 1717.

JAMES, eldest surviving son of **Roger** and **Eliza (Hutchins) Brooke,** *b.* February 21, 1705, "came to housekeeping 25th day of November, 1723," and *m.,* June 21, 1725, **DEBORAH,** eldest *dau.* of **Richard** and **Eliza (Coale) Snowden** (*q. v.*). Issue :

i.   **JAMES,** *b.* in 1731 ; *m.* and had issue at his death, August 21, 1767 :

     i.   **AMOS,** *d.* the same year.
     ii.   **ELIZA,** *m.* **GEORGE ELLICOTT** (*q. v.*).
     iii.   **DEBORAH,** *m.* **GEORGE CHANDLEE** ; *d.* December 31, 1790. Issue :
         Brooke, *b.* in 1785 ; *d.* March 24, 1798.

ii.   **ROGER,** *b.* August 9, 1734, *of whom presently.*
iii.   **RICHARD,** *b.* July 8, 1736 ; *m.* and had issue :

     ELIZA and **ANN.**

iv.   **BASIL,** *b.* December 13, 1738 (*q. v.*).
v.   **ELIZABETH,** *b.* March 22, 1740-41 ; *m.* June 2, 1761, **THOMAS PLEASANTS.** Issue (surname PLEASANTS) :

     i.   **JAMES BROOKE,** *m.* **DEBORAH,** *dau.* of **Basil** and **Elizabeth (Hopkins) Brooke.**
     ii.   **DEBORAH,** *m.* **WILLIAM STABLER** (*q. v.*).
     iii.   **THOMAS SNOWDEN.**
     iv.   **WILLIAM HENRY.**
     v.   **MARY.**
     vi.   **ELIZABETH.**

vi.   **THOMAS,** *b.* March 8, 1743-44.

ROGER, second son of **James** and **Deborah (Snowden) Brooke,** *b.* August 9, 1734; *m.* **MARY MATTHEWS,** who *d.* April 25, 1808. Issue :

i.   **SAMUEL,** *b.* December 9, 1758; *m.* **SARAH GARRIGUES.** Issue :

     i.   **WILLIAM,** *m.,* August 22, 1832, **LYDIA S.,** *dau.* of Bernard and Sarah Gilpin.

     ii.   **ABRAHAM,** *m.,* November 11, 1829, **ELIZABETH,** *dau.* of Samuel and Hannah Y. Lukens. Issue :

         Harriet, *b.* October 18, 1831.

ii.   **MARY,** *b.* July 27, 1760; *m.,* in September, 1791, **THOMAS MOORE,** Patentee of the first refrigerator, about 1803. Laid out as United States Engineer the National road to the West ; from 1818 until his death Civil Engineer of the State of Virginia. Issue :

     i.   **MARY,** *b.* July 8, 1794; *m.* **THOMAS L. REESE** (*q. v.*).

     ii.   **ASA,** *b.* April 25, 1797, *d. u.*

     iii.   **ANN,** *b.* November 17, 1799; *m.* **CALEB B. STABLER** (*q. v.*).

     iv.   **CALEB B.,** *b.* April 26, 1802, *d. s. p.*

iii.   **JAMES,** *b.* March 13, 1762 ; *d.* March 9, 1764.

iv.   **DEBORAH,** *b.* February 6, 1764.

v.   **MARGARET,** *b.* November 23, 1765.

vi.   **SARAH,** *b.* December 29, 1767 ; *m.* **CALEB BENTLEY** (*q. v.*).

vii.   **HANNAH,** *b.* June 5, 1770 ; *m.,* August 27, 1794, **ISAAC BRIGGS,** printer. Issue (surname BRIGGS) :

     i.   **ANNA,** *b.* May 18, 1796.

     ii.   **MARY BROOKE,** *b.* February 17, 1798 ; *m.* **RICHARD BROOKE** (*q. v.*).

     iii.   **DEBORAH,** *b.* August 19, 1799.

     iv.   **SARAH BENTLEY,** *b.* August 9, 1801.

     v.   **ISAAC,** *b.* October 15, 1803.

     vi.   **ELIZABETH,** *b.* October 5, 1807.

     vii.   **MARGARET,** *b.* September 24, 1812.

     viii.   **WILLIAM HENRY,** *b.* May 6, 1815 ; *m.* **HENRIETTA E.,** fourth *dau.* of Samuel and Mary (Howard) Thomas (*q. v.*). Issue :

         i.   Mary Z.

         ii.   Edward Thomas, *m.* Fanny Beckwith. Issue :

            Charles Edward, Samuel Thomas, William, Arthur, Clara.

         iii.   Hannah B.

         iv.   Susan.

         v.   Sarah Ellen.

viii.   **ELIZABETH,** *b.* August 25, 1772 ; *d.* January 21, 1774.

ix.   **ROGER,** *b.* November 24, 1774, *of whom presently.*

x.   **DOROTHY,** *b.* December 24, 1776; *m.* **GERARD T. HOPKINS** (*q. v.*).

ROGER, third son of **Roger** and **Mary Brooke,** *b.* November 24, 1774 ; *m.,* first, August 21, 1804, **MARY PLEASANTS,** *dau.* of **Isaac Younghusband,** who *d.* in 1837 ; and second, May

13, 1840, **SARAH THOMAS,** *dau.* of **Bernard** and **Sarah** **(Thomas) Gilpin** (*q. v.*). By his first wife he had issue :

i.　　**SARAH,** *b.* September 14, 1805 ; *m.* **CHARLES FARQUHAR** (*q. v.*).

ii.　　**MARTHA,** *b.* November 17, 1807, *d. i.*

iii.　　**MARY MATTHEWS,** *b.* January 5, 1809 ; *m.* **ELISHA JOHN HALL ;** both are *d.* Issue :

　　　　i.　　**MARY CATHERINE,** *m.* **SAMUEL A. JANNEY** (*q. v.*).
　　　　ii.　　**LOUISA,** *m.* **GEORGE NESBITT,** of New York. Issue :

　　　　　　i.　　**Louisa.**
　　　　　　ii.　　**George.**
　　　　　　iii.　　**John Hall,** *d. i.*
　　　　　　iv.　　**Thomas,** *d. i.*
　　　　　　v.　　**Roger Brooke,** *d. i.*

　　　　iii. iv. **JOHN** and **MARY,** twins, *d. i.*
　　　　v.　　**MARGARET,** *d. y.*
　　　　vi.　　**JOHN,** *d. i.*

iv.　　**ROGER,** *b.* October 5, 1810, *of whom presently.*

v.　　**GEORGE,** *b.* November 27, 1812 ; *m.*, April 1, 1840, **ELIZA JOR-DAN,** of Norfolk, Va., and *d.* Issue :

　　　　i.　　**LUCY,** *b.* January 23, 1841, *d. i.*
　　　　ii.　　**ALEXANDER JORDAN,** *b.* April 11, 1843 ; *d.* November 20, 1864.
　　　　iii.　　**ALICE,** *b.* July 8, 1845 ; *m.*, December 1, 1870, **JAMES P. STABLER, Jr.** (*q. v.*).
　　　　iv.　　**MARGARET NEWTON,** *b.* December 1, 1847 ; *d.* in December, 1855.
　　　　v.　　**CHARLES F.,** *b.* May 4, 1850.
　　　　vi.　　**ANNIE,** *b.* September 11, 1859.

ROGER, eldest son of **Roger** and **Mary (Younghusband) Brooke,** *b.* October 5, 1810 ; *m.*, first, May 13, 1835, **SARAH,** *dau.* of **Tarlton Pleasants,** of Virginia, and had issue :

i.　　**WILLIAM S.,** *b.* February 4, 1836 ; *m.*, first, March 6, 1862, **MARY HALLOWELL.** Issue :

　　　　i.　　**CAROLINE M.,** *b.* December 29, 1862.
　　　　ii.　　**MARY H.,** *b.* August 30, 1864, *d. u.*

　　　　MRS. MARY H. BROOKE *d.* in November, 1864, and her husband *m.*, second, October 26, 1871, **MARY P. COFFIN.**

ii.　　**MARTHA R.,** *b.* May 22, 1837 ; *m.*, November 6, 1866, **FREDERICK STABLER,** and has issue :

　　　　i.　　**TARLTON BROOKE,** *b.* March 26, 1868 ; *m.* **REBECCA T.,** *dau.* of **William W.** and **Mary E. (Thomas) Moore** (*q. v.*). Issue :
　　　　　　Frederic and **Richard Hallett.**
　　　　ii.　　**ROSE MORRIS,** *b.* May 10, 1867.
　　　　iii.　　**CALEB,** *b.* June 14, 1872.

iii.　　. **MARY P.,** *b.* December 30, 1839.

iv.   **WALTER H.,** *b.* October 24, 1841 ; *m.,* November 24, 1870, **CARO-
      LINE H.,** *dau.* of **Thomas** and **Patience (Haydock) Leggett.**
      Issue :

    i.   **ROBERT H.,** *b.* September 16, 1871.
    ii. **WALTER H.,** *b.* December 1, 1872.
    iii. **GEORGE H.,** *b.* July 9, 1874.
    iv. **WILLIAM,** *b.* October 11, 1876.
    v.   **KATHERINE.**

v.   **TARLTON,** *b.* December 6, 1843 ; *d.* September 28, 1864.
vi.-vii. **ROGER** and **GEORGE,** twins, *b.* August 5, 1846 ; **GEORGE,** *d.* Janu-
      ary 1, 1870 ; **ROGER,** *m.,* September 14, 1871, **LOUISA,** *dau.* of
      Edward and **Lydia Thomas** (*q. v.*).   Issue :

    i.   **EMILIE THOMAS,** *b.* May 30, 1873.
    ii. **SARAH,** *b.* February 9, 1875.
    iii. **JANE PORTER,** *b.* January 28, 1877.
    iv. **ROGER,** *b.* June 14, 1878.
    v.   **EDWARD THOMAS,** *b.* October 18, 1879.

viii. **DEBORAH,** *b.* October 30, 1848, *d. u.*
ix.   **ALBAN,** *b.* September 24, 1850 ; *m.,* January 10, 1878, **SARAH
      PLEASANTS.**

BASIL, fourth son of **James** and **Deborah (Snowden) Brooke,**
b. December 13, 1738 ; *m.,* May 1, 1764, **ELIZABETH,** *dau.*
of **Gerard** and **Mary Hopkins,** who *d.* August 17, 1794, and
her husband *d.* the 22d of the same month.   Issue :

i.   **JAMES,** *b.* May 5, 1766 ; *m.* **HESTHER,** *dau.* of **Isaiah** and **Hannah
      Boone.**   Issue :

    i.   **BASIL,** *b.* October 19, 1798. *d. i.*
    ii. **ISAIAH BOONE,** *b.* December 30, 1800.
    iii. **BASIL,** second, *b.* February 5, 1803.

ii.   **GERARD,** *b.* August 12, 1768, *of whom presently.*
iii. **DEBORAH,** *b.* September 4, 1770 ; *m.* **JAMES BROOKE PLEAS-
      ANTS,** and *d.* February 21, 1835.
iv.   **BASIL,** *b.* April 28, 1772 ; *m.* **MARY ——.**   Issue :

    i.   **ELIZA CUMMINS,** *b.* September 26, 1798.
    ii. **JAMES HARVEY,** *b.* May 15, 1801.
    iii. **THOMAS,** *b.* August 18, 1805 ; *d.* May 19, 1831.
    iv. **DEBORAH,** *b.* July 24, 1807.
    v.   **JANE,** *b.* June 12, 1812.

GERARD, second son of **Basil** and **Elizabeth (Hopkins)
Brooke,** *b.* August 12, 1768 ; *m.,* April 22, 1789, **MARGARET,**
fifth *dau.* of **Richard** and **Sarah (Coale) Thomas** (*q. v.*), who
d. March 5, 1797 ; her husband *d.* in 1821.   Issue :

i.   **RICHARD,** *b.* January 6, 1790, *of whom presently.*
ii.   **JOHN THOMAS,** *b.* November 12, 1791.
iii. **ELIZABETH P.,** *b.* August 12, 1794 ; *m.* **THOMAS P. STABLER**
      (*q. v.*).

RICHARD, eldest son of **Gerard** and **Margaret (Thomas)
Brooke,** *b.* January 6, 1790 ; *m.,* April 21, 1824, **MARY
BROOKE,** second *dau.* of **Isaac** and **Hannah Briggs.** Is-
sue :

i.   **HENRY BRIGGS,** *b.* April 30, 1828.
ii.   **HANNAH BRIGGS,** *b.* September 18, 1829.
iii. **CHARLES H.,** *b.* July 26, 1831 ; *m.,* May 11, 1865, **ANNA FAR-
      QUHAR.** Issue :

    i.   **HENRY,** *b.* September 16, 1866, *d. u.*
    ii. **EDITH,** *b.* May 30, 1869.
    iii. **SARAH B.,** *b.* July 7, 1872.
    iv. **MARY B.,** *b.* May 10, 1875.

iv. **ELIZA,** *b.* December 1, 1834.
v.   **MARGARET,** *b.* January 27, 1838 ; *m.,* May 24, 1864, **DR. WILL-
      IAM EDWARD MAGRUDER.** Issue (surname MAGRUDER) :

    i.   **MARY,** *b.* August 22, 1865.
    ii. **RICHARD BROOKE,** *b.* April 9, 1867.
    iii. **EMMA,** *b.* September 12, 1869.
    iv. **WILLIAM EDWARD,** *b.* June 8, 1873.
    v. **CHARLES BROOKE,** *b.* May 11, 1878.

Authorities : Friends' Records, and family papers.

BROWN

WILLIAM, son of **William Brown,** who *d.* December 28, 1662, was *b.* about 1656, at Puddington, near Willingsborough, Northamptonshire, England, and came to America about 1682, and settled at West Nottingham, in Pennsylvania. He *m.*, first, **DOROTHY** ——, who *d.* at sea on the voyage from England to America; second, in 1684, **ANN MERCER;** third, in 1699, **CATHERINE WILLIAMS,** of Philadelphia; and fourth, in 1711, **MARY MATTHEWS;** and *d.* August 23, 1746. By his second wife he had, with other issue, an eldest son, **MERCER,** *b.* February 27, 1685–86; *m.*, first, in 1710, **JANE RICHARDS,** and second, April 11, 1728, **DINAH,** *dau.* of **John** and **Hannah Churchman,** and *d.* about 1733. His widow *m.*, second, **MORDECAI JAMES,** of Goshen, and *d.*, January 1, 1766, leaving issue by her first husband:

i.   **JOHN,** *b.* in 1729; *m.*, November 21, 1751, **JANE,** *dau.* of John and Jane Pugh.
ii.   **DAVID,** *b.* about 1731; *m.*, first, November 3, 1757, **SARAH,** *dau.* of Joshua and Hannah Brown, of West Nottingham, and second, **ELIZABETH,** who *d.* March 3, 1802, and her husband *d.* about 1781. Issue:

     i.   David, *b.* December 18, 1758.
     ii.   Uriah, *b.* April 18, 1769; *m.,* January 10, 1793, **Mary,** *dau.* of Jacob and Mary Brown, and *d.* Issue: Elizabeth, *b.* August 1, 1794; Sarah, *b.* January 23, 1796; David Uriah, *b.* January 25, 1798; *m.* Rachel, *dau.* of Thomas and Ann Poultney (*q. v.*), and *d. s. p.;* Mary, *b.* June 14, 1800; and Diana, *b.* April 30, 1805.

Authorities: Friends' Records, Cope's Browns of Nottingham, and Mr. Kirk Brown, of Baltimore.

BUCKLEY, OF ROCHDALE, LANCASHIRE

THIS family is of Saxon origin, the name signifying a bleak hill,
according to a pedigree recorded in Sir William Dugdale's "Visitation of the County," 1664–65. It descends from **JOHN DE
BUCKLEY**, whose brother **GEOFFREY** was Dean of
Whalley and Vicar of S. Chad's, Rochdale, and about 1200 wrote
the original grant to Saddleworth Chapel, executed by William
de Stapleton. **JOHN** was Lord of the manor of Buckley in
Hundersfeld, Rochdale, and may have been son of **Geoffrey,**
and grandson of **Adam,** son of **John de Buckeley.** He had
two sons, **GEOFFREY,** killed on the part of King Henry III.,
at the battle of Evesham, and buried in the conventual church
of Evesholme in 1265, and **ADAM,** his heir, who attests deeds in
1323 and 1325 ; *m.* **ALICE,** *dau.* of **Thomas,** son of **William de
Leigh,** and had issue : JOHN, succeeded his father 9 Edward III.,
attests deeds 1339 and 1359, and THOMAS.

ROBERT, son of **John,** living 16 Richard III. (1392–93), had a son
JOHN, attests deeds in 1370 and 1390 ; *m.* **ALICE,** *dau.* and heiress
of **Roger Wolfenden,** 2 Henry IV. Issue : RAFE or RADULPHUS,
his heir, and HENRY, living 9 Henry VI. (1430–31).

RAFE, *m.,* 7 Henry V. (1419), **CATHERINE** ——, and had a son
JAMES, *m.,* 38 Henry VI. (1459–60 ?), **MARGARET** ——. Issue :
ROBERT, and ISABELLA, *m.,* 3 Edward IV. (1463), GILBERT, son
of **Lambert de Leigh.**

ROBERT succeeded 10 Edward IV. (1470), and had two sons, THOMAS, his heir, and JOHN, Vicar of Wasperton, Co. Warwick, 11 Henry VII. (1495–96). THOMAS succeeded, 21 Henry VII. (1505–6), attests a deed May 18, 1507, and had a son and heir, JAMES; succeeds in 1512; *m.*, November 12, 1512, ALICE, *dau.* of ―― Howarth, of Howarth, Lancashire. There is an uncertainty about the next three generations. The Visitation pedigree is certainly wrong in making the great-grandfather of **JOHN BUCKLEY**, born in 1613, a Robert, baptized July 6, 1578. The most probable line runs as follows: **JAMES** and **ALICE (Howarth) BUCKLEY** had issue:

i. ROBERT, *d. s. p.* in 1577, possessed of " messuages, lands, and woods at Buckley Manor and Hundersfeld in Lancashire."
ii. THOMAS, *of whom presently.*
iii. HUGO.
iv. ARTHUR, *m. dau.* of **Henry Hamer**, of Hamer, Lancashire.
v. vi. CATHERINE and ELIZABETH, one of whom *m.* THOMAS CHADWICKE, of Heley, Lancashire.

THOMAS, eventual heir of **James** and **Alice (Howarth) Buckley**, attests deeds May 16, 1561, August 16, 1580, and October 22, 1581; *m.*, 14 Henry VIII., **Margery**, *dau.* of **Ranulph Haworth**, and *d.* August 18, 1588. Issue: A son, ROBERT, baptized July 6, 1578; *m.* GRACE, *dau.* and heiress of John Holt, of Ashworth, Lancashire. Issue: Possibly THOMAS, ELIZABETH, and MARGARET, who make the next generation on the pedigree, as well as ROBERT, *d. u.,* ABELL, his heir, *of whom presently,* and THOMAS, Rector of Damoram, Co. Wilts, *d. u.*

ABELL, second son and heir of **Robert** and **Grace (Holt) Buckley**, was entered at Gray's Inn, November 5, 1602. Rented land from Byron, at Buckley pastures, about 1609; was called to the Bar at Staple Inn, Gray's Inn, June 11, 1617; *m.* **ANNA**, *dau.* and heiress of **Robert Norfolk**, of Barnsley, Yorkshire, and *d.* October 6, 1637. Issue:

i. JOHN, his heir, *of whom presently.*
ii. JOSIAH.
iii. THOMAS.
iv. JONAS.
v. MARIA, *m.*, first, FRANCIS WILFORD; *m.*, second, RICHARD EYRE.

JOHN, son and heir of **Abell** and **Anna (Norfolk) Buckley**, *b.* 1613, was admitted to Gray's Inn August 15, 1628; *m.* **BEA-TRICE**, *dau.* and heiress of **William Browne**, of Mexborough and Swynton, Yorkshire, and, March 11, 1664, had issue :

i. **ABELL**, *b.* 1639 ; *m.* **JUDITH**, *dau.* of **Richard Cokain**, of Bury-Hatley, Bedfordshire. Issue :

                MARGARET, BEATRICE.

ii. **JOHN.**
iii. **EDWARD**, *of whom presently.*
iv. **DOROTHY.**
v. **BEATRICE.**
vi. **FRANCES.**
vii. **GRACE.**
viii. **JUDITH.**

EDWARD, third son of **John** and **Beatrice (Browne) Buckley**, would appear to have become the eventual heir of the property. He was buried in Trinity Church, Rochdale, in 1687, leaving issue :

i. **THOMAS**, *of whom presently.*
ii. A *dau.*, *m.* —— **FOSTER**, of Preston, and had a son, **THOMAS** (heir of his cousin, Captain William Buckley), whose grandson, **Edward**, son of **Thomas Forster-Buckley**, sold the property at Rochdale to Robert Entwistle, of Foxholes, and *d.* in 1816.

THOMAS, son of **Edward Buckley**, had a faculty for the West gallery of S. Chad's Church, December 27, 1693, and *d.* 1697, leaving a son and heir, **CAPTAIN WILLIAM BUCKLEY**. August 9, 1722, he had a dispute with Major Samuel Crooke, of Crooke, over the right of way in a narrow lane at Walton, near Preston, which ended in a duel, in which he killed his antagonist. He was tried at the Lancaster Assizes and found guilty of manslaughter, but escaped with a light sentence. May 9, 1730, he made his will, settling his estates on his cousin, Thomas Foster, and finally on his kinsman, **JOHN BUCKLEY**, of Grotton Hall, Saddleworth, Yorkshire.

The latter, probably descended from **William Buckley**, of Quicke and Saddleworth, Yorkshire, who *d.* in the early part of the reign of Queen Elizabeth ; and was of Grotton in 1712 and 1728; his descendant, **Edmund Buckley**, was of Grotton Hall in 1853. The present building was erected in 1664. Of this family undoubtedly was **Lawrence Buckley**, who, with Edmund Ashton, in 1567, was sued by

Sir John Byron (ancestor of the poet) and others, the inhabitants of Rochdale, about a right of way over property at Butterworth and other rights. Also **Barnarde Buckley,** who contested his inheritance against Roger Gartside and John Holte, in 1569, and there is notice of an **Abell Buckley,** apparently *m.* the *dau.* and *co-h.* of Edward Lord, who brought him lands at Butterworth and Todmorden, and *d.* 1640.

Authorities: Dugdale's Visitation, 1664-65, Ed. Rev. F. R. Raine, *pp.* 60-61. Foster's Collectanea Genealogica, iii., 112. Robertson's History of Rochdale, *pp.* 279-80. Record Commission *Inq. Post-mortem.*

THOMAS LEACH

BUCKLEY, OF NEW YORK

So far as known this family begins with **PHINEAS BUCK-LEY,**[1] of London, a trader to the West India Islands and the North American Provinces, who came in that capacity to Philadelphia in the year 1713. There he *m.* **SARAH,** *dau.* of **Elias Hugg,** of Gloucester Co., New Jersey, then in the nineteenth year of her age. Not long after this he went on a trading voyage to Charleston, S. C., and is said to have died of the yellow fever in that city.

WILLIAM, his only child, was *b.* November 13, 1715, in the city of Philadelphia. Left an orphan during his infancy, parental care seems to have been well supplied by his mother's sister, Elizabeth, and her husband, Ennion Williams, of Bristol, Penn., of which town the latter was Chief Burgess, October 3, 1733, to 1737, and a Justice for Bucks Co., November 22, 1738, and frequently afterward. **WILLIAM BUCKLEY** was educated in Philadelphia, and served his apprenticeship with Joshua Maddock, a noted merchant of that city. Inheriting perhaps from his father some predilection for a seafaring life, he made a few voyages to the West Indies, but it appears he soon became weary of this vocation, and we find it recorded that

---

[1] It is thought he belonged to the family of Buckley of Rochdale, but so far there is no proof of the connection.

he married, May 21, 1741, **RUTH**, *dau.* of **Thomas** and **Sarah (Fry) Leach,**[1] of Newport, R. I., *b.* December 21, 1721. In those early days of our country a journey from Newport to Philadelphia was a momentous event, and family tradition informs us that an elderly gentleman who had accompanied William Buckley to Newport, brought the bride home in his tandem, while the groom rode alongside on horseback. After their marriage William and Ruth Buckley settled at Bristol, and he engaged in the milling business of the place; was Chief Burgess from September 12, 1747, to 1754, and a Justice for Bucks Co., June 9, 1752, to 1757, and it is complained in the latter year that he "refuses to give an oath." The Buckley House, a stone structure on the banks of the Delaware River, was inherited by him, and there is still a Buckley Street in the town. The house was burned a number of years ago, and the present water-tower is on its site. During the American Revolution it was used as a hospital for soldiers. In the year 1759 he entered into a partnership with Reese Meredith, of Philadelphia, and while assisting in taking an account of their stock, which was very large, he was seized with pleurisy, the effect of over-exertion and exposure, and *d.* in Philadelphia, March 3d, of the same year. (His will recorded liber L, fo. 238.) His wife *d.* at Bristol, August 20, 1780. Issue :

i.   **PHINEAS,** *b.* April 6, 1742, *of whom presently.*
ii.   **ENNION,** *b.* February 7, 1743-44, *d.* June 19, 1748.
iii.   **WILLIAM,** *b.* July 19, 1745 (*q. v.*).
iv.   **THOMAS,** *b.* January 9, 1746-47 ; *d.* May 3, 1747.
v.   **ISRAEL,** *b.* April 20, 1748 ; *d.* April 4, 1760.
vi.   **ENNION,** *b.* April —, 1750 ; *d.* September 24, 1751.
vii.   **SARAH,** *b.* November 1, 1751 ; *d.* August 2, 1758.
viii. **ELIZABETH,** *b.* March 25, 1753 ; *d. u.,* November 8, 1826.
ix.   **MARGARET,** *b.* August 10, 1754 ; *d.* December 21, 1754.
x.   **REBECCA,** *b.* January 11, 1756 ; *m.* **JAMES FERGUSON.** Issue
       (surname FERGUSON) :

        i.   **WILLIAM.**
        ii.   **JAMES.**
        iii. **SAMUEL B.,** *m.,* October 14, 1821, **SARAH H.** ——, who *d.* at Bridgeport, Conn., September 5, 1886, her husband having died before her.

[1] Thomas Leach was the son of Thomas and Ann Leach, of Chertsey, in the Co. of Surrey, England ; was *b.* July 16, 1682, serving an apprenticeship in London. He removed to Newport, R. I., arriving November 28, 1706. He *m.,* May 5, 1709, Sarah, *dau.* of Thomas and Mary Fry, *b.* December 23, 1685 ; *d.* at Bristol, Penn., March 31, 1755. The arms engraved are from a book-plate, not certainly his.

xi.   **ELIAS**, *b.* May 22, 1757 ; *d.* April 14, 1760.

xii. xiii. **JOSHUA** and **MARY**, twins, *b.* May 10, 1758, and *d.* the same year.

PHINEAS, eldest son of **William** and **Ruth (Leach) Buckley,** was born at Bristol, April 17, 1742. Having no children of their own, his father's uncle and aunt, Ennion and Elizabeth Williams, adopted him. An interesting memorial of this connection is now in the possession of his great grandson, the compiler of this history. It is a copy of Cranmer's Bible, printed in 1566, given Phineas Buckley by his adopted father, and containing the autographs of its various possessors, beginning with Ennion Williams's father,[1] of the same name, in 1702, and having pasted inside of one cover the original certificate of marriage between Ennion Williams and his first wife, Mary Hugg, dated 21st of second month, 1726. There are also the autographs of Roger Bradbury, 1700 (*q. v.*), and of Jo. Grayson and Jo. Grayson, Jr., whom I have not identified.

Phineas Buckley was carefully educated by his adopted parents in the principles of the Society of Friends, and led a quiet, regular life in accordance therewith. He was Chief Burgess of Bristol, September 24, 1765, and until 1775 ; and during the Revolution he remained loyal to the mother country, it being noted in 1775 that Phineas Buckley and one servant were non-associators. June 27, 1765, the meeting gave its consent, and in December, 1765, he *m.* **MARY ANNA,** *dau.* of **William** and **Mary Rodman,** of Bristol. She only lived six months after her marriage, dying of consumption.

He *m.*, second, May 12, 1768, at Friends' Meeting-House in Wilmington, Del.,[2] **MARY,** *dau.* of **Thomas** and **Mary (Marriott) Shipley,** of Brandywine (*q. v.*). She *d.* very suddenly in New York (whither her husband had removed), October 29, 1795. He survived her thirty-one years, dying in Philadelphia, at the house of his son-in-law, Peter Thomson, November 21, 1826. Issue by his second wife :

i.   **ENNION WILLIAMS,** *b.* October 22, 1769, named for his father's great-uncle, **ENNION WILLIAMS,** Jr., who *d.* February 25, 1780, in the eighty-fifth year of his age. Ennion Buckley *d.* April 2, 1775.

ii.   **THOMAS,** *b.* January 29, 1771, *of whom presently.*

[1] Ennion Williams, Sr., was a cooper and baker ; he probably built the Buckley House, and there is a legend that he laid the foundation of his fortune by the discovery of an iron pot of gold coins when digging the foundations (Davis's Bucks County, 345).

[2] It is said that the first umbrella seen in Wilmington was carried over the head of Mary Shipley as she walked to her marriage. It was spoken of as " a green silk canopy."

iii.   **ELIZABETH WILLIAMS**, *b.* May 10, 1773 ; *m.*, first, in May, 1796,
       SAMUEL UNDERHILL. Issue (surname UNDERHILL) :

   i.   **ANDREW**, *d. s. p.*
   ii.   **MARY BUCKLEY**, *m.*, June 5, 1831, **WILLIAM HUTCHINS**, and had a *dau.*,
         Elizabeth, *d.* in 1846. He *d.* August 15. 1833, and she *m.*, March 25, 1857,
         EDWARD H. BONSALL, and *d. s. p.*, surviving, September 13, 1870.

     MRS. ELIZABETH UNDERHILL *m.*, second, December 16, 1807,
       PETER THOMSON, and *d.* August 5, 1856. Issue (surname
       THOMSON) :

   iii.   **REBECCA**, *d. u.*
   iv.   **SAMUEL**, *d. u.*
   v.   **PETER**, *m.*, November 7, 1843, **CAROLINE BROWNE**.

iv.   **MARY**, *b.* October 22, 1775 ; *d. u.*, July 6, 1788.
v.   **SARAH**, *b.* September 22, 1777 ; *m.* in 1828, **ISRAEL COPE**, of Phila-
       delphia, and *d. s. p.* November 19, 1852.
vi.   **DEBORAH**, *b.* August 24, 1780 ; *d. u.*, February 3, 1796.
vii.   **REBECCA**, *b.* March 10, 1783 ; *d.* August 15, 1783.
viii. **ANN**, *b.* October 1, 1785 ; *d. u.*, October 24, 1857.
ix.   **WILLIAM**, *b.* June 21, 1789 ; *d.* February 19, 1790.
x.   **PHINEAS WILLIAM**, *b.* October 20, 1791 ; *d. u.* at New Orleans, April
       29, 1827.

THOMAS, second son of **Phineas** and **Mary (Shipley) Buckley**,
was *b.* at Bristol, Pa., January 29, 1771. He removed to New
York, August 15, 1790, probably beginning his business life as a
dealer in the flour manufactured by the Brandywine Mills of his
mother's family near Wilmington. At the beginning of the century his firm, Buckley & Abbot, is noted as a large operator in
flour and grain and interested in shipping. In 1800 Mr. Buckley's ship Ariel was captured by the French. In 1809, with his
brothers-in-law, John B. Lawrence and Jacob Schieffelin, he
bought a large tract of land at Manhattanville. Following the
fashion of the day he built [1] himself a country-seat there, on a
commanding site above the Hudson River, in the centre of a plot
of fifteen acres, bounded now by Riverside Drive and the Boule-
vard, and 124th and 128th Streets. This he called Lycoming
Villa, because the purchase-money came from the sale of land
in Lycoming Co., Penn. In 1839 he sold the property to
Daniel F. Tieman, and in 1895 the house was torn down. In
1815, after the severe losses of the War of 1812, he was taxed on
a personal estate of $20,000. He took an active part in city
affairs, mercantile and benevolent, and was called to many posi-

---

[1] Several times recently the New York newspapers have described this house as having been built
in the last century, and the scene of tragic incidents which have no foundation in fact, probably con-
fusing it with one of the older houses in the vicinity.

THOMAS BUCKLEY
BORN 1771, DIED 1846

ANNA (LAWRENCE) BUCKLEY
BORN 1772, DIED 1846

tions of trust and responsibility ; was one of the first directors of the Bank for Savings, established November 29, 1816, and one of its trustees when it began operations in 1819. Longworth's Almanac for 1818 notes that he was a director of the Pacific Insurance Company (office at 49 Wall Street), which commenced business in 1817 ; Secretary of the New York Hospital ; Secretary of the Free School Society, and President of the Bank of America, chartered in 1812, with a capital of $4,000,000, which position he held until advancing years compelled his resignation. A list of the wealthy citizens of New York, printed shortly before his death, estimates his fortune then at $100,000. He *m.*, September 11, 1793, by Friends' ceremony, at their Meeting-house in Pearl Street, New York, **ANNA**, *dau.* of **John** and **Ann (Burling) Lawrence**, who *d.* July 11, 1846. Her husband *d.* in New York City, April 28th of the same year. Issue :

i. **WILLIAM LAWRENCE**, *b.* October 6, 1794 ; *d.* September 9, 1812.
ii. **JOHN LAWRENCE**, *b.* July 31, 1797, *of whom presently.*
iii. **PHINEAS HENRY**, *b.* March 1, 1800 (*q. v.*).
iv. **MARY ANNA**, *b.* July 22, 1802 ; *m.*, May 9, 1821, **WALTER R.**, son of **Jacob** and **Mary Wood**. He *d.* May 19, 1830, and his wife *d.* July 24, 1873. Issue (surname WOOD) :

    i. **ANNA BUCKLEY**, *d. i.*
    ii. **THOMAS BUCKLEY**, *d.* at the age of eight.
    iii. **MARIANA**, *m.* May 9, 1855, **EDWARD THORNTON BROWN**, *d.* March 12, 1889. Issue :

        i. Thornton Edward, *b.* July 24, 1857 ; *d.* October 17, 1876.
        ii. Anna, *b.* February 27, 1863.

    iv. **WALTER RALEIGH**, *b.* May 28, 1830; *m.*, January 17, 1857, **EMILY**, *dau.* of **Charles West Hornor**. Issue :

        i. Mary Ellen.
        ii. Josephine, *m.*, February 1, 1893, Franklin Green Colby.
        iii. Emily, *m.* B. Dorr Schaeffer.

v. **ELIZABETH WILLIAMS**, *b.* July 31, 1805 ; *d. u.* in 1841.
vi. **EFFINGHAM LAWRENCE**, *b.* May 10, 1808 ; *m.*, June 11, 1833, **HANNAH ANN**, *dau.* of **Luke** and **Ann Morris** (*q. v.*), of Philadelphia, and *d.* at Troy, N. Y. ; his widow *d.* September 17, 1889. Issue :

    i. **EDWARD MORRIS**, *m.* **GERTRUDE ONDERDONK**, and *d. s. p.* on the coast of Africa.
    ii. **ANNIE MORRIS**, *m.*, December 3, 1855, her cousin, **ISRAEL W. MORRIS** (*q. v.*).

vii. **JANE LAWRENCE**, *b.* January 14, 1812, at 339 Pearl Street, New York City ; *m.* **DR. JOHN CHEW THOMAS** (*q. v.*).

JOHN LAWRENCE, second son of **Thomas** and **Anna** **(Lawrence) Buckley,** *b.* July 31, 1797 ; *m.*, January 21, 1821, **SARAH ANN TAYLOR,** and *d.* March 13, 1857 ; his wife *d.* May 13, 1878. Issue :

i. **THOMAS CROWELL TAYLOR,** *b.* August 19, 1826, a distinguished lawyer of New York ; *m.*, first, in October, 1859, **JULIETTE ANN GERARD,** of that city, who *d.* July 27, 1866. Issue :

    i. **MARY DICKINSON KEMBLE.**
    ii. **JULIAN GERARD,** *b.* July 3, 1866.

    T. C. T. BUCKLEY, *m.*, second, September 17, 1873, **KATHERINE LEE YOUNG,** of Geneseo, N. Y., and *d.* July 12, 1874, without further issue.

ii. **SARAH TAYLOR,** *m.*, January 14, 1857, **DAVID LORD TURNER,** of New York, and resides at Florence, Italy. Issue (surname TURNER) :

    ELINOR BUCKLEY, JULIET LORD, and JEANIE.

iii. **JOHN LAWRENCE,** *b.* October 1, 1831 ; *m.*, February 22, 1854, **SOPHIE PRICE.** Issue :

    SARAH ANN, FLORENCE, and AGNES, who all *d.* in infancy or childhood ; **MARIE ADELE,** and **FREDERICK.**

PHINEAS HENRY, third son of **Thomas** and **Anna (Law-rence) Buckley,** *b.* March 1, 1800 ; *m.*, first, May 12, 1824, **PHŒBE,** *dau.* of **Townsend** and **Sarah (Vail) McCoun,** of Troy, N. Y., who *d.* March 15, 1838. Issue, born at Troy :

i. **SARAH McCOUN,** *b.* February 14, 1825.
ii. **ANNA LAWRENCE,** *b.* April 19, 1827 ; *m.*, October 17, 1848, at S. Mark's Church, New York City, **ROBERT WALTER RUTH-ERFURD,** of Edgerston, near Belleville, N. J. (*q. v.*).
iii. **TOWNSEND McCOUN,** *b.* May 28, 1829 ; *d.* August 29, 1831.
iv. **TOWNSEND McCOUN,** *b.* September 19, 1831 ; in the C. S. A., at the Battle of Shiloh ; *d.* at Mobile, Ala., September 26, 1862.
v. **THOMAS,** *b.* July 18, 1833 ; *m.*, July 16, 1884, **ALICE WARWICK SLOCUM,** of New Bedford, Mass. Issue : ·

    EFFINGHAM LAWRENCE, *b.* October 14, 1885 ; *d.* February 2, 1892.

vi. **PHEBE McCOUN,** *b.* May 11, 1836 ; *m.*, June 2, 1858, **THOMAS MATTHEW,** son of **Isaac** and **May Lydia (Seaman) Wigham,** of New York City. Issue :

    i. **MAY.**
    ii. **EDITH.**
    iii. **EDGAR CARTERET,** *b.* in December, 1871 ; *d.* in December, 1875.
    iv. **REGINALD EFFINGHAM.**

vii. **ELIZABETH WILLIAMS,** *b.* March 4, 1838 ; *m.*, June 29, 1869, **EASTMAN JOHNSON,** of New York City. Issue :

    ETHEL EASTMAN, *b.* May 2, 1870.

EASTMAN JOHNSON was *b.* July 29, 1834, in the little town of Lovell, near Fryeburg, in Maine. His father was an officer in the employ of the United States Treasury Department. The son was first known to fame as a crayon limner, being so successful in that art that in a few years he was enabled to visit Europe. There he commenced an earnest system of study and began to practise in oil ; at Dusseldorf he remained two years, and then started for Italy, stopping to examine the galleries in Holland. At The Hague he fell in with Mignot, and tarried there ostensibly to copy a remarkable picture in the Royal Collection. His stay lasted four years. He met with flattering success in portraiture, painting many of the wealthy citizens and nearly all of the maids of honor. At The Hague he also painted his first pictures in oil. On his return to the United States he turned his attention with great success to native subjects, ''and no one of our painters,'' says Henry Tuckerman in his '' Book of the Artists,'' '' has more truly caught and perfectly delineated the American rustic and negro, or with such pathetic and natural emphasis put upon canvas bits of household and childish life, or given such bright and real glimpses of primitive human nature.'' A more recent critic declares that '' he always strikes the note which finds a responsive echo in the hearts of the masses.'' Probably no American artist has painted the portraits of so many men of prominence. In 1860 he was elected a member of the National Academy.

PHINEAS HENRY BUCKLEY, *m.*, second, in August, 1843, **JULIA,** *dau.* of **Nathaniel** and **Catherine Lawrence,** of New York City, and *d.* at Newark, N. J. Issue by his second wife, who *d.* December 31, 1854 :

viii.   **KATHERINE LAWRENCE,** *b.* in June, 1844 ; *m.* **LAURENCE YVONNET HOPKINS,** of New York City. Issue (surname HOPKINS) :

     i.   KATHERINE LAWRENCE, *m.*, November 19, 1891, STEPHEN HULL WICKHAM. Issue :

        Katherine Lawrence, *b.* November 3, 1892.

     ii.   JANE LAWRENCE.

ix.   JANE LAWRENCE, *m.*, December 6, 1865, JAMES SHEAFE SATTERTHWAITE (*q. v.*).

WILLIAM, second surviving son of **William** and **Ruth (Leach) Buckley,** *b.* July 19, 1745 ; was a merchant in Philadelphia. The City Directory registers him between 1807 and 1815 as in business with his son, Anthony M., at 147 Front Street, and residing at 87 South Third Street, where his widow was living until her death. He *m.* **SARAH,** *dau.* of **Anthony** and **Sarah**

(Powel) **Morris,** of Philadelphia (*q. v.*), and *d.* October 17, 1815. (Will recorded Liber 6, fo. 360.) His wife *d.* in 1831. Issue :

i.   **ELIZABETH M.,** *b.* July 4, 1772 ; *m.* **LUKE W. MORRIS** (*q. v.*).
ii.   **SARAH POWEL,** *b.* October 4, 1773, *of whom presently.*
iii. **ANTHONY MORRIS,** *b.* December 7, 1777 ; in business with his father, and after his death for some years continued on Front Street, moving in 1820 to 133 South Front Street, and in 1825 having his counting-house at 39½ N. Water Street ; *d. u.*, April 6, 1845.

SARAH POWEL, second *dau.* of **William** and **Sarah (Morris) Buckley,** *b.* October 4, 1773 ; *m.*, first, March 14, 1793, **JO-SEPH COOPER.** Issue (surname COOPER) :

i.   **JOSEPH B.,** *b.* January 17, 1794 ; *m.* **HANNAH WILLS,** and *d.* December 19, 1861. Issue :

    i.   **CHARLES M.,** *m.* **HANNAH W. BROWN.**
    ii.   **SARAH B.,** *d. i.*
    iii. **SAMUEL W.,** *d. i.*
    iv. **JOSEPH B.,** *m.* **ELIZABETH W. KAIGHN,** both *d.* Issue :

        i.   John K., *d. i.*
        ii.   Joseph B., third, *d. i.*
        iii. Rebecca H., *m.* Charles G. Reeve.

MRS. SARAH P. (BUCKLEY) COOPER, *m.*, second, July 17, 1801, **THOMAS HOWARD,** and *d.* November 18, 1847. Issue (surname HOWARD) :

ii.   **CHARLES P.,** *b.* July 25, 1802 ; *m.* **MARY A. MOORE,** and *d.* May 1, 1833. Issue :

    i.   **SARAH P.,** *m.* **CHARLES J. PETERSON,** *d.* Issue (surname PETERSON) :

        i.   Mary, *d. i.*
        ii.   Thomas H., *m.* Mary Connell, and *d.* Issue : Mary H., *d. i.* ; Grace H. ; Maud.
        iii. Thomas B., *d. u.*
        iv. Anthony B., *d. i.*

iii. **EMMA,** *m.* **WILLIAM L. EDWARDS,** since *d.*
iv. **ELIZABETH B.,** *b.* in 1812 ; *m.* **SAMUEL H. EDWARDS** and *d.* January 26, 1893. Issue (surname EDWARDS) :

    i.   **HOWARD,** *m.* **FANNIE CLAXTON.**
    ii.   **ELIZABETH B.,** *m.* **JACOB HOWELL,** *d.* Issue (surname HOWELL) :

        i.   Elizabeth R., *m.* William W. Bacon.
        ii.   Samuel H.
        iii. Emma H.
        iv. Sallie R.

Principal authorities: Bristol and Philadelphia Friends' Records. Old Family Bibles, through Mr. Howard Edwards, of Philadelphia ; a MS. Family Record, in possession of Mrs. Jane L. Thomas, of Baltimore, and Thomas Buckley's Bible.

ANTHONY MORRIS BUCKLEY

From a Portrait by St. Memin

BURLING

EDWARD BURLING, *m.*, in England, **GRACE** ——, and, removing to Long Island about 1680, *d.* there in August, 1697. Issue :

i.   **EDWARD**, *b.* in England, November 4, 1674, *of whom presently.*
ii.   **GRACE**, *b.* in England, October 29, 1676.
iii.   **WILLIAM**, *b.* in England, December 26, 1678 (*q. v.*).
iv.   **REBEKAH**, *b.* in August, 1681.
v.   **JANE**, *b.* July 17, 1684 ; *m.*, May 9, 1717, **JAMES MOTT**, of " Meroneck," Westchester Co.
vi.   **SARAH**, *b.* May 12, 1687 ; *m.*, July 19, 1716, **JOHN WAY.**
vii.   **BENJAMIN**, *b.* February 6, 1689–90 ; *d.* December 21, 1709.

EDWARD, eldest son of **Edward** and **Grace Burling**, *b.* November 4, 1674, was a carpenter ; *m.*, June 11, 1700, **PHEBE**, *dau.* of **John** (*d.* 1715) and **Mary** (*d.* 1704) **Ferris**, of Westchester, and *d.* at New York, May, 1749. Issue :

i.   **JAMES**, *b.* May 9, 1701 ; *m.* **ELIZABETH** ——, and *d.* January 8, 1754. Issue :

    i.   **EDWARD, JR.**, *m.*, October 12, 1757, **DEBORAH VAN WYCK.**
    ii.   **SARAH**, *m.* **CALEB LAWRENCE** (*q. v.*).

ii.   **JOHN**, *b.* August 9, 1703, *of whom presently.*
iii.   **PHEBE**, *b.* October 24, 1705.
iv.   **SARAH**, *b.* July 25, 1712.
v   **EDWARD**, *b.* February 3, 1713–14 ; *m.*, October 20, 1743, **ANN FFARRINGTON**, and *d.* May, 1749. Issue :

    RICHARD, *m.*, April 12, 1761, **CHARITY**, *dau.* of **William Haviland**, of Harrison's Purchase.

vi.   **MARTHA**, *b.* November 29, 1715.

JOHN, second son of **Edward** and **Phebe (Ferris) Burling**, *b.* August 9, 1703 ; *m.*, July 5, 1733, **ANN**, *dau.* of **Thomas** (*deceased*) and **Elizabeth Dobson**, of New York City. (**Mrs. Dobson** *d.* December 5, 1748.) Issue :

i. **JOHN,** Jr., *m.*, January 9, 1767, **HANNAH,** *dau.* of **Benjamin Cornell,** of Scarsdale.

ii. **ANN,** *m.* **JOHN LAWRENCE** (*q. v.*).

WILLIAM, second son of **Edward** and **Grace Burling,** *b.* December 26, 1678; *m.* **REBEKAH ——,** who *d.* April 2, 1729. Issue :

i. **MARY,** *b.* September 15, 1706 ; *d.* August 7, 1727.

ii. **WILLIAM,** *b.* September 18, 1708 ; *m.*, March 12, 1729, **SARAH,** *dau.* of **Samuel** and **Hannah (Smith) Bowne** (*q. v.*) ; lived at Flushing, and *d.* June 7, 1745. Issue :

  i. **HANNAH,** *b.* February 6, 1730-31 ; *d.* May 23, 1732.
  ii. **JOSEPH,** *b.* October 8, 1732.
  iii. **HANNAH,** *b.* April 7, 1734.
  iv. **SARAH,** *b.* June 19, 1736.
  v. **REBECKAH,** *b.* July 30, 1738.

iii. **BENJAMIN,** *b.* November 18, 1710 ; *d.* September 15, 1747.

iv. **REBEKAH,** *b.* February 28, 1711-12 ; *m.*, November 13, 1729, **ROBERT,** son of **Benjamin Field.**

v. **HANNAH,** *b.* December 16, 1713 ; *m.*, August 13, 1730, **ANTHONY,** son of **Benjamin Field.**

vi. **SARAH,** *b.* August 2, 1715.

vii. **EBENEZER,** *b.* August 2, 1717 , *m.*, in 1736, **MARY ——.** Issue :

  i. **REBECKAH,** *b.* July 16, 1737.
  ii. **HANNAH,** *b.* April 4, 1739.

viii. **AMY,** *b.* April 20, 1724 ; *d.* July 12, 1744.

THOMAS and **SUSANNA BURLING,** of this same family, had issue :

i. **ANNE,** *b.* May 30, 1784 ; *d. i.*

ii. **ANNE,** *b.* November 19, 1786.

iii. **MARIA,** *b.* March 15, 1789 ; *d. i.*

iv. **MARIA,** *b.* September 26, 1791.

THOMAS and **HENRIETTA BURLING** had issue :

i. **JOSEPH,** *b.* October 17, 1782 ; *d.* August 15, 1783.

ii. **MARY,** *b.* December 9, 1783.

iii. **ANN,** *b.* November 28, 1785 ; *d.* May 30, 1786.

iv. **JOSEPH,** *b.* August 30, 1787.

v. **ANN,** *b.* April 20, 1789.

vi. **THOMAS,** *b.* August 19, 1791.

Mary, wife of **Edward Burling,** *d.* October 10, 1731. **Mary,** widow of **William Burling,** *d.* October 25, 1747. **Samuel Burling** *d.* November 12, 1757.

Authority: Records of New York Friends' Meeting.

CAREY

JAMES CAREY, *b.* in Baltimore, February 22, 1751–52, was actively engaged in the shipping business and as an importer, and accumulated a considerable fortune. A member of the Society of Friends he was interested in the welfare of the negroes, and one of the organizers and first Vice-president of the Maryland "Society for Promoting the Abolition of Slavery and the Relief of Free Negroes and Others unlawfully held in Bondage." This was the fourth in the United States and the sixth in the world at its organization, September 8, 1798. The town of Baltimore became a city December 31, 1796. He was chosen at the first election under its charter on January, 1797, one of the two Councilmen to represent the First Ward, and held office for a second term. At the November, 1790, session of the Legislature a charter for a bank at Baltimore, under the style of the Bank of Maryland, was granted, and Messrs. James Carey, William Patterson, Robert Gilmor, Thomas Hollingsworth, James Edwards, and Otho H. Williams were appointed a committee to receive subscriptions to its stock, and in two weeks $200,000, being two-thirds of the total capital, was subscribed. Mr. Carey served as a director of the Bank from 1792 until 1817, when he became its President. The Bank was eminently successful, and did a large and conservative business. At the time of his resignation of the presidency, on account of advancing years, it was the principal and most prosperous financial institution in the State.

JAMES CAREY *m.* **MARTHA,** eldest *dau.* of **John** and **Leah (Brown) Ellicott** (*q. v.*), and *d.* October 29, 1834. Issue :

i. **JOHN C.,** *d. i.*
ii. **JOHN ELLICOTT,** *b.* February 22, 1789, *of whom presently.*
iii. **SAMUEL,** *b.* March 6, 1791 ; *m.,* June 22, 1837, **MARTHA,** *dau.* of **John** and **Letitia (Ellicott) Evans,** and *d. s. p.*
iv. **JAMES,** *b.* March 10, 1793 ; *d.* August 8, 1813, at Ballston Springs, N. Y.

v.   HANNAH, *b.* August 7, 1795 ; *m.* WILLIAM E. COALE (*q. v.*).

vi.   MARGARET, *b.* November 22, 1797 ; *m.* GALLOWAY CHES-
       TON (*q. v.*).

vii. GEORGE, *b.* September 9, 1800 (*q. v.*).

viii. MARTHA, *b.* May 12, 1805 ; *m.* DR. RICHARD H. THOMAS (*q. v.*).

JOHN ELLICOTT, second son of James and Martha (Elli-
cott) Carey, *b.* February 22, 1789 ; *m.*, March 2, 1820, ANN, *dau.* of Thomas and Elizabeth (Janney) Irwin, of Alexandria, Va. (*b.* July 29, 1800 ; *d.* May 29, 1846), and *d.* January 16, 1849. Issue :

i.   JAMES, *b.* January 20, 1821 ; for nearly fifty years in mercantile business
        in Baltimore ; *m.* SUSAN B. KIMBER, of Philadelphia, and *d.*
        October 8, 1894. Issue :

    i.   THOMAS KIMBER, *m.* MARY T., *dau.* of Francis T. King (*q. v.*).
    ii.   JOHN ELLICOTT, *m.* SARAH MURDOCK.
    iii. JAMES, JR., *m.* ANNA T., *dau.* of Francis T. King (*q. v.*). Issue:
         Frances.
    iv. MARY IRWIN, *m.* FRANCIS GREENLEAF ALLINSON. Issue (surname
        ALLINSON) :
         Susanne.
    v.   FRANCIS KING, *m.*, April 27, 1886, at Grace Church, Baltimore, ANNE GAL-
        BRAITH, *dau.* of J. Bannister Hall.
    vi   ANTHONY MORRIS, *m.* MARGARET CHESTON, *dau.* of Dr. James
        Carey Thomas (*q. v.*).

ii.   THOMAS IRWIN, *b.* October 19, 1827 ; for some time a cotton-spinner
        in Pennsylvania, since and for a number of years President of the
        Peabody Fire Insurance Company of Baltimore ; *m.*, July 15, 1852,
        MARTHA GRAY, *dau.* of Hon. George Gray and Eliza S.
        (Thomas) Leiper (*q. v.*), of Pennsylvania, who *d.* December 31,
        1890. Issue :

    i.   ELIZA LEIPER, *d. i.*
    ii.   ANN IRWIN, *m.*, November 18, 1885, GEORGE FRANK, son of James and
        Martha Baily. Issue (surname BAILY) :
        i.   Thomas Carey, *b.* April 26, 1887.
        ii. James, *b.* July 24, 1889.
    iii. GEORGE LEIPER, *b.* February 5, 1858 ; *m.*, October 20, 1891, RACHEL HAR-
        RYMAN BROOKS.
    iv. MARY THOMAS.
    v.   THOMAS IRWIN, *b.* October 12, 1862.
    vi.   JAMES, *b.* August 16, 1864.
    vii. MARTHA LEIPER.
    viii. CHARLES HAMILTON, *b.* October 3, 1868.
    ix. x. HELEN HAMILTON and JOHN ELLICOTT, twins, of whom the latter *d. i.*

GEORGE, fifth son of James and Martha (Ellicott) Carey,
b. September 9, 1800 ; *m.*, April, 1830, MARY, *dau.* of Patrick

and **Eleanor (Sanderson) Gibson,** and *d.* January 14, 1865.
Issue : a *dau.,* **ELLEN G.,** and four sons.

GEORGE GIBSON, *m.,* April 10, 1860, **JOSEPHINE C. POE,**
and *d.* May 26, 1894. Issue :

i.   JOSEPHINE GIBSON, *b.* June 10, 1861 ; *m.* DR. HENRY M. THOMAS
     (*q. v.*).
ii.   GEORGE G., *b.* April 4, 1863.
iii.   MARIA GIBSON, *b.* November 29, 1867.
iv.   NEILSON POE, *b.* June 20, 1871.
v.   MARGARET CHESTON, *b.* July 28, 1876.

JAMES, *m.,* June 16, 1869, **MATTIE WARD,** and *d.* Issue :

i.   GEORGE, *b.* March 23, 1870.
ii.   ESTELLA WARD, *b.* May 3, 1871 ; *m.* DR. FREDERICK M. WARREN,
     of Portland, Me.

HENRY GIBSON, *m.,* October 26, 1864, **GRACE GIBSON.** Issue :

i.   WILLIAM G., *b.* August 9, 1866.
ii.   GRACE NOBLE, *b.* August 5, 1868 ; *m.* W. S. GRAFF BAKER.
iii.   HENRY G., Jr., *b.* February 20th ; *d.* August 17, 1876.
iv.   ELLA BARTON, *b.* February 27, 1879.

ALEXANDER GIBSON, *m.,* October 1, 1874, **ELEANORA,** *dau.*
of **William E.** and **Cassandra (Brevitt) Coale.** Issue :

i.   MARY YARNALL, *b.* September 18, 1875.
ii.   ALEXANDER G., *b.* December 2, 1876 ; *d.* August 20, 1877.
iii.   ELEANORA COALE, *b.* February 5th ; *d.* June 3, 1880.

     Authority : Family records, through James Carey, of Thomas, and others.

CARROLL

CHARLES CARROLL, of Carrollton, the last surviving signer of the Declaration of Independence, *m.* **MARY DARNALL,** and had issue a son, **CHARLES.**

CHARLES, son of **Charles** and **Mary (Darnall)** Carroll, *m.,* in 1800, **HARRIET,** *dau.* of Chief-Justice **Benjamin** and **Mary (Galloway) Chew** (*q. v.*), who *d.* at Philadelphia, April 10, 1861. Issue :

i.   **CHARLES,** *b.* July 19, 1801 ; *m.,* **MARY DIGGES LEE,** and *d.* December 2, 1862. Issue :

     i.   **MARY,** *m.* **ELISEO ACOSTA, M.D.,** of Paris.
     ii.   **CHARLES,** *m.* **CAROLINE THOMPSON,** of Staunton, Va.
     iii.   **THOMAS LEE,** *d. y.*
     iv.   **JOHN LEE,** in Senate of Maryland, 1867–75 ; Governor of Maryland, 1876–79 ; *m.,* first, **ANITA,** *dau.* of **Royal Phelps,** of New York, who *d.* March 24, 1873 ; and second, **CARTER THOMPSON.**
     v.   **LOUISA,** *m.* **GEORGE CAVENDISH TAYLOR.**
     vi.   **OSWALD,** *d. y.*
     vii.   **ALBERT HENRY,** in C. S. A.; *m.* **MARY CORNELIA,** *dau.* of **William George** and **Sophia C. (Howard) Read** (*q. v.*), was killed near Martinsburg, Va., September 7, 1862.
     viii.   **THOMAS LEE.**
     ix.   **ROBERT GOODLOE HARPER,** *m.,* first, **ELLINOR THOMPSON;** second, **MARY D. LEE.**
     x.   **HELEN SOPHIA,** *m.* **CHARLES OLIVER O'DONNELL,** of Baltimore, Attorney-at-Law.

ii.   **ELIZABETH,** *m.* **AARON BURR TUCKER, M.D.;** *d.* about 1884. Issue (surname TUCKER) :

     i.   **HARRIET,** *d. y.*
     ii.   **CHARLES** (took surname CARROLL) : *m.* **SUSAN HOWELL,** of Baltimore.
     iii.   **ST. GEORGE.**

iii. **MARY SOPHIA,** *m.* **RICHARD HENRY,** son of James A. Bayard, United States Senator from Delaware, 1804-13, by his wife, **ANNE,** *dau.* of **Richard Bassett,** Governor of Delaware. Mr. Bayard was United States Senator, 1836-37 and 1841-45 ; *Chargé d'Affaires* in Belgium, 1850-53 ; *d.* March 4, 1868. Issue (surname BAYARD) :

    i.   **HARRIET,** *d. y.*
    ii.   **MARY LOUISA,** *m.,* first, **WILLIAM HENRY BECK** ; second, **COLONEL MANLIO BETTARINA.**
    iii. **CAROLINE,** *m.* **HENRY BARING POWEL,** of Philadelphia.
    iv. **ELIZABETH,** *m.* **COLONEL FREDERICK HENRY RICH,** of England.
    v.   **CHARLES CARROLL,** Lieutenant U. S. N., *d. u.*
    vi. **RICHARD BASSETT,** Secretary of Legation to Belgium ; *m.,* December 20, 1860, his cousin, **ELLEN GILMOR HOWARD** (*q. v.*), and *d.* December 25, 1878.
    vii. **HARRIET,** *m.* **CHRISTIAN BÖRS,** Norwegian Consul at Boston, and *d.* 1865.
    viii. **LOUISA,** *m.* **R. ASHURST BOWIE,** of the Philadelphia Bar.

iv. **BENJAMIN CHEW,** *d. y.*, in August, 1806.
v. **BENJAMIN CHEW,** *d. y.*
vi. **HARRIET,** *m.* **JOHN LEE,** of Needwood, Frederick Co., Md. Issue (surname LEE) :

    MARY DIGGES, *m.* **JONATHAN LETTERMAN,** Medical Director U. S. A., and *d.* November 8, 1868.

    Principal authority : Keith's Councillors of Pennsylvania.

CHESTON

DR. DANIEL CHESTON was a merchant, receiving a register for his brigantine the Maryland Merchant sixty-five tons, May 18, 1744, and sloop Chester, fifteen tons, February 26, 1754–55. He *m.* **FRANCINA AUGUSTINA,** *dau.* of **James** and **Ariana (Vanderheyden) Frisby** (*q. v.*), and widow of William Stephenson. She *d.* July ——, 1766. Issue :

i.   **JAMES,** *of whom presently.*
ii.   **DANIEL,** *d. u.*
iii.   **FRANCINA AUGUSTINA,** *b.* in 1752; *m.* **WILLIAM BEN-SLEY,** of England and *d. s. p.*

JAMES, eldest son of **Dr. Daniel** and **Francina A. (Frisby) Cheston,** *b.* in 1747 ; *m.* **ANNE,** *dau.* of **James** and **Anne Galloway** (*q. v.*). Issue :

i.   **DANIEL,** b. 1776, *d. u.,* 1811.
ii.   **FRANCINA AUGUSTINA,** *b.* 1777, *d. s. p.*
iii.   **JAMES,** *b.* 1779, *of whom presently.*

JAMES, youngest son of **James** and **Anne (Galloway) Cheston,** *b.* 1779 ; was a merchant in Baltimore and first President of the Farmers' and Planters' Bank, 1836–43. He *m.* **MARY ANN,** *dau.* of **Colonel Samuel** and **Sarah (Adams) Hollingsworth,** and *d.* 1843. Issue :

i.   **DR. JAMES,** *b.* 1804, *of whom presently.*
ii.   **GALLOWAY,** *b.* 1806, in business with his father as a manufacturer and shipper of flour at the corner of Cable and Patterson Streets, Baltimore ; the firm, James Cheston & Son, being continued fifty-five years. He was a member of the Finance Committee of the Baltimore & Ohio Railroad, and director of many commercial and charitable corporations. His family were church people, and although an attendant on Friends' meeting after his marriage, he never united with the So-

ciety. He *m.* **MARGARET,** *dau.* of **James Carey** (*q. v.*), who *d. s. p.*, and *d.* March 9, 1881, leaving a fortune of $700,000.

iii.   **SAMUEL,** *b.* 1808; *d. u.*, 1875.
iv.   **ANNE,** *b.* 1810; *m.* **DR. CASPAR MORRIS** (*q. v.*).
v.   **SALLY,** *d.*
vi.   **JOHN GALLOWAY,** *d.*
vii.   **BENJAMIN GALLOWAY,** *d.*
viii.   **MARY HOLLINGSWORTH,** *m.*, 1841, **DR. JAMES H. MUR-RAY,** and *d.* 1842. Issue (surname MURRAY):

    i.   **DANIEL,** *b.* 1842; *m.* **MARY C. BROGDEN.** Issue:

       Meta and **Mary Hollingsworth.**

ix.   **ELIZABETH RIDGELY,** *d.*
x.   **JACOB HOLLINGSWORTH,** *d.*
xi.   **FRANCINA HENRIETTA,** *m.* 1845, **DR. JAMES H. MURRAY,** who *d.* 1893. Issue (surname MURRAY):

    i.   **MARY C.,** *m.*, 1870, **DR. M. G. ELLZEY.** Issue (surname ELLZEY):

       J. Murray, M. Graham, Helen, Fanny, and **Mary Preston.**

    ii.   **JAMES CHESTON.**
    iii.   **FANNY.**
    iv.   **ALICE MURDOCH.**
    v.   **MARGARET CHESTON.**
    vi.   **WILLIAM T.**
    vii.   **ELIZABETH C.**
    viii.   **HENRY.**
    ix.   **JAMES H.**

DR. JAMES, eldest son of **James** and **Mary Ann (Hollingsworth) Cheston,** *b.* 1804; *m.*, first, **MARY,** *dau.* of **Philip John** and **Cornelia Thomas** (*q. v.*). Issue:

i.   **CORNELIA,** *d. u.*
ii.   **MARY,** *m.*, 1859, **AUGUSTUS HALL.** Issue (surname HALL):

    i.   **HENRY.** ii. **J. CHESTON.** iii. **EDWARD.** iv. **MARY.** v. **ANNIE.**

iii.   **JAMES,** *b.* 1832; *m.*, 1856, **CHARLOTTE RADCLIFFE,** *dau.* of **Dr. Charles H.** and **Charlotte Steele.** Issue:

    i.   **JAMES,** *m.*, 1892, **CAROLINE C. MORRIS.** Issue:

       James Hamilton.

    ii.   **CHARLES,** *d.*
    iii.   **RADCLIFFE,** *m.*, 1886, **EUGENIA MORRIS.** Issue:

       i.   **George Morris.** ii. **Radcliffe.** iii. **Charles.** iv. **Elizabeth.**

    iv.   **HENRY,** *d.*
    v.   **CHARLOTTE M.**
    vi.   **MARY N. S.**
    vii.   **MARGARET CAREY,** *d.*
    viii.   **HELEN.**

DR. JAMES CHESTON, *m.,* second, **CORNELIA,** another *dau.* of **Philip John Thomas** (*q. v.*), who *d.* 1839.   Issue :

iv.   **NANCY,** *m.,* 1861, **FENWICK HALL.**   Issue (surname HALL) :

    i.   **NANNIE,** *m.,* 1883, **WILLIAM T. MURRAY.**   Issue (surname MURRAY) :

        i.   William. ii. Fenwick. iii. James H. iv. Daniel Hollingsworth, *d.*

    ii.   **CORNELIA T.,** *m.,* 1889, O. W. GOTT, and has a son, Oswald W.
    iii.   **SARAH.**

DR. JAMES CHESTON, *m.,* third, 1841, **SARAH SCOTT,** *dau.* of **Daniel** and **Mary (Dorsey) Murray,** and *d.* 1885 ; his wife *d.* 1891.   Issue :

v.   **DANIEL MURRAY,** a prominent physician of Philadelphia ; *m.,* 1872, . **ELLEN R. RANDALL.**   Issue :

    i.   **KATHARINE WIRT.** ii. **ALEXANDER RANDALL.** iii. **MARGARET.** iv. **DANIEL MURRAY, JR.**

vi.   **SALLY MURRAY.**
vii.   **GALLOWAY,** *m.,* first, 1869, **ELIZABETH RALSTON.**   Issue :

    i.   **SUE WILCOX,** *m.,* 1893, **MORRIS HACKER.**
    ii.   **SALLY MURRAY.**
    iii.   **ROBERT RALSTON,** *d.*
    iv.   **ELIZABETH,** *d.*
    v.   **GALLOWAY,** *d.*
    vi.   **KITTY.**
    vii.   **ELIZABETH.**

       He *m.,* second, 1893, **HENRIETTA S. McCULLOCH.**

viii.   **CAROLINE MURRAY,** *d.*
ix.   **ROBERT MURRAY,** *b.* 1849 ; *m.,* 1887, **MARY DORSEY,** *dau.* of **Henry M.** and **Mary H. (Morris) Murray** (*q. v.*).
x.   **CASPAR MORRIS,** *m.,* 1877, **SALLY C.,** *dau.* of **Colonel Edward** and **Louisa Murray.**   Issue :

    i.   **ELEANOR MURRAY.** ii. **ANNE MORRIS.** iii. **EDWARD MURRAY.** iv. **JAMES.** v. **LOUISA.** vi. **ARTHUR.** vii. **CLEMENCE.**

Authorities : Maryland Records, the late Dr. James Cheston and Mrs. Robert M. Cheston.

CHEW OF BLACKBURN, LANCASHIRE

THE **Chew** family was an ancient freeholding family in that portion of Billington vill, described in charters as the manor of Cho, allied by marriage to the De Bilyngtons, lords of the manor. By an undated deed of the thirteenth century Adam de Bilyngton gave to **Henry,** son of **Hugh del Cho** and **Avicia, his wife,** *dau.* of the grantor, land which Henry and Hugh his father, and their ancestors, had held of the grantor's family. It is now called the Castle Holme, and is the supposed site of a Saxon manor house. **Henry** was father of **Richard del Cho,** who about 1240 granted land to Beatrice de Blackburn, and a little later was seated at Cho Bank, and had a brother, **Thomas,** to whom his father gave lands called the Halgh Billington.

William Choo, of Billington, lived between 1400–1500 ; *d.* before 1523, when "uxor William Chew" was taxed for a royal subsidy. Several tenants of Whalley Abbey of the name occur in a survey of 1538 ; **Richard Chew,** of Benson's Field, also of Olgreave and a fulling mill, **Robert, Adam,** and **Edmund Chowe.**

Richard Chewe, senior, of Billington, taxed 1570, had a son, **Richard,** taxed 1610. **William Chew,** of Olgreave, was taxed, 1663.

ROBERT CHOWE, of Potter Ford, over the Calder, below Whalley Abbey, rebuilt that house in 1562, was living 1575. **EDWARD,** of Potter Ford, possibly his son, *m.* **A——,** and had a son, ROBERT CHEW, Gent., *m.,* May 25, 1618, MARY CROMBLE-HOLME. Issue :

i. RICHARD, *b.* 1619, *of whom presently.*
ii. EDWARD (*q. v.*).
iii. ROBERT, with his sons, were freemen of Bradford ; he *d.* after 1662.

RICHARD, eldest son of **Robert** and **Mary (Crombleholme) Chew,** *b.* 1619, *d.* about 1664, leaving a son, RICHARD, *b.* 1654, *d.* in November, 1721, buried at Whalley Abbey ; left a son, RICHARD, of Whitwams, *m.*, in 1701, CHRISTIANA KENDALL, who *d.* in April, 1763 ; he *d.* in 1726. Issue :

i. KENDALL, *b.* 1703, *of whom presently.*
ii. JOHN, *b.* 1705.
iii. RICHARD, *b.* 1708.
iv. THOMAS, *b.* 1713.
v. ELIZABETH.
vi. DOROTHY.
vii. JENNET.

KENDALL, eldest son of **Richard** and **Christiana (Kendall)** **Chew,** *b.* 1703, was of Elkar, Gent. ; *m.*, May 13, 1736, **ANN** **STONES,** of Haslingden, and *d.* in July, 1764. Issue :

i. RICHARD, of Billington, yeoman ; *m.*, January 5, 1763, SARAH, *dau.* of **Edward Ainsworth**, of Pleasington, Esq., and *d.* in 1782 ; his widow *d.* July 6, 1802. Issue :

    i. KENDALL, *bapt.* August 27, 1766.
    ii. ANN, *bapt.* 1768.
    iii. AINSWORTH, *bapt.* January 23, 1770.
    iv. THEOPHILUS, *bapt.* December 16, 1771.
    v. ELLEN.

ii. ELIZABETH.
iii ELLEN.
iv. ANN.
v. BETTY.

EDWARD CHEW, Gent., of Potter Ford, second son of **Rob-ert** and **Mary (Crombleholme) Chew,** was a governor of Blackburn Grammar School in 1679, still living in 1687 ; *m.*, first, 1656, **ELLEN,** *dau.* of **William Chew,** of Billington ; *m.*, sec-ond, before 1665, **ELIZABETH,** *dau.* of **James Moore,** Gent., of Lower Harrop, Yorkshire. Issue :

i. EDWARD, *of whom presently.*
ii. JAMES, of Poulton, Gent., *d.* before 1722. Issue :

    i. EDWARD, Attorney-at-Law, living 1742.
    ii. THOMAS.
    iii. JAMES.
    iv. CHRISTOPHER.

EDWARD, eldest son of **Edward** and **Elizabeth (Moore)** **Chew,** *bapt.* at Great Harwood Church, January 28, 1674 ; built, in 1702, Chew House, now "the Asylum ; " *m.* **A——,** and was buried April 15, 1743. Issue :

i.   EDWARD, *b.* 1703; *m.* MRS. CATHERINE CROOKE, *dau.* of
     Alexander and Ann (Townley) Chew. Issue :

     TOWNLEY CHEW, Attorney-at-law, of Breston, 1762 ; London, 1782.

ii. ABRAHAM, *bapt.* January 18, 1707–8, was " of Oxfordshire, Gent.,"
     1742 ; *d. u.*, 1767.

iii. RICHARD, *b* 1710.

iv. ELIZABETH, *b.* 1712.

v.   JAMES, *b.* 1713, was of Billington, Surgeon and Gent., *m.* ANN FOTH-
     ERGILL, who *d.* December, 1759 ; he *d.* 1768, leaving issue, for
     which see " Abram's History of Blackburn," 8º , 1877, pages 443 and 444,
     from which the above pedigree is taken. The representatives then
     were WILLIAM CHEW, of Norman Lodge, Shirley, near North-
     ampton, and WILLIAM LAWRENCE CHEW, Solicitor, of
     Manchester.

SIR BRYAN CHEW, Knt., had, at the visitation of London,
in 1568, a *dau.*, ELLEN ; *m.* John Pattenson, Gent., of Cheriburton,
Yorkshire ; and a second son, BRIAN, " Citizen and Vintonner " of
London.

ROBERT CHEW, of Franklin Township, *m.* **TAMZEN**
——. Issue :

i.	**JANE.**
ii.	**SARAH ANN.**
iii.	**THOMAS E.,** *b.* 1818, *of whom presently.*
iv.	**LAFAYETTE.**
v.	**LEVI.**
vi.	**CHARLES.**
vii.	**MARGARET.**
viii.	**ELIZABETH.**
ix.	**ESTHER ANN.**
x.	**BEULAH.**
xi.	**SAMUEL D.**
xii.	**PHEBE.**

THOMAS E., eldest son of **Robert** and **Tamzen Chew,** *b.* 1818, *m.* **ELIZABETH MILLER.** Issue :

i.	**WILLIAM M.**
ii.	**MATTHIAS M.,** *b.* 1842, *of whom presently.*
iii.	**SUSANNA,** *m.* **MASKELL BATES.**
iv.	**SYDNEY,** *d.* before 1883.
v.	**ISABELLA.**
vi.	**ROBERT.**
vii.	**THOMAS.**
viii.	**SARAH.**
ix.	**ELIZABETH;** x. **MARY ELLA;** and xi. **ROSE ELLA,** all three *d.* before 1883.

MATTHIAS M., second son of **Thomas E.** and **Elizabeth (Miller) Chew,** *b.* February 22, 1842, resided at Williamstown, N. J. ; *m.*, December 22, 1864, **MARY ETTA,** *dau.* of **Thomas A.** and **Abigail Ann (Leonard) Chew.** Issue :

i.	**THOMAS J.,** *b.* January 8, 1867 ; *d.* August 4, 1867.
ii.	**MARY ABIGAIL,** *b.* May 21, 1868.
iii.	**ELIZABETH,** *b.* March 8, 1871.
iv.	**EDWARD D.,** *b.* September 11, 1872.
v.	**SAMUEL M.,** *b.* June 18, 1874.

Authority : History of Gloucester, Salem, and Cumberland Counties.

CHEW, OF LONG ISLAND, AND ELSEWHERE

ONDERDONK'S "Hempstead" notices an action of debt against **John Chew**, May 1, 1672, and notes he was dead by July 3, 1672. **Richard Chew** sues Joseph Jennings, January 3, 1677, and there was a **Richard Chew** had at Flushing, N. Y., twelve upland acres of land, *m.* **Frances Woodward,** and in 1698 was at the same place with his wife, **Frances,** and children, **Rich'd, Henry, Tho., Hannah, Charley, Mary,** and **Elizabeth.**

There were *m.* in Gloria Dei Parish, Philadelphia, **Massey Chew** and **James Davis,** February 1, 1758 ; **Michael Chew** and **Judith Heffenin,** December 25, 1791 ; **Rachel Chew** and **Samuel Gibson,** October 30, 1787 ; **Richard Chew** and **Susannah Tomlinson,** October 15, 1785. At the First Baptist Church,[1] Philadelphia, **Joseph Chew** and **Elizabeth Richardson,** July 26, 1794. And at the First Presbyterian Church,[1] Philadelphia, **Charity Chew** and **Michael Fisher,** November 3, 1730 ; **Frances Chew** and **John McCarty,** September 23, 1741 ; **Mary Chew** and **Francis Murray,** January 25, 1745–46, and **Nathaniel Chew** and **Anne Gibbons,** December 16, 1743.

JOHN CHEW, of Alexandria, Va., said to be son of **John** or **Roger Chew,** of Baltimore, Md., had a son, **ROGER,** resided in Loudoun Co., Va., who *m.* ——, and had two sons :

   i.   JOHN A., a Major under John S. Mosby in the C. S. A. during the Civil War.
   ii.   ROGER PRESTON, *b.* April 9, 1843. At eighteen a Lieutenant in the Confederate Artillery, Colonel commanding Chew's Battery, later, commanded all the Horse Artillery of the Army of Northern Virginia. Resides at Charlestown. W. Va. He *m.* LOUISA FONTAINE, *dau.* of Colonel John Augustine Washington, last owner of " Mt. Vernon." His second *dau.*, Virginia, *d.* December 25, 1894, aged sixteen.

There is also a family of **Chew** resident at Chew's Landing and elsewhere in New Jersey at the present time, probably connected with the Maryland family. Franklin Hough in his "Biographical Notices," p. 72, speaks of **William Chew,** during a long period official interpreter at the Tuscarora village, Lewiston, N. Y., of which tribe of Indians he was Grand Sachem. He *d.* December 29, 1857.

[1] Pennsylvania Marriages before 1810, vol. i., 57, 105 ; ii., 13.

CHEW, OF MARYLAND AND PENNSYLVA-NIA

In the Roll's publication, "Materials for a History of English Wars in France under Henry VI.," mention is made of the Serjeantry of Cheux, in Normandy. "Chewton" is a township in the County of Somersetshire. Chew Magna, Chew Stoke, and Chew Mendip are villages in Chewton. At Chew Magna is Chew Court, the manorial mansion. There, also, is the ancient Church of S. Stephen's, commonly called "Chew Church." A few miles farther south is the ruin, Chew Priory, established under royal charter granted in the fourteenth century by Edward the Third, in which charter order was given that the Vicar of Chew should pay an annual stipend for the maintenance of this Priory. The arms ascribed to Chew (in Burke's "General Armory," 1847) are: *Azure*, a catherine wheel, *or*, between three griffins' heads erased, *argent.* Crest: A griffin *sèjant argent gutte't de sang ;* beaked, legged, and winged *sable*, reposing his dexter foot on a catherine wheel *gules*. Granted, September 15, 1703, to William Chew, of Bedfordshire and London, and there was living recently a **George Chew**, chief of the Income-Tax Bureau, Internal Revenue Department, Somerset House, London, who had a family seat in Bedfordshire. An application for his pedigree remains unanswered. The arms engraved are to be found on a seal ring used by Dr. Sam-

BEWDLEY, WORCESTERSHIRE

From an Old Engraving

uel Chew, Chief-Justice of Newcastle, Sussex and Kent Counties, Penna. (now Delaware), at about the same date as the grant of arms in England. Heralds' College, London, reported to the late Mr. Samuel Chew, of Germantown, Pa., that "In a miscellaneous collection of arms is the following entry, evidently written about two hundred and fifty years ago ; CHEW, *ARG.*, A CHEVRON SABLE, ON A CHIEF *AZURE*, 3 LEOPARDS FACES *OR.*" "It is therefore evident that the arms used by your ancestors [in America] (with some difference in the colors) are the same as those borne by the family in England." May 10, 1639, **John Chewe**, late his Majesty's post at Bewdley, Worcestershire, England, peti-

THE CHEW ARMS, FROM A SEAL, 1725

tions the Council, stating at his entrance into said place he paid £100, and has been at continual charge to keep men and horses to perform the service which has obliged him to sell his lands and estate. Is behind in his pay £471, 4s., and is indebted. Is upward of ninety years of age, with many children and grandchildren. Prays he may receive relief or his creditors will cast him into prison.

January 17, 1639-40, his will was proved as John Chewe, Gentleman, in which he speaks of his daughters Dyna, wife of Thomas Berkham; Susan, wife of John Leland; Hester, wife of Edmond Duncombe, and Sarah, wife of John Eldridge. "His loving son, John Chewe," to whom he leaves £5, and names first, and his son Samuel, whom he makes his executor and principal heir. It would seem from this will that John was his eldest son and was provided for, and had no need to share the inheritance, for there is nothing to show that his father was offended with him. It is therefore possible, though still unproved, that he was the John Chewe, of Virginia, ancestor of the family in America.

JOHN CHEWE, with three servants, in 1622, came to Virginia in the Charitie, and landed at Hogg's Island, opposite Jamestown. His wife, **SARAH**, followed him in the Seafloure the next year. Evidently he was a man of some substance, building a house in "James Citie" at once, and styled in the grant of land made to him in 1623, "John Chewe, Merchant." A deed of 1624 granted him "for the better conveniencie and comodotie of his new house," a rood and nine perches of land lying about it. He was a Burgess from Hogg's Island, in 1623, 1624–29, Agent, managing the business of Robert Benet in James City in November, 1622. Governor Harvey, in 1625, calls him one "of the ablest merchants in Virginia." He was commissioned at some time a Colonel of the Provincial Forces, and was a Burgess from York Co., 1642–43–44. A justice of the same Co., 1634 to 1652. In 1651, in view of his intended marriage to Mrs. Rachel Constable, he makes a deed for certain land recorded in that county. In 1668 he appears to be deceased.

His descendant, Joseph Chew, of Montreal, Secretary for Indian Affairs, writing to his cousin, Joseph Chew, of Connecticut, September 28, 1797, states that about 1643 (1653?) he removed to Maryland, notwithstanding Governor Sir William Berkeley, of Virginia, who had a particular regard for him, endeavoured to dissuade him from doing so in letters which the writer declares he had seen among the family papers. He appears to have had two sons, Samuel and Joseph.

JOSEPH, supposed the younger, who was living in York Co., Va., in 1659, may have been the Joseph Chew appointed a Justice of Newcastle on the Delaware, in November, 1674. He *m.*, November 17, 1685, at the house of Ann Chew, in Herring Creek, Md.,[1] **MARY SMITH**, and *d.* in the same province, February 12, 1715–16. He is also said to have married a Miss **LARKIN**, of Annapolis, and to have had by her a son, **LARKIN CHEW** (*q. v.*). Comparing these dates with those of his brother Samuel and his children there would appear to be a discrepancy suggesting that this Joseph Chew was probably a nephew and not a brother of Samuel, but there are no records to decide the question.[2]

SAMUEL CHEW was residing in Maryland as early as 1648, though in Virginia in 1657. In 1659 he was a member of the Maryland House of Burgesses as Samuel Chew, Gent.; December 17, 1669, he was sworn one of the Justices of the Provincial Court and the Court of Chancery as Samuel Chew, Esq.; July 28, 1669, had been commissioned a member of the Governor's Council; sworn in October 22, 1669, and remained as such until his death. He was a prominent member of the provincial government, described the year before his death as "Colonel Samuel Chew, Chancellor and Secretary," a tobacco planter and possessed of land and considerable wealth. He resided at Herring Bay, calling himself

---

[1] Minutes of the West River Yearly Meeting, *p.* 76.

[2] Samuel, son of Colonel Samuel Chew, registers the death of " My onkel, Joseph Chew, 12th of twelfth month, 1715–16, being —— of age," in his Bible.

Samuel Chew, of Herrington, in his will, by which he left the half of his landed estate to his eldest son, dividing the remainder between his two younger sons, and leaving his daughters and other sons shares in his personal property, white and black servants, and tobacco. He also bequeaths to his brother, Joseph Chew, "his seale gold ring." He *m.*, about 1658–59, **ANNE**, only *dau.* and heiress of **William Ayres**, of Nansemond Co., Va., and *d.* March 15, 1676–77. His widow was a prominent member of the Society of Friends, and their monthly meetings were long held at her house on Herring Bay. She *d.* April 13, 1695. Issue :

i.   **SAMUEL**, *b.* in 1660, *of whom presently.*
ii.   **JOSEPH** (*q. v.*).
iii.   **NATHANIEL**, inherited Popping Jay at Lyons Creek, Calvert Co., and *d.* after February 20, 1695–96.
iv.   **WILLIAM.**
v.   **BENJAMIN**, *b.* April 12, 1671 (*q. v.*).
vi.   **JOHN**, *d.* February 19, 1696–97.
vii.   **CALEB**, *d.* May 8, 1698.
viii.   **SARAH**, *m.* a **BURGES.**
ix.   **ANNE**, *d.* January 28, 1699–1700.

SAMUEL, eldest son of **Samuel** and **Anne (Ayres) Chew**, *b.* in 1660, inherited half his father's estate and his right on Poplar Ridge at Herring Creek ; lived at Herring Bay, also owned three hundred acres called Chew's Rest ; *m.*, first, April 14, 1682, **ANNE ——**. Issue by her, who *d.* April 8, 1702 : [1]

i.   **SAMUEL**, *b.* May 28, 1683, *of whom presently.*
ii.   **ANN**, *b.* July 2, 1685 ; *d.* January 28, 1694–95.
iii.   **JOHN**, *b.* April 8, 1687 (*q. v.*).
iv.   v.   **JOSEPH** and **BENJAMIN**, twins, *b.* April 1, 1689 ; the latter *d.* April 18, 1698 ; the former *d.* at London, February 2, 1716–17, and was buried at Ratcliffe.
vi.   **NATHANIEL**, *b.* August 5, 1692 ; *m.* **MARY ——**, who *d.* August 24, 1728 ; he *d.* January 30, 1727–28. Issue :

     i.   **NATHANIEL.**
     ii.   **JOSEPH.**
     iii.   **ANN**, *m.*, in 1727, **AQUILA JOHNS** (*q. v.*).

vii.   **JOSEPH**, *b.* April 28, 1696 ; *m.*, **SARAH ——**, and *d.* in February, 1754. Issue :

[1] This date, and many others on this page, are from a "Chew Family Bible," printed 1683, now at Lebanon, West River, through D. M. Thomas, Esq., of Baltimore. Francis Chew, the then possessor of the Bible, notes : "Sunday, April 12, 1772, this blessed Bible had like to been burnt in Samuel Chew's, Esq., House, where I then lived."

i.   **THOMAS.**
ii.   **ELIZABETH**, *m.* JOHN, son of Samuel and Sarah (Giles) Hopkins (*q. v.*).
iii.   **SUSANNAH.**

SAMUEL CHEW, *m.*, second, June 29, 1704, **MRS. ELIZA**
——, widow of **WILLIAM COALE** (*q. v.*); she *d.* February
27, 1709–10, and **MR. CHEW** *d.*, without further issue, October
10, 1718.

SAMUEL, eldest son of **Samuel** and **Anne** (——) **Chew,** *b.*
May 28, 1683; engaged in commerce, applying, September 24,
1733, for register of his snow Henrietta, eighty tons burden,
and July, 1735, for register of his sloop Boneta, of six tons; he
m., August 26, 1703, **MARY,** *dau.* of Richard and **Elizabeth
Harrison** (*b.* October 10, 1684; *d.* August 24, 1725). **Richard
Harrison** was Burgess from Carroll Co. **SAMUEL CHEW**
d. October 31, 1736. Issue:

i.   **SAMUEL,** *m.* **HENRIETTA MARIA,** *dau.* of Philemon Lloyd,
       who afterward *m.* **HON. DANIEL DULANEY, JR.,** and had
       a son, **LLOYD,** killed in a duel with Rev. Bennett Allen.

       SAMUEL CHEW, *d.* January 15, 1736–37. Issue:

       i.   **SAMUEL,** called of " Herring Bay," a Justice for Anne Arundel Co., May 3, 1740.
       ii.   **HENRIETTA MARIA,** *m.* **EDWARD DORSEY.**
       iii. iv. **PHILEMON LLOYD** and **BENNETT,** twins, the former *d. s. p.*, March 17, 1770,
             leaving his estate on Wye Island to his sister Margaret. The latter *m.* **ANNA
             MARIA,** *dau.* of Edward Tilghman (*q. v.*). Issue:
             Edward (*d. s. p.*).
       v.   **MARGARET,** *m.* **JOHN BEALE BORDLEY** (*q. v.*).
       vi. **MARY,** *m.* **GOVERNOR WILLIAM PACA,** signer of the Declaration of In-
           dependence, and had issue: John.

ii.   **ANN,** *m.*, August 11, 1724, **PHILIP THOMAS** (*q. v.*).
iii. **ELIZABETH,** *b.* October 18, 1709; *d.* July 29, 1719.
iv. **JOHN,** *b.* September 19, 1711; *d.* March 21, 1726–27.
v.   **MARY,** *b.* in 1714; *m.* **JOHN HEPBOURNE**; *d.* August 10, 1770.
vi. **RICHARD,** *b.* in May, 1716, *of whom presently.*
vii. **FRANCIS,** *d.* May 24, 1720.
viii. **FRANCIS,** *b.* in 1721; *m.*, Sunday, February 26, 1749–50, at the house
       of Rev. James Williamson, **MARY LINGAN,** who *d.* February
       12, 1764. He *d.* November 11, 1775. Issue:

       i.   **SAMUEL,** *b.* January 29, 1755.
       ii.   **ANN,** *b.* May 15, 1759.
       iii. **RICHARD,** *b.* October 19, 1761.

ix.   **ELIZABETH,** second, *b.* June 11, 1725; *d.* June 25, 1726.

RICHARD, third son of **Samuel** and **Mary (Harrison) Chew**, *b.* in May, 1716; *m.*, January 5, 1749–50, **MRS. SARAH (LOCK) CHEW**, widow of his cousin, Samuel Chew, of John, and *d.* June 24, 1769; his wife *d.* February 1, 1791, aged seventy years. Issue, by her second husband:

i.   **MARY**, *b.* December 27, 1750; *m.*, first, February 10, 1767, **DR. ALEXANDER HAMILTON SMITH**. Issue:

       i.   **UPTON.**   ii. **SARAH.**

       MRS. SMITH *m.*, second, —— **LLYLES**, and *d.* November 23, 1793.

ii.   **RICHARD**, *b.* April 10, 1753, *of whom presently.*
iii.   **CAPTAIN SAMUEL**, *b.* December 9, 1755; *d.* February 1, 1785.
iv.   **LOCK**, *b.* November 14, 1757; *d. s. p.*, December 9, 1793.
v.   **FRANCIS**, *b.* July 10, 1760.
vi.   **SARAH LOCK**, *b.* November 20, 1761; *m.* —— **LANE.**
vii. **PHILEMON LLOYD**, *b.* July 23, 1765; *m.*, October 28, 1790, **ANN**, *dau.* of **William Bowie**, of Prince George's Co. Issue:

     i.   **MARGARET BOWIE**, *b.* September 17, 1791.
     ii.   **ELIZA**, *b.* January 14, 1793.
     iii.   **WILLIAM BOWIE**, *b.* September 27, 1794.
     iv.   **RICHARD**, *b.* February 6, 1796.
     v.   **ROBERT BOWIE**, *b.* February 21, 1797.
     vi.   **SAMUEL**, *b.* September 18, 1798.
     vii.   **WALTER BOWIE**, *b.* November 23, 1799.
     viii. **HENRY MORTIMER**, *b.* March 17, 1801.
     ix.   **JOHN**, *b.* August 14, 1802; *d.* August 23, same year.
     x.   **SARAH MARIA**, *b.* December 9, 1803.
     xi.   **ANN MARIA**, *b.* October 19, 1806.

RICHARD, eldest son of **Richard** and **Sarah (Lock) Chew**, *b.* April 10, 1753, was a Captain and afterward Major in the Maryland line. July 24, 1776, the soldiers of his company make complaint against him to the Committee of Safety,[1] accusing him of saying, " no poor man was entitled to a vote, and those that would insist upon voting should be put to death." They accuse his brother Samuel of saying " that a poor man was not born to freedom, but to be a drudge on earth." Evidently some of the Revolutionaries did not sympathize with Jefferson's Declaration.

MAJOR CHEW, *m.*, first, February 4, 1773, **MARGARET**, *dau.* of **James John Mackall**, who *d.* May 20, 1779, aged twenty-four. Issue:

i.   **RICHARD**, *b.* October 4, 1773, *of whom presently.*
ii.   **MARY MACKALL**, *b.* September 17, 1776; *m.* —— **BRINGMAN.** Issue:

     MARGARET, *m.* **DR. FRY.**

---

[1] Maryland Archives, printed vol. xii., *p.* 323.

MAJOR CHEW, *m.,* second, May 2, 1780, **FRANCES,** *dau.* of **Thomas Holland,** of Calvert Co., Md.   She *d.* September 26, 1799, and her husband *d.* June 6, 1801.   Further issue :

iii.   **THOMAS HOLLAND,** *b.* October 27, 1781 (*q. v.*).
iv.   **WILLIAM HOLLAND,** *b.* August 7, 1784 ; *d.* September 11, 1799.
v.   **SARAH,** *b.* March 16, 1787 ; *d.* December 28, 1790.
vi.   **PHILEMON,** *b.* February 20, 1789 ; educated at S. John's College, Annapolis ; was a member of the House of Delegates and of the Executive Council of Maryland ; *m.,* February 21, 1813, **ANN MARIA BOWIE,** *dau.* of **General John Brookes,** *b.* November 17, 1789 ; *d.* July 18, 1862. Her husband *d.* September 30, 1850. Issue :

    i.   **RICHARD,** *b.* March 21, 1814 ; *d.* March 30, 1814.
    ii.   **WILLIAM HOLLAND,** *b.* July 10, 1815 ; *d.* in March, 1841.
    iii.   **MARGARET SPRIGG BOWIE,** *b.* January 3, 1818 ; *m.,* June 22, 1843, **JUDGE WILLIAM HALLAM TUCK,** graduated S. John's College, Annapolis, 1827 ; Speaker of the Maryland House of Delegates ; Member State Convention, 1850-51 ; Judge of the Court of Appeals, 1851-61 ; Senator of Maryland, Judge of Second Judicial District, Visitor and Governor of S. John's College. He *d.* March 17, 1884, and his widow *d.* March 12, 1885. Issue (surname TUCK) :

        i.   **Maria Louisa.**
        ii.   **William Hallam,** *d. y.*
        iii.   **Somerville Pinkney,** Judge of the International Court, Alexandria, Egypt. LL.D. by S. John's College, Annapolis, in 1894 ; *m.,* May 14, 1885, **Emily Rosalie Snowden,** *dau.* of Colonel Charles and Emily Rosalie (Andrews) Marshall (*q. v.*). Issue : i. Carola Marshall, *b.* January 27, 1889. ii. William Hallam, *b.* March 9, 1890. iii. Somerville Pinkney, second, *b.* May 21, 1891. iv. Alexander John Marshall, *b.* September 6, 1892.
        iv.   **Frances Chew,** *d. y.*
        v.   **Philemon Hallam.**

    iv.   **MARIA LOUISA,** *b.* January 14, 1820 ; *d.* in October, 1836.
    v.   **BENJAMIN BROOKES,** *b.* February 16, 1823 ; *d.* in 1826.
    vi.   **RICHARD BENJAMIN BROOKES,** *b.* May 14, 1828 ; *m.,* November 23, 1853, **LOUISA DANGERFIELD BROOKES.**   Issue :

        i.   **Eliza Dangerfield,** *b.* November 4, 1854.
        ii.   **Philemon,** *b.* December 3, 1855 ; *d.* December 10, 1855.
        iii.   **Anna Maria Bowie,** *b.* November 22, 1856.
        iv.   **John Brookes,** *b.* January 9, 1859.
        v.   **Richard Benjamin Brookes, Jr.,** *b.* August 8, 1862.
        vi.   **Philemon Walter,** *b.* May 26, 1863.
        vii.   **William Hallam Tuck,** *b.* April 7, 1867.
        viii.   **Sarah Dangerfield,** *b.* August 13, 1870.

vii.   **SARAH LOCK,** *b.* April 28, 1791, *d. i.*
viii.   **FRANCES,** *b.* April 19, 1793.
ix.   **BETTIE HOLLAND,** *b.* September 19, 1795 ; *d.* September 19, 1797.
x.   **SAMUEL LOCK,** *b.* July 27, 1797 ; *d.* February 12, 1798.
xi.   **BETTIE H.,** second, *b.* May 15, 1799 ; *d.* October 18, 1800.

RICHARD, eldest son of **Major Richard** and **Margaret (Mackall) Chew,** *b.* October 4, 1773 ; *m.,* December 20, 1804,

ELIZABETH, *dau.* of **Leonard Hollyday,** and *d.* June 20, 1831. Issue :

i.   **RICHARD,** *b.* September 21, 1805 ; *d. s. p.* September 23, 1832.
ii.   **SARAH AMELIA HOLLYDAY,** *b.* April 21, 1807, *d. u.*
iii.   **MARGARET MACKALL,** *b.* February 1, 1809 ; *m.*, March 20, 1831, **DR. ROBERT W. GLASS.**
iv.   **LEONARD HOLLYDAY,** *b.* November 13, 1810 ; *m.* **AMELIA BEALL HOLLYDAY,** and *d. s. p.*
v.   **JAMES JOHN,** *b.* February 20, 1813, *d. s. p.* October 1, 1847.
vi.   **MARIA LOUISA,** *b.* May 27, 1815 ; *d.* in August, 1838.
vii.   **ROBERT WILLIAM BOWIE,** *b.* March 13, 1819 ; *m.*, May 21, 1846, **MARY VIRGINIA LEVERING,** who *d.* in September, 1863, and her husband *d. s. p.* in April, 1868.
viii.   **MARY ELIZABETH,** *b.* March 17, 1820.

THOMAS HOLLAND, eldest son of **Major Richard** and **Frances (Holland) Chew,** *b.* October 27, 1781 ; *m.*, first, **ELIZABETH,** *dau.* of **Walter Smith,** of Calvert Co., Md., who *d.* December 30, 1825 ; and her husband *m.*, second, February 7, 1828, **MARY DAVIS,** who *d.* August 11, 1829, leaving an only *dau.*, **MARY ELIZABETH F.,** *b.* February 28, 1829 ; *m.*, in 1856, **FREDERICK G. SMITH,** and *d.* 1875, having had issue (surname SMITH): **Philemon Chew,** *b.* in 1857 ; **Mary Evans,** *b.* in 1859 ; **Walter Chew;** and **Susan Freeland,** *d. i.*

THOMAS H. CHEW *d.* March 16, 1840. Issue by his first wife :

i.   **RICHARD,** *b.* September 26, 1806 ; *d.* April 19, 1809.
ii.   **SUSAN SMITH,** *b.* December 5, 1807 ; *d.* September 9, 1809.
iii.   **FRANCES ANN,** *b.* May 2, 1810 ; *d.* August 21, 1822.
iv.   **WALTER SMITH,** *b.* August 13, 1811 ; *m.*, January 7, 1840, **MARTHA J. REID,** of Wilkinson Co., Miss. Issue :

     i.   **ANN REID,** *b.* November 23, 1840.
     ii.   **THOMAS HOLLAND,** *b.* January 29, 1843.
     iii.   **PHILEMON,** *b.* 1845.
     iv.   **SARAH ELLEN,** *b.* May 17, 1848.
     v.   **RICHARD FLOWER,** *b.* April 15, 1851.
     vi.   **ELIZABETH SMITH,** *b.* June 14, 1853.
     vii.   **JAMES REID,** *b.* August 26, 1856 ; *d.* August 15, 1869.
     viii.   **WILLIAM SCOTT,** *b.* September 15, 1858 ; *d.* March 23, 1861.
     ix.   **FREDERICK FREELAND,** *b.* November 9, 1861 ; *d.* May 31, 1863.

v.   **JOSEPH SMITH,** *b.* July 15, 1814 ; *d.* August 27, 1822.
vi.   **PHILEMON,** *b.* July 2, 1816, *of whom presently.*
vii.   **DANIEL RAWLINGS,** *b.* November 25, 1819 ; *d.* July 16, 1820.

DR. PHILEMON, sixth child of **Thomas H.** and **Elizabeth** (**Smith**) **Chew**, *b.* July 2, 1816; *m.*, November 26, 1839, **RE-BECCA CHEW FREELAND.** Issue :

i.   **THOMAS HOLLAND, JR.,** *b.* January 23, 1842.
ii.   **ELIZABETH,** *b.* April 12, 1843; *m.* **DR. T. B. POINTDEXTER.**
iii.   **MARIA LOUISA,** *b.* December 28, 1844; *m.* **SAMUEL G. SMITH.**
iv.   **SUSAN HAWKINS,** *b.* April 21, 1846.
v.   **JOSEPH WALTER,** *b.* March 15, 1849.
vi.   **WILLIAM FREELAND,** *b.* November 20, 1851.
vii.   **EDWARD,** *b.* October 25, 1855; *d.* 1870.
viii.   **MARY CECELIA,** *b.* March 17, 1858; *d.* 1868.

JOHN, second son of **Samuel** and **Anne** (——) **Chew**, and grandson of **Samuel** and **Anne** (**Ayres**) **Chew**, *b.* April 8, 1687; *m.*, in 1708, **ELIZA HARRISON**, who *m.*, second, in 1722, **ELIHU HALL.** Her first husband *d.* the 12th of —— month, 1718. Issue :

i.   **SAMUEL,** *of whom presently.*
ii.   **ANN,** *m.*, August 17, 1727, **JOSEPH,** son of **Gerrard** and **Margaret Hopkins** (*q. v.*).
iii.   **SARAH.**
iv.   **MARY,** probably *m.*, in July, 1727, **GILBERT CROCKETT.**

SAMUEL, only son of **John** and **Eliza** (**Harrison**) **Chew**, *m.* **SARAH**, *dau.* of **Dr. Richard Lock**, and *d.* in London in 1749. Issue :

i.   **SAMUEL LLOYD,** *b.* 1737, *of whom presently.*
ii.   **JOHN** (*q. v.*).
iii.   **WILLIAM,** *b.* 1746 (*q. v.*).
iv.   **ELIZABETH,** *m.*, first, —— **SMITH,** and second, —— **SPRIGG.**

SAMUEL LLOYD, eldest son of **Samuel** and **Sarah** (**Lock**) **Chew**, *b.* in 1737; was a member of the Maryland Revolutionary Convention of 1775; First Lieutenant Third Battalion Flying Camp, June to December, 1776; Captain Third Maryland, December 10, 1776; resigned, February, 1777; *m.*, first, —— **WEEMS.** Issue :

i.   **SAMUEL,** who removed to Kentucky in 1805; was in the State Legislature, and *m.* twice; his second wife, —— **SMITH,** was a sister of the wives of Thomas Holland Chew and General Zachary Taylor. He *d.* about 1820, and is buried at St. Francisville, La. Issue :

     i.   **DR. EDWARD,** *d.* of yellow fever about 1825.
     ii.   **SAMUEL,** who remained in Kentucky, and had a son :
         Dr. Samuel.

SAMUEL CHEW
BORN 1737   DIED 1790
MEMBER OF THE MARYLAND CONVENTION OF 1775

SAMUEL LLOYD CHEW, *m.,* second, **PRISCILLA,** *dau.* of **Rev. Samuel** and **Elizabeth (Gantt) Claggett,** and descended from **Colonel Edward Claggett,** of Canterbury, England, who *m.* **Margaret,** *dau.* of **Sir Thomas Adams,** founder of an Arabic professorship at the University of Cambridge. **SAMUEL LLOYD CHEW** *d.* February 20, 1790. Issue, by second wife :

ii.   **JOHN HAMILTON,** *b.* September 14, 1771, *of whom presently.*

JOHN HAMILTON, only son of **Samuel** and **Priscilla Claggett Chew,** *b.* September 14, 1771 ; *m.* his cousin, **PRISCILLA ELIZABETH,** *dau.* of **Rt. Rev. Thomas John Claggett, D.D.,** first Bishop of Maryland, and the first Bishop of the Protestant Episcopal Church consecrated in the United States, and *d.* March 22, 1830 ; his widow *d.* in 1843. Issue :

i.   **MARY,** *m.* **LA FAYETTE GIBSON.**
ii.   **SAMUEL,** *of whom presently.*
iii.   **THOMAS JOHN,** *m.* **JANE BLAKE.**
iv.   **WILLIAM PACA.**
v.   **PRISCILLA,** *m.* **REV. HENRY WILLIAMS.** Issue   (surname
        WILLIAMS) :

        HENRY, JOHN C., FERDINAND, THOMAS J. C., and SAMUEL.

vi.   **ELIZABETH,** *d. u.*
vii.   **REV. JOHN HILARY,** *m.* **GENEVIEVE CLAGGETT,** and *d.* at
        Washington, D. C., July 6, 1885.

SAMUEL, eldest son of **John Hamilton Chew,** *b.* April 29, 1806 ; was graduated at Princeton College in 1825, and in Medicine, at the University of Maryland in 1829 ; was appointed Professor of Materia Medica in that University in 1841, and transferred to the Chair of Practice of Medicine in 1852. He *m.,* first, **ELIZA M. FITZHUGH.** Issue :

i.   **ELIZA M.**

DR. SAMUEL CHEW *m.,* second, **HENRIETTA S. SCOTT,** and *d.* December 25, 1863. Further issue :

ii.   **ANNA.**
iii.   **SAMUEL CLAGGETT,** was graduated at Princeton College in 1856, and
        in Medicine at the University of Maryland in 1858 ; was appointed to
        the Chair of Materia Medica in the same University in 1864, and to
        that of Practice of Medicine in 1885 ; in 1893 elected Surgeon-General

of the Society of Colonial Wars. He *m.*, first, **MARIA GIBSON.**
Issue :

i.   **SAMUEL,** *d.* 1868.

    He *m.*, second, **AGNES R. MARSHALL.** Further issue:

ii.   **JOHN MARSHALL,** *b.* August 20, 1886.
iii. **SAMUEL CLAGGETT,** *b.* August 31, 1888.
iv.   **HENRY DORSEY,** *b.* January 15, 1891.

iv. **HENRIETTA S.**

JOHN, second son of **Samuel** and **Sarah (Lock) Chew,** *m.* ———
———. There is a letter of his addressed to Captain Richard
Chew, his step-brother, dated March 9, 1776, which may give his
wife's name ; unless the reference is to the Captain's wife. He
writes :

"I am at my moth! now moveing her furnature. there is a
man of war at the mouth of the river and two tenders. I hope
you will let me know by a line how the case is with you. My
mother has sint a boy with six blancoats. From your affect.
Brother,   JOHN CHEW.

"P. S. Peggy & child is well. Mama's love to you all. don't
let Lockey enroll." He *d.* May 26, 1785. Issue :

i.   **JOHN LANE,** *b.* 1762, *of whom presently.*
ii.   **SAMUEL,** *m.*, November 1, 1803, **ANN SMITH.** Issue :

    i.   **WILLIAM PACE,** *b.* November 21, 1806.
    ii.   **SARAH ANN,** *b.* June 21, 1808.
    iii. **HORACE,** *b.* May 12, 1812.
    iv.   **EDWARD R.,** who *d.* November 8, 1829.

iii. **NATHANIEL LANE.**
iv.   **WILLIAM.**

JOHN LANE, eldest son of **John Chew,** *b.* 1762, at the old
homestead, "Lombardy Poplars," Anne Arundel Co., Md., and
resided there. He was educated at Oxford University, England ; *m.* **MARY R. WILSON,** who *d.* in 1802 ; her husband
d. in 1832. Issue :

i.   **ELIZABETH,** *b.* 1788 ; *d. u.,* 1870.
ii.   **JOHN,** *b.* December 3, 1790, *of whom presently.*
iii. **EDWARD,** *b.* 1794. He *m.* **MARY SPARROW** (who afterwards *m.*
    UPTON SCOTT KEY) and *d.* Issue :

    THOMAS EDWARD, *b.* in 1840.

JOHN, eldest son of **John Lane** and **Mary (Wilson) Chew,** *b.*
December 3, 1790 ; entered the United States Navy about 1805,

JOHN CHEW
BORN 1790, DIED 1872

and served for many years, acting as Recruiting Officer in the service, with head-quarters at Philadelphia and New York. He resigned in 1817, and joined the Mexican Expedition of General Espoz y Mina, acting as his Chief of Staff. After the failure of that attempt he returned to the United States and entered the merchant service as captain of a vessel in the trade between Baltimore and the Mediterranean ports. Retired from the sea in 1826, removed to North Mississippi in 1835, and, engaging in cotton-planting, amassed a considerable fortune. He *m.*, May 28, 1828, **MARY ANN SMITH,** of Calvert Co., Md., who *d.* July 10, 1876; her husband *d.* February 24, 1872. Issue, with seven other children, who *d. i.* :

i.   **GLORVINA,** *b.* May 15, 1830 ; *d. u.*

ii.   **JOHN CALHOUN,** *b.* May 28, 1838, residing in New York City ; *m.*, first, July 11, 1861, **ZILPHIA GUTHRIE FULLER.** Issue : **JOHN MARSHALL,** *b.* May 17, 1862, a clergyman of the P. E. Church, Rector of the Church of the Good Shepherd, Newburg, N. Y. **Mrs. CHEW** *d.* August 8, 1863, and her husband *m.*, second, February 1, 1876, **THEODORA R. SEIXAS.**

iii.   **FRISBY FREELAND,** *b.* October 9, 1839 ; resides at Houston, Tex.; *m.*, September 26, 1861, **JULIA A. FULLER.** Issue :

     i.   **FREELAND FULLER,** *b.* May 22, 1863.
     ii.   **ROBERT EDWARD,** *b.* April 11, 1865 ; *d.* April 25, 1865.
     iii.   **FRANK NATHAN,** *b.* March 19, 1866 ; *d. u.*, May 19, 1888.
     iv.   **BEVERLY,** *b.* July 28, 1868.
     v.   **MARY ANN,** *b.* May 17, 1870 ; *m.*, May 3, 1893, **ALBERT STOWE LEE-CRAFT.**
     vi.   **SAM YOUNG,** *b.* January 25, 1873 ; *d.* February 2, 1873.
     vii.   **EDWARD TILGHMAN,** *b.* September 3, 1876.
     viii.   **ZYLPHIA JULIA,** *b.* December 11, 1878 ; *d.* December 27, 1878.
     ix.   **JOHN,** *b.* June 9, 1880.
     x.   **JENNIE,** *b.* September 25, 1886 ; *d.* May 11, 1887.
     xi.   **ANNIE BETH,** *b.* October 9, 1888.

iv.   **ROBERT EDWARD,** *b.* October 28, 1844 : resides at Gibsland, La.; *m.*, October 25, 1865, **MARY PUGH GOVAN.** Issue :

     i.   **JULIA HAWKS,** *b.* June 24, 1866.
     ii.   **EDWARD GOVAN,** *b.* September 9, 1867.
     iii.   **FRISBY FREELAND,** *b.* October 9, 1869.
     iv.   **RALPH,** *b.* September 27, 1872.
     v.   **WILLIAM ROBERTS,** *b.* November 24, 1873 ; *d.* July 15, 1880.
     vi.   **FRANCIS HAWKS,** *b.* May 9, 1875.
     vii.   **CARRIE,** *b.* May 8, 1877.
     viii.   **MARY PUGH,** *b.* October 26, 1879.

WILLIAM, third son of **Samuel** and **Sarah (Lock) Chew,** *b.*

1746; *m.* **ELIZABETH**, *dau.* of **Thomas Reynolds**, who *d.*
April 1, 1801. He *d.* April 9, 1801. Issue:

i.   **SARAH**, *b.* July 11, 1770; *m.*, first, **ALLEN BOWIE**, of Prince
George's Co., Md. Issue:

        A son, **FIELDER.**

    m., second, **DR. FRISBY FREELAND**, of Mississippi; and
third, **BEVERLY R. GRAYSON**, of the same State, and *d.* September 10, 1843.

ii.   **ELIZABETH**, *b.* April 26, 1772; *m.* —— **MOSEBY**, of Kentucky, and
d. in June, 1828.

iii.   **FRANCIS HOLLAND**, *b.* December 12, 1774; *m.* —— **CALVIT**, or
CALVERT, of Mississippi, and *d.* August 24, 1834.

iv.   **MARY**, *b.* June 4, 1776; *m.* **DR. THOMAS REYNOLDS**, of Mississippi, and *d.* May 1, 1821.

v.   **WILLIAM LOCK**, *b.* April 10, 1778, *of whom presently.*

vi.   **ANN REYNOLDS**, *b.* July 19, 1780; *m.* —— **CRAIG**, of Kentucky.

WILLIAM LOCK, only son of **William** and **Elizabeth (Reynolds) Chew**, *b.* April 10, 1778; *m.*, October 22, 1805, **REBECCA**, *dau.* of **Frisby** and **Sarah (Rolle) Freeland**, *b.* April 30, 1785, in Calvert Co., Md.; *d.* June 12, 1840, in Yazoo Co., Mississippi. **WILLIAM L. CHEW** *d.* July 17, 1858, at Bay St. Louis, Miss. Issue:

i.   **WILLIAM**, *b.* July 12, 1806; *d.* July 6, 1807.

ii.   **FRISBY FREELAND**, *b.* April 7, 1808; *m.*, February 28, 1837,
MARIA ANGELICA, *dau.* of **General George W.** and **Ann M. (Hopewell) Biscoe**, of Washington, D. C., and *d.* July 11, 1849. Issue:

    i.   **GEORGE BISCOE**, *b.* December 31, 1837; *d.* August 18, 1840.

    ii.   **WILLIAM LOCK**, *b.* February 4, 1841; *d.* December 2, 1864, in the C. S. A., of
wounds received at the battle of Franklin, Tenn.

    iii.   **MONROE GRAYSON.**

    iv.   **GEORGE BISCOE.**

    v.   **REBECCA FREELAND**, *m.* **CHARLES HUNTINGTON LYMAN, U. S. N.**
Issue (surname **LYMAN**):

        i.   **Charles Huntington**, *b.* September 22, 1875.

        ii.   **Mary Kerr Coffey**, *b.* 1876.

        iii.   **David Hinckley**, *b.* October 14, 1877.

        iv.   **Frisby Freeland**, *b.* 1880.

    vi.   **FIELDER BOWIE**, resides at S. Paul, and is a Gentleman of the Council, Minnesota Society of Colonial Wars, 1896.

iii.   **WILLIAM LOCK**, *b.* February 2, 1810; *m.*, February 10, 1831, **SUSAN MONROE SMITH**, and *d. s. p.* June 8, 1844.

iv.   **FRANCES ANN**, *b.* March 9, 1812; *d.* September 10, 1816.

v.   **SARAH ROLLE**, *b.* July 12, 1814; *m.*, first, July 8, 1830, **MAJOR**

SPENCE MONROE GRAYSON, and second, **GENERAL F. T. GRAYSON**. Issue by her first husband (surname GRAYSON) :

    i.   **THOMAS THORPE**, *b.* March 16, 1835 ; *d.* 1876.
    ii.   **REBECCA FREELAND**.
    iii. **WILLIAM CHEW**, *b.* July 21, 1837.
    iv. **SPENCE MONROE**.

vi.   **AUGUSTIN FREELAND**, *b.* July 23, 1816 ; *d.* July 24, 1816.

vii.   **AUGUSTIN**, *b.* March 22, 1818 ; *m.*, in 1859, **ELIZABETH**, *dau.* of Colonel **Lewis W. Thompson**, of Mississippi.

viii. **BEVERLY GRAYSON**, *b.* January 21, 1820 ; *m.* **ELIZABETH**, *dau.* of Colonel **Frederick Smith**, of Mississippi. Issue :

    i.   **FREDERICK SMITH**, *b.* 1859 ; *m.* **MOLLIE T. BLAKELEY**. Issue :
         Beverly G. ; William Locke ; Pattie Elizabeth Freeland.
    ii.   **WILLIAM LOCK**, *b.* 1861 ; *m.* **ANNA SIMMS**, *d. s. p.* 1889.
    iii. **AUGUSTIN**.

ix.   **EDWARD ROBERT**, *b.* October 12, 1823 ; *d.* June 19, 1826.

x.   **THOMAS REYNOLDS**, *b.* February 22, 1826, *of whom presently.*

xi.   **ROBERT EDWARD**, *b.* January 19, 1829, commander of a regiment in the C. S. A., and killed at the battle of Prairie Grove, Ark., in 1862.

DR. THOMAS REYNOLDS, tenth child of **William Lock** and **Rebecca (Freeland) Chew**, *b.* February 22, 1826 ; resides at San Antonio, Tex.; *m.*, November 7, 1851, **MARY**, *dau.* of **Edward Butler Grayson**, of Washington, D. C. Issue :

i.   **WILLIAM LOCK**, *b.* September 28, 1855.
ii.   **ROBERT EDWARD**.
iii. **SARAH ROLLE**.
iv. **MARY GRAYSON**.
v.   **REBECCA FREELAND**.
vi. **SPENCE MONROVIA**.
vii. **BETTIE**.
viii. **THOMAS REYNOLDS**.
ix. **EDWARD GRAYSON**.

JOSEPH, second son of **Samuel** and **Anne (Ayres) Chew**, inherited " Hambley," four hundred and fifty acres, and *m.* **MRS. ELIZABETH (GASSAWAY) BATTEE**, and *d.* February 1, 1704-5 ; his wife *d.* in May, 1716. Issue by her second husband :

i.   **JOSEPH**, *of whom presently.*
ii.   **HENRY**, *m.* **ELIZABETH ——**. Issue, two sons :

    i.   **HENRY**, who removed to one of the lower counties in Maryland.
    ii.   **JOSEPH**, *b.* August 24, 1719 (*q. v.*).

JOSEPH, eldest son of **Joseph** and **Elizabeth (Gassaway) Chew**, *m*. ——. Issue :

i.   **JOSEPH**, *of whom presently.*
ii.   **HENRY.**
iii.   **ELIZA.**

JOSEPH, the eldest son, *m*. ——. Issue :

i.   **NATHANIEL**, *b*. 1748 ; *d. s. p.* 1827.
ii.   **JOHN**, *m*. ——, and *d*. about 1815, in Prince George's Co., Md. Issue (order of birth uncertain) :

    i.   **ROBERT**, *b*. 1776, *of whom presently.*
    ii.   **NATHANIEL**, *b*. 1785 ; *m*., in 1814, —— ; *d*. 1845. Issue :
       i.   Rev. John W., *m*. —— Bird.
       ii.   Nathaniel, and two others.
    iii.   **WALTER**, *m*. MRS.—— (JONES) COBB. Issue, a son, *d. u.*, under twenty-one.
    iv.   **JOHN**, *d. u.*
    v.   **ANN.**
    vi.   **ELIZABETH.**
    vii.   **ARTRIDGE.**
    viii. **AGNES**, *m*. MASON CLARK, of Montgomery Co., Md.

ROBERT, eldest son of the above **John Chew**, *b*. 1776 ; *m*. **TABITHA WILSON**, of Maryland, and *d*. 1838. Issue :

i.   **MARY ELIZABETH**, *m*. **GABRIEL LANGLEY**, of Washington, D. C.
ii.   **JOHN**, *m*. **ISABELLA STEWART**, of Baltimore.
iii.   **TABITHA ANN**, *d. i.*
iv.   **SPRIGG**, *d. u.*
v. vi.   Twins, **MARCELINA**, *d. i.*, and **ROSINA** ; *m*. **GEORGE MILLER**, of Massachusetts.
vii   **ROBERTA.**
viii.   **ARTRIDGE**, *d. i.*
ix.   **CHRISTINA**, *d. i.*
x.   **ROBERT**, *m*. **MARY CROSS**, of Prince George's Co., Md. No issue.
xi.   **CHRISTOPHER C.**, *b*. 1837 ; *m*. **MARY J. MILES**, of Montgomery Co., Md. Issue :

    i.   **MARY KATHERINE**, *m*. J. H. GILLIGAN, of Massachusetts.
    ii.   **HARRY WINTER**, *m*. LOTTIE C. CALHOUN, of Washington, D. C.
    iii.   **TABITHA E.**, *m*. J. M. BLAIR, of Massachusetts.
    iv.   **JOHN L.**, *b*. December 3, 1866 ; Professor of Mathematics at S. John's College, Annapolis, Md.

JOSEPH, second son of **Henry** and **Elizabeth Chew**, *b*. August 24, 1719 ; resided at Deer Creek, Harford Co., Md. ; *m*., 1745, **SARAH (SHERIDAN ?)**. Issue :

i.   ELIZABETH, *b.* July 18, 1747 ; *m.*, November 24, 1768, JOHN HOP-
     KINS (*q. v.*).
ii. SUSAN, *b.* December 25, 1749 ; *m.* an Englishman, JOSEPH MIL-
     LER, and had a *dau.*, SARAH ; *m.* WILLIAM STUMP, *d. s. p.*
iii. SARAH, *m.*, first, —— YATES ; second, —— BOND.
iv. THOMAS SHERIDAN, *b.* June 8, 1752, *of whom presently.*

THOMAS SHERIDAN, only son of **Joseph** and **Elizabeth**
(——) **Chew,** *b.* June 8, 1752 ; *m.* **ELIZABETH,** *dau.* of
William and **Cassandra Morgan,** and had issue :

i.   WILLIAM, *m.* —— RICHARDSON. Issue :
     CASSANDRA, *m.* SAMUEL HAND.
ii. THOMAS, graduated M.D., in Baltimore ; removed to Natchez, Miss.,
     and *d. u.*
iii. SARAH, *b.* December 1, 1792, *of whom presently.*
iv. CASSANDRA, *d. u.* about 1844.
v.   EDWARD M., *m.*, first, MARGARET HOPKINS, of Deer Creek,
     Md. ; and second, CATHERINE HALL, and *d. s. p.* in 1880.
vi. ELIZA, *m.* JOHN W., son of Samuel and Rachel Hopkins (*q. v.*).
vii. MARGARET, *m.*, 1837, ISAAC WILSON, and *d.* 1865, leaving a
     dau., LAURA M. ; *m.*, 1879, ISAAC WILSON.

SARAH, *b.* December 1, 1792 ; *m.*, April 11, 1809, SAMUEL
WORTHINGTON, of Darlington, Harford Co., Md., and *d.*
November 13, 1821 ; her husband *d.* March 22, 1853. Issue
(surname WORTHINGTON) :

i.   JOHN, *b.* July 29, 1810 ; *d.* June 25, 1817.
ii. ELIZABETH, *b.* March 6, 1812 ; *d.* June 20, 1827.
iii. THOMAS CHEW, *b.* March 25, 1814; *m.*, 1856, CHARLOTTE
     AMOS, and *d.* January 15, 1873.
iv. HENRY WILSON, *b.* December 4, 1815; *m.*, May 31, 1842, ELIZA-
     BETH, *dau.* of Jeremiah and Sarah B. Willits, of Philadelphia,
     and *d.* October 20, 1866.
v.   PRISCILLA, *b.* April 14, 1817 ; *d.* July, 1889.
vi. WILLIAM, *b.* February 24, 1819; *m.*, January 6, 1846, MARY W.,
     dau. of William and Sarah Dallam, of Baltimore, and *d.* October
     4, 1859 ; his widow *d.* September 23, 1888. Issue :
     i.   CHARLES HAMMOND, *b.* November 22, 1846 ; resides at Chester, Pa. ; *m.*, June
          19, 1890, MARY STOKES, *dau.* of Edward H. and Lydia Chapman, of
          St. Louis, Mo.
     ii. ANNIE, *b.* July 8, 1854.
     iii. JOHN DALLAM, *b.* December 2, 1856, removed to Belair, Harford Co., Md. ; *m.*,
          December 28, 1881, THERESE McCORMICK. Issue:
          i.   Malcolm, *b.* 1882.
          ii. Annie L., *b.* 1886.
          iii. Frank, *b.* 1892.
          iv. John, *b.* 1893.

WILLIAM, fourth son of **Samuel** and **Anne (Ayres) Chew,** inherited land within the town of Herrington ; *m.,* December 20, 1690, **SIDNEY,** *dau.* of **Thomas** and **Martha Wynn,** of Pennsylvania, and *d.* February 28, 1709–10. Issue :

An only son, **BENJAMIN,** *of whom presently.*

BENJAMIN, only son of **William** and **Sidney (Wynn) Chew,** removed to Cecil Co., Maryland, in December, 1752 ; was appointed a Justice of the Peace, took the oath of office, and was disowned by Nottingham Quaker Meeting, in October, 1755 ; *m.,* January, 1726–27, **SARAH BOND,** and made his will June 10, 1761, proved January 4, 1763 ; his widow's was proved April 21, 1769. Issue :

i.   **BENJAMIN,** Jr., lived in Cecil Co., Md., may have been Benjamin Chew, Captain of the Baltimore Privateer Chase, 20 men, 6 guns, April 30, 1777. He *m.,* May 1, 1750, **CASSANDRA,** *dau.* of **Richard** and **Ann Johns,** of Baltimore Co. Issue : [1]

         NATHANIEL, one of the first Midshipmen appointed by the Continental Congress, was captured by the British, and confined in the Jersey prison-ships. Survived and attained the rank of Captain. He *m.,* in 1792, **MARGARET,** *dau.* of Commodore John Rodgers, U. S. N. Issue :

         i.   John.
         ii.   Benjamin Franklin.
         iii.   Washington Pinkney, *m.,* January 24, 1831, Mary Hall, who *d.* October 20, 1837 ; he *d.* April 7, 1850. Issue : i. a *dau., d. i.* ii. James White, *b.* January 11, 1833 ; Clerk U. S. Circuit Court, Baltimore. iii. Nathaniel, *b.* May 20, 1835 ; *m.* Gertrude Holliday. iv. William Stokes, *b.* March 9, 1836 ; *m.* Mina A. Barrington. Issue : i. Mary, *b.* November 17, 1869. ii. James Arthur, *b.* June 10, 1871. iii. William, *b.* January 8, 1874.
         iv.   Emeline R.
         v.   Henrietta Mary, *m.* Rev. Cyrus Huntington, D.D.
         vi.   Elizabeth Ann.

ii.   **SARAH,** called in her father's will (1761) "**Sarah Chew,** alias **Johns,**" and in her mother's, seven years later, "**Sarah Johns.**"

iii.   **PHINEHAS,** living in 1768.

iv.   **MARY,** *m.* —— **ELLIOT,** and had a *dau.,* **SARAH** ; *m.* **JOHN O'DON-NELL,** from whom descends **Columbus O'Donnell,** of Baltimore, Md., and **C. O'Donnell Iselin,** of New York City.

v.   **ANN,** *m.* **CAPTAIN ISAAC VAN BIBBER.**

vi.   **HENERITTA** (so named in both her parents' wills), who *m.,* first, about 1778, **HUGH DAVY.** Issue :

         i.   HUGH, *d. u.*
         ii.   ANNE, *d. u.*
         iii.   SARAH, *m.* —— HOTCHKISS.

[1] It seems most probable he also had a son, BENJAMIN ; *m.* SARAH ——, and was father of Henrietta and Sarah, who *m.* sons of Samuel and Ann (Chew) Galloway.

MR. DAVY *d.* about 1783, and about 1785 his widow *m.*, second, **JOHN JAMES**, of Curaçoa, who had removed to Baltimore, Md., and had additional issue (surname JAMES) :

DEBORAH, *m.* **WILLIAM ROBINSON.**

ii.   **MOLLY ELLIOT,** *b.* in 1788 ; *m.*, in 1803, **WILLIAM JACKSON,** of Baltimore, *b.* in 1769 ; afterward a Major of Cavalry ; at the Battle of North Point second in command of the Cavalry, and for several years President of the Old Defenders' Association of Baltimore. He *d.* in 1847, and his widow in 1862.   Issue (surname JACKSON) :

i.   **CHARLES,** *d. i.*
ii.   **HENRY,** *d. y.*
iii.   **ANNE CHEW,** *d. i.*
iv.   **NANCY CHEW,** *d. i.*
v.   **WILLIAM,** *m.*, first, **AMELIA HUTCHINSON,** and second, **ANNE PAT-RICK,** and *d.* in 1866, having had several sons *d.* in early manhood, and Anne, *m.* Montgomery Selden.
vi.   **JOHN,** *m.* **CATHERINE BIER,** and *d.* in 1857.   Issue :

i.   George, *d.* in Brazil, March, 1893.
ii.   Edward Aliment.
iii.   Augusta.

vii.   **BENJAMIN CHEW,** *d. u.*
viii. **ABRAM VAN BIBBER,** *d. u.*
ix.   **JAMES,** *d. u.* in the army during the Mexican War.
x.   **EDWARD,** *m.* **SARAH JOHNSON,** and *d.* in 1842.
xi.   **AMELIA,** *m.* **GEORGE SMITH,** and *d.* in 1850, leaving a *dau.*, Rose ; *m.* David Baldwin.
xii.   **HENRIETTA CHEW,** *m.* **ROBERT M. R. SMITH,** and *d.* in 1846. Issue (surname SMITH) :

i.   Samuel, *d. s. p.* in 1876.
ii.   Louisa, *m.* Perrin Kemp, of Gloucester Co., Va., and *d.* in 1893. Issue (surname KEMP) : i. Henry Greenway. ii. Mary Gibson. iii. Emily Nelson Page.

xiii. **MARY,** *m.* **CAPTAIN JAMES GIBSON,** of Scotland, and *d. s. p.*
xiv.   **FRANCES ELIZABETH,** *b.* in 1827 ; *m.*, October 22, 1852, **JOHN TYLER SEAWELL,** of Sewell's Point, Va.   Issue (surname SEAWELL):

i.   Frances E., *d. i.*
ii.   Molly Elliot, authoress of " Throckmorton," " Maid Marian," " Midshipman Paulding," " Decatur and Somers," " Little Jarvis," " Paul Jones," etc.
iii.   Henrietta Chew.

BENJAMIN, fifth son of **Samuel** and **Anne (Ayres) Chew,** *b.* April 12, 1670–71, *m.* **ELIZABETH BENSON** (who *m.*, second, September 24, 1702, **RICHARD BOND),** and *d.* March 3, 1699–1700.   Issue :

i.   **SAMUEL,** *b.* October 30, 1693, *of whom presently.*
ii.   **ELIZABETH,** *b.* March 13, 1694–95 ; *m.*, in 1710–11, **KENSEY,** son of Richard Johns (*q. v.*).
iii.   **ANN,** *b.* October 14, 1696.
iv.   **MARY,** *b.* December, 1698 ; probably *d. i.*

SAMUEL, only son of **Benjamin** and **Elizabeth (Benson) Chew,** *b.* October 30, 1693, was a physician by profession, signed his name Samuel Chew, of "Maidstone," a plantation of three hundred and fifty acres on the west side of Herring Creek Bay, near Annapolis. He removed, with his second wife, to Dover, on the Delaware, where he had a residence, standing a few years ago, and a plantation some three miles out of town. He was a man of strong character, and obtained great influence in his new home. In 1741 Lieutenant-Governor Thomas appointed him Chief-Justice of the three Lower Counties—Newcastle, Sussex, and Kent—now part of Delaware, but then belonging to the province of Pennsylvania. His first charge to the Grand Jury, in which he set forth the lawfulness of self-defence against an armed enemy, and the duty of every citizen to give money and personal service in the war against Spain, gave great offence to the Quakers. Having a majority in the Assembly of Pennsylvania, they had rejected a bill to put the province in a state of defence. In the Assembly of the Lower Counties a militia law was passed over their votes, and Chew, sustaining it in his charge, they expelled him from the Society. The Chief-Justice replied to the excommunication publicly in a second speech to the Grand Jury, and in an indignant protest printed in the *Gazette*. These publications had great influence among the Quakers and materially aided the government. As a local poet declared :

> " Immortal Chew first set our Quakers right,
> He made it plain they might resist and fight,
> And gravest Dons agreed to what he said
> And freely gave their cash for the king's aid,
> For war successful, or for peace and trade."

DR. CHEW, *m.*, first, October 22, 1715, **MARY,** *dau.* of **Samuel** and **Anne Galloway** (who *d.* May 26, 1734).   Issue :

i. **SARAH,** *b.* July 23, 1716, *d.* in February, 1716–17.
ii. **ANN,** *b.* January 4, 1718–19, *d.* October 2, 1723.
iii. **ELIZABETH,** *b.* November 25, 1720 ; *m.*, in 1749, **COLONEL EDWARD TILGHMAN,** of Wye (*q. v.*).
iv. **BENJAMIN,** *b.* November 29, 1722, *of whom presently.*
v. **ANN,** *b.* April 13, 1725 ; *m.* **SAMUEL GALLOWAY** (*q. v.*).
vi. **MARY,** *b.* June 27, 1727, *d.* May 28, 1728.
vii. **SAMUEL,** *b.* April 29, 1728, *d.* June 29, 1729.
viii. **SAMUEL,** *b.* August 3, 1730, *d.* November 3, 1730.
ix. **HENRIETTA,** *b.* March 17, 1731-32, *d.* in June, 1732.

BENJAMIN CHEW
CHIEF JUSTICE OF PENNSYLVANIA

DR. SAMUEL CHEW, *m.*, second, September 28, 1735, MRS. MARY GALLOWAY, *dau.* of **Aquila Paca,** and widow of **Richard Galloway,** and *d.* June 16, 1744. Further issue :

x.   **SAMUEL,** *b.* August 24, 1737, for many years Attorney-General of the Province of Maryland, and appointed third Judge of the Supreme Court of the three Lower Counties October 30, 1773, and Judge of Oyer and Terminer, November 3, 1773 ; *m.* **ANNA MARIA,** *dau.* of **Peregrine Frisby,** and *d. s. p.* May 25, 1809, at Chestertown, Md.

xi.   **MARY,** *b.* September 6, 1739, *d.* May 1, 1740.

xii.   **JOHN,** *b.* March 21, 1739–40, *d. u.* December 15, 1807. He may have been the John Chew appointed Justice of the Peace for Kent Co., October 24, 1774.

BENJAMIN, eldest son of **Dr. Samuel** and **Mary (Galloway) Chew,** *b.* at West River, November 29, 1722, apparently kept his birthright membership of the Society of Friends until after his second marriage, when his children by his first wife were baptized, together with their next brother, Benjamin, in 1758. He studied law under Andrew Hamilton, of Philadelphia, and after his death, in 1741, went abroad and entered the Middle Temple, Inns of Court, London, having as a fellow-student Sir William Blackstone. He returned to America at his father's death, and was admitted to the bar in 1746. Began to practise law at Dover. In 1751 was a member of the Boundary Commission on the part of the Lower Counties. Was Speaker of the Lower House of the three counties, 1753–58. Removed to Philadelphia about 1754, and January 14, 1755, became Attorney-General of the Province, holding this office until 1769. Recorder of the City of Philadelphia, August 29, 1755, to June 25, 1774 ; Master of the Rolls, August 29, 1755 ; and November 2d, of the same year, appointed a member of the Provincial Council, which office he held until the Revolution. He was one of the Commissioners to put the city in a state of defence against an expected war with Spain in 1761 ; was appointed Register-General of Wills, August 15, 1765, which he held until a change of the system of administration by Act of March 14, 1777. April 29, 1774, succeeded William Allen as Chief-Justice of the province of Pennsylvania. Like other leading men in the colonies he sympathized with the first movements of the Revolution ; signed the non-importation agreement of 1763, and is reported to have

told a Grand Jury that "submission to the mandate of the King
or his ministers when they exceed their constitutional authority
is treason." But he was not prepared to go the length of rebellion and open war against the sovereign to whom he had
sworn allegiance, and took no part in the subsequent proceedings of the Revolutionary party. He was naturally an object of
suspicion to them, and in 1777 was arrested, with his friend John
Penn, the Proprietary ; but when other Philadelphia Friends were
sent to Virginia, they were allowed to retire to his property,
Union Forge, N. J., on parole, and the next year released from
arrest. October 3, 1791, he was appointed Judge and October
4 President of the High Court of Errors and Appeals of Pennsylvania, holding this position until the Court was abolished in
1808. On coming to Philadelphia he resided on Front Street,
above Dock, until he bought, May 3, 1771, from Charles Willing,
the house on Third Street, below Willing's Alley, he built for his
son-in-law, Colonel Byrd. About 1761 he built his country-seat,
"Cliveden," at Germantown. During his exile the battle of
Germantown was fought around his house, which was occupied
by a detachment of British troops. Historians generally consider the delay caused by attempting to take the Chew house
was the occasion of the American defeat, though later researches
would seem to lessen the importance of the attack, and show the
battle was lost independently of it. General Henry Knox is
usually said to have opposed leaving a fortified place in the rear
of the army in its advance. Colonel Pickering differed from
him, but was overruled, while some authorities make General
Joseph Reed responsible for the error. The traces of the attack have been preserved and are still shown to the visitor, including a discoloration on the wall of one chamber, shaped like a
human profile, which is reported to be the mark left by a British
officer's head struck off by a cannon-ball. Probably on account
of the injuries sustained in the battle the Chief-Justice sold the
house, in the fall of 1779, to Blair McClenachan, for £2,500, re-
purchasing it in April, 1797, for £8,500. He *m.*, first, June 13,
1747, **MARY**, *dau.* of **John** and **Mary (Thomas) Galloway,**
who *d.* November 9, 1755, and was buried at Christ Church,
Philadelphia. Issue :

i. **MARY,** *b.* March 10, 1748 ; *m.* **ALEXANDER WILCOCKS** (*q. v.*).
ii. **ANNA MARIA,** *b.* November 27, 1749 ; *d. u.* in November, 1812.

CLIVEDEN, OR CHEW'S HOUSE, AT GERMANTOWN

iiL   **ELIZABETH**, *b.* November 10, 1751 ; *m.* **EDWARD TILGHMAN**
         (*q. v.*).
iv.   **SARAH**, *b.* November 15, 1753 ; *m.* **JOHN GALLOWAY** (*q. v.*).
v.   **HENRIETTA**, *b.* in September, 1755 ; *d.* in 1756.

BENJAMIN CHEW, *m.*, second, September 12, 1757, **ELIZA-
BETH**, *dau.* of **James** and **Mary (Turner) Oswald**, who *d.*
in May, 1819. The Chief-Justice *d.* January 20, 1810, at his
town-house, having had further issue :

vi.   **BENJAMIN**, *b.* September 30, 1758, *of whom presently.*
vii.   **PEGGY**[1] **OSWALD**, *b.* December 17, 1760. At the Meschianza or Tour-
         nament, held during the occupancy of Philadelphia by the British (May
         18, 1778) Major André was her knight. She *m.*, in 1787, **COL-
         ONEL JOHN EAGER HOWARD** (*q. v.*).
viii. **JOSEPH**, *b.* March 9, 1763 ; *d.* in September, 1764.
ix.   **JULIANA**, *b.* April 8, 1765 ; *m.* **PHILIP NICKLIN** (*q. v.*).
x.   **HENRIETTA**, *b.* September 15, 1767 ; *d. u.* March 8, 1848.
xi.   **SOPHIA**, *b.* November 13, 1769 ; *m.* **HENRY PHILIPS** (*q. v.*).
xii.   **MARIA**, *b.* December 22, 1771 ; *d. u.* March 27, 1840.
xiii. **HARRIET**, *b.* October 22, 1775 ; *m.*, in 1799, **CHARLES**, the only son
         of **Charles Carroll**, of Carrollton (*q. v.*).
xiv.   **CATHERINE**, *b.* May 3, 1779 ; *d. u.* May 28, 1831.

BENJAMIN, sixth child of **Chief-Justice Chew**, *b.* September
30, 1758 ; admitted to the bar of Philadelphia in 1786 ; *m.*, December 11, 1788, **KATHERINE BANNING**, *b.* July 6, 1770 ;
d. in 1855 ; he *d.* April 30, 1844. Issue :

i.   **SAMUEL**, *b.* December 8, 1789 ; *d.* March 21, 1795.
ii.   **ELIZA**, *b.* May 4, 1791 ; *d.* March 31, 1795.
iii.   **BENJAMIN**, *b.* December 5, 1793 ; admitted to the bar in Philadelphia in
         1815 ; *m.*, July 11, 1816, **ELIZABETH MARGARET**, *dau.* of
         Chief-Justice Tilghman (*q. v.*), who *d.* June 16, 1817 ; he *d.* Au-
         gust 17, 1864. Issue :

         WILLIAM TILGHMAN, *b.* June 7, 1817 ; *d.* April 6, 1820.

iv.   **SAMUEL**, *b.* June 19, 1795 ; admitted to the bar in Philadelphia, April 8,
         1816 ; *d. u.* August 21, 1841.
v.   **JOHN**, *b.* January 23, 1797. Midshipman, U. S. N. Lost at sea in the
         Epervia, in August, 1815.
vi.   **ELIZA MARGARETTA**, *b.* November 19, 1798 ; *m.*, July 25, 1822,
         Hon. **JAMES MURRAY MASON**, of Virginia, for many years
         U. S. Senator from that State, and Commissioner, with John Slidell,
         from the " Confederate States " to England, whose capture by Cap-

---
[1] So baptized.

tain Wilkes, U. S. Navy, while on their voyage to that country in an English vessel, came so near causing a war between the United States and England. She *d.* February 11, 1874, and her husband *d.* April 29, 1871. Issue :

i.   ANNA MARIA, *m.* JOHN AMBLER, and *d.* 1862.
ii.   BENJAMIN CHEW, *d. u.* 1847.
iii. CATHERINE, *m.* JOHN THOMAS B. DORSEY.
iv.   GEORGE, *m.* ELEANOR WALLACE.
v.   VIRGINIA.
vi.   IDA.
vii. JAMES MURRAY, *m.* ELIZA HILL.
viii. JOHN.

vii.   **HENRY BANNING,** *b.* December 11, 1800, *of whom presently.*
viii. **WILLIAM WHITE,** *b.* April 12, 1803, Secretary of Legation to Hon. George M. Dallas, American Minister to Russia, and Chargé d'Affaires after Mr. Dallas's return ; *d.* November 12, 1851.
ix.   **ANNA SOPHIA PENN,** *b.* March 18, 1805 ; *d. u.* May 9, 1892.
x.   **JOSEPH TURNER,** *b.* December 12, 1806 ; *d.* in 1835.
xi.   **ANTHONY BANNING,** *b.* January 24, 1809 ; *d.* in February, 1854.
xii.   **CATHERINE MARIA,** *b.* May 12, 1811 ; *bu.* October 26, 1811.
xiii. **OSWALD,** *b.* May 23, 1813, drowned while bathing in the Schuylkill River, June 8, 1824.

HENRY BANNING, seventh child of **Benjamin** and **Katherine Chew,** *b.* December 11, 1800 ; *m.* **HARRIET,** youngest *dau.* of **General Charles Ridgely,** of Hampton, who was Governor of Maryland in 1815 ; she *d.* October 20, 1835, and he *m.*, second, March 10, 1839, **ELIZABETH ANN,** *dau.* of **Robert Ralston,** of Philadelphia, by whom he had no issue. He *d.* December 12, 1866. Issue by his first wife :

i.   **CATHERINE,** *b.* April 19, 1823 ; *d.* February 24, 1824.
ii.   **PRISCILLA RIDGELY,** *b.* December 3, 1824 ; *d.* February 11, 1837.
iii. **CHARLES RIDGELY,** *b.* January 20, 1827, *of whom presently.*
iv.   **BENJAMIN,** *b.* May 27, 1828 ; *d.* July 20, 1829.
v.   **BENJAMIN,** *b.* June 21, 1830 ; *d. u.* September 28, 1885.
vi.   **SAMUEL,** *b.* January 28, 1832, lived at " Cliveden," Germantown, Pa. He was admitted to the bar, May 16, 1868, in Philadelphia, *m.*, June 20, 1861, **MARY JOHNSON,** *dau.* of **David S. Brown,** of Philadelphia, and *d.* January 10, 1887. Issue :

i.   ANNA SOPHIA PENN, the third, *b.* June 17, 1862.
ii.   ELIZABETH BROWN, *b.* November 19, 1863.
iii. DAVID SANDS BROWN, *b.* March 3, 1866.
iv.   SAMUEL, JR., *b.* April 28, 1871.
v.   BENJAMIN, *b.* July 31, 1878.
vi.   OSWALD, *b.* May 24, 1880.

vii.   **ACHSAH CARROLL,** *b.* January 22, 1834 ; *d.* July 12, 1834.

viii.   **HENRY BANNING,** *b.* October 19, 1835 ; studied medicine and was graduated at Jefferson College, Philadelphia ; in 1855 appointed Resident Physician to the Baltimore Almshouse, where he was taken ill with typhus fever, and *d.* April 29, 1855.

CHARLES RIDGELY, eldest son of **Henry Banning** and **Harriet (Ridgely) Chew,** *b.* January 20, 1827 ; resided at " Epsom," Baltimore Co., Md. ; *m.,* December 10, 1845, **HARRIET GREEN ;** *d.* October 27, 1875. Issue :

i.   **ELIZABETH ANN,** *b.* February 1, 1847 ; *m.,* December 13, 1877, **J. ALEXANDER GREEN.** Issue (surname GREEN) :

    i.   **CHARLES RIDGELY,** *b.* December 10, 1878 ; *d.* July 14, 1879.
    ii.   **JACOB MILTON,** *b.* July 18, 1880.
    iii. **BESSIE CHEW,** *b.* October 5, 1881.

ii.   **HENRY BANNING, JR.,** *b.* October 28, 1848.

iii. **ANNA SOPHIA PENN,** the second, *b.* November 5, 1850 ; *m.,* October 14, 1875, **WILLIAM GRASON.** Issue (surname GRASON) :

    i.   **MARY CHEW,** *b.* September 3, 1876.
    ii.   **ELIZABETH RIDGELY,** *b.* May 13, 1878.
    iii. **ANDREW STERRETT RIDGELY,** *b.* December 21, 1879.

iv.   **KATHERINE,** *b.* November 7, 1852.

v.   **CHARLES RIDGELY, JR.,** *b.* September 6, 1854.

vi.   **BENJAMIN,** *b.* October 4, 1856.

vii. **HARRIET,** *b.* January 10, 1860.

viii. **SAMUEL,** *b.* January 23, 1862, *d. i.*

Principal authorities : Quaker Records and State papers of Maryland and Pennsylvania ; Keith's Provincial Councillors ; and family papers, through Messrs. Samuel Chew (*dec.*), John C. Chew, Dr. S. C. Chew, and others.

CHEW, OF VIRGINIA

LARKIN CHEW, son of **Joseph** and —— **(Larkin) Chew** (*q. v.*); was in Virginia before 1700, settled in what is now Spottsylvania Co., was a Justice of that county in 1722 ; Member of the House of Burgesses, 1723 and 1726 ; Sheriff, 1727–28 ; *m.* **HANNAH**, *dau.* of **John Roy**, of Port Royal, Va. (**Madam Hannah Chew** appears on the Records in 1724.)   Issue :

i. **JOSEPH**, *d. i.*
ii. **THOMAS**, *of whom presently.*
iii. **ANN**, *m.* **WILLIAM JOHNSTON**, Justice of Spottsylvania Co. Issue :

    i. **JOSEPH.**
    ii. **LARKIN**, *m.* **MARY ROGERS.**
    iii. **JUDITH**, *m.* **ROBERT PARISH**, or Forsyth.
    iv. **ROBERT**, *m.* **ANN COOK.**
    v. **JOHN**, *d. u.*
    vi. **BENJAMIN**, *m.* **DOROTHY JONES.** Issue :
        William, Gabriel, Mary Ann, Benjamin, Sirpey, and Robert.
    vii. **JAMES**, *m.* **MARY WARE.**
    viii. **WILLIAM**, *m.*, first, **ANN FLINT** ; *m.*, second, in 1784, **ELIZABETH**, *dau.* of James Winn, of Fauquier Co., Va.
    ix. **HANNAH**, *m.* **FRANCIS COLEMAN.**
    x. **RICHARD**, *m.*, first, **DOROTHY WALLER**, *dau.* of William Beverley ; and second, **ANN SMITH.**
    xi. **ELIZABETH**, *m.* **JOHN BENGER.**

iv. **JOHN** (*q. v.*).
v. **LARKIN** (*q. v.*).

THOMAS, eldest surviving son of **Larkin** and **Hannah (Roy) Chew**, was a Justice in Spottsylvania Co., in 1722; Sheriff, 1724–25; of Orange, 1745; *m.* **MARTHA**, *dau.* of **Colonel James Taylor**, of York River, Va., and sister of President Madison's grandmother, **Mrs. Ambrose Madison**. Issue:

i. **JOSEPH**, *m.* **GRACE DESHON**, of New London, Conn., was Collector of that Port. Issue:

    i. **JOSEPH**, was probably the Secretary of the Bureau for Indian Affairs under Sir William Johnson, Baronet; *d. u.* in Jamaica.

    ii. **WILLIAM JOHNSTON**, a British officer, killed at Niagara, is said to have descendants on Prince Edward's Island.

    iii. **JOHN**, *d. u.* at Montreal.

    iv. **FRANCES**, *m.* **GABRIEL SISTARE**; *d.* in 1820. Issue (surname SISTARE):

        Joseph, *m.* **Mary Christophers**. Issue: Charles, *m.* —— Bassett.

    v. **GRACE**, *d. u.* at Montreal.

ii. **LARKIN**, was a Lieutenant in Byrd's Second Virginia Regiment in 1754; *d. u.*, in Virginia, in 1776.

iii. **FRANCES**, *m.* **HENRY DOWNS**, of Virginia.

iv. **HANNAH**, *d. u.*

v. **THOMAS**, *d. y.*

vi. **COLEBY**, *d. u.*, at Fort Du Quesne, in 1758.

vii. **ELIZABETH**, *d. u.*

viii. **ALICE**, *m.* her cousin, **ZACHARY TAYLOR**, of Virginia, grandfather of President Taylor; and *d.* in 1796.

ix. **MILDRED**, *m.* —— **COLEMAN**, and *d. s. p.*

x. **SAMUEL**, *of whom presently.*

xi. **JAMES**, *m.*, in 1765, **MARY CALDWELL**, of Virginia.

SAMUEL, fifth son of **Thomas** and **Martha (Taylor) Chew**, was an officer in the American Navy, killed in action in 1779. He *m.*, September 18, 1770, **LUCY MILLER**, of New Haven, Conn. Issue:

i. **COLEBY**, *b.* September 20, 1772, *of whom presently.*

ii. **SAMUEL**, *b.* November 13, 1773 (*q. v.*).

iii. **THOMAS JOHN**, *b.* January 28, 1777; entered the U. S. Navy in 1799; was commissioned Purser, April 25, 1812, and was on the Chesapeake in her fight with the Shannon; and Captain James Lawrence, when mortally wounded and supported in his arms, gave him his dying command: "Don't give up the ship." He was purser of the Washington, a seventy-four gun ship, in 1819, and resigned from the Navy in 1832; *m.*, September 10, 1812, **ABBY HORTENSE HALLAM**; and *d.* in 1846. Issue:

    i. **JAMES LAWRENCE**, *b.* April 3, 1814; *d. u.* October 22, 1829.

    ii. **BETSEY PRENTIS**, *b.* April 19, 1816; *d.* May 11, 1816.

iii. **ELIZABETH HALLAM.**
iv. **LUCY,** *b.* December 13, 1820 ; *d.* January 8, 1821.
v. **ABBY HORTENSE,** *m.,* September 15, 1842, **McREE SWIFT,** of Geneva, N. Y., afterward of New Brunswick, N. J. Issue (surname SWIFT) :

    i. Hortense Hallam, *d.*
    ii. Louisa Walker.
    iii. Elizabeth Chew, *m.* George H. Janeway, of New Brunswick, N. J.
    iv. Alexander Joseph.
    v. Lawrence Chew.
    vi. Thomas Delano.
    vii. Jonathan Williams, *d.*
    viii. Josephine Richards.
    ix. Robert Hallam, *d.*
    x. Mary Lewis.

vi. **MARY HALLAM,** *m.,* April 15, 1844, **GEORGE RICHARDS LEWIS,** of New London, Conn. Issue (surname LEWIS) :

    i. Harriet Richards, *m.* Francesco Barbiellini, Conte d' Amidei, of Rome, Italy. Issue : Elizabetta.
    ii. Hortense, *m.* Rev. Henry Wells Nelson, Jr., D.D., of Boston, Mass., now Rector of Trinity Church, Geneva, N. Y. Issue : Margaret, Howard, George Lewis, Frank Howard, and Mary Hallam Chew.
    iii. Thomas Chew, *d.* January, 1882.
    iv. Mary Elizabeth.

vii. **LUCY CHRISTOPHERS,** *m.,* September 30, 1848, **M. LUDLOW WHIT-LOCK,** of New York City. Issue (surname WHITLOCK) :

    i. Frank Wallace, *m.,* October 4, 1876, Zella A. Kempton, of West Newton, Mass. Issue : Pauline.
    ii. Edward Hallam, *d. i.*
    iii. Edward Bull, *d. y.*
    iv. Lewis Norman, *d. y.*

COLEBY, eldest son of Samuel and Lucy (Miller) Chew, *m.* FRANCES LEARNED, of New London, Conn., who *d.* in 1846. He *d.* in 1803. Issue :

i. **FRANCES,** *b.* in 1800 ; *m.* **LEONARD COIT,** of New London, Conn., and *d.* in 1866. Issue (surname COIT) :

    i. FRANK, *d. u.*
    ii. HORACE, *m.,* February 8, 1870, EMILY, *dau.* of Coleby and Mary C. (Law) Chew. She *d.* in 1881. Issue :
        Coleby Chew, Fanny Learned, Frank, and James Lawrence.
    iii. FANNY, *d. y.*

ii. **COLEBY,** *b.* in 1802 ; *m.,* October 10, 1832, **MARY CECELIA LAW,** of New London, Conn., and *d.* in 1852. Issue :

    i. MARY CECELIA, *m.,* October 21, 1852, WILLIAM CLEVELAND CRUMP, of New London, Conn. Issue (surname CRUMP) :
        i. Eliza Richards.
        ii. John Guy, *m.,* August 28, 1878, Jennie Elizabeth Williams, of New London, Conn. Issue :
            William Cleveland.
    ii. FRANCES, *d. y.*
    iii. COLEBY, *d. y.*

iv.   **RICHARD,** *d. i.*
v.   **ALICE.**
vi.   **JAMES LAWRENCE.**
vii.   **EMILY,** *m.* her cousin, **HORACE COIT.**
viii.   **JULIA BEVERLY,** *d. u.*

SAMUEL, second son of **Samuel** and **Lucy (Miller) Chew,** for many years an officer of the U. S. Navy ; was on the Constitution in the fight with the Guerrière ; *m.* **MARY SABIN,** of New London, Conn., and *d.* in 1834. She *d.* in 1855.   Issue :

i.   **LUCY,** *m.* **JAMES MORGAN SMITH,** of Georgia, and *d. s. p.*
ii.   **SAMUEL COLEBY,** *d. u.* in 1832.
iii.   **THOMAS JOHN,** *b.* December, 1807 ; *m.* **MARGARET A. BEMIS,**
        of Maryland ; no issue ; lived in Iowa ; *d.* July 28, 1892.
iv.   **ANTHONY SANDFORD,** *b.* February 22, 1809, *of whom presently.*
v.   **MARY SABIN,** *m.* **DR. JACOB N. KEELER,** of New Jersey.
        Issue : i. **LUCY.** ii. **COLEBY,** both *d.* in 1895.
vi.   **JAMES SMITH,** *m.* **ELIZABETH KIRK,** of Piqua, O. (who *d. s. p.*), and *d.* June, 1887.

ANTHONY SANDFORD, third son of **Samuel** and **Mary (Sabin) Chew,** *b.* February 22, 1809 ; *m.*, first, **ELIZABETH VAN VECHTEN,** of Fishkill, N. Y.   Issue :   •

i.   **ELIZABETH ANN,** *b.* October 8, 1831 ; *m.* **EDWIN DUDLEY FAY,** of Columbus, O., and has several children.
ii.   **ANTHONY SANDFORD,** *d. i.*

MR. CHEW, *m.*, second, April, 1836, **DELIA,** *dau.* of **Demas Adams,** of Columbus, O.   Issue :

iii.   **THOMAS JOHN, JR.,** *b.* April 8, 1838 ; resides at S. Joseph, Mo. ; *m.*,
        September 19, 1861, **KITTIE M.,** *dau.* of **William E. Forbes,** of
        Brooklyn, N. Y.   Issue :
            A *dau., d. i.*
iv.   **DEMAS A.,** *b.* June 3, 1840.
v.   **DELIA ADAMS,** *b.* September 6, 1852 ; *m.* **JOHN JAY BROWN,**
        of Hannibal, Mo.   Issue, several children.

JOHN, second surviving son of **Larkin** and **Hannah (Roy) Chew,** Justice of Spottsylvania Co., 1731 ; *m.* (License June 26, 1729) **MARGARET,** *dau.* of **Colonel Robert Beverley,** Clerk of the Council of Virginia, in 1679, and author of the " History of Virginia," by R. B., Gent., published in 1705.   Issue :

i.   **ROBERT,** *of whom presently.*

ii.   **MARY BEVERLEY**, *m.* Colonel **JOHN**, son of **Joseph Brock**, of
"Poplar Neck," Spottsylvania, Va.   Issue (surname BROCK) :

    i.   JOHN, *m.* ANN CURTIS.
    ii. ELIZABETH, *m.*, first, J. T. LEWIS ; and second, BEVERLEY STUBBLE-
          FIELD, Cadet in Captain Towles's Virginia Company, February 10, 1776.
    iii. MARY, *m.* JOHN CARTER.
    iv. CATHERINE, *d. u.*
    v. JOSEPH, a Captain in the United States Army, *m.* ANN, *dau.* of John and Ann
          (Fox) Chew.   Issue :
          i.   Julia Ann Chew, *m.* Silas Wood, of New York.
          ii. Cadwallader William, *d. u.*
          iii. Mary, *d. i.*
    vi. WILLIAM, *m.*, first, —— BARNES ; and second, BETSEY TOWLES.
    vii. SUSAN, *m.* BEVERLY ROBINSON.

iii.   **MARGARET**, *d. y.*
iv.   **JOHN** (*q. v.*).
v.   **HANNAH**, *m.* **JOHN CARTER.**

ROBERT, eldest son of **John** and **Margaret (Beverley) Chew,**
m. **MOLLY**, *dau.* and heiress of **Richard Perrott** or **Parrott,**
of " Parrotts Neck," Middlesex.   Issue :

i.   **ROBERT BEVERLEY**, clerk of Spottsylvania Co.; Lieutenant in
    Continental Line ; *d. u.*, 1791.
ii.   **JOHN**, *of whom presently.*
iii.   **HENRY**, *d. u.*
iv.   **ELIZABETH**, *m.* **Captain LARKIN STANARD**, of " Stanfield,"
    Spottsylvania Co.
v.   **JOSEPH** (*q. v.*).

JOHN, eldest surviving son of **Robert** and **Molly (Parrott)**
Chew, was cadet in Captain Towles's Virginia Company, Feb-
ruary 14, 1776 ; Clerk of Spottsylvania Co., 1787–1802 ; and
Clerk of the Corporation Court of Fredericksburg, 1787–1806 ; *m.*
ELIZABETH SMITH.   Issue :

i.   **ROBERT SMITH**, Clerk of Spottsylvania Co., 1802–18, and Clerk of the
    Corporation Court of Fredericksburg, 1806–26.   He *m.* **ELIZA-**
    BETH FRENCH, and *d.* November 23, 1826.   Issue :

    i.   JOHN JAMES, Clerk of Corporation Court of Fredericksburg, 1826 to 1870, with an
         interregnum of two years during the reconstruction era.   He *m.* ELEANOR,
         sister of Judge John M. Patton.   Issue:
         i.   Ann Mercer, *m.* Frank Forbes.
         ii. Robert S., *b.* 1828, was a colonel in the Thirtieth Virginia Infantry, C.
             S. A., and Clerk of the Corporation Court of Fredericksburg from
             1870 to August, 1886, when he died, having nearly completed a
             century of that office held by the family of Chew.
         iii. Eliza F., *d. i.*
         iv. Ellen Patton.

   v. **Hugh Patton.**
   vi. **Eliza French.**
   vii. **Margaret H.**
 ii. **GEORGE FRENCH,** *d. u.*
 iii. **ANN ELIZA,** *m.* **LIEUTENANT GEORGE MINOR,** United States Navy.
    Issue :

    John Chew.

 iv. **ROBERT SMITH,** *b.* 1811, was Chief Clerk of the United States State Department
    for nearly a quarter of a century, and in the Department over
    fifty years ; *m.* **ELIZABETH R. SMITH,** and *d.* August 3,
    1873. Issue :
   i. Richard Smith, *b.* December 4, 1843 ; graduated at Annapolis Naval
     Academy, 1861 ; Lieutenant United States Navy, 1864 ; on the
     Minnesota in the fight with the Virginia and in the battle of Mo-
     bile Bay, Md. ; *m.* —— Nourse, and *d.* April 10, 1875.
   ii. Elizabeth F., *d. u.*
   iii. Harriet P.
   iv. Robert S.
   v. John James.
   vi. Louis F.
   vii. Walter H.
   viii. Leonard C.

ii. **MARY BEVERLEY,** *m.* **SETH BARTON.**
iii. **ELIZABETH,** *m.* **DR. JAMES FRENCH.**

JOSEPH, youngest son of **Robert** and **Molly (Parrott) Chew,**
 m. **MARY WINSLOW,** and had issue :

i. **ROBERT BEVERLEY,** *d. u.*
ii. **JOHN WINSLOW,** *m.* **ANN THORNTON VOSS.** Issue :

 i. **MARY WINSLOW,** *m.* **J. B. TERRY.** Issue (surname TERRY) :
   i. **Emelia R.,** *m.* **Dr. George Buchanan.**
   ii. **Junius Adrian,** *d. y.*
   iii. **Adriana,** *m.* **C. W. Towner.**
   iv. **Mary W.,** *d. y.*
   v. **Elizabeth R.,** *d. u.* in 1870.
   vi. **Josephine,** *d. y.*
   vii. **Catherine.**
   viii. **Joseph.**
   ix. **Augusta.**
   x. **Roberta Lee.**
 ii. **ROBERT BEVERLY.**
 iii. **ALEXANDER VOSS,** *d. u.* in 1851.
 iv. **AUGUSTA WASHINGTON,** *d. y.*
 v. **JOSEPH.**
 vi. **HENRY,** *d. y.* in 1833.
 vii. **ELIZABETH.**
 viii. **THOMAS ROLLINS.**
 ix. **JOHN,** *d. y.*
 x. **ALBERT G.,** *m.* **RACHEL MURPHY.** Issue :
   i. Elizabeth, *d. y.*
   ii. Mary.
   iii. Emma.
 xi. **FRANCIS THORNTON,** *m.* **MARY W. WINSOR.**

iii.   **ALBERT GALLATIN**, *m.* **NANNIE NORRIS,** of Pennsylvania ;
    and *d.* May 20, 1883.   Issue :

    i.   **MARY MILLER,** *m.* **G. W. E. ATKINS.**   Issue (surname ATKINS):

       i.   **George Chew,** *b.* January 3, 1880.
      ii.   **John Norton,** *b.* August 4, 1881.

    ii.   **NANNIE M. N.,** *m.,* April 29, 1885, **DARWIN GEORGE BREED,** of Louisville,
       Ky.   Issue (surname BREED).

       i.   **John Chew,** *b.* January 20, 1886.
      ii.   **James Norris,** *b.* December 23, 1891.

iv.   **ADELINE W.,** *m.,* first, **JAMES VAUGHN.**   Issue :

    JAMES ALBERT, *m.* **SALLIE LEWIS.**

    ADELINE (CHEW) VAUGHN, *m.,* second, **WILLIAM McCON-
    NELL.**   Issue :

    MARY C., *m.* **J. W. LANCASTER.**

v.   **JOSEPH,** *m.,* first, **MARY LAMME.**   Issue :

    i.   **VERNON TILFORD,** *m.* **ANNA WILLIAMS.**
    ii.   **MARIA HELEN,** *m.* **E. M. SLOAN.**
    iii.   **SAMUEL,** *d. i.*
    iv.   **JOSEPH,** *d. u.* in California in 1864.

    He *m.,* second, **MARY BROWN.**   Issue :

    i.   **ADELINE W.,** *m.* —— **MORRIS,** of Montana.
    ii.   **THOMAS,** *d. i.*
    iii.   **HENRY.**
    iv.   **VIRGINIA.**
    v.   **GEORGE,** *d. i.*
    vi.   **JOHN,** *d. y.*
    vii.   **MARY PRICE.**
    viii.   **ROBERT LEE.**

vi.   **WILLIAM R.,** *m.* **HELEN M. WARE,** of Kentucky.   Issue :

    i.   **EMMA WINSLOW,** *m.* **D. S. SNODGRASS.**
    ii.   **SALLIE PARRISH,** *m.* **JUDGE M. D. ECTOR.**
    iii.   **ELLEN,** *m.,* first, —— **PINKERTON ;** second, **DR. EDWARD INGLIS.**
    iv.   **MARY ADELINE,** *m.* **GEORGE A. PEETE.**
    v.   **ANNA BEVERLY,** *m.* **DR. L. S. RAYFIELD.**
    vi.   **WILLIAM BARTLETT.**
    vii.   **JAMES EDMOND.**
    viii.   **JOSEPH JOHNSON.**

JOHN, second son of **John** and **Margaret (Beverley) Chew,** was
a Colonel in the Revolutionary Army, wounded at the battle of
Camden, S. C. ;   *m.,* in 1772, **ANN,** *dau.* of **Thomas Chew** and
Philadelphia Cole (Claiborne) Fox, and *d.* in 1799 ; his wife
d. in 1821, aged sixty-six.   Issue :

i.   **BEVERLY,** *b.* in 1773, *of whom presently.*
ii.   **JOHN,** *d. u.* in 1838.

BEVERLY CHEW
BORN 1773, DIED 1851

iii. PHILADELPHIA CLAIBORNE, *m.* BOOKER WALLER.
iv. ANN, *m.* her cousin, CAPTAIN JOSEPH BROCK, United States Army (*q. v.*).
v. THOMAS, *d. u.* in Kentucky.
vi. ELIZABETH, *m.* ROBERT CAMMACK.
vii. ROBERT, *m.* LOUISE, *dau.* of Antonio Wickliffe De Marcellon, and *d. s. p.*
viii. CLAIBORNE, *d. u.*, January 29, 1817, at Richmond, Va.
ix. MARY, *d. u.* in 1871.
x. LUCY, *d. u.* at Fredericksburg, Va., in 1815.
xi. CAROLINE MATILDA, *m.* COLONEL JOHN STANARD (*q. v.*).
xii. MARGARET, *d. i.*

BEVERLY, eldest son of **John** and **Ann (Fox) Chew,** *b.* in 1773, removed to New Orleans in 1797, was Collector of the Port from 1817 to 1829, President of the Branch Bank of the United States, and Vice Consul of Russia. He *m.*, January 14, 1810, **MARIA THEODORA,** *dau.* of **Colonel W. Duer,** of New York City, and *granddau.* of **Lord Stirling,** of the Revolutionary Army, and *d.* in 1851. Issue :

i. BEVERLY, *d. u.* in 1828.
ii. CAROLINE, *d. u.* in 1823.
iii. LUCY, *m.* WILLIAM, son of **Judge John Duer,** of New York City.
iv. JOHN WILLIAM.
v. KATHERINE A., *m.* JUDGE THOMAS KENNEDY, and *d.* in 1863.
vi. ROBERT, *d. i.*
vii. ALEXANDER LAFAYETTE, *of whom presently.*
viii. MARY VIRGINIA, *m.* MARTIN G. KENNEDY, and *d.* in 1863.
ix. MORRIS ROBINSON, *m.*, April 10, 1860, **MARY MEDORA KENNEDY,** of New Orleans, La. Issue :

    i. MARY MEDORA, *b.* in 1861.
    ii. JOSEPH WITHERS, *b.* in 1862.
    iii. JOSEPH BEVERLY, *b.* in 1865.
    iv. MARY ROSE, *b.* in 1868.
    v. MARY VIRGINIA, *b.* in 1869.
    vi. MORRIS ROBINSON, *b.* in 1874 ; *d.* the same year.

ALEXANDER LAFAYETTE, seventh child of **Beverly** and **Maria Theodora (Duer) Chew,** *b.* October 4, 1824 ; *m.*, in 1849, **SARAH AUGUSTA,** *dau.* of **Phinehas Prouty,** of Geneva, N. Y. Issue :

i. BEVERLY, *b.* March 5, 1850 ; Librarian of the Grolier Club, Secretary of the Metropolitan Trust Company of New York City, and Vice-Chancellor of the New York Chapter of the Colonial Order ; *m.*, December 11, 1872, CLARISSA, *dau.* of **Rev. Job Pierson, D.D.,** of Ionia, Mich., who *d.* May 30, 1889.

ii.   **HARRIET HILLHOUSE,** *b.* December 8, 1851 ; *m.*, in 1874, **ER-NEST CLEVELAND COXE,** son of Rt. Rev. A. Cleveland Coxe, Bishop of Western New York. Issue :
        ARTHUR CLEVELAND, *b.* in April, 1876.

iii.   **PHINEAS PROUTY,** *b.* February 1, 1854 ; *m.*, October 15, 1879, **MARGUERITE,** *dau.* of **Philip Pistor,** of New York. Issue :
        THEODORA MARGUERITE, *b.* August 28, 1880.

iv.   **THOMAS HILLHOUSE,** *b.* May 26, 1856.

v.   **ALEXANDER DUER,** *b.* September 21, 1858.

vi.   **KATE ADELAIDE,** *b.* April 17, 1861.

vii.   **THEODORA AUGUSTA,** *b.* February 12, 1863 ; *d.* in 1874.

viii. **LILLIAN BEVERLY,** *b.* February 19, 1866.

LARKIN, third son of **Larkin** and **Hannah (Roy) Chew,** was Sheriff of Spottsylvania Co., Va., in 1739 and 1756 ; *m.*, in 1733, **MARY,** *dau.* of **Captain Harry Beverley**[1] and **Elizabeth,** *dau.* and heiress of **Robert Smith,** of Brandon, Middlesex Co. Issue :

i.   **ELIZABETH BEVERLEY,** *m.*, first, **BEVERLEY STANARD** (*q. v.*) ; *m.*, second, **COLONEL MORDECAI BUCKNER.**
    Issue (surname BUCKNER) :

    i.   BALDWIN, *m.* FANNY, second *dau.* of Major John May Burton. Issue, with others :
        Elizabeth Beverley, *m.* Anaalem Brock. Issue (surname BROCK) :
          i.   Joseph Baldwin. Chief Surgeon of Exchange to General Robert E. Lee during the Civil War, *d.* 1870.
          ii. Charles W. P., Medical Director Confederate States Army, President of the Virginia Surgical and Medical Association in 1883.
          iii. Sarah A., *m.* Rev. Richard Fletcher Putnam of the Protestant Episcopal Church.
          iv. Elizabeth Beverley, *m.* Joseph Reinhart, of Virginia.

    ii. JOHN, *d. u.*

ii.   **MARY,** *m.*, first, **JOHN SMITH,** of Fredericksburg, Va. ; *m.*, second, **COLONEL OLIVER TOWLES.**

Authorities : Virginia Records and family papers through Beverly Chew, of New York, Major Thomas J. Chew, of St. Louis, Mrs. R. F. Putnam, of Brooklyn, and others.

[1] He was captain of a sloop captured by the Spaniards, probably treasure hunting, and escaped before August, 1717. Justice in Middlesex Co., 1700. Will proved February 2, 1730-31. Son of Major Robert Beverley, who *d.* 1687, by Mary, widow of George Keeble. His brother Robert was the historian of Virginia.

CLARK

WILLIAM NEWTON CLARK, *b.* March 30, 1796 ; *m.*, September 25, 1827, **MARY THERESA,** *dau.* of **Henry H.** and **Maria T. (Bradhurst) Schieffelin** (*q. v.*), and *d.* September 17, 1867 ; his widow *d.* August 13, 1886. Issue :

i.   **MARY LAWRENCE,** *b.* July 28, 1828 ; *d. u.* March 23, 1849.
ii.   **WILLIAM NEWTON,** *b.* August 14, 1832, *of whom presently.*
iii. **HENRY SCHIEFFELIN,** *b.* April 8, 1834 ; *d.* October 6, 1850.
iv.   **JOHN STILWELL,** *b.* April 21, 1836 ; *m.* **ELIZABETH BAGA-LEY.** Issue :
      ELIZABETH, *m.* CHARLES S. EATON.
v.   **SAMUEL BRADHURST,** *b.* March 3, 1838 ; *m.* **ELIZA R. TRACEY.**
vi.   **MARIA THERESA,** *b.* November 14, 1839.
vii. **CATHERINE ANN,** *b.* April 14, 1841.
viii. **THOMAS LAWRENCE,** *b.* June 11, 1843.
ix.   **LAWRENCE,** *b.* July 28, 1845.
x.   **EUPHEMIA,** *b.* May 26, 1847 ; *m.*, June, 1887, **JAMES H. STEBBINS, M.D.**

WILLIAM NEWTON, eldest son of **William N.** and **Mary Theresa (Schieffelin) Clark,** *b.* August 14, 1832, is a partner in the drug firm of William H. Schieffelin & Co. ; *m.*, May 20, 1858, **H. MATILDA ANDERSON** (*b.* 1832). Issue :

i.   **SMITH ANDERSON,** *b.* and *d.* March 3, 1859.
ii.   **MARY THERESA,** *b.* November 15, 1860 ; *d.* January 1, 1861.
iii. **HENRY SCHIEFFELIN,** *b.* February 25, 1862, is a Councillor of the Colonial Order ; *m.*, April 9, 1891, **MARY DOUGLASS** (*b.* May 31, 1870). Issue :
      HENRY SCHIEFFELIN, JR., *b.* December 2, 1892.
iv.   **HARRIET ANDERSON,** *b.* December 22, 1863 ; *m.*, June 16, 1891, **WILLIAM GORDON VERPLANCK** (*b.* April 15, 1861). Issue (surname VERPLANCK) :
      MARGARITA SCHUYLER, *b.* October 17, 1892.
v.   **MATILDA SCHUYLER,** *b.* May 3, 1866.
vi.   **HELEN MARGARETTA,** *b.* March 26, 1873 ; *d.* April 14, 1873.

Authority : Family papers, through Mr. W. N. Clark.

SKIPWITH ARMS

COALE

WILLIAM COALE, of Anne Arundel Co., Md., was an eminent Minister of the Society of Friends, and the minute-book of the "Meeting at the Clifts" contains a number of testimonies to his memory, recorded at the time of his death. He *m.*, first, **HESTER ——**. Issue :

i.   **WILLIAM,** *b.* September 21, 1655, *of whom presently.*

WILLIAM COALE, *m.*, second, **HANNAH ——**, who *d.* November 20, 1669. Issue :

ii.   **WILLIAM,** *b.* October 20, 1667 (*q. v.*).

WILLIAM COALE, *m.*, third, **ELIZABETH,** *dau.* of **Philip** and **Sarah (Harrison) Thomas** (*q. v.*)—who *m.*, second, **EDWARD TALBOT** (*q. v.*)—and *d.* October 30, 1678.[1] Further issue :

iii.   **ELIZABETH,** *b.* August 30, 1671 ; *m.* **NATHAN,** second son of **Thomas Smith, Sr.,**[2] merchant, of Calvert Co., Md., and **Alice,** his wife. He *d.* 1711 (will, November 23, 1710 ; probate, January 30, 1710–11 ; Liber W. B., No. 5, folio 146). Issue (surname SMITH)—order uncertain :

---

[1] Will made October 26, 1678, proved February, 1678–79. Liber W. B., folio 92, names "wife Elizabeth ;" "son William, begotten of Hester, his wife ; son William, begotten of Hannah, his second wife ; sons Samuell and Philip and *dau.* Elizabeth, begotten of his wife Elizabeth."

[2] Will, January 13, 1685 ; his wife's, May 4, 1698.

i. JOSEPH, *m.*, May 4, 1710, LAURANA or LEURANIA, *dau.* of Daniel and
    Elizabeth Richardson (*q. v.*).
ii. NATHAN.
iii. WILLIAM.
iv. THOMAS.
v. PHILIP.
vi. ELIZA or ELIZABETH.
vii. SAVANA or SUSANNA.
viii. SARAH.
ix. MARY.
x. CASSANDRA, *m.*, January, 1722–23, JOHN GILES, JR. Issue (surname
    GILES):

    i. Sarah, *b.* December 26, 1723 ; *m.* Samuel, son of Gerrard and Margaret
    (Johns) Hopkins (*q. v.*).
    ii. Elizabeth, *m.* —— Bankster.

iv. **PHILLIP,** *b.* September 6, 1673 (*q. v.*).
v. **SAMUELL,** *b.* April 9, 1676

WILLIAM, son of **William Coale,** by his first wife **Hester,**
m., between December 18, 1683, and August, 1685, **ELIZA,**
relict of **SIR GEORGE SKIPWITH** (who afterward *m.*
SAMUEL CHEW) (*q. v.*), and *d.* 1700. (Will made June 4,
1700, as William Cole, of Annarundell ; proved October 28, 1700.
Liber H. 397.) Issue :

    WILLIAM, *b.* April 2, 1686 ; *d.* September 11, 1687.

WILLIAM, JR., son of **William Coale** by his second wife,
Hannah, *m.,* July 30, 1689, **ELIZABETH,** *dau.* of **Thomas**
and **Eliza (Kinsey** or **Kensey) Sparrow,** and *d.* 1715 [1] (his
widow *m.,* second, **RICHARD JOHNS**) (*q. v.*). Issue :

i. **ELIZA JANE,** *b.* December 3, 1692 ; *m.* **RICHARD SNOWDEN**
    the youngest (*q. v.*).
ii. **MARY,** *b.* April 11, 1697 ; *m.,* about July, 1716, **JOHN CROCKETT.**
iii. **WILLIAM,** *b.* April 11, 1697.
iv. **HANNAH,** *b.* July 14, 1699.
v. **SAMUEL,** *b.* August 24, 1701.
vi. **PRISCILLA,** *b.* October 5, 1703.
vii. **THOMAS,** *b.* March 1, 1705–6 ; *m.* **MARY,** *dau.* of **Joseph** and **Sarah**
    (Thomas) Richardson (*q. v.*) and lived at Bush River, Baltimore Co.
viii. **SARAH,** *b.* February 25, 1706–7.
ix. **ANN,** *b.* August 10, 1709 ; *m.* **WILLIAM,** son of **William** and **Mar-**
    garet Richardson (*q. v.*).
x. **MARGARET,** *m.,* May 26, 1730, **RICHARD,** son of **Richard** and
    Margaret Richardson (*q. v.*).

PHILIP, eldest son of **William** and **Elizabeth (Thomas) Coale,**
b. September 6, 1673, is said to have been an officer in the British

---

[1] Will made July 17, 1713; proved June 24, 1715. Liber W. B., No. 6, folio 62.

Army. He *m.*, April 6, 1697,[1] **CASSANDRA** (*b.* October 29, 1678), *dau.* of **Sir George Skipwith,** Baronet,[2] by his wife, **Elizabeth** ——. Issue :

i.   **CASSANDRA.**
ii. **ELIZABETH.**
iii. **SKIPWITH**, *of whom presently.*

SKIPWITH, only son of **Philip** and **Cassandra (Skipwith) Coale,** removed to Baltimore Co. in 1732, was Sheriff in 1742, *m.* **MARGARET HOLLAND,** and *d.* before 1759. Issue— order uncertain :

i.   **PHILIP.**
ii.   **WILLIAM,** *of whom presently.*
iii. **SKIPWITH,** *m.,* August 25, 1759, SARAH, *dau.* of **Joseph** and **Ann Hopkins,** of Deer Creek, Md.
iv.   **SAMUEL.**
v.   **CASSANDRA.**
vi.   **SARAH,** *m.* **RICHARD THOMAS** (*q. v.*).
vii. **SUSAN.**

WILLIAM, second son of **Skipwith** and **Margaret (Holland) Coale,** *m.* **SARAH WEBSTER,** and settled in Harford Co. Issue :

i.   **JOHN.**
ii. **ISAAC,** a farmer and miller at Deer Creek, in Harford Co., *m.,* September 7, 1786, **RACHEL,** *dau.* of **William** and **Mary (Goldhawk) Cox,** of that Co., but originally of Egham, in England. Issue :

    i.   **SKIPWITH.**
    ii.   **WILLIAM ELLIS,** *of whom presently.*
    iii. **SARAH.**
    iv.   **ELIZABETH.**
    v.   **JOHN WEBSTER.**
    vi.   **MARY.**
    vii. **SUSAN HOLLAND.**
    viii. **ISAAC.**

WILLIAM ELLIS, second son of **Isaac** and **Rachel (Cox) Coale,** *b.* September 25, 1795, was in business in Baltimore, of the firm of Tompkins, Coale & Co., afterward teller in the Union Bank and cashier of the Susquehanna Bridge and Banking Company of the same city. He resided at "Loudoun," which place

---

[1] West River Marriage Book, folio 25.

[2] Sir George Skipwith was grandson of Sir Henry Skipwith, of Prestwould, Leicestershire ; created a Baronet December 20, 1622. For his *dau.* see West River Register, *p.* ii., line 13, in Pedigrees and Notes, by L. B. Thomas, 1883.

his first wife inherited from her father. He *m.*, first, April 16, 1823, **HANNAH ELLICOTT**, *dau.* of **James** and **Martha** (Ellicott) **Carey**, who *d.* March 13, 1837. Issue :

i. **JAMES CAREY**, *b.* May 25, 1825 ; for many years in the insurance business in Baltimore ; *m.*, August 2, 1847, **KATHARINE**, *dau.* of **George Baily**, of Chester Co., Penn. ; *d.* April 13, 1891. Issue :

> **ELIZABETH BAILY**, *b.* April 24, 1848 ; *m.* **EDWARD BLAKE BRUCE**, of Boston, Mass. Issue (surname BRUCE) :
>
> i. Edward Skipwith, *b.* August 1, 1877.
> ii. James Carey Coale, *b.* December 14, 1879 ; *d.* August 23, 1882.
> iii. Katharine Baily, *b.* August 1, 1881.
> iv. Rosalind, *b.* December 24, 1883.
> v. John Marshall Hills, *b.* March 24, 1886.

ii. **ISAAC, JR.**, *b.* April 10, 1827 ; *m.*, first, April 30, 1851, **MARY GABLE**. Issue :

> i. **ALFORD G.**, *b.* March 22, 1852 ; *m.*, October 25, 1891, **ELSIE JAUNCEY RAY**, of New York.
> ii. **JAMES CAREY**, *b.* November 27, 1858, and *d.* August 4, 1867.

> **MR. COALE** *m.*, second, October 22, 1868, **HELEN McDOWELL**, and *d.* December 31, 1873 ; his widow *d.* December 19, 1887. Issue :

> iii. **HELEN C.**, *b.* November 30, 1869 ; *m.*, June 1, 1893, **DR. HENRY B. THOMAS**, of Baltimore, formerly of S. Mary's City, S. Mary's Co., Md.

iii. **MARY**, *b.* November 15, 1829 ; *m.*, June 5, 1855, **FRANCIS COPE YARNALL**, of Overbrook, Pa., who *d.* June 26, 1890 ; his widow *d.* March 30, 1891. Issue (surname YARNALL) :

> i. **MARGARET CHESTON**, *b.* February 20, 1856 ; *m.*, June 2, 1887, **ALFRED COPE**.
> ii. **CAROLINE COPE**, *b.* April 30, 1859 ; *m.*, June 12, 1884, **EDWARD AUGUSTUS CASEY**. Issue (surname CASEY) :
>
> > i. Mary Yarnall, *b.* August 16, 1885.
> > ii. Edward Augustus, Jr., *d. i.*
> > iii. Francis Yarnall, *b.* December 4, 1889.
> > iv. v. Theodore Murdoch and Herbert Stephen, twins, *b.* December 26, 1893.
>
> iii. **EDWARD**, *b.* November 16, 1864.

iv. **WILLIAM ELLIS, JR.**, *b.* November 17, 1831 ; *m.* October 9, 1858, **LOUISA SCHMIDT**, who *d.* December 30, 1873, and he *d.* November 3, 1880. Issue :

> i. **WILLIAM ELLIS**, *b.* February 7, 1860 ; *m.*, April 2, 1891, **ANNE ESTHER**, *dau.* of Captain Frederick M. and Clara C. COLSTON, of Baltimore.
> ii. **MARY YARNALL**, *b.* September 26, 1862.
> iii. **THOMAS ELLICOTT**, *b.* May 19, 1865 ; *m.*, November 20, 1890, **NANNIE EULALIA MURPHY**.
> iv. **LOUISA**, *b.* March 8, 1868.
> v. **LILIAN**, *b.* March 8, 1868, now **LILIAN COALE ALDERSON**, having been adopted by Mr. and Mrs. William Charles Alderson, of Overbrook, Pa.

v.   **THOMAS ELLICOTT**, *b.* March 31, 1833, *of whom presently.*
vi.   **MARTHA CAREY**, *b.* June 11, 1835, *d. i.*
vii.   **HANNAH ELLICOTT**, *b.* February 27, 1837 ; *m.*, February 28, 1861, **DAVID SCULL, JR.** (*q. v.*).

WILLIAM ELLIS COALE *m.*, second, November 29, 1841, **CASSANDRA ANN**, *dau.* of **Surgeon Joseph Brevitt**, of the British Army, who *d.* April 5, 1888 ; her husband *d.* September 13, 1865. Issue :

viii.   **MARGARET CHESTON**, *b.* August 17, 1842 ; *m.*, October 1, 1868, **BARTHOLOMEW W. BEESLY**, of Philadelphia, Pa. Issue (surname BEESLY) :

    i.   HANNAH COALE, *b.* November 11, 1870.
    ii.   CHARLTON WISTAR, *b.* April 1, 1878.

ix.   **SKIPWITH HOLLAND**, *b.* August 27, 1845, *d. u.* February 9, 1878.
x.   **ELEANORA E.**, *b.* March 9, 1848 ; *m.* **ALEXANDER G. CAREY** (*q. v.*).
xi.   **EDWIN BREVITT**, *b.* May 16, 1856 ; *d. u.* March 7, 1887.

THOMAS ELLICOTT, fourth son of **William Ellis** and **Hannah E. (Carey) Coale**, *b.* March 31, 1833 ; *m.*, January 18, 1855, **CECELIA HARVEY**. Issue :

i.   **WILLIAM ELLIS**, *b.* October 14, 1856 ; *m.*, May 8, 1878, **MARY ELLA**, *dau.* of **H. B. Baily**, of Covington, Ky. Issue :

    i.   EDITH BAILY, *b.* July 30, 1879.
    ii.   GRIFFITH BAILY, *b.* May 21, 1890.
    iii. WILLIAM ELLIS, *b.* March 8, 1891.

ii.   **HARVEY**, *b.* March 31, 1858 ; *m.*, October 27, 1881, **LAURA E. COLMARY**. Issue :

    i.   HARVEY MORTON, *b.* December 4, 1882.
    ii.   ELIZABETH L., *b.* September 21, 1884.

iii.   **ISAAC, JR.**, *b.* June 2, 1861.
iv.   **THOMAS ELLICOTT**, *b.* January 29, 1863.
v.   **HELEN C.**, *b.* December 8, 1866 ; *m.*, July 17, 1890, **HENRY CREW**. Issue (surname CREW) :

    ALICE H., *b.* March 11, 1892, and another child, *b.* January 6, 1894.

vi.   **CAREY**, *b.* September 7, 1868.

Authorities : Friends' Records and family papers, in this issue, through Mr. William E. Coale, of Baltimore.

COWMAN

JOSEPH COWMAN, of Parshlow Crag, in Cumberland, England, and a seaman by profession, *m.*, March 5, 1723–24, **MRS. SARAH HILL,** widow, and had with other issue two sons: **JOHN,** *of whom presently*, and **JOSEPH,** who engaged in the iron business with his father-in-law, Richard Snowden, and *m.*, April 4, 1754, **ELIZABETH,** youngest *dau.* of **Richard** and **Elizabeth (Thomas) Snowden** (*q. v.*). Issue:

    i.   **RICHARD,** *b.* September 12, 1777; *m.* **ANN DARE,** and *d.* in March, 1784, leaving three *daus.*, Ann, Elizabeth, and Mary.
    ii.   **JOSEPH,** *m.* **ELEANOR HALL.**
    iii.   **ELIZABETH.**
    iv.   **SAMUEL.**
    v.   **SARAH,** *m.* **RICHARD HALL.**
    vi.   **THOMAS,** *m.* **HENRIETTA HARWOOD.**

JOHN, eldest son of Joseph and Sarah Cowman, *b.* in 1737; *m.*, September 27, 1757, **SARAH,** *dau.* of **Gerard Hopkins** (*q. v.*), and *d.* September 15, 1808. Issue:

    i.   **JOSEPH,** *b.* September 8, 1758, *of whom presently*.
    ii.   **MARY,** *b.* April 18, 1760; *m.* **SAMUEL THOMAS** (*q. v.*).
    iii.   **GERARD,** *b.* May 6, 1762; *d.* December 31, 1789.
    iv.   **JOHN,** *b.* March 10, 1764; *m.*, before June 21, 1793, **MARY PLUMMER,** and *d.* August 10, 1826.
    v.   **SARAH,** *b.* February 9, 1766; *m.*, December 28, 1786, **WILLIAM GOVER.** Issue (surname GOVER):

        i.   **SARAH,** *b.* November 2, 1787.
        ii.   **MARY COWMAN,** *b.* February 24, 1789.
        iii.   **WILLIAM ALEXANDER,** *b.* February 16, 1791.
        iv.   **AUGUSTUS FREDERICK,** *b.* January 18, 1793.
        v.   **ELIZABETH,** *b.* December 22, 1794.
        vi.   **MARGARET,** *b.* September 10, 1796.
        vii. **JOHN,** *b.* March 17, 1798.
        viii. **ELIZA,** *b.* May 31, 1800.
        ix.   **ANN MARIA,** *b.* August 1, 1802.
        x.   **CAROLINE,** *b.* September 4, 1804.
        xi.   **ROBERT,** *b.* November 1, 1806.

vi.   **MARGARET,** *b.* May 22, 1769.
vii. **ANN,** *b.* July 24, 1771 ; *m.,* November 22, 1792, **THOMAS NORRIS.**
viii. **ELIZABETH,** *b.* March 12, 1774.
ix.   **RICHARD,** *b.* September 12, 1777.

JOSEPH, eldest son of **John** and **Sarah (Hopkins) Cowman,** *b.*
September 8, 1758 ; *m.,* February 3, 1786, **MARY,** third *dau.* of
Samuel and **Elizabeth (Thomas) Snowden** (*q. v.*), and *d.* in
August, 1825 ; his wife *d.* August 15, 1834.   Issue :

i.   **ELIZABETH,** *b.* December 29, 1786 ; *d.* in August, 1822.
ii.   **SARAH,** *b.* May 28, 1789.
iii. **GERARD,** *b.* November 9, 1791.
iv.   **SAMUEL SNOWDEN,** *b.* February 9, 1794; *m.* and had a son,
      THOMAS W., *b.* in 1827 ; *d.,* August 5, 1829.
v.   **JOHN G.,** *b.* April 22, 1796.
vi.   **MARY,** *b.* in 1798 ; *d. u.* August 9, 1817.
vii. **JOSEPH,** *b.* May 22, 1801.

Authority : Maryland Friends' Records.

DE ZENG

BARON DE ZENG, of Rücherswalde Wolkenstein, near Marien-
burg in Saxony, Lord Chamberlain to the Duchess of Saxe-Weis-
senfels, and High Forest Officer to the King of Saxony, *m.* **LADY
JOHANNA PHILLIPINA VON PONICKAU,** of Alten-
berg. Issue :

> **FREDERIC AUGUSTUS,** *b.* 1756; *m.*, in 1784, **MARY,** *dau.* of **Caleb**
> and **Sarah Lawrence** (*q. v.*), who *d.* 1836; her husband *d.* April 26,
> 1838. Issue :

> > i. **GEORGE SCRIBA,** *m.* **ELIZA SMITH,** and *d. s. p.*
> > ii. **ERNESTINE FREDERICA AUGUSTA JEANNETTE,** *m.* **JAMES
> >   HOUGHTELING,** M.D., of Kingston, N. Y. (*q. v.*).
> > iii. **RICHARD LAWRENCE,** *m.* his cousin, **SARAH,** *dau.* of **Richard** and **Mary
> >   Lawrence** (*q. v.*).
> > iv. **PHILIP MARK,** *m.* **LUCRETIA SEARS,** of Bainbridge, N. Y.
> > v. **WILLIAM STEUBEN,** *m.* **CAROLINE C.,** *dau.* of Major **James Rees,** of
> >   Philadelphia.
> > vi. **ARTHUR NOBLE,** *d. s. p.*
> > vii. **SARAH,** *m.* her cousin, **RICHARD L. LAWRENCE** (*q. v.*).
> > viii. **AMELIA CLARISSA,** *m.* **ADDISON GRISWOLD,** of Syracuse.
> > ix. **MARIA,** *m.* **WILLIAM S. STOW,** of Clyde, N. Y.

Authority : New York Biographical and Genealogical Record.

ELLICOTT

ANDREW, son of **Andrew** and **Elizabeth (Hodge) Elli-cott,**[1] of Collumpton, Devonshire, England, *m.,* February 10, 1707, **MARY,** eldest *dau.* of **Francis Fox,** of S. Germans, Cornwall, by his second wife, **Tabitha Croker,** and with his eldest son, **ANDREW,** came to America, in 1730.

ANDREW ELLICOTT the third, *b.* July 11, 1708; *m.,* June 17, 1731, **ANN BYE,** of Bucks Co., Pa., and settled there, dying in June, 1741. Issue:

i.   **JOSEPH,** *b.* October 8, 1732, *of whom presently.*

ii.   **ANDREW,** *b.* January 22, 1734 (*q. v.*).

iii.   **NATHANIEL,** *b.* February 17, 1736; *m.* **LETITIA HARVEY,** and *d. s. p.*

iv.   **THOMAS,** *b.* March 16, 1738; *m.,* first, October 26, 1763, **ANNE ELY.** Issue:

       RUTH, JOHN, SARAH, ANNE, PAMELIA, THOMAS, JOSEPH, and LETITIA.

       He *m.,* second, **MRS. REBECCA WILKINSON,** and had further is-sue:

       GEORGE and RACHEL.

       He *m.,* third, November 16, 1791, **JANE KINSEY,** by whom he left a *dau.,* HANNAH, at his death, in 1799.

v.   **JOHN,** *b.* December 28, 1739 (*q. v.*).

[1] A hawk, with wings expanded and belled; all proper; is said by some authorities to be the true crest of Ellicott.

JOSEPH, eldest son of **Andrew** and **Ann (Bye) Ellicott,** *b.* October 8, 1732 ; was Sheriff of Bucks Co. in 1768–69. In 1771 he followed his brother, John, to Maryland, and with their other brother, Andrew, bought water rights and land on the Patapsco River, about ten miles west of Baltimore, where Ellicott City now stands. By 1774 they had completed their first flour-mill, which was burned in 1809. In 1783, their trade increasing, they bought their first water lot in the town of Baltimore, and built a wharf at the corner of Pratt and Light Streets, in order to export their flour to England.

They, and their family after them, carried on an extensive milling business for a number of years, and were largely interested in the early progress of the Baltimore & Ohio Railroad and other works of public utility. In 1837 the mill property was sold to Colonel Charles Carroll, and in 1844 the firm became Charles A. Gambrill & Co.

JOSEPH ELLICOTT, *m.*, in 1753, JUDITH BLEAKER,

and *d.* in 1780 ; she *d.* July 9, 1809. Issue :

i.   **ANDREW,** *b.* January 24, 1754 ; *m.*, in 1775, **SARAH BROWN.** Issue :

     i.   **ANDREW A.,** *m.*, in 1801, **SARAH WILLIAMS.**
     ii.   **GEORGE,** *d. s. p.*
     iii.   **JANE J.,** *m.*, first, **THOMAS R. KENNEDY** ; and second, **JOHN REYNOLDS.**
     iv.   **MARY,** *m.* **NATHANIEL C. GRIFFITH.**
     v.   **LETITIA M.,** *m.* **JOHN BLISS.**
     vi.   **JOSEPH,** *m.* **ELIZA SHERMAN.**
     vii.   **SARAH,** *m.* **HENRY BALDWIN.**
     viii.   **ANNA E.,** *m.*, in 1815, **DAVID B. DOUGLASS.**
     ix.   **RACHEL B.,** *m.* **TRUMAN H. WOODRUFF.**
     x.   **JOHN B.,** *m.*, in 1822, **HELEN GRIFFITH.**

ii.   **SARAH,** *b.* July 19, 1755 ; *d. u.*, July 18, 1779.
iii.   **DAVID,** *b.* December 26, 1756 ; *m.*, in 1777, **MARTHA,** *dau.* of **William** and **Martha (Hough) Evans.** Issue :

     SARAH, ELIZABETH, JOSEPH, and **JOHN,** who all *d. i.*

iv.   **ANN,** *b.* December 3, 1758 ; *m.*, in 1777, **JOSEPH EVANS.** Issue (surname EVANS) :

     MARTHA, JOSEPH E., ALICE, JUDITH, MARY ANN, BENJAMIN, SARAH, JOHN, and **ELIZABETH.**

v.   **JOSEPH,** *b.* November 1, 1760 ; *d.* in New York in 1826.
vi.   **LETITIA,** *b.* November 19, 1762 ; *m.*, in 1778, **JOHN EVANS.** Issue (surname EVANS) :

WILLIAM, *m.*, January 8, 1807, MARTHA RANDALL. Issue:
  i.　　Charles W.,[1] *b.* in 1816.
  ii.　　Rachel.
  iii.　　Lewis E.
  iv.　　Ann.
  v.　　Martha, *m.* Samuel Carey (*q. v.*).
  vi.　　Letitia, *b.* in 1792; *d. u.* in 1815.

vii.　BENJAMIN, *b.* April 17, 1765.
viii.　RACHEL, twin of the above, *b.* April 17, 1765; *m.*, in 1787, LEWIS
　　　EVANS. Issue (surname EVANS):

　　　DAVID E., ELIZABETH, and HANNAH.

ix.　MARY, *b.* May 10, 1769; *m.*, in 1785, THOMAS BROWN. Issue:
  i.　　SARAH.
  ii.　　MARY, *b.* in 1789; *d. u.* in 1817.

ANDREW, second son of **Andrew** and **Ann (Bye) Ellicott**, *b.*
January 22, 1734, *m.*, first, in 1755, **ELIZABETH**, *dau.* of
Thomas Brown. Issue:

i.　JONATHAN, *b.* November 9, 1856, *of whom presently.*
ii.　ELIAS, *b.* December 27, 1757; *d. i.*
iii.　ELIAS, *b.* January 5, 1759 (*q. v.*).
iv.　GEORGE, *b.* March 28, 1760; *m.*, December 29, 1790, ELIZABETH,
　　　dau. of **James** and **Deborah Brooke** (*q. v.*), and *d.* in 1832. Issue:

  i.　　JAMES, *b.* January 3, 1792; *d. i.*
  ii.　　ELIZABETH, *b.* December 5, 1793; *m.*, in 1812, THOMAS LEA.
  iii.　　MARTHA, *b.* September 13, 1795, a woman of remarkable abilities and authoress of
　　　　a history of the Ellicott's Mills settlement; *m.* NATHAN TYSON (*q. v.*).
  iv.　　GEORGE, *b.* July 16, 1798; *m.*, in 1842, AGNES B. IGLEHART.
  v.　　MARY, *b.* May 14, 1801; *m.*, October 19, 1825, THOMAS TYSON (*q. v.*).
  vi.　　ANNA B., twin of MARY, *m.*, in 1836, THOMAS TYSON, as his second wife,
　　　　and *d.* July 16, 1839.
  vii.　　SARAH, *b.* November 3, 1803; *d.* August 31, 1804.
  viii.　　EDWARD.
  ix.　　THOMAS.

v.　BENJAMIN, *b.* October 16, 1761; *d. u.* in 1838.
vi.　NATHANIEL, *b.* January 10, 1763; *m.*, in 1790, ELIZABETH, *dau.*
　　　of **John** and **Leah (Brown) Ellicott** (*q. v.*). Issue:

  i.　　JOHN A., *m.* MARY, widow of John Ross, of Kent Co., Md. Issue:
　　　　i.　　Joseph P., *b.* in 1818, residing in Boston.
　　　　ii.　　Edward S., *b.* in 1820; *d.* at Havana in 1856.
　　　　iii.　　Frances A., *b.* in 1824; *m.* Dr. S. H. Henry, of Baltimore.

　　　　MRS. JOHN A. ELLICOTT, *m.*, second, GEORGE POE.

  ii.　　HANNAH, *m.* JAMES J. SYMINGTON, and *d. s. p.* in 1835.
  iii.　　NATHANIEL H., *m.* ELIZABETH, *dau.* of John and Mary Ross, of Kent
　　　　Co., and *d.* in 1833. Issue:

　　　　A *dau.*, Mary, *d. y.*

---

[1] Author of the History of the Fox, Ellicott, and Evans families, in 1882, from which much of
this Ellicott pedigree is taken.

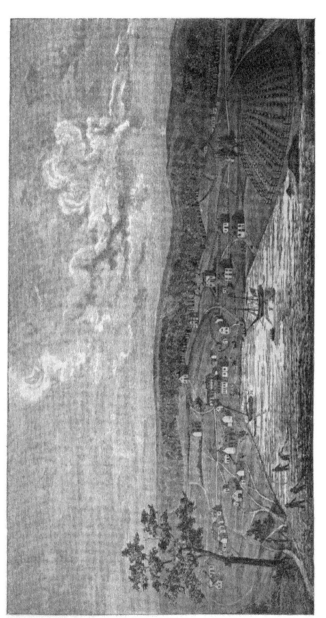

BALTIMORE IN THE EIGHTEENTH CENTURY

After a Drawing by Moule, 1752

iv. CASSANDRA, *d. y.*
v. MARY, *d. u.* in 1830.
vi. JONATHAN, *d. u.* in 1831.
vii. ANDREW, *d. u.* in 1852.

vii. ANDREW, *b.* December 9, 1764 ; *d.* May 23, 1766.
viii. ELIZABETH, *b.* January 18, 1766 ; *d.* May 23, 1766.

ANDREW ELLICOTT, *m.*, second, in 1767, **ESTHER BROWN,** and *d.* June 20, 1809. Further issue :

ix. JOSEPH, *b.* June 22, 1768 ; *d.* September 16, 1771.
x. TACY, *b.* May 3, 1770 ; *m.*, October 20, 1796, as his third wife, **ISAAC McPHERSON,** and *d.* in 1829.
xi. JAMES, *b.* August 24, 1772 ; *m.* **HENRIETTA,** *dau.* of Philip William Thomas, and *d.* July 12, 1820, leaving an only son **CHARLES,** *d. s. p.* August 18, 1841.
xii. ANDREW, *b.* October 2, 1775 ; *m.*, March 4, 1812, **HANNAH TUNIS,** and *d.* in January, 1823. Issue :

   i. JANE TUNIS, *b.* February 14, 1813 ; *m.* THOMAS, son of Thomas and Ann Poultney (*q. v.*).
   ii. ELIZA R., *b.* October 31, 1814 ; *m.* BENJAMIN POULTNEY (*q. v.*).
   iii. MARIA, *b.* December 26, 1816 ; *d. u.* in July, 1839.
   iv. ANDREW, *b.* June 25, 1819 ; *d. y.*

xiii. THOMAS, *b.* November 18, 1777 (*q. v.*).
xiv. JOHN, *b.* February 2, 1780 ; *m.* **MARY MITCHELL,** and *d.* in 1813. Issue :

   i. RACHEL, *b.* April 6, 1804.
   ii. ANN, *b.* October 16, 1805.
   iii. MARY, *b.* June 23, 1810.

JONATHAN, eldest son of **Andrew** and **Elizabeth (Brown) Ellicott,** *b.* November 9, 1756, was a man of stalwart frame, strongly marked Roman features, keen gray eyes, plain in speech and manners, and with a decided genius for mechanical invention. He was the projector and first President of the Frederick Turnpike, leading from the town of Baltimore, by the flour-mills of his family, to Frederick City ; and was the first President of the Baltimore Water Company. He *m.* **SARAH HARVEY,** of Bucks Co., Pa., and *d.* in 1826. His wife was *b.* May 20, 1764, was petite and delicate in figure, and remarkable for the fineness of her complexion at an advanced age, the great kindness of her disposition and profuse hospitality, combined with economy and careful housewifery. She *d.* in 1840. Issue :

i. NATHANIEL, *b.* in 1782 ; *d.* in 1786.
ii. SAMUEL, *b.* December 13, 1783 ; *d. u.* December 13, 1843.

iii. **ELIZABETH,** *b.* December 5, 1785 ; *m.* **WILLIAM TYSON** (*q. v.*).
iv. **FRANCES,** *b.* December 5, 1785 ; *d.* in 1790.
v. **NATHANIEL H.,** *b.* April 26, 1791 ; *m.*, October 2, 1828, **THOMAS-INE TRIMBLE,** of New York, and *d.* in 1860. Issue :

    i. JANE, *b.* September 26, 1829 ; *m.*, June 17, 1852, JOSEPH P. WILLSON, and *d.* April 4, 1877. Issue (surname WILLSON) :
      Cornelia, Mary, and Henry.
    ii. FRANCES H., *b.* 1832 ; *d.* 1837.
    iii. RICHARD T., *b.* January 18, 1842.

vi. **WILLIAM,** *b.* October 15, 1793 ; *m.*, in 1833, **MARY ELEONORA NORRIS,** and *d. s. p.* March 22, 1836.
vii. **SARAH,** *b.* February 27, 1796 ; *m.* **WILLIAM E. GEORGE** (*q. v.*).
viii. **FRANCES,** *b.* July 24, 1798 ; *d.* in 1814.
ix. **JONATHAN H.,** *b.* January 20, 1801 ; *d.* March 3, 1881.
x. **LETITIA H.,** *b.* July 27, 1803 ; *m.*, November 18, 1829, **THOMAS R. FISHER,** of Philadelphia. Issue (surname FISHER) :

    i. SARAH E., *b.* October 4, 1830 ; *d.* February 18, 1832.
    ii. WILLIAM LOGAN, *b.* July 4, 1832 ; *d.* December 8, 1858.
    iii. GEORGE L., *b.* May 17, 1835 ; *d.* July 2, 1836.
    iv. MARY R., *b.* August 20, 1838 ; *m.*, February 1, 1860, GEORGE W. CARPEN-TER. Issue (surname CARPENTER) :
      i. Letitia E., *b.* April 7, 1861 ; *m.*, April 18, 1881, William Redwood Wright.
      ii. Elizabeth R. F., *b.* February 17, 1870.
    v. ELLICOTT, *b.* May 30, 1840.
    vi. HARVEY, *b.* November 4, 1843.

xi. **MARY ANN,** *b.* February 10, 1806 ; *d. u.*, March 22, 1843.
xii. **BENJAMIN H.,** *b.* February 6, 1809 ; *m.*, February 22, 1838, **MARY WARFORD.** Issue :

    RACHEL C., BENJAMIN WARFORD, GEORGE WARFORD.

ELIAS, third son of **Andrew** and **Elizabeth (Brown) Ellicott,** *b.* January 4, 1759 ; *m.*, April 26, 1786, **MARY,** *dau.* of **Evan** and **Rachel Thomas** (*q. v.*), of Mount Radnor. Issue :

i. **ELIZABETH,** *b.* February 17, 1787 ; *m.* **LEWIN WETHERED** (*q. v.*).
ii. **EVAN THOMAS,** *b.* September 17, 1788 ; *d.* August 10, 1791.
iii. **RACHEL,** *b.* February 17, 1791 ; *m.*, January 15, 1812, **JOHN,** son of **Edward** and **Mary Hewes,** first President of the Fireman's Insurance Company of Baltimore. Issue (surname HEWES) :

    i. EDWARD, *b.* October 9, 1812 ; *d.* November 13, 1836.
    ii. ELIAS ELLICOTT, *b.* March 9, 1814.
    iii. HENRY, *b.* February 20, 1816.
    iv. MARY ELLICOTT, *b.* April 9, 1818 ; *d.* July 13, 1838.
    v. JAMES ELLICOTT, *b.* August 10, 1820.
    vi. BENJAMIN ELLICOTT, *b.* January 16, 1823 ; *d. i.*
    vii. JOHN, Jr., *b.* March 10, 1827.
    viii. WILLIAM G., *d. i.*

iv.   **EVAN THOMAS**, *b.* December 6, 1793, a prominent civil engineer ; *m.* **HARVEY M. BOND**, and *d. s. p.* She *d.* June 14, 1881.

v.   **TACY**, *b.* January 14, 1795 ; *m.* **JOSEPH KING** (*q. v.*).

vi.   **BENJAMIN**, *b.* November 13, 1796 ; *m.*, January 15, 1837, **MARY A.**, *dau.* of **William Carroll**, descended from **Daniel Carroll**, of Duddington. Issue :

     i.   **HENRIETTA M.**, *b.* June 2, 1841 ; *m.*, August 3, 1864, **CHARLES M. BACHE.**
     ii.   **WILLIAM C.**, *b.* October 13, 1842 ; *m.*, June 29, 1868, **ISABELLA PIERCE.**
     iii.   **CHARLES J. F.**, *b.* December 6, 1844.
     iv.   **EUGENE**, *b.* December 8, 1846 ; *m.*, January 16, 1877, **MAGGIE I.**, *dau.* of Richard W. Tyson (*q. v.*). Issue :
         Mary C., *b.* January 1, 1880.
     v.   **FREDERICK A.**, *b.* April 27, 1849 ; *d.* August 3, 1854.
     vi.   **SALVADOR**, *b.* July 8, 1852.
     vii.   **MARY DOLORES**, *b.* August 20, 1854 ; *d.* October 21, 1854.
     viii.   **MARY G.**, *b.* June 5, 1856 ; *d.* July 6, 1856.

vii.   **ANN**, *b.* August 24, 1798 ; *d.* January 15, 1799.

viii.   **THOMAS**, *b.* December 11, 1799 ; *m.*, May 17, 1825, **LOUISA McFADON.** Issue :

     i.   **MARY.**
     ii.   **PRISCILLA.**
     iii.   **JOHN.**
     iv.   **JAMES F.**, *m.* **ELVIRA A. JONES**, of S. Mary's Co., Md. Issue :
         i.   John Morris, *b.* September 4, 1859.
         ii.   Rose, *b.* in 1861.

ix.   **ANDREW**, *b.* December 23, 1801 (*q. v.*).

x.   **JAMES**, *b.* January 3, 1804.

xi.   **JOHN**, *b.* January 18, 1805 ; was much interested in genealogy ; had a tree of the Fox family made ; *d. u.* in 1860.

xii.   **SAMUEL**, *b.* August 11, 1806 ; *m.*, October 31, 1833, **MARY ANN**, *dau.* of **Joseph E.**[1] and **Eliza Todhunter**, who *d.*, 1894, leaving issue :

     i.   **ELIZA TODHUNTER.**
     ii.   **MARIAN.**
     iii.   **JOSEPH TODHUNTER**, *b.* October, 1842 ; *m.*, September 4, 1866, **LAURA ELDER.**
     iv.   **FRANCIS FOX**, *b.* March 28, 1848.
     v.   **NANNIE POULTNEY.**

xiii.   **ELIAS**, *m.* **SARAH**, *dau.* of **Dudley** and **Deborah Poor**, and *d.* in 1873. Issue :

     i.   **SARAH**, *m.* September 10, 1867, **HENRY TRACY ARNOLD**, of New York.
     ii.   **ADELAIDE VICTORIA.**
     iii.   **HENRY**, *d. i.*
     iv.   **MARGARET**, *m.*, 1868, **DR. ALFRED A. WOODHULL**, U. S. A., Author of a valuable report on the Medical Department of the British Army, published by the United States Government in 1895.
     v.   **MARY LOUISA**, *d.* May 12, 1873.

[1] Joseph Todhunter *m.* Eliza Onion. Issue : i. Mary Ann, *m.* Samuel Ellicott ; ii. Eliza, *m.* Evan Philip Thomas (*q. v.*) ; iii. Kate, *m.* Jonathan Thompson, of New York, and *d.* May 9, 1878 ; iv. Edmondson, *m.* Emma Frances Keyworth. Issue : Joseph, *d. i.* ; Mary G., Stephen, and Robert ; v. Joseph, *d. s. p.* ; vi. Charles ; vii. William ; viii. Alison, *m.* —— Cleveland.

xiv.　**HENRY**, *d. u.* in August, 1833.
xv.　**PHILIP T.**, *d. u.*

ANDREW, fifth son of **Elias** and **Mary (Thomas) Ellicott**, *b.* December 23, 1801, *m.*, December 4, 1823, **EMILY A. McFADON.** They both died in 1866. Issue :

i.　**HENRY WILLIAM**, *b.* in 1824, *of whom presently.*
ii.　**JAMES P.**, *b.* August 22, 1826 ; *m.*, October 30, 1845, **FANNIE ADELAIDE INCE**, and *d.* in 1873, leaving, with other issue :

EVAN T., *b.* February 14, 1853 ; *m.*, September 4, 1878, **ALICE STELLA McCORMICK. Issue :**

Gilmor Meredith, *b.* June 20, 1879.

iii.　**EVAN THOMAS**, *b.* in 1828 ; *d. s. p.* in 1867.
iv.　**JOHN E.**, *b.* in 1832 ; *d.* in 1833.
v.　**HARVEY BOND**, *m.*, August 30, 1859, **ROBERT T. MACCOUN,** U.S.N.
vi.　**CAROLINE.**
vii.　**EMILY**, *b.* November 30, 1837 ; *d.* in 1848.

HENRY WILLIAM, eldest son of **Andrew** and **Emily A. (McFadon) Ellicott**, *b.* September 11, 1824 ; *m.*, October 4, 1849, **ELIZABETH Y. BARNEY.** Issue :

i.　**EMILY**, *b.* in 1851 ; *d.* in 1853.
ii.　**ADELE E.**, *b.* May 15, 1854 ; *m.* **REV. ISAAC L. NICHOLSON,** now Bishop of Milwaukee.
iii.　**HENRY WILLIAM, JR.**, *b.* August 23, 1856.
iv.　**ELIZABETH B.**, *b.* March 26, 1862.
v.　**MARY**, *b.* January 14, 1864.
vi.　**CHARLES RIDGELY**, *b.* December 15, 1867.

THOMAS, eleventh son of **Andrew** and **Esther (Brown) Ellicott**, *b.* November 18, 1777 ; was Cashier and afterward President of the Union Bank of Maryland, at Baltimore, a prominent merchant, and much interested in the family history, for which he made collections of great value. He *m.*, December 11, 1806, **MARY MILLER**, who *d.* May 30, 1855, and *d.* October 6, 1859. Issue :

i.　**WILLIAM MILLER**, *b.* September 30, 1807, *of whom presently.*
ii.　**SARAH ANN**, *b.* January 21, 1809 ; *m.*, August 19, 1858, **JACOB LINDLEY**, and *d. s. p.* January 19, 1874.
iii.　**HANNAH**, *b.* August 21, 1810 ; *m.* **RICHARD B. GILPIN.** Issue :
　　THOMAS ELLICOTT.

iv.   **LYDIA,** *b.* February 11, 1812 ; *m.* **DR. FREDERICK TURNPEN-NY.** Issue :

      MARY ELLICOTT, *m.* JOHN LAMBERT.

v.   **MARY THOMAS,** *b.* September 10, 1813.
vi.   **ESTHER B.,** *b.* November 12, 1814 ; *d.* January 17, 1827.
vii.   **REBECCA M.,** *b.* March 6, 1816.
viii. **CATHERINE S.,** *b.* November 9, 1817 ; *m.*, October 4, 1847, **JACOB LINDLEY,** and *d.* April 9, 1856. Issue (surname LINDLEY) :

   i.   MARY ELLICOTT, *d. y.*
   ii.   THOMAS ELLICOTT, *b.* January 14, 1851 ; *m.*, April 30, 1879, IDA F. LOCKWOOD. Issue :

      Elizabeth Downing, *b.* October 16, 1885.

   iii.   SARAH HAVARD, *d. y.*
   iv.   DR. HAVARD, *b.* December 10, 1853, resides in St. Louis, Mo. ; *m.*, October 25, 1883, ELLA PHILLIPS. Issue :

      John Marshall, *b.* November 15, 1889.

   v.   JACOB, *b.* March 13, 1856 ; *m.*, June 1, 1882, FANNIE, *dau.* of Isaac and Fannie (Thornton) Tyson (*q. v.*).

ix.   **ELIZABETH,** *b.* January 1, 1822 ; *m.*, June 5, 1855, **JAMES S. PIKE,** United States Minister at the Hague under President Lincoln.

WILLIAM MILLER, eldest son of **Thomas** and **Mary (Miller) Ellicott,** *b.* September 30, 1807 ; *m.*, November 11, 1829, **SARAH,** *dau.* of **Thomas** and **Ann Poultney** (*q. v.*), who *d.* May, 1891. Issue :

i.   **THOMAS POULTNEY,** *b.* September 25, 1830, *of whom presently.*
ii.   **WILLIAM MILLER, JR.,** *b.* January 16, 1834 ; *m.*, November 15, 1860, **NANCY MORRIS,** *dau.* of **Charles** and **Mary Ellis** (*q. v.*), of Philadelphia, and resided in that city, both *d.* Issue :

   i.   CHARLES ELLIS, *b.* November 3, 1861.
   ii.   WILLIAM MILLER, 3d, *b.* May 5, 1863.
   iii.   LINDLEY, *b.* August 20, 1864 ; *d.* May 7, 1876.
   iv.   MARY MORRIS, *b.* February 1, 1867.
   v.   EDITH, *b.* August 8, 1871.
   vi.   LYDIA, *b.* October 12, 1872.

iii.   **DR. LINDLEY,** *b.* January 26, 1836 ; *d. u.* August 29, 1876.
iv.   **MARY MILLER,** *b.* March 10, 1838 ; *m.*, June 20, 1871, **JOHN B. ROBERTS.** Issue :

      WILLIAM MILLER, *b.* May 15, 1872.

v.   **NANNIE POULTNEY,** *b.* April 13, 1840 ; *d.* June 27, 1854.
vi.   **DAVID B.,** *b.* July 20, 1844.
vii.   **SARAH POULTNEY,** *b.* May 21, 1847 ; *d.* January 20, 1853.
viii. **CHARLES LEWIS,** *b.* December 19, 1849.

THOMAS POULTNEY, eldest son of **William M.** and **Sarah (Poultney) Ellicott**, *b.* September 25, 1830 ; *m.*, September 19, 1855, **CAROLINE MACKEY ALLEN.** Issue :

i.   **THOMAS**, *b.* June 18, 1856.
ii.   **SUSAN ALLEN**, *b.* March 31, 1858.
iii.   **FRANCIS ALLEN**, *b.* March 19, 1860.
iv.   **SARAH POULTNEY**, *b.* August 12, 1863.
v.   **WILLIAM MILLER**, *b.* August 17, 1865 ; *d.* December 14, 1878.
vi.   **PHILIP P.**, *b.* February 16, 1868 ; *d.* August 4, 1868.
vii.   **RACHEL POULTNEY**, *b.* February 23, 1870 ; *m.*, December 27, 1894, **EDWARD L. MATTHEWS**, of Atlanta, Ga.
viii. **NANCY POULTNEY**, *b.* February 17, 1872.
ix.   **JAMES POULTNEY**, *b.* December 26, 1876.

JOHN, youngest son of **Andrew** and **Ann (Bye) Ellicott**, *b.* December 28, 1739, was the pioneer in the settlement of Ellicott's Mills, Maryland ; *m.*, first, **LEAH BROWN**, and second, **CASSANDRA**, *dau.* of **Samuel** and **Sarah (Giles) Hopkins** (*q. v.*), who *d. s. p.* By his first wife he had :

i.   **MARTHA**, *b.* November 7, 1761 ; *m.* **JAMES CAREY** (*q. v.*).
ii.   **ELIZABETH**, *b.* in 1763 ; *m.* **NATHANIEL ELLICOTT** (*q. v.*).
iii.   **JOHN**, *m.*, in 1814, **MARY KIRK**, and *d.* about 1820. Issue :

     i.   SAMUEL, *b.* November 22, 1814 ; *m.*, September 18, 1862, SARAH E., *dau.* of Dr. James Duck, and *d.* November 3, 1880. Issue :

         i.   Mary Sophia, *b.* November 2, 1863 ; *m.* Walter W. Thomas (*q. v.*).
         ii.   Sarah Amelia, *b.* May 25, 1867.

     ii.   RACHEL, *b.* April 11, 1816 ; *m.*, in 1851, ALBAN GILPIN. Issue :
         Mary Ellicott.

iv.   **HANNAH**, *m.*, January 2, 1793, as his second wife, **ISAAC McPHERSON.**
v.   **SAMUEL**, *d. u.*

Authorities : As stated in the Pedigree and Friends' Records.

FAIRFAX

THIS family was seated at Towcester in Northumberland, at the Conquest, and is supposed to be of Saxon stock. The pedigree begins with **RICHARD DE FAIRFAX,** son of **John,** and grandson of **Henry Fairfax,** of Shapenbeck, who in 1204 possessed the Manor of Askham and other lands in Yorkshire; he had issue, a son and heir, WILLIAM, living in 1212–13, *m.* ALICE, *dau.* and heiress of Nicholas de Bugthorpe, and had a son and heir, WILLIAM, High Bailiff of York in 1249; bought the Manor of Walton, and *m.* MARY, widow of WALTER FLOWER, and had a son and heir, Thomas, living in 1284; *m.* Anne, *dau.* and heiress of Henry de Sezevaux, Mayor of York. Issue: i. William. ii. Bego, *d. s. p.* iii. John, living in 1312, *of whom presently.*

JOHN, third son of **Thomas** and **Anne Fairfax,** *m.* **CLARA,** *dau.* and *co-h.* of **Roger Brus,** of Walton, and had a son and heir, THOMAS, *m.* MARGARET, *dau.* of John Malbis, and had a son and heir, WILLIAM, *of whom presently;* and two daughters; ANN, *m.* ——— MARTIN, and CLARE, *m.,* first, ——— PALMS, and second, SIR WILLIAM MALBIS.

WILLIAM, son of **Thomas** and **Margaret (Malbis) Fairfax,** *m.* ELLEN, *dau.* of **John Roucliffe,** of Roucliffe. Issue:

i. THOMAS, was living in 1350; *m.* ELIZABETH, *dau.* of Sir Ivo Etting, Knt., of Gilling. Issue:

303

   i.   **WILLIAM**, his heir, *of whom presently.*
   ii.   **THOMAS.**
   iii.   **GUY.**
   iv.   **JOHN.**
   v.   **RICHARD.**

ii.   **JOHN.**
iii.   **MARGARET**, Prioress of Muncton.
iv.   **MARY**, nun of Sempringham.
v.   **ALICE**, nun of Sempringham.

WILLIAM, son of **Thomas** and **Elizabeth Fairfax**, *m.* **CONSTANCE**, sister and *co-h.* of **Peter**, fourth **Baron de Mauley.**[1] Issue:

i.   **THOMAS**, his heir.
ii.   **RICHARD.**
iii. **BRYAN**, who was Parson of Longtoft, and Precentor of York Minster in
      1423-24.

THOMAS was living between 1385 and 1396; *m.* **MARGARET**, widow of **Sir Robert Roucliffe, Knt.**, and sister and heiress of **Richard Friston**, of Marston. Issue:

   i.   **RICHARD**, his heir, *of whom presently.*
   ii.   **GUY.**
   iii.   **GEORGE.**
   iv.   **THOMAS.**
   v.   **JOHN.**
   vi.   **NICHOLAS.**

RICHARD, son of **Thomas** and **Margaret Fairfax**, living between 1400 and 1430; *m.* **EUSTACE**, *dau.* and heiress of **John Carthorp**, by his wife **Elisabeth**, *dau.* and *co-h.* of **Sir William Ergham.** Issue:

i.   **WILLIAM**, *of whom presently.*
ii.   **BRYAN**, a priest.
iii.   **SIR GUY** (*q. v.*).
iv.   **RICHARD**, a priest.
v.   **SIR NICHOLAS**, a Knight of Rhodes.
vi.   **MILES.**
vii.   **MARGARET.**
viii. **ANN.**
ix.   **ELLEN**, a nun of Muncton.

WILLIAM, son of **Richard** and **Eustace Fairfax**, *d.* in 1452-53, leaving a son **THOMAS**, *d.* in 1504-05, leaving a son, **SIR THOMAS, K.B.**, *d.* in 1520-21, leaving a son, **Sir Nicholas**, *of whom presently.*

---

[1] The present Lord Fairfax is eldest *co-h.* to this barony, created in 1295.

SIR NICHOLAS, son of **Sir Thomas Fairfax, K. B.,** *d.* in 1570, leaving a son, **SIR WILLIAM,** whose son, SIR THOMAS, was created, in 1629, Viscount Fairfax of Emely, in the peerage of Ireland. He *m.* CATHERINE, sister of Sir Henry Constable, of Burton and Halsham, Yorkshire, first Viscount Dunbar, and *d.* 1636. Issue :

    i.   Thomas, *of whom presently.*
    ii.   Henry (*q. v.*).

THOMAS, second Viscount Fairfax, *m.* **ALATHEA,** *dau.* of **Philip Howard,** and had a son, **THOMAS,** third Viscount, whose only son, CHARLES, *m.*, November 17, 1729, ELIZABETH, *dau.* of Hugh, second Lord Clifford of Chudleigh, and widow of William, fourth and last Viscount Dunbar, and issue became extinct in the male line in the same century.

HENRY, second son of the first **Viscount Fairfax,** had a son, **HENRY,** of Hurt, Berkshire, whose only *dau.* and heiress FRANCES, *m.*, in 1697, DAVID ERSKINE, Earl of Buchan.

We now return to **SIR GUY,** third son of **Richard** and **Eustace (Carthorp) Fairfax,** who was appointed Judge of the Court of King's Bench, September 29, 1478, built the Castle of Steeton, *m.* **MARGARET,** *dau.* of **Sir William Rither,** of Rither, and *d.* in 1495. Issue :

i.   **SIR WILLIAM,** his heir.
ii.   **THOMAS,** a Sergeant-at-law.
iii. **GUY.**
iv. **NICHOLAS.**
v.   **ELLEN,** *m.* **SIR NICHOLAS WELSTROP.**
vi. **MAUD,** *m.* **SIR JOHN WATERTON,** Master of the Horse to King Henry VI.

SIR WILLIAM, was appointed a Judge of the Court of Common Pleas, May 21, 1510 ; *m.* **ELIZABETH,** sister of **Thomas Manners,** first Earl of Rutland, and granddaughter of Anne, Duchess of Exeter, the sister of King Edward IV., and *d.* in 1514–15.

i.   **SIR WILLIAM,** his heir.
ii.   **ELLEN,** *m.* **SIR WILLIAM PICKERING,** Knight Marshal of England.
iii. **ELIZABETH,** *m.* **SIR ROBERT OUGHTRED.**
iv. **ANNE,** *m.* **SIR ROBERT NORMANVILLE, KNT.,** of Kilnwick.
v.   **DOROTHY,** *m.* —— **CONSTABLE,** of Hexby.

SIR WILLIAM, eldest son of **Sir William** and **Elizabeth (Manners) Fairfax**, was High Sheriff of York in the reign of Henry VIII.; *m.*, in 1518, **ISABEL THWAITES**, who brought him the Manor of Denton and Askwith in Wharfedale, and Bishop Hill and Davy Hall within the walls of York. He joined the Pilgrimage of Grace, but appears to have been pardoned for his share in that outbreak, and *d.* October 31, 1557. Issue :

i.   **GUY**, *d. s. p.*
ii.   **THOMAS**, *of whom presently.*
iii.   **FRANCIS.**
iv.   **EDWARD.**
v.   **HENRY.**
vi.   **GABRIEL** (*q. v.*).
vii.   **ANNE**, *m.* **SIR HENRY EVERINGHAM**, of Saxton.
viii.   **MARY**, *m.* **ROBERT ROCKLEY**, of Rockley.
ix.   **BRIDGET**, *m.* **SIR COTTON GARGRAVE**, of Nostell.
x.   **URSULA**, *m.* **RALPH VAVASOR**, of Hazlewood.
xi.   **AGNES**, *m.* **EDWARD ELLOFT**, of Farnell and Nottingley.

THOMAS, eldest son of **Sir William** and **Isabel (Thwaites) Fairfax**, was Sheriff of Yorkshire, 1571 ; knighted by Queen Elizabeth, 1576 ; *m.* **DOROTHY**, *dau.* of **George Gale**, of Askham Grange, and *d.* 1599. Issue :

> **THOMAS**, his heir ; **CHARLES**, a pupil of Sir Francis Vere, killed at the siege of Ostend ; and **EDWARD**, of Newhall, translator of Tasso's "Jerusalem Delivered," *d.* 1632.

THOMAS, the eldest son, *b.* in 1560, fought in the Low Country Wars, and was knighted by Lord Essex for gallant conduct before Rouen. He served Elizabeth as a Diplomatist, was one of the Council of the North, under the Presidency of Lord Sheffield, from 1602–19, and October 18, 1627, was created Baron Fairfax, of Cameron, in the Peerage of Scotland. He *m.*, in 1582, **ELLEN**, *dau.* of **Robert Aske**, of Aughton, and *d.* May 1, 1640. Issue :

i.   **FERDINANDO**, *of whom presently.*
ii.   **HENRY**, a clergyman (*q. v.*).
iii.   **WILLIAM**, a soldier in the Low Country Wars, killed at the siege of Frankenthal, in 1621.
iv.   **CHARLES**, a lawyer, the antiquary who compiled the pedigree, and left a large collection of MSS.

After an Original by William Faithorne

v.   **JOHN**, a soldier, killed with his brother William, in 1621.

vi.   **PEREGRINE**, Secretary to the Ambassador, at Paris, and killed at the siege of Montauban, in 1621.

vii.   **THOMAS**, a merchant adventurer, *d.* at Scanderoon in the same fatal year, 1621.

viii.   **DOROTHY**, *m.* **SIR WILLIAM CONSTABLE.**

ix.   **ANNE**, *m.* **SIR GODFREY WENTWORTH.**

x.   **MARY**, *b.* in 1588 ; *d. u.*

And three other sons, *d. y.*

FERDINANDO, succeeded his father as second Lord Fairfax ; was *b.* March 29, 1584 ; fought on the side of the Parliament in the Civil War ; *m.*, first, in 1607, **LADY MARY SHEFFIELD**, *dau.* of the first **Earl Mulgrave** ; *m.*, second, in September, 1646, **RHODA**, *dau.* of **Mr. Chapman**, of London, and widow of **Thomas Hussey**, by whom he had a *dau.*, **URSULA**, *m.* **WILLIAM CARTWRIGHT**, of Aynho. Issue (surname CARTWRIGHT) :

i.   **WILLIAM.**

ii.   **RHODA**, *m.* **LORD HENRY CAVENDISH.**

Lord Fairfax *d.* March 14, 1647–48. Issue by his first wife :

i.   **THOMAS**, third Lord, *of whom presently.*

ii.   **CHARLES**, a Colonel in the Parliamentary Army, mortally wounded at the Battle of Marston Moor, in 1644, and *d. s. p.* a few days afterward.

iii.   Another son, who *d. i.*

iv.   **URSULA**, *b.* in 1609.

v.   **ELLEN**, *b.* in 1610 ; *m.* **SIR WILLIAM SELBY**, of Twizell.

vi.   **FRANCES**, *b.* in 1612 ; *m.* **THOMAS WIDDRINGTON**, of York.

vii.   **ELIZABETH**, *b.* in 1614 ; *m.* **SIR WILLIAM CRAVEN**, of Lenchwicke, who *d.* October 12, 1655, having had a son, **WILLIAM**, *b.* 1649 ; *d.* August 3, 1665.

viii.   **MARY**, *b.* in 1616 ; *m.* **HENRY ARTHINGTON.**

ix.   **DOROTHY**, *b.* in 1617 ; *m.* **EDWARD HUTTON**, of Poppleton.

THOMAS, the eldest son, *b.* January 16, 1611–12, succeeded as third Lord Fairfax, and was the great Parliamentary General of the Civil War ; he was also largely instrumental in effecting the restoration of King Charles II. For the incidents of his life see the Biography by C. R. Markham, published at London, in 1870. He *m.*, June 20, 1637, **ANNE**, *dau.* and *co-h.* of **Lord Vere**, of Tilbury, who *d.* October 16, 1665. Lord Fairfax *d.* November 12, 1671, leaving an only *dau.*, **MARY**, *b.* July 30, 1638 ; *m.*, September 15, 1657, **GEORGE VILLIERS**, second Duke of Buckingham, son of the favorite of James I. She *d. s. p.*, October 20, 1704, and the estates of the family were inherited by the heir of line for whom we must return to **HENRY**, brother of the second Lord Fairfax. He was *b.* in 1587, was in holy orders, and the Rector of Bolton Percy. He *m.* **MARY**, *dau.* of Sir **Henry Cholmley**, and *d.* April 6, 1665. Issue :

i.　　**HENRY**, fourth Lord, *of whom presently*.

ii.　　**BRYAN**, *b.* October 6, 1633 ; *m.*, April 22, 1675, **CHARLOTTE**, only *dau.* and heiress of **Sir Edmund Cary**, by **Anne**, sister of the Earl of Macclesfield, who *d.* November 14, 1709 ; her husband *d.* September 23, 1711. Issue (who all *d. s. p.*) :
　　　　i.　**BRYAN**.
　　　　ii.　**FERDINANDO**.
　　　　iii.　**CHARLES**, M.A. Christ Church College, Oxford, in 1712.

HENRY, fourth Lord Fairfax, *b.* December 30, 1631 ; *m.*, **FRANCES**, *dau.* of **Sir Robert Barwicke**, of Tolston, and *d.* in April, 1688. Issue :

i.　　**THOMAS**, fifth Lord, *of whom presently*.

ii.　　**HENRY** (*q. v.*).

iii.　　**BRYAN**, Commissioner of Customs, *d.* January 9, 1747-48.

iv.　　**BARWICKE**.

v.　　**DOROTHY**, *m.*, first, **ROBERT STAPLETON**, of Wighill ; *m.*, second, **BENNET SHERRARD**, of Whissenden, and *d.* in January, 1743-44.

vi.　　**FRANCES**, *m.* —— **RYMER**.

vii.　　**ANNE**, *m.*, September 2, 1690, **RALPH**, son of **Sir Ralph Car**, of Cocken, and *d.* July 3, 1699.

viii. ix.　**URSULA** and **MARY**, who both *d. u.*

THOMAS, fifth Lord Fairfax, took an active part in promoting the Revolution of 1688, and the accession of William III. and Mary to the throne of England ; *m.* **CATHERINE**, *dau.* and heiress of **Thomas Lord Colepepper**, of Thoresway, by **Margaret**, *dau.* of **Jean de Hesse**, with whom he obtained the estate of Leeds Castle, in Kent, and over five million acres of land in Virginia. Lord Fairfax *d.* in January, 1709–10. Issue :

i.　　**THOMAS**, sixth Lord Fairfax, *b.* in 1690. He was obliged to alienate Denton Hall and the Yorkshire property in order to save Leeds Castle, and the Kentshire estates. In 1747 he removed to America, alienated his English estates in favor of his brother Robert, and built " Belvoir " and " Greenway Court," in Virginia. He is said to have met with a disappointment in love which prevented his ever marrying, was one of the writers of the " Spectator," and the friend and patron of Washington. He *d. s. p.* at Greenway Court, December 9, 1781.

ii.   HENRY COLEPEPPER, *d. u.*, October 14, 1734.

iii.   MARGARET, *m.* REV. DAVID WILKINS, D.D., and *d. s. p.*

iv.   FRANCES, *b.* in 1703 ; *m.* DENNY MARTIN, and *d.* December 13, 1791. Issue : DENNY, a clergyman ; and PHILIP, general in the army ; who both assumed the name of " FAIRFAX," and inherited, in succession, the English estates of the family.

v.   ROBERT, *b.* in 1706, succeeded as seventh Lord Fairfax, was a Major in the Life Guards, M. P. for Kent in 1754 and 1761 ; *m.*, first, April 25, 1741, MARTHA, *dau.* and *co-h.* of Anthony Collins, of Baddow. She *d.* in 1744, leaving a son who *d.* in 1747 ; and her husband *m.*, second, in 1749, a *dau.* of Thomas Best, of Chatham, who *d. s. p.* in 1750 ; and Lord Fairfax, *d. s. p.*, July 15, 1793, leaving his English estates, by will, to his nephew, Rev. Denny Martin.

HENRY, second son of the fourth Baron Fairfax, was Sheriff of Yorkshire in 1691 ; *m.* ANNE, *dau.* and *co-h.* of Richard Harrison, and *d.* in 1708. Issue :

i.   HENRY, *bapt.* September 15, 1685, *d. s. p.* at York, November 22, 1759.

ii.   THOMAS, *bapt.* March 13, 1687, *d. i.*

iii. RICHARD, *bapt.* July 31, 1690 ; *bu.* October 29, 1690.

iv. WILLIAM, *of whom presently.*

v.   BRYAN.

vi. DOROTHY.

vii. ANNE.

WILLIAM, son of Henry and Anne (Harrison) Fairfax, *b.* in 1691 ; was Virginia Agent of his cousin, the sixth Lord Fairfax ; *m.*, first, in 1723, SARAH, *dau.* of Major Walker, of the Bahamas. Issue :

i.   GEORGE WILLIAM, *b.* 1724; *m.* SARAH CARY, and *d. s. p.* at Bath, April 3, 1787.

ii.   THOMAS, entered the Royal Navy and was killed on the Harwich, under Captain Cartaret, at a sea-fight in the West Indies, June 26, 1746.

iii. SARAH, *m.* MAJOR JOHN CARLYLE, of Alexandria, Va., and had a *dau.*, *m.* WILLIAM HERBERT (*q. v.*).

iv. ANNE, *b.* at Salem, Mass. ; *m.*, first, July 19, 1743, MAJOR LAWRENCE WASHINGTON, of Mount Vernon, eldest brother of George Washington, and had four children, *d. y. ; m.*, second, COLONEL GEORGE LEE, before 1756, by whom she had three sons.

WILLIAM FAIRFAX *m.*, second, DEBORAH CLARKE, of Salem, Mass., and *d.* September 3, 1757. Further issue :

v.　　WILLIAM HENRY, Lieutenant Twenty-eighth Regiment of Regulars;
　　　　d. s. p. of wounds received at the siege of Quebec in 1759.

vi.　　HANNAH, *m.*, about 1764, WARNER WASHINGTON.

vii.　　BRYAN, who succeeded as eighth Lord Fairfax.

BRYAN, eighth Lord Fairfax, was a clergyman of the Church of
England; *m.*, first, ELIZABETH, youngest *dau.* of Wilson
Cary. Issue:

i.　　THOMAS, *of whom presently.*

ii.　　FERDINANDO (*q. v.*).

iii.　　ELIZABETH, *m.* DAVID GRIFFITH.

LORD FAIRFAX *m.* a second time, and had a *dau.*, ANNE, *m.*
CHARLES CATLETT.

THOMAS, eldest son of the eighth lord, *b.* in 1762, succeeded his
father in the title, resided at Vaucluse, Fairfax Co., Va.; he *m.*,
first, MARY AYLETT; *m.*, second, LOUISA WASH-
INGTON; *m.*, third, MARGARET, *dau.* of William Herbert, and *d.* April 21, 1846. Issue only by his third wife:

i.　　ALBERT, *m.*, April 8, 1828, CAROLINE ELIZA, *dau.* of Richard
　　　　and Eliza Snowden (*q. v.*), and *d.* in the life-time of his father.
　　　　His widow *m.*, March 1, 1838, CAPTAIN SANDERS. Issue
　　　　only by her first husband:

　　i.　　CHARLES SNOWDEN, succeeded as tenth lord, *m.*, in 1855, ADA, *dau.* of
　　　　　　Joseph S. Benham, of Cincinnati, O.; resided at Ranche San Marin, Cal.;
　　　　　　d. s. p. in 1869; his widow *d.* September 26, 1888.

　　ii.　　DR. JOHN CONTEE, *b.* in 1830, the present and eleventh Baron Fairfax, of
　　　　　　Cameron, though his Republican sentiments make him refuse to bear the title.
　　　　　　He *m.*, in 1857, MARY, *dau.* of Colonel Edward Kirby, United States
　　　　　　Army. Issue:

　　　　　i.　　Albert Kirby, *b.* June 23, 1870.
　　　　　ii.　　Charles Edmund Kirby, *b.* 1876.
　　　　　iii.　　Caroline, *b.* 1858.
　　　　　iv.　　Josephine, *b.* 1865.
　　　　　v.　　Mary, *b.* 1871.
　　　　　vi.　　Frances, *b.* 1878.

ii.　　HENRY, *b.* May 4, 1804; *m.*, 1827, ANN CAROLINE, eldest *dau.* of
　　　　John C. Herbert (*q. v.*); *d.* August 14, 1847.

iii.　　ORLANDO, *b.* 1809; *m.*, May 21, 1829, MARY R. CARY.

iv.　　RAYMOND, *d.* in 1813.

v.　　EUGENIA, *m.*, first, EDGAR MASON; *m.*, second, CHARLES
　　　　K. HYDE.

vi.　　ETHELBERT, *d.* in 1827.

vii.　　AURELIA, *m.*, 1852, COLONEL JAMES W. IRWIN.

viii.　　LAVINIA, *d.* in 1822.

ix.　　MONIMIA, *m.*, November 15, 1828, ARCHIBALD, son of Wilson

Jefferson and Virginia (Randolph) Cary, of Carysbrook, Va., who *d.* 1854. A *dau.* of this marriage, CONSTANCE CARY, *m.* BURTON HARRISON, and is author of " The Bachelor Maid," " The Anglomaniacs," " Helen of Troy," " Bric-à-brac Stories," etc.

x.   REGINALD, *b.* 1822 ; *d. u.* July, 1862.

FERDINANDO, second son of **Rev. Bryan** and **Elizabeth (Cary) Fairfax,** *m.* ELIZABETH BLAIR CARY, and *d.* September 24, 1820. Issue, with others :

i.   GEORGE WILLIAM, *b.* November 5, 1797 ; *m.*, November, 1815, ISABELLA, *dau.* of **Major W. Gibbs McNeill,** of New York. Issue, with others :

> DONALD McNEILL, Admiral United States Navy, *m.* VIRGINIA, *dau.* of Thomas Ragland, of Virginia, and *d.* leaving a son, William McNeill.

ii.   · WILSON MILES CARY, *b.* December 1, 1798 ; *m.*, March 2, 1824, ANNA GRIFFITH, and *d.* August 8, 1860. Issue, with others :

> i.   WILSON, *b.* December 13, 1833.
> ii.   FREDERICK, *b.* September 26, 1835.
> iii. EMILY CARY, *m.*, May 15, 1848, REV. FRANCIS McNEECE WHITTLE, now Bishop of Virginia.

iii. FERDINANDO, *b.* January 9, 1803 ; a physician ; *m.*, first, January 11, 1831, MARY ANNE JETT ; *m.*, second, November 28, 1855, MARY JANE JETT, and *d.* December 30, 1873.

iv.   ARCHIBALD BLAIR, *b.* May 22, 1809, was in the United States Navy, and during the Civil War a Commander Confederate States Navy ; *m.*, first, November, 1832, SARAH CARLYLE, *dau.* of **John C. Herbert** (*q. v.*), who *d.* January 23, 1850. Issue surviving :

> ARCHIBALD CARLYLE, *b.* August 24, 1843 ; served in Confederate States Army ; *m.*, April 30, 1873, VIRGINIA CAROLINE, *dau.* of William H. Redwood. Issue :
> i.   John Carlyle, *b.* December 27, 1874.
> ii.   William Redwood, *b.* December 3, 1876.

> COMMANDER A. B. FAIRFAX *m.*, second, March 2, 1852, ELIZA MARY, *dau.* of **Rev. Oliver Norris,** and *d.* January 3, 1867.

v.   CHRISTINE, *m.* THOMAS RAGLAND.

vi.   LOUISA, *m.* —— TAPSCOTT.

GABRIEL, youngest son of **Sir William** and **Isabella (Thwaites) Fairfax,** under his father's will inherited Steeton, Bolton Percy, and the greater part of the property. He *m.* ELIZABETH, *dau.* of **Robert Aske,** and had a son and heir, SIR PHILIP FAIRFAX, *b.* 1586, extravagant and dissipated ; sold Bolton to his cousin, the first Lord Fairfax, and dying in 1613, left a son and heir, SIR WILLIAM, who was a parliamentarian in the Great Rebellion, Colonel of a regiment of foot under Lord Essex, fought at Edgehill, the storming of Leeds, the siege of Lathom House, the Battle of Marston Moor, and was killed at the head of his men before the walls of Montgomery Castle, Wales, leaving a son, Thomas, a General in the Army, and William, *of whom presently.* This **WILLIAM FAIRFAX** succeeded to the estate, had a son, **ROBERT**, an Admiral in the Navy ; built a house at New-ton Kyme, and made it the family seat ; he also acquired the manor of Bilbrough. THOMAS, his son, succeeded in 1725, was the author of " The Complete Sportsman," published in 1760. John, his son, succeeded in 1803, and in 1811 was followed by his son, Thomas Lodington Fairfax : **THOMAS FAIRFAX,** his son, succeeded in 1840, and *d.* in 1875. **THOMAS FER-DINAND**, his son, Lieutenant-Colonel of the Guards, was an en-thusiastic sportsman, Master of the York and Ainsty Hunt. April 14, 1869, he *m.* **EVELYN SELINA**, second *dau.* of Sir William Milner, of Nun Appleton, and *d.* in 1883. Issue :

GUY, BRIAN, and EVELYN.

SIR WILLIAM G. FAIRFAX, flag-captain to Admiral Duncan at the Battle of Camperdown, was probably of this branch of the family. He *m.* a *dau.* of **Samuel Charters**, Solicitor of Cus-toms for Scotland, and had a son, **HENRY**, *b.* 1790, Colonel in the Army, November, 1841. Created a Baronet as Fairfax of Holmes Roxburghe, in 1836, in recognition of his father's services in the Navy ; *m.*, 1830, the third *dau.* of Thomas Williamson Ramsay, and had a son and heir WILLIAM GEORGE HERBERT TAYLOR, *b.* 1831.

Authorities : Fairfax Correspondence, Neill's Fairfaxes, etc., and Joseph Foster's Peerage, 1883.

FARQUHAR

CHARLES FARQUHAR, *m.* **SARAH,** eldest *dau.* of **Roger**
and **Mary P. Brooke,** since *d.* Issue :

i.   **ANNA,** *b.* October 30, 1834 ; *m.* **CHARLES H. BROOKE** (*q. v.*).

ii.   **ROGER BROOKE,** *b.* October 4, 1837 ; *m.* **CAROLINE MILLER.**
      Issue :

    i.   **GEORGE BROOKE,** *b.* October 5, 1868 ; *m.* **EDITH B.,** *dau.* of Edward .P.
          and Mary (Bentley) Thomas (*q. v.*).

    ii.   **ANNA MILLER,** *b.* January 30, 1871.

    iii.   **SARAH B.,** *b.* September 4, 1872.

    iv.   **ROBERT MILLER,** *b.* May 2, 1874.

    v.   **ROGER B.,** *b.* December, 1876.

    vi.   **ALICE,** *b.* August 24, 1878.

    vii.   **MALCOLM.**

    viii.   **HARRY.**

iii.   **MARY EDITH,** *b.* April 3, 1839.

iv.   **CHARLES HENRY,** *b.* May 24, 1841.

v.   **GRANVILLE,** *b.* March 22, 1843 ; *m.,* in 1877, **MARTHA,** *dau.* of
      William John Thomas (*q. v.*). Issue :

    i.   **WILLIAM JOHN THOMAS,** *b.* September 8, 1878.

    ii.   **FAITH.**

    iii.   **MARY WILLIS.**

    iv.   **ELGAR.**

vi.   **ELIZA E.,** *b.* March 20, 1845.

FERRIS

BENJAMIN, son of **Jonathan** and **Rachel (Deane) Ferris,** *b.*
at Peekskill, N. Y., November 9, 1771, was a prominent lawyer
in New York City, held several commissions in the State Militia,
was member of the Assembly in 1806–7–8, and 1824, and Sheriff
of New York in 1808–10–11–13 ; *m.,* August 13, 1780, at New
York, **ANNA MARIA,** *dau.* of **Jacob** and **Hannah (Lawrence) Schieffelin** (*q. v.*), who *d.* October 24, 1848, and *d.* at
New York, February 19, 1832. Issue :

i.   **EMILY MATILDA,** *b.* in 1810; *m.* **EDWARD C. RICHARDS,**
       and *d. s. p.* January 1, 1892.

ii.   **LAURA MARY,** *b.* in 1812 ; *m.,* first, **CORNELIUS M. GAUL;**
       m., second, **REDFORD A. WATKINSON,** *d. s. p.*

iii.   **HANNAH M.,** *b.* in 1814; *m.* **DR. SAMUEL BLOIS,** and *d.* in
       1881. Issue (surname BLOIS) :

     i.   **EUGENE S.,** *b.* in 1845; *m.* **LILIAN LA BARR,** *d. s. p.* in 1893.
     ii.   **EMILY M.,** *m.* **DR. HENRY A. DUBOIS,** and has several children.

iv.   **BENJAMIN CLINTON,** *b.* in 1817 ; *d. u.*

v.   **CAROLINE EUDORA,** *b.* in 1819 ; *m.* **HOMER MORGAN,** and *d.*
       in 1882. Issue (surname MORGAN) :

     i.   **ALMA,** *m.* **COL. CLIFFORD CODDINGTON,** and has several children.
     ii.   **ANNIE T.**

vi.   **JULIA,** *b.* in 1823 ; *m.* **S. B. NOBLE,** and *d.* in 1879. Issue :

     CORA, *b.* in 1845; *m.* **JAMES C. NICOLL,** and *d.* in 1880, leaving several chil-
     dren.

vii.   **ADELAIDE,** *b* in 1825 ; *m.* **WILLIAM HOWLAND PELL** (*q. v.*).

viii.   **ELLEN,** *b.* in 1828 ; *m.* **COLUMBUS BEMENT ROGERS,** and
       d. in 1892. Issue (surname ROGERS) :

     i.   **ELLA A.**
     ii.   **EDITH J.,** *m.* **JOHN GELLATLY.**

Authorities : Family papers, through Mr. Howland Pell.

FITZHUGH, OF VIRGINIA

HENRY MAYNADIER, son of **Daniel Dulany** and **Margaret (Maynadier) Fitzhugh** and descended from **Colonel William,** son of **Henry Fitzhugh,** of Bedford, England, who emigrated to Virginia before 1674, was *b.* at " Windsor," Baltimore Co., Md., June 29, 1815; *m.*, first, June 8, 1843, **ANNE,** *dau.* of **William E.** and **Sarah (Ellicott) George** (*q. v.*), who *d.* August 7, 1867. Issue :

i. **MARGARET MAYNADIER,** *b.* March 23, 1844; *d.* May 7, 1845.
ii. **SARAH ELLICOTT,** *b.* August 29, 1845; *d. u.*, December 16, 1863.
iii. **MARY DULANY,** *b.* May 30, 1847; *m.*, June 28, 1864, **DEXTER ANGELL BALLOU,** who *d.* October 23, 1882. Issue (surname BALLOU) :

    i. **ANNE GEORGE,** *b.* September 26, 1867.
    ii. **WALLING ANGELL,** *b.* November 14, 1869.
    iii. **ISABEL ADELAIDE,** *b.* August 8, 1871.
    iv. **DEXTER FITZHUGH,** *b.* January 26, 1873; *d.* February 13, 1881.
    v. **LUCY TYSON,** *b.* January 13, 1875.

iv. **ANNE GEORGE,** *b.* October 22, 1848; *m.*, November 29, 1882, **CHARLES,** son of **Charles C.** and **Jane Fitzhugh.** Issue :

    i. **JANE,** *b.* November 15, 1887.
    ii. **WALTER DULANY,** *b.* December 14, 1889.
    iii. **CHARLES,** *b.* December 9, 1890.

v. **HENRIETTA MAYNADIER,** *b.* April 20, 1850; *m.*, June 29, 1878, in New York, **FRANK SMITH.** Issue (surname SMITH) :

    i. **ANNE FITZHUGH,** *b.* March 16, 1880.
    ii. **GRAFTON FITZHUGH,** *b.* December 6, 1884.

vi. **DANIEL DULANY,** *b.* January 31, 1852; *m.*, November 9, 1882, in Bay City, Mich., **ELEANOR LOUISE,** *dau.* of **Dabney Terrel** and **Eliza C. (English) Carr.** Issue :

    i. **MARGARET MURRAY MAYNADIER,** *b.* August 26, 1883.
    ii. **MARY DULANY,** *b.* March 21, 1886.
    iii. **DABNEY CARR,** *b.* August 14, 1889.
    iv. **WILLIAM HENRY,** Jr., *b.* August 30, 1892.

vii.   **WILLIAM·HENRY,** *b.* June 28, 1854 ; *m.,* July 2, 1878, **MARY
        ENGLISH,** *dau.* of **Dabney Terrel** and **Eliza (English) Carr.**
viii.   **SEVERNE WALLIS,** *b.* July 8, 1856 ; *d.* October 8, 1859.

MR. FITZHUGH *m.,* second, February 1, 1872, **LUCY,** *dau.* of
   Nathan and **Martha (Ellicott) Tyson** (*q. v.*).   Issue :

ix.   **HENRY MAYNADIER,** *b.* September 16, 1875, at Bay City, Mich.

Authorities : Family papers, through Mrs. Lucy (Tyson) Fitzhugh.

PEMBERTON ARMS

GALLOWAY

RICHARD GALLOWAY, of London, England, was probably in Maryland December 4, 1662, when " Galloway," two hundred and fifty acres of land in Anne Arundel Co., was surveyed for him. He afterward possessed Ewen's addition, ninety acres, and Ewen upon Ewenton, four hundred more. He *m.* **HANNAH** ——. Issue :

i.   **SAMUEL,** *b.* October 7, 1659, *of whom presently.*
ii.   **RICHARD,** *b.* January 28, 1663-64 (*q. v.*).

SAMUEL, eldest son of **Richard** and **Hannah Galloway**, of London, *b.* October 7, 1659 ; *m.*, first, **SARAH** ——, by whom he had issue, at her death, February 25, 1685–86, four children, of whom **HANNAH** *m.*, against her father's will and out of Meeting, in 1710, **WILLIAM FORDE**, or **FOORD**, and was disowned by Friends ;[1] and **SAMUEL,** *b.* October 8, 1682, was of Calvert Co., Md. ; *m.* ——, and *d.* in 1723.[2] Issue :

[1] Her experience does not encourage runaway matches. October 26, 1711, she requested to be received again, saying, " I did run out with my now Husband to ye priest and were married, for wch frds did therupon publickly disown and denny us, wch I did at first think very hard it being stricter discipline then had formerly been used in ye like cases." July 29, 1737 : " Meeting has under consideration the scandalous behaviour of William Foord and his wife unto each other. Seven friends are to visit and reconcile them ' if Posiable.' " They succeeded in doing so.

[2] Will proved April 20th. Liber W. B., No. 1, folio 74.

317

i. **SAMUEL.**
ii. **RICHARD.**
iii. **JOSEPH.**
iv. **MARY.**
v. **ELIZABETH,** *m.* **JOHN,** son of Edward and Elizabeth (Thomas) Talbot (*q. v.*).
vi. **SARAH.**
vii. **ANN.**
viii. **SOPHIA.**

SAMUEL GALLOWAY, *m.,* second, in April, 1689, at London, England, **ANNE,** *dau.* of **Borrington Webb,** and *d.* April 13, 1720,[1] at London, and was buried in Friends' burying-ground, Bunfields. Issue, by this second wife, who *d.* March 20, 1722–23 :

i. **RICHARD,** *b.* at London, January 5, 1689–90 ; the West River Register says : "Desest ye 16 of the 8 mo. 89."
ii. **PETER,** *b.* at West River, July 12, 1690 ; "*d.* 7 weeks old."
iii. **JOHN,** *b.* January 14, 1692–93, and *d.* "10 months and 2 weeks old."
iv. **JOHN,** *b.* February 6, 1693–94 ; *m.,* first, July 31, 1718, **MARY,** *dau.* of **Samuel** and **Mary (Hutchins) Thomas** (*q. v.*). Issue :

    i. **SAMUEL** (*q. v.*).
    ii. **MARY,** *m.* **CHIEF JUSTICE BENJAMIN CHEW** (*q. v.*).
    iii. **JOSEPH,** *m.* **ANN COOKSON.**

    JOHN GALLOWAY *m.,* second, **MRS. JANE (ROBERTS) FISH-BOURNE,** *dau.* of **Edward Roberts,** and widow of **William Fishbourne,** by whom she had two children (surname FISHBOURNE), **SAM-UEL** and **SARAH** ; by her second husband, who *d.* in October, 1747 (she *d.* in June, 1748), she had a *dau.* **JANE,** *m.,* September 29, 1768, **JOSEPH,** son of **Edward** and **Sarah (Plymley) Shippen** of Philadelphia, Secretary of the Province of Pennsylvania, who *d.* February 10, 1810, and his wife February 17, 1801.

SHIPPEN ARMS

v. **ANN,** *b.* April 11 or 12, 1695 ; *m.* **ISAAC,** son of **Richard** and **Elizabeth (Kinsey) Johns** (*q. v.*).
vi. **PETER BINDS** or **BINES,** *b.* April 25, 1696, *of whom presently.*
vii. **MARY,** *b.* July 15, 1697 ; *m.* **DR. SAMUEL CHEW** (*q. v.*).
viii. **UNNAMED,** *b.* in October, 1698, and *d. i.*
ix. **JOSEPH,** *b.* October 8, 1699 ; *m.,* August 8, 1749, **ANNE HARRIS,** and *d.* in December, 1752. Issue :

    ANN, *b.* September 5, 1750 ; *m.* JOSEPH PEMBERTON, from whom descended Henry Pemberton, of Philadelphia, and the late General John C. Pemberton.

[1] Will proved January, 1720–21. Liber T. B., No. 5, folio 393.

MRS. GALLOWAY afterward *m.* PHILIP THOMAS (*q. v.*).

x.   SARAH, *b.* January 15, 1700–1 ; *m.*, first, March 9, 1720–21, HENRY HILL ; *m.*, second, JOSEPH COWMAN (*q. v.*).

xi.   RICHARD, called "of Cumberstone," *b.* January 10, 1701–2 ; *m.* MARY, *dau.* of Aquila Paca, and *d.* February 28, 1731–32, leaving an only *dau.*, SUSANNAH. His widow *m.* DR. SAMUEL CHEW (*q. v.*).

xii.   NAMELESS, *b.* October 12, 1702 ; *d. i.*

xiii.   SAMUEL, *b.* April 7, 1705.

xiv.   SAMUEL, *b.* August 9, 1707.

xv.   An unnamed son, *b.* and *d.* in November, 1709.

PETER BINDS, or BINES, sixth child of Samuel and Ann (Webb) Galloway, *b.* April 25, 1696 ; *m.*, January 19, 1715–16, ELIZABETH, *dau.* of John and Elizabeth Rigbie. Issue :

JOSEPH, *b.* about 1730, the celebrated Loyalist, a member of the Assembly of Pennsylvania in 1757 and almost continuously till the Revolution, a leader against the Proprietaries, Speaker of the House, 1766–74, Delegate to the first Continental Congress, proposed a scheme for the government of the colonies by a Federal system, preserving the connection with the Mother Country, which, if adopted, would have averted the Revolution, and possibly not a few other evils from which America suffers. It was rejected by the close vote of six colonies to five, the prime agents in the agitation seeing no hope of their advancement except by a separation from England. After this Mr. Galloway withdrew from Congress, refused Benjamin Franklin's entreaty that he would join the Revolutionists, and in 1776 went for his personal safety within the British lines. During their occupation of Philadelphia he was at the head of the civil government, and the October following their evacuation of the city he went to England. In June, 1779, he was examined before a committee of the House of Commons on the state of affairs in America, and his evidence has been printed. March 6, 1778, the Assembly of Pennsylvania attainted him of high treason, and confiscated his estate, worth over £40,000. In 1802 and 1803 he published Commentaries on the Book of Revelation, showing great ingenuity and ability in his scheme of prophecy. October 18, 1753, he had *m.* GRACE, *dau.* and *co-h.* of Lawrence Growdon, Councillor of Pennsylvania, and his wife, Elizabeth Nicholls. Her father was grandson of Lawrence Growdon, Gent., of Trevose, Cornwall, and principal owner of the early iron works at Durham, Pa. He *d.* April 1, 1770, leaving a large estate, Mrs. Galloway's portion in 1779 being valued at £113,478 13*s.* 9*d.* She remained in Pennsylvania after the evacuation of Philadelphia, and the Supreme Court exempted her estate from her husband's attainder. She *d.* February 6, 1782, and her husband *d.* at Watford, Herts, England, August 29, 1803. Issue :

i.   JOSEPH L. GROWDON, *d. y.*

ii.   LAWRENCE GROWDON, *d. y.*

iii.   ELIZABETH, *m.* WILLIAM ROBERTS, ESQ., of Portman Square, London, and *d.* April 7, 1815, leaving an only *dau.*, Ann Grace, *m.*, May 30, 1819, Lieutenant Benjamin Burton, of the Nineteenth Lancers, son of Sir Charles Burton, of Pollacton, and *d.* December 12, 1837, leaving descendants.

SAMUEL, eldest son of **John** and **Mary (Thomas) Galloway**, *m.*, about 1745, **ANNE**, *dau.* of **Dr. Samuel Chew** (*q. v.*). He *d.* in November, 1785. Issue:

i. **MARY**, *m.* **THOMAS RINGGOLD** (*q. v.*).
ii. **ANNE**, *m.* **JAMES CHESTON** (*q. v.*).
iii. **BENJAMIN**, *m.* **HENRIETTA**, *dau.* of Benjamin and Sarah Chew, of Cecil Co. (*q. v.*).
iv. **JOHN**, *m.*, October 23, 1796, **SARAH**, *dau.* of Benjamin and **Mary** Chew, and *d.* in June, 1810, leaving an only *dau.*, **MARY**, who *m.* **HON. VIRGIL MAXCY.** Issue (surname MAXCY):

    i. **SARAH**, *m.* **COLONEL GEORGE W. HUGHES.**
    ii. **MARY**, *b.* 1812; *m.* **FRANCIS MARKOE**, and *d.* March 19, 1878. Issue (surname MARKOE):

        i. **Francis**, resides in Baltimore, *m.* **Maria Perry**, *dau.* of Governor Philip F. Thomas (*q. v.*).
        ii. **Sophie**, *m.* Professor **Samuel F. Emmons**, of the United States Geological Survey.
        iii. **Mary Galloway.**
        iv. **Virgil Maxcy.**

RICHARD GALLOWAY, SR., *b.* February 28, 1663–64, second son of **Richard** and **Hannah Galloway**; *m.*, first, December 10, 1686, at West River, **MRS. ELIZABETH (TALBOT) LAWRENCE**, only *dau.* of **Richard Talbot**; *m.*, second, July 30, 1719, **MRS. SARAH (SMITH) SPARROW**,[1] who afterward *m.*, November 14, 1738, **HENRY HILL**, and *d.* February, 1755, aged eighty-three.

RICHARD GALLOWAY, SR., *d.* October 28, 1736. (Will, Liber T. and D., folio 804.) Issue, by first wife:

    RICHARD, JR., *of whom presently.*

RICHARD, son of **Richard** and **Elizabeth (Talbot) Galloway**, *m.*, September 29, 1715, **SOPHIA**, *dau.* of **William** and **Margaret (Smith) Richardson** (*q. v.*), (*b.* May 7, 1696; *d.* January 27, 1781), and *d.* 1741. (Will proved October 28, 1741. Liber D. D., No. 1, folio 410.) Issue:

    ELIZABETH, *b.* January 16, 1721–22; *m.*, December 14, 1737, **THOMAS SPRIGG**, *b.* 1714; *d.* December 29, 1781. Issue (surname SPRIGG):

        RICHARD (only one on the Register), *b.* December 16, 1739.

Authorities: West River Records, C. P. Keith's Councillors of Pennsylvania, and Maryland land papers.

[1] She was sister of Nathan Smith, *m.* Elizabeth Coale (*q. v.*), and her Will, Liber B. T., No. 1, folio 334, is very valuable genealogically.

GEORGE

ROBERT and **ANN GEORGE**, of Kent Co., Md., of whom the former was descended originally from the **George** family of Scotland, and in the female line from **William Edmundson**, the well-known Quaker preacher of the seventeenth century, had issue : Twelve children, of whom only three lived to maturity ; they were **WILLIAM EDMUNDSON**, *of whom presently ;* **ELIZA**, who *m.* **PHILIP E. THOMAS** (*q. v.*) ; and **SARAH**.

WILLIAM EDMUNDSON, surviving son of **Robert** and **Ann George**, removed to Baltimore with his sister, and resided mainly with her until his own marriage. At the age of twenty-one he was taken into partnership by his brother-in-law, and continued in business with him or his sons until within a few years of his death. He was distinguished for urbanity, courtesy, strict adherence to principle, and a generous hospitality. He *m.*, in 1812, **SARAH**, *dau.* of **Jonathan** and **Sarah Ellicott** (*q. v.*), and *d.* in 1839. Issue :

i. **SARAH**, *d. i.*

i. **ELIZA**, *b.* in 1815 ; *m.*, June 12, 1839, **JOHN D. EARLY**, and *d.* July 6, 1892. Issue (surname EARLY) :

 i. **JOHN D.**, *b.* March 25, 1840 ; for many years Cashier of the Commercial and Farmers' National Bank of Baltimore ; *m.*, April 27, 1865, **MAUD G. RIEMAN**, and has issue :

  i. **Eliza George**, *b.* March 6, 1866 ; *m.*, January 20, 1892, **George Dyer Burgess**, of Indianapolis, Ind. Issue (surname BURGESS) :
   John Early, *b.* January 1, 1893.

321

  ii. Evaline, *b*. August 5, 1868.
  iii. Alexander Rieman, *b*. February 22, 1870 ; *m*., October 29, 1891.
     Frances Elder Moale. Issue :
       Alexander Rieman, *b*. September 11, 1892.

ii. **WILLIAM GEORGE,** *b*. June 1, 1843.
iii. **JOSEPH D.,** *b*. May 26, 1846; *d*. August 9, 1850.

iii. **PHILIP THOMAS,** *of whom presently.*
iv. **ANNE,** *m*., June 8, 1843, **HENRY M. FITZHUGH** (*q. v.*).
v. **JONATHAN ELLICOTT,** *b*. January 20, 1801 ; *d. u*. March 3, 1881.
vi. **ROBERT,** living at San Francisco, Cal. ; *m*., December 8, 1858, **JO-SEPHINE BOSTON.** Issue :

 i. **ROBERT HARVEY,** *b*. November 18, 1859.
 ii. **JONATHAN ELLICOTT,** *b*. March 2, 1861.
 iii. **ALICE CECILIA,** *b*. November 26, 1863.
 iv. **ANNE JOSEPHINE,** *b*. July 12, 1866.
 v. **MARTHA T.,** *b*. July 4, 1868.

vii. **SARAH HARVEY,** *d. u*. August 25, 1883.
viii. **FRANCES E.,** *m*., in 1854, **HENRY LATIMER.**
ix. **MARY ANN,** *m*., in 1851, **MARK W. JENKINS.** Issue :

 i **JULIANNA E.,** *b*. August 18, 1853.
 ii. **BASIL,** *b*. October 12, 1854 ; *d*. June 7, 1855.

x. **WILLIAM E.,** *b*. in 1829 ; *m*., in 1866, **MARGARET HAMIL-TON** ; *d*. March 3, 1882. Issue :
  ANNE, *d. i.*

PHILIP THOMAS, eldest son of **William E.** and **Sarah (Ellicott) George,** *m*., in 1847, **ELLEN JENKINS.** Issue :

i. **MARY ELLEN,** *b*. February 20, 1848 ; *d*. February 20, 1856.
ii. **SAMUEL ELLICOTT,** *b*. December 18, 1849 ; *m*. **CATHERINE M. DAVIS.** Issue :

 i. **PHILIP THOMAS,** *b*. February 2, 1870.
 ii. **MARY E.,** *b*. May 7, 1873.
 iii. **ANNE E.,** *b*. December 7, 1875.

iii. **SARAH I.,** *b*. May 29, 1852 ; *m*., July 15, 1874, **RICHARD CROM-WELL, JR.** Issue (surname CROMWELL) :

 i. **PHILIP THOMAS GEORGE,** *b*. February 2, 1875.
 ii. **JOSIAH J.,** *b*. July 1, 1876.
 iii. **JAMES HERBERT,** *b*. November 22, 1879.
 iv. **ELIZABETH,** *b*. February 7, 1881.
 v. **SARAH I.,** *b*. May 20, 1889.

iv. **JOSIAS J.,** *b*. March 9, 1853 ; *m*., in 1878, **MINNIE JENKINS,** of Lebanon, Ky. Issue :

 i. **ELLEN JENKINS,** *b*. July 11, 1879.
 ii. **WILLIAM EDMONDSON,** *b*. August 7, 1883 ; *d*. September 27, 1887.
 iii. **SARAH I.,** *b*. October 28, 1886.
 iv. **HARVEY ELLICOTT,** b. October 7, 1889.

Authorities : Family papers, principally through Mr. Philip T. George and Mrs. Josias J. George.

GIFFARD, CLARE, AND MARSHALL

GIFFARD ARMS

Osbern de Bolebec, Lord of Longueville in Normandy, had a son, **WALTER GIFFARD,** *b.* before 1015, knight, 1053, furnished thirty ships for the invasion of England, 1066, a commander in the Norman Army at the Battle of Hastings, October, 1066, Councillor to William I., created Earl of Buckingham before 1071 ; *m.* **AGNES,** *dau.* of **Gerard Fleitel,** and *d.* before 1084, leaving a son and heir, **WALTER,** *b.* before 1064, knight, founder and patron of Longueville Priory, Justiciar or Commissioner for the Survey and Valuation of England, 1085, commander in the Royal Army in Normandy and the Vexin, 1097, witness to King Henry I. Charter of Liberties, 1101. " A vigorous Baron and leader of great bravery and shining piety ; " *m.* **AGNES,** sister of **Anselm de Ribemont,** and *d.* July 15, 1102, leaving a son and heir, **WALTER,** knight, 1119, commander in the Royal

Army at Brémule, August 20, 1119, founder and patron of Nutley Abbey, Bucks, called Chief Marshal of the King's Court or Marshal of England ; *m.* ERMENTRUDE DE —, and had a *dau.*, Rohais, *m.* Richard de Clare, Earl of Pembroke, *of whom presently.*

RICHARD FITZ GILBERT DE CLARE,[1] Knight, *b.* before 1035, sometimes styled Richard de Bienfaite, was Lord of Bienfaite and Orbecq in Normandy, 1053 ; councillor in Normandy in 1066 ; a commander in the

BEAUMONT ARMS

army of the Conqueror, and received one hundred and seventy-six Lordships in England (*vide* Domesday Book); Joint Chief Justiciar of England, 1074 ; Lord of Clare and Tunbridge ; founded Tunbridge Priory, perhaps called " Earl " of Clare ; *m.* **ROHAIS**, *dau.* of **Walter Giffard**, third Earl of Buckingham (as above said), and *d.* before 1090, having had a second son, **GILBERT**, *b.* before 1066 ; styled in 1088 Gilbert Fitz Richard ; succeeded as second Lord or Earl of Clare in 1090, and founded Clare Priory that year. Knighted 1095 ; commanded forces against the Welsh, 1107 ; and was created Lord of Cardigan by Henry I.; is called by Ordericus Vitalis " a knight potent and rich ; " *m.* **ADELIZA**, *dau.* of **Hugh**,[2] Count of Clermont, and *d.* 1116, leaving, with other issue : a third son, GILBERT, *b.* before 1116, knight, Lord of Striguil and Chepstow, succeeded as Lord of Netherwent and Pembroke, 1138, was created Earl of Pembroke that year, and Marshal of England by King Stephen. Was Patron of Tintern Abbey, Monmouthshire, and S. Neot's Priory, Huntingdonshire, joint founder of Usk Nunnery, Monmouthshire ; *m.* ELIZABETH, *dau.* of Robert de Beaumont,[3] Earl of Leicester, by Isabel, *dau.* of Hugh Capet, Count of Vermandois, a descendant of Charlemagne, and niece of Philip I., King of France. Issue :

Richard, *of whom presently.*

[1] Descended from Godfrey, eldest natural son of Duke Richard the Fearless, of Normandy.

[2] Renaud, Count of Clermont in Beauvaisis, living in 1087, had a son Hugues, *m.* Marguerite de Roucy, *dau.* of Hilduin, Count of Montdidier, and Alix, Countess de Roucy, and had a son Renaud, and *dau.* Adeliza, as above.

[3] Robert de Beaumont, *b.* 1049, was son of Roger, Lord of Beaumont, Brionne, and Pontaudemer in Normandy, by Adeline, *dau.* of Waleran, Count of Mellent or Meulan.

RICHARD, son of **Gilbert** and **Elizabeth (Beaumont) de Clare,** *b.* before 1135, was called "Strongbow." He was Hereditary Marshal of England, styled Earl of Striguil; November 6, 1153, was a witness to the compromise between King Stephen and Henry, Duke of Normandy; December 19, 1154, Marshal of England at the coronation of King Henry II.; 1167, Joint Ambassador to Germany. Gerald de Barri describes him as "a man with reddish hair and freckled face, bright gray eyes, delicate, even feminine features, a high voice, and a short neck, stature above the average. Freehanded, and mild of disposition. What exertion could not effect he obtained by suavity of speech. In private life more ready to be led by others than to lead. In war rather a tactician than a fighter. If supported by advice he would dare anything, but he never relied on his own judgment in ordering an attack, nor staked all on mere personal valour. During an engagement where his standard waved was ever a firm rallying point or a safe refuge for his men. In victory or defeat he displayed the same equanimity, the same unwavering purpose." Having come into disgrace with the king, he was deprived of his estate, and in hope of repairing his fortunes became leader of an expedition into Ireland to aid

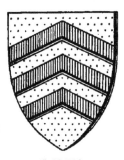

CLARE ARMS

Dermot, King of Leinster, in 1170, and, marrying his daughter, held the kingdom for a year. In July, 1171, was Constable or Steward of Ireland, 1173 Governor of Gisors, 1174 Justiciar of Ireland, and Governor of Dublin, Waterford, and Wexford, and founded Kilmainham Priory. He *m.* **EVA,** *dau.* and heiress of **Dermot MacMurchad,** King of Leinster about August 26, 1170, and *d.* April 5, 1176. Issue, an only *dau.* and heiress :

> ISABEL, *m.*, before September 3, 1189, WILLIAM, son of John Le Mareschal or Marshall, *of whom presently.*

WILLIAM MARSHALL, *b.* before 1153; was knighted April 15, 1173; took the cross as a crusader June 11, 1183; joint ambassador to France, August, 1188. Founded Cartmel Priory that year; Earl of Striguil and Steward of Leinster (*Jure Uxoris*),

September 3, 1189. Earl of Pembroke, June 7, 1199 ; Constable of the castles of Nottingham, Lillebonne, S. Briavel's, Carmarthen, Cardigan. Founded many priories in Ireland, was a Councillor of Regency, February, 1191 ; joint guardian of England, April and May, 1199 ; Warden of the Marches of Normandy, May, 1201 ; Lieutenant of Ireland, 1210-; joint surety for King John, May, 1213 ; witness to his surrender of England and Ireland to the Pope's Legate, May 15, 1213 ; Guardian and Governor of King Henry III. and Regent of England, October 12, 1216, to May, 1219, and one of the most powerful barons of

MARSHALL ARMS

his time. He *m.*, before September 3, 1189, **ISABEL DE CLARE**, as above said (who *d.* after June 18, 1219), and *d.* May 14, 1219. Issue (with others) :

i.   **WILLIAM,** *b.* before 1190, Joint Warden of Bamborough Castle, Newcastle-on-Tyne and the County of Northumberland, August 20, 1212, one of the twenty-five guardians of Magna Charta, June, 1215, and held many other offices ; *d. s. p.* April 24, 1231.

ii.   **MAUD,** *m.*, first, **HUGH BIGOD** (*q. v.*) ; *m.*, second, **WILLIAM DE WARRENNE,** Earl of Surrey ; *m.*, third, **WALTER DE DUNSTANVILLE.**

iii.   **EVA,** *co-h.* with her sisters, *m.* **WILLIAM DE BRAOSE** (*q. v.*).

Authorities : G. T. Clark's Earls of Pembroke. Tenby, 1880, *pp.* 9-75 ; F. P. Barnard's Strongbow's Conquest of Ireland, 1888 ; Doyle's Official Baronage, i. 251 ; ii. 335 ; iii. 1, 2, 6, 714 ; Moréri Grand Dictionnaire (1740), iii. 464. National Dictionary of Biography, vol. x., 375-383.

GILPIN

BERNARD, son of **Gideon** and **Sarah Gilpin,** *m.,* August 21, 1793, at Sandy Spring Meeting-house, in Montgomery Co., Md., **SARAH,** third *dau.* of **Richard** and **Sarah (Coale) Thomas** (*q. v.*), who *d.* April 29, 1805. Issue :

i. **SARAH,** *b.* May 30, 1794 ; *m.* **ROGER BROOKE** (*q. v.*).
ii. **ELIZABETH,** *b.* November 21, 1795 ; *m.* **JAMES P. STABLER** (*q. v.*).
iii. **ANN ROBINSON,** *b.* July 1, 1797; *m.* **EDWARD STABLER** (*q. v.*).
iv. **THOMAS,** *b.* February 10, 1799.
v. **SAMUEL,** *b.* March 28, 1801, *of whom presently.*
vi. **HANNAH,** *b.* May 20, 1803 ; *m.,* February 5, 1835, **ANDREW,** son of **Whitson** and **Rachel Birdsall,** of Loudoun Co., Va.
vii. **LYDIA S.,** *b.* April 16, 1805 ; *m.* **WILLIAM BROOKE** (*q. v.*).

BERNARD GILPIN *m.,* second, August 26, 1807, **LETITIA GILBERT,** *dau.* of **Whitson Canby.** Further issue :

viii. **WILLIAM HENRY,** *b.* August 10, 1808.
ix. **JOSHUA CANBY,** *b.* April 12, 1810.
x. **MARY B.,** *b.* June 24, 1812.
xi. **GIDEON EDWARD,** *b.* December 21, 1814.
xii. **GEORGE FOX,** *b.* April 4, 1817.
xiii. **CHARLES CANBY,** *b.* November 11, 1819 ; *d.* August 9, 1820.
xiv. **JAMES STABLER,** *b.* April 12, 1821.
xv. **CANBY,** *b.* December 1, 1823.
xvi. **BERNARD,** *b.* March 5, 1826.

SAMUEL, second son of **Bernard** and **Sarah** (**Thomas**) **Gilpin,** *b.* March 28, 1801 ; *m.* **RACHEL GOVER.** Issue :

i.   **EDWARD CANBY,** *m.,* February 23, 1854, in Philadelphia, **ANNIE FEAST.** Issue :

    i.   **LIZZIE FEAST,** *b.* December 30, 1854 ; m., June 5, 1888, **NATHANIEL B. HOGG,** JR., of Brownsville, Pa. Issue (surname HOGG) :

        i.   **Florence N.,** *b.* April 27, 1889.
        ii. **Anna,** *b.* February 10, 1892.

    ii. **WILLIAM H.,** *b.* April 4, 1856.
    iii. **SAMUEL,** *b.* September 1, 1858 ; *d.* September 4, 1859.
    iv. **JOSEPH,** *b.* October 21, 1860 ; *d.* April 22, 1862.
    v.   **ELWOOD,** *b.* November 4, 1863 ; *d.* August 1, 1865.
    vi. **MARY A.,** *b.* September 16, 1865.
    vii. **CLARENCE LEA,** *b.* July 21, 1870 ; *m.,* October 11, 1893, **ROSE M.,** *das.* of **Frederick** and **Martha R. Stabler.**

ii.   **FRANCES A.,** *m.,* October 19, 1865, **EDWARD J.,** son of **Thomas** and **Deborah A. Lea.** Issue :

    i.   **EDWARD S.,** *b.* September 16, 1867.
    ii. **FRANK T.,** *b.* June 6, 1869.
    iii. **ALBERT G.,** *b.* August 13, 1872.

iii. **MARY A.,** *m.* **EDWARD REESE** (*q. v.*).
iv.   **EMILY,** *m.* **JOHN TURNBULL,** of Scotland.
v.   **JOSEPH B.**
vi.   **ALBERT** ; and others whose names are unknown.

Authorities : Friend's records and family papers.

OWEN GLENDOWER

BLEDDYN ap Cynfen, Prince of Wales, was a patron of the Bards and revised the laws of Howell the Good. He *m.* **HAER,** *dau.* and *co-h.* of **Cilyn,** and was murdered in 1073. Their son, **MEREDITH,** Prince of Powys, *m.* **HUNYDD,** *dau.* of **Efnydd Gwernwy,** Lord of Duffryn Clwyd, and *d.* 1133, leaving a son, MADOC, last Prince of Powys, *m.,* first, **SUSANNA,** *dau.* of Gruffyd ap Cynan; *m.,* second, **EPA,** *dau.* of **Madoc ap Urien,** and *d.* 1160, leaving a son, Gruffyd Maelor, *of whom presently.*

This **GRUFFYD MAELOR,** Lord of Bromfield, *m.* **ANGHARAD,** *dau.* of **Owen Gwynedd,** and *d.* 1191. Their son **MADOC,** Lord of Bromfield, Yale, and Chirk, *m.* **GLADYS,** descended from **Jestin ap Gwrgant,** and *d.* 1236, leaving a son and heir **GRIFFITH,** Lord of Dinas Bran, *of whom presently.*

GRIFFITH, Lord of Dinas Bran, *m.* **EMMA,** *dau.* of **Henry,** second Lord **Audley** (*q. v.*), and *d.* 1270. Issue :

i.   **MADOC,** *m.* **MARGARET** ——, and *d. s. p.* before December 10, 1278.
ii. **LLEWELLYN,** living November, 1282, drowned in the River Dee.
iii. **OWAIN,** Rector of Blanchebir, January 11, 1283.
iv. **GRYFFYD,** *of whom presently.*

GRYFFYD, youngest son and heir of **Griffith,** is called "Gryffyd y Barwn Gwyn," and "Griffith Vychan." He was Lord of Yale ; *m.,* it is said, a *dau.* of **John le Strange,** of Knockin, and had a son **MADOC,** *m.* **GWENLLIAN,** *dau.* of **Ithel Vychan,** of Nor-

thop and Mostyn in Englefield, and *d.* November 11, 1305, leaving a
son GRIFFITH, *b.*[1] November 23, 1298 ; was steward of **Oswestry**
under Richard, Earl of Arundel, 1347 ; *m.,*[2] July 8, 1304, **ELIZABETH**,
dau. of Lord Strange, of Knockin (*q. v.*), by Maud, *dau.* of Roger d'Eiville ;
was steward of Oswestry in 1347, and left a son and heir, Griffith Vychan,
of whom presently.

This **GRIFFITH VYCHAN** *m.* **ELA**, or **HELEN**, *dau.* and
  co-h. (with her sister **Margaret**, who *m.* **Tudor ap Grono**, ancestor of **Henry VII.**) of **Thomas ap Llewellyn**, *heir* of
  the Princes of South Wales (*vide Appendix I.*).   Issue :

i.   **OWEN**, *of whom presently.*
ii.   **TUDOR**, inherited Gwyddelwern in Merionethshire.
iii.   **LOWRY**, *m.* **ROBERT PULESTON**, of Emral.
iv.   **MORVYDD**, *m.* **RICHARD CROFT.**
v.   ——, *m.* **DAVID ap Ednyfed Gam.**

OWEN GLENDOWER, Glyndyrdy or Glendourdy, as he
wrote it himself, the eldest son and heir, was *b.* May 28, 1359.   He
received a liberal education, went to London, entered one of the Inns
of court and became a Barrister, but left the profession of the law for
arms.   He was a witness in the Scrope and Grosvenor Controversy,
September 3, 1386, and squire of the body to Richard II. ; knighted
by him in 1387, and was one of his attendants when he was seized at
Flint Castle August 20, 1399, but was allowed to return to his home,
Sychart, near Corwen.

   Lord Grey, of Ruthin, one of the Lords marchers, presuming on
his influence as a zealous Lancastrian, seized some lands of Glendower's.   Owen's appeal to Parliament was disregarded, and Grey
obtained the grant of a further portion of his estate, but was himself captured in attempting to take possession.   The Welsh were in
arms and called upon Owen as the great-grandson and heir of
Llewelyn, the last native prince, to lead them.   This he did with
vigor and success.   In his first incursion into England he defeated
and made prisoner Sir Edmund Mortimer, uncle of the Earl of
March, Yorkist heir of the English throne.   He captured many
strong castles in the marches—Conway, Ruthin, Radnor, and Oswestry—and soon formally assumed the title of Prince of Wales, was
crowned at Machynlleth, and entered into a treaty with the Morti-
mers and Percys, having for its object the overthrow of Henry IV.

[1] *Inq. P. M.*, 14 Edward II., No. 13.   [2] *Rotuli Parl.*, vol. i., 306.

This alliance was dissolved by the battle of Shrewsbury; but Glendower maintained the contest. He repelled three formidable armies led by Henry in person, and captured many of the most considerable "English" towns and castles in Wales. Though he was attainted and proclaimed an outlaw by the English Parliament in 1403, he exercised the rights of sovereignty in Wales, expelled bishops and appointed others, and was recognized as prince by the King of France, Charles VI., who made a formal alliance with him, June 14, 1404, and sent troops to his assistance. With them he marched as far as Worcester, and though Henry of Monmouth had some success against him he failed to effect his subjugation. Several years after, when he was about to embark on his invasion of France, unwilling to leave so active an enemy behind him, he began negotiations with Glendower, looking toward a peace. While they were in progress Owen died at Monnington, in Herefordshire, September 20, 1415, having for fifteen years kept up his struggle against England. He married, early in life, **MARGARET,** *dau.* of **Sir David Hanmer** (*q. v.*), of Hanmer, in Flintshire, one of the justices of the King's Bench, by whom he had five sons and five daughters. Most of the sons fell in the field of battle, and the daughters eventually became *co-h.* of their father. **ALICIA,** or **ELIZABETH,** one of them, *m.* **SIR JOHN SCUDAMORE,** Knight of Ewyas and Home Lacey (*q. v.*).

OWEN GLENDOWER. FROM HIS GREAT SEAL ENGRAVED IN THE ARCHÆOLOGIA

Authorities: Thomas's Life of Glendower; *Rotuli Walliæ*, Edward I., 6, 9, etc.; Williams's Enwogion Cwmru, 173; Annals of England, ii., 16, 17; Calendarium Genealogicum, i., 360; Yorke's Royal Tribes, 62; Bridgeman's Princes of South Wales, 250.

GODEY

WALTER GODEY, *m.,* in 1818, **CHARLOTTE** (*q. v.*), eldest *dau.* of **John** and —— **(Berry) Thomas** (*b.* in 1800 ; *d.* 1863). Issue :

i. **THOMAS,** *of whom presently.*
ii. **HENRY,** *b.* in 1821 ; *d. u.*
iii. **A DAUGHTER,** *d. i.*

MRS. GODEY *m.,* second, **DR. JOHN WOLFENDEN.** Issue :

SARAH, *d. u.* in 1858.

THOMAS, her eldest son by her first marriage, *b.* December 22, 1819; *m.,* January 29, 1846, **SARAH ANN NORRIS** (*d.* February 13, 1879). Issue :

Besides **FRANK, THOMAS WALTER, EDWARD, CHARLES,** and **ROBERT,** who *d. i.*

i. **MARY CHARLOTTE,** *b.* February 28, 1847 ; *m.,* October 10, 1867, **HENRY W. WARNER.** Issue :

   i. **MARY GODEY,** *b.* June 25, 1871.
   ii. **JULIA ROGERS,** *b.* January 7, 1876.
   iii. **HENRY MICHAEL,** *b.* October 20, 1880.

ii. **HARRY,** *b.* April 9, 1849 ; *m.,* November 3, 1875, **M. LOUISE WILSON.**

iii. **THOMAS,** *b.* March 9, 1861 ; *m.,* November 20, 1883, **MARY R. RASIN.** Issue :

THOMAS RASIN, *b.* September 7, 1884.

Authority : Family papers, through Mrs. H. W. Warner.

GRAY, OF GRAY'S FERRY, PHILADELPHIA

GEORGE, son of **George Gray,** of Barbadoes, came to Philadelphia in 1691 ; *m.,* as his fourth wife, **MARY,** *dau.* of **Alexander Beardsley,** and had a son **GEORGE,** *b.* in 1714; *m.,* first, **MARY HILL,** and had a son, ᴳᴱᴼᴿᴳᴱ, *of whom presently ; m.,* second, **MRS. MARY EWING,** whose *dau.* by her first husband, ᴱᴸᴵᶻᴬᴮᴱᵀᴴ, *m.,* March 13, 1735, ᴄᴼᴸᴼᴺᴱᴸ ᴶᴬᴹᴱˢ ᴄᴼᵁᴸᵀᴬˢ, High Sheriff of Philadelphia Co., October, 1755, to October, 1758. Judge of the Orphans' Court, Quarter Sessions, and Common Pleas, 1765 ; who built the older part of Whitby Hall, on Gray's Lane, in 1741, and *d. s. p.*

GEORGE, son of **George** and **Mary (Hill) Gray,** *b.* October 26, 1725, was active in the troubled politics of the province previous to the Revolution, and a leader of the popular party. Was a member of the Assembly, 1772 to 1787, at one time its speaker. In 1775 author of the " Treason Resolutions," a member of the Committee of Safety, 1776–77, a member and chairman of the Board of War of the revolted colony, and a member of the Constitutional Convention of 1790. He *m.,* November 25, 1752, **MARTHA,** *dau.* of **Robert** and **Margaret (Coultas) Ibbetson** (*b.* January 28, 1734), and *d.* 1800. Issue, with others :

i.   **ELIZABETH COULTAS,** *b.* August 20, 1762 ; *m.* **THOMAS LEIPER** (*q. v.*).
ii.   **MARGARET GRAY,** *b.* November 28, 1766 ; *m.* **JAMES KNOWLES,** (*q. v.*).
iii. **MARTHA,** *b.* November 23, 1771 ; *m.* **EVAN WILLIAM THOMAS** (*q. v.*).

Authority : Family papers, through Mrs. W. Harpar Thomas and Dr. R. P. Robins, of Philadelphia.

JAMES AP GRIFFITH

A SISTER of Sir Rhys ap Thomas, K.G., *m.* **Griffith ap Howell,** and had issue : **James,** who in his exile assumed the name of **Robert Brampton** or **Brancetour.** In 1516 we find him, through the influence of his uncle, a Gentleman Usher of the Royal Household.

After the death of Sir Rhys he seems to have returned to Wales and resided there, probably in some office under his cousin, Rice ap Griffith. After the arrest of Rice, James ap Griffith held out for some time against the King's officers, and we find Henry VIII. addressing a special warrant to Lord Ferrars as Justice in South Wales, dated October 7, 1531, directing the arrest of James ap Griffith ap Howell, who had fortified himself in the Castle of Emlyn.[1] This was accordingly done, and he was imprisoned in the Tower of London. From this he escaped some time in 1533, and going to Wales, collected a few of the old servants of his House, and taking his wife and daughter went to Scotland. July 2, 1533, Lord Dacre writes to the King that a gentleman of Wailes, his wife and eight persons with them, were landed at St. Ninian's, in Scotland, and that he was uncle to Ryse, of Wailes. In reply, Dacre and Wharton, Henry's agents, were ordered to watch him. A later letter says he had a daughter with him, and named himself **Ryse,** and that the party was well favorably arrayed and appointed. He was ordered to a castle S. W. of Edinburgh, and visited there by King James. Afterwards he came to Edinburgh and was much resorted to by the Courtiers, but had no audience of the King. Finally went to the Emperor, and is noticed as being at Antwerp in December, 1533, and at Lubeck in the following May. After this we hear nothing of him until 1539, when he appears in Paris in the train of Charles V. Henry at once instructed his Ambassador, Sir Thomas Wyatt, to demand his arrest. Wyatt informed the Constable Montmorency that he was an English subject who had robbed his Master and afterwards conspired against the King, had him watched to his lodgings by a spy, and in Decem-

[1] These notices of James ap Griffith come from the Calendars of State Papers, Domestic Series, published by the Master of the Rolls, England.

ber, 1539, taking with him a Provost Marshal's guard, surrounded the house at night. Wyatt entered Griffith's room where he sat writing at a table. He says in his report to the King that "Brancetour's colour changed as soon as he heard my voice ; and with that came in the Provost and set hand on him. I reached to the letters he was writing, but he caught them afore me and flung them backwards into the fire. I overthrew him and cracked them out ; but the Provost got them." Upon this Brancetour declared himself the Emperor's servant, and taking other papers from his pocket placed them in the Provost's hands. The Provost, leaving a guard with Wyatt and Brancetour, went to the Chancellor for instructions. Wyatt then attempted to persuade the prisoner to submit to him, but he made the Emperor his master and refused. "Once he told me," says Wyatt, "that he had heard me oft times say that kings have long hands ; but God, quoth he, hath longer." The Provost, returning, took charge of Brancetour till the morning. After breakfast the next day, Wyatt saw Cardinal Granvelle and the Chancellor, and finally the matter was referred to the Emperor. He was extremely angry. The man, he said, "was his servant, and had been in Perse, and had followed him in all his viages in Affrica, in Province, in Italy and France these ten or twelve years past." Wyatt answered that Brancetour was his master's subject, and had of his own knowledge committed treason in Spain, and insisted that he should be surrendered in accordance with previous treaties in regard to persons guilty of treason. The Emperor cared nothing for treaties, Brancetour was his servant and should go free, and Wyatt was compelled to let him do so. Griffith returned to Germany in the train of the Emperor, and we next hear of him in a letter written by Sir Thomas Seymour at the siege of Buda, August 8, 1542, who says "there lately came to Vienna James Griffith up Powell, who calls himself Robert Brampton, and hath a letter from the Pope to the King of Hungary, to be captain of two hundred howshereres or light · horse of Hungary." May 6, 1549, Cardinal Pole writes to Bishop Ceneda, Papal Envoy in France, recommending Captain Griffith, who, with Dr. Hilliard, were the Cardinal's Envoys to the Protector of England. This appears to be the last mention of his name in the English state papers. Evidently he was an active emissary of the Pope in his attempts to regain England. More fortunate than Fathers Campian, Parsons, and Garnet, he seems, in spite of the vigilance of King Henry's officers, to have escaped his vengeance.

ARMS OF HANMER

HANMER AND MACCLESFIELD

SIR THOMAS DE MACCLESFIELD, descended maternally from **John de Hanmere,** of the Fennswood, Flintshire, in 1198, assumed the name of **HANMER** in the reign of Henry III. **SIR JOHN HANMER,** his son, was Constable of Carnarvon Castle under King Edward III., *m.* **HAWYSE,** or Alicia ——, of Powys. **PHILIP,** their third son, was of Hanmer, *m.* **AGNES,** *dau.* and heiress of **David ap Rivid ap Rhys Sais,** descended from **Tudor Trevor,** who was living in 907, and had a son, **Sir David,** *of whom presently.*

SIR DAVID, son of **Philip** and **Agnes Hanmer,** was a judge of the King's Bench, sixth Richard III.; *m.* **AGNES,** *dau.* of **Llewellyn Ddu ap Griffith ap Jorwerth Voel,** and had a *dau.* **MARGARET,** *m.* **OWEN GLENDOWER** (*q. v.*).

Authorities : Thomas's Life of Glendower, and Burke's Peerage, 1886.

HARRIS AND WILLSON

WILLIAM, third son of **William** (*b.* February 10, 1688–89 ; *d.* January, 1732) and **Margaret Harris,** and grandson of William Harris, who *d.* March 21, 1694–95, *m.*, after 1735, **MARGARET,** fifth *dau.* of **Samuel** and **Mary (Hutchins) Thomas** (*q. v.*). She *d.* April 23, 1766, and her husband, July 16, 1782. Issue :

i.   **WILLIAM,** *b.* July 31, 1744 ; *d.* January 7, 1746-47.

ii.   **SAMUEL,** *b.* February 24, 1746-47 ; *m.*, April 2, 1771, **RACHEL,**[1] *dau.* of **Henry Willson,** who *m.*, second, **GERARD,** son of **Samuel** and **Sarah Hopkins** (*q. v.*). Issue :

     i.   **WILLIAM,** *m.* **MARY CONSTABLE.**
     ii.   **SAMUEL,** *b.* September 17, 1774, *m.* **ELIZA CONKLING.**

iii.   **MARGARET,** *b.* June 27, 1749 ; *m.*, January 3, 1771, **HENRY WILLSON.**[1] Issue (surname WILLSON) :

     i.   **HENRY,** *m.* **ANTOINETTE POUJARD.**
     ii.   **WILLIAM.**
     iii.   **SAMUEL.**
     iv.   **PRISCILLA,** *m.* **JOHN McFADON.**
     v.   **MARGARET,** *m.* **ROBERT ANDREWS.**
     vi.   **RICHARD.**
     vii. **JOHN.**
     viii. **THOMAS.**
     ix.   **GERARD.**
     x.   **ELIZABETH,** *m.* —— **WILLSON.**

iv.   **ELIZA,** *b.* March 25, 1752 ; *m.*, May 13, 1775, **JOHNS,** Jr., son of **Johns Hopkins** (*q. v.*).

v.   **MARY,** *m.*, May 29, 1770, **RICHARD ROBERTS.** Issue :

     i.   **RICHARD,** *m.* —— **KENT.**
     ii.   **MARGARET.**

Authority : West River Friends' Records.

[1] Henry Willson, of Baltimore Co., had issue : Henry, *b.* June 19, 1747 ; Priscilla, *b.* October 29, 1749 ; *m.*, November 7, 1769, John Worthington ; Rachel, *b.* November 9, 1751 ; Elizabeth, *b.* March 13, 1754.

337

HERBERT, OF ALEXANDRIA, VA.

WILLIAM HERBERT, of the family seated at Muckross Abbey, on the Lakes of Killarney, in Ireland, came to America, and was President of the Bank and Mayor of Alexandria. He *m.* a *dau.* of **John** and **Sarah (Fairfax) Carlyle,** of Virginia. Issue :

i.   **JOHN CARLYLE,** *of whom presently.*
ii.   **WILLIAM,** *m.* a sister of John P. Dulany, of Virginia.
iii.   **MARGARET,** *m.* **THOMAS,** ninth Lord Fairfax (*q. v.*).
iv.   **SARAH,** *m.* **REV. OLIVER NORRIS,** of Philadelphia.
v.   **ANN,** *d. u.*
vi.   **ELIZA P.,** *d. u.* in 1865.
vii. **LUCINDA,** *d. y.*

JOHN CARLYLE, eldest son of **William Herbert,** graduated at S. John's College, Annapolis, Md., 1794 ; was a Representative in Congress from Maryland, Senator of the State, Speaker of the House of Delegates, Presidential Elector from Maryland, 1825. He *m.* **MARY,** *dau.* of **Major Thomas Snowden** (*q. v.*). Issue :

i.   **DR. THOMAS SNOWDEN,** *of whom presently.*
ii.   **ANN CAROLINE,** *m.* **Hon. HENRY FAIRFAX** (*q. v.*).
iii. **ALFRED,** a graduate of West Point, brevetted first Lieutenant July 27. 1836, for gallantry in the Florida War ; resigned his commission June 30, 1837 ; Civil Engineer from 1837 to 1842 ; Superintending Engineer of several Southern Railroads ; Professor in State Military Academy, S. C., 1843–46 ; in U. S. Ordnance Bureau, 1846–53 ; U. S. Assistant or Principal Examiner of Patents, 1853–57.

iv.   **SARAH,** *m.* **CAPTAIN ARCHIBALD FAIRFAX,** U. S. N. (*q. v.*).
v.   **WILLIAM FAIRFAX.**
vi.   **EMMA,** *m.* **REV. W. BRYANT,** of Virginia.
vii.   **MARY VIRGINIA,** *m.* **CAPTAIN THOMAS T. HUNTER,** U. S. N., who resigned his commission at the beginning of the Civil War, and entered the Confederate Navy ; both *d.* Issue (surname HUNTER) :

     i.   **DR. FREDERICK,** *m.* —— **LIPSCOMB.**
     ii.   **THOMAS,** in the Confederate Navy during the Civil War.
     iii.   **MADELINE,** *m.* **MAJOR EDMONDSTONE,** of South Carolina.
     iv.   **JULIA,** *m.* **LIEUTENANT-COLONEL FRANKLIN HARWOOD,** U. S. A.
     v.   **WILLIAM.**
     vi.   **CHARLES.**
     vii.   **SARAH.**
     viii.   **MINNIE.**

viii.   **JULIA.**
ix.   **EUGENIA.**
x.   **LUCINDA,** *m.* **JOHN EVERSFIELD.**
xi.   **ELIZA P.,** *d. u.* May 18, 1883.
xii.   **EDWARD,** *m.* **MARY H. BARRETT.** Issue :

     WILLIAM PINKNEY, *m.* **REBECCA,** *dau.* of Robert Beverly.

DR. THOMAS SNOWDEN, eldest son of **John C.** and **Mary (Snowden) Herbert,** *m.,* first, **CAMILLA HAMMOND ;** *m.,* second, **ELIZABETH DUER,** who *d. s. p.* Issue, by his first wife :

i.   **JOHN CARLYLE.**
ii.   **JAMES R.,** served as a Confederate Colonel of Infantry during the Civil War, leading the Maryland line in a charge at Gettysburg, when out of five hundred in the ranks three hundred were either killed or wounded ; was a Brigadier-General in the Maryland Militia, and one of the Police Commissioners of Baltimore City ; *m.* **ELIZABETH COLEMAN,** *dau.* of **Mark Alexander,** of Mecklenburg Co., Va., who *d.* June, 1895. Issue :

     i.   **ANN GORDON.**
     ii.   **CAMILLA HAMMOND.**
     iii.   **MARK ALEXANDER.**
     iv.   **MARY COLEMAN,** who *d.* in 1877.

iii.   **MATTHIAS HAMMOND.**

     Authority : Family papers through Colonel James R. Herbert.

HERBERT, OF TROY HOUSE

HERBERT, OF WALES

SIR WILLIAM AP THOMAS, of Ragland Castle, Monmouthshire, *m.* **GWLADYS,** *dau.* of **Sir Davy Gam,** and widow of **Sir Roger Vaughan,** and had, with other issue :

i. **WILLIAM,** *of whom presently.*
ii. **RICHARD,** of Coldbrook (*q. v.*).
iii. **ELIZABETH,** *m.*, first, **SIR HARRY STRADLING, Knt.,** of S. Donat's Castle, Glamorganshire ; *m.*, second, **SIR RHYS AP THOMAS, K.G.** (*q. v.*).

SIR WILLIAM HERBERT, the eldest son, was a leading adherent of the House of York, *b.* before 1430, knighted by King Henry VI. December 25, 1449, confirmed Sheriff of Glamorgan and Morgannoc, and Steward of the Lordship of Abergavenny, Dynas, Usk, Ellewys, Ewyas Lascey, and Caerleon, February 5, 1460. Privy Councillor, March 3, 1461 ; Chief Justice and Chamberlain of South Wales, May 8, 1461 ; created Baron Herbert, of Herbert, July 26, 1461 ; K. G., March 21, 1462 ; Lord of Dunster, June 16, 1463 ; High Forester of the Royal forests in South Wales for life ; and Constable for life of the Castles of Usk, Carleon, Dynas, Builth, and Clifford, September 26, 1466 ; Chief Justice of North Wales, August 28, 1467 ; Earl of Pembroke, September 8, 1468 ; Constable of Beaumaris, Conway, Denbigh, Cardigan, Hardlegh, and Caermarthen Castles. July 27, 1469, with his brother Richard, defeated at the battle of Banbury and beheaded at Northampton. He *m.*, before July, 1460, **ANNE,** *dau.* of **Walter Devereux,** and sister of the first **Lord Ferrers of Chartley.** Issue :

340

SIR WILLIAM AP THOMAS, OF RAGLAND

From the Effigy on his Tomb

i.   **WILLIAM,** *b.* March 5, 1461 ; created Baron Herbert, of Dunster, September, 1466 ; succeeded his father as Earl of Pembroke and Hereditary Chief Justice, Forester and Constable of castles in Wales. Surrendered his Earldom to King Edward IV., and was created Earl of Huntingdon, July 4, 1479. He *m.*, first, in September, 1466, **MARY,** fifth *dau.* of Richard Woodville or **Wydeville, Earl Rivers,** and had a *dau.,* **ELIZABETH,** *m.* **SIR CHARLES SOMERSET,** natural son of Henry Beaufort, Duke of Somerset, descended from John of Gaunt, from which marriage descend the present Dukes of Beaufort. The Earl *m.*, second, March 3, 1484, **LADY KATHARINE PLANTAGENET,** *dau.* of **KING RICHARD III.,** and *d.* 1491.

ii.   **SIR WALTER.**

iii.   **JOHN,** *m.* the third *dau.* of **Thomas ap Gruffyd Nicholas,** and had a *dau.* and heiress, **ANN,** *m.* **ANDREW NORTON.**

By **MAUD,** *dau.* and heiress of **Adam ap Howell Graunt, WILLIAM,** the first Earl of Pembroke, had a numerous illegitimate issue, of whom **SIR RICHARD HERBERT,** of Ewyas, was ancestor of the present Earls of Pembroke seated at Wilton House, the Earls of Montgomery and of Caernarvon, the Marquises of Powis and the distinguished statesman, Sidney, Lord Herbert, of Lea.

SIR WILLIAM HERBERT, another son of the first **Earl of Pembroke** and **Maud ap Adam,** was of Troy House, Monmouthshire, and according to the visitation of Hunts, in 1613, *m.* **BLANCHE,** *dau.* and *co-h.* of **Simon Milbourne** (*q. v.*). Issue :

i.   **SIR CHARLES,** *of whom presently.*

ii.   **THOMAS,** of Wynestowe, Co. Monmouth, *m.* **ANNA,** *dau.* of Sir **William Lucy, Knt.,** of Charlecote, Warwick. Issue :

    i.   **HENRY,** of Wynestowe, or Wonastow House, *m.* **LUCY,** *dau.* of William, **Earl** of Worcester. Issue :

        i.   **William,** *d. y.*

        ii.   **Ellen,** *m.* **William Rawlins,** of Treregave.

        iii.   **Christiana,** *m.* ——— **Milborne.**

        iv.   **Elizabeth,** *m.* **Charles Herbert,** of Hadnock.

        v.   **Johanna,** *m.* **Lewis de St. Pier.**

    ii.   **ELIZABETH,** *m.,* first, **WALTER VAUGHAN** ; *m.,* second, **JOHN BREYNTON.**

    iii.   **CHARLES,** of Covington, Co. Hunts, living and signs the pedigree in 1613, *m.* **MARIA TETLOWE,** of Lancashire. Issue :

        i.   **Charles,** *b.* 1585.

        ii.   **Francis,** of London, *m.* **Elizabeth Negoose,** of Bedfordshire.

        iii.   **Edward.**

        iv.   **John.**

        v.   **George.**

        vi.   **Elizabeth,** *m.* **William Hawkes.**

iv.   **EDMUND.**

v. BLANCHE, *m*. WALTER POWELL.
vi. BARBARA, *m*. —— WALSHE or WELCHE.

SIR CHARLES, eldest son of **Sir William** and **Blanche (Milbourne) Herbert,** was of Troy House, High Sheriff of Monmouthshire, 1541 and 1549 ; *m*. **ELIZABETH,** *dau*. of **Sir Griffith ap Rhys, Knt.,** and *d*. 1557. Issue :

i. **BLANCHE,** *m*. **OLIVER LLOYD,** of Leighton, Montgomeryshire.
ii. **JOAN,** *m*. **GEORGE JAMES,** of Penrose.

He also had a natural son, **WALTER HERBERT, ESQ.,** of Skenfrith Castle, Monmouthshire, High Sheriff in 1552 ; *m*. **CATHERINE,** *dau*. and *co-h*. of **Thomas Powel Prichard,** of the Goytre. Issue :

i. **CHARLES.**
ii. **ALICE,** *m*. **LEWIS HENRY DAVID,** of Llanwenarth.
iii. **ELIZABETH,** *m*. **SAUNDERS ap REES ap PHILIP WILLIAMS.**
iv. **A DAUGHTER,** *m*. **WALTER SPICER,** of Monmouth.
v. **GWENLLIAN,** *m*. **JOHN ap PHILIP THOMAS,** of Grosmount (*q. r.*).
vi. **A DAUGHTER,** *m*. **WILLIAM JOHN POWEL HAWKINS.**
vii. **CATHERINE,** *m*. **PHILIP ap WILLIAM THOMAS NICHOLAS,** of Skenfrith.

SIR RICHARD HERBERT, of Coldbrook, younger brother of the first Earl of Pembroke, *m*. **MARGARET,** eldest *dau*. of **Thomas ap Gruffyd Nicholas,** of Abermarlais, and was beheaded with his brother after the battle of Banbury, leaving a younger son, **SIR RICHARD,** who was ancestor of Edward, Lord Herbert of Chirbury, the Philosopher, the pious George Herbert, Rector of Bemerton, and author of "The Temple ;" Admiral Herbert, Earl of Torrington, Chief Justice Sir Edward Herbert, and the extinct Earls of Powis, with whom ended the legitimate male line of descent.

Authorities: Sandford and Townsend's Great Governing Families, Clark's Morgan and Glamorgan, and Doyle's Official Baronage, III., 15-38.

ARMS OF THE EARL OF PEMBROKE

HERMAN AND RANDOLPH

AUGUSTINE HERMAN, of Prague, *b.* about 1608, son of
Ephraim Augustine Herman, and **Beatrice,** *dau.* of **Caspar Redel,** served under Wallenstein, and was at Lutzen Battle, where the noble Gustavus Adolphus, of Sweden, was killed.
Afterward entered the service of the Dutch West India Company and came to America. He was one of the " nine men " of
New Amsterdam, 1647–49 and 1650. In September, 1659, he
was sent to Maryland as a Commissioner on the boundary line
of that Province, and between 1660 and 1670 was engaged in
making the surveys for his great map of Maryland and Virginia, which was engraved in four folio sheets by William Faithorne, in 1670 (a reduced copy is in the Virginia and Maryland
Boundary Report, 1873). In consideration of this survey Lord
Baltimore granted him Bohemia Manor, Cecil Co., and others.
The first patent is dated June 11, 1662. The year after he
moved his family to the Province. **ANNA MARGARETTA,** one
of his daughters, *m.* **MATTHIAS VANDERHEYDEN,** of Albany, N. Y., and had issue : several sons, all of whom *d. s. p.*, and
the following daughters :

i. **JANE,** *m.* —— **COUTS,** of Scotland. Issue :
     James.
ii. **FRANCINA,** *m.,* first, **EDWARD SHIPPEN,** of Philadelphia, and had a *dau.,*
     Margaret, *m.* John Jekyll, of Boston.
     MRS. SHIPPEN, *m.,* second, **COLONEL HYNSON,** of Chestertown, Md.

iii.   **AUGUSTINA**, *b.* in 1685 ; *m.* **JAMES HARRIS**, and *d.* in 1775. **Issue :**
       Matthias.

iv.   **ARIANA**, *b.* in 1690 ; *m.*, first, February 9, 1712-13. **JAMES FRISBY**, *of whom presently.*

JAMES and ARIANA (VANDERHEYDEN) FRISBY had
issue (surname FRISBY) :

i.   **SARAH**, *b.* December 7, 1714 ; *m.*, September 9, 1730, **JOHN BRICE.**
       Issue :

    i.   **ARIANA**, *b.* June 19, 1732 ; *m.*, September 4, 1750, **DR. DAVID ROSS.**
    ii.   **SARAH**, *b.* June 3, 1735 ; *m.*, in 1761, **JOHN HENDERSON.**
    iii.   **JOHN**, *b.* September 22, 1738.
    iv.   **ANN**, *b.* in 1744.
    v.   **JAMES**, *b.* in 1746.
    vi.   **BENEDICT**, *b.* in 1749.
    vii.   **EDMUND**, *b.* in 1751.
    viii. **ELIZABETH**, *b.* in 1757 ; *m.*, first, **LLOYD DULANY** ; and second, **WAL-
              TER DULANY.**

ii.   **ARIANA MARGARET**, *b.* September 18, 1717 ; *m.* **WILLIAM
       HARRIS**, and had a son, **JAMES**, *d. s. p.*

iii.   **FRANCINA AUGUSTINA**, *b.* August 16, 1719 ; *m.*, first, in 1738,
       WILLIAM STEVENSON, and had a son, **WILLIAM** ; *m.*, sec-
       ond, **DR. DANIEL CHESTON** (*q. v.*).

MRS. ARIANA FRISBY, *m.*, second, THOMAS BORD-
LEY (*q. v.*) ; *m.*, third, in November, 1728, **EDMUND JEN-
INGS**, of Annapolis, where they resided until 1737 when they
removed to England. **MRS. JENINGS**, having been inocu-
lated for the small-pox, died of that disease in April, 1741. Issue, by her third husband :

iv.   **EDMUND**, *b.* in 1731 ; *d.* in 1819.

v.   **ARIANA**, *m.* **JOHN** (*of whom presently*), son of **Sir John Randolph,
       Knt.**, and Attorney-General of Virginia, who *d.* in 1784, at London,
       having removed to England at the breaking out of the Revolutionary
       War, being a prominent loyalist.

JOHN and ARIANA (JENINGS) RANDOLPH had issue
(surname RANDOLPH) :

i.   **EDMUND**, *of whom presently.*
ii.   **SUSAN BEVERLY**, *m.* **MAJOR GRIMES.**
iii.   **ARIANA JENINGS**, *m.* **CAPTAIN JAMES WORMELEY**, de-
       scended from Ralph Wormeley, of " Rosegill," President of the Coun-
       cil, and Secretary of State of Virginia, who *d.* 1701. Issue, with
       others :

i.   **RALPH RANDOLPH,** *b.* October 29, 1785, a Rear Admiral in the English Navy,
     who *d.* June 26, 1852, at Utica, N. Y., leaving issue :

    i.   **Mary Elizabeth,** *b.* in London, July 26, 1822, a well-known novelist ;
          authoress of "Forest Hill," "Annabel," "Our Cousin Veronica,"
          and numerous magazine articles ; *m.* **Randolph Latimer,** of Bal-
          timore, and resided at Newport, R. I.

    ii. **Katherine Prescott,** *b.* January 14, 1830, made for Messrs. Roberts
          Brothers, of Boston, a translation of Balzac's novels, which has been
          very highly praised by the critics.

EDMUND, only son of **John** and **Ariana (Jenings) Randolph,**
b. August 10, 1753, espoused the side of the Colonies in the
Revolution ; appointed by Washington his Aide, August 15,
1775 ; Attorney-General of Virginia in 1776 ; elected a delegate to Congress in 1779, and took an active part in its proceedings until 1782 ; was Governor of the State of Virginia from
1786–88 ; a member of the Convention that formed the Federal
Constitution in 1787, opposed that instrument as then proposed,
but magnanimously gave it his support after its adoption, and
when it was submitted to the Virginia Convention voted in its
favour ; was Attorney-General of the United States, 1789–90,
and Secretary of State in Washington's Cabinet, 1794–95. He
m., August 29, 1776, **ELIZABETH,** *dau.* of **Robert Carter
Nicholas,** and *d.* September 13, 1813. Issue :

      LUCY, PEYTON, EDMONIA, and **SUSAN BEVER-
          LY.**

Authorities : Magazine articles and Colonel G. A. Hanson's Old Kent.

HOPKINS, OF MARYLAND

There are found in the province of Maryland, at early dates, the following persons of the name of Hopkins :

ROBERT and **THOMAS,** in 1562 ; **WILLIAM,** who owned Hopkins's plantation on Greenberry's Point, among the Men of Severn, in 1657 ; **GERARD,** in 1658, *of whom presently ;* **DENNIS,** who was from England and settled on the Eastern Shore about 1660, from whom descended, in the seventh generation, **Robert George Hopkins,** father of Mrs. J. Barclay Jones, of Camden, N. J. ; **JOSEPH,** of Baltimore Co., in 1664, who *m.* **SARAH** ——, and *d.* in 1685. Issue :

i.   **ANN,** *m.* **GEORGE TEARNER.**
ii.   **JUDITH.**
iii.   **SARAH.**
iv.   **JOSEPH,** a minor, in 1685.
v.   **JONATHAN,** of Talbot Co., in 1669.

GERARD or **GARRARD HOPKINS,** of Anne Arundel Co., made his will October 12, 1691 (Liber 2, folio 233), proved between June, 1692, and February 2, 1693–94, in which he leaves land adjoining that of William Coale, Jr., in Anne Arundel Co., calls himself "Planter," and mentions his wife "**THOMSIN,** his son **GARRARD,** and daughters, **ANN, THOMSON,** and **MARY.**"

346

I have little doubt it was his son **GERRARD HOPKINS,** of Anne Arundel Co., who *m.*, in January, 1700–1, **MARGARET,** *dau.* of **Richard** and **Elizabeth (Kinsey) Johns** (*q. v.*) (*b.* October 8, 1683), and *d.* in January, 1743–44.[1] Issue :

i. **MARGARET,** *m.* **AQUILA JOHNS** (*q. v.*).
ii. **ELIZABETH,** *b.* June 13, 1703 ; *m.*, January 10, 1723–24, **LEVIN HILL,** and *d.* February 27, 1772. Issue :
    Priscilla and **Mary.**
iii. **JOSEPH,** *b.* November 2, 1706 ; *m.*, August 17, 1727, **ANN,** *dau.* of **John** and **Eliza Chew** (*q. v.*). Issue :
    i. **Joseph,** *m.* **Elizabeth Gover** ; and probably
    ii. **Sarah,** *m.* **Skipwith Coale** (*q. v.*).
    iii. **Elizabeth,** *m.*, March 6, 1760, Samuel, son of John Hill.
iv. **GERRARD,** *b.* March 7, 1709, *of whom presently.*
v. **PHILIP,** *b.* August 9, 1711 ; *m.*, in 1736, **ELIZABETH HALL.** Issue :
    i. **Samuel,** *m.* **Mary Gover,** of Harford Co., Md.
    ii. **Gerrard.**
vi. **SAMUEL,** *b.* January 16, 1713–14 (*q. v.*).
vii. **RICHARD,** *b.* December 15, 1715 ; *m.* **KATHERINE TODD.** Issue :
    i. **Nicholas,** *b.* May 12, 1747 ; *m.* **Mary Brian.** Issue : i. Katherine, *m.* George Stevenson, of Baltimore Co. ; ii. Mary, *m.* Charles Bowen ; iii. Nicholas, *m.* Ann Stevenson ; iv. Sarah, *m.* Joseph Entler ; v. Ellen, *m.* Isaiah Stevenson, of Baltimore Co.
    ii. **Rachel,** *b.* January 31, 1749–50.
    iii. **Richard,** *b.* February 15, 1750–51.
    iv. **Sarah,** *b.* September 20, 1751 ; *m.* **Charles Rodgers.**
    v. **Katherine,** *b.* January 20, 1753 ; *d.* September 27, 1763.
    vi. **Gerrard,** *b.* February 21, 1754 ; *d.* December 2, 1757.
    vii. **Samuel,** *b.* September 25, 1756 ; *d.* December 2, 1757.
    viii. **Elizabeth,** *b.* September 17, 1758 ; *m.* Israel Cox, of Harford Co., Md. Issue : George, *m.* Eliza, *dau.* of Joseph and Sarah Hopkins (*q. v.*).
    ix. **Joseph,** *b.* April 9, 1761 ; *m.* **Sarah Hopkins.** Issue : i. Charlotte ; ii. Sophia ; iii. Eliza, *m.* her cousin, George Cox (*q. v.*) ; iv. Richard, *m.* Mary Ann Gover.
viii. **WILLIAM,** *b.* August 8, 1717 (*q. v.*).
ix. **JOHNS,** *b.* December 30, 1720 (*q. v.*).

GERRARD, second son of **Gerrard** and **Margaret (Johns) Hopkins,** *b.* March 17, 1709, settled at South River, and *m.*, May 7, 1730, **MARY HALL,** a Roman Catholic, who joined Friends about 1733. He *d.* July 3, 1777. Issue :

i. **MARGARET,** *b.* January 11, 1730–31 ; *m.* **JOHN,** son of John and **Elizabeth Thomas** (*q. v.*).
ii. **GERARD,** *b.* August 25, 1732.
iii. **MARY,** *b.* November 11, 1734 ; *m.*, August 11, 1761, **PHILIP GOVER.**
iv. **SARAH,** *b.* September 20, 1737 ; *m.* **JOHN COWMAN** (*q. v.*).
v. **RICHARD,** *b.* February 7, 1739–40, *d. i.*
vi. **ELIZABETH,** *b.* November 3, 1741 ; *m.* **BASIL BROOKE** (*q. v.*).
vii. **RACHEL,** *b.* December 30, 1742 ; *m.* **EVAN THOMAS** (*q. v.*).

[1] Will proved February 2, 1743–44, Liber D. D., No. 1, *p.* 302.

viii. **JOSEPH**, *b.* January 11, 1744-45, *of whom presently.*
ix. **RICHARD**, *b.* March 20, 1747-48 (*q. v.*).
x. **HANNAH**, *b.* August 29, 1749.
xi. **ELISHA**, *b.* October 15, 1752, practised medicine; *m.*, first, June 27, 1777, **HANNAH HOWELL**, of Philadelphia. Issue:

    i. **ISAAC HOWELL**, *b.* March 31, 1781.
    ii. **DEBORAH**, *b.* July 8, 1782.
    iii. **PATIENCE HOWELL**, *m.* **GERARD R. HOPKINS** (*q. v.*).
    iv. **ELIZABETH HOWELL**, *m.*, July 2, 1812, **JOSEPH**, son of Joseph and **Hannah (Jones) Janney**, and *d.* Issue:

        Hannah Ann, m. Robert Hull, of Baltimore. Issue: William Janney.

    v. **HANNAH HOWELL**, *m.*, as his second wife, **JOSEPH JANNEY**, both *d.* Issue:

        i. **Elizabeth**, *m.* J. M. Sewell.
        ii. **Rebecca**, *m.* Joseph Merrefield. Issue: i. Joseph Janney; ii. William Janney; iii. Elizabeth, *m.* Henry Cox; iv. Rebecca Janney.

    iii. **William Janney.**

JANNEY ARMS

DR. ELISHA HOPKINS *m.*, second, November 24, 1796, **SARAH**, *dau.* of **Samuel** and **Elizabeth (Thomas) Snowden** (*q. v.*), and *d.* September 30, 1809. Further issue:

    vi. **SAMUEL SNOWDEN**, *b.* November 6, 1797.
    vii. **BASIL BROOKE**, *b.* November 6, 1799.
    viii. **HENRIETTA ANN**, b. July 30, 1801.
    ix. **THOMAS SNOWDEN**, *b.* June 18, 1803.
    x. **JOHN SNOWDEN**, *b.* May 16, 1805.
    xi. **RICHARD SNOWDEN**, *b.* September 1, 1807.

JOSEPH, third son of **Gerrard** and **Mary (Hall) Hopkins**, *b.* January 11, 1744-45; *m.* **ELIZABETH HOWELL**, who *d.* November 4, 1810, and her husband September 11, 1825. Issue:

i. **ISAAC HOWELL**, *b.* December 19, 1770.
ii. **PATIENCE**, *b.* November 5, 1771; *m.* **PHILIP SNOWDEN** (*q. v.*).
iii. **GERARD**, *b.* January 22, 1775; *m.*, first, October 14, 1804, **HENRIETTA**, *dau.* of **Samuel** and **Elizabeth (Thomas) Snowden** (*q. v.*); *m.*, second, December 23, 1818, **MARY**, *dau.* of William Gover.
iv. v. **HANNAH** and **MARY**, twins, *b.* April 12, 1777.
vi. **MARGARET**, *b.* March 2, 1779.

vii. viii. **JOSEPH** and **ELIZABETH**, twins, *b.* March 10, 1781.
ix.　　**ISAAC GRAY**, *b.* June 16, 1783.
x.　　**PRISCILLA**, *b.* October 24, 1785.
xi.　　**MARY**, *b.* April 9, 1788.
xii.　　**SAMUEL**, *b.* April 9, 1790 ; *m.* **RACHEL WORTHINGTON.**
xiii.　　**SARAH**, *b.* September 3, 1792.

RICHARD, fourth son of **Gerrard** and **Mary (Hall) Hopkins**, *b.* March 20, 1747–48 ; *m.*, December 23, 1774, **ANN**, *dau.* of **Samuel** and **Elizabeth (Thomas) Snowden** (*q. v.*), who *d.* March 16, 1818, and her husband *d.* September 20, 1823.　Issue :

i.　　**ELIZABETH**, *b.* November 20, 1775 ; *m.* —— **PLUMMER**, and *d.* June 25, 1806.
ii.　　**GERARD R.**, *b.* August 10, 1777, *of whom presently.*
iii.　　**MARY**, *b.* September 1, 1779.
iv.　　**SAMUEL SNOWDEN**, *b.* July 15, 1783.
v.　　**HENRIETTA SNOWDEN**, *b.* January 20, 1786 ; *m.* —— **PLUM-MER**, and *d.* December 19, 1862.
vi.　　**ANN**, *b.* June 29, 1789, *d. u.* October 8, 1864.
vii.　　**RICHARD**, *b.* December 26, 1791 ; *d. u.* August 2, 1872.
viii.　　**SARAH**, *b.* April 16, 1793, *d. u.* in 1874.
ix.　　**MARY JANET**, *b.* October 6, 1796.

GERARD R., eldest son of **Richard** and **Ann (Snowden) Hopkins**, *b.* August 10, 1777 ; *m.* **PATIENCE HOWELL**, *dau.* of **Dr. Elisha** and **Hannah (Howell) Hopkins.**　Issue :

i.　　**LOUISA MARIA.**
ii.　　**EMMELINE PATIENCE.**
iii.　　**ROBERT BARCLAY**, lived in Louisville, Ky. ; *m.* **CATHERINE MOORE EWING.**　Issue :
　　i.　　**ROBERT.**
　　ii.　　**KATIE**, *m.* —— **THOMPSON.**
　　iii.　　**THOMAS BUTLER.**
　　iv.　　**SALLIE.**
　　v.　　**MARSHALL EWING.**
iv.　　**ALFRED THOMAS**, lived in Louisville, Ky. ; *m.* **LOUISA XAVIER ROBINSON.**　Issue :
　　i.　　**MARGARET HOWELL.** ii. **NANNIE.** iii. **SUSAN.** iv. **ROBINSON.** v. **LOUISA.**

SAMUEL, fourth son of **Gerrard** and **Margaret (Johns) Hopkins**, *b.* January 16, 1713–14 ; *m.*, September 2, 1740, **SARAH**, *dau.* of **John** and **Cassandra (Smith) Giles** (*q. v.*), who *d.* May 15, 1795.　Issue :

i. **GERRARD,** *b.* April 26, 1742 ; *m.*, first, —— **DAWES.** Issue :

   i. **MARGARET,** *m.* **THOMAS SAUNDERSON.** Issue :
      i. **Kitty.**
      ii. **Nancy.**
      iii. **Sarah,** *m.* **Severn Savage** and had an only *dau.* Margaret, *m.* Henry Alnutt, of Baltimore, Md., and had a son, E. Severn, *m.* Annie Coulter.

   GERRARD HOPKINS, *m.*, second, December 19, 1778. **RACHEL (WILLSON),** widow of **Samuel Harris,** and *dau.* of **Henry Willson** (*q. v.*), and *d.* April 18, 1800. Further issue :

   ii. **HENRY,** *b.* September 23, 1779.
   iii. **PRISCILLA,** *b.* December 4, 1780 ; *m.* **ABRAHAM BARKER,** of Philadelphia. Issue :
      i. **Sarah,** *m.* **Saunderson Robert.**
      ii. **Henry.**
      iii. **Ann,** *m.* **William Fell Johnson.** Issue : Kate, Marshall, and Robert.
   iv. **GERARD,** *b.* June 27, 1786 ; *d.* August 6, 1807.
   v. **RICHARD,** *b.* December 9, 1791.

ii. **SAMUEL,** *b.* December 9, 1743, removed to New York and *m.* there. Issue :

   i. **SALLIE,** *m.* **WILLIAM SHOTWELL.**
   ii. **ELIZABETH,** *m.* **EDWARD KING.**
   iii. ——, *m.* **JOSEPH JAMES.**
   iv. ——, *m.* —— **HARTSHORNE.**
   v. **NANCY.**

iii. **JOHN,** *b.* January 4, 1745–46 ; *m.*, November 24, 1768, **ELIZABETH,** *dau.* of **Joseph** and **Sarah Chew** (*q. v.*), who *d.* September 25, 1806, having had issue :

   i. **SARAH,** *m.* **JOSEPH HOPKINS** (*q. v.*).
   ii. **HARRIET,** *m.* **CHARLES BRIAN.**
   iii. **THOMAS,** *b.* December 19, 1774 ; *d.* at sea, July 16, 1798.

iv. **MARGARET,** *b.* September 2, 1747 ; *m.*, in 1771, **JOB HUNT.** Issue :

   i. **JOHNS,** *m.* **SARAH BOSLEY.**
   ii. **MIRIAM,** *m.* **LEWIS EVANS.**
   iii. **SARAH,** *m.* **JOHN DEVER.**
   iv. **JESSE,** *m.* **MARGARET YONDT.**
   v. **ELIZABETH,** *m.* **DANIEL STANSBURY.**
   vi. **JOB.**

v. **PHILIP,** *b.* September 30, 1749 ; *m.* ——. Issue :
   SARAH, *m.* **THOMAS MATTHEWS.**

vi. **ELIZABETH,** *b.* August 17, 1751 ; *m.*, in 1803, **ISAAC WEBSTER,** and *d. s. p.*

vii. **JAMES,** *d. u.*

viii. **CASSANDRA,** *b.* January 6, 1755 ; *m.*, first, **JOHN ELLICOTT** (*q. v.*), who *d. s. p.* ; *m.*, second, before 1794, **JOSEPH THORNBURGH,** and *d.* March 24, 1812. Issue :

i. **ELIZABETH,** *m.* **EDWARD DENNISON.**
ii. **SARAH,** *m.* **DR. McCAULEY.**
iii. **DEBORAH,** *m.* **JOHN WEBSTER.**
iv. **MARGARET.**

ix. **RICHARD,** *b.* August 31, 1756, *d. y.*

x. **JOSEPH,** *b.* September 2, 1758 ; *m.* and had a *dau.,* **ELIZA,** *m.* **JOSEPH ZANE.**

xi. **WILLIAM,** *b.* July 23, 1760 ; *m.* —— **TWINING.** Issue :

    SARAH, *m.* —— **LYON.**

xii. **NICHOLAS,** *d. y.*

xiii. **JOHNS,** *b.* June 6, 1764, *of whom presently.* •

JOHNS, youngest son of **Samuel** and **Sarah (Giles) Hopkins,** *b.* June 6, 1764 ; *m.* **ELIZABETH BRIAN.** Issue :

i. **SAMUEL,** *m.* **MARY ANN HILL,** of Harford Co., Md., and *d. s. p.*

ii. **JAMES,** *b.* November 9, 1802 ; *m.* **ELIZA JACQUETTE,** and both *d.* since 1878. Issue :

    i. **VIRGINIA,** *m.* **JOHN P. RAU,** of Baltimore. After his death his widow removed to York, Pa., and *d.* Issue (surname RAU) :

        i. **James,** *d. u.*
        ii. **Adèle Virginia,** *d. u.*
        iii. **Philip Johns,** Attorney-at-Law, of York, Pa.

    ii. **ELIZA,** *m.* **JAMES McCALMONT JOHNS,** of Delaware. Issue (surname JOHNS) :

        i. **Frank.** ii. **Clayton.** iii. **Virginia Hopkins.**

    iii. **REBECCA,** *m.* **JACOB SMALL,** of York, Pa., who *d.* Issue (surname SMALL) :

        i. **Charles Hopkins.** ii. **Jacob Etler.**

    iv. **JOHNS GERARD.**
    v. **SAMUEL.**

iii. **WILLIAM,** *m.* **MARY ANN DUER,** and their issue *d. i.*

iv. **GERARD,** *m.* **ANN CHANDLER.** Issue :

    i. **ANNA,** *m.* —— **UNDERHILL,** of New York.
    ii. **GERARDINE.**
    iii. **FRANK.**
    iv. **ZAYDEE,** *m.* **GEORGE A. POPE,** of the iron firm of Pope, Cole & Co., of Baltimore, Md.

v. **JOSEPH,** *m.* ——. Issue :

    i. **CAROLINE.** ii. **FRANK.** iii. **JOHNS.**

vi. **SARAH,** *m.* **HENRY McELDERRY,** of Baltimore Co., Md., who *d.* Issue (surname McELDERRY) :

    i. **ANNIE,** *m.* **JOHN W. DONN,** of the United States Coast Survey. Issue (surname DONN) :

        i. **John.** ii. **Bessie.** iii. **Henry.**

    ii. **MARY,** *m.* **CAPTAIN WILLIAM KNOWER,** United States Army, and had two sons, Henry and William.

    iii. **HENRY,** of the United States Army.

iv.   **ELIZABETH.**
v.   **THOMAS.**
vi.   **JEAN.**
vii.   **HUGH.**

vii.   **MARGARET,** *m.* **HENRY BOGGS** and *d. s. p.*

viii.   **MARY,** *m.* **CHARLES WORTHINGTON HOPKINS,** of Harford Co., Md.   Issue :

    i.   **RACHEL.** ii. **ELIZABETH.** iii. **JOHN.**

ix.   **EDWARD,** *m.* **ANNA WEED,** of Connecticut.   Issue :
    JOSEPHINE.

WILLIAM, sixth son of **Gerrard** and **Margaret (Johns) Hopkins,** *b.* August 8, 1717 ; *m.* **RACHEL ORRICK.**   Issue :

i.   **GERRARD,** *m.* ———.   Issue :
    LEVIN, FRANCES, WILLIAM, SUSAN, GRACE, and **EMILY.**

ii.   **ELIZABETH,** *m.* **WILLIAM HUSBAND.**   Issue (surname HUSBAND) :

    i.   **ELIZABETH,** *m.* **JOHN QUARLES.**
    ii.   **RACHEL,** *m.* ——— **WEAVER.**
    iii.   **POLLY,** *m.* ——— **KELLY,** Attorney-at-Law, Baltimore, Md., and had a *dau.,* **Maria.**
    iv.   **SUSANNA,** *m.* **WILLIAM BAGLEY.**

iii.   **RACHEL.**

iv.   **SUSANNAH,** *m.,* December 4, 1778, **GEORGE MASON,** of Philadelphia.   A memoir of his life and some of her letters were edited and published by her *dau.,* **RACHEL.**   She *d.* October 13, 1805.   Issue (surname MASON) :

    i.   **WILLIAM,** *b.* September 27, 1779 ; *d.* June 22, 1796.
    ii.   **RACHEL,** *b.* October 16, 1783 ; *d. u.* April 8, 1849.
    iii.   **GEORGE,** *b.* January 1, 1782 ; *d. u.* March 27, 1869.
    iv.   **SUSANNAH HOPKINS,** *b.* May 18, 1785 ; *d.* June 26, 1796.

v.   **WILLIAM,** *d. u.*
vi.   **JOHN.**
vii.   **LEVIN,** *m.,* May 18, 1780, **FRANCES WALLACE.**   Issue :

    i.   **ELIZABETH,** *d. u.*
    ii.   **JOEL,** *m.* **HARRIET (HARGROVE)** ———, widow, and *d. s. p.*

viii.   **HANNAH MOORE,** *m.,* first, **RICHARD,** son of **Samuel** and **Elizabeth Snowden** (*q. v.*) ; *m.,* second, December 25, 1788, **EDWARD WATERS.**

ix.   **CHARLES,** *m.* **ANN JENKINS,** widow.   Issue :
    FRANCIS, entered the Jesuit Order.

x.   **SAMUEL,** *b.* March 10, 1764, *of whom presently.*

SAMUEL, youngest son of **William** and **Rachel (Orrick) Hopkins,** *b.* March 10, 1764, settled in Harford Co., Md. ; *m.,* in December, 1790, **SARAH,** *dau.* of **Joseph** and **Mary (Pusey) Hus-**

band; her mother afterward *m.* a Mifflin ; and her brother, Samuel Husband, *m.* Rachel Snowden (*q. v.*).

SAMUEL HOPKINS, *d.* May 2, 1839 ; and his wife, March 8, 1841, aged seventy-one years. Issue :

i. **RACHEL,** *b.* August 27, 1793 ; *d.* March 28, 1805.
ii. **MARY,** *b.* July 26, 1794; *m.,* November 25, 1824, **JOSHUA MAT-THEWS,** and *d.* November 8, 1843. Issue :

   i. **ANNA HUMPHREY,** *b.* April 4, 1827 ; *m.,* January 16, 1851, **ALPHEUS P. SHARP,** of Baltimore, and *d.* March 7, 1894. Issue :
     George Matthews, *b.* November 17, 1851, Attorney-at-Law.
   ii. **SAMUEL HOPKINS,** *b.* November 18, 1828, resides in the house which Gerrard Hopkins built for his son, William, about 1740 ; *m.,* in September, 1860, **RUTH HANNAH,** *dau.* of Joseph and Tacy Branson. Issue :
     Tacy, Joshua H., and Mary.
   iii. **SARAH H.,** *b.* April 22, 1831 ; *d. u.* in May, 1853.
   iv. **LYDIA HOPKINS,** *b.* April 20, 1834 ; *m.* **JOSEPH H. KENT,** and *d.* February 8, 1875. Issue :
     i. **Maria.**
     ii. **Anna M.**
     iii. **George M.,** *d. i.*

iii. **ELIZABETH,** *b.* October 8, 1795, *d. i.*
iv. **JOSHUA,** *b.* February 12, 1797 ; *d.* June 14, 1863.
v. **JOSEPH,** *b.* February 24, 1798 ; *d.* October 22, 1869.
vi. **HANNAH,** *b.* February 27, 1800 ; *m.,* April 24, 1851, **GEORGE HAT-TON,** who *d. s. p.*
vii. **LYDIA,** *b.* February 28, 1802 ; *d.* April 10, 1839.
viii. **WILLIAM,** *b.* March 29, 1804 ; *m.,* June 24, 1844, **MARGARET,** *dau.* of Joshua and Margaret Husband, and *d.* January 23, 1866.
ix. **LEVIN HILL,** *b.* March 16, 1807 ; *d.* January 20, 1833.
x. **ELIZA H.,** *b.* November 26, 1807 ; *m.,* October 22, 1844, **AMOS B.,** son of Aaron and Susannah Shaw, and *d.* October 6, 1854. Issue :
   JOSHUA HOPKINS, *b.* August 13, 1845; *m.* **LOUISA SULLIVAN,** and *d.* in 1874. Issue :
     George J.
xi. **SARAH ANN,** *b.* March 1, 1810 ; *d.* January 21, 1826.

JOHNS, youngest son of **Gerrard** and **Margaret (Johns) Hop-kins,** *b.* October 30, 1720 ; *m.,* first, in May, 1744, **MARY GIL-LISS,** and had one son, **EZEKIEL,** *b.* May 11, 1747. After his first wife's death **JOHNS HOPKINS** *m.,* second, November 14, 1749, **MARY,** *dau.* of **Joseph Richardson** (*q. v.*), and widow of **Colonel John Crockett,** of the British Army, and had a son, **JOHNS,** *b.* July 8, 1751, who *m.,* first, May 15, 1775, **ELIZABETH,** *dau.* of **William** and **Margaret (Thomas) Harris** (*q. v.*) ; *m.,* second, April 13, 1779, **CATHERINE HOWELL,** of

Philadelphia, and removed to Charleston, S. C. **JOHNS HOPKINS, Sr.,** *m.,* third, February 16, 1758, **ELIZABETH,** *dau.* of **Samuel** and **Mary (Snowden) Thomas.** Issue by her :

i.   **SAMUEL,** *b.* February 3, 1759 (*q. v.*).

ii.   **PHILIP,** *b.* September 24, 1760 ; *m.,* March, 21, 1787, **MARY,** *dau.* of **Isaiah Boone,** and *d.* July 25, 1814. His wife *d.* September 15, 1816, aged forty-six years. Issue :

    i.   **HANNAH,** *b.* April 10, 1788 ; *m.,* July 2, 1807, **JACOB JANNEY,** and *d.* November 1, 1819. Issue :

        i.   **Philip Hopkins,** *b.* June 20, 1808.
        ii.   **Lewis,** *b.* April 14, 1810.
        iii.   **Mary,** *b.* January 27, 1812.
        iv.   **Henry,** *b.* April 27, 1814.

    ii.   **JOHNS,** *b.* May 28, 1790.
    iii.   **ELIZABETH,** *b.* June 3, 1791.
    iv.   **ISAIAH BOONE,** *b.* July 25. 1793.
    v.   **SUSANNAH,** *b.* October 2, 1795 ; *d.* April 2, 1817.
    vi.   **EZEKIEL,** *b.* December 7, 1797.
    vii.   **HESTHER,** *b.* April 4, 1800.
    viii. **MARY,** *b.* December 10, 1800 ; *d. u.* September 14, 1824.
    ix.   **ANN,** *b.* May 10, 1805.
    x.   **RACHEL,** *b.* May 2, 1808.
    xi.   **RICHARD,** *b.* July 28, 1810.
    xii.   **SARAH,** *b.* July 20, 1812.

iii.   **RICHARD,** *b.* March 2, 1762 ; *m.* **HANNAH HAMMOND.**
iv.   **MARY,** *b.* January 7, 1764 ; *m.,* in March, 1787, **SAMUEL PEACH.**
v.   **MARGRIT,** *b.* February 20, 1766 ; *m.* **JESSE TYSON** (*q. v.*).
vi.   **GERARD T.,** *b.* October 24, 1769, *of whom presently.*
vii.   **ELIZABETH,** *m.,* March 26, 1825, **JOHN,** son of **Joseph** and **Hannah Janney.**
viii. **EVAN,** *b.* November 30, 1772 ; *m.,* January 25, 1810, **ELIZABETH,** *dau.* of **Joseph** and **Elizabeth Hopkins.** Issue :

    i.   **ELIZABETH,** *b.* October 26, 1810.
    ii.   **JOSEPH,** *b.* November 26, 1812.

ix.   **ANN,** *b.* February 26, 1775 ; *m.,* November 5, 1801, **THOMAS,** son of **Caleb** and **Grace Shrieves.** Their descendants now live in California.
x.   **RACHEL,** *b.* September 7, 1777 ; *m.,* March 29, 1804, **ROBERT,** son of **Joseph** [1] and **Mary (Tompkins) Hough,** of Pennsylvania. Issue (surname HOUGH) :

    i.   **SAMUEL HOPKINS,** *b.* June 21, 1806 ; *m.* **MARGARETTA JOHNSON.**
    ii.   **MARY,** *m.* **JOHN BROOKS.** Issue (surname BROOKS) :

        i.   **Rachel Hough,** *m.* **Richard Stockett Mathews,** and had a *dau.,* Mary Eliza.
        ii.   **Mary Alice.**
        iii.   **Isaac, Jr.,** Attorney-at-Law.

    iii.   **ROBERT,** *m.* **MARY GORDON DICKINSON.**

xi.   **WILLIAM.**

[1] Great-grandson of Richard Hough, Provincial Councillor of Pennsylvania, in 1693 and 1700.

GERARD T., third son of **Johns** and **Elizabeth (Thomas) Hopkins**, *b.* October 24, 1769 ; *m.*, April 6, 1796, **DOROTHY**, *dau.* of **Roger** and **Mary Brooke** (*q. v.*), and *d.* in 1834. Issue :

i.   **MARY,** *b.* August 12, 1797 ; *m.*, May 12, 1817, **BENJAMIN P. MOORE.** Issue (surname MOORE) :

    i.   **ELIZABETH,** *m.* **SAMUEL B. WALTON,** of Omaha City, Neb.
    ii.   **ROBERT,** *d. s. p.*
    iii.   **DEBORAH.**
    iv.   **BENJAMIN P.,** *m.*, in 1876, **FLORENCE,** *dau.* of Jared Sparks, the historian. Issue :
        Jared Sparks, *b.* September 29, 1879.
    v., vi., vii.   **REBECCA, WILLIAM,** and **GERARD,** who all *d. s. p.*

ii.   **EDWARD,** *b.* December 9, 1798 ; *d.* March 9, 1800.
iii.   **DEBORAH,** *b.* November 27, 1800, *d. s. p.* in 1830.
iv.   **ELIZABETH,** *b.* March 31, 1802 ; *d. u.* December 9, 1890.
v.   **SARAH,** *b.* December 8, 1805, *d. s. p.*
vi.   **THOMAS,** *b.* May 19, 1811, *d. u.* February 17, 1886.
vii.   **WILLIAM,** *b.* July 5, 1813 ; *d. u.* May 27, 1881.
viii.   **GERARD T.,** *b.* October 5, 1815 ; *m.* **ELIZABETH COATES.** Issue :

    i.   **FRANCIS NEVILLE,** *m.* **FANNY MONROE,** and *d.* February 16, 1879.
    ii.   **ANNA ROBERTS,** *m.* **EVAN POULTNEY** (*q. v.*).
    iii.   **BESSIE.**
    iv.   **JOHNS,** removed to Philadelphia, was active in street railway affairs ; *m.*, December 30, 1885, —— ——, and *d.* 1895. Issue :
        Johns, *b.* May 5, 1893.
    v.   **GERARD T.**
    vi.   **ROGER BROOKE.**

ix.   **MARGARET,** *b.* August 26, 1817 ; *m.*, August, 1839, **MEREDITH HELM JOLLIFFE** (descended from John Jolliffe, who was of Norfolk Co., Va., January 22, 1662) both *d.* Issue :

    i.   **THOMAS HOPKINS,** *m.*, first, April 16, 1878, at the residence of General Francis C. Barlow, New York City, **ELLA N. BARLOW,** of Boston ; *m.*, second, **AGNES BLAKE,** *dau.* of Moses Blake Williams, of Boston, Mass.
    ii.   **WILLIAM HOPKINS,** *m.*, first, **LUCY MATTHEWS,** who *d.* January 15, 1878 ; *m.*, second, **MARY C.,** *dau.* of Dr. Hamilton Scott, of Baltimore.
    iii.   **ELIZABETH,** *m.*, May 13, 1869, **NATHANIEL B. CRENSHAW,** of Virginia, now of Germantown, Pa. Issue :

        i.   Margaret, *b.* 1874.
        ii.   John Meredith, *d. i.*
        iii.   Nathaniel B., *d. i.*
    iv.   **FANNIE,** *m.* **WILLIAM GILMOR.**

x.   **RACHEL,** *b.* May 19, 1822 ; *d. u.* May 17, 1891.

SAMUEL, eldest son of **Johns** and **Elizabeth (Thomas) Hopkins**, *b.* 1759 ; *m.*, in August, 1792, **HANNAH,** *dau.* of **Joseph** and **Hannah (Jones) Janney,** and *d.* February 9, 1814. Issue :

i.   **JOSEPH JANNEY,** *b.* August 28, 1893 ; *m.* **ELIZABETH SCO-FIELD.** Issue :

    i.   **LEWIS NEILL,** *m.,* first, **JOSEPHINE HOGE,** of Virginia, who *d.* leaving issue :

        i.   **Josephine E.**

        He *m.,* second, **LUCY T.,** *dau.* of General Corbin Braxton, of Chericoke, Va. ; further issue :

        ii.   **Lucy B.**

        iii.   **Elizabeth C.**

        iv.   **Mary T.,** *d. i.*

    ii.   **GERARD,** *m.,* October 6, 1874, **EMILY R.,** eldest *dau.* of **Nicholas** and **Henrietta Snowden** (*q. v.*), who *d.* April 29, 1886. Issue :

        i.   **Joseph Waverly,** *b.* July 15, 1875.

        ii.   **Mary Blanche,** *b.* September 23, 1876.

        iii.   **Nicholas Snowden,** *b.* September 23, 1877.

    iii.   **SAMUEL,** *m.,* in 1877, **MARTHA,** *dau.* of John M. and Elizabeth Smith (*q. r.*), and *d.* February 15, 1893. Issue :

        i.   **Samuel Harold,** *b.* June 7, 1878.

        ii.   **Matthew Smith,** *b.* December 30, 1879.

        iii.   **Elizabeth Scofield Brooke,** *b.* December 1, 1888.

        iv.   **Alda Tyson,** *b.* March 13, 1891.

    iv.   **JOSEPH S.,** *m.* **ANNETTE,** *dau.* of John Hopkins of Haddonfield, N. J. Issue :

        i.   **Helen Rolfe.** ii. **Marian.**

    v.   **JOHNS,** *d. i.*

ii.   **JOHNS,** *b.* May 19, 1795, *of whom presently.*

iii.   **ELIZA,** *b.* May 19, 1797 ; *m.* **NATHANIEL CRENSHAW,** of Virginia.

iv.   **SARAH,** *b.* February 27, 1799 ; *m.* **RICHARD M.,** son of Abijah and Jane (McPherson) Janney, who *d.* Issue (surname JANNEY) :

    i.   **JOHNS HOPKINS,** *m.* **CAROLINE SYMINGTON.** Issue :

        i.   **Lena.** ii. **Richard.** iii. **Johns.**

    ii.   **SAMUEL ABIJAH,** *m.* **MARY CATHERINE,** *dau.* of Elisha John Hall. Issue :

        i.   **Mary Brooke.** ii. **John Hall.** iii. **Sarah.** iv. **Samuel A.** v. **Joseph Elliott.** vi. **Richard Mott.**

    iii.   **JANE,** *m.* **FRANCIS WHITE** (*q. r.*).

    iv.   **HANNAH.**

    v.   **MARGARET,** *m.* **JOSEPH ELLIOTT.**

v.   **HANNAH,** *b.* November 19, 1801, *d. u.*

vi.   **SAMUEL,** *b.* November 20, 1803 ; *m.* **LAVINIA JOLLIFFE.** Issue :

    i.   **JOHN J.,** *m.* **ELIZABETH BEARD** and *d. s. p.*

    ii.   **ELLA W.,** *m.* **JAMES MONROE MERCER,** of Cedar Park, Md., who *d.* June 22, 1878. Issue (surname MERCER) :

        i.   **Samuel H.** ii. **Mary.** iii. **George Douglas.** iv. **Margaret W.**

    iii.   **DR. ARUNDEL,** *d. u.* at Paris.

    iv.   **MAHLON.**

vii.   **MAHLON JANNEY,** *b.* June 18, 1805.

viii.   **PHILIP,** *b.* May 31, 1807.

ix.   MARGARET, *m.*, being his second wife, MILES WHITE, of North
       Carolina, and *d.* March, 1891 ; he *d.* in March, 1876. Issue by his
       first wife (surname WHITE) :

   i.   DR. ELIAS, *d. s. p.*
   ii.   FRANCIS, *m.* JANE, *dau.* of Richard M. and Sarah Janney (*q. v.*). Issue :

      i.   Miles, *m.*, April, 1890, Virginia Purviance, *dau.* of Stephen Bonsal,
         of Baltimore.
      ii.   Sarah, *d. u.*
      iii. Francis.
      iv.   Richard.

x.   GERARD, *b.* November 26, 1809.
xi.   MARY, *b.* October 8, 1811.

JOHNS, second son of **Samuel** and **Hannah (Janney) Hopkins,** *b.* May 19, 1795, began his career in Baltimore as a clerk.
With his uncles' assistance he branched out in business for himself,
and entered upon a career of money-making that monopolized all his
time and energy. He became the financial authority of the city ;
furnishing capital for its business. Close in his dealings, indif-
ferent in his dress, and curt in his manner, he was a man of un-
doubted breadth of mind and soundness of judgment ; and although
he is largely remembered in Baltimore for his parsimony, he did
much good in a charitable way that the public never knew of. He
was an influential factor in the prosperity of the Baltimore & Ohio
Railroad during John W. Garrett's presidency, and it was his cool-
ness that saved the banks of Baltimore in 1873. He *d.*, December
24, 1873, leaving a fortune of upwards of $8,000,000, which he had
accumulated by persistent thrift and judicious investment. Mr.
Hopkins left about $1,000,000 to his relatives, and devoted the
remainder of his great fortune to the establishment of a university
and a hospital to bear his name. To the university he gave about
$3,000,000 and his country-seat ; to the hospital, which he intended
to be the finest institution of its kind in the world, he gave more, the
endowment being worth about $3,400,000, and including fourteen
and a-half acres of ground on Broadway—a splendid elevation on
one of the most beautiful thoroughfares of Baltimore.

The university was opened on October 3, 1876, with a corps of
professors and associates of eminent attainments, and is already one
of the chief seats of learning and culture in the country. By the
provisions of the will, twenty free scholarships were founded, open
to students from Maryland, Virginia, and North Carolina. The
trustees have also founded ten fellowships for meritorious students,
and five free scholarships open to candidates from any part of the

country. The will also provided for Schools of Law, Medicine, and Agriculture, as parts of the University.

Mr. Hopkins in his will directed that the hospital should be for the " indigent sick of the city [Baltimore] and its environs, without regard to sex, age, or color." A home for convalescents will be built in the country, and an orphan asylum of large capacity, for colored children, will also be established, both being in connection with the same trust. The work on the hospital was begun in 1879 and it was opened on May 7, 1889, leaving two buildings yet to be erected, but these will not be begun until the hospital is in full operation and there is a demand for more room. On the buildings, including heating and ventilation, $1,570,000 have so far been spent, and the total expenditures upon buildings and grounds reach $2,050,000—or an average of $9,150 for each free bed. All this vast sum has been taken from the income, and the original endowment has not only remained untouched, but has been increased over $200,000.

JOHN W., son of **Samuel**[1] and **Rachel Hopkins**, *m.* **ELIZA**, *dau.* of **Thomas S.** and **Elizabeth (Morgan) Chew** (*q. v.*). Issue :

i.   **ELLEN**, *m.* **THOMAS DALLAM**, *d. s. p.*

ii.   **THOMAS**, *m.* **MARGARET MATTHEWS**, of Baltimore Co. Issue :

        LAURA WILSON, STANLEY, and HERBERT.

iii. **FRANCIS**, *m.*, June 10, 1863, **ANNIE ELLEN**, *dau.* of **Samuel** and **Hannah Harper.** Issue :

    i.   LILLIE M., *b.* 1864; *m.*, April 19, 1894, BENJAMIN H. SILVER.
    ii.   ELLEN GENETTE, *b.* 1865; *m.* HORACE GREELEY BROWN.
    iii. MAGGIE CHEW, *b.* 1866.
    iv. ALICE HARPER, *b.* 1868; *d.* 1881.
    v.   FRANCIS WATSON, *b.* 1870.
    vi. JOHN WORTHINGTON, *b.* 1873.
    vii. ANNA JAY, *b.* 1878.
    viii. GRACE, *b.* 1884.

iv. **SAMUEL**, *m.* **LUCY**, *dau.* of **Fletcher** and **Helen Jones.** Issue :

    i.   EDWIN, *b.* 1877.
    ii.   JOHN FLETCHER, *b.* 1879.
    iii. SAMUEL ROWLAND, *b.* 1884.
    iv. ALLAN LESLEY, *b.* 1889.
    v.   CARROLL CRESWELL, *b.* 1890.
    vi. BESSIE, *b.* and *d.* 1891.
    vii. HELEN, *b.* 1892.

Authorities : Maryland Friends' Records and family papers, with some help from wills before 1776.

[1] Probably son of Joseph and Elizabeth (Howell) Hopkins (*q. v.*), and *b.* 1790.

HOUGHTELING

The first of this name in America was **JAN WILLEMSEN HOOGTEYLING,** who settled at Esopus (now Kingston), N. Y., in 1661. Five generations in unbroken descent lived and died there before **JACOBUS** or **JAMES HOUGHTE-LING,** Doctor of Medicine, who *m.,* February 26, 1807, **ERNESTINE FREDERICA JEANNETTE** (*q. v.*), eldest *dau.* of **Baron Frederic Augustus De Zeng** by **Mary Lawrence,** his wife, and *d.* December 22, 1849, at Clyde, N. Y. His widow *d.* April 9, 1859. Issue :

i.   **MARY MATILDA,** *b.* November 11, 1808, at Kingston ; *d.* May 12, 1824, at Geneva, N. Y.

ii.   **CATHERINE ARRIETTA,** *b.* July 19, 1810, at Kingston.

iii.   **SUSAN AMELIA,** *b.* March 30, 1812, at Kingston ; *m.*, June 5, 1837, at Geneva, N. Y., **CHARLES D. LAWTON,** and *d.* July 24, 1886, at Berkeley, Cal., the first death from natural causes in her generation of the family for sixty-two years. Issue (surname LAWTON):

    i.   **JAMES H.,** *dec.*
    ii.   **CHARLES A.,** *m.,* and has four children.
    iii.   **WATSON.**
    iv.   **GEORGE,** *dec.*
    v.   **WILLIAM H.,** *m. s. p.*
    vi.   **FRANK,** *m.,* with three children.

iv.   **LAURA LOUISE,** *b.* December 16, 1813, at Bainbridge, N. Y. ; *m.,* March 27, 1833, at Geneva, N. Y., **HIRAM REYNOLDS,** *d.* July 27, 1892, at Kenosha, Wis. Issue (surname REYNOLDS):

    i.   **ERNESTINE,** *m.,* December 18, 1866, at Chicago, Ill., **AUGUSTINE LAWRENCE McCREA.**
    ii.   **AGNES.**
    iii.   **LOUISE,** *m.,* July 31, 1873, at Chicago, **GEORGE K. SHOENBERGER.**

v.   **JAMES LAWRENCE,** *b.* August 27, 1815, at Bainbridge ; *m.,* 1837, **ZILMENA ADELLE,** and was accidentally killed in Louisiana, May 30, 1852.

vi.   **CAROLINE DE ZENG,** *b.* July 8, 1817, at Bainbridge ; *m.,* December 18, 1838, at Clyde, **CHARLES S. DE ZENG.** Issue (surname DE ZENG):

i. **JAMES REES.**
ii. **VIRGINIA,** *d.*
iii. **LAURA,** *m.* May 10, 1861, **DR. WILLIAM HEISE,** and *d.* March 27, 1871.
iv. **ROBERT,** *d.*
v. **CHARLES M.**
vi. **JOSEPHINE.**
vii. **LAWRENCE.**
viii. **WILLIAM.**

vii. **WILLIAM DE ZENG,** *b.* August 23, 1819, *of whom presently.*

viii. **AUGUSTA ANNA,** *b.* July 27, 1821, at Geneva; *m.,* October 19, 1842, at Clyde, N. Y., **JOHN A. RHODES,** and *d.* April 8, 1892, at Chicago. Issue (surname RHODES).

i. **JAMES HOUGHTELING,** *m.,* November 20, 1869, at Rockford, Ill., **CLARA KEYT.**
ii. **MARY WRIGHT,** *m.,* 1864, **WILLIAM B. SMITHELL,** *d. s. p.* 1874.
iii. **CATHERINE HOUGHTELING,** *m.,* first, 1865, **EDWARD LA COSTE;** *m.,* second, December, 1881, **HENRY G. OBERG.**
iv. **LOUISE AUGUSTA,** *m.,* November 18, 1872, at Chicago, **AMBROSE S. DELEWARE,** and has four children.

ix. **JANE ROSE,** *b.* September 8, 1823, at Geneva; *m.,* June 28, 1852, **CYRUS GROSVENOR PERKINS,** of La Fayette, Ind., and *d.* March 4, 1892, at San Francisco. Issue (surname PERKINS):

i. **JANET RUSSELL.**
ii. **ERNEST,** *d.*

x. **ABRAM,** *b.* September 27, 1825; *m.,* October 5, 1853, **ELIZA STOUT McGINNIS,** of Battle Creek, Mich., and was accidentally killed January 22, 1872. Issue:

AMELIA, CAROLINE DE ZENG, and **MARGARET.**

xi. **SARAH LAWRENCE,** *b.* March 27, 1828, at Geneva; *m.,* May 2, 1854, at Clyde, **EDMUND B. HENDRICK.** Issue (surname HENDRICK):

MARY ERNESTINE, *m.,* 1893, **CLARENCE P. BARTLETT,** of Los Angeles, Cal.

WILLIAM DE ZENG, second son of **Dr. James** and **Ernestine F. A. J. (De Zeng) Houghteling,** *b.* August 23, 1819, at Geneva, N. Y., removed to Chicago, Ill., in 1855 and became one of the leading merchants of that city. He has taken an active interest in field sports, and in his seventy-sixth year still rides to hounds. He *m.,* 1853, at Allegan, Mich., **MARCIA E.,** *dau.* of **Dr. John Stockbridge,** of Bath, Me., whose ancestor settled at Scituate, Mass., in 1635; by his wife, **Eliza,** *dau.* of **John Russell,** publisher of the *Columbian Centinel,* of Boston. Issue:

i. **ELIZA RUSSELL,** *m.,* 1878, at Chicago, **OWEN F. ALDIS,** and *d.* 1888, leaving a son, **OWEN WILLIAM.**
ii. **JAMES LAWRENCE,** *of whom presently.*

iii.   **JOSEPH,** *d. i.*
iv.   **JOSEPHINE,** *m.,* 1887, at San Francisco, Cal., **A. CASS CAN-FIELD.** Issue (surname CANFIELD) :

        LAURA and **MARY.**

v.   **LAURA,** *d. u.*
vi.   **WILLIAM,** *d. i.*

JAMES LAWRENCE, only surviving son of **William De Zeng** and **Marcia E. (Stockbridge) Houghteling,** is (in 1895) about forty years old, the only male of his generation with male issue, as was his father and grandfather before him. He is a graduate of Yale College and a partner in the banking-house of Peabody, Houghteling & Co., of Chicago, an active member of the Protestant Episcopal Church, and a vestryman of S. James's Parish, Chicago ; but above all else, on S. Andrew's Day, 1883, the founder of the Brotherhood of S. Andrew, which has already done such a great work among the young men of the Church. If kept upon its original lines and devoted with a single eye to the spread of Christ's kingdom among men by the faithful observance of its twofold Rule of Prayer and Service, many future generations of churchmen will rise up and call its founder blessed. **MR. HOUGHTELING** *m.,* September 20, 1879, at Chicago, **LUCRETIA TEN BROECK,** *dau.* of **Francis Bolles** and **Harriot Cutter (Ten Broeck) Peabody.**[1] Issue :

i.   **FRANCIS STOCKBRIDGE.**
ii.   **JAMES LAWRENCE,** Jr.
iii.   **HARRIOT PEABODY.**
iv.   **WILLIAM.**
v.   **LEILA.**

Authorities : Records of the Old Dutch Church at Kingston, N. Y., and family papers, through J. L. Houghteling, Esq., and Miss Agnes Reynolds.

[1] Mrs. Peabody was descended from Governor Peter Stuyvesant, of New Amsterdam, and in 1683 her direct ancestor, Wessels ten Broeck, stood godfather to Dina, granddaughter of the first Hoogteling, and Johannes Ten Broeck, in 1717, did like duty for Sara, a niece of Dina Hoogteling, the friendship between the families being thus two hundred years old.

HOWARD, OF BELVIDERE, MD.

JOHN EAGER, son of **Cornelius Howard,** of the " Forest," Baltimore Co., by his wife, **Ruth Eager,** of "Belvidere," *b.* June 4, **1752,** entered the Revolutionary Army as a Captain in 1776, appointed Colonel of the Second Maryland Regiment in 1777, afterwards a General ; distinguished himself by great bravery during the war, especially at the battle of Cowpens, S. C. Was a member of the Continental Congress in 1787 ; Governor of Maryland, 1788–91 ; United States Senator from Maryland, 1796–1803, and President, *pro tem.,* of the Senate during part of the Sixth Congress. He *m.,* May 18, 1787, **MARGARET OSWALD,** *dau.* of **Chief-Justice** Chew (*q. v.*). She *d.* May 29, 1824, and her husband *d.* October 12, 1827. Issue :

i.   **JOHN EAGER,** *b.* June 25, 1788 ; *m.* **CORNELIA ANNABELLA READ,** December 20, 1820, and *d. s. p.,* surviving December 23, 1862.

ii.   **GEORGE,** *b.* November 21, 1789, *of whom presently.*

iii.   **BENJAMIN CHEW,** *b.* November 5, 1791 (*q. v.*).

iv.   **WILLIAM,** *b.* December 16, 1793, of high scientific attainments ; *m.,* April 14, 1828, **REBECCA ANN KEY,** and *d.* August 25, 1834.

v.   **JULIANA ELIZABETH,** *b.* May 3, 1796; *m.,* December 7, 1818, **JOHN McHENRY,** of Sudbrooke, Baltimore Co., son of **James** and **Margaretta (Caldwell) McHenry.** She *d.* May 22, 1821, and her husband *d.* October 9, 1822.

vi.   **JAMES,** *b.* December 17, 1797 (*q. v.*).

vii.   **SOPHIA CARROLL,** *b.* March 6, 1800 ; *m.,* April 7, 1825, **WILLIAM GEORGE READ,** and *d.,* leaving issue, November 22, 1880.

viii.   **CHARLES,** *b.* April 26, 1802 ; *m.,* November 9, 1825, **ELIZABETH**

GENERAL JOHN EAGER HOWARD, U.S.A.

From a Portrait by Harding

PHŒBE, *dau.* of **Francis Scott Key, Esq.,** author of the " Star-Spangled Banner," by his wife, **Mary T. Lloyd,** and *d.* June 18, 1869. Issue :

i.   **FRANCIS KEY,** *m.* **LYDIA E. H. MORRIS,** and *d.* May 29, 1872.
ii.   **JOHN EAGER.**
iii.   **CHARLES,** *m.* **MARY C. WINDER.**
iv.   **MARY LLOYD,** *m.* **EDWARD LLOYD.**
v.   **JAMES.**
vi.   **ALICE KEY,** *d. u.* 1880.
vii. **EDWARD LLOYD,** *d. u.* September 5, 1881.
viii. **McHENRY,** Attorney-at-Law, a Captain in Confederate States Army, *m.* **JULIA D.,** *dau.* of General C. G. Coleman, of Jerdone Castle, Louisa Co., Va.
ix.   **ELLEN KEY,** *m.* **CHARLTON HUNT MORGAN.**
x.   **ELIZABETH GRAY,** *d. i.*
xi.   **ANNA ARNOLD KEY,** *d. u.*

GEORGE, second son of **John Eager** and **Margaret (Chew) Howard,** *b.* November 21, 1789 ; was acting Governor of Maryland, 1831 ; Governor, 1832–33 ; *m.,* December 26, 1811, **PRUDENCE GOUGH,** *dau.* of **General Charles Ridgely,** of Hampton, Md., and *d.* August 2, 1846 ; his wife *d.* July 5, 1847. Issue :

i.   **JOHN EAGER,** *d. u.* July 3, 1838.
ii.   **PRISCILLA RIDGELY,** *m.* **EUGENE POST,** and *d.* May 5, 1837.
       Issue : a son, **EUGENE HOWARD,** *m.* **MARY ADAMS.**
iii. **MARGARET ELIZABETH,** *m.,* as his second wife, **EUGENE POST.** Issue (surname POST) :

   i.   **MARY MAGDALENE.**
   ii.   **JOHN E. H.,** *m.* **REBECCA L. NICHOLSON,** *d. s. p.* February 12, 1876.
   iii. **SOPHIA HOWARD,** *m.,* June 4, 1858, **RIDGELY DUVALL.**
   iv. **GEORGE HOWARD,** *b.* 1845, *d. i.*
   v.   **RICHARD BAYLEY,** *b.* January 8, 1847, Secretary of the Peabody Fire Insurance Company of Baltimore, *m.,* November 1, 1866, **ELLA,** *dau.* of Alexander Hamilton and Elizabeth Bordley Stump. Issue :
      i.   **Elizabeth Bordley,** *b.* August 22, 1867.
      ii.   **Alexander Hamilton Stump,** *b.* November 6, 1870.
      iii. **Martha Goldsborough,** *b.* September 24, 1880.
   vi. **WILLIAM EDWARD VOSS,** *b.* June 7, 1850 ; *m.,* April 15, 1876, **MARY ELIZABETH,** *dau.* of James and Mary Elisabeth Boyce. Issue :
      i.   **Mabel Howard,** *b.* August 20, 1878.
      ii.   **James Boyce,** *b.* January 13, 1881.

iv. **CHARLES RIDGELY,** entered United States Navy ; *m.,* December 24, 1844, **ELIZABETH ANN WATERS,** and *d.* at Panama, January 30, 1859.
v.   **SOPHIA CATHARINE,** *m.,* May 12, 1840, **RICHARD NORRIS,** he *d. s. p.* in 1879.
vi. **GEORGE,** *d.* July 7. 1876.
vii. **JACOB H.,** *d. i.*
viii. **WILLIAM,** *m.* **OCTAVIA DUVALL.**

BENJAMIN CHEW, third son of **John Eager** and **Margaret (Chew) Howard,** *b.* November 5, 1791, commanded a company at the Battle of North Point in 1814; Reporter of the United States Supreme Court from February 1, 1843, publishing twenty-four volumes of Reports; *m.,* February 24, 1818, **JANE GRANT GILMOR,** and *d.* March 6, 1872. Issue:

i. **LOUISA SHERLOCK,** *m.,* June 1, 1841, **GEORGE BRICE HOFF-MAN,** and *d.* 1876; he *d.* 1879, *s. p.* surviving.
ii. **ROBERT GILMOR,** *d. i.* December 26, 1821.
iii. **SOPHIA,** *d. u.* May 23, 1852.
iv. **MARIAN.**
v. **ANN WILLIAMS.**
vi. **JANE GILMOR,** *m.* **JOSEPH KING** (*q. v.*).
vii. **WILLIAM GILMOR,** *d. i.* March 16, 1829.
viii. **JULIANA McHENRY,** *m.* **RICHARD W. TYSON** (*q. v.*).
ix. **ELLEN GILMOR,** *m.,* December 20, 1860, **RICHARD BASSETT BAYARD** (*q. v.*).
x. **WILLIAM GILMOR,** *m.,* first, **ANNIE,** *dau.* of John Doyle, of Darjeeling, East Indies; *m.,* second, **LUCY BRENT,** and *d.* January 2, 1877.
xi. **BENJAMIN CHEW,** *d. u.*
xii. **CHARLES GILMOR,** *d. i.* 1839.

JAMES, fifth son of **John Eager** and **Margaret (Chew) Howard,** *b.* December 17, 1797; *m.,* first, **SOPHIA GOUGH,** *dau.* of **General Charles Ridgely,** of Hampton. Issue:

i. **JULIANA ELIZABETH,** *d. u.*
ii. **REV. CHARLES RIDGELY,** clergyman of the Protestant Episcopal Church; *m.* **MARY HOLLY AUSTIN,** and *d. s. p.* 1862. Memorial Church, Baltimore, is a joint memorial to him with the **Rev. H. V. D. Johns, D.D.**
iii. **MARGARET SOPHIA,** *m.* **CHARLES RIDGELY,** of Hampton, since *d.* Issue surviving (surname RIDGELY):

    i. JOHN, *m.* HELEN STEWART.
    ii. HOWARD, *m.* HELEN MORRIS, *dau.* of William A. Tucker.
    iii. OTTO EICHELBERGER, *m.* ETTA, *dau.* of Captain Thomas.
    iv. ELIZA.
    v. JULIANA ELIZABETH HOWARD.
    vi. MARGARET.

JAMES HOWARD, *m.,* second, **CATHERINE M.,** *dau.* of **William** and **Catherine W. (Johnson) Ross,** and *d.* March 19, 1870, leaving further issue.

Authorities: Family papers and Keith's Provincial Councillors of Pennsylvania.

HOWARD, OF EFFINGHAM, ENGLAND

THOMAS PLANTAGENET, surnamed "De Brotherton," eldest son of **King Edward I.**, of England, by his second wife, **Margaret**, *dau.* of Philip III., of France, *b.* June 1, 1300, was created Earl of Norfolk and Suffolk, Lord of Chepstow and Netherwent, Lord of Catherlagh and Rospont in Ireland, December 13, 1312, and Marshal of England, February 10, 1315–16, styled the Earl Marshal, July 15, 1333, being the first so designated. He *m.*, first, **ALICE**, *dau.* of **Sir Roger Halys, Knt.**, of Harwich. Issue :

i. **MARGARET**, *of whom presently.*
ii. **ALICE**, *m.* **EDWARD de MONTACUTE**, and had a *dau.*, JOAN, who *m.* **WILLIAM UFFORD**, Earl of Suffolk, and *d. s. p.*

THOMAS PLANTAGENET, *m.*, second, **MARY**, Baroness Braose, of Brembre, *dau.* of **William Lord Roos**, and widow of William Le Brus, and *d.* in August, 1338, having had a son, who became a monk at the Abbey of Ely.

MARGARET, eldest *dau.*, and eventually heiress of **Thomas Plantagenet**, *b.* about 1320, was created Duchess of Norfolk for life, September 19, 1397, and *m.*, first, before December 15, 1338, **JOHN**, sixth **LORD SEGRAVE**, who *d.* in 1353. Issue :

i. **ANNE**, a nun, Abbess of Barking.
ii. **ELIZABETH**, *of whom presently.*

MARGARET, Duchess of Norfolk, *m.*, second, **WALTER LORD de MANNY**, K.G., and *d.* May 24, 1398, having had a *dau.*, ANNE, who *m.* **JOHN HASTINGS**, Earl of Pembroke.

ELIZABETH, *dau.* and *co-h.* of **Margaret,** Duchess of Norfolk, *m.* **JOHN,** eighth Baron Mowbray of Axholme, who had issue, with others :

i.   **JOHN,** ninth Baron, *b.* 1364, created, July 15, 1377, Earl of Nottingham, *d. s. p.* February 10, 1383.

ii.   **THOMAS,** tenth Baron, created Earl of Nottingham, February 12, 1383, and Duke of Norfolk, September 29, 1397, Earl Marshal, February 10, 1397, and K.G. in 1383 ; *m.,* in 1385, **ELIZABETH,** *dau.* and *co-h.* of **Richard Fitz-Alan,** Earl of Arundel, and *d.* in 1413. Issue :

> **MARGARET,** eventually a *co-h.* of her cousin, John Mowbray, fourth Duke of Norfolk; *m.* **ROBERT,** son and heir of Sir John Howard, Knt.,[1] and had a son, John, *of whom presently.*

SIR JOHN, son of **Robert** and **Margaret (Mowbray) Howard,** *b.* 1422, was summoned as Baron de Howard, October 15, 1470, created Earl Marshal and Duke of Norfolk, June 28, 1483, K.G., April 24, 1472 ; Admiral of England, Ireland, and Aquitaine, July 25, 1483. Slain at Bosworth Field, August 22, 1485, and being attainted all his honors were forfeited. He had issue by his first wife, **CATHERINE,** *dau.* of **William Lord Molines,** with several daughters, an only son and heir, **THOMAS,** *b.* in 1443, created Earl of Surrey, June 28, 1483, attainted with his father, but restored to the Earldom of Surrey in 1489, and was Lieutenant-General of the North and Warden of the Scotch Marches about the same time. He commanded at the Battle of Flodden, September 9, 1513, which resulted in the death of James IV. and utter defeat of the Scottish army. February 1, 1514, he was created Duke of Norfolk and Earl Marshal. He was also Lord Treasurer and K.G., and *d.* May 21, 1524, having had issue by his second wife, **AGNES,** sister and heiress of **Sir Philip Tilney, Knt.,** of Boston, with others, an eldest son, **WILLIAM,** who was created Baron Howard, of Effingham, and was the father of the Lord High Admiral who defeated the Spanish Armada in 1588 ; and a sixth *dau.,* **CATHERINE,** *m.* **RICE AP GRIFFITH** (*q. v.*).

Authorities : Sandford and Townsend's Great Governing Families ; Doyle's Official Baronage, and Sharpe's Peerage, 1829.

---

[1] He was descended from Sir William Howard, or Haward, one of the special justices appointed by Edward I. to hold assizes throughout the realm in 1293.

THOMAS HOWARD, EARL OF SURREY
From an Ancient Book of Heraldry, 1597

HOWARD, OF WASHINGTON, D. C.

SIR HENRY HOWARD, of England, came to the Province of Maryland in 1706, and *m.* **SARAH,** *dau.* of **John** and **Honor (Elder) Dorsey.** Issue :

i.   **JARED,** or **GERARD.**
ii.   **DR. JOHN DORSEY.**
iii.   **JOSHUA,** *of whom presently.*
iv.   **EPHRAIM.**
v.   **SARAH.**
vi.   **RACHEL.**
vii. **HONOR ELDER DORSEY.**

JOSHUA, son of **Sir Henry** and **Sarah (Dorsey) Howard,** *m.,* first, **REBECCA OWINGS ;** *m.,* second, a **MRS. WARFIELD.** By his first wife he had issue :

i.   **SARAH,** *m.* —— **WINCHESTER.**
ii.   **MARY,** *m.* **SAMUEL THOMAS** (*q. v.*).
iii.   **RACHEAL,** *m.* **SAMUEL ROBERTSON.**
iv.   **SAMUEL,** *m.* —— **D'ARCEY,** and was father of **ELI HOWARD,** of Baltimore, and grandfather of **Mrs. John Leary, Mrs. Fannie Saltzer,** and **Emma Howard.**
v.   **JOSEPH,** *of whom presently.*
vi.   **BEALE.**
vii. **DEBORAH,** *m.* —— **D'ARCEY.**
viii. **JOSHUA.**
ix.   **HENRY** (*q. v.*).

JOSEPH, second son of **Joshua** and **Rebecca (Owings) Howard,** *m.* **MARY,** fourth *dau.* of **Samuel** and **Mary (Cowman) Thomas.** Issue :

i.   **SAMUEL,** *d. s. p.*
ii.   **MARIA,** *m.* —— **IRVINGS.**
iii. **MARY,** *m.* **JAMES THORNTON.**

iv.   FLODOARDO, *of whom presently.*
v.   SARAH ANN, *m.* —— TIBBALS, and *d.*   Issue :

    i.   DR. WILLIAM F., of Cincinnati, O.
    ii.   ANNIE.

vi.   HENRIETTA, *m.* —— McKENZIE.
vii. ELIZABETH, *m.* —— THORNTON.
viii. LAWRENCE.

FLODOARDO, second son of **Joseph** and **Mary (Thomas) Howard**, *b.* May 11, 1811, was a physician ; *m.*, June 11, 1833, **LYDIA MARIA**, *dau.* of **Samuel Robertson**, and *d.*   Issue :

i.   FLODOARDO WILLIAM, *b.* May 14, 1834 ; *m.*, first, October 23, 1860, SARAH ROSANNA, *dau.* of Robert Henning, who *d.* Issue :

    i.   WILLIAM ROBERT, *b.* August 31, 1861.
    ii.   FLODOARDO BENNETT, *b.* May 27, 1866 ; *d.* June 9, 1871.
    iii.   LYDIA MARY, *b.* July 2, 1873.

    FLODOARDO W. HOWARD, *m.*, second, November 14, 1876, ANNA M., *dau.* of Alexander Brown.
ii.   SAMUEL ROBERTSON, *b.* March 24, 1837 ; *d.* September 29, 1838.
iii. LYDIA MARY, *b.* March 6, and *d.* October 16, 1838.
iv.   GEORGE ROBERTSON, *b.* August 22, 1839 ; *d.* September 13, 1840.
v.   LAURA ROBERTSON, *b.* October 11, 1841 ; *m.*, May 28, 1873, **G. HERBERT**.   Issue :

    i.   MILDRED, *b.* April 30, 1874.
    ii.   LYDIA ROSE, *b.* May 14, 1876.

vi.   JOSEPH LAWRENCE, *b.* August 19, 1844 ; *d.* July 26, 1850.
vii. ROBERTSON, A.M., M.D., LL.B., *b.* December 12, 1847 ; a member of the Maryland and District of Columbia Bar ; *m.*, June 8, 1875, **ISOLINA**, *dau.* of **Samuel Carusi**.   Issue :

    JOSEPH THORNTON, *b.* April 10, and *d.* June 11, 1876.

viii. EDWIN, *b.* October 5, 1850.

HENRY, fifth son of **Joshua** and **Rebecca (Owings) Howard**, *b.* May 28, 1791, an M.D. and Professor of Medicine ; *m.*, first, **HANNAH**, *dau.* of **James Snowden Pleasants**, who *d.* Issue :

i.   VIRGINIA PLEASANTS, *m.* PROFESSOR COURTENAY, and *d.*   Issue :

    i.   HENRY HOWARD.
    ii.   DAVID, *d. s. p.*
    iii.   ALEXANDER DALLAS BACHE.

ii.   **DR. MARSHALL PLEASANTS**, *m.* **ANNA NORMAN Mc-CENEY**, and *d.* Issue :

    i.   MARGARET V., *m.* ELISHUA RIGGS.
    ii.   LAURA V., *m.* SAMUEL RIGGS.
    iii.   HENRY PLEASANTS.
    iv.   MARSHALL PLEASANTS.

iii.   **LAURA PLEASANTS**, *m.* **PROFESSOR WILLIAM H. Mc-GUFFEY**, LL.D., of the University of Virginia. Issue :

    ANNA, *d. s. p.*

iv.   **DR. HAMILTON PLEASANTS**, *m.*, September 4, 1855, **MARIA ELLEN**, *dau.* of **Archibald Chisolm** and **Eliza Lucretia** (Hayden) **Gibbs**, and *d.* December 29, 1863. Issue :

    i.   IDA, *d. s. p.*
    ii.   HAMILTON.

PROFESSOR HENRY HOWARD, *m.*, second, **ELIZA**, *dau.* of **Joseph Elgar**, since deceased, and *d.* March 2, 1874. Further issue :

v.   **ELIZA ELGAR.**
vi.   **ANNA ELGAR.**

Authorities : Family papers, through Robertson Howard, Esq.

JOHNS AND HUTCHINS

RICHARD JOHNS, *b.* March 29, 1649–50, at Bristol, England, removed to the Province of Maryland, and settled at the Clifts in Calvert Co., in 1675 ; he became of great influence among the Friends, or Quakers, and was highly respected by his neighbours. He *m.*, July 7, 1676, **ELIZABETH,** youngest *dau.* of **Hugh** and **Margaret Kensey,** and widow of **Thomas Sparrow,** and *d.* December 16, 1717. His wife *d.* February 1, 1715–16. Issue :

i. **ABRAHAM**, *b.* June 24, 1677 ; *m.* **MARGARET HUTCHINS** (*q. v.*), and *d.* December 10, 1707 ; his widow *m.*, second, August 24, 1712, **NEHEMIAH BIRCKHEAD,** who *d.* March 11, 1719-20, and she *m.*, third, May 10, 1727, **JOHN ENGLAND,** and *d.* June 10, 1733.

ii. **AQUILLA,** *b.* September 30, 1679 ; *bu.* May 11, 1682.

iii. **PRISCILLA,** *b.* March 21, 1681–82 ; *m.* (intentions declared, December 3, 1703) **ROBERT,** son of **Hugh** and **Jane (Owen) Roberts,** and *d.* April 1, 1725.

iv. **MARGARET,** *b.* October 11, 1683 ; *m.* **GERRARD HOPKINS** (*q. v.*).

v. **AQUILLA,** *b.* February 5, 1684-85 ; *m.*, at Cecil Meeting, November 16, 1704, **MARY,** second *dau.* of **Henry Hozier,** and *d.* January 16, 1709. His widow *m.*, September 7, 1712, **RICHARD HALL,** and *d.* May 14, 1762.

vi. **RICHARD,** *b.* April 4, 1687 ; *m.*, in 1707, **PRISCILLA,** *dau.* of **Francis** and **Elizabeth Hutchins** (*q. v.*), and *d.* August 16, 1719 ; his widow *m.* a **BECKIT,** or **BIRCKHEAD,** and *d.* March 24, 1766, aged seventy-six.

vii. **KENSEY,** *b.* July 12, 1689 ; *m.*, in 1711, **ELIZABETH,** *dau.* of **Benjamin** and **Elizabeth (Benson) Chew** (*q. v.*), and *d.* April 2, 1729 ; his wife *d.* February 9, 1726-27 ; his son, **KENSEY,** *m.*, November 15, 1749, **SUSANNA,** *dau.* of **Richard** and **Mary (Paca) Galloway** (*q. v.*).

viii. **ISAAC,** *b.* May 10, 1692 ; *m.*, December 25, 1712, **ANN,** *dau.* of **Samuel** and **Ann (Webb) Galloway** (*q. v.*), who *d.* November 29, 1728 ; her husband *m.*, second, January 22, 1730-31, **ELIZA HARRIS,** and *d.* February 17, 1733-34.

BRISTOL IN THE SEVENTEENTH CENTURY

(Reproduced from "Speed's Map")

ix. ELIZABETH, *b.* May 26, 1694 ; *m.*, first, August 14, 1711, **HENRY,**
son of **William Troth,** of Talbot Co., Md., and his wife, **Mrs.
Isabel Harrison,** widow, from whom descends **Samuel Troth,** the
genealogist of Philadelphia. **HENRY TROTH,** *d.* October 30,
1728, and his widow *m.*, second, in August, 1732, **JOHN STE-
VENS,** who *d.* about 1742 ; she *d.* December 19, 1772, and is buried
in the Meeting-House Yard, corner of Fourth and Arch Streets, Philadelphia, Pa.

By her first husband, **THOMAS SPARROW,** who *d.* 1674–75,
MRS. RICHARD JOHNS had issue :

i. **THOMAS,** *m.*, first, June 8, 1697, **ANN,** *dau.* of **Colonel William** and
Ursula Burges, who *d.* July 25, 1697 ; *m.*, second, November 28,
1698, **SOPHIA RICHARDSON** (*q. v.*).
ii. **ELIZABETH,** *m.*, July 30, 1689, **WILLIAM COALE** (*q. v.*).

FRANCIS HUTCHINS was commissioned a Justice, and
of the Quorum for Calvert Co., Md., in 1678. He was a Burgess for
the Co., May 1681 ; still in the Lower House in 1689. In 1690 he
is named in a list of the nineteen " most substantial Protestants in
the Province."

He was one of nine commissioners at a County Court, held February
7, 1692, at Waringtown, for laying out parishes in Calvert
Co., also at Leonardtown, February 14th, of the same year.
He made his will, February 20, 1698–99 ; proved July 14, 1699
(Liber H., 104) ; in which he names his wife, **ELIZABETH,**
son-in-law,[1] **SAMUEL THOMAS** (*q. v.*), son, **JOHN,** and six
daughters as follows (all under sixteen years of age in 1699) :

i. **MARGARET,** *m.* **ABRAHAM JOHNS** (*q. v.*).
ii. **ELIZA,** *m.* **ROGER BROOKE** (*q. v.*).
iii. **SARAH,** *m.*, 1706, **NEHEMIAH BIRCKHEAD.**
iv. **FRANCES.**
v. **PRISCILLA,** *b.* August 12, 1690 ; *m.* **RICHARD JOHNS** (*q. v.*).
vi. **MARY,** *m.* **BENJAMIN HANCE.**

Authorities : Records of West River and Nottingham Meetings, and family papers, through Rev.
Horace E. Hayden, of Wilkes-Barre, Pa., and Mr. Samuel Troth, of Philadelphia, Pa., and the late
Rev. J. Owen Dorsey.

[1] As Samuel Thomas unquestionably *m.*, in 1688, a Mary Hutchins, and their certificate is signed,
first, by Francis Hutchins (see West River Marriage Book, *p.* 19), she must have been the child of a
former marriage, her sister of the same name marrying Benjamin Hance.

JOHNSON

THOMAS JOHNSON, a lawyer of Poole, near Garmouth, in England, *m.* **MARY**, *dau.* of **Roger Baker**, of Liverpool, and a ward in Chancery, and is said to have emigrated to Maryland about 1660. This date is evidently incorrect; it was about thirty years later that he settled in Calvert Co., in that State, and trafficked in furs with the Indians.

Early in the following century he attempted to return to England, and appears to have set sail in a vessel whose cargo represented his hard-earned fortune. The vessel was captured by the Spaniards, and he lost his all. After a long imprisonment he escaped, and returned to America in a Canadian vessel. From Canada he travelled on foot to his home in Maryland. The fatigue and hardships of the journey seriously injured his health, and in 1714, shortly after his return, he died. His wife died in a few months, leaving an only child, **THOMAS**, *b.* February 19, 1701-2.

THOMAS, son of **Thomas** and **Mary (Baker) Johnson**, was *m.*, March 30, 1725, by Rev. Jonathan Ray, to **DORCAS**, *dau.* of **Joshua** and **Elizabeth Sedgewick**, of Connecticut, who *d.* December 11, 1770. Her husband *d.* April 12, 1777. Issue:

i.   **THOMAS**, *b.* December 13, 1725, *d. i.*
ii. **BENJAMIN**, *b.* July 6, 1727; *d.* in May, 1786.
iii. **MARY**, *b.* August 5, 1729; *m.* **WALTER HELLEN**, and *d.* in 1801.

iv.   **REBECCA,** *b.* November 8, 1730; *m.* **THOMAS McKENZIE,** and *d. s. p.* March 11, 1767.

v.   **THOMAS,** *b.* November 4, 1732, *of whom presently.*

vi.   **JAMES,** *b.* September 30, 1736, a Colonel in the Continental Army ; *m.* **MARGARET SKINNER.** Issue :

          JAMES, THOMAS, and REBECCA.

vii.   **ELIZABETH,** *b.* September 17, 1739; *m.* **CAPTAIN GEORGE COOK,** of the Maryland Navy.

viii.   **JOSHUA,** *b.* June 25, 1742 (*q. v.*).

ix   **DR. JOHN,** *b.* August 9, 1745.

     BAKER, *b.* September 30, 1747, a colonel in the Continental Army, *m.,* December 9, 1784, **CATHERINE,** *dau.* of **Colonel Nicholas Worthington** and *d.* June 18, 1811. Issue, with others :

     i.   .   JULIANNA, *m.* Right Reverend Bishop JOHN JOHNS, of Virginia.

     ii.   CHARLES WORTHINGTON, *b.* September 28, 1805, *m.* ELEANOR MURDOCK, *dau.* of Dr. Bradley and Harriet (Murdock) Tyler. Issue :

         i.   Harriet, *m.,* 1849, Charles Schley.

         ii.   Bradley Tyler, General in the C. S. A., *m.,* June 25, 1851, Claudia, *dau.* of Hon. Romulus N. and Anna Hayes (Johnson) Saunders, and has a son Bradley Saunders.

xi.   **ROGER,** *b.* March 18, 1749 (*q. v.*).

THOMAS, third son of **Thomas** and **Dorcas (Sedgewick) Johnson,** *b.* November 4, 1732, with his brothers, **James, Baker,** and **Roger,** engaged extensively in the manufacture of iron, establishing Catoctin Furnace ; Johnson, near the mouth of the Monocacy River ; Potomac Furnace, in Loudoun Co., Va. ; Bloomsburg, on Bennet's Creek ; and one on Bush Creek, which supplied cannon, shells, etc., to the Revolutionary Army. In 1775 he erected powder-mills at the Catoctin Furnace. June 22, 1774, he was elected a Delegate to the Colonial Congress ; and June 15, 1775, it was upon his motion that George Washington was made Commander-in-Chief of the Revolutionary Army. Being absent on account of illness, he did not sign the Declaration of Independence. While still a member of Congress, January 6, 1776, he was elected the first Brigadier of the Provincial Militia, and Commander of the Maryland Flying Camps. February 13, 1777, he was elected the first Governor of the State by the Assembly, and re-elected twice, being ineligible to a fourth term by the law. August 5, 1791, appointed a Justice of the United States Supreme Court. He presided over a meeting held at Frederick, Md., to thank President John Adams for his course in the troubles with England and France, and February 22, 1800, made an oration at the ceremonies in eulogy of Washington, at the German Reformed Church, in Frederick.

He *m.*, February 16, 1766, **ANN**, only *dau.* of **Thomas Jenings,** of Annapolis, and *d.* October 26, 1819.　Issue :

i.　　**THOMAS.**
ii.　　**ANN,** *m.* **MAJOR JOHN GRAHAM.**
iii.　　**REBECCA,** *m.* **THOMAS JOHNSON.**
iv.　　**DORCAS.**
v.　　**JOSHUA.**

JOSHUA, fifth son of **Thomas** and **Dorcas (Sedgewick) Johnson,** *b.* in 1742, removed to France, and engaged in mercantile life at Nantes.　He afterward removed to London, and was appointed Consular Agent of the United States.　He *m.* **CATHERINE NUTH.**　Issue : eight children, among whom were **THOMAS BAKER,** *d. u.,* and **LOUISA CATHERINE,** *b.* February 12, 1775 ; *m.,* July 27, 1797, at London, **JOHN QUINCY,** son of **President John Adams,** and removed with him in the autumn of that year to Berlin, Mr. Adams having been appointed Minister to that Court.　In 1824 he was elected President of the United States, and served one term.　He *d.* February 23, 1848, issue surviving (surname ADAMS) : **CHARLES FRANCIS,** *b.* August 18, 1807, at Boston, was graduated at Harvard College in 1825, admitted to the Boston Bar in 1828 ; a member of the Massachusetts Legislature, 1831–36 ; Member of Congress from Massachusetts, 1859–61 ; Minister to England from 1861–68, and acted with consummate ability in that position, especially during the critical period of the Civil War.　He *m.*, in 1829, the youngest *dau.* of Peter C. Brooks, of Boston, and *d.* November 21, 1886.　Issue : John Quincy, *b.* September 22, 1833, a prominent politician of Massachusetts, resides at Quincy.　Charles Francis, Jr., *b.* May 27, 1835 ; admitted to the Bar in 1858 ; served through the Civil War, mustered out with the brevet rank of Brigadier-General. Henry Brooks, *b.* February 16, 1838 ; Private Secretary to his father while Minister to England, in 1870 ; Assistant Professor of History at Harvard College, and Editor of the *North American Review.*

ROGER, youngest son of **Thomas** and **Dorcas (Sedgewick) Johnson,** *b.* March 18, 1749, was a Major in his brother James's battalion ; *m.,* February 4, 1781, by Rev. Francis Lander, to **ELIZABETH,** eldest *dau.* of **Richard** and **Sarah (Coale) Thomas** (*q. v.*), who *d.,* September 7, 1837, her husband having *d.* March 3, 1831.　Issue :

i.   **RICHARD**, *b*. November 9, 1781 ; *m*. **JULIANNA DORSEY**, and *d*.
       July 14, 1839. Issue, with others :

    i.   RICHARD DORSEY, who *m*. NANNIE SIMMS, and has issue :
            Richard.
    ii.   MARION, *m*. DR. DUVALL.
    iii. FLORA, *m*. —— WILLIAMS.
    iv.   EDITH MAY, *m*. THOMAS MORGAN, and another *dau*. unmarried.

ii.   **GEORGE**, *b*. July 25, 1783 ; *m*. **ELIZABETH DUNLOP**, and had
       ten children, of whom were living in 1879 :

    i.   ELIZABETH DORCAS, *m*. GEORGE LOWRY.
    ii.   THOMAS, *m*. HENRIETTA JOHNSON. Issue :
        i.   William. ii. Roberta.
    iii. ROBERTA, *m*. ROBERT, eldest son of Major George Peter, of Montgomery
        Co., Md.

iii. **SAMUEL.**
iv.   **HENRIETTA**, *b*. in November, 1784, *d. u.*
v.   **WILLIAM THOMAS**, *b*. October 4, 1787 ; *m*. **DOLLY MAC-
       TIER**, and *d. s. p.*
vi.   **SARAH**, *b*. December 26, 1788 ; *m*. **ELI DORSEY**, and *d*. August
       25, 1834, leaving five children.
vii. **JOSEPH**, *b*. October 30, 1790 ; *m*. **ELEANOR HILLEARY**, and *d*.
       March 4, 1835. Issue :

    i.   THOMAS ROGER. ii. DR. WILLIAM HILLEARY. iii. NETTIE.

viii. **CHARLES**, *b*. February 18, 1792, *d. u.* October 16, 1867.
ix.   **DORCAS**, *b*. May 14, 1793 ; *m*. **HENRY MACTIER**, and *d. s. p.*
       December 4, 1815.
x.   **DR. JAMES THOMAS**, *b*. November 12, 1794 ; *m*. **EMILY NEW-
       MAN**, and *d*. September 4, 1867. Issue :

    i.   DR. JAMES T.
    ii.   OTIS.
    iii. ELIZABETH R., *m*. WILLIAM RICHARDSON.
    iv.   SUSAN BIRD, *m*. JOHN V. WHITE.

xi.   **ELIZA**, *b*. August 8, 1796 ; *m*. **REV. WILLIAM ARMSTRONG.**
       Issue (surname ARMSTRONG) :

    i.   WILLIAM J., *d*. leaving issue :
        William J. Eliza. Nettie.
    ii.   ANNA TOWNSEND, *m*. DR. READ, of Accomac Co., Va.
    iii. HENRIETTA, *m*. THOMAS PARRAMORE, of the same State.

Authorities : George A. Hanson's Old Kent, Frederick County Records, and family papers through
    Mrs. Robert Peter and the late Hon. Charles F. Adams.

JONES, OF MARYLAND

DAVID JONES, who was a nephew of Nicholas Sluby, of Sweden ; *m.* **MARIA,** *dau.* of **Richard S.** and **Mary Thomas** (*q. v.*). Issue :

i.   **DEBORAH,** *m.*, February 29, 1838, **COLONEL EDWARD WILKINS,** of Kent. Issue :

     i.   **JULIANA,** *m.* **CAPTAIN ROBERT S. EMORY.** Issue :
         Edward Wilkins, Maria Ella, Julia, Isabelle, and Robert Julienne.
     ii.   **EDWARD MIFFLIN,** *m.* **MARY ANNA MERRITT.** Issue :
         Susan Carter, Fanny Louise, and Jenny.
     iii.   **MARIA DEBORAH,** *m.* **JAMES RUSSELL,** of Baltimore City. Issue :

         James, Olive, and Maria.

ii.   **ANN MARIA,** *m.* **JAMES WHITAKER,** who *d.*, leaving issue :

         HARRIET, FRANK, JAMES, ANNIE, and **MIFFLIN.**

iii.   **MARY LOUISA,** *m.* **A. W. SPARKS.** Issue :

     i.   **BENJAMIN FRANKLIN,** *b.* November 5, 1833 ; *d.* in 1844.
     ii.   **DAVID WARNER,** *b.* July 24, 1834 ; *d.* February 22, 1843.
     iii.   **HENRY ABSALOM,** *b.* December 15, 1837 ; *m.*, February 11, 1863, **FANNY SHAW.** Issue :

         Linwood, *b.* February 7, 1864.

     iv.   **MARY ELIZABETH,** *b.* October 19, 1839 ; *m.*, October, 1866, **REV. JOHN D. KINZER.**
     v.   **JOHN THOMAS,** *b.* June 15, 1843 ; *d.* September 4, 1844.
     vi.   **EMMA,** *b.* September 27, 1845.

iv.   **OLIVER PERRY,** *m.* **MARY BROWN,** and *d.* in 1868. Issue :

         EDWARD, HIRAM, DAVID PAUL, and two daughters.

v.   **RICHARD.**
vi.   **THOMAS,** *m.*, September 10, 1840, **FANNIE ISABELLE,** *dau.* of **R. T. Jones.** Issue :

     i.   **MARIA THOMAS** (Lilly T. Armstrong).
     ii.   **THOMAS BROWN,** *b.* February 7, 1845.
     iii.   **JAMES ARMSTRONG,** *b.* August 20, 1851.
     iv.   **MARY BROWN.**
     v.   **NICHOLAS SLUBY,** *b.* April 16, 1853.

      Authority: Family papers, through Miss L. T. Armstrong and Colonel E. Wilkins.

376

ELISHA KENT KANE, M.D., U. S. NAVY

From a Daguerreotype by Brady

KANE

JOHN KINTZING, son of **Elisha** and **Alida (Van Rens-selaer) Kane,** was *b.* at Albany, N. Y., May 16, 1795. He was a graduate of Yale College, studied law with Judge Hopkinson, and was admitted to the Philadelphia Bar in 1817. Member of the Academy of Fine Arts ; Member of the Musical Fund Society, and President of the latter, 1854–56 ; Vice-President of the Pennsylvania Institute for Blind ; Member of the American Philosophical Society, 1825, and President of same ; Member of the Pennsylvania Legislature ; City Solicitor, 1828–30 and 1832 ; Attorney-General of Pennsylvania, 1844–46. In June, 1846, succeeded Judge Archibald Randall, as Judge of Admiralty of the United States District Court of Eastern District of Pennsylvania.

He *m.* **JANE DUVAL,** *dau.* of **Thomas Leiper** (*q. v.*), and *d.* February 21, 1858. Issue :

i.   **DR. JOHN K.,** *m.* a sister of **Hon. Thomas F. Bayard,** of Delaware.
ii.   **ROBERT PATTERSON,** of the Philadelphia Bar.
iii. **GENERAL THOMAS LEIPER,** Colonel of the Forty-second Pennsylvania Volunteers in the Civil War.
iv.   **ELIZABETH.**
v.   **DR. ELISHA KENT,** *b.* February 3, 1820, *of whom presently.*

DR. ELISHA K. KANE was educated at the University of Virginia for the profession of a Civil Engineer, but was compelled to leave that Institution, in 1838, owing to a disease of the heart, from which he never fully recovered. The next year he began the study of medicine, at the University of Pennsylvania, and October 19, 1840, while still an undergraduate, and not of age, he was elected Resident Physician to the Pennsylvania Hospital. In May, 1843, having obtained the post of Surgeon in the United States Navy, he sailed in the frigate Brandywine, with Commodore Parker, as Physician to the Embassy to China. After the Embassy left, he remained six months in Whampoa, practising his profession. Between 1843 and 1846 he travelled extensively in the Philippines, Borneo, Sumatra, and India, passed through Persia, Egypt, and Syria, crossed Greece on foot, travelled on the Continent and in England, and returned to the United States in 1847. In May of that year he visited Africa, and afterward took part in the Mexican War. In these travels he met with numerous adventures, and displayed undaunted courage and persistence in his plans despite all obstacles. In 1850 he accompanied Lieutenant De Haven's Arctic Expedition as its Surgeon and Naturalist, publishing an account of the Expedition in 1854. In 1853, Mr. Henry Grinnell and Mr. George Peabody were instrumental in fitting out another Arctic expedition, to which Dr. Kane contributed his pay (about three thousand dollars), and the proceeds of Lectures which he delivered in 1852–53. He was appointed the Commander of the Expedition, which sailed from New York, May 30, 1853, in the Advance. The surviving officers and men returned October 11, 1855, having been compelled to abandon their vessel in the ice, and to travel with sledges and dogs for eighty-four days to the Danish settlements on the coast of Greenland, where they met Captain Hartstene, who had been sent to their relief. The story of the expedition was most graphically told by Dr. Kane in two volumes, published by Childs & Peterson, of Philadelphia, in 1856. Gold medals were awarded him by Congress, the Legislature of New York, and the Royal Geographical Society of London. His health again gave way, and after a visit to London he sailed for the West Indies, February 17, 1856. On the voyage he suffered a paralytic stroke, and *d.* at Havana, December 25th, of the same year.

KING

WILLIAM KING, living in the north of England, *m.*, in 1674, **JANE,** *dau.* of **James Halliday,** who *d.* August 16, 1726. Issue :

i.	**JAMES,** *b.* June 8, 1675.
ii.	**JOHN,** *b.* March 8, 1677.
iii.	**MARY,** *b.* January 1, 1679–80 ; *m.* **GEORGE ALLOTT.**
iv.	**WILLIAM,** *b.* December 13, 1681.
v.	**TREFENY,** *b.* in May, 1683.
vi.	**JANE,** *b.* March 29, 1686.
vii.	**HANNAH,** *b.* June 11, 1689 ; *m.* **THOMAS DUNLOP.**
viii.	**JOSEPH,** *b.* December 11, 1692, *of whom presently.*
ix.	**BENJAMIN,** *b.* June 9, 1694.

JOSEPH, fourth son of **William** and **Jane (Halliday) King,** *b.* December 11, 1692 ; *m.*, August 15, 1717, **HANNAH HER-RON.** Issue :

i.	**JAMES,** *b.* June 7, 1718, *of whom presently.*
ii.	**JOSEPH,** *b.* November 22, 1719 (*q. v.*).
iii.	**ELINOR,** *b.* September 4, 1721.
iv.	**HANNAH,** *b.* November 30, 1723.
v.	**JANE,** *b.* May 28, 1726 ; *m.*, January 20, 1755, **JOSEPH GASKIN.**

JAMES, eldest son of **Joseph** and **Hannah King,** *b.* November 22, 1719 ; *m.*, October 21, 1755, **ANN GOLDSBOROUGH.** Issue :

i.	**JOSEPH,** *b.* June 10, 1756, *of whom presently.*
ii.	**ANN,** *b.* December 23, 1757 ; *d.* September 12, 1827.
iii.	**JAMES,** *b.* February 20, 1760 ; *d.* November 2, 1777.
iv.	**HANNAH,** *b.* May 15, 1763.

JOSEPH, eldest son of **James** and **Ann KING,** *b.* June 10, 1756 ; *m.* **MARY,** *dau.* of **John Harrison,** of Darlington, and *d.* March 5, 1796. Issue :

i.   **JOHN,** *b.* June 2, 1786 ; *m.,* October 16, 1816, **ELEANOR WADKIN.**
Issue :

    i.   **SAMUEL,** *b.* July 11, 1817.
    ii.   **JOHN,** *b.* November 13, 1819 ; *m.,* June 5, 1856, **FRANCES FELL.** Issue :

        i.   Leonard, *b.* September 21, 1857.
        ii.   Goldsborough.
        iii.   Alfred John, *b.* February 14, 1859.

    iii.   **ELEANOR,** *b.* September 12, 1821 ; *m.,* in 1857, **THOMAS GARRICK,** and *d.* June 15, 1858. Issue : John Arthur.
    iv.   **MARY,** *b.* August 20, 1823.
    v.   **ELIZABETH,** *b.* October 20, 1824.
    vi.   **JOSEPH HARRISON,** *b.* December 16, 1827 ; *m.* **SARAH ROOKE.**
    vii.   **ANN,** *b.* April 28, 1830 ; *d.* in June, 1830.
    viii.   **THOMAS BARRON,** *b.* June 22, 1832 ; *m.,* April 5, 1860, **MARGARET ROOKE.**
    ix.   **WILLIAM,** *b.* January 31, 1835.

ii.   **JOSEPH,** *b.* October 31, 1787 ; *m.* **SARAH AROMACK.**
iii.   **UNNAMED SON,** *b.* and *d.* December 30, 1788.
iv.   **ANN,** *b.* September 29, 1790 ; *m.* **MILES B. FOSTER.**

JOSEPH, second son of **Joseph** and **Hannah (Herron) King,** *b.* September 22, 1719 ; *m.,* August 4, 1752, **ANN,** *dau.* of **Thomas Reay,** *b.* in 1719. Issue, *b.* in England :

i.   **ANN,** *b.* June 3, 1756 ; *d.* August 24, 1834.
ii.   **JOSEPH,** *b.* July 6, 1757.
iii.   **THOMAS,** *b.* at Kenton, April 2, 1758 ; *m.* **JANE E. STOREY,** of Newcastle-on-Tyne. Issue :

    i.   JOSEPH, *b.* August 10, 1784, *of whom presently.*
    ii.   ELIZA.
    iii.   THOMAS.
    iv.   JANE.

JOSEPH KING removed to America, and had further issue :

iv.   **HANNAH.**
v.   **JOHN.**
vi.   **JAMES.**
vii.   **ELEANOR.**
viii.   **REAY.**

JOSEPH, Jr., son of **Thomas** and **Jane E. (Storey) King,** *b.* August 10, 1784 ; *m.,* December 17, 1817, **TACY,** *dau.* of **Elias** and **Mary (Thomas) Ellicott** (*q. v.*), and *d.* in 1865. She *d.* in 1872. Issue :

i.   **FRANCIS THOMPSON,** *b.* February 25, 1819, for many years a member of the firm of King, Carey & Howe, and amassed a large fortune. For over fifteen years he devoted himself to charitable work, and the administration of his duties as president of the Board of Trustees of the Johns Hopkins Hospital and as director of the Johns Hopkins University. He was an executor of the estate of the philanthropist, Thomas Wilson, and was president of the Thomas Wilson Sanitarium. He was a director of the Samuel Ready Orphan Asylum, the founder of the Central Savings Bank, president of the Board of Trustees of Bryn Mawr College, Philadelphia, and a director in a number of insurance companies, banks, and trust companies. For many years he was president of the Maryland Bible Society. He *m.*, January 8, 1846, **ELIZABETH TABER,** who *d.* in March, 1856. Issue :

i.   **MARY T.,** *b.* December 8, 1847 ; *m.* **THOMAS K. CAREY** (*q. v.*).
ii.   **ANNIE T.,** *b.* in 1848 ; *m.* **JAMES CAREY,** Jr. (*q. v.*).
iii.   **BESSIE T.,** *b.* in 1855.
iv., v. Two other children, who *d. i.*

ii.   **THOMAS,** *b.* July 19, 1820 ; *d. u.*
iii.   **MARY ELLICOTT,** *b.* September 2, 1823 ; *m.*, November 17, 1853, **GEORGE A. WARDER,** and *d.* in April, 1856. Issue :

      MARY K.

iv.   **JOSEPH,** *b.* July 17, 1825 ; *m.*, June 1, 1869, **JANE GILMOR,** *dau.* of Hon. Benjamin C. and Jane Grant (Gilmor) Howard (*q. v.*).
v.   **ELIAS E.,** *b.* February 28, 1823 ; *d. u.* May 28, 1876.

    Authority : Family papers, through the late Francis T. King.

KIRKBRIDE AND MARRIOTT

JOSEPH, son of **Mahlon** [1] and **Magdalen Kirkbride,** of Kirkbride, in Cumberland, England, *b.* in 1662, emigrated to Pennsylvania on the ship Welcome, with William Penn, in 1682 ; was
a Justice of the Peace in Bucks Co., March 6, 1708, and again in
1722, and a member of the Provincial Assembly five terms, from
1698–1716. He *m.,* first, March 14, 1688, **PHEBE,** *dau.* of
Randal, or **Randulph,** and **Alice Blackshaw** (*q. v.*) ; *m.,*
second, February 17, 1702–3, **SARAH,** *dau.* of **Mahlon Stacy.**
By his first wife he had issue :

> **MARTHA,** *m.* **THOMAS MARRIOTT,** member of the Assembly
> from Bristol in 1734 and 1738. Issue (surname MARRIOTT) :
>> **MARY,** *b.* November 1, 1719 ; *m.* **THOMAS SHIPLEY** (*q. v.*).

RANDULPH BLACKSHAW, of Hallingee, Cheshire, Eng-
land, arrived, with his wife, **ALICE,** in Maryland, November 2, 1682,
in the ship Submission, of Liverpool. He removed to Pennsylvania,
arriving at Appoquinamine, January 15, 1682–83, with his *dau.* **PHEBE,**
who *m.* **JOSEPH KIRKBRIDE** (*q. v.*), and Roger Bradbury and Sarah
Bradbury, to serve four years and then to have fifty acres of land ;
Elenor, wife to Roger, and Roger, Jacob, and Joseph, his sons, Mr.
Blackshaw sold in Maryland. May 9, 1683, **ALICE BLACK-
SHAW,** her other children, and Martha Bradbury, arrived also in
Pennsylvania.

Authorities : Davis's Bucks Co., *pp.* 67 and 109, and MS. Records at Bristol, Pa.

[1] Of the ancient family of that name in Cumberland, descended from Richard Kirkbride, who *m.*
Euphemia, *dau.* and *co-h.* of Adam de Levington, Baron of Levington, who *d.* A.D. 1210–11. See
Nicholson and Burne's Cumberland, etc., ii., 361–62, and N. H. Nicholas, Roll of Caerlaverock.

KNIGHT AND CANBY

THE earliest known ancestor was **GILES KNIGHT,** of Gloucestershire, England, *b.* 1653, who was an Elder of the Society of Friends, and came to America in 1682, leaving England in the ship Welcome, with William Penn, August 30th of that year, and landing at Newcastle, on the Delaware, some time in October. He *m.* **MARY ENGLISH** before leaving England, was frequently a member of the Provincial Assembly, and *d.* August 20, 1726. His only son, **JOSEPH,** *b.* in 1680, *m.* **ABIGAIL ANTILL,** and *d.* April 26, 1762 ; his wife *d.* November 19, 1764, aged eighty-two years. GILES, their son, was *b.* November 17, 1719, *m.* ELIZABETH JAMES February 24, 1738, and *d.* July 13, 1799, at Bensalem, Pa. Israel, their tenth child, was *b.* March 4, 1760 ; *m.,* November 26, 1782, Sarah, *dau.* of Isaac and Esther Tyson (*q. v.*), of **Pennsylvania,** and *d.* January 31, 1810, his wife *d.* April 8, 1824, aged sixty-six years. Issue, with others : Isaac, *of whom presently.*

ISAAC, second son of **Israel** and **Sarah (Tyson) Knight,** was *b.* September 14, 1785 ; *m.,* September 24, 1811, at Sandy Spring Meeting House, **JULIANNA MARIA,** *dau.* of **Samuel** and **Anna (Warfield) Thomas** (*q. v.*). He was a man of considerable engineering ability, and the inventor of Knight's Box for the wheels of railroad cars. He *d.* April 1, 1855, and his wife February 20, 1868. Issue :

i.   **SARAH,** *d. i.*
ii.   **CHARLES ALEXANDER,** *b.* November 11, 1812 ; *d.* July 12, 1848.
iii.   **ELIZA SNOWDEN,** *d.* October 15, 1880.
iv.   **DR. SAMUEL THOMAS,** *of whom presently.*
v.   **WILLIAM HENRY,** *b.* January 20, 1820 ; *d.* October 31, 1847.
vi.   **ANN REBECCA,** *d.* October 8, 1880.
vii. **MARIA LOUISA** (*q. v.*).
viii. **MARY VIRGINIA.**
ix.   **GRANVILLE SHARP,** *b.* July 18, 1828 ; *d.* October 2, 1851.

DR. SAMUEL THOMAS, fourth child of **Isaac** and **Julianna (Thomas) Knight,** *b.* December 20, 1817, was graduated in Medicine at the University of Maryland in 1835, and practised in Baltimore. He *m.,* first, November 12, 1839, **REBECCA JANE,** *dau.* of **Joseph E.** and **Lucretia (Gibbons) Moore.** She *d.* August 22, 1851. Issue :

i.   **JULIA.**
ii. **LUCY GIBBONS,** *m.* **JAMES ATLEE,** since *d.*
iii. **DR. LOUIS WILLIAM,** *b.* October 21, 1844.
iv. **EMMA.**
v.   **MARTHA THOMAS,** *m.* **REV. WILLIAM L. AUSTIN,** of Virginia. Issue (surname AUSTIN) :

    i.   **JULIA.** ii. **LUCY.** iii. **MARTHA.** iv. **BERTHA.** v. **PAUL C.**

vi. **DR. SAMUEL THOMAS, Jr.,** *b.* April 7, 1850 ; at the age of seventeen was graduated in Medicine at the University of Maryland, and obtained the position of Clinical Recorder in the University Hospital. He *d.* February 12, 1870, from disease contracted there.

    DR. SAMUEL T. KNIGHT *m.,* second, September 2, 1825, **MARY,** *dau.* of **William** and **Tabitha McConkey,** and *d.* January 20, 1881.

MARIA LOUISA, seventh child of **Isaac Knight,** *m.,* May 11, 1848, **Samuel Canby,** who *d.* August 21, 1878 ; his widow *d.* November, 1891. Issue :

i.   **WILLIAM THOMAS,** *b.* April 13, 1849 : *m.,* May 28, 1870, **IDA L. FISH,** of Boston, a niece of Honourable Hamilton Fish, Secretary of State of the United States, and *d.* having had one child, **CLARENCE S.**
ii. **EDWIN KNIGHT,** *b.* December 6, 1853 ; *m.,* November, 1879, **MAE BLACKMAN,** *d.* November 9, 1880.
iii. **ALBERT HENRY,** *b.* October 7, 1856 ; Business Manager of Francis Wilson's Opera Company ; *m.,* April 14, 1890, **JESSIE QUIGLEY.**

Authorities : Martindale's Byberry and Moreland, 1867, and family papers, through Dr. S. T. Knight and his sisters.

KNOWLES

DR. WILLIAM GRAY, son of **James** and **Margaret (Gray) Knowles,** *b.* February 16, 1811 ; *m.,* October 27, 1835, at " Longwood," Maryland, **MARTHA ANN,** *dau.* of **Dr. Gustavus** and **Mary (Thomas) Warfield** (*q. v.*), and *d.* January 11, 1890. Issue :

i. **GEORGE GRAY,** *b.* March 12, 1837, at Darby, near Philadelphia ; *m.,* April 28, 1864, by the Rev. Halsey Dunning, to **MARY ELIZABETH WHITE ;** she *d.* March 11, 1875.

ii. **MARY WARFIELD,** *b.* April 15, 1839 ; *m.,* December 31, 1863, **WILLIAM HARRISON HORNER,** and *d.* February 25, 1875. Issue :

    i. **MARTHA THOMAS,** *b.* April 1, 1895 ; *m.,* January 31, 1889, **BENJAMIN FRANKLIN BEATTY.**
    ii. **MARY WARFIELD,** *b.* March 5, 1867.
    iii. **WILLIAM,** *b.* October 25, 1873 ; *d.* June 14, 1874.
    iv. **EMMA CROZER,** *b.* February 25, 1876 ; *d.* June 9, 1876.

iii. **GUSTAVUS WARFIELD,** *b.* March 12, 1841 ; *m.,* March 29, 1870, by Rev. Dr. Benjamin Griffith, to **EMMA,** *dau* of **John P. Crozer,** of Upland. Issue :

    i. **WILLIAM GRAY,** *b.* December 14, 1870.
    ii. **HENRY CROZER,** *b.* April 22, 1872 ; *d.* January 13, 1874.
    iii. **SALLY,** *d. i.*
    iv. **LUCY CROZER,** *b.* 1877 ; *d.* 1882.
    v. **EVA CROZER,** *b.* 1878 ; *d.* 1882.
    vi. **FRANK CROZER,** *b.* January 26, 1881.
    vii. **HERBERT CROZER,** *b.* 1883 ; *d.* 1887.
    viii. **ELSIE CROZER,** *b.* April 16, 1885.
    ix. **FLORENCE CROZER,** *b.* February 10, 1888.

iv. **LOUISA VICTORIA,** *b.* August 19, 1843 ; *m.,* October 27, 1868, at her father's residence in Baltimore, by Rev. Dr. Thomas J. Shepherd, to **CLARENCE ALBERTUS EVANS.** Issue :

    i. **DR. WILLIAM KNOWLES,** *b.* August 10, 1869.
    ii. **EMMA CROZER,** *b.* June 12, 1874.

Authority : Family papers, through Mrs. William G. Knowles.

LARGE

JOHN LARGE, of Bristol, Pa., *b.* about 1698 ; *m.*, 1721, **SARAH,** *dau.* of **William Corker,** and had a son, **WILLIAM,** member of councils in Bristol, 1749–63 ; *m.*, May 31, 1744, **SARAH ALLEN.** Issue :

> **EBENEZER,** *b.* March 26, 1750, a prominent merchant of Philadelphia ; *m.* **DOROTHY,** *dau.* of **James Sparks,** and *d.* January 11, 1810, leaving a son, **James,** *of whom presently.*

JAMES, son of **Ebenezer** and **Dorothy (Sparks) Large,** *b.* November 10, 1786 ; *m.*, January 15, 1817, **ELIZABETH,** *dau.* of **Thomas** and **Ann (Thomas) Poultney** (*q. v.*), who *d.* April 12, 1833. He *d.* December 2, 1862. Issue :

i.　**THOMAS POULTNEY,** *b.* February 12, 1819 ; *m.*, June 26, 1837, **MARY STRICKLAND,** and *d.* July 27, 1852. Issue :

> **ELIZABETH POULTNEY,** *d. u.* December, 1872.

ii.　**MARY,** *b.* October 7, 1820 ; *m.*, October 31, 1839, **ROBERT H. LARGE.** Issue :

> i.　**SALLIE,** *b.* October 15, 1840 ; *m.*, March 1, 1870, **DR. THEODORE FASSITT.**
> ii.　**JAMES,** *b.* August 23, 1842.
> iii.　**JOHN B.,** *b.* March 7, 1846 ; *m.,* April 10, 1872, **SARAH W.,** *dau.* of **General George G.** and **Margaret (Sergeant) Meade,** and *d.* November 1, 1892. Issue :
>> i.　**George Gordon Meade,** *b.* August 26, 1873.
>> ii.　**Robert H.,** *b.* October 31, 1875.
>> iii.　**Margaretta Sergeant,** *b.* February 27, 1877.
>> iv.　**Mary,** *b.* December 6, 1878.
>> v.　**Henrietta Meade,** *b.* October 12, 1880.
>> vi.　**John Baldwin,** *b.* August 18, 1882.
>> vii.　**William Mifflin,** *b.* August 12, 1884 ; *d.* July 15, 1885.
>> viii.　**Spencer Sergeant,** *b.* November 30, 1887.

iii.　**ANN POULTNEY,** *b.* October 31, 1822 ; *m.*, February 4, 1839, **WILLIAM MIFFLIN** (*q. v.*).

iv.　**SARAH M.,** *b.* May 24, 1827, *m.* **SAMUEL H. TAGART,** Attorney-at-Law, of Tagart & Steele, Baltimore, since *d.*, and *d.* May 6, 1891.

> Authority : Family papers and Mifflin Genealogy.

LAWRENCE, OF CALVERT COUNTY, MD.

THE earliest colonial notice of this name I find in Liber B, Maryland Archives, No. 2, folio 570, where is record of **RICHARD LAWRENCE** setting over to John Cage, on December 20, 1649, one hundred acres of land due him because he transported himself to the province about seven years since. Later a **BENJAMIN LAWRENCE**, of "The Deserts," Calvert Co., September 26, 1674, proves his rights for 500 acres of land (Liber 18, folio 39) ; he had to wife **ANN ——**, and sons **BENJAMIN** and **NEHEMIAH. BENJAMIN,** his son was of Calvert Co. and of "Benjamin's Fortune," 115 acres in Anne Arundel Co. He *m.* **ELIZABETH,** *dau.* of **Richard Talbot** (*q. v.*), and made his will[1] January, 1684–85 (Liber G, 142), in which he names his *dau.* ELIZABETH, son BENJAMIN, *of whom presently,* dau. LUCY, and his brother **THOMAS LAWRENCE,**[2] sister **LUCY SMITH,** brother-in-law, **EDWARD GIBBS,** and sister-in-law, **JANE SIMMONDS.**

BENJAMIN, son of **Benjamin** and **Elizabeth (Talbot) Lawrence,** was a Quaker ; *m.,* 1701, **RACHEL,** *dau.* of **Edward** and **Honor Marriarté,** of Anne Arundel Co., Md., and *d.* before 1728. His widow *m.* **THOMAS NORWOOD.** Issue, by first husband :

i.   **ELIZABETH,** *b.* December 8, 1702.
ii. **BENJAMIN,** *b.* January 27, 1704–05 ; *m.* **RUTH,** *dau.* of **John Dorcey.**
iii. **SOPHIA,** *b.* June 2, 1707.
iv. **JOHN,** *b.* November 11, 1709.
v.   **LEVIN,** *of whom presently.*
vi. **MARGARET,** *b.* January 11, 1716–17.

[1] His dying testimony was read at West River Quaker Meeting, April 17, 1685.
[2] Could this be Sir Thomas Lawrence, Bart., of the Chelsea family (*q. v.*) ?

LEVIN, youngest son of **Benjamin** and **Rachel (Marriarté)**, **Lawrence**, *b.* March 6, 1711–12, was reared among Friends, but *m.* into a church family, and from 1749 until his death from an accident in the hunting-field, was a vestryman of Christ Church, Queen Caroline Parish. He resided at "Poplar Spring Garden," part of a tract inherited by his wife, twelve miles southwest of Ellicott City on the Frederick Turnpike. The house was built in 1741. He *m.* **SUSANNA**, *dau.* of **John** and **Honor (Elder) Dorcey**, *b.* December 12, 1717, and *d.* 1756. Issue :

i.   **BENJAMIN**, *of whom presently.*
ii.   **JOHN**, of Valley Farm, Linganore Hills.
iii. **LEVIN**, a first lieutenant in the Flying Camp, 1776.
iv.   **RACHEL**, *m.*, first, **CAPTAIN PHILEMON DORSEY** ; *m.*, second, **NATHAN HARRIS.**
v.   **RUTH**, *b.* 1745 ; *m.*, 1760, **THOMAS OWINGS.**
vi.   **ELISABETH.**
vii. **MARGARET**, *b.* 1751 ; *d.* 1835.
viii. **RICHARD**, *b.* 1757, served under General Otho H. Williams in the Revolutionary War ; was thrice married. A granddaughter is **Mrs. S. H. Kerfoot**, of Chicago.

BENJAMIN, eldest son of **Levin** and **Susanna (Dorcey) Lawrence**, *b.* May 17, 1741, removed to Kentucky in 1799 ; *m.*, January 26, 1762, **URITH RANDALL**, *dau.* of **Samuel** and **Urith (Randall) Owings**, of Owings's Mills, Baltimore Co., Md., *b.* July 7, 1738 ; *d.* September, 1807, and was buried with her husband at "Eden," Ky. Issue :

i.   **SAMUEL**, *b.* September 28, 1764, *of whom presently.*
ii.   **MARY**, *b.* February 20, 1767 ; *m.*, first, **ELIAS DORSEY** ; *m.*, second, **WILLIAM CHAMBERS.**
iii. **SUSANNA**, *b.* May 4, 176– ; *m.*, first, **EDWARD DORSEY** ; *m.*, second, **JOHN WILLIAMSON.**
iv.   **REBECCA**, *b.* July 4, 1770 ; *m.* **RICHARD WINCHESTER.**
v.   **LEVIN**, *b.* April 8, 1774 ; *m.* **MARY**, *dau.* of **Elias Dorsey.**
vi.   **ELISABETH**, *b.* May 2, 1778 ; *m.* **WILLIAM ROSE HINES.**

SAMUEL, eldest son of **Benjamin** and **Urith R. (Owings) Lawrence**, *b.* September 28, 1764 ; *m.*, June 29, 1790, **SARAH**, *dau.* of **Nicholas**[1] and **Elisabeth (Cummins) Hobbs**, of Linganore Hundreds, *b.* July 3, 1769 ; *d.* September 19, 1828 ; her husband *d.* September 17, 1822. Issue :

i.   **URITH OWINGS**, *b.* June 27, 1791, *of whom presently.*

[1] Member of the Committee of Observation, 1775.

ii.   BENJAMIN, *m.* SUSANNA DORSEY HOWARD.
iii.   ELIAS DORSEY, *m.* MARY ANN PEACHY FRY.

URITH OWINGS, eldest child of **Samuel** and **Sarah (Hobbs) Lawrence,** *b.* June 27, 1791, in Baltimore Co., Md., was *m.* September 25, 1809, by Rev. David Ward, to **JAMES**, son of **James** and **Elizabeth (Clarkson) Brown,** of "Bear Grass," Ky., and *d.* January 2, 1854 ; her husband, *b.* November, 1780, *d.* April 15, 1853. Issue, arrived at middle life (surname BROWN) :

i.   SARAH LAWRENCE, *b.* 1810 ; *m.* PATRICK HENRY POPE.
ii.   CAROLINE, *of whom presently.*
iii.   MARY ANN, *m.* THOMAS SEABROOK FORMAN.
iv.   THEODORE, *m.*, first, SALLY BRYAN ; *m.*, second, SUE PAGE
       MEADE.
v.   JAMES LAWRENCE, *m.*, first, EMILY T. MOORE ; *m.*, second,
       MARY BOSWELL.
vi.   ARTHUR, *b.* June, 1834 ; *m.* MATILDA E. GALT.

CAROLINE, second child of **James** and **Urith O. (Lawrence) Brown,** *b.* December 25, 1813 ; *m.*, January 15, 1833, **JAMES, Jr.,** son of **James** and **Sarah (Bell) Anderson,** *b.* January 1, 1798, at Cool-collet Hill, Glaslough, Co. Monaghan, Ireland ; *d.* July 1, 1882, at Louisville, Ky. ; his wife *d.* December 30, 1850, at the same place. Issue (surname ANDERSON) :

i.   EDMONIA POPE ANDERSON. *b.* February 17, 1834.
ii.   LOUISA ALEXANDER, *b.* August 4, 1838 ; *m.*, January 10, 1865, by
       Rev. Francis M. Whittle (now Bishop of Virginia) at S. Paul's, Louis-
       ville, to DR. ANDREW CARR KEMPER, Captain and Assist-
       ant Adjutant-General of United States Volunteers, member of the
       Loyal Legion, etc., son of David Rice and Sarah Hall (Fulton)
       Kemper, of East Walnut Hills, Cincinnati, O., *b.* July 11, 1832 ;
       resides at 303 Broadway, Cincinnati. Issue (surname KEMPER) :

    i.   CAROLINE ROGERS, *b.* December 8, 1865; *m.*, March 19, 1894, by Rt. Rev.
        Boyd Vincent, Assistant Bishop of Southern Ohio, to LOUIS CARLETON,
        son of Philemon C. and Mary (Moody) Bulkley, of S. Louis, Mo. Issue :
        Louise, *b.* February 28, 1895.
    ii.   CARR LAWSON, *b.* March 19, 1867 ; *d.* October 26, 1874.
    iii. SARAH HALL, *b.* July 15, 1870 ; *d.* October 31, 1874.
    iv.   JAMES BROWN, *b.* January 6, 1876.

iii.   CAROLINE BROWN, *b.* November 9, 1840 ; *m.* WILKINS G. AN-
       DERSON.
iv.   ELISA JANE LONGWORTH, *b.* July 21, 1842.
v.   BROWN, *b.* January 25, 1844 ; *m.* SARAH MITCHELL.
vi.   MARY LAWRENCE, *b.* Sept. 10, 1845 ; *m.* THOMAS SUTTON.

Authority : Family papers, through Mrs. Andrew C. Kemper, of Cincinnati.

LAWRENCE, OF CHELSEA, MIDDLESEX

THOMAS LAWRENCE, of London, *d.* October 28, 1594, is *bu.* with many of his family in the Lawrence Chapel, S. Luke's Church, Chelsea.

JOHN, his son was of Chelsea, and Delaford, in Iver, Bucks; created a Baronet October 9, 1628; *m.* **GRISSELL,** *dau.* and *co h.* of **Gervase Gibbon,** of Benenden, in Kent, and was *bu.* November 13, 1638, aged fifty. His grandson, the third Baronet, was SIR THOMAS LAWRENCE, who was Secretary of the Colony of Maryland. September 20, 1698, letters appointing Sir Thomas Lawrence Baronet revoked and Thomas Lawrence, Esq., appointed during pleasure. This was his son, who *d.* April 14, 1701, and July 11th his father was reappointed Secretary of the Province. The colonial records show that his position was made a very trying one by the local authorities, every possible objection being raised to his claims. He returned to England and was *bu.* at Chelsea, April 25, 1714. He *m.* ANNE. *dau.* of Mrs. E. English, who was *bu.* at Chelsea in 1710. Issue: Anne, *bapt.* there May 4, 1675, and John. *bapt.* there November 5, 1676. ANNE LADY LAWRENCE was *bu.* at Chelsea November 2, 1723. John. heir apparent of Sir Thomas and Anne, his wife, sold an estate at Chelsea, March 26, 1706; his wife, Elizabeth, was *bu.* there

RESIDENCE OF SIR JOHN LAWRENCE
LORD-MAYOR OF LONDON, 1665

August 7, 1701, but the Secretary Baronet appears to have left but small estate, and the family[1] disappears from notice in this generation.

SIR JOHN LAWRENCE, Knt., of S. Helen's, Bishopsgate Street, London, was of Dutch extraction, despite the shields with the cross raguly which are seen on his house. He claimed connection with the Chelsea family, was Lord Mayor of London in 1665, and accumulated a large fortune. His *dau.*, **MARTHA,** *m.* **SIR STEPHEN ANDERSON**, of Eyworth, Bedfordshire, in 1673.

A certain **SIR OLIVER LAWRENCE** bought Crick Grange, in Steple Parish, Dorset, in 1540; *m.* **ANNE,** sister of **Henry Wriothesley,** Earl of Southampton ; had two sons :

i.   **EDWARD,** *m.*, first, **ALICE,** *dau.* of **Thomas Trenchard** ; *m.*, second, **JOYCE HUDLESTONE.**
ii.   **AUGUSTINE,** *m.* **ANNE,** *dau.* of **Francis Kelwaye.**

(For this family see Harleian MS., 1451, and the Visitations of Dorset, in 1565 and 1623.)

Another family was of Cirencester, Gloucestershire, descended from **DR. WILLIAM LAWRENCE,** *b.* September 11, 1753, son of **William Lawrence,** of Burford, Oxfordshire, represented now by SIR JAMES JOHN TREVOR LAWRENCE, Bart., *b.* December 30, 1831, son of **William Lawrence,** a distinguished surgeon, author of " Lectures on the Physiology, etc., of Man," 1819, and other works ; President of the College of Surgeons, 1846–55 ; created a Baronet, April 30, 1867. (See the Dictionary of National Biography and the Baronetages.)

Authorities : Faulkner's Chelsea, Maryland State papers, and some genealogical articles.

[1] Henry Kingsley introduces this family as the Hillyars, in his novel, " The Hillyars and the Burtons."

LAWRENCE, OF LANCASHIRE, ENGLAND

JAMES LAWRENCE, living 37 Henry III. (1252), by some
called son of **Sir Robert Lawrence**; *m.* **MATILDA,** *dau.*
and heiress of **John de Washington,** of Washington, Lancashire. Issue :

> **JOHN,** living in 1283 ; *m.* **MARGARET,** *dau.* of **Walter de Chesford.**
> Issue :
>
> i.   **JOHN,** presented to the Church at Washington in 1326; *m.* **ELIZABETH
> HOLTE,** of Stabley, Lancashire, and *d.* 1360. From him most of the English
> families of the name claim to be descended through a supposed son, **Robert.**
> ii.   **WILLIAM,** *of whom presently.*

WILLIAM, son of **John** and **Margaret (de Chesford)
Lawrence,** was probably the William Lawrence who held in 1311
lands at Ashton, on the Ribble, near Preston, in right of his wife, who
was a *dau.* and *co-h.* of **Heydock,** or **Eyedock,** of Haydock, in
the same county. This seems to dispose of the crusading **Sir Robert Laurens,** of Ashton Hall, making the property come to the
Lawrence family by this marriage. William Lawrence was a Burgess
in Parliament, 1326, and living in 1341. His son, **JOHN,** succeeded
him in his estate in 1368. His inquisition in 1399 reads : John, son
of William Lawrence, *dec.* 1368, "*feoffavit Laurencium de Myerch
cap ..de omnibus terris suis in Ribbleton, Ashton, Preston, Laton et Thorn-*

ton. idem Johannes obiit die ante Ascensionem 1398." WILLIAM, his son and heir, aged eighteen years ; mother, Margaret. In 1344 another **WILLIAM DE LAWRENCE** was seneschal of Henry, Earl of Lancaster, Steward of Blackburnshire, 1351–54. He *m.* **ALICE,** *dau.* of **Sir Nicholas de Stapylton,** by **Sybil,** *dau.* of **Sir John de Bella Aqua** and **Laderine,** who was *dau.* of **Peter Brus,** of Skelton, and **Helwyse de Lancaster.** William and Alice (Stapylton) Lawrence had a son and heir, **SIR EDMUND,** who *m.* **MARY** ——. Had a manor "*ex dimisione*" from his grandfather, **Sir Nicholas de Stapylton,** and was summoned to a Parliament at Westminster, in 1362, about the affairs of Ireland, as one of the heirs of Camville holding land in Ireland. As he was not again summoned, it is held that no barony was created by this writ. His heir, apparently, was **Sir Robert Lawrence,** of Ashton Hall, Escheator of Lancashire in 1403 ; Sheriff of Lancashire, 1407 and 1420 ; proved his arms, 1419, 1427, 1429 ; *d.* 18th Henry VI. (1440).

According to Harleian MS. No. 6, 159, a copy of the Visitation of Lancashire in 1567 with additional pedigrees, he was the son of **Edmund Lawrence,** and had brothers **James** and **William,** who both *d. s. p.*

The best supported version of this pedigree as revised by the Rev. R. Gwynne Lawrence, with corrections from my own researches, is as follows :

SIR ROBERT LAWRENCE aforesaid, who may have been Robert Lawrence, Esq., who, with two men at arms and six foot archers, was of the retinue of King Henry V., in 1417 (see Nicholas's "Agincourt," *p.* 381), possibly *m.* **MARGARET HOLDEN,** of Lancashire. Issue :

i.   **ROBERT,** *b.* in 1400, *of whom presently.*
ii.   **EDMUND,** who had issue :

> i.   **THOMAS,** *d. s. p.*
> ii.   **ROBERT.**
> iii.   **JOHN,** father of John.
> iv.   **NICHOLAS,** *d. s. p.*
> v.   **JAMES,** *d. s. p.*

iii.   **THOMAS** (*q. v.*).

ROBERT, the eldest son of **Sir Robert** and **Margaret (Holden) Lawrence,** *m.* **MARGARET,** *dau.* of **John Lawson** or **Lawrence,** of Rixton or Raxton, and *d.* 1450. Issue :

i.   **SIR JAMES, Knt.**, of Ashton, aged twenty-two at his father's inqui-
     sition, who *d.* 1490 ; *m.*, first, **CECILIA ·BOTILER ;** *m.*, second,
     ELEONORA, *dau.* of **Lord Welles** and widow of **Lord Hoo**
     and **Hastings** (Lord Hoo *d.* 1455), by whom he had no issue ; by
     his first wife he had :

     i.   **SIR THOMAS,** K.B., 1501, *d.* before 1513 ; his only son, John, *d. s. p.* abroad
          before his father. Some say a *dau.*, Cecilia, *m.* William Gerard, ancestor
          of the Lords Gerard.
     ii. **SIR JOHN,** *m.* but *d. s. p.* at Flodden in 1513, being the last male of the main line.

ii. **ROBERT,** killed at Bosworth in 1485, leaving issue : only daughters (who
     were co-heiresses of their cousin, Sir John Lawrence of Ashton) :

     i.   **AGNES,** *m.* —— **SKILLICORNE.**
     ii. **MARGARET,** *m.* **JOHN RIGMAYDEN.**
     iii. **ELIZABETH,** *m.* —— **BUTLER,** of Rawcliffe.
     iv. **ALICE,** *m.* **CUTHBERT CLYFTON,** of Clifton.

THOMAS, third son of Sir Robert Lawrence, of Ashton Hall, *m.*
MABILLA, *dau.* and heiress of **John Redmayne,** of Yeland
Redmayne.   Issue :

i.   **EDMUND,** *of whom presently.*
ii.   **JOHN,** *d. s. p.*
iii. **WILLIAM,** *d. s. p.*
iv.   **ROBERT,** *d. s. p.*
v.   **RICHARD,** *d. s. p.*
vi.   **JAMES,** *d. s. p.*
vii. **ELIZABETH,** *m.* **JOHN NAUSIER,** and had a *dau.*, **AGNES ;** *m.*
      WILLIAM PRESTON·

EDMUND, the eldest son of **Thomas** and **Mabilla (Redmayne)
Lawrence,** had issue at his death, 6th Henry VIII. : **LANCE-
LOT. LANCELOT LAWRENCE** was heir male of the family
and *d.* 26th Henry VIII., leaving issue : **THOMAS ;** and **SIR
OLIVER,** knighted at the Battle of Musselburg in 1547, *d. s. p.* ;
THOMAS, the eldest son, *d.* 35th Henry VIII., leaving an only son
and heir, Robert, who *m.* Anne, *dau.* of Thomas Bradley, of Bradley, and
d., in the second year of the reign of Philip and Mary, possessed
of lands at Yeland Redmain, Dylake, Heysham, Myddleton, Bolton, Warton, Skirton Hutton, Flokborow, and Sylverdale in Lancashire.   He left an only *dau.*, Anne, aged ten at her father's inquisition, who was the sole heiress of the family, and *m.* Walter,
third son of Sir John Sydenham, of Brampton, Co. Somerset.   This
seems to be the full history of the Lawrence family of Lancashire, though many pedigrees of doubtful authenticity will be

STRINGER LAWRENCE Esq.ʳ

THE FATHER OF THE EAST INDIAN ARMY

From a Painting by Sir Joshua Reynolds

found in print and manuscript, setting forth its later history and recording the great alliances the family has made. A writer in the *European Magazine* for 1796, vol. 29, page 275, calls the family cousins to Dudley, Duke of Northumberland, and to his rival, the Earl of Warwick, to Lord Guilford Dudley, Lady Jane Grey's hapless husband, to Leicester, and to Sir Philip Sidney, and therefore to "Sidney's sister, Pembroke's mother," celebrated by Ben Jonson, though some of these exalted claims need proving. An examination of the coats of arms used by nearly all of the name who have attained distinction will show that they claim descent from this Lancashire family. Among the more prominent of the name may be noted General **Stringer Lawrence**, *b.* at Hereford, England, in 1697, called the "Father of the Indian Army," whose skilful generalship in the last century expelled the French from India and laid the foundation of English rule in that country. Also the sons of Lieutenant-Colonel Alexander William Lawrence and Catherine Knox, who did so much to preserve it to the empire.

i. **SIR GEORGE ST. PATRICK**, *b.* at Trincomalee, Ceylon, March 17, 1804 ; *d.* November 16, 1884.

ii. **SIR HENRY MONTGOMERY**, *b.* at Madura, Ceylon, June 28, 1806 ; *d.* at Lucknow, July 4, 1857.

iii. **JOHN LAIRD MAIR**, *b.* at Richmond, Yorkshire, March 24, 1811, created Lord Lawrence of the Punjaub in 1869, Governor-General of India, 1863–69 ; *d.* June 27, 1879.

Authorities : Rev. R. G. Lawrence's article in the Herald and Genealogist, viii., 212, and references, most of which I have verified ; also Record Publications, especially Ducatus Lancastriæ, i., 11, 28, 32, 40, etc. ; Parliamentary Writs, i., 3d, 1084, and various printed pedigrees.

LAWRENCE, OF MONMOUTH COUNTY, N. J.

WILLIAM LAWRENCE, owning land at Middleborough, now Newtown, L. I.,[1] came to Monmouth Co., N. J., about 1667 ; settled at Hop River, where he had a house, a fulling mill, and orchard. He owned land at Middletown and Wakake. Was an overseer at Middletown in 1668 and 1670–71 ; and in 1669 and 1673 was a Deputy to the Legislature. He made his will December 3, 1701 ; proved, May 22, 1704 (Liber I, 56, Secretary of State's office, Trenton) ; naming his wife **ELIZABETH,** sons **JAMES, WILLIAM** (*of whom presently*), **BENJAMIN, ELISHA, JOHN** (*q. v.*), and **JOSEPH,** his grandsons, **JAMES GROVER, WILLIAM,** son of **WILLIAM, WILLIAM,** son of **ELISHA** (*q. v.*), and the eldest son of **JOSEPH,** his granddaughters, **ELIZABETH,** *dau.* of **JAMES, DEBORAH, MARY, HANNAH, ELIZABETH, SUSANNAH,** and **REBECCA GROVER.**

WILLIAM, son of **William** and **Elizabeth Lawrence,** *b.* 1658 : *m.,* June 24, 1686, **RUTH,** *dau.* of **Richard Gibbons.** Issue :

i.   **WILLIAM,** *b.* November 1, 1688.
ii.   **ELIZABETH,** *b.* December 3, 1690 ; *m.,* between 1716 and 1718, **WILLIAM HARTSHORNE,** and *d.* April 18, 1751.[2]
iii.   **ROBERT,** *b.* September 25, 1692.
iv.   **RICHARD,** *b.* July 11, 1694.
v.   **JOHN,** *b.* August 22, 1696, *of whom presently.*
vi.   **MARY,** *b.* December 28, 1698.
vii.   **HANNAH.**
viii.   **THOMAS,** *d. u.*

JOHN, son of **William** and **Elizabeth Lawrence,** made his will as of Monmouth, April 4, 1719 (Liber A, 153) naming his wife **RACHEL** (probably **GIBBONS**), sons **JOHN, GIBBONS,** and

---

[1] According to papers in possession of H. L. Everit, of Philadelphia, Pa.
[2] Her *dau.* Elizabeth *m.* Tylee Williams, and had a *dau.* Elizabeth, *m.* Joseph Parker, whose granddaughter, Elizabeth Williams Parker, *m.* Walter Tallman Westervelt, of New York City.

CAPTAIN JAMES LAWRENCE, U.S.N.

From a Painting by Stuart

BENJAMIN, daughters **CONSTANT, RACHEL, HANNAH, MARY,** and **DORCAS.**

ELISHA, said to be second son of **William** and **Elizabeth Lawrence,** made his will April 14, 1722; proved in May, 1724 (Liber A, 292), names his wife **LUCY,** sons **ELISHA, JOHN,** and **JOSEPH,** daughters **ELIZABETH,** *m.* **JOHN SALTER, SARAH,** *m.* **JOHN FINLAY, HANNAH,** *m.* **RICHARD SALTER,** second, and **REBECCA LAWRENCE.**

ELISHA, the eldest son, was father of **JOHN BROWN LAWRENCE,** whose son **JAMES** served in the United States Navy, with distinction, during the war of 1812, attained the rank of Post Captain, and while in command of the frigate Chesapeake engaged the Shannon, commanded by Captain Broke, on June 1, 1813, though his ship was quite unprepared, and in consequence lost both his vessel and his life.

Authorities: New Jersey Historical Collections, and family papers, through Mr. W. T. Westervelt.

LAWRENCE, OF S. ALBANS, ENGLAND, NEW YORK AND LONG ISLAND

A **John Lawrence** was chief Burgess of S. Albans in 1553, and Mayor in 1567 and 1575, and may have been father of William Lawrence, with whom the proven pedigree of this family begins. This **WILLIAM LAWRENCE**, of S. Albans, Hertfordshire, England, *m.*, November 25, 1559, **KATERIN BEAUMONT**. Issue:

i. **JOHN**, *bapt.* January 12, 1561-62, *of whom presently.*
ii. **ELIZABETH**, *bapt.* September 16, 1572. And possibly
iii. **THOMAS LAWRENCE**, who *m.*, November 9, 1589, **MARIE WILKINSON.**

JOHN, son of **William** and **Katerin (Beaumont) Lawrence**, *bapt.* January 12, 1561-62, had by an early marriage (wife's name unknown):

i. **WILLIAM**, *bapt.* December 4, 1580 ; probably the William Lawrence who *m.* at S. Stephen's Church, near S. Albans, February 16, 1617-18, **JOAN BROOKE**, or **BROCKE**. (She may have been *dau.* of John Brocke and **Joan Lawrence**, *m.* August 26, 1564.)
ii. **EDWARD**, *bapt.* June 18, 1582.

JOHN LAWRENCE, *m.*, second, January 25, 1586-87, **MARGARET ROBERTES**. Issue :

iii. **RICHARD**, *bapt.* July 26, 1587, who was a "Sargeant ; " *d.* May 21, 1616.
iv. **THOMAS**, *bapt.* February 2, 1588-89, *of whom presently.*

ST. ALBANS, HERTFORDSHIRE

From an Old Engraving

THOMAS, second son of **John** and **Margaret (Robertes)
Lawrence,** *bapt.* February 2, 1588–89, probably Chief Burgess
of S. Albans in 1622 ; *m.,* October 23, 1609, **JOANE,** *dau.* of
Walter and **Jane (Arnolde) Anterbus** or **Antrobus** (*q. v.*).
He *d.* March 20, 1624–25, having had issue :

i.	**JOANE,** *bapt.* August 29, 1610 ; *d.* August 31, 1610.
ii.	**JANE,** *bapt.* December 18, 1614, *m.* **GEORGE GIDDINGS.**
iii.	**MARIE,** *bapt.* November 17, 1616 ; *d.* November 28, 1616.
iv.	**JOHN,** *bapt.* July 26, 1618, *of whom presently.*
v.	**THOMAS,** *bapt.* March 8, 1619–20 (*q. v.*).
vi.	**WILLIAM,** *bapt.* July 27, 1622 (*q. v.*).
vii.	**MARIE,** *bapt.* April 10, 1625. Came to America with her mother and may have returned with her.

Shortly after her husband's death, probably in 1627, **JOAN
(ANTROBUS) LAWRENCE,** of S. Albans, *m.* **JOHN TUT-
TELL,** a mercer, of Ipswich.   April 2, 1635, the list of passengers to
New England on board the ship Planter, Nicholas Trarice master,
contains the following :

John Tuttell, a mercer, aged thirty-nine years.
Joan Tuttell, aged forty-two years.
John Lawrence, aged seventeen years.
William Lawrence, aged twelve years.
Marie Lawrence, aged nine years.
Abigail Tuttell, aged six years.
Simon Tuttell, aged four years.
Sara Tuttell, aged two years.
Jo. Tuttell, aged one year.
Joan Antrobus, aged sixty years (mother of Mrs. Tuttell).
George Giddings, aged twenty-five years.
Jane Giddings, aged twenty years (*dau.* of Mrs. Tuttell).

John Tuttell, *b.* 1596, was a freeman, March 13, 1639 ; Representative in 1644, when he was at Ipswich, Mass. Lieutenant in the
Provincial forces, a member of the Artillery Company ; probably had
more children in America, as Simon and Mary. After a few years
Savage says he went home and established himself to advantage in
Ireland, whither, in 1654, his wife followed him. He *d.* December 30,
1656, at Carrickfergus, whence his widow writes in 1689 to George
Giddings. There is little known of the New England life of the
emigrant Lawrences. The sister, **Marie,** disappears from sight.
The second brother, **Thomas,** came over at a later date. Landing

at Plymouth first, they afterward removed to Ipswich, and at about 1644 appear to have gone to Long Island, **John,** possibly going first and his brothers following him.

JOHN, eldest son of **Thomas** and **Joan (Antrobus) Lawrence,** *bapt.* July 26, 1618 ; emigrated in 1635, in the Planter, to New England. He must have attained some eminence in the Massachusetts Colony before removing to New Amsterdam, as Governor Endicott writes, September 15, 1658, specially commending him. November 16, 1644, we find him as one of the original corporators of " The Great Plains " (afterward Hempstead, L. I.), and October 10, 1645, of Flushing. February 1, 1648, he is one of the committee asking that a minister shall be settled at Flushing. In 1658 removed to New Amsterdam and engaged in business there ; July 23, of that year, the Council inquires concerning " goods removed from the house of Cornelis Steenwyck by John Laurens, an English merchant." He owned a small trading vessel called The Adventure, with which he traded up the Hudson to Albany and on both sides of Long Island. He was very successful in his affairs, became a Burgher of the city and gained the good-will of the Dutch. Governor Stuyvesant, speaking of him, June 10, 1664, as " well affected to the Dutch." May 29, 1664, he buys a negro for three hundred and forty-five florins. In October, 1663, with two others, is sent as a Commissioner to the General Assembly at Hartford, Conn. March 1, 1664–65, he is Attorney for Flushing in a boundary dispute. After the capture of the province by the English he is one of the first aldermen appointed, June 12, 1665, holding office until 1667, and again 1670–72, the latter year he is elected Mayor. August 18, 1673, " the Burgomasters and Schepens resolve that the mace, gowns, and city seal of the late Mayor, John Lawrence, be brought in, and the late Mayor reappearing delivers up his gown or cloak, with the city seal and mace." November 1, 1673, is one of three guardians of the estate of Richard Morris, brother of Colonel Lewis Morris. In the Dutch recapture of the city, in 1673, his house was not plundered. February 19, 1674, in a valuation of the best and most affluent inhabitants of New Amsterdam, John Lawrence has ten thousand florins, Holland currency, only ten others having as much or more. Is again Alderman of New York in 1680, and

NEW AMSTERDAM, NOW NEW YORK

From a Dutch Map of 1656

until 1684. September 29, 1683, he has at Flushing " 1 male, 12 acres upland, 10 of meadowes, 1 horse, 5 cowes, 6 young cattle, 1 pig, and is taxed 7 shills. 5d." The same year has at Newtown " 10 acres of lande, 4 cowes, and 3 three-year oldes." In 1674 is appointed a member of the Governor's Council. The same year he has, in New York City, a house of the first class, and property valued at $10,000, on the west side of Pearl Street, called the Water Side, between Wall and William Streets, and a house of the fourth class, and property valued at $1,500, on the west side of Pearl Street, between Franklin Square and Wall Street. In 1687 is Alderman of the East Ward of New York. August 20, 1689, appointed a Justice of the Peace for New York City. March 26, 1690, he is one of the Special Commission to try Jacob Leisler and his confederates after their unsuccessful revolution, and as such signs and seals Leisler's commitment. A facsimile of his signature will be found in General J. Grant Wilson's "Memorial History of New York." March 27, 1691, with Colonel Richard Townley, who had married his brother's widow, he is reappointed to the Governor's Council, and the same year is again Mayor of New York. April 20, 1693, he is one of the Justices of the Supreme Court of the colony. September 28, 1698, Governor Bellomont writes that " he has suspended from the Council Colonel Bayard, Colonel Minvielle, Colonel Willet, and Mr. Lawrence, because they were always resty and perverse in everything that I proposed for the King's service, tho' such sycophants as to comply with Colonel Fletcher in all parts of his corrupt administration," while the third head of the bill of complaints against the Governor, dated March 11, 1700, declares that " upon frivolous pretences he suspended ten of the most considerable for estates and parts and experience in busynesse (Mr. Lawrence named amongst them) and placed six of the Leislerian faction in their room." October 21, 1698, as further excuse for his action the Governor writes he is superannuated, being eighty-two years of age. His will, proved January 7, 1698–99, recorded Liber 5, p. 346, names " his *dau.*, Martha, widdow of Thomas Snowsell (deceased above seventeen years ago), his sons, John and Thomas, daughters, Martha as aforesaid, Susanna, wife of Gabriel Monvielle, his *dau.*, Withingham's children, and his son Joseph's *dau.*" and states that he was a patentee in Hempstead and Flushing and the only survivor in both. He has given to every one of his children a considerable part of his estate, they being all of full age and marriageable. Ends : "Soe I pray God Bless them as my children, & make them his children, by faith and love in Christ Jesus. Amen." His wife, Susanna and Gabriel Monvielle are executors. He *m.* SUSANNA ——, who survived him. Issue :

i. JOHN, in several papers called his eldest son, *of whom presently.*

ii. JOSEPH, said to have *d.*, leaving a *dau.*, *d. y.* There is no trace of him outside the mention in his father's will.

iii. THOMAS, may possibly be the Thomas Lawrence taxed at Flushing, October 9, 1675, on thirty-two acres, and is said to have *d. u.*

iv. MARTHA, *m.* (License dated August 22, 1675) THOMAS SNOW-SELL, who *d. s. p.*, in 1682.

v. SUSANNA, *m.*, first (License, January 25, 1676-77), GABRIEL MINVIELLE, or MONVIELE, Mayor of New York and Member of the Governor's Council. Made his will March 8, 1697-98; proved, October 1, 1702. Executors, Robert Livingston and John Barbarie, his nephew. He leaves his wife,[1] " All his servants, household stuff, silver plate, gold chains, pearles, dyamonds, gold rings and other jewells ; " the rest of the estate to his nephews and nieces.

She *m.*, second (by License, dated December 22, 1702), WILLIAM SMITH, Alderman of New York, and *d. s. p.*

vi. MARY, *m.* WILLIAM WHITTINGHAME, graduated at Harvard University, in 1660, and had a *dau.* MARY, of some literary culture, a liberal benefactor of Harvard and Yale Colleges ; *m.* GORDON SAL-TONSTALL, Governor of Connecticut, and *d.* in 1730. See a notice in Knapp's Female Biography, *p.* 453.

JOHN, eldest son of John and Susanna Lawrence, must have been born 1644, at latest, as in 1664 it is noted that John, son of John Lourens, English merchant and Burgher at the Manhattans, was sent to New England for provisions by Governor Stuyvesant, and brought back some three or four tons. In 1680 he was witness to a deed given by his aunt, Mrs. Elizabeth Carteret, September 29th (possibly this may be his cousin of the same name). By marriage license dated November 20, 1682, he *m.* SARAH, *dau.* of Thomas Cornell, and widow successively of Thomas Willett, first English Mayor of New York (*m.*, September 1, 1643), and Charles Bridges, by whom he appears to have had no issue. March 4, 1697-98, Will Book 5, p. 278, records that " John Lawrence, Esq., of his Majesty's Council, having a son *non compos mentis*, married, and

---

[1] The nature of this bequest is interesting when we learn that Minvielle was shrewdly suspected of being concerned in the early piratical voyages out of New York.

has an estate at Jamaica, in Queen's Co.; his wife, lately deceased, is appointed guardian to his son's person and estate, by Governor Benjamin Fletcher." As late as 1712 he was still alive, and insane.

THOMAS, second son of **Thomas** and **Joan (Antrobus) Lawrence,** of S. Albans, England, was *bapt.* there March 8, 1619–20. He appears to have emigrated after the rest of the family, but the date is not known. The first notice I find speaks of him as being at New Haven, August 24, 1651, with money of Governor Stuyvesant's to which the New England authorities laid claim and arrested him. After his release he joins with his brothers in the patent of Middleburgh, afterward Newtown, L. I., in 1655, and appears to have settled there; on July 10, 1662, being owner of two lots. August 23, 1665, he receives license, as Captain Thomas Lawrence, to purchase of the Indians " Round Island near Helgate," about eight or nine acres of land. This purchase is disputed by William Hallett, in 1667, but confirmed by the Governor. March 14, 1669–70, he is one of the road surveyors at Newtown.

In September, 1675, he has at Newtown forty acres of land, 2 horses, 4 oxen, 8 cows, 12 younger cattle and 8 swine. Three years later he has 4 persons, forty acres, 10 horses, 2 oxen, 8 cows, 22 younger cattle, 20 sheep and 12 swine. December, 1677, he has a patent of Anneke Jans's farm on Hellgate Neck. February 16, 1689–90 he is spoken of as Major Thomas Lawrence of Queen's County, on December 24th, of that year, having been commissioned by Jacob Leisler as Major of horse for the Co. This branch of the family adhered to the cause of Leisler. William Lawrence was one of the Committee of Safety. John and Daniel had commissions in the Co. militia from the rebel governor. His first wife's name is unknown. November 9, 1692, Thomas Lawrence, widower, of Newtown, has a license to marry Mary Ferguson. His will was made February 5, 1703; proved, April 25, 1703 (Liber 7, *pp.* 134, 135). He leaves " his son Thomas the great neck of land with the island, his wife Mary, the third part of his movable estate, his son Johnathan (*sic*) that lot of land which was—(*illegible*) the house he now lives in ; to his sons William and Johnathan the piece of Salt Medow bought of Robert Beacham, to son Daniel, Trains Medows, names also his grandchild Elizabeth Saunders and four sons—Thomas, William, John, and Johnathan." Spells his surname Lawrance. January 27, 1704–5, Mary, his widow, complains of ill-treatment at the hands of William Lawrence,

her stepson. February 5th, 10th, and 17th there are further depositions in the case, and April 3d she complains also against John his
brother. By his first wife **MAJOR LAWRENCE** had issue (the
order of birth is uncertain, but probably was) :

i. THOMAS, for whose descendants see Thomas Lawrence's Genealogy of
    the family (1858) *pp.* 84–87.
ii. WILLIAM, *of whom presently.*
iii. JOHN (*q. v.*).
iv. JOHNATHAN, see Lawrence Genealogy as above for his issue.
v. DANIEL, commissioned Cornet of a troop of horse by Governor Bello-
    mont. His issue, if any, is unknown.
vi. ELIZABETH, *m.*, by license dated July 26, 1683, JOHN SAUN-
    DERS, and had a *dau.* ELIZABETH, living in 1703.

WILLIAM, second son of **Major Thomas Lawrence,** was
an adherent of Jacob Leisler, probably a member of the Committee of
Safety. A comparison of the terms in which this William Lawrence
and his cousin of Flushing are spoken of by Governors Bellomont
and Cornbury, will show that politics in the Province differed little
in their amenities of speech from those of the present State of New
York. January 16, 1700–1, Lord Bellomont adds to the Council
William Lawrence, of Newtown, Queen's Co., on Nassau Island, "an
honest understanding man. He has a good estate and must be distinguished by the place of his dwelling from another of the same
name and surname, who has not so good a character." (Historical MSS.,
New York, iv. 834.) April, 1701, Paroculus Parmiter, an attorney,
(afterward Attorney-General of Pennsylvania), exhibits a bill of costs
against him. December 27, 1702, he complains to the Council, and
expresses surprise that he has not received authority to sue him, "as
the way to justice ought to be like the way to hell, smooth and
broad." December 31, 1702, he writes again enclosing two bills of
costs to the Council. January 14, 1703, he makes an affidavit regard-
ing his claim, and February 19th asks relief in equity against Lawrence and others. October 22, 1704, he writes to Thomas Cardale,
Sheriff of Queen's Co., in relation to John and William Lawrence, and
November 6th there are affidavits of the sheriff and Christopher
Rousby as to his proceedings. There is no record that he ever obtained the satisfaction he sought (" New York Colonial Historical
MSS.," English, 282, 305, 307, 333). January 23, 1703, William Lawrence writes excusing his absence from the Council on account of
sickness.

"November 8, 1673, he met Jacob Wiltse, of Newtown, on the highway near the late Thomas Lawrence's, and assaulted him with a stake which he suddenly took up and smote him with that violence and blows that he broke his arm; under the pain and bruises of which," it is shortly after testified, "he now languishes." But Lawrence being of his Majesty's Council, Wiltse "can get no satisfaction unless he presents him to the Council." This he does the next day (Colonial MSS., vol. 48, in Onderdonk's "Queen's County," *p.* 15). August 10, 1706, Lord Cornbury, the Governor, writes to the Commissioners for Trade and Plantations : "I must acquaint your Lordships that I have been forced to dismiss Mr. William Lawrence from the Council after having borne with him upwards of three years in many irregularities. One time having a complaint against him for assaulting a man upon the highway I sent for him and told him if he would not cease committing those irregular proceedings that he had been guilty of, I should be forced to remove him. He promised to amend his ways, but instead, in a few weeks, I had a complaint by some of the justices of Queen's Co., where he lives, that he, and some other persons moved by him, had committed a riot. The Council were all of opinion that he ought to be dismissed. Therefore I did dismiss him ("New York Historical MSS.," IV., 1181)." The aforesaid riot may refer to the case of William, John, Daniel, and Jonathan Lawrence, on December 12, 1705, cutting down the fence of William Hallett, of Newtown, with axes (Onderdonk, *p.* 16), or the assault on George Hallett by William Lawrence and John White, about which Hallett and Joseph Moore make depositions on March 6 and 7, 1706. In spite of the governor's bad opinion of him, June 26, 1706, he had been appointed one of the Commissioners about a claim of the Mohegan Indians. After his dismissal from the Council he drops out of public notice. December 3, 1731, he made his will as of Newtown, proved the following February 11 (Liber 11, *p.* 218). He leaves to his wife **ELIZABETH** his best bed and furniture, to his eldest son **WILLIAM**, his plate, with £5 in money, the rest of his estate in equal proportions to his wife, his sons **WILLIAM, SAMUEL, JOHN,** and the child his wife is now pregnant with if a son, but if a daughter then £5 to her. His uncles and friends, James Hazard and Nicholas Berrien, to be executors.

The descent of this line of the family has never been traced.

JOHN, third son of **Major Thomas Lawrence,** of Newtown, *b.*

1668, was commissioned captain of the troop of horse in the Queen's Co. Regiment by the Earl of Bellomont (who *d.* March 5, 1701) (New York Papers, N. O.; O. 14); with his brother Daniel in September, 1698, was fined £3 each for burning a hovel valued at £12 2*s.*, which William Hallett, after digging a cellar, had set up on land they claimed as theirs. He was sheriff of Queen's Co. in 1698. He *m.* **DEBORAH,** *dau.* of **Richard Woodhull,** one of the patentees of Brookhaven (*b.* 1659, *d.* January 6, 1742), and *d.* December 17, 1729. Issue :

i.   **JOHN,** *b.* 1695, *of whom presently.*
ii.   **THOMAS,** *m.*, January 3, 1730, **DEBORAH WOOLSEY,** and *d.* 1752.
      See Lawrence genealogy (1858) for his issue.
iii. **NATHANIEL** (*q. v.*).

JOHN, eldest son of **John** and **Deborah (Woodhull) Lawrence,** *b.* at Newtown, September 9, 1695, was in the county magistracy for a number of years. He *m.*, December 6, 1720, **PATIENCE,** *dau.* of **Joseph Sackett** (*b.* April 29, 1701 ; *d.* October 24, 1772), and *d.* May 7, 1765. (Will proved August 9, 1765, Liber 25, *p.* 108). Besides two sons and a *dau. d. y.*, he had issue :

i.   **JOHN,** *b.* 1721, *of whom presently.*
ii.   **JOSEPH,** *b.* 1723, commander of the sloop Wheel of Fortune, July 19. 1763 ; *m.* **PATIENCE,** aunt of **Bishop Benjamine Moore,** of New York. Issue.
      i.   **RICHARD,** *d. s. p.*
      ii. **ANN,** *m.* **SAMUEL RIKER,** member of the Assembly, 1784. Issue (surname RIKER).
           i.   Richard, Recorder of New York City.
           ii.   John Lawrence, author of a "History of Newtown," etc.
           iii. Jane, *m.* Dr. William James Macneven.
iii. **RICHARD,** *b.* 1725, captain of horse in the militia of Queen's Co., May 10, 1776, resigned on account of ill-health ; *d. s. p.* 1781, a prisoner of the British at New York.
iv.   **NATHANIEL,** *b.* 1727 ; *d. u.* at St. Eustatia in the West Indies, 1761, whither he had probably gone as commander of the privateer Catherine.
v.   **WILLIAM** (*q. v.*).
vi.   **SAMUEL,** *b.* 1735 ; *m.*, but early lost his wife and child, and *d. s. p.*, 1810.
vii. **JONATHAN,** *b.* 1737 (*q. v.*).
viii. **DANIEL,** *b.* 1739, served as a member of the Assembly of New York from Queen's Co. ; through the Revolution he was commissioned a colonel in the militia ; *m.* **EVA VAN HORNE,** and *d.* 1807, leaving issue.
ix.   **THOMAS,** *b.* 1743 (probably 1733), engaged in privateering, and in 1758 commanded the ship Tartar, sixteen guns, of which his brother John

was part owner. (The date of his commission would imply an error in that given for his birth.) In this pursuit he accumulated wealth, and purchasing land on Flushing Bay settled there. In 1784 commissioned a County Judge; *m.* **ELIZABETH,** *dau.* of **Nathaniel Fish,** of Newtown, L. I., and *d.* in 1816, leaving issue.

JOHN, eldest son of **John** and **Patience (Sackett) Lawrence,** *b.* 1721, became one of the leading merchants of New York City. He entered into partnership with Lawrence Kortright, and engaged extensively in what was then the legitimate and profitable business of privateering. September 28, 1756, with John Jauncey, Mariner, he petitions for a commission for Richard Harris Captain of the Privateer, Charming Sally, 26 guns, and in case of his death to James Lilley, First, and Stephen Skinner, Second Lieutenant. October 4, 1764, the firm ask for a commission for Peter Healy as Captain, Thomas Duren, First, and Thomas Hays, Second Lieutenant, of the Harlequin 18 guns. January 3, 1757, the same vessel as a sloop with 8 guns is to be commanded by Captain Doran. September 27th, Henry Lane is to be Captain. November 29th, James Wright is to be Captain, and 2 guns have been added to the armament. July 10, 1758, John Lawrence, Jr., of New York, merchant, owner of the Brigantine, Catherine, 10 guns, applies for a commission for Nathaniel Lawrence (his brother) as its commander. September 28th, with Kortright he applies for a commission for Nathaniel Slooe to command the Harlequin, 10 guns, and John Harrison as commander of the Ship Hunter, 18 guns, of which they are owners. October 5th, with his father-in-law, Philip Livingston, he applies for a commission for Thomas Lawrence (his brother) to command their ship, Tartar, 16 guns. April 19, 1760, with others, owners of the Privateer, De Lancey, commanded by Stephen Skinner, he petitions for the release of the vessel and crew, which had been taken by the Dutch of Curaçoa. April 25th, Governor De Lancey writes to Governor Rodier, of Curaçoa, and orders Captain John Van Ranst, of Schooner Polly, to demand their release. Mr. Lawrence resided on Dock Street and was Alderman of the Dock Ward. He *m.,* in 1759, **CATHERINE,** *dau.* of **Philip Livingston,** and sister of Governor William Livingston, of New Jersey (who survived him) and *d. s. p.* August 3, 1764. George Whitefield preached his General Sermon in the Presbyterian Meeting-house, and he was buried in Lord Stirling's vault in Trinity Churchyard. His will, made August 11, 1761, proved September 25, 1764, Liber 24, 481, distributes his large estate among his relatives, and is valuable for its numerous statements of relationship. "On the Friday before April 13, 1747, Captain John Lawrence, late of the Privateer Rainbow, being in a bit of lunacy, ran himself through the body with his sword. Had been subject to these fits. Came to himself and died very penitent."[1] Evidently he was of this branch of the family, though I have not identified him.

WILLIAM, fifth son of **John** and **Patience (Sackett) Lawrence,** *b.* about 1729; possibly commissioned Captain, Newtown District, August 14, 1776 ("New York Archives," I., 286); a magistrate of Queens Co.; had apparently by his first wife, **ANN BRINCKERHOFF,** with other issue, a son, ISAAC, *b.* 1768, *of whom presently.*

ISAAC, youngest son of **William** and **Ann (Brinckerhoff) Lawrence,** *b.* 1768, was a merchant in New York City, and for several years President of the United States Branch Bank there; *m.* **CORNELIA,** *dau.* of **Rev. Abraham Beach, D.D.,** Rector of Trinity Church, and *d.* 1841. Issue:

i.   **WILLIAM BEACH,** *b.* October 23, 1800; Chargé d'Affaires at London, in 1827; settled at Ochre Point, Newport, R. I. Was Lieutenant-Governor of the State in 1850, afterward Governor. For many years Vice-President of the New York Historical Society. Was member of the Institute of the Law of Nations, a statesman, Diplomat, and International Jurist of the first rank. Wrote (in French) a "Commentary on International Law," and many pamphlets; edited, with extensive notes, Wheaton's "International Law;" translated Marbois's "History of Louisiana," from the French; *m.* ——, and *d.* in 1881. Issue:

      i.   **ALBERT GALLATIN,** *b.* 1835, graduated at Harvard and studied law at the Cambridge Law School, obtained the position of Secretary of the American Legation at Vienna, but left that post at the outbreak of the war. After serving on General Stahl's staff in the Eleventh Army Corps and as a recruiting officer he went to the field as a Captain of colored troops. In the assault on Fort Fisher he received three wounds, one of which resulted in the loss of his left arm. For his gallantry he was thanked by the General commanding and the Legislature of Rhode Island, while the War Department gave him the brevet rank of Colonel, which was raised to Brigadier-General. 1866-68 he was appointed Minister to Costa Rica, by President Johnson. During a visit to Washington he engaged in a duel with an attache of the Prussian Legation, who had cast a slur upon the American flag. The Prussian fired and missed, and General Lawrence fired into the air. The sensation caused by the affair and criticisms from official quarters caused General Lawrence to resign his post. His only subsequent public service was a report which he made, after investigation, upon the Sitting Bull and other Indian troubles. He *m.* ——, and *d.* in January, 1887. Issue:

         Esther Grace, *b.* 1873.

[1] Valentine's New York Manual, 1865, *p.* 811.

WILLIAM BEACH LAWRENCE, LL.D.

From a Portrait Engraved for General James Grant Wilson

ii. **JAMES GORE KING,** Secretary of the Coney Island Jockey Club, and prominent in Turf circles ; *d.* June 22, 1895.

ii. **CORNELIA A.,** *m.* **JAMES A. HILLHOUSE,** of " Sachem Wood," New Haven, Conn. Author of " Hadad," " Percy's Masque," and other poems.

iii. **HARRIET,** *m.* **DR. JOHN A. POOL,** of New Brunswick, N. J.

iv. **JOSEPHINE C.,** *m.* **DR. BENJAMIN McVICKAR** (*q. v.*).

v. **JULIA B.,** *m.* **THOMAS L. WELLES.**

vi. **MARIA E.,** *m.* **REV. WILLIAM INGRAHAM KIP,** Rector of S. Paul's Church, Albany, N. Y. ; *b.* October 3, 1811 ; Bishop of California, October 28, 1853 ; author of " The Double Witness of the Church," the " Catacombs of Rome," " Holy Week in Rome," " Some Unnoticed Things of Scripture," " Olden Times in New York," etc. ; *d.* April 7, 1893.

vii. **HANNAH E.,** *m.* **HENRY WHITNEY,** and *d.* 1844.

JONATHAN, seventh surviving son of **John** and **Patience (Sackett) Lawrence,** *b.* October 4, 1737, at Newtown, L. I., was in business as a partner of the firm of Watson, Murray & Lawrence, of New York. Prospering himself and inheriting largely from his brother, John, he purchased the original estate of his emigrant ancestor, at Hellgate, and retired from business. In 1772 was commissioned Captain in the local militia, but joined the Revolutionary party and, 1774, was a member of their Committee, at Newtown. In 1775 elected a member of the Congress at New York, and again in 1776 and 1777. In 1776–77 member of the Constitutional Convention, and appointed Major of the Militia of Queens and Suffolk Counties, of which Nathaniel Woodhull was Commander. Was Captain of a company in the regiment of Lieutenant-Colonel John Harper ;[1] and April 14, 1777, Captain in the regiment of Colonel Albert Pawling,[1] one of sixteen additional of the Line, authorized by Congress. This company was one of four made up of refugees from New York and Long Island. He was an active member of the Revolutionary party in New York, and held many important positions on committees and commissions for the carrying on of the war. Was member of the New York Senate, 1777–83 ; and in 1783, with two other senators alone, opposed the passage of the iniquitous bill declaring those described therein, who had been loyal to the Crown, to have been aliens from the date of the Declaration of Independence. This Bill, clearly in violation of the provisional treaty of peace, and introducing endless confusion into the land titles on Long Island and

[1] New York Archives, I., 413.

elsewhere, was delayed by the greater discretion of the Council of revision after passing both Houses of the Legislature, and at the next session was repealed.

MAJOR LAWRENCE *m.*, first, **JUDITH**, *dau.* of Nathaniel Fish, who *d.* aged eighteen. Among their descendants were William Anson Lawrence, a merchant of Canton, China, whose monument is one of the sights of Greenwood Cemetery, Brooklyn, and Jonathan Lawrence, a lawyer, *d. y.*, the author of a volume of essays and poems. **MAJOR LAWRENCE** *m.*, second, August 7, 1768, **RUTH** (*b.* November 18, 1746, *d.* October 9, 1818), *dau.* of Andrew Riker, Esq., of Riker's Island, and *d.* September 4, 1812. Issue, with others :

i.   **RICHARD M.**, *b.* January 12, 1778, merchant at Savannah and in the trade to Cadiz, Lisbon, and Calcutta.

ii.   **ABRAHAM R.**, *b.* December 18, 1780, President of the New York & Harlem Railroad Company, 1836-40.

iii.   **JOHN L.**, *of whom presently.*

JOHN L., seventh son of **MAJOR JONATHAN** and **RUTH (RIKER) LAWRENCE**, *b.* October 2, 1785, in New York City, practised law there from 1806 ; was attorney for the United States Branch Bank. In 1814, Secretary of Legation to Sweden and became Chargé d'Affaires ; returning was a member of Assembly ; in 1821, member of the State Constitutional Convention ; 1824, appointed Assistant Register of the New York Court of Chancery ; 1840, a presidential elector ; 1847-49, State Senator, was Treasurer of Columbia College, and in 1850 appointed Comptroller of the City. He *m.*, June 2, 1816, **SARAH AUGUSTA TANGIER**, only *dau.* of **General John Smith**, of S. George's Manor, Suffolk Co., and his wife **Elizabeth**, only *dau.* of General Nathaniel Woodhull. **MRS. LAWRENCE** was *b.* May 19, 1794, and *d.* in New York City, November 13, 1877. Her husband *d.* July 24, 1850. Issue :

i.   **ELIZABETH**, *m.* **ALFRED N. LAWRENCE** (*q. v.*).

ii.   **JOHN SMITH**, practised law in New York City ; *m.* **SARAH MAURAN**, of Providence, R. I. Issue :

    i.   **GRACE**, *d. y.*

    ii.   **ELIZABETH MAURAN.**

    iii.   **EMMA McALLISTER.**

    iv.   **JOHN S.**, *m.* **SARAH WYNN**, of Philadelphia. Issue :
        John S., Sarah, and Caroline.

    v.   **FRANCIS MAURAN.**

iii.   **SARAH**, *d. u.*

iv.   **MARGARET R.**, *m.* **JAMES W. WALSH**. Issue (surname WALSH) :

     i.   **J. LAWRENCE**, *d. u.*
     ii.   **RICHARD MONTGOMERY LAWRENCE**.
     iii.   **ELIZABETH ROBERTSON**.
     iv.   **JAMES W.**, *m.* **SUSAN N.**, *dau.* of Newbold Lawrence (*q. v.*). Issue :
         Margaret and **James W.**, Jr.

v.   **ANNIE MIDDLETON**, *m.* **JOHN R. SUYDAM**. Issue (surname SUYDAM) :

     i.   **JANE**, *m.* **WALTER L. SUYDAM**. Issue :
         Walter Lispenard.
     ii.   **JOHN R.**, *m.* **HARRIET COCHRAN**, of Philadelphia. Issue :
         John R. and Lisa.

vi.   **RICHARD MONTGOMERY**, *d. y.* at Manilla, East Indies.

vii.   **CHARLES W.**

viii.   **MARY**, *d. y.*

ix.   **WILLIAM THOMAS**, *m.* **SOPHIE TILLEY**. Issue :

     i.   **SARAH**, *d. y.*
     ii.   **SOPHIA ST. GERMAIN**.
     iii.   **ALICE MADISON**, *d. u.*, July 20, 1895.
     iv.   **MARGARET WOODHULL**.

x.   **ABRAHAM RIKER**, *b.* September 19, 1832 ; Justice of the Supreme
        Court of the State of New York, elected 1873 ; Chancellor of the New
        York Society of Colonial Wars, 1895. He *m.*, 1860, **ELIZA
        WILLIAMS**, only *dau.* of **Dr. William** and **Julia Caroline**
        (**Williams**) **Miner**, of New York. Issue :

     i.   **WILLIAM MINER**, Member of Assembly, 1891, *m.* **LAVINIA OLIVER.** Issue :
         Oliver.
     ii.   **RUTH**.

xi.   **LYDIA S.**, *m.* **WILLIAM THURSTON HORN**. Issue : (surname HORN).

     i.   **ANNIE LAWRENCE**.
     ii.   **JAMES THURSTON**.
     iii.   **SARAH LAWRENCE**.
     iv.   **MARY THURSTON**.

NATHANIEL, third son of **John** and **Deborah (Woodhull)
Lawrence**, *m.*, May 23, 1728, **SUSANNA**, *dau.* of **Thomas
Alsop**, of Newtown. Issue :

i.   **DEBORAH**, *b.* March 3, 1728–29.

ii.   **ELIZABETH**, *b.* January 24, 1730–31.

iii.   **NATHANIEL**, *b.* October 18, 1732, *of whom presently.*

iv.   **RICHARD**, *b.* April 5, 1735, *d. s. p.*

v.   **HANNAH**, *b.* May 16, 1737.

vi.   **MARY**, *b.* June 29, 1739.

vii. **SUSANNA**, *b.* January 3, 1742–43.
viii. **JOHN**, *b.* March 25, 1745; *m.* **CATHERINE**, *dau.* of **Colonel Van Horne Beekman.** Issue :

    i.   **JOHN**, *d. s. p.* at sea.
    ii.   **CATHARINE**, *m.*, first, **JOHN BOWNE HICKS** ; and second, **NATHANIEL LAWRENCE** (*q. v.*). By her first husband, issue (surname HICKS) :
        i.   **Mary Lawrence**, *b.* 1794 ; *m.* Robert B. Van Zandt (her granddaughter is Marie Van Zandt, the cantatrice).
        ii.   **Louisa**, *m.* John C. Clarkson.

NATHANIEL, eldest son of **Nathaniel** and **Susanna (Alsop) Lawrence**, *b.* October 18, 1732 ; *m.* **MARTHA DUNCAN.** Issue :

    i.   **JAMES DUNCAN**, sailing-master of a 74-gun ship in the British Navy. *d. s. p.*
    ii.   **NATHANIEL**, *b.* 1763 ; *m.* **CATHERINE**, *dau.* of John and Catherine (Beekman) Lawrence (*q. v.*). Issue :
        i.   **CAROLINE**, *m.*, first. —— **ABEEL** ; *m.*, second, —— **GOULD.**
        ii.   **CATHERINE**, *m.* **CAPTAIN GALLAGHER, U. S. N.** Issue : Dr. Charles Gallagher, of Baltimore, Md.
        iii.   **ELIZABETH**, *m.* **CHARLES CLARKSON.**
        iv.   **JULIA**, *m.* **PHINEAS HENRY BUCKLEY** (*q. v.*).
        v.   **CORNELIA.**
        vi.   **CHARLOTTE.**
        vii.   **JOHN C.**, in the navy, *d.* at sea.
        viii.   **CHARLES**, Lieutenant U. S. N. *d. s. p.* abroad.

WILLIAM, third son of **Thomas** and **Joan (Antrobus) Lawrence**, *b.* at S. Albans, Hertfordshire, England, and *bapt.* there July 27, 1622 ; was brought to New England in the ship Planter, by his step-father, John Tuttell, in 1635. Ten years later, with his brother John, October 10, 1645, he was one of the eighteen original incorporators of Flushing on Long Island, and seems to have made that his permanent residence thereafter. April 22, 1655, William Lawrence, Thomas Saul, and Edward Ffarrington were appointed Magistrates of Flushing. March 25, 1656, he was elected by the Council Presiding Magistrate of the town.

January 26, 1657–58, with Tobias Feke and Robert Ferry, deputies to the Council about the encroachments of Hempstead upon their boundaries. The following letter from him to Governor Stuyvesant is on record :

" HONORED SIR :

"Wearas divers of our inhabittants having Cases depending in our Courtt att Vlissing (Flushing) and desiering Isheeuw in ther cases.

Edw. Farrintton and William Nobell in regard of ther latte trubell are nott willing to proseed aney ferrder without your honeres forder order this is to request you would be pleased to maniffest your mind in this case to this bearrer W^m. Nobell so that wee may ether proseed or forbeare so I shall remain

" Your humbell Saruantt

" WILLIAM LAWRENCE.

" Vlishinge
" Jenewarey
" the 20th 1658."

July 10, 1662, with his brothers, John and Thomas Lawrence, and his father-in-law, Richard Smith, he is among the taxables at Middleburgh (Newtown), Long Island. January 7, 1664, some Indians complain that they were summoned to a conference about some land at Flushing by him, but he was not present when they came. In 1665, Captain of the Queen's Co. Militia. September 27, 1666, was one of the jury in a lawsuit between Gravesend and Flatbush. The same year Rev. Francis Doughty, Minister of Flushing, in a suit about his unpaid salary, states that his contract of salary was burnt one year before the trial by William Lawrence's wife, who " put it under a pye in an oven." He claimed back salary, and the defence was made that Governor Stuyvesant forced them to call him. His son recovered, in 1669, six year's salary, each party to pay their own costs. December 18, 1666, William Lawrence, of Flushing, for seditious words is fined £15, and to make an apology to the Court.

February 24, 1670–71, " Captain William Lawrence, with consent of the major part of the inhabitants of Flushing, receives a patent of his land where hee lives, with an addition of a piece of swampy meadow ground lyeing within that Neck." Consent of Thomas Willett and others to this patent was given February 15, 1670–71. September 29, 1672, one of his negroes at Flushing is complained of as a thief. August 31, 1673, he is schout or sheriff of Flushing, and several letters to him in that capacity are among the Historical MSS. of the State of New York. The same year commanded the " Flushing Foote Companie," at the surrender of New York to the Dutch. In 1674 either he or his son of the same name has a house of the second class, valued at $2,000, on the east side of Broadway between Beaver and Wall Streets, in New York. May 19th of that year, it is complained that " Richard Smith of Nessequack, with the aid of his son-in-law, William Lawrence, the Sheriff," in a lawsuit, "had chosen such jury as were favourable to him." September 14, 1675, it is ordered by the Council that Captain William Lawrence be "added to ye justices of ye peace of the North Riding of Long Island." In October, 1677, judgment is entered against him in a suit for £6 19s. 5d. May 7, 1678, the constable and others complain of Captain William Lawrence fencing in the highway. April 29, 1679, his negro, Andreas, is convicted of the murder of a squaw ; verdict, "conditionally manslaughter." Early in the next year he died, his estate being administered March 25, 1680, by his " widow Elizabeth and eldest son (by a former venter) William Lawrence." The principal items of the inventory returned by Richard Cornell, John Bowne, John Lawrence, and Abraham Whorley on April 19, 1680 (recorded Lib. 2, *pp.* 212–223) are :

Tew's Neck houses, etc.	£1250.
250 acre lots at Whitestone	60.
50 acre lot No. 13	20.
50 acre lot at Newton's Neck	15.
10 four acres in the town	60.
640 acres " Sinken Meddowes"	150.
6 shares at Westchester	16.
Silver money	135.
Plate	7.
12 leather chairs	48.
6 rush chairs	7.16
One great looking-glass	1.
Negroes John, Andreas, Tenny, Harry, Mingo, and Peter, etc.	
Total valuation	4,432.1.10¼.

CAPTAIN WILLIAM LAWRENCE had a first wife whose name is unknown, by whom he had issue, two sons :

i. **WILLIAM,** *of whom presently.*
ii. **JOHN** (*q. v.*).

By license dated March 4, 1664, he *m.*, second, **ELIZABETH,** *dau.* of **Richard Smith,** of Nessequack, patentee of Smithtown, L. I., and had further issue :

iii. **MARY,** *b.* in 1665 ; *m.*, first, in 1682 or 83, **JAMES EMOTT,** Secretary of the Province of New Jersey ; Clerk of the Council, in 1683 : Deputy-Secretary, 1684 ; Captain-Lieutenant of a foot company at Perth Amboy, December 11, 1686. He was Counsel for the celebrated pirate, Captain Richard Kidd, and *d.* at New York in April, 1713, leaving his widow with four sons, and a fortune of £2,000. She *m.*, second, in 1714, **REV. EDWARD VAUGHAN**, Missionary of the Society for the Propagation of the Gospel, at Elizabeth, who *d.* October 12, 1747.

iv.   **JOSEPH** (*q. v.*).

v.   **THOMAS**, *b.* 1668 ; *d.* October 26, 1687.

vi.   **RICHARD**, at school, a pupil of Rev. John Harriman, Puritan pastor at Elizabeth, between 1695 and 1702 ; *m.* (license, September 24, 1699), **CHARITY**, *dau.* of **Thomas Clerke**, or **Clarke**, of Brookhaven, Gent. ; and had a *dau.*, **CHARITY**, *m.* —— **DAYTON**.

vii.   **SAMUEL**, *b.* 1672 ; *d.* August 16, 1687, and with his brother, **THOMAS**, was buried in the rear of the Meeting-house, at Elizabeth. Their graves are now covered by the First Presbyterian Church, and their monuments adorn the rear wall of the building, the most ancient stones in the cemetery.

viii.   **SARAH**, *m.* **JAMES TILLETT.**

ix.   **JAMES**, of whom nothing is known.

After the death of **CAPTAIN WILLIAM LAWRENCE,** his widow *m.*, second, in April, 1681, the **HON. CAPTAIN PHILIP CARTERET,** *b.* 1639, Seigneur of the Manor of La Houque, Parish of S. Peter, Island of Jersey, and Governor of the Province of East and West Jerseys, and removed to Elizabeth with her seven children. Like many of the Provincial Governors he was involved in disputes with the local authorities, and by high-handed injustice on their part even imprisoned.

He *d.* between December 10 and 20, 1682, leaving his estates in Jersey to his mother, and to "his most deare wife Elizabeth Carteret and her heirs," all his estate in New Jersey and all his negroes and other servants "except Black Jack who is to be set free." After his death she occupied for over a year and claimed as her own, in her husband's right, the Government house and property at Elizabeth. May 29, 1684, the Council speak of her "many clamours made against the proprietors and late Governor on pretence of Rong Don her." In her petition presented to the Hon. Gawen Laurie, Deputy-Governor of the Province of East New Jersey and his Council, she claims :

"1st, her husbands sallery for being Governor amounteing to the sume of 1000 lb.

"2d. A patent for 3,596 acres in Elizabeth Towne bounds as expressed in 2 patents when Robert Vicars was Secretary.

" 3d. Patent for lot of land on Rareton River purchased by her husband of the Indians.

" 4th. That the house, lot, and orchard in Elizabeth Towne, now in possession of the proprietors, be delivered to her."

" The Bord " answer to 2d and 4th : " patents of that date are voided." 3d, deny Carteret's having paid for the land.   1st, " is not in their province," so that her complaints failed to procure her any redress.   September 29, 1683, in the list of taxables at Flushing, appears Widow Cartwright (Carteret) " with 4 males, 30 upland acres, and 50 meadows, 2 horses, 14 oxen, 3 cowes, 4 younger cattle, taxed £1. 3s. 9d." In 1685 she *m.*, third, **COLONEL RICHARD TOWNLEY**, eighth son of **Nicholas Townley**, of Littleton, Middlesex, England, a junior branch of the Lancashire family of Towneley, of Towneley, and *d.*, 1712.[1] Colonel Townley emigrated to Virginia in the suite of the Earl of Effingham, Governor of that province in 1683 ; the following year removed to East New Jersey. May 27, 1685, was appointed Justice of the Court of Common Right. Member of the Council, October 20, 1686, and also on his return to the province, February 5, 1710.   Captain of Foot Company at Elizabeth, December 11, 1686.   Was of the New York Council in 1692–1697, though accused in the latter year of not attending its meetings. Was presiding Judge of Quarter Sessions, when he *d.* in April, 1711.

WILLIAM, eldest son of **Captain William Lawrence**, the Emigrant, by his first wife, was prominent in the troubled politics of New York of the end of the seventeenth century.   He was probably the William Lawrence who signs and seals first of the Committee of Safety on the commission dated August 16, 1689, appointing Captain Jacob Leisler Commander-in-chief of the Province.   December 11, 1689, he was named of Leisler's Council, and was frequently present at its sessions.   December 14th, the same year he was one of the justices of peace for Orange Co.   In March, 1691, with other Councillors is imprisoned by Leisler.   September 9, 1692, being confined on treasonable charges, petitions for release.   There is some uncertainty whether his cousin William, son of Thomas Lawrence, of Newtown, may not be the Councillor.

September 29, 1683, Captain William Lawrence has at Flushing " 2 males, 20 upland acres, 50 of meadow, 4 horses, 2 oxen, 5 cowes, 9 younger cattle and 10 swine, and is taxed 19 shills. 9d."   August 19, 1697, he bought 1,000 acres of land near Percassin, Bucks Co., Penn.,

[1] Will made March 8, 1711-12, recorded at Trenton, N. J.

which he afterward sold. In the 1698 list of inhabitants of Flushing, third in rank is " Major William Lawrence, Deborah his wife, eleven (*sic*) children, William, Richard, Obadiah, Daniell, Samuell, John, Adam, Deborah, Sarah, ——; and six negroes, James, Tom, Lew, Bess, and two children." May 5, 1699, with John Barbaree, recommended by his uncle, John Lawrence, as guardians of his idiot son, John. July 20, 1703, John Embree, of Flushing, asks for an injunction against him for trespassing on his land. August 2d of that year, William makes a counter-complaint against John Embree, of intrusion on part of his estate called Tew's Neck, Flushing. May 31, 1704, with others, is complained of as surveying the common lands in the town of Flushing. He appears to have been removed from the guardianship of his lunatic cousin, for on January 20, 1709, he petitions to be restored to it ; and again, March 1, 1711, there are further proceedings in reference to it. April 27, 1711, he renders an account, and March 20, 1711–12, there is a report upon it. July 28, 1719, he made his will ; proved March 16, 1719–20 (Liber 9, *p.* 152), leaving " his wife Deborah half his household stuff and farm, half to his *dau.* Elizabeth Lawrence, to his son Joshua a bond for £57 10*s.* New York money, to his son Caleb," my farm I now live on in Tew's Neck, to his son Stephen 500 acres of land at a place called " on Springhill in East and West Jerseys I bought of the Underhills," to his sons Obadiah, Daniel, Sam^ll, Joshua and Adam Lawrence, and son-in-law Joseph Rodman, " right of land in Smithtown Patent which Father Smith gave me in his Will, all rest of moveables and 2 lotts at New York, bought of Coster Larenson, lying on William Street, to all his children."

He *m.*, by license dated June 1, 1680, **DEBORAH,** *dau.* of **Richard Smith,** Patentee of Smithtown. Issue :

i.   **WILLIAM,** not mentioned in his father's will.
ii.   **RICHARD,** *m.*, April 26, 1716, **ALICE** ——, and *d.* 1766. Issue :
iii.   **OBEDIAH,** *m.* **SARAH RODMAN,** and *d.* in 1733 (will proved March 27, 1733, Liber 11, *p.* 475). Issue :
    i.   **DEBORAH.**
    ii. **MARY,** *d. u.*
    iii. **SARAH,** *m.* **JOSEPH BOWNE** (*q. v.*).
    iv. **DR. WILLIAM.**
    v.   **SAMUEL JORDAIN.**
    vi. **OBEDIAH.**

iv.   **DANIEL,** *m.* **MARY,** *dau.* of **Abraham Redwood,** of Antigua, West Indies, and Newport, R. I., who *d.* 1763 ; he *d.* 1757. (Will proved August 18, 1757, Liber 20, folio 322). Issue :

i.   **MARY.**
ii.   **MEHITABEL.**
iii.   **LONGFORD.**
iv.   **ABRAHAM** (ancestor of Lieutenant Daniel Lawrence Braine, U. S. N.).

v.   **SAMUEL,** *m.* **MARY HICKS,** and settled at Black Stump, L. I. From
       him descends **Franklin C. Paxson,** of Philadelphia, Pa.
vi.   **JOSHUA.** *d. u.,* abroad.
vii.   **ADAM,** High Sheriff of Queen's Co. ; *d.* 1780.
viii. **DEBORAH.**
ix.   **SARAH,** *m.,* before 1719, **JOSEPH RODMAN.**
x.   **STEPHEN,** *m.,* July 4, 1734, **AMY,** *dau.* of **John** and **Mary (Cock)**
       Bowne, *d.* 1781 (*q. v.*). Issue :

       i.   **SUMMERSET,** *b.* May 7, 1735.
       ii.   **LANSELOTT,** *b.* June 7, 1737.
       iii.   **DEBORAH,** *b.* August 8, 1739.
       iv.   **LENNERD,** *b.* September 17, 1741 ; *m.* **MARGARET DOUGHTY.**

xi.   **ELIZABETH,** *m.* (license, October 15, 1737), **THOMAS WIL-**
       LETT.
xii.   **CALEB,** *d. u.* in the West Indies in 1723.

JOHN, second son of **Captain William Lawrence** by his first
wife, was probably the John Lawrence admitted to the Council
of the Colony by Royal Mandamus, dated August 10, 1702. He
is named in the list of inhabitants of Flushing of 1698, with his
wife Elizabeth, and children William, Richard, Eliza, Mary, and
Deborah. He *m.* **ELIZABETH,** *dau.* of **Richard Cornell**
(who was *b.* 1662), and made his will September 29, 1712, proved
February 21, 1714–15 (Liber 8, *pp.* 332–33). In it he leaves to his
wife Elizabeth, his houses, etc., until his son Richard is twenty-
one, then he is to have half, " other half the widow for life, then
to son Benjamin at twenty-one, after which they shall pay the
widow £20 per annum." He gives negroes to his daughters,
Charity Lawrence, Sarah Lawrence, Elizabeth Fford, and Mary
Briggs. His brother, William Lawrence, is an executor. Issue :

i.   **WILLIAM** (will probably 1758, Liber 21, *p.* 24).
ii.   **RICHARD.**
iii.   **ELIZABETH,** *m.* —— **FFORD.**
iv.   **MARY,** *m.* —— **BRIGGS.**
v.   **DEBORAH.**
vi.   **BENJAMIN.**
vii.   **CHARITY.**
viii. **SARAH.**

JOSEPH LAWRENCE, eldest son of **Captain William,** and **Elizabeth (Smith) Lawrence** (*q. v.*), *b.* about 1666. September 10, 1684, was commissioned an Ensign in the New York Provincial troops. March 14, 1685–86, there is a capias against him recorded, for a debt of £20.0.0. In 1701 he signs a petition of the inhabitants of East Jersey, addressed to the King, and does the same again in 1717, with his brother Richard, also John Bowne, John and Benjamin Lawrence. In 1698 he is recorded at Flushing, with his wife Mary and children, Richard and Thomas. December 8, 1754, he made his will, proved April 18, 1759, recorded Liber 22, *p.* 7. Mentions his wife, his sons Richard and John, and *dau.* Elizabeth Bowne, Sarah Lawrence, Hannah Molynex, and Abigail Forbes. Unvarying family tradition marries him to a **MARY TOWNLEY,** who was probably a *dau.* of his mother's third husband, **Colonel Richard Townley,** of New Jersey. There appears to be no legal proof of his wife's name, and the early records of the first Presbyterian Church of Elizabeth where the marriage was probably performed, have been destroyed. In this connection it may be well to note, that even though it were proven Mrs. Lawrence was a *dau.* of **Colonel Town-ley,** that would not make her descendants heirs of any great English estate, for two good and sufficient reasons : first,[1] Colonel Townley was eighth son of a younger branch of the family and the elder line **Towneley,** of Towneley, has never lacked direct male heirs until 1879, when the three daughters and co-heiresses of **Colonel Charles Towneley,** elder brother of **Colonel John Towneley,** the last male, carried the property into the families of their respective husbands **Lord Norreys, Lord Lennox,** and **Lord O'Hagan.** A second reason[2] why there is no English fortune for her heirs, is the non-existence of any such enormous unclaimed sums of money in the possession of the British Court of Chancery, or the Bank of England, and the passage of an Act in 1869 by Parliament which escheated to the Crown all unclaimed

TOWNELEY ARMS

---

[1] See Frank Alden Hill, the Mystery Solved, 1888 (address P. O. Box 242, Hampton, N. H.), for a complete pedigree of Townley, and a thorough exposé of the myths and frauds connected with the so-called Lawrence-Townley, or Chase-Townley estate.

[2] See James Usher's Lawrence, Chase, Townley, New York, 1884.

funds which had been in Chancery for over sixteen years, in all only £2,327,823.

JOSEPH and MARY (TOWNLEY?) LAWRENCE, had issue :

i. RICHARD, *b.* about 1691, *of whom presently.*

ii. THOMAS, living at Flushing in 1698, but not mentioned in his father's will.

iii. ELIZABETH, *m.* JOHN BOWNE (*q. v.*).

iv. JOHN, *b.* in 1703 ; removed to Newport, R. I., and *d.* November 10, 1781. Among his descendants were **Joseph Lawrence,** *b.* 1729, founded the Insurance business in Rhode Island. His son **Thomas Lawrence,** *b.* May 21, 1792, I think was the author of the " Lawrence Genealogy," printed in 1858. The **Lawrence** family of Hudson, N. Y. **Laura Gardinier,** *m.* **Theodore S. Fay,** *b.* in 1809 ; United States Minister to Switzerland ; author of " Norman Leslie," " Hoboken," etc. ; and **Eugene Lawrence,** *b.* October 4, 1823, author of " Lives of the British Historians," etc. ; *d. u.*

v. SARAH, unmarried in 1754.

vi. HANNAH, *m.* MOSES MOLYNEUX, of Westchester. Issue :

    i. MARY, *b.* March 26, 1723.

    ii. JOSEPH, *b.* September 5, 1724.

vii. ABIGAIL, *m.* MAJOR ALEXANDER FORBES, of the British Army, from whom descends the present **James Parker, Esq.,** of Perth Amboy, N. J.

RICHARD, eldest son of **Joseph and Mary (Townley) Lawrence,** *b.* 1691, resided at Flushing ; *m.,* April 6, 1717, at Friends' Meeting-House, in Flushing, **HANNAH,** *dau.* of **Samuel** and **Mary (Becket) Bowne** (*q. v.*), and *d.* in 1781. Issue :

i. MARY, *b.* April 2, 1718 ; *m.* EDWARD BURLING.

ii. ELIZABETH, *b.* June 15, 1719 ; *m.* JOHN EMBREE. Issue (surname EMBREE) :

    i. LAWRENCE, member of the New York Committee of Safety, May 1, 1775 ; *d. s. p.*

    ii. GEORGE, *m.* ABIGAIL, *dau.* of SAMUEL and ABIGAIL (BURLING) BOWNE (*q. v.*), and had a *dau.*, Sarah, *m.* Andrew Cock.

    iii. EFFINGHAM, a prominent merchant of New York, one of the original founders of the Tontine Coffee-House ; a watch and clock maker ; *m.,* December 26, 1780, MARY, *dau.* of John and Ann (Burling) Lawrence (*q. v.*), who *d.* September 16, 1831. Issue :

        i. John Lawrence, *m.* Deborah Lawrence.

        ii. Effingham Lawrence, *m.* Eliza Hartman.

        iii. Lawrence Effingham, *m.* Sarah Franklin.

        iv. Jane, *m.* John Wines.

        v. Mary Ann, *m.* Gilbert Hicks.

        vi. Hannah Matilda, *m.* Daniel Wright ; and after his death, Thomas U. V. P. Mercereau.

iv. ELIZABETH, *m.* —— CORNELL.

iii.   **JOSEPH**, *b.* September 10, 1721 ; *d. y.*
iv.   **CALEB**, *b.* February 10, 1723–24, *of whom presently.*
v.   **HANNAH**, *b.* April 2, 1726 ; *m.* **ABRAHAM WILLETT.**
vi.   **LIDDYA**, *b.* September 29, 1728 ; *m.*, in 1745, **STEVANUS HUNT** (for their descendants see T. Lawrence's "Lawrence Family," *pp.* 40–45).
vii.   **JOHN**, *b.* January 31, 1730–31, lived nine days.
viii.   **JOHN**, *b.* January 22, 1731–35 (*q. v.*).
ix.   **EFFINGHAM**, *b.* February 11, 1734–35 (*q. v.*).
x.   **NORRIS**, *b.* January 6, 1737–38 (*q. v.*), and **JOSEPH**, his twin, *d. i.*
xi.   **JOSEPH**, *b.* August 23, 1741, inherited, under his father's will, the estate at Bayside ; *m.* **PHŒBE**, *dau.* of **Henry Townsend**, of Oyster Bay. Among his descendants were **Cornelius W. Lawrence**, member of the firm, Hicks, Lawrence & Co., New York City ; President of the Bank of the State of New York ; Mayor of the City, etc. ; and **Jeanne Nuola**, the Cantatrice, *dau.* of **Effingham** and **Jane (Osgood) Lawrence**, of Louisiana.

CALEB, second son of **Richard** and **Hannah (Bowne) Lawrence**, *b.* February 10, 1723–24 ; *m.*, June 7, 1754, at Flushing, **SARAH**, *dau.* of **James**, *dec'd.*, and **Elizabeth Burling** (*q. v.*). Issue :

i.   **MARY**, *m.*, 1784, **BARON FREDERIC A. DEZENG** (*q. v.*).
ii.   **RICHARD**, *of whom presently.*
iii.   **ELIZABETH**, *d. u.*
iv.   **SARAH**, *m.* **CALEB NEWBOLD.**
v.   **CHARLOTTE**, *d. u.*
vi.   **HANNAH**, *d. u.*
vii.   **ESTHER**, *m.* **CAPTAIN JOHN CLARK.**

RICHARD, only son of **Caleb** and **Sarah (Burling) Lawrence**, *m.* **MARY**, *dau.* of **Dr. William Lawrence** (*q. v.*).   Issue :

i.   **WILLIAM**, *m.* **JANE**, *dau.* of John Hutchinson.
ii.   **CALEB**, *d. u.*, 1847.
iii.   **MARY ANNE**, *m.* **ALEXANDER COLDEN.**
iv.   **RICHARD L.**, *m.* **SARAH**, *dau.* of Baron Frederic De Zeng (*q. v.*).
v.   **SARAH**, *m.* **RICHARD DE ZENG** (*q. v.*).
vi.   **ELIZABETH.**
vii.   **JANE.**
viii.   **EMMA**, *m.* **CHARLES McCULLY.**

JOHN, fourth son of **Richard** and **Hannah (Bowne) Lawrence**, *b.* January 22, 1731–32 ; *m.*, August 13, 1755, **ANN**, *dau.* of **John** and **Ann Burling** (*q. v.*), and *d.* in New York City, July 26, 1794 ; his wife *d.* at the same place, February 14, 1821.   Issue :

i.   **EDWARD BURLING,** *b.* June 13, 1756; *m.* **ZIPPORAH,** *dau.* of
      Dr. **William Lawrence,** of Oyster Bay and *d.* April 16, 1832.
      Issue :

    i.   **EDWARD L.,** *b.* June 13, 1780; *m.* **MATILDA WHITING.** Issue :

       i.   **Robert,** lost at sea.
       ii.   **Ann Maria,** *m.* **Martin Baker.**
       iii. **Sarah,** *m.* **Joshua Baker.**

    ii.   **PHŒBE,** *m.* **THOMAS WHITING.**
    iii. **JOHN L.,** *m.* **ADELINE TUPPER.**
    iv.   **WALTER,** *m.* **MALVINA DANIELS.**
    v.   **CORNELIA,** *m.* **THOMAS TREADWAY.**
    vi.   **JANE,** *m.* **HENRY B. FOWLER.**

ii.   **HANNAH,** *b.* July 8, 1758, *m.* **JACOB SCHIEFFELIN** (*q. v.*).
iii. **EFFINGHAM,** *b.* July 6, 1760, *of whom presently.*
iv.   **MARY,** *b.* September 11th, and *d.* November 13, 1762.
v.   **MARY,** *b.* October 17, 1763; *m.*, December 26, 1780, her cousin **EFFING-
      HAM EMBREE** (*q. v.*):
vi.   **CATHERINE,** *b.* May 15, 1765; *d. u.* May 9, 1834.
vii. **JANE,** b. September 2, 1768; *m.* **ISAAC LIVESAY,** and *d. s. p.*
      August 24, 1854.
viii. **PHEBE,** *b.* December 24, 1770; *d.* July 2, 1771.
ix.   **ANNA,** *b.* May 22, 1772; *m.* **THOMAS BUCKLEY** (*q. v.*).
x.   **JOHN BURLING,** *b.* October 21, 1774 (*q. v.*).
xi.–xii. **PHEBE** and **CORNELIA,** twins, *b.* March 17, 1778; the latter *d.* March
      27th of the same year, and her sister, August 8, 1780.

EFFINGHAM, second son of **John** and **Ann (Burling) Lawrence,** *b.* June 6, 1760; began mercantile life for himself in 1781,
and retiring with an ample competency thirteen years afterward,
purchased a house in Flushing, L. I., and resided there until his
death. He *m.*, about 1785, **ELIZABETH (Watson) MER-
RITT,** widow of **Lieutenant Merritt,** and *dau.* of **Thomas
Watson,** of New Jersey, and *d.* December 13, 1800. Issue :

i.   **WATSON EFFINGHAM,** *of whom presently.*
ii.   **EFFINGHAM WATSON,** was in business about 1830, with Gideon
      Freeborn, as Freeborn & Lawrence, but subsequently removed to
      Flushing, L. I. He *m.* **REBECCA,** *dau.* of **Benjamin Prince.**
      Issue :

    i.   **WILLIAM HENRY,** *b.* July 25, 1824.
    ii.   **REV. FRANCIS EFFINGHAM,** D.D., *b.* in Flushing. L. I., May 12, 1827.
       Educated under Dr. Muhlenberg at S. Paul's School. Graduate of General
       Theological Seminary, 1852. Ordained Deacon in 1853 by Bishop Chase, and
       Priest in 1854 by Bishop Wainwright. 1854-1859, Assistant Minister of Church
       of the Holy Communion, New York. 1859-1879, Pastor of the same. *d. s.*
       June 10, 1879.
    iii. **FREDERICK,** *b.* November 12, 1830.

iii.   **MARY WATSON,** *b.* in March, 1787 ; *m.*, in 1808, **JAMES T. TALL-MAN** ; her granddaughter *m.* **Dr. Charles H. Burnet,** of Philadelphia. Issue.

      MARY TALLMAN and **MAUD LAWRENCE,** twins.

iv.   **ANNA WATSON,** *b.* in 1792 ; *d.* in June, 1868.
v.   **JOHN WATSON,** *b.* in 1798 (*q. v.*).

WATSON EFFINGHAM, eldest son of **Effingham** and **Elizabeth (Watson) Lawrence,** *b.* August 13, 1788, went into business in New York in 1808.   In 1819 removed to Flushing, where he resided for several years.   Between 1825 and 1827 he was engaged in the banking business in New York with Charles Lawton.   After the dissolution of their partnership Mr. Lawrence had an intimation from his friend Judge Wright, engineer of the Delaware & Hudson Canal Company, that he had, in his survey of the route of the canal, discovered large beds of hydraulic limestone in Ulster Co.   Mr. Lawrence having some knowledge of mineralogy examined the stone, and satisfied of its quality, made large investments in the manufacture of cement from it, and removing to that district became the founder of Lawrenceville.   Through his friends, General Joseph G. Totten and Colonel De Russey, he succeeded in introducing his Rosendale cement into general use, and many of the government works have been constructed with it.   Mr. Lawrence furnished numerous articles on genealogical or antiquarian subjects to Thompson's " Long Island," and similar works, was a prominent member of the Protestant Episcopal Church, and is buried in Trinity Churchyard, New York City. He *m.*, January 3, 1810, **AUGUSTA MARIA,** *dau.* of **John Nicoll,** of New Haven, Conn., and a lineal descendant of the first English Governor of New York, and *d.* September 16, 1872.   Issue :

i.   **JANE NICOLL,** *b.* November 14, 1810 ; *m.*, September 13, 1831, **JOHN GEORGE ANDERSON,** of Florida.   Issue :

    i.   **JAMES EFFINGHAM,** *b.* October 24, 1838.
    ii.   **LAWRENCE MEL,** *b.* July 21, 1841 ; *d.* April 6, 1862.
    iii.   **AUGUSTA LAWRENCE,** *b.* October 6, 1845 ; *m.*, first, **EDWARD HOUSE-TOWN,** who *d. s. p.*; *m.*, second, September 20, 1870, **WILLIAM G. POOLE.** Issue :
        Lawrence Anderson, *b.* December 17, 1871.

ii.   **EFFINGHAM NICOLL,** *b.* August 30, 1812, *of whom presently.*
iii.   **ELIZABETH WATSON,** *b.* April 3, 1814 ; *m.* **LAWRENCE P. HILL,** and *d. s. p.* October 10, 1867.

iv.   **JOHN NICOLL**, *b.* November 17, 1816; *d.* March 27, 1817.

v.   **AUGUSTA NICOLL**, *b.* May 8, 1818; *d.* November 16, 1820.

vi.   **ANNA WATSON**, *m.*, June 18, 1839, **MANDEBERT CANFIELD**

vii.   **CHARLOTTE AUGUSTA**, *b.* April 3, 1823; *d. u.* May 16, 1858.

viii.   **WATSON AUGUSTUS**, *b.* December 31, 1825; *d.* July 13, 1841.

ix.   **MARY TALLMAN**, *b.* July 2, 1828; *m.*, February 5, 1861, **RICHARD MANSFIELD EVERIT.** Issue:

      i.   **RICHARD LAWRENCE**, *b.* December 19, 1861.

      ii.   **EMMA AUGUSTA**, *b.* October 27, 1863; *d.* July 27, 1864.

      iii.   **ANNIE COLEY**, *b.* May 14, 1867.

      iv.   **EDWARD HOTCHKISS**, *b.* August 5, 1870.

x.   **EMMA AUGUSTA**, *b.* April 27, 1832.

xi.   **CHARLES EDWARD**, *b.* November 30, 1836; *m.*, April 17, 1860, **LEILA HOMEYARD.** Issue:

      i.   **ASHTON CLEVELAND**, *b.* October 7, 1861.

      ii.   **LEILA HOMEYARD**, *b.* February 23, 1863.

      iii.   **ERNEST MINTURN**, *b.* May 10, 1869.

      iv.   **LAURA EFFINGHAM**, *b.* May 16, 1875.

EFFINGHAM NICOLL, eldest son of **Watson E.** and **Augusta Maria (Nicoll) Lawrence**, *b.* August 30, 1812; *m.*, first, February 6, 1837, **MARGARET CLENDINNING**, *dau.* of **Horace W.** and **Margaret Bulkley**; *m.*, second, November 30, 1853, **MARGARET**, *dau.* of **William** and **Sarah Hogan**, who *d. s. p.* Issue, by his first wife:

i.   **CLENDINNING NICOLL**, *b.* January 19, 1838; *d.* March 15, 1843.

ii.   **THEODORE**, *b.* September 1, 1839; *d.* December 21, 1861.

iii.   **GEORGE ANDERSON**, *b.* March 24, 1841; *m.*, November 28, 1866, **CHARLOTTE L.**, *dau.* of **Randolph M.** and **Louisa Cooley.** Issue:

      i.   **RANDOLPH MORGAN**, *b.* November 23, 1867.

      ii.   **MARGARET CLENDINNING**, *b.* September 20, 1869.

      iii.   **KATE CHESTER**, *b.* October 26, 1870.

      iv.   **BERTHA EFFINGHAM**, *b.* July 29, 1875.

iv.   **WATSON EFFINGHAM**, *b.* September 26, 1842; *d.* September 9, 1844.

v.   **EFFINGHAM BULKLEY**, *b.* March 30, 1844; *d.* October 13, 1844.

vi.   **CHESTER BULKLEY**, *b.* September 15, 1845; *m.*, January 9, 1867, **CATHERINE COVELL**, *dau.* of **George C.** and **Kate Peters.** Issue:

      i.   **KATE EFFINGHAM**, *b.* October 9, 1867; *d.* June 7, 1868.

      ii.   **GEORGE COVELL**, *b.* May 10, 1869.

      iii.   **CHESTER BULKLEY, Jr.**, *b.* June 13, 1872.

vii.   **MARGARET CLENDINNING**, *b.* September 3, 1847; *d.* January 16, 1849.

viii.   **AUGUSTA MARIA**, *b.* November 29, 1849; *d.* December 2, 1849.

ix.   **EDWIN**, *b.* October 19, 1850; *d.* October 22, 1850.

x.   **ALBERT EFFINGHAM**, *b.* November 12, 1851.

JOHN WATSON, third son of **Effingham Lawrence** and **Elizabeth Watson,** *b.* in 1800, served a clerkship in the office of Samuel Hicks. When of age he associated himself with William Howland in the shipping and commission business, as Howland & Lawrence. He was a director of the old United States Branch Bank of New York, was a member of the State Legislature in 1840 and 1841, a member of Congress from the First District in 1846 and 1847, and President of the Seventh Ward Bank of New York, 1847 to 1854, when he resigned that position and retired from business. In 1826 he *m.* **MARY KING,** *dau.* of **Walter** and **Eliza (Southgate) Bowne** (*q. v.*). She *d.* in 1873, and her husband January, 1889. Issue :

i.   **CAROLINE,** *m.,* in October, 1847, **HON. HENRY BEDINGER,** of Virginia. He was a member of Congress from that State, and afterward United States Minister to Denmark, June 29, 1854, to August 10, 1858. He *d.* in 1859 and his wife ten years afterward. Issue :

      i.   **MARY,** *m.,* June 29, 1871, **CAPTAIN JOHN F. B. MITCHELL,** who had been an officer in the United States Army during the Civil War. She *d.* March 22, 1896.

      ii.   **Rev. HENRY,** *b.* in 1853, a clergyman of the Protestant Episcopal Church, *m.,* April 18, 1876, **ADA,** *dau.* of W. N. Doughty, of Flushing.

      iii. **CAROLINE DANSKE,** *b.* in Denmark, author of "Joy and Other Poems," 1888, and "Rose Brake," 1890; *m.,* May 3, 1877, **A. STEPHEN DANDRIDGE,** of Virginia.

ii.   **ELIZA SOUTHGATE,** *m.,* in 1849, **GENERAL ARMISTEAD T. M. RUST,** of Virginia, and *d.* in 1858. Issue :

      i.   **LAWRENCE,** *b.* May, 1850; educated at Washington and Lee University, graduated M.A. with honors, 1875 ; Professor of Greek at Kenyon College, Ohio, 1875-85 ; LL.D. from his *Alma Mater*, 1885. The same year, with Mr. H. N. Hills he took charge of Kenyon Military Academy, and in 1887 founded Harcourt Place Seminary for girls. About 1880, was seized with sclerosis in a mixed form, but with heroic fortitude labored on, and met with great success at both schools. Was ordained Deacon in the Protestant Episcopal Church, but prevented by his illness from receiving the priesthood. He *m.,* April, 1876, **EVELYN,** *dau.* of Rev. William F. Junkin, D.D., of Montclair, N. J., and *d.* April 15, 1895.

      ii. **REBECCA,** *m.,* in October, 1875, **EDMUND LEE,** of Virginia.

iii.   **MARY BOWNE,** *m.,* November 5, 1853, **HENRY A. BOGERT.** Issue :

      i.   **MARY LAWRENCE,** *b.* January 19, 1855 ; *m.,* June 3, 1873, **WILLIAM ELLIMAN,** and had a son, *b.* September 11, 1876.

      ii. **HENRY LAWRENCE,** *b.* January 20, 1857.

      iii. **JOHN LAWRENCE,** *b.* October 27, 1858.

      iv. **EMILY ELOISE,** *b.* October 29, 1860 ; *d.* April 8, 1864.

      v. **EDWARD LUDLOW,** *b.* December 19, 1862 ; *d.* October 21, 1863.

      vi. **WALTER LAWRENCE,** *b.* December 7, 1864.

      vii. **JAMES LAWRENCE,** *b.* March 31, and *d.* July 21, 1867.

    viii.   **MARSTON TAYLOR**, *b.* April 18. 1868.

    ix.   **FRANCIS LAWRENCE**, *b.* July 11, 1869; *d.* July 19, 1870.

    x.   **FANNY LAWRENCE**, *b.* September 8, 1870.

    xi.   **THEODORE LAWRENCE**, *b.* June 24, 1875.

iv.   **EMILY**, *m.*, in December. 1874, **CHARLES H. SHEPARD.**

v.   **ANNA LOUISA**, *m.*, in 1862, **REV. THOMAS AUGUSTUS JAGGAR**, consecrated Bishop of Southern Ohio, in 1875.

vi.   **WALTER BOWNE**, *b.* in 1839; *m.*, in October, 1866, **ANNA TOWNSEND.**

vii.   **REBECCA**, *d.* in childhood.

viii.   **ISABELLA**, *m.* **LEMUEL P. DANDRIDGE.**

ix.   **FANNY**, *m.*, July 2, 1873, **REV. FREDERICK B. CARTER**, a clergyman of the Protestant Episcopal Church, Rector of S. Luke's Church, Montclair, N. J. Issue :

    i.   **GERTRUDE MAY**, *b.* May 10, 1874.

    ii.   **MARY LAWRENCE**, *b.* November 12, 1876.

    iii.   **LOUISA**, *b.* June 3, 1878.

x.   **ROBERT**, *b.* December 1, 1852 ; *m.* **ETTIE**, *dau.* of **Dr. B. A. CLEMENTS**, U. S. A.

JOHN BURLING, third son of **John** and **Ann (Burling) Lawrence**, *b.* October 21, 1774, was a merchant and wholesale druggist of New York City ; the firm being Lawrence, Keese & Co. Described shortly before his death as "a model man of the Old School gentlemen merchants." Though inheriting a large fortune from his father he pursued business with the ardor of youth, and doubled and trebled his property. His estate was estimated at $300,000 in 1845. His business is still carried on by his grandsons, Emlen N. and John B. Lawrence, Jr. He *m.*, February 15, 1804, **HANNAH**, *dau.* of **Caleb Newbold**, of Philadelphia, and his wife, **Sarah Haines**, of New Jersey, and *d.* October 8, 1844. Issue :

i.   **EDWARD NEWBOLD**, *b.* February 12, 1805 ; *m.* **LYDIA ANNA**, *dau.* of Hon. **Effingham** and **Anna (Townsend) Lawrence**, of Flushing ; and dying at Liverpool, England, October 21, 1839, was buried at Bayside, L. I. Issue :

    FREDERIC NEWBOLD, *b.* February, 28, 1834 ; *m.* **ELIZABETH**, *dau.* of Kerr Boyce, of South Carolina, and has a *dau.* Mary Lawrence, *m.*, first, **Frank Worth White** ; *m.*, second, December 10, 1892, Foxhall, son of James R. Keene.

ii.   **GEORGE NEWBOLD**, *b.* October 20, 1806, a distinguished ornithologist ; one of the founders of the New York College of Pharmacy, and their last survivor. He *m.*, October 23, 1834, **MARY ANN**, *dau.* of **George Newbold**, and *d.* January 17, 1895 ; his wife *d.* January 12, 1895. Issue :

i. **EMLEN NEWBOLD,** *b.* December 24, 1836.
ii. **JOHN BURLING,** Jr., *b.* in 1844; *m.* **KATHERINE D.,** *dau.* of Gabriel Wisner, of New York City.

iii. **MARY NEWBOLD,** *b.* October 31, and *d.* November 15, 1808.
iv. **NEWBOLD,** *b.* October 23, 1809; *m.*, October 21, 1851, at Philadelphia, **ANNA H.,** *dau.* of **Joseph Trotter,** of that city. Issue:

   i. **CAROLINE TROTTER,** *b.* August 25, 1852.
   ii. **ANNIE TROTTER,** *b.* December 10, 1853.
   iii. **NEWBOLD TROTTER,** *b.* May 6, 1855; *m.*, December 6, 1887, **ISABEL,** *dau.* of **Mrs. N. Halleck Gillett.**
   iv. **SUSAN NEWBOLD,** *b.* July 27, 1856; *m.*, April 25, 1882, **JAMES W. WALSH,** Jr. (*q. v.*).
   v. **MARY GERTRUDE,** *b.* March 27, 1860; *m.*, October 26, 1886, **DR. FRANCIS N. MURRAY.**

v. **ALFRED NEWBOLD,** *b.* July 10, 1813, at one time a drygoods merchant, afterward a wholesale druggist; *m.*, June 30, 1837, **ELIZABETH,** *dau.* of Hon. **John L. Lawrence** (*q. v.*), of New York City (*d.* May, 1884); and *d.* April, 1884. Issue:

   i. **WOODHULL,** *b.* April 19, 1850; *d.* July 7, 1870.
   ii. **HANNAH NEWBOLD,** *b.* April 9, 1852.
   iii. **JOHN L.,** *b.* June 22, 1857; *m.*, November 21, 1895, **ALICE WARNER,** *dau.* of J. Henry Work.

vi. **CAROLINE AUGUSTA,** *b.* August 18, 1815; *m.* her cousin **WILLIAM EFFINGHAM LAWRENCE,** of Bayside, L. I.; *d.* April 20, 1841, leaving one son, **EDWARD N.,** *b.* April 15, 1841; *d.*, at Madeira, of consumption.
vii. **JOHN B.,** *b.* December 30, 1817; *m.* **MARY ADELINE FURMAN,** of Maspeth, L. I.
viii. **THOMAS NEWBOLD,** *b.* January 15, 1820; *d. u.*, July 9, 1889, leaving a fortune of $4,000,000.

EFFINGHAM, fifth son of **Richard** and **Hannah (Bowne) Lawrence,** *b.* February 11, 1734–35, Captain of the ship Lord Dunmore, 1771; June 9, 1773, carried General Gage and others to England; removed to London and became an eminent merchant there. He *m.* **CATHERINE FARMER,** *d.* in 1806. (Will made December 14, 1803; proved September 3, 1806.) Issue.

i. **WILLIAM EFFINGHAM,** partner in business with his father.
ii. **JOHN CURZON,** settled in Bengal.
iii. **EFFINGHAM CALVERT,** in East India Navy.
iv. **EDWARD BILLOP,** *b.* 1791.
v. **CATHERINE MARY,** *m.*, April 20, 1816, **JOHN THOMAS,** eldest son of **John**[1] and **Mary (Roberts) Jones,** *b.* March 25, 1783;

[1] Descended from Daniel Jones of a family long settled at Sunny Hill, Caermarthenshire, through his son David, *b.* in 1678.

Commissioned Second Lieutenant Royal Engineers, August 30, 1798 : was Chief of Engineer Staff in the Walcheren expedition, June,

1809 ; employed on the lines at Torres Vedras in 1810, and, as Brigade Major of Engineers, all the details of the service in the Peninsula passed through his hands. In 1814, with Sir Alexander Bryce, was appointed by Wellington to report defences for the Netherlands. In 1816 was sole Inspector of these defences, and Commandant at Woolwich, England. September 30, 1831, was created a Baronet, as of Cranmer Hall, Fakenham, Norfolk ; Major - General, January 10, 1837 ; K.C.B., in 1838. Requested to devise a scheme of coast defence for Great Britain in 1839. He

JONES ARMS

is ranked among the first military engineers of his time. A statue to his memory by Behnes was erected in the south transept of S. Paul's Cathedral by the officers of the Royal Engineer Corps. He was author of a Journal of the sieges in Spain, and other military works, and *d.* at his residence, Pittville, Cheltenham, February 25, 1843. Issue (surname JONES) :

i. LAWRENCE, second Baronet, killed by Greek brigands while travelling between Macri and Smyrna, and *d. s. p.* November 7, 1845.
ii. WILLOUGHBY, *b.* November 24, 1820, *of whom presently.*
iii. HERBERT WALSINGHAM, *b.* October 10, 1826, *m.,* April 23, 1850, CATHERINE RACHEL, *dau.* of Daniel Gurney, of North Runcton, Norfolk, and Lady Harriet Hay, second *dau.* of William, fifteenth Earl of Erroll.
iv. EMILY FLORENCE, *m.,* December 27, 1849, WILLIAM FRANKS, Jr., of Woodhill, Hertfordshire.

WILLOUGHBY, second son of **Sir John Thomas** and **Catherine Mary (Lawrence) Jones,** *b.* November 24, 1820 ; succeeded as third Baronet in 1845 ; *m.,* April 15, 1856, his cousin **EMILY,** *dau.* of **Henry S. Jones,** and *d.* August 20, 1884. Issue :

i. SIR LAWRENCE JOHN, *b.* August 16, 1857, fourth Baronet, M. A., late Captain Third Volunteer Battery, Norfolk ; *m.,* April 13, 1882, EVELYN MARY, *dau.* of James Johnstone Bevan, of S. Edmundsbury. Issue.

    i. WILLOUGHBY JOHN, *b.* March 19, 1884.
    ii. LAWRENCE EVELYN, *b.* April 6, 1885.
    iii. BERTRAM EDWARD, *b.* October 1, 1886.
    iv. MAURICE HERBERT, *b.* December 8, 1888.
    v. HESTHER.
    vi. CATHERINE.
    vii. RACHEL MARGARET.

JOSEPH RODMAN DRAKE
From a Portrait by Rodgers

i.   **REV. HERBERT EDWARD,** *b.* April 6, 1861 ; *m.*, July, 1888, **MADELINE,** *dau.* of **Edward L. Fox, M.D.**

ii.   **MARY FLORENCE.**

NORRIS, sixth son of **Richard** and **Hannah (Bowne) Lawrence,** *b.* January 6, 1737–38 ; *m.* (license, January 6, 1765) **ANN,** *dau.* of **Caleb Pell** (*q. v.*) (*b.* December 23, 1743), and *d.* in early manhood. Issue :

    MARY, *b.* October 10, 1765.

i.   **HANNAH,** *b.* October 21, 1767 ; *m.* **JONATHAN DRAKE.** Issue (surname DRAKE) :

> **DR. JOSEPH RODMAN,** *b.* August 7, 1795, author of "The Culprit Fay," "American Flag," and other poems ; and with Fitz-Greene Halleck, of the "Croaker Papers," a notable series of social satires. He was a physician, and his early death was caused by consumption. His brother poet wrote of him,
>
> > " None knew thee but to love thee,
> > Nor named thee but to praise."
>
> He *m.*, 1818, **SARAH,** *dau.* of Henry Eckford, of New York, builder of some of the finest ships of the United States Navy, and *d.* September 21, 1820. Issue, a *dau.,* **Janet Halleck,**[1] *b.* January 3, 1819 ; *m.*, September, 1833, **Commodore George Coleman de Kay** (*b.*, 1802 ; *d.*, 1849). Issue (surname DE KAY) :

    i.   Katharine Coleman, *m.* Arthur Bronson.

    ii.   Joseph R. Drake, *d.* 1886.

    iii.   Julia.

    iv.   George C., killed at Baton Rouge, 1862.

    v.   Sidney, *m.* M. Craven and *d.* 1890.

    vi.   Sarah Helena Drake, *m.*, June 3, 1874, Richard Watson Gilder, Author of " The New Day" and other poems of a high order, and Editor of the *Century Magazine.* Issue (surname GILDER) : Rodman Drake de Kay, *b.* 1877 ; Dorothea de K., *b.* 1882 ; George C. de K., *b.* 1885 ; H. Francesca, *b.* 1888, and Janet Rosamond, *b.* 1891.

    vii. Charles, Author and Poet, *m.*, June, 1888, Edwalyn L. Coffey.

Authorities : Parish Records at S. Albans, through Mrs. Frank Alden Hill ; Savage's Dictionary, and S. G. Drake's Founders of New England. New York and New Jersey State papers ; Documentary history of New York ; Onderdonk's Queen's County ; Wills in the Surrogate's Office, New York City, Quaker Records of New York and Flushing, family papers through the late Messrs. Effingham N. and Newbold Lawrence ; Mrs. Danske (Bedinger) Dandridge, Miss Ruth Lawrence and others ; the family history by Thomas Lawrence, New York, 1858, and Old Merchants of New York, five volumes, *v. d.*

    [1] Fitz-Greene Halleck was her godfather.

LAWRENCE, OF S. IVES, HUNTINGDON-SHIRE

THE first of this line on record was an **EDMUND LAW-RENCE,** called fourth son of **Sir Robert Lawrence,** of Ashton Hall. (This seems merely an attempt to make a connection with the Lancashire family, as there is no evidence offered to substantiate the claim.) **EDMUND** had issue : i. **RICHARD,** who had a son, JOHN ; and ii. **JOHN LAWRENCE DE WURDEBOYS,** who was Abbot of Ramsey Abbey, in Huntingdonshire, from 1507 ; in 1539 he was not only very forward in procuring his own abbey to be surrendered to the king when the Vicar-General Cromwell sent out his visitors, but influenced others to submit, for which service he obtained, according to Dug-dale, the large pension of £266 13s. 6d. per annum. In his will, dated in 1541, and proved in November, 1542 (Registro Spert), he makes considerable bequests to the churches of S. Ives, Ramsey, and Bur-well, leaves £10 among twenty paupers, and his silver plate, etc., to his cousin, William Lawrence. He desires to be buried in S. Mary's, Burwell, and appoints William Lawrence of S. Ives one of his execu-tors.

JOHN, son of **Richard,** and nephew of the Lord Abbot, styled in all evidences " generosus," d. in 1538, leaving by his will (Registro Dingley), besides considerable donations to the Church, two of his best mares to my Lord of Ramsey for supervising his will. He had issue : **EMMA,** m. **GABRIEL,** third son of **Richard Throckmorton,** of Higham Ferrers, Seneschal of the Duchy of Lancaster ; **AGNES,** m. **GILBERT SMYTH,** of Fenton ; and **WILLIAM,** who settled at S. Ives, was High Sheriff of Cambridge and Hunts at the death of Queen Mary, and was buried at S. Ives, December 20, 1572. By his will (Registro Peter) he bequeaths to his son HENRY his armour, the plate he inherited from his uncle the Abbot of Ramsey, and "the iron chest in the library, containing papers which had been particu-larly mentioned in the will of his father."

He *m.*, first, **FRANCES HOUSTON,** and had issue by her :

   i.   **HENRY,** *of whom presently.*
   ii.   **WILLIAM** (ancestor of the Lawrences of Chichester and Aldingbourne).

WILLIAM LAWRENCE, *m.*, second, **MARGARET,** *dau.* of **Edward Kaye,** of Woodson, in Yorkshire and had further issue :

   iii.   **ROBERT,** *d.* in 1597 (ancestor of the Lawrences of Norfolk).
   iv.   **LEWIS.**
   v.   **ELIZABETH,** *m.,* **JOHN HUTTON,** of Cambridge.

HENRY, son of **William** and **Frances (Houston) Lawrence,** probably entered Gray's Inn from Barnard's Inn in 1569 ; *m.* **ELIZABETH,** *dau.* of **John Hagar,** of Bourne Castle, Cambridgeshire, and was buried at S. Ives, February 25, 1580–81, having had a son and heir, **JOHN,** who entered Gray's Inn, April 24, 1597, was knighted by James I., in 1603, at Windsor ; *m.* **ELIZABETH,** sole *dau.* and heiress of **Ralph Waller,** of Beaconsfield, who after his death, and before 1646, *m.*, second, **Robert Bathurst,** Sheriff of Gloucestershire, whose son Edward was created a Baronet in 1643. **SIR JOHN LAWRENCE** was buried at S. Ives, February 10, 1604. In his will (made January 10th, proved February 9, 1604, Registro Hayes) he mentions his two sons, HENRY and JOHN (*q. v.*). HENRY was then aged three years, two months, and four days (Cole's Escheats, Harl. MS., 760). He entered Emanuel College, Cambridge, in 1622, as a fellow-commoner ; B.A. 1623 ; M.A., 1627. Had been registered at Gray's Inn August 7, 1617. In 1641 was in Parliament as a Knight of the Shire for Westmoreland. Milton, in his "Second Defence of the People of England," calls him "a man of the highest ability and best accomplishments," and addresses his son in a sonnet, "Lawrence of virtuous father, virtuous son." He is also said to have assisted him in writing his treatise "On Angels." He was M.P. for Westmoreland, 1645 ; one of the Commissioners to keep peace with Scotland, 1646 ; was at Arnheim, in Flanders, December, 1645, and at Altona, January 21, 1646. From a preface to a work of his, printed in 1646, it appears that he was abroad at the beginning of the Civil War : "The warre found me abroad, not sent me thither, and I have beene onely wary without a just and warrantable reason to ingage my selfe in that condition from which a providence seem'd to rescue mee." He found such reason shortly thereafter, as he appears as a Member of Parliament for Hertfordshire in 1653, and, July 14th of that year, is added to the Coun-

cil of State by Cromwell; July 27th is on the Committee of Foreign
Affairs, was present at seventeen sittings of the Council in November
and December, 1653, and at one hundred and sixty-four in 1654, being
the only member present at all the sittings. December 19, 1653, Cromwell appointed him Lord President of the Council for one month from
date. January 16, 1653-54, there was an order by the Protector that
" Hen. Lawrence be continued President of the Council until further
order; " February 9, 1654, we find him paid £300, apparently his
salary. Notices of his action as Lord President may be found in Domestic State Papers for 1653–54, and he is not unfavourably mentioned
by Clarendon in his history. He was elected M.P. for Colchester and
Carnarvonshire in 1656, and chose to sit for the latter shire. In December, 1657, he was gazetted a Lord of the other House, Cromwell's
attempt at a life peerage. As Lord President he took the responsibility of proclaiming Richard Cromwell as his father's successor, but on
the Restoration of Charles II. was allowed to return to private life.
He opposed the execution of Charles I., and there is in Thurloe's
" State Papers " a letter to him from the Queen of Bohemia, Elizabeth
Stuart, wife of Frederick Elector Palatine and mother of Prince Rupert,
recommending Lord Craven to his good graces, and saying she knew
he had only accepted office in order to render services to those who
needed them. He published at Amsterdam, in 1646, " Militia Spirit-
ualis, a Treatise of our Communion and Warre with Angels ; " in the
same year an anonymous treatise " On Baptism; " in 1649 a " Vindi-
cation of the Scriptures," and in 1652 " Gospel Ordinances." The author has a copy of the third edition of the first treatise " On Angels,"
formerly in the possession of the Woollaston-White family, heirs of the
President's grandson, Sir Edward Lawrence, Bart. Afterward in that
of Major J. H. Lawrence-Archer, who has made some MS. memoran-
da relating to the Lawrence genealogy, of which I have made use in
the above sketch of the Lord President's ancestry, in connection with
the Memoir written by Sir James Lawrence, Knight of Malta, and the
English State Papers. Major Archer also had a photograph made of
the unique drawing in the Queen's copy of Clarendon's " Rebellion," at
Windsor Castle, from which the engraved portrait of the President
was copied. He m. AMY, dau. of Sir Edward Peyton Bart., of Iselham, in
Cambridgeshire, and d. August 8, 1664, intestate. Major Archer says
the records of the Probate Court show his widow was administra-
trix ; but Sir James Lawrence states that his son Henry administered
the estate. According to his gravestone (visible in 1802) in the

HENRY LAWRENCE
PRESIDENT OF CROMWELL'S COUNCIL OF STATE
From the Portrait in the Possession of the Queen at Windsor Castle

chapel at S. Margaret's Als Thele, in Hertfordshire, the President had issue seven sons and six daughters :

i.   **HENRY**, M. P. for Carnarvonshire in 1656, *d.* in 1679, leaving issue :

     i.   **HENRY**, *d. u.*

     ii.   **EDWARD**, created a Baronet, with remainder to his sister's son, and *d.* May 2, 1749.

ii.   **EDWARD**, M. P. for Pembrokeshire in 1656, and *d.* in 1657.

iii.   **JOHN**, emigrated to Jamaica, *of whom presently.*

iv. v.   **WILLIAM** and **MARTHA**, naturalized as born abroad, November 27, 1656 ; the latter *m* **RICHARD**, Earl of Barrymore.

vi.   **ELIZABETH**, *d.* in February, 1662, aged thirty.

vii.   **THEODOSIA**, *d.* September 2, 1664, aged twenty.

viii.   **HENRIETTA**, *d.* September 30, 1664, aged thirteen.

The others I have not been able to trace. Hotten's "Original Lists of Emigrants," etc., New York, 1874, notices that Henry Lawrence owned ten acres of land and six negroes in S. James's Parish, Barbadoes, December 20, 1629. This may have been the Lord President.

JOHN, supposed son of **President Henry Lawrence** (*q. v.*). Emigrated to the West Indies, settling first on Barbadoes Island, removing afterward to Jamaica. He may have been Captain John Lawrence, mentioned in a letter, March 10, 1682–83, as commanding a ship expected to sail to the Leeward Islands. He made his will May 10, 1690 ; *m.* **MRS. JANE (COLLINS) DUNN**, and had three sons and six daughters.

JOHN, eldest son of the emigrant, John Lawrence, *m.* **SUSAN-NAH PETGRAVE**, and *d.* in 1725. Their *dau.*, SUSANNA, *m.* **LAWRENCE LAWRENCE** (Will, 1743), and had RACHEL. *m.* LIEU-TENANT-COLONEL HARRY GORDON (Will, 1787). Their *dau.*, Ann, *m.* Alexander Edgar, of Lanarkshire (Will, 1820), and had Mary, *m.* J. H. Archer, of the Umberslade family (Will, 1840), whose son was Lieutenant-Colonel J. H. Lawrence-Archer. (See also Roby's "History of the Parish of S. James, Jamaica," Part 3d.) Of this family was **(Major) John Lawrence**, *d.* January 7, 1718–19, in the forty-sixth year of his age, a buccaneering commander under Sir Henry Morgan ; and **Rev. Richard Brisset Lawrence**, *d.* October 13, 1831, aged thirty-one years and three months.

The **HON. COLONEL JAMES LAWRENCE**, third son of John Lawrence the emigrant, was of Fairfield, Jamaica, *bu.* June 15, 1756, in the forty-seventh year of his age, who *m.* **MARY**, *dau.* of **Colonel Richard James**, and had an eldest son, RICHARD

JAMES, who *m.* MARY, fourth *dau.* of Thomas Hall, of Kirkpatrick, and *d.* November 8, 1830, having had five sons :

i.	Sir James, Knight of Malta, author of the " Nobility of the British Gentry," " The Prisoner of Verdun," " Empire of the Nairs," etc.
ii.	George, of Cowsfield House, Wilts.
iii.	Charles, of Mossley Hall, Lancashire.
iv.	Henry, Barrister-at-Law.
v.	Frederick Augustus, a Gentleman of the Privy Chamber.

JOHN, younger brother of **President Henry Lawrence,** *d.* in 1670, leaving an only son, THOMAS, Physician-General of the Army, Physician to Queen Anne and four other crowned heads. He *d.* in 1714, leaving an eldest son, THOMAS, a Captain in the Royal Navy ; *m.* ELIZABETH, *dau.* of Gabriel Soulden, of Kinsale, and widow of a Colonel Piers. Their second son, Thomas, *b.* May 25, 1711, was Dr. Samuel Johnson's physician, President of the Royal College of Physicians, and an author. He *m.,* May 25, 1744, Frances, *dau.* of Dr. Charles Chauncey, of Derby, who *d.* January 2, 1780 ; her husband *d.* June 6, 1783, leaving a son, Sir Soulden Lawrence, *b.* 1751, Justice of the Common Pleas, and knighted in March, 1794 ; promoted to the King's Bench, June of the same year; *d. u.* July 8, 1814. Of this family were the **Lawrences** of Studley Royal and Fountains Abbey, whose heiress *m.* a **Mr. Aislabie,** in the middle of the present century.

Authorities: As stated in the text, the Biographical Dictionaries, and R. Cooke's Visitation of Cambridge, 1575.

LEIPER

ACCORDING to family tradition **THOMAS LEIPER**, living at Strathaven, in Clydesdale, Scotland, at the beginning of the eighteenth century, was descended from a Frenchman who came to Scotland in 1561 in the suite of Mary Queen of Scots. This **THOMAS LEIPER** *m.* **HELEN**, *dau.* of **Hamilton**, of Kype (she *m.*, second, before 1771, —— Scott)[1], and great-grand-daughter of **John Hamilton**, of Stanehouse, and dying in 1763 left issue :

i.   **ROBERT**, inherited the homestead and left descendants living there in 1856.
ii.   **DR. JAMES HAMILTON**, *of whom presently.*
iii.   **THOMAS**, *b.* December 15, 1745 (*q. v.*).
iv.   **NANCY**, living in 1771.
v.   **JANET**, living in 1771.
vi.   **ANDREW**, *b.* in 1750, a graduate of the Medical School of the University of Edinburgh ; emigrated to Virginia, and practised medicine at Richmond. Served through the Revolutionary War as surgeon, *m.* **FRANCES**, *dau.* of **Alexander Trent**, of " Warehill," Chesterfield Co., Va., and *d.*, October 17, 1798, of yellow fever contracted while attending a sailor in the hold of a vessel in Richmond Harbour, and is *bu.* in S. John's Churchyard under a handsome tombstone erected by his wife. Issue :

     i.   **ANDREWETTA HAMILTON**, *b.* 1797 ; *m.* **Dr. GEORGE WILLIAMSON**, of "Woodlawn," Henrico Co., Va., and *d.* December 25, 1833, leaving issue.
     ii.   **FRANCES ANN**, *m.* **RICHARD CROUCH**, and left issue.

JAMES HAMILTON, second son of **Thomas** and **Helen (Hamilton) Leiper**, was educated at the Medical School of the University of Edinburgh, is said to have come to Maryland and settled in Prince George's Co. before 1763, but in his will, dated in 1771, calls himself " surgeon, and resident of London." He *m.*, according to his will, **ELIZABETH**, sister of **General William Small-**

---

[1] The will of her son, Dr. James H. Leiper, names her as " my mother Helen Scott," at that date.

435

wood, a prominent officer of the Revolutionary forces and Governor of Maryland, 1785–88. November 15, 1771, being about to voyage to Lisbon for his health he made his will, which was proved December 2, 1771. In it he names his children, **GEORGE ROBERT LEIPER,** who *d. u.*, and **LUCY ANN HEBBARD,** who is said to have married **BERNARD MOORE,** son of Bernard Moore, of Chelsea, Va., by his wife Anne Catherine, *dau.* of Major-General Alexander Spotswood, Governor of Virginia, and *d.* leaving issue. **ELIZABETH** *m.* **WILLIAM PENN TAYLOR,** of " Hayfield," Caroline Co., Va.

THOMAS, third son of **Thomas** and **Helen (Hamilton) Leiper,** *b.* at Strathaven, December 15, 1745, was educated at Glasgow and Edinburgh, his father's intention being that he should become a minister of the Scotch Kirk. This was not to his taste, and in 1763, at his father's death, he followed his brothers to America. According to a MS. account, written by him, now in the possession of one of his descendants, he sailed from Scotland in April, 1763, landed in Maryland in June, went to Port Tobacco and resided as assistant in Mr. John Semple's store. In the fall was compelled by the fever and ague to go to Occoquan. The fever remained with him through the winter, but in the spring " taking up his line of march for Frederick County," it left him without the aid of medicines. From Frederick, in the spring of 1765, he went to Philadelphia, attracted by an advantageous offer of employment made him by his cousin Gavin Hamilton, who was extensively engaged in the storage and shipment of tobacco to Europe. In a few years he left him and went into business for himself. At the breaking out of the Revolution, the leading tobacco house being interdicted, he seized the opportunity to push his business, and became the principal factor in Philadelphia. He also engaged in the manufacture of snuff and other tobacco commodities. By ability, energy, and business tact, he soon accumulated a considerable fortune. At the Revolution he took sides against the mother country, contributed largely of his means to the cause, and was an active member of the " First Troop of City Light Horse," and present with them at the battles of Princeton, Trenton, Brandywine, and Germantown, besides several skirmishes. He was graded first as Orderly Sergeant, afterward as Lieutenant ; as Treasurer of the Troop he carried the last subsidies of the French to the army before Yorktown. After the war he acted with the corps in quelling several civil insurrections and riots, notably the whiskey insurrection, of 1794, and in the attack upon the residence of James Wilson, at the

THOMAS LEIPER

From a Painting by Otis

southwest corner of Walnut and Third Streets, where he was one of the seven troopers who charged and routed the mob of two hundred rioters. He was active in politics, taking a position of opposition to Washington and the Federalists, and during the violent party quarrels which arose he was Major of the "Horse of the Legion," raised to oppose the "Black Cockade" forces of the friends of Mr. Adams's Administration, and it was said recruited and equipped the first company of troopers at his own expense. He built and equipped the first permanent tramway in America (one for temporary purposes being used in Massachusetts, in 1807), from his quarries, on Crum Creek to tide-water, a distance of three-quarters of a mile. He was a Presidential Elector in 1809, and in 1825 Director of the Banks of Pennsylvania and the United States, Commissioner for the Defence of the City in the War of 1812 ; a member, and ultimately President (1801-5, 1808-10, 1812-14) of the Common Councils of the city of Philadelphia. Was one of the Executive Committee of the S. Andrew's Society ; Secretary in 1774, and Vice-President from 1804 to 1810, and 1812 to 1816. Active in his business affairs, there was hardly an industry which he did not turn to profit. He was also enterprising and progressive in the adoption of new machines and improvements in agricultural implements long before his neighbours forsook the time-worn appliances they had inherited from their fathers. "In personal attributes [1] Thomas Leiper was noticeable for comeliness of countenance and grace of figure. Slightly above the medium height, with a square and compact frame, and finely proportioned limbs. His countenance exhibited an ample and perfectly fair forehead, dark brows, bright, but thoughtful eyes of a hue between a hazel and dark blue, finely cut and expressive features, with a remarkably clear and ruddy complexion, traits combining to produce a visage indicative of intelligence, firmness, and benignity. This manly beauty of face and form obtained for him the cognomen of the 'handsome Scotchman.' His habits were particular nearly to fastidiousness, being daily shaved, head powdered, and hair dressed with a short queue, tied with black ribbon. These services were performed by a German barber, who had formerly been Trumpeter to the City Troop. As to dress, he retained the style in vogue during his earlier days, consisting of a blue or black dress coat, with bright brass buttons, vest of cloth or marseilles, according to season, breeches buckled at the knee, where they where joined by hose of silk, cotton, or wool, as circumstances demanded,

---

[1] From Dr. R. P. Robins, The First Tramway in America.

the whole terminating in shoes ornamented with broad silver buckles for in-door wear, or yellow top-boots for out-door service. Hat, a low-crowned, broad-brimmed, white or black beaver. Naturally of a quick and impulsive temper, he had it under much control, never indulging in long-lived anger or harbouring malice. He was reverent and punctual in attendance upon religious services, being a pew-holder in both the First and Second Presbyterian Churches."

He *m.*, November 3, 1878, **ELIZABETH COULTAS**, *dau.* of **George** and **Martha (Ibbetson) Gray**, of Gray's Ferry (*q. v.*) (*b.* August 26, 1762, and *d.* August 12, 1829), her husband *d.* July 6, 1825 (an eulogistic obituary appeared in the Philadelphia *Aurora* of July 8th). Issue :

i.   **THOMAS**, *b.* September 17, 1780 ; *d.* same day.
ii.   **THOMAS**, *b.* June 9, 1782 ; *d.* June 9, 1782.
iii. **MARTHA GRAY**, *b.* February 3, 1786 ; *m.* **JACOB J.**, son of **George** and **Effie (Ten Eyck) Janeway** ; a graduate of Columbia College in 1793 ; licensed to preach November 30, 1797 ; Pastor of Second Presbyterian Church, Philadelphia ; Vice-President of Rutger's College, and a Trustee of Princeton College ; *d.* June 25, 1857, leaving issue.
iv.   **GEORGE GRAY**, *b.* February 3, 1786, *of whom presently.*
v.   **ELIZABETH COULTAS**, *b.* June 28, 1788 ; *m.* **ROBERT TAY-LOR**, and *d.* September 13, 1832. Issue :

> **DR. GEORGE GRAY, JAMES LEIPER, SAMUEL LEIPER,** and **THOMAS LEIPER.**

vi.   **THOMAS**, *b.* March 2, 1790 ; *d.* May 23, 1792.
vii. **HELEN HAMILTON**, *b.* April 20, 1792 ; *m.*, April 20, 1814, **DR. ROBERT M. PATTERSON**, son of **Robert** and **Amé Hunter (Ewing) Patterson**, of Philadelphia, *b.* March 23, 1787. Graduated M.D., University of Pennsylvania, 1808 ; was Acting Consul-General at Paris, 1809 ; Professor of Natural Philosophy and Chemistry, University of Pennsylvania, 1813–28 ; Vice-Provost, 1814–28 ; Trustee, 1836 ; Professor of Natural Philosophy and Chairman of Faculty, University of Virginia, 1829–35 ; Member of American Philosophical Society, 1809 ; President, 1845–53 ; one of the Founders of the Franklin Institute, Philadelphia, 1823 ; Director United States Mint at Philadelphia, 1835–53 ; Member of American Academy of Arts and Sciences, 1839 ; a Founder of the Musical Fund Society, Philadelphia, and President, 1845. He *d.* September 5, 1854. His widow *d.* December 14, 1871, leaving issue.
viii. **JAMES GRAY SPROAT**, *b.* July 21, 1794 ; *m.* **ANN**, *dau.* of **Pierce** and **Christiana Crosby**, and *d.* March 18, 1821. Issue :

> **ELIZABETH GRAY**, *m.* **JOHN HOLMES**, of Philadelphia, and *d.* February 1, 1873, leaving issue.

JOHN KINTZING KANE

From a Family Portrait

ix.   JANE DUVALL, *b.* November 10, 1796; *m.* JUDGE JOHN K. KANE (*q. v.*).

x.   ANN GRAY, *b.* December 18, 1789; *m.* GEORGE GRAY THOMAS (*q. v.*).

xi.   JULIANA DUNLAP, *b.* January 11, 1801; *m.*, June 9, 1825, COLO-NEL HENRY, son of John and Lucy (Perrin) Taylor, of Caroline Co., Va., and *d.* February 21, 1883, leaving issue.

xii.   WILLIAM JONES, *b.* April 17, 1803. Graduate University of Pennsylvania, A.B., 1823; A.M., 1824; Member City Troop, May 5, 1823; Honorary Member, December 15, 1832; *d. u.* September 27, 1860.

xiii.   SAMUEL McKEAN, of Avondale, *b.* August 20, 1805. Graduate University of Pennsylvania, A.B., 1822; A.M., 1825; Member Philadelphia City Troop, April 19, 1829; Honorary Member, May 19, 1833; *m.*, 1831, MARY, *dau.* of Dr. Charles S., and Mary (Irvine) Lewis, and *d.* February 17, 1854. Issue:

    i.   ELIZABETH LEWIS, *d. i.*

    ii.   THOMAS IRVINE, First Lieutenant of United States Volunteers, September 13, 1861; Adjutant Fifty-eighth Pennsylvania Volunteers, May 1, 1862; Captain Company A, June 14, 1862; honourably discharged at expiration of term, October 24, 1864; *m.* EMMA, *dau.* of Young S. Walter, of Chester. Issue:

        Mary, *m.* William Addison Magee, Virginia, Ann de B., Letitia, *d. i.*, and Charles Lewis.

    iii.   MARY LEWIS, *m.*, February 2, 1859, to EDWARD McFUNN, son of William M. and Julia (Montgomery) Biddle.

    iv.   JANE, *d. i.*

    v.   CHARLES LEWIS, mustered in United States Volunteers September 7, 1861, promoted from First Lieutenant Company C, to Captain Company L, November 20, 1862; wounded at Beverly Ford, Va., June 9, 1863, and at Old Church, May 30, 1864; Major, September 1, 1864, and Lieutenant-Colonel, February 1, 1865; Colonel, March 20, 1865; Brevet Brigadier-General, March 13, 1865; transferred to Second Provisional Cavalry, June 17, 1865; Member City Troop, May 9, 1861; Honorary Member, February 6, 1862. GENERAL LEIPER *m.* HENRIETTA MARIA, *dau.* of Lucius Witham and Catharine (Stockton) Stockton. Issue:

        Samuel McKean and Katherine Stockton.

    vi.   CALLENDER IRVINE, *m.* MARGARET, *dau.* of the Rev. James W. Dale, D.D. Issue:

        Callender Irvine, Mary G., and Margaret D.

    vii.   SARAH IRVINE, *d. i.*

    viii.   WILLIAM JONES.

GEORGE GRAY, eldest son of **Thomas** and **Elizabeth (Gray) Leiper**, *b.* February 3, 1786, lived at Lapidea, near Leiperville, Delaware Co., Pa., was a member of Congress, 1829–31; Associate Judge (lay) of the Delaware Co. Circuit Court. He served numerous terms in the Pennsylvania Legislature, and at one time was waited upon by a delegation of distinguished Democratic politicians, who pressed him to become their candidate for Governor of Pennsylvania, but he told them he would have to

decline the nomination, as his private interests had already suffered too much, in his service to his State and country, every
office he had ever held making him a poorer man. He was
intimately acquainted with all the public men of his day, and his
house was one of open hospitality, and one where numerous
public men were wont to stop on their way to and from the
Capitol. He was a personal friend of Andrew Jackson, and supported him warmly when he ran for President, making a large
number of speeches in his behalf throughout the country. When a
member of the Pennsylvania Legislature, he met James Buchanan,
and an intimacy sprang up which lasted throughout their lives.
He completed the canal which was projected by his father for
the purpose of conveying stone on boats from his quarries, and
it continued in use until 1852. He had large mills, quarries, and
numerous farms, and was equally as active as his father had
been in the management of his business interests. He was also
a member of the Philadelphia City Troop. Judge Leiper *m.*, May
3, 1810, **ELIZA SNOWDEN**, *dau.* of **John Chew** and **Mary
(Snowden) Thomas** (*q. v.*), and *d.* November 17, 1868, having
celebrated his golden wedding-day eight years previously. His
wife *d.* September 28, 1868. Issue :

i.   **ELIZABETH COULTAS**, *of whom presently.*
ii.   **THOMAS GRAY**, *b.* July 16, 1807 ; *d.* April, 1896.
iii.   **ANNE**, *b.* June 16, 1817 ; *m.* **DR. JESSE BONSALL**, and *d. s. p.*
       June 6, 1847.
iv.   **JOHN CHEW** (*q. v.*).
v.   **HENRIETTA**, *d. y.*
vi.   **MARY THOMAS**, *b.* December 19, 1826 ; *m.* **JOHN HENRY
       THOMAS** (*q. v.*).
vii.   **MARTHA GRAY**, *b.* November 22, 1828 ; *m.* **THOMAS IRWIN
       CAREY** (*q. v.*).
viii. **GEORGE GRAY**, *m.* **SALLIE HAMILTON**, and *d.* Issue :
       ELIZA SNOWDEN.

ELIZABETH COULTAS, eldest child of **Judge Leiper**, *b.*
June 16, 1815 ; *m.*, December 14, 1843, **THOMAS MIFFLIN
SMITH**, who *d.* in 1857 ; his wife *d.* January 15, 1888. Issue
(surname SMITH) :

i.   **MARY THOMAS**, *m.*, December 7, 1871, **COLONEL ARCHER
       NEVINS MARTIN**, and *d.* October 5, 1894 ; her husband *d.*
       January, 1895. Issue :

i.   **AUBREY HENRY**, *b.* March 30, 1873; *m.*, April 17, 1895, **JULIA KINGS-BURY**, second *dau.* of James Robertson Pitcher, of Short Hills, N. J.

ii. iii. **ROBERT NEVINS** and **CHARLES LAWRENCE**, *b.* May 31, 1875 (the former *d.* January 24, 1877).

iv.   **ELIZABETH LEIPER**, *b.* May 11, 1879.

v.   **CLARENCE CLARK**, *b.* January 19, 1882.

ii. **ELIZA LEIPER**, *m.*, September 28, 1865, **JAMES EDWARD FARNUM**, of Media, Pa., who *d.* Issue :

    i.   **PAUL**, *b.* August 18, 1867.

    ii.   **EDWARD**, *b.* May 2, 1869.

    iii. **GEORGE LEIPER**, *b.* May 10, 1872.

    iv. **ELIZABETH**, *b.* April 1, 1875.

    v.   **MARY**, *d. y.*

iii. **ANNE LEIPER**, *m.*, June 7, 1868, **ROBERT MARTIN**. Issue :

    LILLY LEIPER, ADELAIDE NEVINS, ROBERT, FANNY, and ARCHER N.

iv. **GEORGE LEIPER**, *d. y.*

v.   **JOHN MILLER**, *m.* **MARY BARTOL**.

vi. **HARRIET J.**, *m.*, 1880, **WILLIAM H. DE FOREST**, Jr., of New York City.

JOHN CHEW, second son of **George G.** and **Eliza (Thomas) Leiper**, member of the Philadelphia City Troop, February 6, 1850; resigned December 31, 1859; *m.*, March 24, 1852, **MARY LEWIS**, *dau.* of **Peter** and **Rebecca (Irvine) Fayssoux**, of Philadelphia, and *d.* 1889. Issue :

i.   **GEORGE GRAY**, *b.* January 23, 1853.

ii.   **MARTHA F.**, *d. i.*

iii. **REBECCA FAYSSOUX**, *b.* May 29, 1856; *m.*, December 12, 1877, **DR. RANDOLPH** (*b.* October 23, 1852), son of **Dr. Caleb** and **Jane (Parry) Winslow**, of Baltimore, now Professor of Anatomy and Clinical Surgery in the University of Maryland. Issue :

    NATHAN, *b.* November 17, 1878. JOHN LEIPER, *b.* March 7, 1880. FITZ RANDOLPH, *b.* July 2, 1881. EDWARDS FAYSSOUX, *b.* November 23, 1883. MARY FAYSSOUX, *b.* July 7, 1885. JANE PARRY, *b.* November 7, 1886. CALEB, *b.* July 1, 1889. ELIZA LEIPER, *b.* February 10, 1891. GEORGE LEIPER, *b.* March 4, 1893.

iv. **EDWARDS FAYSSOUX**, Lieutenant U. S. N. ; *m.*, October 15, 1891, **MARY J. ASHURST**.

v.   **ELIZA SNOWDEN**.

vi. **BARNARD BEE**, *b.* April 21, 1863.

vii. **JOHN HENRY THOMAS**, *b.* December 23, 1867.

Authority : Family papers, through Mr. James Carey of Thomas, Baltimore, and Dr. R. P. Robins.

McCOBB, OF MAINE

JAMES McCOBB, with his brother **GEORGE,** of Aberdeen, Scotland, emigrated to America early in the eighteenth century, and became active citizens of Bath, Me. **JAMES** was appointed to raise recruits for the French and Indian War, 1746; commissioned Captain; and *m.* **BEATTRICE ——.** Issue:

i. **JOHN,** *b.* October 8, 1738.
ii. **ISABELLA,** *b.* March 21, 1739-40.
iii. **GEORGE,** *b.* March 23, 1741-42.
iv. **SAMUEL,** *b.* November 20, 1744, *of whom presently.*
v. **JAMES,** *b.* July 9, 1746. In 1776 of the Revolutionary Committee of Correspondence; Captain of Company 4, of his brother's regiment, 1778.
vi. **BEATTRICE,** *b.* January 13, 1749.
vii. **THOMAS,** *b.* October 7, 1751.
viii., ix. **FRANCES** and **MARGARET,** *b.* July 2, 1755.
x. **ANN,** *b.* April 16, 1756.

SAMUEL, third son of **Captain James** and **Beattrice McCobb,** *b.* November 20, 1744, was active in town affairs, and through his marriage became one of the leading men in Bath. He was Town Clerk, 1773-75; Delegate to Congress from Arrowsic Island, 1775, and Town Treasurer, 1778-79; commissioned Captain in the Provincial Forces, May 17, 1775; Colonel, February 14, 1776. Was of the Committee of Correspondence, 1776. Later was Brigadier-General. He *m.,* 1768, **RACHEL,** *dau.* of **Major Samuel Denny,** by his second wife, **Mrs. Rachel (Loring) White,** *b.* about 1752.

MAJOR SAMUEL DENNY, of the family of **Sir Anthony Denny, Knt.,** of Huntingdonshire, England, was third son of **Thomas** and **Grace Denny,** of Coombs Manor House, Suffolk, *b.* in 1689; emigrated, 1717. His sister, **DEBORAH,** *m.* the **REV. THOMAS PRINCE,** the historian of New England. **SAMUEL**

DENNY became the leading man in the settlement at Georgetown, was Town Clerk from 1738 to 1771 ; *d.* June 2, 1772 ; he *m.*, first, **SARAH,** widow of his partner, a **Mr. Robinson,** who *d.* in 1750 ; *m.*, second, in 1751, **MRS. RACHEL (LORING) WHITE,** who *d.* leaving an infant *dau.* RACHEL, *m.* **GENERAL McCOBB.**

GENERAL SAMUEL and **RACHEL (DENNY) McCOBB**
   had issue :

i.   **DENNY,** *b.* February 13, 1770, *of whom presently.*
ii.   **BEATTRICE,** *b.* October 1, 1772 ; *m.*, before 1800, **COLONEL AN-DREW REED.**
iii.   **RACHEL,** *b.* June 24, 1774.
iv.   **NANCY,** *b.* February 1, 1777.
v.   **JOHN,** *b.* February 9, 1779 (*q. v.*).
vi.   **JANE,** *b.* April 7, 1781.
vii.   **SALLY,** *b.* May 15, 1783.
viii. **PARKER,** *b.* March 30, 1785 ; *d.* in 1845 or 1846.

DENNY, eldest son of **General Samuel** and **Rachel (Denny) McCobb,** *b.* February 13, 1770 ; was Town Clerk, 1792 to 1805 ; was Lieutenant-Colonel, May 10, 1798 ; commissioned Colonel Maine and New Hampshire Volunteers, December 23, 1812 ; Colonel Thirty-seventh Infantry, March 26, 1814 ; transferred to United States Forty-fifth Infantry, April 14th, and called "the bravest officer in the army under General Henry Dearborn." A Brigadier-General of the State Militia. He *m.* **HANNAH,** youngest *dau.* of **Isaiah** and **Hannah (Harding) Crooker,** who *d.* in 1856. Issue :

i.   **RACHEL,** *b.* December 1, 1799 ; *d.* February 12, 1801.
ii.   **SAMUEL,** *b.* January 19, 1801 ; *d.* August 25, 1802.
iii.   **SAMUEL,** *b.* October 6, 1802.
iv.   **SALLY,** *b.* October 16, 1803.

JOHN, second son of **General Samuel** and **Rachel (Denny) McCobb,** *b.* Feb. 9, 1779 ; *m.* **SARAH WESTON,** of Virginia, and *d.* 1848 ; leaving a son, **THOMAS FARRELL,** *of whom presently.*

THOMAS FARRELL, son of **John** and **Sarah (Weston) McCobb,** *m.* **MARION L.,** *dau.* of **Tolemiah** and **Mary Berry,** of Virginia, who *d.* 1880. Issue :

i.   **MARION L.,** *m.* **JOHN W. TURTLE,** in 1873. Issue surviving :
        SARAH ELIZABETH, MARION BERRY, and **MARIE ADÈLE.**
ii.   **JOHN PARKER,** killed in the Confederate States Army.
iii.   **MARY BERRY,** *m.* **REV. LAWRENCE BUCKLEY THOMAS** (*q. v.*).

Authorities : Parker McCobb Reed's History of Bath, Me. ; Parish Records of Georgetown, Me., and family papers, through Mr. Thomas F. McCobb.

McVICKAR

ARCHIBALD McVICKAR, Gent., younger son of an Irish gentleman, was admitted as a freeman of New York City, October 3, 1769. He is noticed as an importer, November 22, 1776. **MRS. ELIZABETH McVICKAR**, probably his widow, *m.*, second, October 16, 1797, **ANDRUS WATSON. JOHN**, a nephew of **ARCHIBALD McVICKAR**, in Ireland, *of whom presently*, being ill-treated by his step-mother, came over to his uncle, at the age of seventeen, and settled in New York. His brother, **NATHANIEL**, emigrated, also, in 1798; *m.* **CATHERINE**, *dau.* of —— **Bucknor**, by his wife, a **Miss Goelet**, and *d.* 1827. Issue:

  i.   **WILLIAM H.**, *m. a dau.* of Thaddeus Phelps.
  ii.   **NATHAN.**

JOHN McVICKAR may have been the young man named Mc-Vickar complained of as communicating with the British, March 8, 1777, and was certainly in business in New York City before 1786. He was an importer and ship-owner; a director of the Bank of New York from 1793–1810; Vice-President of S. Patrick's Society, in 1797; a vestryman of Trinity Church from 1801–12; a director of the Western and Northern Coal Company, in 1805; a member of the Friendly Club, and had two shares in the celebrated Tontine Coffee-house. He is described as a "tall, sharp featured, courtly man, with a kindly eye, a smile of singular sweetness and a mouth and chin indicative of unbending will." He was rich and respected, able and generous; noted for his liberality in building churches, was constantly aiding the clergy and unobtrusively assisting young merchants in difficulties. He *m.* **ANN**, *dau.* of **John Moore**, of Long Island (*b.* 1761), a first cousin of **Bishop Moore**, and sister to **Lady Dongan**, and *d.* 1812. Issue (order of birth uncertain):

444

i.   **JAMES**, *m.* **EURETTA**, *dau.* of **William Constable**. Issue :

> JOHN A., M.D., living in 1863, whose son is the Rev. William Neilson McVickar, D.D., Rector of Holy Trinity Church, Philadelphia.

ii.   **ARCHIBALD**, a lawyer, *m.*, August 30, 1809, **CATHERINE AUGUSTA**, *dau.* of **Henry Brockholst Livingston**.

iii.   **JOHN**, *b.* 1787, a clergyman of the Protestant Episcopal Church, author and Professor. He *m.*, in 1809, **ELIZA**, *dau.* of **Dr. Samuel Bard**, and *d.* October, 1868. Issue :

> i.   REV. WILLIAM A., D.D., of New York City.
> ii.   BARD, *d.* 1838.

iv.   **HENRY**, began mercantile life in 1814.

v.   **EDWARD**, *m.* **MATILDA**, *dau.* of **William Constable**.

vi.   **NATHAN**, *d. u.*

vii.   **BENJAMIN**, *m.* **JOSEPHINE C.**, *dau.* of **Isaac** and **Cornelia (Beach) Lawrence** (*q. v.*).

viii.   **ELIZA**, *m.* **WILLIAM CONSTABLE**.

ix.   **AUGUSTA**, *m.* **JUDGE WILLIAM JAY**, youngest son of Chief Justice **John Jay**.

Authorities : Martha J. Lamb, "History of New York," *pp.* 469, 517, 520 ; " Old Merchants of New York," II., 281-291 ; " New York Genealogical and Biographical Record ;" and family papers, through the Rev. Dr. McVickar, of Philadelphia.

MIFFLIN

JOHN MIFFLIN, *b.* in 1637, and his son **JOHN,** *b.* in 1661, came
to America from Warminster, in Wiltshire, England, about 1677,
or 1678, being at Burlington, N. J., in 1679. In 1684, William
Penn confirmed them in possession of 300 acres of land on the
east bank of the Schuylkill River, afterward called " Fountain
Green," which **JOHN MIFFLIN,** Jr., bought of his father in 1698,
when the latter removed to Merion, Pa., dying in Philadelphia
September 4, 1716. **JOHN MIFFLIN,** Jr., *b.* in 1661 ; *m.,* February 6, 1683–84, **ELIZABETH HARDY,** from Derby, England,
and *d.* in Philadelphia, June 4, 1714. Issue, with others :

i.   **EDWARD,** *b.* in 1685 ; *m.,* and *d.* in Virginia about 1743.
ii.   **GEORGE,** *b.* 1688, *of whom presently.*

GEORGE, second son of **John** and **Elizabeth (Hardy) Mifflin,**
b. 1688 ; *m.,* February 29, 1713, **ESTHER,** *dau.* of **Hugh** and
Deborah Cordery, and *d.* at Philadelphia, April 13, 1758, leaving, with other issue, an eldest son, **JOHN,** *b.* January 18, 1714–15,
a prominent and wealthy merchant of Philadelphia. In 1747 Common Councilman ; 1751 an Alderman ; May 20, 1752, Commissioned Justice of Courts of Common Pleas, Quarter Sessions, and
Orphans' Court ; November 2, 1755, a Privy Councillor. He *m.,*
first, **ELIZABETH BAGNELL,** and after her death. second, in

MAJOR-GENERAL THOMAS MIFFLIN

From a Portrait in the Possession of his Great Nephew, William Mifflin

1755, **SARAH,** *dau.* of **William** and **Sarah (Roberts) Fishbourne,** and *d.* February 10, 1759, leaving surviving issue by his first wife :

i. THOMAS, *b.* January 10, 1744, *of whom presently.*
ii. GEORGE, *b.* about 1746 (*g. v.*).

THOMAS, eldest son of **George** and **Esther (Cordery) Mifflin,** *b.* January 10, 1744 ; *m.* **SARAH MORRIS,** and *d. s. p. m.,* at Lancaster, Pa., January 20, 1800. In 1772 he was chosen one of the two representatives of the city of Philadelphia in the Provincial Legislature, and took an active part in the debates of that Assembly, and in the proceedings out of doors which preceded the Revolution. In 1775 was commissioned a Major in the Pennsylvania troops, became Aide-de-Camp to Washington at Boston, in August, 1775, Quartermaster-General, and shortly afterward Adjutant-General ; May 19, 1776, commissioned a Brigadier-General ; February 19, 1777, Major-General. In 1782 elected a Delegate to the Continental Congress, and as President of that body in 1783 received the resignation of Washington as Commander-in-Chief of the Army. In 1785 he was a member and Speaker of the Pennsylvania Legislature, a delegate to the Convention to form the Federal Constitution in 1787 ; President of the Supreme Executive Council from October, 1788, to December, 1790 ; President of the Pennsylvania Constitutional Convention, 1790, and inaugurated the first Governor of the State thereunder, December 21, 1790. He was re-elected twice, serving until December, 1799.

GEORGE, second son of **John** and **Elizabeth (Bagnell) Mifflin,** *b.* 1746, was a prominent merchant of Philadelphia, Paymaster of the Fifth Pennsylvania Battalion in the Revolution, Colonel Robert Magaw, Commander ; under the Act of July 25, 1775, was appointed one of the gentlemen to sign the Continental Currency. He *m.,* July 10, 1772, **MARTHA,** *dau.* of **Joseph** and **Martha Morris** (*b.* 1751, *d.* January 9, 1793), and *d.* at Philadelphia, July 14, 1785. Issue :

i. JOSEPH, *b.* 1773 ; *d.* 1775.
ii. ELIZABETH, *b.* 1775 ; *m.,* November 28, 1798, CASPAR WISTAR, M.D., and *d.* in 1844.
iii. THOMAS, *b.* in 1777, *of whom presently.*

THOMAS, only surviving son of **George** and **Martha (Morris) Mifflin,** *b.* in 1777, was a merchant of Philadelphia ; member of First City Troop, May 12, 1798 ; resigned, January 31, 1810 ;

m., June 20, 1799, **SARAH,** *dau.* of **Ebenezer** and **Dorothy (Sparks) Large** (*p.* 386), *b.* in 1779, and *d.* December 7, 1856; her husband *d.* April 1, 1820.   Issue :

i.   **JAMES LARGE,** *b.* June 26, 1800 ; *d.* September 25, 1872.
ii. **GEORGE,** *b.* May 2, 1802 ; *d.* October 25, 1837.
iii. **MARY,** *b.* December 26, 1804 ; *d.* February 3, 1873.
iv. **MARTHA,** *b.* November 7, 1807 ; *d.* May 2, 1867.
v.   **THOMAS,** *b.* March 5, 1811 ; *d.* August 29, 1870.
vi. **PHŒBE MORRIS,** *b.* March 12, 1814 ; *d.* April 10, 1872.
vii. **JOHN LARGE,** *b.* April 23, 1817 ; *d.* July 8, 1859.
viii. **WILLIAM,** *b.* January 22, 1820 ; *m.*, February 4, 1839, **ANN POULT-NEY,** *dau.* of **James** and **Elizabeth (Poultney) Large** (*q. v.*), *b.* October 31, 1822.   Issue :

    i.   JAMES, *b.* in Philadelphia, August 2, 1840 ; Deputy Governor-General of the Society of Colonial Wars, on the part of Pennsylvania, 1893-96 ; *m.*, November 29, 1871, LILY STURGIS, *dau.* of Edward and Caroline Frances (Stimson) Wight, of New York City and Dedham, Mass. (*b.* October 2, 1850), and *d.* in 1895.

    Authorities : Mifflin Genealogy and W. H. H. Davis's History of Bucks County, Pa.

MORRIS ARMS

MORRIS AND PEROT

ANTHONY, son of **Anthony Morris,** *b.* in London in 1654, came to Philadelphia with Penn in the ship Welcome in 1682; in 1687 he purchased a lot on Front Street, below Walnut, facing the river, and erected a brewery and malt-house thereon. He was Presiding Justice of the Court of Common Pleas at Philadelphia, May 29, 1693, and Mayor of the city, October 12, 1703 and 1704. He *d.* 1721, leaving a son **ANTHONY,** *b.* 1682, Member of the Assembly 1722–24; *m.* **PHEBE GUEST,** and had a son ANTHONY, *b.* 1705, *of whom presently.*

ANTHONY, the fourth son of **Anthony** and **Phebe (Guest) Morris,** *b.* 1705, built the brewery and malt-house still standing at the corner of Pear and Dock Streets, and *m.* **SARAH POWEL,** who *d.* 1780. Issue, with others :

i.　**THOMAS,** his grandson **Anthony Saunders Morris,** had a *dau.* Elizabeth M., *m.* Francis Perot, who succeeded to the business in 1823, and founded what is now the centenary firm of **Francis Perot's Sons Malting Company.**
ii.　**SAMUEL,** *of whom presently.*
iii.　**JOSEPH.**
iv.　**SARAH,** *m.* **WILLIAM BUCKLEY** (*q. v.*).

SAMUEL, son of **Anthony** and **Sarah (Powel) Morris,** was Sheriff of Philadelphia Co., 1752–60, and Captain of the First City Troop at the end of the Revolution. He was Register of Wills, March 14, 1777, and High Sheriff of Philadelphia Co., March 6, 1752 to 1755. He *m.,* December 11, 1755, **REBECCA WISTAR.** Issue :

i.　**BENJAMIN.**
ii.　**ANTHONY.**

449

iii.   **CASPAR.**
iv.   **SARAH,** *m.* **RICHARD WISTAR.**
v.   **LUKE,** *of whom presently.*
vi.   **ISAAC.**
vii.   **CATHERINE.**
viii.   **ISRAEL WISTAR** (*q. v.*).

LUKE, fourth son of **Samuel** and **Rebecca (Wistar) Morris,** *b.* 1767 ; *m.,* first, **ELIZABETH,** *dau.* of **William** and **Sarah (Morris) Buckley.** Issue :

i.   **SAMUEL BUCKLEY,** *of whom presently.*

He *m.,* second, **ANN PANCOAST,** and *d.* 1793.   Further issue :

ii.   **ELIZABETH,** *m.* **THOMAS WISTAR.**
iii.   **MARY,** *m.* **CHARLES ELLIS** (*q. v.*).
iv.   **SARAH,** *m.,* June 5, 1827, **JOSEPH PEROT,** of Philadelphia, and *d.* March 7, 1855. He *d.* January 19, 1876. Issue (surname PEROT) :

    i.   JOHN, *b.* June 4, 1828 ; *d.* July 23, 1857.
    ii.   ANN MORRIS, *b.* May 6, 1830 ; *d.* January 24, 1863.
    iii.   JOSEPH SANSOM, *b.* September 8, 1832 ; *m.,* December 4, 1856, SALLIE A. LEA, and has seven children.
    iv.   ELLISTON LUKE, *b.* November 5, 1834 ; *m.,* December 4, 1862, JULIA E. BARLOW.
    v.   EFFINGHAM BUCKLEY, *b.* August 10, 1837 ; *m.,* February 11, 1868, MARY ELENA, *dau.* of Horatio Nelson Burroughs.
    vi.   HANNAH, *b.* April 28, 1839 ; *m.* GALLOWAY C. MORRIS (*q. v.*).

v.   **HANNAH ANN,** *m.* **EFFINGHAM L. BUCKLEY** (*q. v.*)..

SAMUEL BUCKLEY, only son of **Luke** and **Elizabeth (Buckley) Morris,** *b.* December 27, 1791 ; *m.* **HANNAH PEROT,** and *d.* January 23, 1859. Issue :

i.   **SAMUEL,** *m.* **LYDIA SPENCER.** Issue :
    i.   HANNAH PEROT.
    ii.   LUKE W., *d.* aged sixteen.
    iii.   GEORGE SPENCER.

ii.   **BEULAH SANSOM,** *m.* **CHARLES RHOADS.** Issue :
    MARY M., *d. i.*

iii.   **ELLISTON PEROT,** Attorney-at-Law, *m.* **MARTHA CANBY.** Issue :
    i.   MARRIOTT C.
    ii.   ELIZABETH C.
    iii.   SAMUEL B., *d.* June 20, 1866.
    iv.   ELLISTON P., *d.* March 16, 1881.

iv.   **MARY HOLLINGSWORTH,** *b.* 1835 ; *m.,* 1856, **HENRY MAYNADIER,** son of **Daniel** and **Mary (Dorsey) Murray,** of West River, Md. Issue (surname MURRAY) :

i.   CORNELIA, *b.* 1857; *m.*, 1880, CHARLES M. COLHOUN. Issue (surname COLHOUN) :

H. Maynadier, C. Forbes, and Adelaide.

ii. MARY DORSEY, *b.* 1859; *m.* ROBERT M. CHESTON (*q. v.*).

iii. ROBERT, *b.* 1861; *m.*, 1889, OLIVIA S. WILSON. Issue:

Olivia S.

iv. EMILY HOLLINGSWORTH, *b.* 1863.

v.   SALLY CHESTON, *b.* 1865.

vi. ANNE CHESTON, *b.* 1866.

vii. HENRY M., *b.* 1870; *d.* 1876.

viii. FRANCIS KEY, *b.* 1877; *d.* 1880.

ISRAEL WISTAR, youngest son of **Samuel** and **Rebecca** **(Wistar) Morris,** *m.* **MARY,** *dau.* of **Levi Hollingsworth,** and had, with other issue, a son, **CASPAR,** *of whom presently.*

CASPAR, son of **Israel W.** and **Mary (Hollingsworth) Morris,** was a prominent physician of Philadelphia, connected with numerous charitable institutions, and one of the founders of the Episcopal Hospital there.   He *m.*, 1829, **ANNE,** eldest *dau.* of **James** and **Mary (Hollingsworth) Cheston** (*q. v.*), who *d.* November 28, 1880 ; her husband *d.* March 17, 1884.   Issue :

i.   JAMES CHESTON, a physician, translated Lehmann's Manual of Chemistry, 1856 ; *m.*, first, HANNAH ANN, *dau.* of Isaac and Hannah (Wood) Tyson (*q. v.*).   Issue :

ISAAC TYSON, CASPAR, J. CHESTON, and HENRY V. D. JOHNS.

DR. MORRIS *m.*, second, MARY E. JOHNSON.   Further issue :

LAWRENCE, WILLIAM STEWART, MARY, and ISRAEL WISTAR.

ii. ISRAEL WISTAR, *m.*, December 3, 1855, ANNE MORRIS, *dau.* of Effingham L. and Hannah Ann (Morris) Buckley (*q. v.*).   Issue :

EFFINGHAM BUCKLEY, *b.* August 23, 1856, President of the Girard Trust Company, of Philadelphia, *m.*, November 5, 1879, ELLEN DOUGLAS, *dau.* of H. Nelson Burroughs.   Issue :

i.   Rhoda Fuller, *b.* November 5, 1880.

ii.   Eleanor Burroughs, *b.* October 6, 1881.

iii. Caroline Mitchell, *b.* June 24, 1886.

iv.   Effingham Buckley, *b.* August 26, 1890.

iii. GALLOWAY CHESTON, *m.*, November 21, 1861, HANNAH, *dau.* of Joseph and Sarah Perot (*q. v.*).   Issue :

i.   ELLISTON JOSEPH, *b.* September 28, 1862 ; *m.*, April 28, 1892, ELISE CAROLINE HEYDECKER.   Issue:

Elliston Joseph, Jr., *b.* January 23, 1893.

ii.   JOHN PEROT, *b.* August 26, 1864 ; *d.* March 3, 1866.

iii. HERBERT, *b.* Dec. 23, 1866 ; *m.*, Sept. 3, 1891, FANNY LOUISE HAWS. Issue:

Hannah Perot, *b.* July 12, 1892.

iv.   CASPAR MORRIS, *b.* November 7 ; *d.* November 9, 1869.

Authorities : "Centenary Firms of America," and family papers, through the late Dr. Caspar Morris and Mrs. E. B. Perot.

MORTIMER

ROGER DE MORTIMER, said to be related to **William the Conqueror,** and by some called a son of **William de Warrenne** or **Walter de S. Martin,** his brother, had a son **RALPH,** who fought in the Norman Army at Hastings, and dispossessing Edric at Wigmore Castle, Hereford, became a Baron by tenure and *m.* **MILLICENT** ——. His son, **HUGH,** apparently held Wigmore, Cleobury, and Bridgenorth, rebelled against Henry II. in 1155. He *m.* **MAUD,** *dau.* of **William Longespee,** of Normandy, and *d.* at Cleobury, 1185, leaving a son and heir, **Roger,** *of whom presently.*

ROGER, son of **Hugh and Maud (Longespee) Mortimer,** was continually at war with his Welsh neighbours ; *m.,* first, **MILLI-CENT,** *dau.* of **Robert Ferrers Earl of Derby** ; *m.,* second, **ISABEL,** *dau.* of **Walchelin,** son of **Robert Earl of Derby,** and *d.* 1215. Issue, by first wife :

i.　**HUGH,** *m.* **ANNORA,** *dau.* of **William de Braose** (*q. v.*) a strong partisan of King John ; *d. s. p.* 1227.

By his second wife :

ii.　**RALPH,** *of whom presently.*

SIR RALPH, son of **Roger** and **Millicent (Ferrers) Mortimer,** *m.* **GWLADYS DDU,** *dau.* of **Llewellyn ap Jorwerth,** Prince Paramount of Wales and widow of **Reginald de Braose** (*q. v.*), and had a son, **ROGER,** *b.* 1225–26 ; fought in Gascony and Wales ;

was on the side of Henry III. in the Barons' War ; planned the escape of Prince Edward from Hereford Castle, and commanded the third division of his army at the battle of Evesham. He held a great tournament at Kenilworth Castle. 7th Edward I., was Sheriff of Herefordshire, and some say an Earl, *m.* **MAUD,** second *dau.* and *co-h.* of **William de Braose,** Lord of Brecknock (*q. v.*). He *d.* at Kingston, October 28, 1282. Issue, with others :

i.   **SIR RALPH,** Knt., *d. v. p.*, Lord of Wigmore.

ii.   **EDMUND,** *b.* 1255 ; the heir, was summoned to Parliament from 1294-1302 ; *m.* **MARGARET,** *dau.* of **William de Fendeles,** nearly related to Queen Eleanor, of Castile, and *d.*, fighting against the Welsh, 1303, leaving, with other issue :

    i.   **Roger,** his heir, *b.* about April 29, 1286, favourite of Queen Isabella ; was Earl of March, Baron Mortimer of Wigmore, Lord of Mellenith, Kedy and Ewyas, held many high offices in England, Wales, and Ireland ; *m.* before 1308, **Joan,** *dau.* and heiress of **Peter de Genevil,** Lord of Trim in Ireland (*d.* 1356), and was hanged at Tyburn, November 29, 1330. One of his daughters, **Joan,** *m.* **James,** Lord Audley (*q. v.*), and his great-grandson, **Edmund Mortimer,** *m.* **Philippa,** *dau.* and heiress of **Lionel, Duke of Clarence,** third son of King Edward III., and became ancestor of the Yorkist Kings of England.

    ii.   **Maud,** *m.* **Theobald de Verdon** (*q. v.*).

Authorities : Sir T. C. Banks, Baronage of England, II. 364-370. Doyle's Official Baronage, II. 466-469.

NICKLIN AND DALLAS

PHILIP NICKLIN, merchant of Philadelphia ; *m.*, April 1, 1793, **JULIANA**, *dau.* of Chief Justice **Benjamin** and **Mary (Galloway) Chew** (*q. v.*), and *d.* in November, 1806 ; his widow *d.* August 11, 1845. Issue :

i.   **ELIZABETH**, *b.* February 18, 1794 ; *d.* November, 1813.
ii.   **WILLIAM**, *b.* 1796 ; *d.* November, 1811.
iii.   **SOPHIA CHEW**, *b.* June 25, 1798, *of whom presently.*
iv.   **MARIA HENRIETTA**, *b.* February 14, 1800 ; *m.* **EDMUND CARMICK WATMOUGH** ; who *d.* February 23, 1848 ; his widow *d.* November 30, 1864. Issue (surname WATMOUGH) :

    i.   JULIANA NICKLIN, *d. u.*, January 16, 1880.
    ii.   MARIA CHEW, *d. y.*, June 10, 1838.
    iii.   SOPHIA DALLAS, *m.* HON. MARTIN RUSSELL THAYER, and *d.* October 27, 1881.
    iv.   GEORGIA DALLAS, *d. y.*, July 5, 1838.
    v.   MARY ELIZABETH CARET LORD, *m.* RICHARD A. GILPIN.
    vi.   WILLIAM NICKLIN, *m.* SARAH ELIZABETH, *dau.* of Rear-Admiral Joshua R. Sands, U. S. N.
    vii.   MARGARETTA SERGEANT, *d. i.*

SOPHIA CHEW, eldest *dau.* of **Philip** and **Juliana (Chew) Nicklin**, *b.* June 25, 1798 ; *m.* **GEORGE MIFFLIN**, son of **Alexander James** (*d.* January 16, 1817) and **Arabella Maria (Smith) Dallas** (*d.* August 9, 1837).

GEORGE M. DALLAS, *b.* July 10, 1792, was Private Secretary to Albert Gallatin on his mission to Russia in 1813 ; appointed by President Jackson District Attorney, 1829 ; Attorney-General of Pennsylvania, October, 1833 ; Minister to the Court of S. Petersburg, 1837–39 ; elected Vice-President of the United States, March 4, 1845. Under Presidents Pierce and Buchanan, Minister to the Court of S. James ; *d.* December 31, 1864 ; his widow *d.* January 11, 1869. Issue (surname DALLAS) :

i. **ALEXANDER JAMES,** *d. y.*, September 30, 1826.
ii. **JULIANA MARIA.**
iii. **ELIZABETH NICKLIN,** *m.* **DR. DAVID HUNTER TUCKER,** of Richmond, Va., since deceased, leaving issue.
iv. **SOPHIA PHILIPS.**
v. **PHILIP NICKLIN,** *b.* August 13, 1825, Secretary of Legation to his father, in England ; *d. u.*, March 14, 1866.
vi. **CATHERINE CHEW,** *m.* **FITZ-EUGENE DIXON,** and *d.* August 18, 1878 ; he *d.* January 22, 1880. Issue (surname DIXON) :

    i. **ALEXANDER JAMES DALLAS,** *m.* **MARGARETTA,** *dau.* of William Sergeant.
    ii. **THOMAS FRASER,** *m.* **JANE EMMA,** *dau.* of Colonel Charles J. Biddle.
    iii. **SOPHIA DALLAS,** *m.* **FRANCIS J. ALISON,** of the Philadelphia Bar. Issue (surname ALISON) :

        Catherine Dallas and Mary Elizabeth.

    iv. **MARY HOMER,** *m.* her cousin, **GENERAL RUSSELL THAYER.**
    v. **GEORGE DALLAS,** *m.* **MARY Q.,** *dau.* of William H. Allen, LL.D., President of Girard College.
    vi. **THOMAS HENRY.**
    vii. **WILLIAM BOULTON.**
    viii. **CATHERINE EUGENIA.**
    ix. **HARRIET.**
    x. **SUSAN DALLAS,** *m.*, December 4, 1888, **THOMAS WILSON SHARPLESS.**
    xi. **MATILDA WILKINS.**
    xii. **CARY SANDERS,** *b.* November 23, 1871 ; *d.* July 4, 1872.

vii. **SUSAN.**
viii. **CHARLOTTE BYRON,** *m.* **CARLOS ENRIQUE MORRELL,** of Cuba, deceased, leaving issue.

    ALEXANDER JAMES DALLAS, U. S. N., probably another son, *d.* at Callao, Peru, June 3, 1844.

Authorities : Family papers, through the late Samuel Chew, Esq., of Germantown, and Keith's " Provincial Councillors of Pennsylvania."

PAGANEL, SOMERIE, AND STRANGE

RALPH PAGANEL, or **PAINELL,** living in 1089, held divers Lordships at the time of the Great Survey; whereof some fifteen were of Yorkshire and fifteen of Co. Lincoln. His son and heir,

ALBINI ARMS

FULK, in the reign of William Rufus, probably *m.* a *dau.* of **William Fitz Ausculf,** Lord of Dudley Castle and many manors in Domesday, as he held the castle and much of the land. His son, **RALPH,** was of Dudley Castle, Stafford, in 1138, and a partisan of the Empress Maud in her contest with King Stephen. He left six sons; Gervase, the eldest, succeeding as Lord of Dudley, founded a priory there about 1161; held fifty-six knight's fees in 1166; was living in 1181; *m.* Elizabeth, *dau.* of Robert le Bossu,[1] Earl of Leicester, and had a son, Robert, *d. s. p.*

in his father's lifetime; and a *dau.,* Hawyse, his heir, *of whom presently.*

HAWYSE PAGANEL *m.* **JOHN,** son of **Stephen de Somerie,** and had a son and heir, **JOHN RALPH DE SOMERIE;** *m.* **MARGARET ——,** and *d.* 1208, leaving an heir, **WILLIAM,** whose

---

[1] From S. Arnoul, of Burgundy, *d.* August 16, 640, descended through Charles Martel and the Emperor Charlemagne, Herbert IV., Count of Vermandois, who *m.* Adela, *dau.* of Raoul, Count of Crespy and Valois, and had a *dau.* and heiress, Adelaide; *m.* Hugh, Count of Vermandois (son of Henri I. of France, and Anne, *dau.* of Jaroslav, Grand Duke of Russia). Their *dau.,* Isabel, *m.* Robert de Bellomont or Beaumont. Issue: Robert, as above, and Elizabeth, *m.* Gilbert de Clare (*q. v.*). This descent well illustrates the ease with which any fairly good English pedigree can be carried back to royalty through female lines.

son, Nicholas, *d. s. p.* 1229 ; and a younger son, ROGER, *of whom presently.*

This **ROGER,** son of **John Ralph Somerie,** inherited the estates,
was. an active participant in the affairs of the stormy reign of
Henry III. ; taken prisoner at the Battle of Lewes ; in 1267 one
of the three commissioners to complete the peace with Llewellyn, Prince of Wales ; *m.,* second, AM-
ABELL ——, and *d.* 1273, leaving by
her a son and heir, **ROGER,** then eighteen years of age, who *m.* **NICHOLA,**
dau. and *co-h.* of **William de Albini,** Earl
of Sussex,[1] and *d.* 19 Edward I. (1292),
leaving an heir ROGER, *b.* 1280, *d. s. p. ;*
and JOHN, his brother, under age, in
1300 succeeded him ; was knighted, with
Prince Edward and many others, 34 Ed-
ward I. (1305) ; between 1300 and 1312 was seven times in the
Scottish wars. It was complained " that he did so domineer in
Staffordshire that no man could enjoy the benefit of law or reason ; that there was no abiding for any man thereabouts unless
they did bribe him in contributing largely toward the building
of his castle at Dudley." He *d. s. p.* before the end of 1321,
leaving as his *co-heirs* his sisters :

L'ESTRANGE ARMS

i.   **MARGARET,** aged thirty-two, wife of **JOHN DE SUTTON.**
ii.   **JOANE,** aged twenty-nine, then wife of **THOMAS BOTETORT.** She *m.,* second, **JOHN LE STRANGE,**[2] Lord of Knockin. Issue:

> John, *b.* 1254 ; summoned to Parliament as Johanni Extraneo from Decem-
> ber 29, 1299, and as Johanni Lestrange de Knokin, March 4, 1309.
> He *m.* **Maud,** *dau.* and heiress of **Roger D'Eiville,** and *d.* 1310.
> Issue, with others :
>
>> A *dau.,* Elizabeth, *m.* Griffith ap Madoc, of Yale (*q. v.*).

Authorities : Twamley's " Dudley Castle " (London, 1867), pp. 3–11. Courthope and Nicolas's
" Historic Peerage," pp. 168, 370, 436, 452. Eyton's " Historic Itinerary of Henry II.," pp. 80, 198.
Louis Morèri's " Grand Dictionnaire," viii., 81. Smith and Wace's " Dictionary of Christian Biogra-
phy," i., 455 ; iv., 398.

[1] He was son of William, who *d.* October 12, 1176, and grandson of William Fitz William de Albini, Lord of Buckenham, Norfolk, by Adeliza of Louvain, widow of King Henry I., who brought
him in dower Arundel Castle.

[2] Guy, called third son of the Duke of Brittany, had a son, John le Strange, Lord of Nesse and
Cheswardine, Shropshire ; *d.* about 1217; his son, John, *m.* Amice ——, and had a son, John, father
of John, who *m.* Joan de Somerie.

PELL

JOHN PELL, B.A., at Cambridge in 1594, was son of **John Pell,** of the ancient family of **Pell** of Water Willoughby, in Lincolnshire; became Rector of Southwick, near Brighton, Sussex; *m.* **MARY HOLLAND**, of Kent, and *d.* in 1616. Issue:

i. **THOMAS**, *b.* in 1608, a gentleman of the Bedchamber to King Charles I., emigrated to America, was a surgeon in the Pequot War, and served with Lion Gardiner at Fort Saybrook. He settled at Fairfield, Conn., and was a Deputy to the General Court, 1664-65. He purchased what became the Manor of Pelham, Westchester Co., N. Y., from the Indians in 1654, and *d. s. p.* in 1669, leaving all his property to his nephew, **John Pell**, of London.

ii. **JOHN**, *b.* at Southwick, in Sussex, March 1, 1609-10, entered Trinity College, Cambridge, at the age of thirteen; B.A. in 1630; afterward became D.D.; in 1643 elected Professor of Mathematics at Amsterdam, where he attained a high reputation. From 1654 to 1658 Cromwell's Minister Resident to the Protestant cantons of Switzerland. After the restoration of Charles II. became Rector of Fobbing, Laindon, and Orset, in Essex; May 20, 1663, elected Fellow of the Royal Society. Nearly all his private and public papers are at the British Museum in over ten volumes of MSS. He *m.*, in 1632, **ITHAMARIA REGINOLLES**, and *d.* in 1685, leaving a son, **JOHN**, *of whom presently.*

JOHN, son of **Dr. John** and **Ithamaria (Reginolles) Pell,** *b.* February 3, 1643, commonly called **SIR JOHN**; inheriting his uncle's property, came to America and became second Lord of the Manor in 1669. Appointed Captain of horse, 1684, and Major in the French and Indian War, 1692. First Judge of the Court of Common Pleas in Westchester Co., 1688, and first Member for the County in the Provincial Assembly in 1691-95. He *m.* **RACHEL PINCKNEY**, and *d.* in 1702, leaving a son, **THOMAS**, third Lord of the Manor.

This **THOMAS PELL** *m.* **ANNA**, by tradition said to be *dau.* of **Wampage**, an Indian Sachem. Issue:

458

i.   **CALEB,** *m.* **MARY FERRIS,** and *d.* in 1768 ; his wife *d.* in 1772. So far as known their male line is extinct.

ii.   **PHILIP,** *of whom presently.*

iii.   **JOSHUA** (*q. v.*).

iv.   **DAVID,** *d. s. p.* about 1735.

v.   **JOHN,** *b.* in 1702 ; *m.* —— **TOTTEN,** and *d.* in 1773, leaving issue.

vi.   **THOMAS,** *b.* 1704 ; *m.* **DOROTHY WARD,** and *d.* in 1753, leaving issue.

vii.   **JOSEPH,** *b.* in 1715 ; *m.* **PHŒBE DEANE,** and *d.* in 1752, leaving issue.

PHILIP, second son of **Thomas** and **Anna Pell,** *m.*, February 28, 1731, **PHŒBE FITCH.** Issue :

> **PHILIP,** *b.* November 22, 1732 ; *m.* **GLORIANNA TREDWELL,** and *d.* in 1788. Issue :
>
> i.   **PHILIP,** *b.* July 7, 1753 ; *d.* May 1, 1811 ; Judge Advocate in the Continental Army, Surrogate of Westchester Co., Member of Congress, and Honorary Member of the Society of the Cincinnati. No known living descendants.
>
> ii.   **SAMUEL,** *b.* July 26, 1755 ; Major Second New York Regiment of the Continental Line, Member of the Society of the Cincinnati, his name standing fourth on the original list. He *d. s. p.* December 29, 1786.
>
> iii.   **COLONEL DAVID,** *b.* January 13, 1760 ; *m.* **HESTER SNEDEN,** and *d.* August 8, 1823, leaving issue.

JOSHUA, third son of **Thomas** and **Anna Pell,** *m.* **PHEBE PALMER,** made his will in 1758, proved in 1781, and *d.* leaving with other issue a son, **BENJAMIN,** *of whom presently.*

BENJAMIN, son of **Joshua** and **Phebe (Palmer) Pell,** *m.*, Nov. 25, 1778, **MARY ANNA FERRIS;** *d.* March, 1828. Issue :

i.   **WILLIAM FERRIS,** *b.* in 1779, *of whom presently.*

ii.   **ALFRED S.,** *b.* in 1786 (*q. v.*).

iii.   **COLONEL FERRIS,** *m.* **MARIANA CHANNING,** and *d.* in 1850, leaving several daughters.

WILLIAM FERRIS, eldest son of **Benjamin** and **Mary Anna (Ferris) Pell,** *b.* in 1779 ; *m.*, November 17, 1802, **MARY SHIPLEY,** of London, Eng., and *d.* October 28, 1840. Issue :

i.   **ARCHIBALD MORRIS,** *b.* in 1803 ; *m.* **CATHERINE RUTGERS,** and *d.* in 1839. Issue :

> i.   **CORNELIA,** *m.* **HENRY MORGAN.**
>
> ii.   **CLEMENTINE,** *m.* **EDWARD A. LE ROY.**

ii.   **ALFRED,** *b.* in 1805 ; *m.*, first, **ELIZA CRUGER.** Issue :

> i.   **WILLIAM CRUGER.**
>
> ii.   **ALFRED.**
>
> iii.   **ARTHUR,** *d.* 1894.
>
> iv.   **ROBERT S.,** *d.* in 1868.

> He *m.*, second, **ELIZA WOOD,** and *d.* May 21, 1869, leaving a *dau.*
>
> v.   **EDITH,** *m.* **MARTIN ARCHER SHEE,** of England.

iii.　DUNCAN CAMPBELL, *b.* in 1807, was Lieutenant-Governor of Rhode
Island ; *m.* ANNA CLARKE, and *d.* January 16, 1874.　Issue :

　　i.　LESLIE, changed his name to LESLIE PELL-CLARKE, and *m.* HENRI-
ETTA TEMPLE.
　　ii.　DUNCAN ARCHIBALD, Colonel of the United States Volunteers, *m.* CARO-
LINE CHEEVER, and *d.* October 21, 1874.　Issue :
　　　　i.　Duncan C., *m.* Anna O. Pendleton.
　　　　ii.　H. Archibald, *m.* Sadie D. Price.
　　　　iii.　Alexander Mercer.

iv.　WALDEN, *b.* in 1808 ; *m.* ORLEANNA R. ELLERY, and *d. s. p.*
March 14, 1863.
v.　MORRIS SHIPLEY, *b.* in 1810, *of whom presently.*
vi.　ECROYDE, *b.* in 1811, *d. y.*
vii.　MARY S., *b.* in 1813 ; *m.* CAPTAIN FRANCIS S. HAGGER-
TY, U. S. N., and *d. s. p.* June 5, 1884.
viii.　SOPHIA, *b.* in 1815 ; *m.* JAMES DUANE PELL (*q. v.*).
ix.　EMMA, *b.* in 1817 ; *d. u.* October 24, 1875.
x.　JAMES K., *b.* in 1819 ; *d. u.* November 24, 1874.
xi.　CLARENCE, *b.* in 1820 ; *m.* ANNIE CLAIBORNE, and *d.* June 8,
1865.　Issue :

　　i.　JAMES K., Jr., *b.* in 1852 ; *d.* March 27, 1885.
　　ii.　HERBERT C., *m.* CATHERINE KERNOCHAN.　Issue :
　　　　Herbert C. and Clarence Cecil.
　　iii.　CLARA, *m.* CAPTAIN THOMAS G. TOWNSEND, U. S. A.
　　iv.　EMILY, *m.* CHARLES H. COSTER.
　　v.　CHARLOTTE L.

MORRIS SHIPLEY, fourth son of William Ferris and Mary (Shipley) Pell, *b.* February 24, 1810 ; *m.,* 1830, MARY RODMAN HOWLAND, and *d.* February 4, 1881.　Issue :

i.　JOHN HOWLAND, *b.* in 1831 ; Captain United States Volunteers ; *m.,*
first, CORNELIA CORSE.　Issue :

　　i.　RODMAN CORSE, *b.* March 31, 1861 ; enlisted Company I, Seventh Regiment,
N. G. S. N. Y., 1883 ; *m.* ANTOINETTE G. PELL.　Issue :
　　　　Rodman, C., Jr.
　　ii.　FLORENCE C., *m.* NATHAN E. BROWN, of Portland, Me.

　　CAPTAIN JOHN H. PELL *m.,* second, CAROLINE E. HYATT,
and *d.* October 6, 1882.　Further issue :

　　iii.　HOWLAND (now HOWLAND PELL HAGGERTY).
　　iv.　STEPHEN H.
　　v.　SAMUEL O.
　　vi.　MARY H.
　　vii.　THEODORE R.
　　viii.　HORACE P.

ii.　WILLIAM HOWLAND, *m.* ADELAIDE, *dau.* of Benjamin and
Anna Maria (Schieffelin) Ferris (*q. v.*).　Issue :
HOWLAND, *of whom presently.*

HOWLAND, son of **William Howland** and **Adelaide (Ferris) Pell**, *b.* at Flushing, N. Y., March 19, 1856. In 1872 entered the School of Mines, Columbia College ; in 1874 left to engage in business. June 7, 1875, enlisted in Company I, Seventh Regiment, N. G. S. N. Y. ; September 7, 1881, honorably discharged. February 8, 1884, commissioned Second Lieutenant Company E, Twelfth Regiment ; June 3, 1884, First Lieutenant Company G ; August 25, 1885, Captain Company A. In 1892, resigned his commission, but has since re-enlisted in Company K, Seventh Regiment. Is a member of the New York Genealogical and Biographical Society, of the New York Historical Society, the S. Nicholas Society, the Seventh Regiment Veteran Association, and the Union, United Service, and Larchmont Yacht Clubs ; Treasurer of the Badminton Club, Secretary of the Society of Colonial Wars in the State of New York, and elected May 10, 1893, Secretary-General of the National Society. He *m.*, April 12, 1887, **ALMY GOELET**, *dau.* of **Frederic** and **Almy Goelet (Gerry) Gallatin.** Issue :

i.   **GLADY AMY HOWLAND**, *b.* in 1888, and **HOWLAND GAL-LATIN**, *b.* in 1889.

ALFRED S., second son of **Benjamin** and **Mary Anna (Ferris) Pell**, *b.* 1786 ; *m.* **ADELIA DUANE**, and *d.* 1831. Issue :

i   **ROBERT L.**, *m.* **MARIA L. BRINCKERHOFF**, and *d.* February 13, 1880. Issue :

    i.   **ROBERT T.**, *d. w.* in 1868.
    ii.   **JAMES B.**, *d. w.* in 1870.
    iii.   **ADÈLE.** *m.* **JOHN B. IRELAND.**

ii.   **JAMES DUANE**, *m.* **SOPHIA**, *dau.* of **William F.** and **Mary (Shipley) Pell** (*q. v.*), and *d.* in 1881 ; his widow *d.* August 20, 1885. Issue :

    i.   **WALDEN**, *m.* **LILLY HYATT.** Issue :
       i.   Frederick T., *d.* November 6, 1887.
       ii.   Francis Livingston.
       iii.   James D.
       iv.   Walden, Jr.
       v.   Zelia, *m.* Eben Wright.
    ii.   **MARY DUANE.**
    iii.   **FREDERICK**, *d. w.*

iii.   **JOHN A.**, *m.* **SUSAN FIELD** (who *d.* 1893), and *d.* 1894. Issue :
    ELEANOR L., *m.* **CHARLES HARRIS PHELPS.**

iv.   **RICHARD M.**, *m.* **FANNY JONES**, and *d. s. p.* April 22, 1882.

v.   **GEORGE W.**, *m.* **MARY BRUEN.** Issue :
    ALFRED DUANE.

Authority : Family papers, through Howland Pell, Esq., New York City.

PENROSE

RICHARD ALEXANDER FULLERTON, second son of **Hon. Charles Bingham** and **Valeria F. (Biddle) Penrose,**[1] *b.* Carlisle, Pa., March 24, 1827 ; educated at Dickinson College ; LL.D., 1875 ; M.D., 1849, University of Pennsylvania. Resident Physician of the Pennsylvania Hospital three years. A leading practitioner in Philadelphia ; in 1856 one of the founders of the Children's Hospital ; in 1863 elected Professor of Obstetrics and the Diseases of Women and Children in the University of Pennsylvania ; resigned May 1, 1888. He was a very popular lecturer and successful teacher in the medical school, and has contributed a number of papers to professional journals. He *m.*, September 28, 1858, **SARAH HANNAH,** *dau.* of **Jeremiah S. H.** and **Mary Frances Caroline (Thomas) Boies** (*d.* March 31, 1881) (*q. v.*). Issue :

i.   **BOIES,** *b.* October 12, 1859 ; *d.* July 20, 1860.
ii.   **BOIES,** *b.* November 1, 1860, graduated with honors at Harvard University, 1881 ; read law with Wayne McVeagh and George T. Bispham ; admitted to the Bar of Philadelphia, 1883, and formed the firm of Page, Allison & Penrose ; Member of the House of Representatives in 1885 ; with E. P. Allison wrote a " History of Philadelphia Municipal Government " for the Johns Hopkins University studies ; member of the State Senate, November, 1886 ; re-elected in 1890 ; President, January 6, 1891. In 1892 was the mover of a bill to abolish the Public Buildings Commission. Was described in 1894 as " a quiet, reserved man, the typical picture of the gentleman in politics."
iii.   **CHARLES BINGHAM,** *b.* February 1, 1861 ; a physician ; *m.*, November 17, 1892, **KATHERINE,** *dau.* of the late **Joseph W. Drexel.**
iv.   **RICHARD A. F., Jr.,** *b.* December 17, 1863.
v.   **SPENCER,** *b.* November 2, 1865.
vi.   **FRANCES BOIES,** *b.* August 2, 1867.
vii.   **PHILIP THOMAS,** *b.* March 10, 1869.

Authority : Family papers, through Professor R. A. F. Penrose.

[1] Descended from Bartholomew Penrose, a sea-captain, who emigrated to Pennsylvania about 1700.

PHILIPS AND MONTGOMERY

HENRY PHILIPS, of Philadelphia, second son of **John Philips,** of Bank Hall, Lancashire, England, *m.*, October 3, 1796, **SO-PHIA,** *dau.* of **Chief Justice Benjamin Chew,** who *d.* September 3, 1841. Issue :

> **ELIZABETH HENRIETTA,** *b.* August 31, 1797 ; *m.*, November 25, 1817, **JOHN CRATHORNE,** third son of **John** and **Mary (Crathorne) Montgomery,** of Philadelphia, and lineally descended from **Roger, Count of Montgomerie,** in Normandy, in the tenth century, his nephew, **John T. Montgomery,** being the male representative of the family. **MRS. ELIZABETH H. (PHILIPS) MONT-GOMERY** *d.* July 11, 1850, and her husband *m.*, second, November 27, 1855, **CAROLINE,** only *dau.* of **Nehemiah Rogers,** of New York, and *d.* August 5, 1857. Issue, by first wife :

i.   **JOHN PHILIPS,** *b.* September 28, 1818 ; *m.*, November 13, 1851, **ANNA BOWKER,** *dau.* of **James L. Claytor.** Issue :

     i.   **Octavia Claytor,** *d. u.* 1890.
     ii.   **Elizabeth Philips,** *d. y.*
     iii.   **James Claytor,** *d. u.*
     iv.   **Virginia,** *d. u.*

ii.   **HENRY EGLINTON,** *b.* December 9, 1820 ; a clergyman of the Protestant Episcopal Church ; *m.*, September 10, 1846, **MARGARET AUGUSTA,** *dau.* of Judge **James Lynch,** and *d.* October 15, 1874. Issue :

     i.   **Janet T.**
     ii.   **John H.,** *m.* **Annie G.,** *dau.* of Dr. James Fitch.
     iii.   **James Lynch.**
     iv.   **Edward Livingston,** *m.* **Mary W.,** *dau.* of William M. Goodrich.
     v.   **Sophia Elizabeth,** *m.* **Woodbury G. Langdon,** of New York City.
     vi.   **Adelaide Henrietta.**
     vii.   **Elizabeth Henrietta Philips.**
     viii.   **Henry Eglinton.**
     ix.   **Hardman Philips Alan.**

iii. **OSWALD CRAYTHORNE**, *b.* August 24, 1822 ; *m.*, October 3, 1849, **CATH-ERINE GERTRUDE**, *dau.* of James W. Lynch, *d.* January 19, 1871. Issue :

    i.   **Charles H.**
    ii.   **Thomas E.**
    iii.   **Thomas L.**

iv. **AUSTIN JAMES**, *b.* October 27, 1824 ; *m.*, November 10, 1858, **SARAH COR-DELIA**, *dau.* of **Charles Swift Riche.**

v. **JAMES EGLINTON**, *b.* September 20, 1826 ; Captain United States Army ; served with distinction in the Civil War ; *m.*, first, November 10, 1851, **NINA**, *dau.* of James Tilghman ; *m.*, second, **MARY S.**, *dau.* of **Thomas Walker**, of Utica, N. Y. Issue :

    i.   **Lloyd P.**
    ii.   **Elizabeth Philips.**
    iii.   **Arthur E.**
    iv.   **Hugh E.**

vi. **CHARLES HOWARD**, *b.* September 27, 1828 ; *d.* May 8, 1848.

vii. **SOPHIA HENRIETTA CHEW**, *b.* October 16, 1830 ; *d.* December 22, 1836.

viii. **BENJAMIN CHEW**, *b.* January 3, 1833 ; *d.* July 16, 1856.

ix. **HARDMAN PHILIPS**, *b.* September 25, 1834.

x. **MARY CRATHORNE**, *b.* January 20, 1837 ; *m.*, April 26, 1859, **EUGENE TILLOTSON LYNCH.** Issue (surname LYNCH) :

    EUGENE TILLOTSON and **ELIZABETH HENRIETTA.**

Authorities : Thomas H. Montgomery, history and pedigree of the family, and the late James C. Montgomery.

POULTNEY

RICHARD POULTNEY, of England, *m.,* about 1710, **MARY,** *dau.* of **Anthony** and **Alice Neutby,** of London, and had five children, of whom **JOHN,** *b.* in 1714, came to America about 1736, lived in Virginia, *m.* —— **WORKER,** and had issue : **AN-THONY, SARAH,** and **MARY. THOMAS,** the second son, *b.* April 25, 1718, at London, arrived at Philadelphia in the fall of 1730 with his father. Lived for about three months with William Tidmarsh. In 1743 removed to Lancaster, Pa.; *m.,* first, December 18, 1744, **ELEANOR,** *dau.* of **John Scarlet.** Issue :

    i.   **BENJAMIN,** *b.* October 27, 1745.
    ii.   **JOSEPH,** *b.* September 23, 1747.
    iii. **HANNAH,** *b.* March 1, 1749.
    iv. **THOMAS,** *b.* March 13, 1751 ; *d.* July 10, 1758.
    v.   **JOHN,** *b.* June 16, 1753 ; lived about sixteen months.
    vi. **ELEANOR,** *b.* July 5, 1754 ; lived about five months.

MRS. POULTNEY, *d.* September 13, 1754, of consumption, and her husband *m.,* second, in July, 1757, **ELIZABETH STOCKTON,** *dau.* of **James Smith,** and had further issue :

    vii. **ELEANOR,** *b.* March 2, 1758.
    viii. **JOHN,** *b.* January 20, 1750.
    ix. **THOMAS,** *b.* September 29, 1762, *of whom presently.*
    x.   **WILLIAM,** *b.* September 16, 1764.
    xi. **ALICE,** *b.* January 22, 1768 ; *m.* —— **TODD,** and *d.* in the one hundredth year of her age.
    xii. **JAMES,** *b.* October 13, 1769.

THOMAS, second son of **Thomas** and **Elizabeth (Smith) Poultney,** *b.* September 29, 1762 ; *m.,* April 21, 1790, **ANN,**

second *dau.* of **Evan** and **Rachel (Hopkins) Thomas** *(q. v.)*, who *d.* February 4, 1858. Issue :

i.   **ELIZABETH**, *b.* December 2, 1792 ; *m.* **JAMES LARGE** *(q. v.)*.
ii.   **EVAN THOMAS**, *b.* March 22, 1795 ; *m.* **JANE TUNIS**, and *d.* Issue :

    i.   **ANN**, *m.* **WILLIAM T. RIGGS**, and *d.* November 28, 1890.
    ii.   **THOMAS**, *m.* **SUSAN CARROLL**, and *d.* in April, 1887. Issue :

        Carroll, Evan, and Thomas.

    iii. **JANE**, *m.* **HON. JOHN BIGELOW**, Author, Associate Editor of the New York *Evening Post*, and in 1865 and 1866 Minister at the Court of France, and *d.* 1889. Issue (surname BIGELOW) :

        i.   **Grace.**
        ii.   **Poultney**, *d. i.*
        iii. **John.**
        iv.   **Poultney**, a well-known traveller and essayist.
        v.   **Jenny**, *m.*, March 28, 1886, **Charles Edward Tracy**.
        vi.   **Annie**, *m.*, October 23, 1889, **Butler K.**, son of **George Harding**, of Philadelphia, who *d.* in a few months.
        vii. **Ernest**, *d. i.*
        viii. **Flora**, *m.* **Charles S. Dodge** *(q. v.)*.

iii. **SAMUEL THOMAS**, *b.* June 16, 1797, *of whom presently*.
iv.   **PHILIP**, *b.* May 18, 1799 ; *m.*, April 23, 1847, **ANN ELIZABETH McNEIR**, of Annapolis, and *d.* September 10, 1869. Issue :

    EVAN, *b.* in 1848 ; *m.*, November 25, 1873, **ANNA R.**, *dau.* of Gerard T. and Elizabeth Hopkins, who *d.* July 15, 1885 *(q. v.)*.

v.   **RACHEL THOMAS**, *b.* July 14, 1801 ; *m.* **DAVID U. BROWN** *(q. v.)*.
vi.   **MARY ANN**, *b.* June 16, 1804 ; *m.*, February 24, 1842, **DR. WILLIAM W. HANDY**,[1] and *d.* February 4, 1891 ; her husband *d.* January 27, 1864. Issue (surname HANDY) :

    THOMAS POULTNEY, *m.*, October 31, 1865, **MARIA**, *dau.* of Benjamin and Eliza (Ellicott) Poultney *(q.v.)*, and *d.* in 1876. Issue :

        i.   **William Winder**, *b.* April 3, 1871.
        ii.   **Mary Ann**, *b.* April 14, 1872 ; *m.*, October 8, 1890, **Francis Ellicott.** Issue : May Poultney, *b.* May 4, 1891.

vii. **SARAH CRESSON**, *b.* July 8, 1806 ; *m.* **WILLIAM M. ELLICOTT** *(q. v.)*.
viii. **THOMAS**, *b.* December 7, 1808 ; *m.*, November 24, 1830, **JANE T.**, *dau.* of **Andrew** and **Hannah (Tunis) Ellicott** *(q. v.)*, and *d.* September 25, 1832. Issue :

---

[1] Samuel Handy came to America from England about 1635, and *d.* in Somerset Co., Md., in 1721. He was the father of Colonel Isaac Handy, whose son, Henry, *m.* Jane, *dau.* of Captain William Winder, and sister of Levin Winder, Governor of Maryland, and had a son, Dr. William Winder Handy, *m.* Mary Ann Poultney.

i.   HANNAH T., *b.* September 15, 1831; *m.*, March 1, 1853, HENRY D. FAR-
NANDIS. Issue (surname FARNANDIS):

     i.   Annie, *b.* October 23, 1853.
     ii.   Elizabeth D., *b.* April 12, 1855.

ii.   THOMAS.

ix.   LYDIA, *b.* September 25, 1810; *m.* DR. WILLIAM H. DAVIS, and
d. s. p.

x.   LUCY, *b.* December 13, 1812; *m.*, January 28, 1845, DR. SEPTIMUS
DORSEY. Issue (surname DORSEY):

     i.   NANNIE POULTNEY, *m.*, April 15, 1868, CHARLES D. FISHER. Issue
(surname FISHER):

        i.   Lucy, *b.* February 25, 1869; *m.*, April 26, 1892, Herbert M. Brune, and
has a *dau.*, Nancy Fisher, *b.* October 22, 1893.
       ii.   Sally Tagart, *b.* December 13, 1870.
       iii.   Nannie Poultney, *b.* July 30, 1873.

ii.   WILLIAM, *d. s. p.*
iii.   LYDIA, *d. s. p.*

xi.   BENJAMIN, *b.* September 18, 1815; *m.*, October 10, 1844, ELIZA,
dau. of Andrew and Hannah Ellicott (*q. v.*), and *d.*, leaving issue:

     MARIA, *b.* January 10, 1846; *m.* THOMAS P. HANDY (*q. v.*).

SAMUEL THOMAS, fourth son of Thomas and Ann (Thomas) Poultney, *b.* June 16, 1797; *m.*, September 30, 1828, ELLIN MOALE CURZON (who *d.* December 5, 1880), and *d.* Issue:

i.   ELIZABETH MOALE, *b.* June 29, 1829; *m.*, November 26, 1856,
RICHARD HALL PLEASANTS. Issue (surname PLEAS-
ANTS):

     i.   JOHN PEMBERTON, *b.* September 4, 1857; *m.*, February 4, 1886, KATHE-
RINE LAWRENCE, *dau.* of Dr. Charles Gallagher (*p.* 412). Issue:

        Lawrence Pemberton, *b.* March 4, 1888.

     ii.   RICHARD CURZON, *b.* December 14, 1859; *d. i.*
     iii.   ELLIN CURZON.
     iv.   WILLIAM ARMISTEAD.
     v.   RICHARD HALL.
     vi.   SAMUEL POULTNEY, *d. i.*
     vii.   ELIZABETH.
     viii. JACOB HALL.

ii.   THOMAS, *b.* October 23, 1832; *m.*, first, May 8, 1859, GEORGIANNA
VIRGINIA McCLELLAN, who *d.* Issue:

     i.   RICHARD CURZON, *b.* January 25, 1861.
     ii.   ARTHUR EMMETT, *b.* August 2, 1863; *m.*, June 7, 1892, EMILY CHAPMAN
BLACKFORD.
     iii.   JOHN McCLELLAN, *d. i.*

THOMAS POULTNEY, *m.*, second, January 3, 1867, **SUSAN MEADE WARD,** of Virginia, and *d.* December 26, 1893. Further issue :

iv. **HARRIET FITZHUGH,** *b.* January 26, 1868.
v. **ELLIN CURZON,** *b.* September 23, 1870 ; *d.* April 15, 1879.
vi. **WILLIAM DAVIS,** *b.* September 21, 1873.
vii. **ANNIE WARD,** *b.* November 17, 1874.

iii. **RICHARD CURZON,** *b.* February 8, 1835 ; *d.* February 10, 1855.

iv. **NANCY THOMAS,** *b.* April 27, 1837 ; *m.*, November 12, 1863, **A. SMITH FALCONAR,** who *d.* April 15, 1886 ; his widow *d.* July 22, 1893.

v. **SAMUEL EUGENE,** *b.* December 22, 1839 ; *m.*, November 4, 1869, **LEILA LIVINGSTON MINIS.** Issue :

i. **EUGENE,** *b.* October 23, 1871.
ii. **JOHN LIVINGSTON,** *b.* January 25, 1875.
iii. **EDGAR CURZON,** *b.* March 11, 1881.

vi. **WALTER DE CURZON,** *b.* November 4, 1845.

Authorities : Family papers, through Mr. W. DeC. Poultney and others.

REESE

THOMAS L. REESE, *m.*, first, November 24, 1813, **MARY MOORE**; *m.*, second, in November, 1840, **MARY McCOR-MICK,** who *d. s. p.* He *d.* April 11, 1863. Issue, by his first wife:

i.   **MARY BROOKE,** *b.* August 12, 1814, *d. y.*

ii.   **ANN,** *b.* May 21, 1816; *m.*, September 23, 1840, **CALEB S. HALLO-WELL.** Issue (surname HALLOWELL):

    i.   **MARY JANE,** *d. y.*
    ii.   **CHARLES,** *m.* **FANNY FERRIS.** Issue:

        i.   **William Ferris.**
        ii.   **Charles.**
        iii.   **Benjamin Shoemaker,** *d. i.*
        iv.   **Lewis Bush.**

    iii.   **AMELIA BIRD.**
    iv.   **EMMA.**
    v.   **ROBERT SHOEMAKER.**
    vi.   **THOMAS REESE.**
    vii.   **ELIZABETH MOORE.**
    All five of whom *d.* in infancy or youth.

iii.   **GERARD HOPKINS,** *b.* September 8, 1818; *m.*, September 18, 1845, **SARAH JANE JANNEY.** Issue:

    i.   **THOMAS LACEY, Jr.,** *d.*
    ii.   **ELIZABETH MOORE.**
    iii.   **MARY ANNA,** *d. s. p.*
    iv.   **CORNELIA STABLER.**

iv.   **THOMAS MOORE,** *b.* July 18, 1820; *m.*, September 8, 1840, **MAR-THA,** *dau.* of Henry and Eliza Stabler (*q. v.*). Issue:

    i.   **FRANK,** *d. s. p.*
    ii.   **HENRY STABLER,** *m.*, January 19, 1876, **BELLE LIPPINCOTT.** Issue:

        Gordon Lippincott, Howard Hopkins, and Edith.

    iii.   **WALTER,** *m.*, April 17, 1877, **JANET D. BARRETT,** and *d.* April 22, 1880.
    iv.   **LAWRENCE MOORE,** *m.* **MARY SNOWDEN.**

v.   **CHARLES,** *b.* June 16, 1823; *m.*, May 12, 1847, **SUSAN WETHER-ALD.** Issue:

    i.   **PERCY MEREDITH**, *m.* **ELIZABETH McCORMICK.** Issue :
            Percy M. and Guy Harrison.

    ii.   **MARY WALTON**, *m.* W. **BURR.** Issue :
            Agnes, Susan, and David.

    iii.   **ANNE HALLOWELL.**
    iv.   **ESTELLE EVANGELINE.**
    v.   **WARREN HASTINGS.**
    vi.   **ALICE MAUD MURIELLE.**
    vii. **FREDERICK HERMANN.**
            The last five *d. y.*

vi.   **EDWARD**, *b.* June 16, 1825 ; *m.*, in May, 1854, **MARY A. GILPIN.**
         Issue :

    i.   **JULIET CANBY.**
    ii.   **FANNY GILPIN.**
    iii.   **CATHERINE STABLER.**
    iv.   **JAMES STONE**, *m.* **ALICE GORE.** Issue :
            Edward.

vii.   **DEBORAH**, *b.* June 26, 1827.
viii.   **HENRY**, *b.* May 21, 1830 ; *m.*, July 16, 1857, **MARY ANNA MIL-
        LER.** Issue :

    i.   **CAROLINE MILLER.**
    ii.   **HELEN**, *m.* **JAMES JANNEY SHOEMAKER.** Issue (surname SHOE-
            MAKER):
            Clarice, Edith, Ruth, and Henry Reese.

    iii.   **ROBERT MILLER.**
    iv.   **ANNE LACEY.**
    v.   **ARTHUR LACEY**, *d.* 1894.
    vi.   **ALBERT MOORE.**
    vii. **MABEL MEREDITH.**

ix.   **SAMUEL BROOKE**, *b.* May 7, 1832 ; *d. i.*

      Authorities : Family papers, through Thomas L. Reese, Jr., Henry Reese, and others.

RICE, OF DYNEVOR

GRIFFITH, only son of **Sir Rhys ap Thomas, K.G.** (*q. v.*), by his first wife, **Eva ap Gwilym,** *m.*, about 1504, **KATHE-RINE,** *dau.* of **Sir John St. John,** and *d.* September 29, 1521. Issue, with others :

> **RICE,** his heir, *m.* **LADY KATHERINE HOWARD** (*q. v.*), *dau.* of the second **Duke of Norfolk,** and was executed January 4, 1531–32. Issue :
>
> i.　**GRIFFITH,** *of whom presently.*
> ii.　**AGNES.**

GRIFFITH RICE, son of **Rice ap Griffith,** was restored in blood in the reign of Philip and Mary, but not to the estates of his attainted father. He was High Sheriff of Caermarthenshire in 1567 and 1583, and *m.* **ELEANOR,** *dau.* of **Sir Thomas Johnes, Knt.,** of Abermarlais. Issue :

ST. JOHN ARMS

i.　**WALTER,** *of whom presently.*
ii.　**BARBARA,** *m.* **DAVID FLUDD (LLOYD ?).**
iii.　**MARY,** *m.* **WALTER VAUGHAN,** of Golden Grove ; High Sheriff, 1585 ; their son **JOHN** was created Earl of Carbery.

SIR WALTER, son and heir of **Griffith** and **Eleanor (Johnes) Rice,** was M.P. for the county of Caermarthen in 1585, High Sheriff in 1586, and M.P. for the town of Caermarthen 1601 and 1603. He *m.* **ELIZABETH,** eldest *dau.* of **Sir Edward Mansel, Knt.,** of Margam (*b.* 1531, *d.* August 5, 1585), by

Jane, *dau.* of **Edward Somerset,** Earl of Worcester.   Issue (order of birth uncertain) :

i.   ,HENRY, *of whom presently.*
ii.   THOMAS.
iii.   ANTHONY, a Captain R. N., commanding the Antelope in 1628 ; afterward of the Ninth Lion's Whelp.
iv.   EDWARD.
v.   JANE, *m.* JOHN LLOYD, Esq., of Llanvair Clydoga ; High Sheriff of Cardiganshire in 1603.
vi.   ELEANOR, *m.* DAVID EVANS, High Sheriff of Glamorganshire, 1632.
vii.   BARBARA.
viii.   MARY, *m.* SIR THOMAS BUTTON, Knt.,[1] who was at sea in 1592. August, 1609, was Captain R. N. ; 1610 one of the incorporated Discoverers of the Northwest Passage, of which Prince Henry was the patron ; in 1612–13 commanded an expedition for that purpose, exploring Hudson's Bay and wintering there.   On his return was appointed Admiral of the King's ships on the coast of Ireland.   Was Rear Admiral of the expedition against Algiers in 1620 on the Rainbow ; 1631–1634 was in trouble with the Admiralty over the S. Jehan, of Dunkirk, captured by him, but finally cleared himself.   He *d.* April, 1633–34.   Issue :

    i.   MILES, *m.*, first, BARBARA MEYRICK ; *m.*, second, FLORENCE, *dau.* of Sir Nicholas Kemys, of Cefn Mably, who *d. s. p.*, December 3, 1711, aged ninety-three.
    ii.   ELIZABETH, *m.* COLONEL JOHN POYER.
    iii.   WILLIAM, Captain R. N., of the Garland.

ix.   ELIZABETH.
x.   JOAN.
xi.   LETTICE.

HENRY, eldest son of **Sir Walter Rice, Knt.,** had issue a son, SIR HENRY, to whom Charles I. relinquished all the family estates in the possession of the crown.   He lived at Newton, *m.* **MARY,** *dau.* of Sir Thomas Lewys, Knt., of Penmark.   Issue :

i.   SIR EDWARD, Sheriff ; 1663, *d. s.*
ii.   WALTER, *m.* ELIZABETH DEER, widow of Richard Games, of Llanelly. Issue :
    i.   Griffith, *of whom presently.*
    ii.   Henry, *d.i.*
    iii.   Walter, *d.i.*
    iv.   Elizabeth, *m.* Richard Middleton, of Middleton Hall.

GRIFFITH, second son and heir of **Henry Rice,** of Newton, was Sheriff, 1694, a member of Parliament for Caermarthenshire

---

[1] Sir Thomas was the fourth son of Miles Button, of Worlton, otherwise Duffryn, in Glamorgan ; Sheriff of that county in 1564 and 1570 ; by Margaret, *dau.* of Edward Lewis, of Van.   See his Life, by G. T. Clark, Dowlais, 1883.

CHARLES, BARON TALBOT OF HENSOL
LORD HIGH CHANCELLOR

in the reigns of King William III. and Queen Anne, and is said to have given the casting vote which in 1701 carried the Act of Succession, limiting the throne of England to the Protestant descendants of Sophia Electress of Hanover. He *m.*, September 6, 1722, **KATHERINE**, second *dau.* and *co-h.* of **Philip Hoby,** of Neath Abbey, and *d.* September 26, 1729. Issue :

i. **EDWARD,** *of whom presently.*
ii. **PHILIP,** *d. i.*
iii. **ELIZABETH,** *m.* **THOMAS LLOYD,** of Altecadnoe.
iv. **KATHERINE,** *m.* **WILLIAM BRYDGES,** of Tyberton.
v. **MARIA,** *d. u.*
vi. **ALBINIA,** *d. u.*
vii. **ARABELLA,** *d. i.*

EDWARD, only son of **Griffith** and **Katherine (Hoby) Rice,** was M.P. for Caermarthenshire ; *m.*, September 6, 1722, **LUCY,** *dau.* of **John Morley Trevor,** of Glynde in Sussex, and his wife **Lucy,** sister of **Charles,** first Earl of Halifax, and *d.* April 5, 1727. Issue :

i. **GEORGE,** *of whom presently.*
ii. **LUCY,** *d. u.*
iii. **KATHERINE,** *d. i.*

GEORGE, only son of **Edward** and **Lucy (Trevor) Rice,** *b.* 1726 ; heir to his grandfather, **Griffith Rice** ; was a member of Parliament in 1754, 1761, 1768, and 1770 to 1779, a Privy Councillor, Lord Lieutenant, and Colonel of the Militia of the county of Caermarthen. He *m.*, August 16, 1756, **LADY CECIL TALBOT,** *b.* July, 1735, only *dau.* and heiress of **William,** first Earl Talbot, eldest son of the much honoured and respected Lord Chancellor, **Charles, Baron Talbot of Hensol. Earl Talbot** *m.* **Mary,** *dau.* and heiress of **Adam de Cardonnel,** Secretary at War, and was created, October 17, 1780, **Baron Dynevor,** with remainder to his *dau.* and her issue.

GEORGE RICE, *d.* August 3, 1779, and **LADY DYNEVOR,** *d.* March 14, 1793. Issue :

i. **HENRIETTA CECILIA,** *b.* September 28, 1758 ; *m.*, December 16, 1788, **MAGENS DORRIEN MAGENS,** M.P. for Caermarthen in 1796, who *d.* in 1849. Issue :
   CECILIA, GEORGE WILLIAM, and **MARIA.**

ii.   **LUCY,** *b.* May 29. 1763 ; *d. u.*

iii.   **GEORGE TALBOT,** *b.* October 8, 1765, *of whom presently.*

iv.   **WILLIAM,** *b.* April 1, 1769 ; *d.* April 20, 1780.

v.   **MARIA,** *b.* April 5, 1773 ; *m.,* November 17, 1796, **JOHN MARK-HAM,** Rear Admiral of the White, and *d.* in 1810.

vi.   **EDWARD** (*q. v.*).

GEORGE TALBOT, eldest son of **George Rice** and the **Baroness Dynevor,** *b.* October 8, 1765, succeeded his mother as third Baron Dynevor in 1793, and assumed the name of **De Cardonnel** under his grandmother's will. In 1817 he had license to resume the name of **Rice.** Was Lord Lieutenant of Caermarthenshire and Colonel Commandant of the County Militia, M.P. for the county in 1790, and *m.,* October 20, 1794, **FRANCES,** third *dau.* of **Thomas Townshend,** first Viscount Sydney, and *d.* April 9, 1852 (his widow *d.* August 13, 1854). Issue, one son :

> **GEORGE RICE,** *b.* August 5, 1879, *of whom presently,* and six daughters, **FRANCES CECIL, HARRIET LUCY, CAROLINE MARY, KATHERINE SARAH,** and **MARIA ELIZABETH.**

GEORGE RICE, only son of the third **Baron Dynevor,** *b.* August 5, 1795, succeeded his father as fourth Baron, assumed the additional name of **"TREVOR,"** on inheriting the estates of the Trevors, of Glynde, in Sussex, becoming **GEORGE RICE RICE-TREVOR.** He was Honorary Colonel of the Caermarthenshire Militia ; D.C.L., June 11, 1834 ; M.P. for the county in 1820, 1826, 1830, and 1832-52, *m.,* November 27, 1824, **FRANCES,** *dau.* of **General Lord Charles Fitzroy** by his second wife, **Frances Ann,** *dau.* of **Robert Stewart,** Marquis of Londonderry, and *d.* October 7, 1869. Issue :

i.   **FRANCES EMILY,** *m.,* May 1, 1848, **EDWARD FFOLLIOTT WINGFIELD,** and *d.* November 26, 1863.

ii.   **CAROLINE ELIZABETH ANNE,** *m.,* February 24, 1849, **Sir THOMAS BATESON,** Bart.

iii.   **EVA GWENTHAM,** *d. u.* July 28, 1842.

iv.   **SELINA,** *m.,* November 12, 1862, **Sir WILLIAM LYGON PAKENHAM,** third Earl of Longford.

v.   **ELEANOR MARY.**

EDWARD, third son of **George** and **Lady Cecil (Talbot) Rice,** *b.* November 19, 1776 ; in Holy Orders and Dean of Gloucester;

m., July 9, 1800, **CHARLOTTE**, *dau.* of **General Francis Lascelles,** by his wife **Anne Cately,** a celebrated singer, and *d.* August 5, 1862.   Issue, order of birth uncertain :

i. **EDWARD**, *d. s. p.* June 5, 1820.
ii. **FRANCIS WILLIAM**, *b.* May 10, 1804, *of whom presently.*
iii. **GEORGE ROBERT**, *d. s. p.* May 12, 1854.
iv. **HENRY**, Rector of Great Rissington ; *m.*, December 12, 1837, **EMMA,** *dau.* of **W. F. Lowndes-Stone,** of Brightwell Park.   Issue, order of birth uncertain :

OLD DYNEVOR CASTLE

i. **EDWARD**, *b.* in 1855.
ii. **HENRY**, *b.* in 1862.
iii. **FRANCES EMMA**, *m.*, April 23, 1861, **CECIL CHARLES,** only son of Sir Peter Van Notten Pole, Bart.
iv. **CATHERINE.**
v. **CECIL LOUISE.**
vi. **FLORENCE MARIA.**
vii. **GEORGIANNA.**
viii. **AMY AUGUSTA.**
ix. **BEATRICE.**

v. **JOHN TALBOT,** *m.*, first, October 13, 1846, **CLARA LOUISA,** *dau.* of **Sir John Chandos Reade,** Bart., who *d.* August 11, 1853 ; *m.*, second, October 24, 1855, **ELIZABETH LUCY,** *dau.* of **Robert Boyd.**
vi. **CHARLOTTE,** *m.*, September 1, 1835, **Rev. A. CAMERON.**
vii. **CECIL,** *m.*, January 4, 1837, **COLONEL CHARLES AUGUSTUS ARNEY,** and *d.* June 2, 1852.
viii. **MARIA,** *m.*, September 3, 1839, **Rev. CANON EDWARD BANKES.**
ix. **ELIZA,** *d. u.* October 7, 1828.

x.   **LUCY HORATIA,** *m.*, June 7, 1832, **Rev. WILLIAM ESCOTT.**
xi.   **FRANCES EMMA,** *m.*, March 29, 1842, **Rev. WILLIAM WIGGIN,** and *d.* May 1, 1860.
xii. **MARIA LOUISA,** *d. u.* February 21, 1845.

REV. FRANCIS WILLIAM, second son of **Dean Edward** and **Charlotte (Lascelles) Rice,** *b.* May 10, 1804 ; Vicar of Fairford, Gloucestershire, 1827–1878 ; in 1869 succeeded his cousin, the fourth Lord, as fifth Baron Dynevor ; *m.*, first, February 3, 1830, **HARRIET IVES,** *dau.* of **Daniel Raymond Barker,** who *d.* July 22, 1854. Issue :

i.   **ARTHUR De CARDONNEL,** *b.* in 1836, *of whom presently.*
ii.   **ELLEN,** *m.* **Rev. J. G. JOYCE.**

REV. F. W. RICE *m.*, second, November 18, 1856, **ELIZA AMELIA,** *dau.* of **Rev. Henry Carnegie Knox,** and *d.* August 3, 1878. Further issue :

iii. **FRANCIS CARNEGIE,** *b.* July 18, 1858.
iv.   **WILLIAM TALBOT,** *b.* March 24, 1861.
v.   **CECIL MINA.**
vi.   **ALICE.**
vii. **MARY.**

ARTHUR DE CARDONNEL, eldest son of **Rev. Francis William Rice,** fifth **Baron Dynevor,** *b.* January 24, 1836, matriculated at Christ Church, Oxford, October 17, 1855 ; B.A., 1861 ; M.A., 1865 ; succeeded his father as sixth Baron Dynevor in 1878 ; *m.*, February 4, 1869, **SELINA,** *dau.* of **Hon. Arthur Lascelles** and **Caroline Frances,** *dau.* of **Sir Richard Brooke, Bart.,** who was *b.* May 7, 1841 ; and *d.* at Dynevor Castle, December 16, 1889. In 1883 the family estates comprised 7,208 acres in Caermarthenshire, 3,299 acres in Glamorgan, and 231 in Oxford, Wilts, and Gloucestershire, in all 10,728 acres, worth £12,562 per annum according to the new Doomsday Book of England.

Authorities : The New Peerage, by G. E. C. ; Report of Owners of Land, etc., 1883, and T. Nicholas's Annals of Wales.

RICHARDSON

ROBERT RICHARDSON, of Somerset Co., in Maryland; *m.*
SUSANNA ——, removed to Anne Arundel Co., and *d.* in
November, 1682. Issue:

i.   **WILLIAM,** *of whom presently.*
ii.   **ELIZABETH.**
iii.   **SUSANNA.**
iv.   **ROBERT.**
v.   **TABITHA.**
vi.   **SARAH.**
vii.   **CHARLES.**

WILLIAM, eldest son of **Robert** and **Susanna Richardson,**
was apparently a Minister of the Society of Friends; fined as a
Quaker, November 10, 1662; *m.* **ELIZABETH (EWEN),**
widow of **Richard Talbot** (*q. v.*), and *d.* November 2, 1697;[1]
his wife *d.* January 1, 1703-4. Issue:

i.   **WILLIAM,** *b.* August 26, 1668, *of whom presently.*
ii.   **DANIEL,** *b.* March 13, 1670-71 (*q. v.*).
iii.   **SOPHIA ELIZABETH,** *b.* July 4, 1675; *d.* September 2, 1678.
iv.   **JOSEPH,** *b.* April 3, 1678 (*q. v.*).
v. vi.   **SAPPHIRA** and **ELIZABETH,** twins, *b.* July 27 (?), 1680.

WILLIAM, eldest son of **William** and **Elizabeth (Ewen) Richardson,** *b.* August 26, 1668; *m.,* July 15, 1689, **MARGARET,**
sister of **Nathan Smith**; who *d.* in February, 1756, aged eighty-
three. He *d.* July 13, 1744. Issue:

i.   **WILLIAM,** *b.* July 1, 1690, *of whom presently.*
ii.   **ELIZABETH,** *b.* July 31, 1692.
iii.   **SAMUEL,** *b.* May 14, 1694; *d.* October 16, 1697.
iv.   **SOPHIA,** *b.* May 7, 1696; *m.* **RICHARD GALLOWAY,** Jr. (*q. v.*).
v.   **SARAH,** *b.* —— 26, 1698.

[1] Will proved January 15, 1697-98, Liber K, folio 259.

vi.   **JOSEPH**, *b.* January 31, 1701–2.

vii.   **SAMUEL**, *b.* September 13, 1703 ; *d.* April 24, 1722.

viii. **DANIEL**, *b.* December 25, 1705 ; *d.* August 9, 1756.

ix.   **RICHARD**, *b.* —— 12, 17—.

x.   **NATHAN**, *m.*, first, **ELIZABETH**, *dau.* of **John Crockett**, of Baltimore Co., who *d.* July 10, 1746.   Issue :

> i.   **WILLIAM**, *b.* November 7, 1736.
> ii.   **ELIZABETH**, *b.* December 26, 1740.
> iii. **NATHAN**, *b.* August 26, 1744.

> He *m.*, second, April 20, 1749, **MRS. HANNAH GOVER**, widow, *dau.* of **Isaac Webster**, and had a son, **DANIEL**, *b.* January 12, 1749–50.

xi.   **THOMAS**, *b.* November 20, 1715 ; *d.* at his house, in Kent Co., June 14, 1745.

WILLIAM, eldest son of **William** and **Margaret (Smith) Richardson**, *b.* July 1, 1690 ; *m.*, before 1708, **MARGARET**, *dau.* of **William** and **Mary Harris**, who *d.* in 1760. He *d.* February 22, 1731–32.   Issue :

i.   **WILLIAM**, *m.* **ANN**, *dau.* of **William Coale** (*q. v.*).   Issue :

> i.   **JOSEPH**, *b.* November 24, 1744.
> ii.   **ANN**, *b.* September 27, 1747.

ii.   **RICHARD**, *m.*, May 26, 1730, **MARGARET**, *dau.* of **William** and **Elizabeth Coale** (*q. v.*).   Issue :

> i.   **SAMUEL**, *b.* April 6, 1732.
> ii.   **SOPHIA**, *b.* June 9, 1735.
> iii. **JOSEPH**.
> iv. **DANIEL**, *m.*, November 12, 1754, **MARGARET**, *dau.* of **Gerard Hopkins** (*q. v.*).
> v.   **RICHARD**, *of whom presently*.
> vi. **NATHAN**.

iii.   **SOPHIA**.

RICHARD, son of **Richard** and **Margaret (Coale) Richardson** ; *m.*, August 13, 1754, **ELIZABETH**, *dau.* of **John** and **Elizabeth (Snowden) Thomas** (*q. v.*), and *d.* in April, 1804. Issue :

i.   **ELIZABETH**, *b.* September 14, 1756 ; *d.* March 20, 1762.

ii.   **RICHARD**, *b.* January 8, 1758 ; *d.* January 17, 1775.

iii.   **MARY**, *b.* April 20, 1760 ; *m.*, November 12, 1780, at West River, **SAMUEL ELLIOTT**.

iv.   **ANN THOMAS**, *b.* February 5, 1763 ; *m.* **FREDERICK MILLS**.

v.   **JOHN THOMAS**, *b.* May 28, 1765 ; *m.*, in 1790, **JEMIMA SHECKELLS**.

vi.   **WILLIAM,** *b.* August 12, 1767 ; *m.* —— **PLUMMER.**
vii. **JOSEPH,** *b.* July 17, 1770.
viii **REBEKAH,** *b.* August 26, 1772 ; *m.* **GASSAWAY WATKINS,**
      Commander of a company in the Fifth Maryland Regiment during the
      Revolution. Was President of the Maryland Society of the Cincin-
      nati. He *d.* in July, 1817, leaving a son, **RICHARD GASSAWAY.**
ix.   **DEBORAH SNOWDEN,** *b.* August 11, 1775 ; *m.* —— **SHECK-**
      ELLS, and removed to the Genesee Country before 1804.

DANIEL, second son of **William** and **Elizabeth (Ewen) Rich-**
ardson, *b.* March 13, 1670–71 ; *m.* **MRS. ELIZABETH**
WATSON, who *d.* in April, 1710. Issue, by her first husband
(surname WATSON) :

i.   **WILLIAM.**
ii.   **JAMES.**

       Issue, by her second husband :

i.   **JOHN,** *b.* September 30, 1692 ; *d.* about four months after.
ii.   **LEURANIA,** or **LAURANA,** *b.* January 22, 1693 ; *m.* **JOSEPH,** son
      of **Nathan** and **Elizabeth (Coale) Smith** (*q. v.*).
iii. **DANIEL,** *b.* March 3, 1695–96.
iv.   **JOHN,** *b.* March 7, 1697–98 ; *d.* April 12, 1722.

JOSEPH, third son of **William** and **Elizabeth (Ewen) Rich-**
ardson, *b.* April 3, 1678 ; *m.*, October 25 1705, at West River
Meeting-House, **SARAH,** eldest *dau.* of **Samuel** and **Mary**
(Hutchins) Thomas (*q. v.*), who *d.* January 27, 1724; and her
husband *d.* August 18, 1748. Issue :

i.   **SAMUEL,** *b.* July 6, 1706 ; *m.* —— **CROWLEY.**
ii.   **JOSEPH,** *b.* September 19, 1708 ; *m.* —— **BUCE.**
iii. **MARY,** *b.* September 13, 1710 ; *m.* **THOMAS COALE** (*q. v.*).
iv.   **WILLIAM,** *b.* December 26, 1712, was a Colonel in the Provincial Forces ;
      m. **ISABEL,** *dau.* of the **Marquis de la Calmes,** of Clarke Co.,
      Va., a Huguenot exile. Issue :
      JOHN CROWLEY, Captain in the Revolution.
v.   **PHILIP,** *b.* March 29, 1716 ; *m.* —— **BEART.**
vi.   **ELIZABETH,** *b.* March 18, 1716–17 ; *m.*, January 19, 1737–38, **FRAN-**
      CIS, son of **Charles** and **Sidney (Winn) Pierpont,** and had a
      dau., **MARY** ; *m.*, January 24, 1755, **BENJAMIN POWELL.**
vii. **SARAH,** *b.* May 3, 1719; *m.* **NEHEMIAH,** son of **Nehemiah Birck-**
      head.
viii. **JOHN,** *b.* March 19, 1720–21 ; *m.* —— **WILLIAMSON.**
ix.   **RICHARD,** *b.* May 5, 1723 ; *d.* September 22, 1736.

Authority : The West River Quaker Register of Births and Burials.

RINGGOLD

THOMAS RINGGOLD *m.* **MARY**, eldest *dau.* of **Samuel** and **Anne (Chew) Galloway**, and *d.* October 26, 1776 ; his wife *d.* February 21, 1817. Issue :

i.   **THOMAS**, *b.* September 4, 1768 ; *m.* February 10, 1795, **MARY GIT-TINGS**, and *d.* in 1818.

ii.   **SAMUEL**, *b.* January 15, 1770, *of whom presently.*

iii.   **ANNA MARIA**, *b.* March 9, 1772 ; *m.*, March 24, 1795, **COLONEL FRISBY TILGHMAN**, and *d.* February 21, 1817.

iv.   **BENJAMIN**, *d. u.* August 24, 1798.

v.   **TENCH**, *b.* March 6, 1776 ; *m.*, April 10, 1799, **MARY CHRISTIAN LEE**.

SAMUEL, second son of **Thomas** and **Mary (Galloway) Ringgold**, *b.* January 15, 1770, was a Major-General in the United States Army ; *m.*, May 3, 1792, **MARIA**, *dau.* of **General John** and **Elizabeth (Lloyd) Cadwalader**, descended from **John Cadwalader**, admitted Freeman of the city of Philadelphia, July 13, 1705, and **Dr. Thomas Wynne**, Speaker of the first three General Assemblies of the Province. General Ringgold was an M. C. from Maryland, and resided at Fountain Rock, Washington Co. Issue :

i.   **ANNA MARIA**, *b.* July 10, 1793 ; *d. u.* March 4, 1828.

ii.   **JOHN**, *b.* November 15, 1794 ; *d. u.*

iii.   **SAMUEL**, *b.* October 16, 1796, Captain of the United States Army, 1836 ; served in the Florida War with the Seminoles ; Brevet-Major, 1842 ; commanded Light Artillery Troop in the Mexican War ; killed at the Battle of Palo Alto, in 1846 ; *d. u.*

iv.   **MARY ELIZABETH**, *b.* December 18, 1798 ; *d. u.* March 9, 1836.

v.   **ANN CADWALADER**, *b.* January 10, 1801 ; *m.*, September 28, 1854, **WILLIAM SCHLEY**, of the Baltimore Bar ; *d.* June, 1870. Issue (surname SCHLEY) :

    i.   **ANN CADWALADER**, *b.* 1830 ; *m.*, 1857, **WILLIAM WOODVILLE**, Jr. Issue (surname WOODVILLE) :

    i.   **William,** *b.* 1859.
    ii.   **Middleton,** *b.* 1866.
    iii.   **Cadwalader,** *b.* 1875.

  ii.   **AGNES,** *b.* 1831 ; *m.* **WILLIAM KEY HOWARD.**
  iii. **SAMUEL RINGGOLD,** *b.* 1836 ; *d. u.* 1871.
  iv. **WILLIAM CADWALADER,** *b.* 1840, officer in the Confederate service on the staff of General Fitzhugh Lee ; *m.,* December 17, 1868, **ELLEN,** *dau.* of St. George W. Teackle. Issue :

    i.   **Anne Teackle,** *b.* January 8, 1870.
    ii.   **William Cadwalader,** *b.* March 18, 1871.
    iii.   **St. George Teackle,** *b.* August 23, 1872.

vi.   **CADWALADER,** *b.* August 20, 1802 ; Lieutenant of the United States Navy, 1828 ; Commander of the brig Porpoise, in Wilkes's exploring voyage, 1838–42 ; Commodore, 1862 ; Rear-Admiral, 1867 ; *d. u.* April 29, 1867.

vii.   **CORNELIA,** *b.* September 2, 1805 ; *m.,* November 16, 1826, **GEORGE M. POTTS,** and *d.* 1868.

viii. **CHESTER,** *b.* January 17, 1809 ; *d. s. p.* 1837.

ix.   **FREDERICK,** *b.* July 22, 1811 ; *m.,* 1846, **LOUISA ADAMSON.**

And there were other children, who died quite young.

Authorities : Hanson's "Old Kent," Judge H. H. Goldsborough, and Keith's "Provincial Councillors."

RUSSELL AND SEWALL

THOMAS RUSSELL was of Greenhill, Cecil Co., Md., and the Principio Iron Company (so called because it was the first organized for the working of iron in the American Colonies). He *m.* **ANN,** *dau.* of **Samuel** and **Mary Thomas.** Issue :

i.   **MARIA,** *d. u.*

ii.   **FRANCES,** *m.,* October 28, 1797. **WILLIAM E. SEWALL.** Issue :

    i.   **ANN,** *b.* in 1798; *m.* **THOMAS S. THOMAS** (*q. v.*).

    ii.   **FRANCES,** *d. u.*

    iii.   **MARTHA S.** *d.*

    iv.   **WILLIAM,** *b.* September 26, 1805 ; *m.,* in 1836, **ADELAIDE HUMBERT,** of New York (*d.* 1840), and *d.* October 8, 1861. Issue :

        William Russell and Fanny Jane.

    v.   **DR. THOMAS,** *b.* January 22, 1808 ; *m.,* April 15, 1845, **REBECCA MAULDIN.** Issue :

        i.   **Thomas Russell.**

        ii.   **Mary Adelaide,** *m.,* September 3, 1874, **William H. Fisher.**

        iii.   **Charles.**

    vi.   **BASIL,** *b.* January 7, 1810 ; *m.,* January 13, 1836, **CAROLINE L. HASLETT,** of Westchester, Pa., who *d. s. p.*

    vii.   **MARIA,** *d. u.* March, 1891.

iii.   **NANCY,** *d. u.*

iv.   **THOMAS,** *d.* in early manhood.

v.   **WILLIAM,** *d. s. p.*

ANN (THOMAS) RUSSELL afterward *m.* **DANIEL,** only son of **Thomas** and **Ann Sheridine,** and *d.* without further issue.

Authorities : Family papers and wills, and the Pennsylvania Historical Magazine, XI., pp. 63, 190, and 288, for the Principio Company.

From an Old Engraving, 1705

RUTHERFURD

SIR JOHN RUTHERFURD descended from **Robert, Lord de Rutherford,**[1] witness to a charter given by David the First of Scotland, in 1140; *m.*, in 1710, **ELIZABETH CAIRN-CROSS,** of Colmslie, and had nineteen children, of whom one son, **ROBERT,** was a Baron of the Russian Empire.

WALTER, another son, removed to America, spelled his surname "Rutherfurd;" was a Major in the British army; in 1756 one of the founders of the S. Andrew's Society of New York; Treasurer, 1761; President, 1766. On the revival of the Society after the Revolution, 1785, he was Vice-President, and, 1792–98, President; 1771 one of the incorporators of the New York Hospital, and one of its Governors; 1774–78 was a merchant of prominence, and *m.* **CATHERINE,** third *dau.* of **James Alexander** and sister of **Major-General William Alexander,** of the American Revolutionary army, who claimed and assumed the titles of Earl of Stirling and Viscount of Canada, as heir male of **William,** first Earl of Stirling, the Scottish Poet of the reign of James I., through **Henry,** fifth Earl and Viscount, who *d. s. p.* December 4, 1759. **WALTER RUTHERFURD** *d.* about 1803, leaving a son, **JOHN,** *b.* in 1760, graduated at the College of New Jersey in 1776; was one of the first Presidential Electors, and a Senator of the United States from New Jersey from 1791 to 1798. In 1807 he was the principal member of a Commission appointed to lay out the streets of New York. He *m.* **HELENA,** *dau.* of **Lewis Morris,** the signer, and niece of **Staats Long Morris** (who was an officer of the British Army, and *m.* the Dowager Duchess of Gordon), and of the cel-

[1] See L. B. Thomas, Genealogical Notes, 1877, *pp.* 130, 131.

ebrated **Gouverneur Morris**. **JOHN RUTHERFURD** *d*. February 23, 1860. Issue, with others :

i.   **ROBERT WALTER,** *b*. in May, 1778, *of whom presently.*
ii.   **MARY,** *b*. in 1784 ; *d. u.* June 16, 1863.
iii. **ANNA,** *m*. **DR. JOHN WATTS.**
iv.   **HELENA,** *m*. **PETER G. STUYVESANT,** a descendant of the last Dutch Governor of New York.

ROBERT WALTER, only son of **John** and **Helena (Morris)** Rutherfurd, *b*. in May, 1778 ; *m*. his cousin **SABINA,** *dau*. of **Lewis Morris, Jr.,** and his wife, **Ann Elliott,** of South Carolina, and *d*. Issue :

i. **WALTER,** *m*. **ISABELLA BROOKS,** and *d*. in 1868. Issue :

    i.   **JOHN ALEXANDER.**
    ii.   **WALTER,** *m*. **LOUISE LIVINGSTON,** *dau*. of Ohver H. Jones.
    iii. **FRANK MORRIS.**
    iv.   **WILLIAM WALTER.**

ii. **JOHN,** *m*. **CHARLOTTE LIVINGSTON,** and *d*. in 1871. Issue :

    HELEN MORRIS, LIVINGSTON, and **ARTHUR.**

iii. **LEWIS MORRIS,** a distinguished astronomer and scientist, *m*. **MARGARET STUYVESANT CHANLER.** Issue :

    i.   **STUYVESANT,** who changed his name to **RUTHERFURD STUYVESANT,** in accordance with the will of his great uncle, P. G. Stuyvesant, whose heir he was, and *m*. **MARY E.,** *dau*. of H. E. Pierrepont, since *d*.
    ii.   **MARGARET,** *m*. **HENRY WHITE,** Secretary of Legation to the United States Embassy at London.
    iii. **LOUISA.**
    iv.   **LEWIS M.,** *m*., June 16, 1890, at London, the second *dau*. of **Oliver Harriman,** of New York.
    v.   **WINTHROP.**

iv. **ROBERT WALTER,** *b*. July 14, 1819 ; *m*., October 17, 1848, **ANNA LAWRENCE,** *dau*. of **Phineas Henry** and **Phœbe Buckley** (*q. v.*). Issue :

    i.   **ROBERT WALTER,** *b*. August 12, 1849, at Morrisania, drowned in the Passaic River, August 5, 1852.
    ii.   **SABINA ELLIOTT,** *b*. August 4, 1851, at Edgerston Cottage, New Jersey.
    iii. **SARAH,** *b*. July 29, 1853, at Edgerston ; *d. i.*
    iv.   **MARY,** *b*. December 18, 1855, at Edgerston.
    v.   **ROBERT ALEXANDER,** *b*. July 13, 1860, at Edgerston.
    vi.   **HENRY LAWRENCE,** *b*. June 4, 1862, at Fairlawn Cottage, near Belleville, N. J. ; *m*., September 8, 1892, at Innsbruck, in the Tyrol, Austria, **HARRIET COLWELL FULTON.**
    vii. **ELIZABETH,** *d. i.*

Authorities : Sir Robert Douglas's Peerage of Scotland, articles in the New York Genealogical and Biographical Record, and family papers.

RUTLAND

THOMAS RUTLOND was sub-prior of S. Alban's Monastery. He *d.* 1521, and his tomb is in the south transept of S. Alban's Abbey, Hertfordshire (Nicholson's "S. Albans," *p.* 64). **George Rutland** is the earliest of the name I find in Maryland, having a case in court in 1646 (Maryland Land Records, Liber I, 216). A **Thomas Rutland** patents a lot forty-nine and one-half feet on Mulberry Street, Philadelphia, June 21, 1683, for Randall Maylin.

THOMAS RUTLAND, of South River, Anne Arundel Co., Md., *m.*, January 13, 1695, **JANE LINTHICUM.** He *d.* December 12, 1731. Will, proved December 24, 1731 (Liber C, C, No. 3, folio 471), names a *dau.*, **ELIZABETH STUARD,** and friend, Richard Snowden. Other issue:

i. **ELIZABETH,** *b.* January 22, 1696; *d.* 1707.
ii. **JANE,** *b.* 1698; *m.*, December 18, 1715, **JOSEPH BREWER.**
iii. **MARY,** *b.* 1699; *m.*, January 30, 1717, **THOMAS SAPPINGTON.**
Issue, a son, **THOMAS.**
iv. **ANN,** *b.* 1701; *m.* **LEONARD WAYMAN.** Issue, a *dau.*, **JEANE.**
v. **THOMAS,** *b.* 1703, *of whom presently.*

THOMAS, only son of **Thomas** and **Jane (Linthicum) Rutland,** *b.* 1703; *m.* **ANNE DORSEY,** and *d.* before February, 1774. His widow made her will August 25, 1773 (her husband then living); proved January 23, 1776; Elizabeth Rutland a witness. She gives Mary Snowden, *dau.* of Eliza Snowden, a pair of gold sleeve-buttons, but leaves the bulk of her property to her sister, Elizabeth Dorsey's children.

THOMAS and **ANNE (DORSEY) RUTLAND** had issue:

i. **THOMAS,** *m.* **ANN,** and made his will 1790 (Liber J G, No. 1, folio 181). Issue:

THOMAS, apparently *d. s. p.* The story goes he declared "that if he had sat upon the seashore and thrown his fortune to the waves, he could not have gotten rid of it faster." When his corpse was to be laid in the tomb of his ancestors, tradition records " that the ashes of his father rose against him."

ii.   **ELIZA,** *m.* **RICHARD SNOWDEN** (*q. v.*).

The will of **THOMAS RUTLAND,** of Anne Arundel Co., was proved August 15, 1781 (Liber T G, No. 1, folio 31); wife, **COMFORT**; sole heir, son THOMAS, under age November 10, 1780; Joseph Howard, Jr., uncle of the heir ; and **ELIZABETH,** *dau.* of **Edmond** and **Elizabeth Rutland,** *b.* August 7, 1758 ; *m.,* July 7, 1778, **NICHOLAS,** son of Colonel Nicholas and Catherine (Griffith) Worthington.

Authorities : Annapolis wills and register of All Hallows Parish, South River.

SCHIEFFELIN

THE family of **Schieffelin** can be traced back to the thirteenth century, when it had large properties in Germany and founded a Chapel in Nordlingen, at a place called the Wine Market, in the year 1269. There was a branch of the family existing in Switzerland in the middle of the fifteenth century, and it has been claimed, seemingly with little authority, that the Swiss was the elder branch. However this may be, **CONRAD**, the son of **Franz Schieffelin,** of Nordlingen and Nuremburg (for in 1476 the latter kept up residences in both places), migrated to the Canton of Geneva, Switzerland, and in consideration of his near relative, the Lord Syndic **Besançon Huges,** he was admitted to citizenship February 14, 1518, gratis, and became possessed of the Fief de la Moliere, July 6, 1527. He left descendants prominent in the cantonal affairs of Switzerland for several generations. In 1543 **HANS LEONARD SCHIEFFELIN,** second, the nephew of **Conrad,** being the son of his brother, **Hans Leonard,** also moved from Germany to Switzerland, making Friburg his residence. A picture painted in 1538 is still extant, representing the elder **Hans Leonard Schieffelin** and his two sons worshipping the Paschal Lamb, which is also the crest of the family in this country. The first of the family to visit America was **JACOB SCHIEF-FELIN,** of Weilheim an der Deck, in Germany. The family had a dwelling in Weilheim and a seat in the country, with the perpetual right vested in the family of sending the eldest son to the College. **JACOB SCHIEFFELIN** died 1746, and in the same year his son, also named **JACOB,** came over to Philadelphia and settled in this country, bringing his family Bible, printed in 1560, with him, which is still in the possession of the family.

JACOB SCHIEFFELIN, second, was *b.* February 4, 1732; *m.,* September 16, 1756, **REGINA MARGARETTA KRAF-TEN RITSCHAURIN** (*b.* in Milhaus an der Ense, Germany, September 9, 1739), and *d.* 1769.   Issue :

i.   **JACOB**, *b.* August 24, 1757, *of whom presently.*
ii.   **MELCHIOR**, *b.* August 16, 1759.
iii.   **JONATHAN**, *b.* July 16, 1762.
iv.   **THOMAS.**

JACOB, son of **Jacob** and **Regina Margaretta Schieffelin,** was *b.* in Philadelphia, August 24, 1757, and baptised by the Rev. Mr. Muhlenberg, of the Lutheran Church.   While still a young man he went to Detroit as Secretary of the Province, and owned considerable property in that town.   He came to New York, holding a commission in the British army, early in 1780, and August 16, 1780, *m.* **HAN-NAH,** oldest *dau.* of **John** and **Ann (Burling) Lawrence** (*q. v.*), one of the handsomest women of her time, and a distinguished poetess (*d.* October 3, 1838).   He afterward removed to Montreal, where his two eldest sons were born.   Taking his wife back to New York, he left her there and spent some time in London.   Returning to Montreal, his wife joined him in that ancient city.   About 1794 he returned to New York, and went into business with his brother-in-law, John B. Lawrence.   Five years afterward they dissolved partnership to allow Mr. Schieffelin to engage in ship-owning, which Mr. Lawrence considered too hazardous.   Jacob Schieffelin continued to carry on business at No. 195 Pearl Street, and in 1805 his son, Henry Hamilton, was taken into partnership.   In 1814 Jacob Schieffelin retired, and the firm was carried on until 1849 under the title of H. H. Schieffelin & Co.   Only by extreme care and perseverance was the business at times continued successfully.   There were the troubles caused by the wars of the great Napoleon, England with its Orders in Council, France with its Berlin Decrees, the piracies of the Barbary Powers, and the Great Panic of 1837.   Through all these, as well as the later financial crises of 1857, 1861, and 1873, the house has been guided with sagacity and success.   In 1849 Henry H. Schieffelin retired, leaving as his successors his four sons, by whom the business was carried on until 1865, when the firm name became William H. Schieffelin & Co., under which title it continues a flourishing existence in New York, having agencies in London, Chicago, and San Francisco.   A pamphlet, recently published in commemoration of the centennial of

LIEUT. JACOB SCHIEFFELIN

HANNAH (LAWRENCE) SCHIEFFELIN

the house, entitled "One Hundred Years of Business Life," has attracted much attention. Jacob Schieffelin resided for many years at the old Walton House, on Pearl Street. He also had a country-seat near Manhattanville ; and that village was laid out by him in conjunction with his brothers-in-law, Thomas Buckley and John B. Lawrence. He *d.* at his residence in New York, April 16, 1835.

JACOB and HANNAH (LAWRENCE) SCHIEFFELIN had issue :

i. **EDWARD LAWRENCE**, *b.* September 13, 1787, *d.* October 5, 1850, at Lyme, Conn. He *m.*, January 1, 1802, **SUSAN ANNA**, *dau.* of **Alexander Stewart.** Issue :

> **EDWARD ANNA**, *b.* in 1809 ; *m.*, in 1830, **FRANK NICOLL SILL**, who *d.* in 1848. She then *m.* **DR. JOHN NOYES**, who *d.* in 1854. After his death she *m.* **CAPTAIN S. CHADWICK**, of Lyme, and *d. s. p.*

ii. **HENRY HAMILTON**, *b.* June 20, 1783, *of whom presently.*

iii. **ANNA MARIA**, *b.* April 11, 1788 ; *m.*, April 4, 1808, **BENJAMIN FERRIS** (*q. v.*).

iv. **EFFINGHAM**, *b.* February 17, 1791 ; a prominent lawyer of New York ; member of the Common Council ; Assistant for the Ninth Ward, 1818–1825, and the Twelfth Ward in 1826. He *m.*, September 9, 1813, **MARY**, *dau.* of **Caspar Lander**, and *d.* at East Chester, July 14, 1863. Issue :

> A son, **EDGAR**, who has three daughters and two sons, and a grandchild by another son, Charles M. Schieffelin, who *m.* Mary, *dau.* of William Chisolm, and niece of Rev. Dr. William A. Muhlenberg. Issue :
>> Two daughters and a son.

v. **JACOB**, *b.* April 20, 1793 (*q. v.*).

vi. **JOHN LAWRENCE**, *b.* February 25, 1796 ; *m.*, August 19, 1844, **MATHILDE THERESE BOWEN**, and *d.* at New Haven, April 22, 1866. Issue :

> **MARY T.**, *m.* **HENRY J. SAYERS**, of New York.

vii. **RICHARD LAWRENCE**, *b.* November 9, 1801 (*q. v.*).

HENRY HAMILTON SCHIEFFELIN, second son of **Jacob** and **Hannah (Lawrence) Schieffelin**, *b.* June 20, 1783 ; was graduated from Columbia College in 1801, and shortly afterward admitted to the Bar, but soon abandoned the profession for mercantile pursuits, becoming in 1805 partner with his father and in 1814 head of the firm. He was a remarkable man, who seemed to have a knowledge of every science and art. He *m.*, April 19, 1806, **MARIA THERESA**, *dau.* of **Dr. Samuel Bradhurst**, who *d.* May 22, 1872. Issue :

i.　**MARY THERESA**, *b.* January 14, 1807 ; *m.*, in 1827, **WILLIAM N. CLARK** (*q. v.*).

ii.　**HENRY MAUNSELL**, *b.* August 7, 1808, was for many years a member of the firm of H. M. Schieffelin & Fowler, merchants, of New York. · He was a man of large benevolence and especially interested in the advancement of the negroes, being for a number of years a director of the New York Colonization Society. He *m.*, first, in 1835, **SARAH LOUISA**, *dau.* of **David Wagstaffe**, who *d. s. p. ; m.*, second, June 14, 1859, **SARAH M. KENDALL**, of Maine, and *d.* at Alexandria, Egypt, July 23, 1890.　Issue :

　　i.　FANNY, *b.* September 16, 1860 ; *m.*, October 12, 1881, **ERNEST HOWARD CROSBY.** Issue :

　　　　i.　Margaret Eleanor, *b.* April 25, 1884.
　　　　ii.　Maunsell Schieffelin, *b.* February 14, 1887.

　　ii.　MARY BRADHURST, *b.* July 18, 1862.

iii.　**SAMUEL BRADHURST**, *b.* February 24, 1811, *of whom presently.*

iv.　**JAMES LAWRENCE**, *b.* in 1813.

v.　**PHILIP**, *b.* in 1815 ; *m.* **ELIZABETH**, *dau.* of **Richard Townley Haines**, of Messrs. Halstead, Haines & Co., New York City, and of Elizabethtown, N. J. ; *d.* before 1889.　Issue :

　　i.　MARIA THERESA, *m.* REV. WILLIAM T. SABINE, and *d.* February 19, 1892. Issue (surname SABINE) :

　　　　i. Edith Schieffelin.　ii. Elizabeth Haines.　iii. William Tufnell.　iv. Philip Schieffelin.　v. Alice Winifred.　vi. Gustavus Arthur.　vii. Julia Hannah Tufnell.　viii. Maunsell Schieffelin.　ix. Samuel Schieffelin.　x. Mary Theresa Schieffelin.

　　ii.　ELLA, *d. u.*

vi.　**SIDNEY AUGUSTUS**, *b.* in 1818, resided at Geneva ; *m.* **HARRIET SCHUYLER**, of Belleville, and *d.* 1894.　Issue :

　　Two sons and three daughters.

vii.　**JULIA**, *b.* in 1821 ; *m.*, in 1840, **CLEMENT REMINGTON**, and *d.* September 15, 1871.　Issue :

　　i.　MARY THERESA, *m.* WILLIAM CHAMBERLAIN.
　　ii.　JULIA, *m.* CHARLES MORGAN.

viii.　**BRADHURST**, *m.* twice.　Issue :

　　i.　LAURA G., *m.*, in 1875, DAVID BARTON CUSHING.
　　ii.　EMILY.

ix.　**EUGENE**, *b.* in 1827, an artist of some distinction, though calling himself an amateur ; *m.* **CATHERINE**, *dau.* of **Valentine G. Hall**.

SAMUEL BRADHURST, second son of **Henry H.** and **Maria T. (Bradhurst) Schieffelin**, *b.* February 24, 1811, was author of " Foundations of History," an illustrated volume on the early history of the world, and of " Milk for Babes," and other catechisms and religious manuals. He *m.*, in 1835, **LUCRETIA HAZARD.** Issue :

i.   **WILLIAM HENRY,** *b.* in 1836, *of whom presently.*
ii.   **ALICE HOLMES,** *b.* in 1838 ; *m.*, in 1859, **RUSSELL STEB-BINS.** Issue (surname STEBBINS) :

     i.   GRACE, *m.* ALFRED C. CHAPIN. Issue (surname CHAPIN) :

         Grace and Beatrice.

     ii.   SAMUEL SCHIEFFELIN.
     iii.   RUSSELL HAZARD.

iii.   **MARY THERESA BRADHURST,** *b.* in 1840 ; *m.*, in 1863, **GENERAL CHARLES CLEVELAND DODGE.** Issue (surname DODGE) :

     CHARLES STEWART, *m.* FLORA, *dau.* of Hon. John Bigelow (*q. v.*). Issue :

     i.   Lucy Bigelow.
     ii.   Ethel, *m.* William Cary Sanger, and has a son, William Cary, Jr.

WILLIAM HENRY, eldest son of **Samuel Bradhurst** and **Lucretia (Hazard) Schieffelin,** *b.* in 1836, was a member of the Seventh New York Regiment at the beginning of the Civil War, and went to the front with it. Commissioned Major of the First New York Mounted Rifles, he completed the regiment by the enlistment of four hundred men, and served for some time in Virginia under General Wool. He became a member of his father's firm in 1859, and its head on his father's retirement in 1865, which position he occupied at the time of his death. He *m.*, in 1863, **MARY,** *dau.* of the late **Hon. John Jay,** and *d.* June 21, 1895. Issue :

i.   **ELEANOR JAY.**
ii.   **WILLIAM JAY,** *of whom presently.*
iii.   **SAMUEL BRADHURST,** Jr., *d. y.*
iv.   **JOHN JAY,** *d. y.*
v.   **GEOFFREY,** *d. y.*

WILLIAM JAY, eldest son of **William Henry** and **Mary (Jay) Schieffelin,** *m.*, February 5, 1891, **MARIA LOUISA,** *dau.* of **Colonel Elliot F.** and **Margaret (Vanderbilt) Shepard.** Issue :

i.   **WILLIAM JAY,** Jr.
ii.   **MARGARET LOUISE.**

JACOB,[1] fourth son of **Jacob** and **Hannah (Lawrence) Schieffe-lin,** *b.* April 20, 1793, at New York City, removed to Tioga Co., Pa., about 1830 ; *m.* **ELIZABETH CHAPMAN,** and *d.* December 27, 1880, at Tioga, Pa. ; his widow *d.* January 27, 1881, at the same place, aged eighty-four.   Issue :

i.   **CLINTON,** *b.* February 16, 1823, *of whom presently.*
ii.   **ALFRED,** *b.* September 23, 1827, at New York City.
iii.   **ELIZABETH,** *b.* May 23, 1829, at New York.
iv.   **LAURA,** *b.* September 2, 1831, in Tioga Co., Pa. ; *m.* **O. B. LOWELL,** and *d.* September 18, 1866.
v.   **CORNELIA,** *b.* February 4, 1834, in Tioga Co.
vi.   **JACOB B.,** *b.* March 25th ; *d.* July 7, 1836.
vii.   **EDWARD GIRARD,** his twin brother, *b.* March 25, 1836.
viii.   **JACOB, Jr.,** *b.* April 18, 1838, at Charleston, Tioga Co. ; *m.*, February 1, 1866, **EMILY P. RYON,** of Elkland, Pa. (*b.* July 23, 1843, at Knoxville, Pa.).   Issue :

    i.   **LILA GERTRUDE,** *b.* November 11, 1868, Doctor of Medicine.
    ii.   **EDWARD EFFINGHAM,** *b.* September 21, 1872.
    iii.   **THOMAS LAWRENCE,** *b.* July 31, 1874.
    iv.   **JAY HOYT,** *b.* April 22, 1876.

ix.   **HANNAH LAWRENCE,** *b.* March 6, 1840.

CLINTON, eldest son of **Jacob** and **Elizabeth (Chapman) Schieffelin,** *b.* February 16, 1823, at New York City, removed to the Pacific Coast and settled in Oregon.   In 1880 took up his residence in East Los Angeles, Cal., on property purchased and given to him by his son Edward.   He *m.* **JANE ——,** and *d.* suddenly April 15, 1884.   Issue :

i.   **LAFAYETTE,** *b.* August 1, 1843 ; *d.* April 8, 1844.
ii.   **EDWARD L.,** *b.* October 8, 1847, the discoverer of the silver mines at Tombstone, Ariz.
iii.   **ALBERT EUGENE,** *b.* August 27, 1849.
iv.   **JANE ELIZABETH,** *b.* September 2, 1851.
v.   **EFFINGHAM L.,** *b.* November 5, 1857.
vi.   **CHARLOTTE,** *b.* November 27, 1859 ; *m.* **EDWARD DUNHAM.**
vii.   **RICHARD CHARLES (?),** *b.* April 26, 1862.
viii.   **JACOB,** *b.* October 1, 1865 ; *d.* May 10, 1867.
ix.   **THEODORE,** *b.* October 6, 1867 ; *d.* September 17, 1881.
x.   **JAY L.,** *b.* July 15, 1870.

RICHARD LAWRENCE, youngest son of **Jacob** and **Hannah (Lawrence) Schieffelin,** *b.* November 9, 1801, immediately on

---

[1] This account of Jacob Schieffelin, Jr., and his descendants, is from his family Bible, through Mr. Jay Hoyt Schieffelin, of Tioga, Pa.

graduating from Columbia College in the class of 1819 (he was its oldest living alumnus at the time of his death), entered the law office of his brother-in-law, Benjamin Ferris, and in due course was admitted to the Bar. He continued in active practice until 1843.

Upon retiring from active business, Mr. Schieffelin devoted himself to the care and oversight of his private interests. He indulged to a limited extent in the excitements of political life, accepting an election to the Common Council and serving as President of the Board during 1843–44. Upon the expiration of his term of office he declined a nomination for Congress. He was a prominent member of the Protestant Episcopal Church, and in 1823 drew up the articles of incorporation of the church of S. Mary, Manhattanville, which is built upon land donated by his father; was a vestryman or warden of the church from that time until 1889, and at the time of his death its Senior Warden. He enjoyed the distinction of representing the church in the Diocesan Convention for more than sixty years. He also served S. Thomas's Church as vestryman for a considerable period, and for many years was prominently identified with Grace Church, in the city of New York.

In early life he was much interested in the militia of the State of New York, holding the commission of Brigadier-General.

MR. SCHIEFFELIN was a Trustee and Director in a number of charitable and financial institutions. He had marked literary tastes and abilities, contributed extensively to the press, and inherited in no slight degree the poetic talent of his mother. He *m.*, August 3, 1833, **MARGARET HELEN,** *dau.* of **Captain George Knox McKay,** United States Artillery, and *d.* November 21, 1889. Issue :

i.   **SARAH SOPHIA,** *b.* June 22, 1834 ; *m.*, January 30, 1858, **REV. CUTHBERT COLLINGWOOD BARCLAY,** Rector of All Saints' Church, New York (who *d.* February 7, 1863), and *d. s. p.* March 5, 1886.

ii. **GEORGE RICHARD,** *b.* July 27, 1836, *of whom presently*.

iii. **HELEN MARGARET,** *b.* May 7, 1841 ; *m.*, June 21, 1866, **WILLIAM IRVING GRAHAM.** Issue (surname GRAHAM):

   i.   **HELEN MARGARET,** *b.* April 26, 1867.
   ii. **JULIA IRVING,** *b.* September 18, 1870.

   Mr. Graham *d.* August 21, 1871, and his widow *m.*, April 7, 1875, **ALEXANDER ROBERT CHISOLM.** Issue by him :

   iii. **RICHARD SCHIEFFELIN,** *b.* September 4, 1876.

GEORGE RICHARD SCHIEFFELIN, son of **Richard Lawrence** and **Margaret Helen (McKay) Schieffelin**, *b.* July 27, 1836, was graduated from Columbia College in 1855, and shortly afterward admitted to the Bar in New York ; elected Deputy-Governor of the New York Society of Colonial Wars in 1895 ; *m.*, May 19, 1866, **JULIA MATILDA**, *dau.* of **Hon. Isaac C. Delaplaine.**   Issue :

i.   **JULIA FLORENCE**, *m.*, December 4, 1888, at New York City, **JOSEPH BRUCE ISMAY**, of Liverpool, England, one of the leading owners of the White Star Steamship Company.   Issue (surname ISMAY) :

MARGARET BRUCE and THOMAS BRUCE.

ii.   **MARGARET HELEN**, *m.*, December 10, 1890, **HENRY GRAFF TREVOR.**   Issue (surname TREVOR) :

GEORGE SCHIEFFELIN and MARGARET ESTELLE.

iii. **MATILDA CONSTANCE.**
iv.   **SARAH DOROTHY.**
v.   **GEORGE RICHARD DELAPLAINE.**

Authorities : Family papers, chiefly through the late Richard L. Schieffelin and Messrs. Eugene and George R. Schieffelin, of New York City.

SCUDAMORE ARMS

SCUDAMORE, OF HEREFORDSHIRE, ENGLAND

S. SCUDAMORE, so called from his shield of a cross and motto, "*Scutum amoris divini,*" is said to have been of the invading army of William the Conqueror in 1066, and to have had a son, **SIR ALAN,** in the reign of William Rufus, who *m.* **JOAN,** *dau.* and heiress of **Sir Alexander Catchmay, Knt.,** of Troy and Bigswear, Monmouthshire, and had a son, **SIR TITUS,** *m.* **JOYCE,** *dau.* of **Sir Robert Clifford,** Lord of Clifford. Issue:

i.   **Sir Wilcock,** *m.* **Eleanor,** *dau.* and heiress of **Sir Brian Trowhek, Knt.**
ii.   **Jenkin,** *m.* **Agnes** or **Alice,** *dau.* and heiress of **Sir Robert Ewyas, Knt.**
       Issue:

          Sir John, *of whom presently.*

SIR JOHN, son of **Jenkin** and **Agnes (Ewyas)** Scudamore, *m.* **JOANE,** *dau.* of **Sir Walter Baskerville, Knt.,** of Eardisley. Issue:

       SIR JOHN, *m.* **JOYCE,** *dau.* and *co-h.* of **Sir Robert Marbery, Knt.,** and had a son, **SIR JENKIN,** *m.* **ALICE,** *dau.* and *co-h.* of **Sir Walter Pedwarden.** Issue:

          i.   **Sir John,** *of whom presently.*
          ii.   **Philip,** ancestor of the Holme or Home Lacy branch, was probably executed by the English in 1408, as an officer of Owen Glendower.

SIR JOHN, eldest son of **Sir Jenkin** and **Alice (Pedwarden)** Scudamore, was of Ewyas and Kentchurch, *m.* **ALICIA** or **ELIZABETH,** *dau.* and *co-h.* of **Owen Glendower** (*q. v.*), and had a son, **SIR JOHN,** *m.* **MAUD,** *dau.* of **Griffith ap Nicholas,**

of Dynevor (*q. v.*), and had a son, **PHILIP**, *m.* **AGNES**, *dau.* and heiress of John Huntercombe (*q. v.*).   Issue :

> George, *m.* —— Burghill. Issue :
>   i. Philip, *of whom presently.* ii. William.

PHILIP, eldest son of **George Scudamore**, was Mayor of Hereford, 1482 ; *m.* ——, *dau.* and heiress of —— **Osbourne**, of London.   Issue :

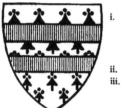

i.   **WILLIAM**, *m.* **ALYS**, *dau.* of Richard Minors, of Treago. Issue :

      i. **JAMES**, *of whom presently.*
      ii. **JOHN** (*q. v.*).

ii.   **EDWARD**.
iii. **ANNE**, *m.* **JOHN SCUDAMORE**, of Rolston.

HUNTERCOMBE ARMS

JAMES, eldest son of **William and Alys (Minors) Scudamore**, was of Kentchurch, *m.* **JOANE** or **SIBELL**, *dau.* of **Sir Walter Baskerville**, of Eardisley. Issue :

i.   **JOAN**, inherited Kentchurch ; *m.* **PHILIP SCUDAMORE**, of Rolston. Her descendant, **John Lucy Scudamore**,[1] represented the family in 1847, and *m.* the eldest *dau.* of **Sir Harford Jones Bridges**, **Bart.**

ii.   **ELEANOR**, *m.* **MILES AP HARRY**, of Newport.

JOHN, younger son of **William** and **Alys (Minors) Scudamore**, was a Gentleman Usher to King Henry VIII., *m.* **SIBILL**, *dau.* of **Walter Vaughan**, of Hergest (*q. v.*), and *d.* September 25, 1571, leaving, with other issue :

i.   **SIR JOHN** ; was standard-bearer to the Band of Gentlemen Pensioners under Queen Elizabeth ; *m.* **LADY MARY SKELTON**, and had a son, **SIR JAMES**, Knt., the " **SIR SCUDAMORE** " of Spenser's " Faerye Queen."   Issue :

VAUGHAN ARMS

    i.   **John**, was created a Baronet, June 1, 1620, Baron of Dromore and Viscount Scudamore of Sligo, in the Peerage of Ireland, July 2, 1628. Titles extinct December 2, 1716.

    ii.   ——, *m.* **Sir John Scudamore**, of Ballingham, Herefordshire ; created a Baronet, July 23, 1644. Title extinct between 1718 and 1727.

        [1] See Burke's Landed Gentry for the pedigree.

ii.   **PHILIP,** fourth son, *m.* **JOAN,** *dau.* of **Richard Warnecombe** and widow of Walter Kyrle, and had a *dau.*, **SYBELL,** *m.* **PHILIP AP THOMAS** (*q. v.*).

There was also a family at Norton Scudamore and Upton Scudamore, Hunts, descended from **WALTER,** nephew of Sir Peter Esscudemore, Knt., living 1316–17. Another branch was in Kent, descended from **Robert Scudamore,** *b.* 1601, Rector of Stoke Edith, Herefordshire ; many of this line were physicians. (See W. Berry's Kent., *pp.* 34, 35.)

Authorities : Harleian MS. 615 ff. 9, 10. Cooke's Visitation of Herefordshire, *pp.* 62–64 ; C. J. Robinson's Herefordshire, 142 ; W. Camden's Visitation of Hunts, *pp.* 82–85 ; Lodge's Irish Peerage, and Courthope's Baronetage, *p.* 177.

SCULL

THE brothers, **JOHN** and **NICHOLAS SCULL,** claiming connection with the family of Scull, of Much Cowarne, Herefordshire, England, emigrated to America in the ship Bristol Merchant, John Stephens, Master, in company with Colonel Jaspar Farmer, who took up eight thousand acres near what is now Chestnut Hill, Philadelphia. They arrived September 10, 1685.

NICHOLAS SCULL remained in Pennsylvania, bought and laid out four hundred acres called Springfield Manor, and *d.* in 1703.

JOHN SCULL was an owner of whalers, is said to have removed from Long Island to Great Egg Harbour, N. J., about 1690. He owned five hundred and fifty acres of land there, still called Scullville ; *m.,* before his arrival in New Jersey, **MARY** ——. and *d.* 1744–45. Issue :

i.	**JOHN,** stolen by the Indians in infancy and never recovered.
ii.	**ABEL.**
iii.	**PETER.**
iv.	**DANIEL.**
v.	**BENJAMIN.**
vi.	**MARGARET,** *m.* **ROBERT SMITH.**
vii.	**CAROLINE,** *m.* **AMOS IRELAND.**
viii	**MARY.**
ix.	**RACHEL,** *m.* **JAMES EDWARDS.**
x.	**JOHN RECOMPENSE,** *m.* **PHEBE DENNIS.**
xi.	**GIDEON,** *of whom presently.*

xii.   **ISAIAH,** *m.* **ANN ——.**
xiii.   **DAVID,** *d.* January 10, 1741-42.

GIDEON, seventh son of **John** and **Mary Scull,** *b.* 1722, *m.* **JU-DITH,** *dau.* of **James** and **Margaret Smith (Bellanger),** and both *d.* of small-pox in 1776.   Issue :

i.   **PAUL.**
ii.   **HANNAH,** *m.* **DAVID DAVIS.**
iii.   **MARY,** *m.* **DAVID BASSETT.**
iv.   **JUDITH,** *m.* **DANIEL OFFLEY.**
v.   **JAMES,** *m.* **SUSANNAH LEEDS.**
vi.   **GIDEON,** *of whom presently.*
vii.   **RUTH,** *m.* **SAMUEL REEVE.**
viii.   **MARGERY,** *m.* **DANIEL LEEDS.**
ix.   **RACHEL,** *m.* **SAMUEL BOLTON.**
x.   **MARK,** *m.* **MARY BRANNING.**

GIDEON, second son of **Gideon** and **Judith (Bellanger) Scull,** *b.* 1756, sold his paternal estate to his brother Mark and removed to Salem Co. to a place called Sculltown for some sixty years, now Auburn.   He *m.*, April 29, 1784, **SARAH,** *dau.* of **James James,** by his wife **Abigail,** youngest *dau.* of **Samuel** and **Mary (Hicks) Lawrence,** of Black Stump, Long Island (*b.* 1759, *d.* 1836), and *d.* 1825.   Issue :

i.   **ABIGAIL,** *d. i.*
ii.   **ABIGAIL,** *d. u.* 1867.
iii.   **JAMES,** *d.* at sea.
iv.   **GIDEON,** *m.* **LYDIA ANN ROWAN,** of Salem, N. J.
v.   **JONATHAN,** *d. y.*
vi.   **OFFLEY.**
vii.   **SARAH,** *d. u.*
viii.   **HANNAH,** *m.* **WILLIAM CARPENTER,** of Salem, N. J.
ix.   **DAVID,** *of whom presently.*
x.   **PAUL,** *m.* **HOPE KAYE.**

DAVID, fifth son of **Gideon** and **Sarah (James) Scull,** *b.* December 8, 1799, *m.*, first, 1823, **Lydia,** *dau.* of **Joshua** and **Ester Davis Lippincott**[1] (*b.* September 16, 1801 ; *d.* August, 1854). He *m.*, second, **HANNAH DAVIS,** *dau.* of **Richard** and **Elizabeth (Bacon) Wood,** and *d.* December 24, 1884.   Issue, by first wife :

---

[1] Dorothea, youngest *dau.* of Thomas and Jane (Knatchbull) Scott, of Egerton Hall, Kent, *m.*, first, Major Daniel Gotherson. Dorothea, her younger *dau.*, *m.* John Davis, a Welsh singing Quaker, of Oyster Bay, Long Island, who moved to Salem Co., N. J., about 1705. Their son, David Davis, Judge of the Salem Co. Courts, was grandfather of Ester Davis, who married Joshua Lippincott.

i. **GIDEON DELAPLAINE**, *b.* August 13, 1824; author of "Voyages of Peter Esprit Radisson, 1654-84," in publications of the Prince Society; "The Evelyns in America;" "Dorothea Scott," 1883; "Genealogical Notes Relating to Scull Family," 1876. He settled in England; *m.*, April 7, 1862, at Leipzig, Saxony, **ANNA**, *dau.* of **Thomas Holder**, *dec.*, of Temple Grafton, Warwickshire, England, and *d.* April 22, 1889. Issue:

    i. **WALTER DELAPLAINE**, *b.* at Bath.
    ii. **EDITH MARIA**.
    iii. **LYDIA**, *b.* at Malvern, England.

ii. **CAROLINE**, *d. y.*
iii. **HANNAH**, *d. u.*
iv. **JANE L.**, *m.* **WILLIAM D. BISPHAM.** Issue:

    DAVID S.

v. **LYDIA L.**, *d. i.*
vi. **DAVID**, *of whom presently.*
vii. **MARY**, *m.* **PASCHALL HACKER.**
viii. **EDWARD LAWRENCE**, *m.* **SARAH MARSHALL**, and *d.* June 14, 1884. Issue:

    EDWARD MARSHALL and **JOHN LAWRENCE.**

DAVID, second son of **David** and **Lydia (Lippincott) Scull**, *b.* at Sculltown, N. J., January 17, 1836; removed to Philadelphia, and engaged in the wool business. Is prominent in many educational, charitable, trust and reform boards; *m.*, February 28, 1861, **HANNAH ELLICOTT**, *dau.* of **William E. Coale** (*q. v.*). Issue:

    WILLIAM ELLIS, *b.* March 3, 1862, in Philadelphia; a partner in the publishing house of John C. Winston & Company; *m.*, February 16, 1887, **FLORENCE MOORE**, *dau.* of Hon. **Edwin T. Prall**, of Paterson, N. J., seventh in descent from **Aaron Prall**, one of the founders of the Huguenot Colony on Staten Island, who came from Holland in 1660.

Authorities: Thomas Shourd's "History of Fenwick's Colony, N. J.," 1876, *pp.* 218-23, and family papers, through Mr. William Ellis Scull.

SHEAFE AND SATTERTHWAITE

SAMPSON, son of **Edmund Sheafe**, *b.* at Boston in 1650, was Assistant and Secretary of Massachusetts Colony, 1698 ; Commissary of the New England expedition against Quebec, 1711 ; *m.* **MEHITABLE**, *dau.* of Jacob Sheafe, of Boston, and *d.* in 1724, leaving a son, **SAMPSON**, Jr., *b.* in 1681, member of the Council of New Hampshire, 1740–61 ; *m.* **SARAH**, *dau.* of Colonel Theodore Walton, and *d.* in 1772, leaving a son, JACOB, *b.* in 1715 ; *m.,* in 1740, HANNAH, *dau.* of Colonel Shadrach Seavy, and *d.* leaving a son, James, *of whom presently.*

JAMES, son of **Jacob** and **Hannah (Seavy) Sheafe**, *b.* November 17, 1755, was of Portsmouth, N. H. His cousin, **Roger Hall**, son of **William Sheafe**, *b.* 1763, was created a Baronet in 1813. **JAMES SHEAFE**, *m.,* July 13, 1800, as his second wife, **SARAH**, *dau.* of **John Fisher** by **Ann**, *dau.* of **Hon. Mark Hunking Wentworth,**[1] and *d.* December 5, 1829. His wife *d.* February 7, 1863, aged eighty-eight years. Issue :

i.   **ANN FISHER**, *of whom presently.*
ii. **LOUISA**, *b.* in 1803 ; *m.* **ALFRED W. HAVEN,** and *d.* in 1828. Issue :

  A *dau.,* LOUISA SHEAFE, *m.* MARK FREEMAN, who *d.* October, 1894.

iii. **ELIZABETH WENTWORTH**, *d. u.* in 1814.
iv. **JOHN FISHER**, *m.* **MARY**, *dau.* of Robert Lennox, of New York, and *d.* November, 1881.
v.   **GEORGE**, *b.* and *d.* in 1825.
vi. **JAMES EDWARD**, *b.* in 1810 ; *d.* at St. Augustine, Fla., in 1830.

ANN FISHER, eldest *dau.* of Hon. James and Sarah (Fisher) Sheafe, *b.* in 1801 ; *m.,* in 1837, **THOMAS WILKINSON**, son of **Thomas Wilkinson** and **Catherine (Bache) Sat-**

[1] He was of the family of Earl Strafford and the colonial governors of the name.

terthwaite, descended from **Thomas Wilkinson Satterthwaite,** of London, England. They resided at Nutley, N. J., where she *d.* March 1, 1890 ; her husband *d.* November 12, 1878, aged eighty-one. Issue (surname SATTERTHWAITE) :

i.   **ELIZABETH WENTWORTH,** *b.* in 1839; *m.,* in 1863, **JOHN S. CONDIT,** who *d.* 1869. Issue :

    i.   **WENTWORTH,** *b.* June 6, 1865.
    ii.   **ELSIE A.,** *b.* 1867.
    iii.   **JOHN PAUL,** *b.* July, 1869.

ii.   **JAMES SHEAFE,** *b.* 1840, *of whom presently.*

iii.   **SARAH FISHER,** *m.,* 1879, **REV. WILLIAM ROBINSON NAIRN,** Rector of Grace Church, Nutley, N. J., until his death, in October, 1889. Issue :

    i.   **ARCHIBALD ROBINSON,** *b.* 1880 ; *d.* 1886.
    ii.   **LOUISA FISHER,** *b.* 1881.
    iii.   **ELIZABETH WENTWORTH,** *b.* 1882.
    iv.   **WALTER GEOFFREY,** *b.* February 29, 1884.
    v.   **TACIE,** *b.* May, 1887.

iv.   **DR. THOMAS EDWARD,** *b.* 1844 ; *m.,* November, 1884, **ISABELLA,** *dau.* of James Lenox Banks.

v.   **JOHN FISHER,** *b.* 1845.

JAMES SHEAFE, eldest son of **Thomas W.** and **Ann F. (Sheafe) Satterthwaite,** *b.* 1840, was of the Marine Insurance firm of Catlin & Satterthwaite, New York City ; a man of remarkably high and noble character, and his early death was greatly to be lamented. He *m.,* December 6, 1865, **JEANIE LAWRENCE,** *dau.* of **Phineas Henry** and **Julia (Lawrence) Buckley** (*q. v.*), who *d.* January 30, 1891 ; and *d.* suddenly himself September 6, 1884. Issue :

i.   **KATHERINE BACHE,** *b.* November 6, 1866 ; *m.,* September 2, 1891, **ADRIAN HOFFMAN LARKIN,** and has a son, **JAMES SATTERTHWAITE,** *b.* May, 1893.

ii.   **JULIA LAWRENCE,** *b.* July 1, 1867 ; *m.,* June 25, 1890, **ERNEST ROLLIN TILTON,** and has a son, **ERNEST ROLLIN,** *b.* September 27, 1893.

iii.   **ANNE FISHER,** *b.* June 6, 1870 ; *m.,* December 9, 1891, **PETER WILLIAM LUDVIG STRÖM,** Architect, of New York City.

iv.   **JAMES SHEAFE,** *b.* January 8, 1873 ; *m.,* April 7, 1896, **LILLIE BUTMAN,** *dau.* of the late **Francis Alexander Marden,** of Nutley, N. J.

v.   **THOMAS WILKINSON,** *b.* December 25, 1876.

Authorities : Wentworth Genealogy, I., 557 ; II., 307-315, and family papers, through the late James S. Satterthwaite and Mrs. P. W. L. Ström.

SHIPLEY

WILLIAM SHIPLEY, *b.* in 1693, in Leicestershire, England ;
early in 1725 sailed from Bristol, England, and came to Philadelphia. He settled first at Ridley, in Delaware Co., Pa. In 1735 he
purchased twelve acres of land in Willingtown, Del., and removed
there with his family in the fall of the same year. A man of
wealth, enterprise, and influence, and a prominent member of the
Society of Friends, he exerted himself successfully in behalf of
the little town in which he lived. He induced emigrants to settle there ; in 1736 built the market-house on the corner of Fourth
and Market Streets, and in 1740 was one of the most active in
building a vessel (the Wilmington) for foreign trade, the first
which ever sailed from Willingtown, now Wilmington, September 8, 1740. At the first election for municipal officers, November 23, 1739, he was elected Chief Burgess, or Mayor, and again
September 12, 1743. He *m.*, in England, about 1717, **MARY,**
dau. of **Robert** and **Ann Tatnall,** who *d.* in 1727. Issue :

i.   **THOMAS,** *b.* in 1718, *of whom presently.*
ii.   **ANN,** *b.* in 1720 ; *m.* **JOSEPH MARIS,** and settled at Springfield, Dela-
        ware Co., Pa.
iii.   **ELIZABETH,** *b.* in 1722 ; *m.*, April 12, 1744, **OLIVER CANBY,** of
        Brandywine, and *d.* November 16, 1789.

After his first wife's death **WILLIAM SHIPLEY** *m.*, second,
in 1728, **ELIZABETH,** *dau.* of **Samuel Levis,** of Springfield, Pa.
She was a very remarkable woman, and one of the most eminent
ministers of the Society of Friends in America. The novelist, Charles
Reade, has introduced her in his "Wandering Heir." Soon after her
marriage she had a dream, in which she supposed herself to be travelling, on horseback, with a guide, some distance from her home, through
a wild, unsettled region of country. Coming to the summit of a little
hill a beautiful landscape lay before her, and the guide told her that
she was to remove there with her husband, and they would become

the instruments of great benefits to the place and people. Several years afterward, travelling on a religious mission to the Friends on the peninsula between the Delaware and Chesapeake Bays, she passed through the little village of Willingtown. The road crossed a hill on the west of the town, and when she reached its summit, through a vista in the woods she saw the landscape of her dream. On her return home she persuaded her husband to visit the place, and his sagacious eye noting the capabilities of the situation, decided him to remove there, and become one of the most active agents in the growth of what is now the flourishing city of Wilmington, Del.

During the fall of 1777, in the darkest days of the American Revolution, Mrs. Shipley was confined to her bed with her last illness. One evening, a few friends being by her bedside, she desired her nurse to raise her up, and addressed the company on the existing state of public affairs and the general distress of the country, expressing strong sympathy with the Revolutionary party, and ending with this prophecy : " But I have seen, in the light of the Lord, that the invader of our land shall be driven back ; for the Arm that is mighty to save and able to deliver from the hand of the oppressor is stretched forth for the deliverance of this nation, which, I am firm in the faith, will secure its independence." Soon after uttering this prophecy she *d.*; her husband *d.* December 19, 1768. Issue :

i.　　**MARY,** *b.* in 1727 ; drowned, in attempting to cross the Brandywine River, in 1753.

ii.　　**SARAH,** *b.* in 1729 ; *m.,* December 6, 1750, **ROBERT RICHARD-SON,** and *d.* June 29, 1793.

iii.　　**WILLIAM,** *b.* in 1731 ; *m.,* December 27, 1753, **SARAH RUMFORD,** and *d.* November 19, 1794.

THOMAS, eldest son of **William** and **Mary (Tatnall) Shipley,** *b.* June 24, 1718, in Leicestershire, England, came to America with his parents in 1725. He did not remove to Wilmington until 1755, when he purchased, on the Brandywine River, the mill property erected some time before by Oliver Canby, and valuable water privileges which became the source of great wealth to his family. He built the famous old Shipley mill, and in 1762 associated Joseph Tatnall with him in the business. Eight years later the latter withdrew and formed a partnership with Thomas Lea, now represented in the Centenary Association of business firms by the William Lea & Sons Company (see

Centenary Associations, etc., *p.* 17). November 15, 1744, the meeting authorized his marriage to **MARY**, *dau.* of **Thomas** and **Martha (Kirkbride) Marriott** (*q. v.*), who was *b.* November 1, 1719, at Bristol, Pa., and *d.* February 21, 1771. Her husband *d.* November 1, 1789. Issue :

i.   **WILLIAM,** *b.* May 9, 1746 ; *d. u.* February 14, 1816.
ii. **SAMUEL,** *b.* August 30, 1747 ; *d. i.*
iii. **MARTHA,** *b.* October 2, 1748 ; *d.* February 6, 1748–49.
iv. **MARY,** *b.* September 2, 1750 ; *m.* **PHINEAS BUCKLEY** (*q. v.*).
v.   **THOMAS,** *b.* September 9, 1751 ; *d. i.*
vi. **JOSEPH,** *b.* November 11, 1752, *of whom presently.*
vii. **SARAH,** *b.* September 6, 1758 ; *m.*, in 1790, **CYRUS NEWLIN,** of
       Philadelphia, Pa., and *d.* in 1834. Issue (surname NEWLIN) :
   i.   **MARY.**
   ii. **THOMAS SHIPLEY,** *m.* **CATHARINE WHITE,** and *d.* February 8, 1879.
viii. **ANN,** *b.* January 29, 1758 ; *m.*, in 1792, **JOHN JONES,** and *d.* in 1808.
       Issue (surname JONES) :
   i.   **CYRUS.**
   ii. **LYDIA,** *m.* **THOMAS BYRNES** (*q. v.*).
ix. **ANNA,** *b.* August 22, 1760 ; *m.* **WILLIAM BYRNES,** and *d.* in
       1805. Issue :
       THOMAS, *m.* **LYDIA JONES** (*q. v.*).

JOSEPH, fourth son of **Thomas** and **Mary (Marriott) Shipley,**
b. November 11, 1752, inherited the mill property on the Brandywine, and pursued the business with probity and success. He
m. **MARY,** *dau.* of **Samuel Levis,** of Springfield, Pa., and *d.*
in 1832 ; his wife *d.* December 11, 1843. Issue :

i.   **SAMUEL,** *b.* February 12, 1777 ; engaged in the milling business with his
       father, and continued it until the failure of his health obliged him to
       retire. He *m.* **ELIZABETH,** *dau.* of **Captain James Jefferiss,**
       and *d.* in 1844. Issue :

       THOMAS and SARAH.

ii. **MARY,** *b.* December 27, 1778 ; *m.* **JOHN DIXON,** of Wilmington,
       and *d.* in 1844. Issue (surname DIXON) :

       JOSEPH, ISAAC, SAMUEL, THOMAS, MARY ANNA, and
       SARAH.

iii. **THOMAS,** *b.* September 30, 1780 ; engaged in the flour and shipping
       business in Philadelphia. On a visit to the south of France he was
       prostrated by a sunstroke, from which he never recovered, and *d.* in
       1813 of apoplexy.

iv. **JOHN,** *b.* December 25, 1782 ; engaged in the milling business with his
       father and brother, and *d. u.* August 1, 1863.

v.   **ANNA,** *b.* July 26, 1788 ; *d. u.* in 1852.
vi.   **ELIZABETH,** *b.* June 10, 1789 ; *d. u.* in July, 1865.
vii. **SARAH,** *b.* March 3, 1791 : *d. u.* August 27, 1872.
viii. **MARGARET,** *b.* December 18, 1793 ; *d. u.* in 1832.
ix.   **JOSEPH,** *b.* April 12, 1795, *of whom presently.*
x.   **HANNAH,** *b.* May 3, 1801 ; resided at the late residence of her brother **JOSEPH,** " Rockwood," in Brandywine Hundred.

JOSEPH, youngest son of **Joseph** and **Mary Shipley,** *b.* April 12, 1795 ; entered the counting-house of Samuel Canby in Philadelphia at the age of eighteen. In 1819 he went to England in the employ of John Welsh, of Philadelphia, father of the United States Minister to that country in 1878. While there he was offered a partnership by William Brown, of Liverpool, which he accepted, and the firm became that so well known under the name of Brown, Shipley & Company, of Liverpool and London. He continued in active business for thirty years, and was largely instrumental in the success of the firm, and in the building up of its reputation for ability and uprightness. His health failing, he withdrew from business, and in 1851 returned to his native State, and purchasing a large property in Brandywine Hundred, built a handsome mansion on it, to which he gave the name of " Rockwood." He *d. u.* May 9, 1867.

Authorities : Family papers, through Miss Hannah Shipley, and Benjamin Ferris's " Settlements on the Delaware."

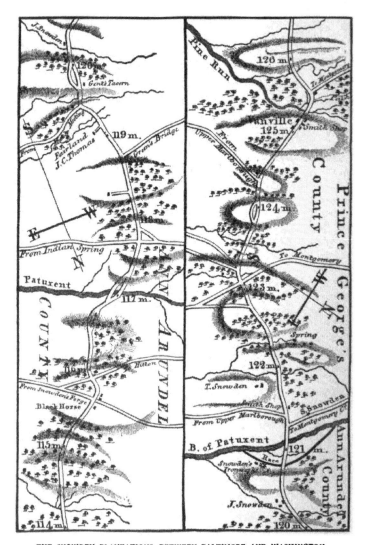

THE SNOWDEN PLANTATIONS, BETWEEN BALTIMORE AND WASHINGTON

From the Traveller's Directory, 1804

SNOWDEN, OF MARYLAND

There is no clear trace of this family in England or Wales, and but few notices of any bearing the name. I find only the following in the printed English State Papers : **Richard Snowden**, Merchant, is taken prisoner by the rebels in Ireland in July, 1529. **John Snowden**, who returned to England in 1591 (which he had left in 1582) was a priest, born in Worcester, a spy of Burleigh's, but would not "inform against a Catholic for religion but only for treason." "A mean fellow **Dr. Robert Snowden** made Bishop of Carlisle in 1616" (*d.* May 15, 1621). **George Snowden** of Ashe, Co. Kent, mentioned May 7, 1622. **Thomas Snowden** has a grant of an alms-room in S. Stephen's, Westminster, October 15, 1631. **Luke Snowden,** aged twenty-one years, having a certificate from the Minister of Gravesend, embarked in the Primrose for Virginia, July 27, 1635.[1] **Rutland Snoden,** Justice of the Peace, Co. Lincoln, June 30, 1686. Ditto, a delinquent, April 22, 1648 (see Seventh Report Historical MSS. Commission).

In the middle of the eighteenth century there was a Quaker family of the name at Gisborough, in Yorkshire, of whom **John Snowden** signs a testimonial of the meeting, March 28, 1754, and **Mary Snowden** *d.* in sixth month, 1745, in the fifty-seventh year

---

[1] See J. C. Hotten's Lists of Emigrants to America.

of her age.　**George Snowden** was a banker of Stockton-on-Tees, Durhamshire, in 1800.

Henry Snowden, of Talbot Co., Md., in his will[1] dated March 7, 1698–99, proved June 20, 1699, mentions his "Wife Elenor, sons William and Henry, daughters Rachel and Henrietta, Maria and child his wife was now pregnant with."

RICHARD SNOWDEN, of Wales, said to have held a major's commission under Oliver Cromwell, came to Maryland in the seventeenth century.　His son, **RICHARD SNOWDEN**, Sr., is mentioned as a well-known owner of land near South River, Md., in a deed dated October 13, 1679.　At Treadhaven, West River, meeting, October 8, 1684, the Friends appointed to visit him report "that he disownes friends' practices, and that he denyes friends before they deny him, and abuses several friends and said yt he had not lately been at a meeting at John Lynam's and that John Lynam[2] and his company were honest people and that they lived in the fear of God & friends had done them honest people wrong."　August 1, 1686, a tract of land containing 10,500 acres was patented to him. October 13, 1688, William Parker deeded him certain land for £306. April 12, 1704, he presented to the West River meeting a paper of condemnation "of the spirit that led him to accept the office of Captain."[3]　May 20, 1711, he was buried, leaving a son, RICHARD, Jr., *of whom presently.*

RICHARD SNOWDEN, Jr., was one of the Quakers who sympathised with the rebel, Richard Clarke, for November 5, 1707, he brought to Herring Creek quarterly meeting a paper on his giving the government occasion against him on that account.　He *m.*, before 1690, **MARY ——**, and both were living December 19, 1717, when they signed their son's certificate of marriage.

This son, **RICHARD SNOWDEN,** "the youngest," as he is called in his marriage certificate, was *b.* about 1690, and early in life began to take an active interest in affairs.　His father probably was the builder of Birmingham Manor-house in 1690, destroyed by fire August 20, 1891 ; but the son added very largely to the lands of the Manor, ten thousand acres and over being patented to him in 1719, and at his death it included the plantations now known as Birmingham, Snowden Hall, Fairland, Montpelier, Oakland, Snow Hill, Avon-

---

[1] Liber H, folio 267.　The first Snowden will on record, at Annapolis, Md.

[2] He was disciplined for comparing the meeting to a jury, and its head to the foreman, and refusing to retract his statement.

[3] In the provincial forces from 1700 to 1703.　*Vide* Thomas's Gen. Notes, II., for facsimile.

dale, Woodland Hill, Alnwick, Elmwood, Brightwood, and Maple Grove, and part, if not all, of the town of Laurel. Before 1736 he engaged in the manufacture of iron, September 29th of that year land being patented to the " Patuxent Iron Work Company," in which were partners " Richard Snowden, owning 11–16, Edmund Jennings, of Annapolis, owning 2–16, and John Galloway and Joseph Cowman, of Annarrundel, and John Pritchard, mariner, then of London, each owning 1–16."

This business Richard Snowden continued until his death, at which time it appears by his will [1] he was sole owner of the works, and was engaged in building a new forge. These iron works were among the first ever operated in Maryland. It has been noted that " Birmingham Manor-house was preserved through all the generations owning it without modernizing or destroying its antique elegance. The site was commanding. The grounds were extensive and the approaches impressive. The house was built in the old English style of bricks to the second story, where shingles formed sidewalls with a leaning toward the roof. There were recessed windows to the second story. There was a porch in front, through which the massive front door was reached, and the door opened into a quaint hall. There were large old-fashioned fireplaces in the rooms and in the hall, and the house was a most interesting souvenir of colonial days. The house had near it a terrace and a quaint old garden, edged with immense borders of box, and a family burial-ground is on the place."

RICHARD SNOWDEN *m.*, first, May 19, 1709, **ELIZA**, *dau.* of **William** and **Eliza (Sparrow) Coale** (*q. v.*). Issue :

i.   **DEBORAH**, *m.* **JAMES BROOKE** (*q. v.*).
ii. **ELIZA**, *m.* **JOHN THOMAS** (*q. v.*).
iii. **MARY**, *b.* in 1712 ; *m.* **SAMUEL THOMAS** (*q. v.*).

MRS. ELIZA (COALE) SNOWDEN *d.* about 1713, and her husband *m.*, second, December 19, 1717, **ELIZABETH**, *dau.* of **Samuel** and **Mary (Hutchins) Thomas** (*q. v.*). Issue by her (who *d.* in 1775) : [2]

iv. **RICHARD**, *b.* in 1719-20 ; *m.*, before October 31, 1748, **ELIZABETH**, only *dau.* of **John**,[3] and **Miriam Crowley**, or **Croley**, of Prince George's Co., Md., and *d. s. p.* March 18, 1753 (will proved April 11, 1753. Liber D D, No. 7).

[1] Proved March 12, 1763. Liber D D, No. 1, folio 1011.
[2] Will proved August 9, 1775. Liber W F, No. 1, folio 407.
[3] His will recorded, Liber D D, No. 5, folio 100.

v.   **THOMAS,** *of whom presently.*

vi.   **ANN,** *m.* **HENRY WRIGHT CRABB.**   Issue (surname CRABB):

    i.   **RICHARD.**
    ii.   **ELIZABETH,** *m.,* March 29, 1771, **WILLIAM,** son of Samuel Robertson.
    iii.   **JEREMIAH,** *m.* **ELIZABETH GRIFFITH.**
    iv.   **RALPH.**
    v.   **JOHN.**

vii.   **MARGARET,** *m.* **JOHN CONTEE,** and had issue (surname CONTEE)

    i.   **ELIZABETH,** *m.* **JAMES KEITH.**
    ii.   **JEAN.**
    iii.   **RICHARD,** *m.* **ELIZABETH SANDERS.**
    iv.   **ANN,** *m.* **DENIS MAGRUDER.**

viii.   **SAMUEL,** *b.* in 1728 (*q. v.*).
ix.   **ELIZABETH,** *m.* **JOSEPH COWMAN** (*q. v.*).
x.   **JOHN** (*q. v.*).

THOMAS, eldest surviving son of **Richard** and **Elizabeth (Thomas) Snowden,** *b.* about 1722; resided in Prince Georges Co.; *m.*, before 1744,[1] **MARY,** *dau.* of **Henry Wright.** Henry Wright was *b.* in England, and sent to America when a boy. An annuity was regularly paid to the gentleman who had charge of his education, and after his death to Henry himself. At his marriage he received a handsome service of silver marked with the letter W., and soon after this event the annuity ceased. Once previously he attempted to discover his parentage, but immediately received a letter through the channel by which his annuity came, notifying him that it would cease unless he desisted from his attempt. He *m.* **ELIZABETH,** *dau.* of **Colonel Edward Sprigg,** member of the House of Delegates for Prince Georges Co., January 25, 1739, and *d.* 1750–52, leaving two *daus.,* Margaret, unmarried, and Mary, who *m.* Thomas Snowden. The latter *d.* in 1770.[2] Issue:

i.   **HENRY,** *d. s. p.* (will proved April 22, 1775. Liber W F, No. 1, folio 260).
ii.   **RICHARD,** *m.* **ELIZA,** *dau.* of **Thomas** and **Ann Rutland** (*q. v.*), who *m.*, second, —— **ORME,**[3] and *d.* in 1775; her first husband *d.*, leaving an only *dau.,* **MARY,** *b.* August 28, 1770, who was left an orphan at an early age by the death of her mother, and was brought up at her uncle, Major Thomas Snowden's residence, "Montpelier." She *m.* JOHN CHEW THOMAS (*q. v.*).

[1] Will made February 22, 1744, proved October 31, 1750.   Liber D D, No. 6, folio 379.
[2] Will proved May 24, 1770.   Liber W D, No. 3, folio 2.
[3] See Harris & Johnson, Maryland Chancery Reports, iv., 271.

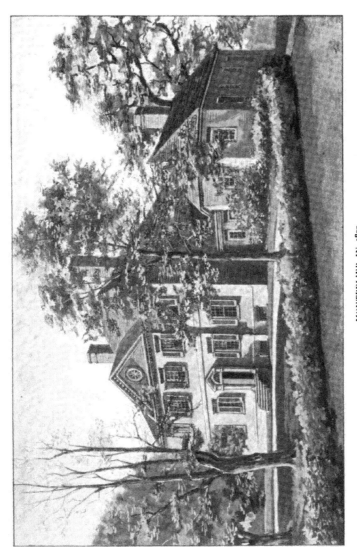

MONTPELIER IN 1800

RESIDENCE OF MAJOR THOMAS SNOWDEN

iii.   **THOMAS,** *b.* in 1751, was a Captain in the Revolutionary army and commissioned, March 18, 1776, Second Major of the Twenty fifth Battalion of Militia, Prince Georges Co. In November, 1774, was a County Commissioner to enforce the "association" of the Continental Congress. He lived at "Montpelier," which was on the great Northern and Southern Post-road, and entertained great numbers of people who were then continually passing upon it, and, in accordance with the hospitable customs of the day, would not hesitate to stop at his residence for the night. Washington himself once spent a night there, and the bed in which he slept is still preserved. **MAJOR SNOWDEN** *m.* **ANN,** *dau.* of **Colonel Henry**[1] and **Anne (Dorsey) Ridgely,** a great heiress, and *d.* in 1803; his wife *d.* on Good Friday of 1834. Issue:

    i.   **RICHARD,** *of whom presently.*
    ii.   **THOMAS,** lived at Summerville, and *d. n.*
    iii.   **MARY,** *m.,* at "Montpelier," **JOHN C. HERBERT,** of Walnut Grange, Va. (*q. v.*).
    iv.   **NICHOLAS,** *b.* October 21, 1786 (*q. v.*).
    v.   **CAROLINE,** *d.* at the age of eight years.

RICHARD, eldest son of **Major Thomas** and **Ann (Ridgely) Snowden,** who inherited from his parents the estate of "Oakland," *m.,* first, February 13, 1798, at "Bushy Park," **ELIZA,** *dau.* of **Dr. Charles Alexander** and **Eliza (Ridgely) Warfield** (*q. v.*), and was secondly *m.,* May 18, 1818, by Rev. Oliver Norris, to **LOUISA VICTORIA WARFIELD** (*d.* July 30, 1820), sister of his first wife, who *d. s. p.* He *d.* September 3, 1823. Issue, by his first wife, who *d.* July 26, 1817:

i.   **ANN LOUISA,** *b.* August, 1800; *m.* **JOHN CONTEE,** who *d.,* having had issue eight daughters, who were dead in 1879, and two sons (surname CONTEE).

    i.   **CHARLES SNOWDEN,** *m.* **BETTY BOLLING.**
    ii.   **RICHARD,** *m.* **ANNA BOLLING.**

ii.   **THOMAS,** *b.* March 7, 1802, *m.,* November 30, 1824, **ANN REBECCA NICHOLLS.** Issue:

    i.   **NICHOLAS,** *d.*
    ii.   **CHARLES A.**
    iii.   **ELLA,** *m.* **DR. A. M. SNOWDEN** (*q. v.*).
    iv.   **JONATHAN HUDSON,** *d.*
    v.   **THOMAS,** *d.*

[1] On May 20, 1776, he has a long petition to the Council of Safety from Elkridge, Ann Arundel Co., protesting against being compelled to serve in the militia, which very well exhibits the self-seeking spirit of "the patriots." He says that he commanded a company of rangers on the western border after Braddock's defeat in 1755; afterward commanded the Elkridge Troop of Horse; was Major of the Co. in 1761, Lieutenant-Colonel in 1773; formed a company there in 1774; did the same in the neighbourhood of Thomas Dorsey in 1776, declining the command of both; thinks he might be excused.

vi.   **SARAH REBECCA.** *m.* **COLONEL CHARLES MARSHALL** (*q. v.*).
vii. **CAROLINE.**

iii. **CHARLES ALEXANDER,** *b.* April 6, 1805 ; *d.* at " Oakland," in 1823.

iv.   **CAROLINE ELIZA,** *b.* April 21, 1807, *m.*, April 8, 1828, the **HON. ALBERT FAIRFAX** (*q. v.*).

v.   **EMILY ROSEVILLE,** *b.* April 21, 1807 ; *m.*, October 21, 1828, **COLONEL TIMOTHY P. ANDREWS,** U. S. A. (*q. v.*).

vi.   **HARRIET,** *d. i.*

vii. **RICHARD NICHOLAS,** *b.* at " Oakland," July 19, 1815 ; *m.*, at " Longwood," January 1, 1835, **ELIZABETH RIDGELY,** *dau.* of Dr. **Gustavus Warfield** (*q. v.*), and *d.* in California. Issue ·

  i.   **GUSTAVUS WARFIELD,** *b.* July 27, 1836.
  ii.   **RICHARD,** *b.* October 13, 1837.
  iii. **GEORGE THOMAS,** *b.* August 29, 1840.
  iv.   **EVAN WARFIELD,** *b.* November 5, 1842.
  v.   **MARY THOMAS,** *b.* October 30, 1844.
  vi.   **ELIZABETH WARFIELD,** *b.* September 1, 1849 ; *m.*, April 11, 1872, **WILLIAM J. DORSEY,** of Howard Co., Md. Issue (surname DORSEY) :

    i.   Mary Thomas, *b.* February 20, 1873.
    ii. Louisa Victoria, *b.* June 2, 1876.

NICHOLAS, third son of **Major Thomas** and **Ann (Ridgely) Snowden,** *b.* at " Montpelier," October 21, 1786 ; *m.*, at Roxbury Mills, October 7, 1806, **ELIZABETH WARFIELD,** *dau.* of **Samuel** and **Anna Thomas** (*q. v.*), and *d.* March 8, 1831, at " Montpelier." His wife *d.* at Avondale, June 16, 1866. Issue :

i.   **ANN ELIZABETH,** *b.* at Roxbury Mills, July 31, 1808 ; *m.*, first, at " Montpelier," September 23, 1828, **FRANCIS M. HALL.** Issue (surname HALL) :

  i.   **FRANCIS,** *b.* in August, 1829 ; *m.* **EUGENIA CONTEE.**
  ii. **ELIZABETH SNOWDEN,** *b.* January 28, 1831 ; *m.* **RICHARD HILL.**

    MR. HALL *d.* at Collington Meadows, September 3, 1831, and his widow *m.*, at " Montpelier," October 4, 1836, **CHARLES HILL,** and *d.* July 15, 1847. Further issue (surname HILL) :

  iii. **LAURA BROOKE,** *b.* in August, 1837.
  iv.   **NICHOLAS,** *b.* in 1839.
  v.   **EUGENE,** *b.* in February, 1841.
  vi.   **AUGUSTINE,** *b.* in August, 1842 ; *d.* in 1866.
  vii. **NORMAN,** *b.* in 1847.

ii.   **THOMAS J.,** *b.* at Roxbury, February 12, 1810 ; *d.* at Magnolia, Fla., July 3, 1835.

iii. **LOUISA,** *b.* at " Montpelier," June 3, 1811 ; *m.* there, June 5, 1834, **COLONEL HORACE CAPRON,** and *d.* at Laurel, March 27, 1859. Issue (surname CAPRON) :

i. **NICHOLAS SNOWDEN.**
ii. **HORACE.**
iii. **ADELINE.**
iv. **ALBERT B.**, *m.*, October 20, 1869, **AMELIA DOOLITTLE.** Issue:

    i. **Horace**, *b.* August 27, 1872.
    ii. **Florence**, *b.* November 18, 1873.
    iii. **Albert**, *b.* February 8, 1877.

v. **ELIZABETH SNOWDEN**, *m.* **GEORGE G. MAYO**, of Peoria, Ill. Issue (surname MAYO):

    Two boys, *d. y.*; **Mary, Louisa**, and **Adeline.**

v. **JULIANNA MARIA**, *b.* at Laurel, January 28, 1813; *m.*, at "Montpelier," June 23, 1835, **DR. THEODORE JENKINS**; he *d.* at the same place December 15, 1866. Issue:

i. **THEODORE**, *b.* April 19, 1838; killed at the Battle of Cedar Mountain, August 9, 1862.
ii. **ELIZABETH SNOWDEN.**
iii. **LOUIS WILLIAM**, *b.* June 16, 1842.
iv. **FRANCIS XAVIER**, *b.* September 29, 1844.
v. **MARY ELIZA**, *b.* November 5, 1846.
vi. **ANN LOUISA**, *d.* in childhood.
vii. **ARTHUR**, *b.* in 1852.

v. **ADELINE**, *b.* at Laurel, October 9, 1814; *m.*, September 1, 1836, **WALTER WILLIAM WEEMS BOWIE**, and *d.* at Eglington, January 8, 1865. Issue (surname BOWIE):

i. **WALTER**, *b.* June 25, 1837; a Captain in Mosby's Guerillas during the civil war; killed on a raid in Maryland, October 6, 1864.
ii. **NICHOLAS DE WILTON**, *b.* January 27, 1839; *d.* May 15, 1845.
iii. **THOMAS RICHARD**, *b.* November 23, 1840; drowned June 20, 1853, trying in vain to rescue two of his companions.
iv. **ELIZABETH**, *b.* October 25, 1842; *d.* April 30, 1845.
v. **HENRY BRUNE**, *b.* January 26, 1845; fought on the side of the Confederacy during the civil war; *m.*, November 4, 1872, **FLORENCE REESE**.
vi. **ROBERT**, *b.* December 22, 1852; *m.*, in June, 1873, **ALICE EARL**'.
vii. **AMELIA.**
viii. **MARY**, *m.*, in October, 1870, **THOMAS FRANKLIN**, C. E.
ix. **ADA**, *m.*, November 24, 1874, **PROFESSOR B. MAURICE.**
x. **REGINALD.**
xi. **EMILY**, who *d. i.*

vi. **EDWARD**, *b.* at Laurel, October 29, 1816; *m.*, June 29, 1841, at "Longwood," **MARY THOMAS**, *dau.* of **Dr. Gustavus Warfield** (*q.v.*), and *d. s. p.* June 21, 1890.

vii. **DR. DE WILTON**, *b.* August 19, 1818, *of whom presently.*

viii. **HENRY**, *b.* September 29, 1820, at Laurel; *m.*, first, April 27, 1847, at Alexandria, Va., **MARY C. COWMAN**, who *d. s. p.*; *m.*, second, December 12, 1878, **M. VICTORIA BIRKEY**, and *d.* January 16, 1894. Issue:

LAWRENCE WILMER, *b.* October 22, 1880.

ix. **ELIZA**, *b.* April 8, 1822, at Laurel; entered the Georgetown Convent in 1847.

x.   **EMILY ROSEVILLE**, *b.* June 24, 1824, at "Montpelier;" *m.*, April 29, 1845, at Avondale, **CHARLES C. HILL.** Issue (surname HILL):

    i. ii.   **ANN ELIZABETH** and **CHARLES**, twins; ANN *d.* July 15, 1847.
    iii.   **IDA.**
    iv.   **EDWARD.**
    v.   **FRANCIS SNOWDEN.**
    vi.   **EMILY ROSEVILLE.**
    vii.   **EDITH.**
    viii.   **ALBERT.**

xi.   **NICHOLAS**, *b.* April 7, 1828, at "Montpelier;" *m.*, May 28, 1850, at Philadelphia, **HENRIETTA**, *dau.* of William Henry and Eliza (Thomas) Stabler, and *d.*, near Harrisonburg, Va., June 6, 1862. Issue:

    i.   **EMILY ROSEVILLE**, *b.* April 7, 1851; *m.* GERARD HOPKINS (*q. v.*).
    ii.   **MARION**, *b.* June 28, 1853; *d.* January 7, 1857.
    iii.   **LUCY**, *b.* March 13, 1855.
    iv.   **HELEN**, *b.* April 7, 1857.
    v.   **FRANCIS**, *b.* March 19, 1859.
    vi.   **MARY**, *b.* June 3, 1861; *m.*, November 17, 1886, **CHARLES D. WARFIELD** (*q. r.*).

xii.   **DR. ARTHUR MONTEITH**, *b.* December 30, 1830, at "Montpelier;" *m.*, May 19, 1867, at Laurel, **ELLA**, *dau.* of Thomas and Ann Rebecca (Nicholls) Snowden (*q. v.*). She *d.* in Greenbrier Co., Va., April 11, 1858, and her husband *m.*, secondly, June 5, 1866, **MARY VAUX**, of Northumberland Co., Va. He was a Surgeon in the Confederate States Army, and falling overboard from the steamer Wenonah, on the Chesapeake Bay, was drowned, August 28, 1869.

DR. DE WILTON, seventh child of Nicholas and Elizabeth (Warfield) Snowden, *b.* August 19, 1818, at Laurel; *m.*, March 8, 1839, at Easton, Md., EMMA C. CAPRON, who *d.* April 30, 1878. Issue:

i.   **NICHOLAS**, *b.* February 20, 1842, at Avondale; *d.* in September, 1849, at Upper Marlboro.

ii.   **JOHN C.**, *b.* June 29, 1843, at Bacon Hall; *m.*, October 24, 1867, **MARIA GRIFFITH.**

iii.   **ELIZABETH THOMAS**, *b.* June 22, 1844, at Avondale; *d.* April 29, 1845, at Laurel.

iv.   **HENRY**, *b.* June 17, 1846, at Laurel; *d.* August 29, 1846, at Laurel.

v.   **DE WILTON BOWIE**, *b.* June 12, 1848, in Chesterfield Co., Va.; *m.*, July 30, 1873, **ALMIRA HEATH**, and had one child, **STANLEY HEATH**, *b.* July 28, 1875; *d.* in July, 1877.

vi.   **ELIZABETH**, *b.* March 29, 1851, at Upper Marlboro, and *d.* there October 29, 1855.

vii.   **ARTHUR**, *b.* July 8, 1853, at Upper Marlboro, and *d.* there July 28, 1853.

viii.   **AMELIA CHEW**, *b.* May 7, 1855, at Laurel.

ix.   **ADELINE,** *b.* May 28, 1858, at Washington, D. C. ; *d. i.*

x.   **MARY THOMAS,** *b.* August 11, 1860, at Washington, D. C.

SAMUEL, third son of **Richard** and **Elizabeth (Thomas) Snowden,** *b.* November 2, 1728 ; in November, 1774, was member of the Prince Georges Co. Committee to carry into execution the association of the Continental Congress. He *m.* **ELIZABETH,** *dau.* of **Philip** and **Ann (Chew) Thomas** (*q. v.*), and *d.* June 27, 1801 ; his wife had *d.* January 30, 1790. Issue :

i.   **RICHARD,** *m.,* August 2, 1782, **HANNAH MOORE,** *dau.* of William and Rachel (Orrick) Hopkins (*q. v.*).

ii.   **ANN,** *m.* **RICHARD HOPKINS** (*q. v.*).

iii.   **ELIZABETH,** *b.* in 1758 ; *d.* August 25, 1793.

iv.   **PHILIP,** *of whom presently.*

v.   **MARY,** *m.* **JOSEPH COWMAN** (*q. v.*).

vi.   **SAMUEL,** *b.* in 1766 (*q. v.*).

vii.   **HENRIETTA,** *m.,* October 14, 1804, **GERARD HOPKINS** (*q. v.*).

viii.   **SARAH,** *m.* **ELISHA HOPKINS** (*q. v.*).

ix.   **JOHN,** *b.* in 1774 ; *d.* January 26, 1790.

PHILIP, second son of **Samuel** and **Elizabeth (Thomas) Snowden,** *m.,* December 1, 1791, **PATIENCE,** *dau.* of **Joseph Hopkins** (*q. v.*) ; she *d.* October 16, 1822. Issue :

i.   **ELIZABETH,** *b.* October 8, 1792 ; *d.* November 7, 1795.

ii   **SAMUEL,** *b.* January 13, 1794, *of whom presently.*

iii.   **MARY ANN,** *b.* May 28, 1796 ; *m.* —— **HUSBANDS,** and *d.* August 10, 1824.

iv.   **JOSEPH HOPKINS,** *b.* April 26, 1798 ; *d.* October 14, 1801.

v.   **RICHARD,** *b.* March 19, 1800 (*q. v.*).

vi.   **ELIZABETH,** second, *b.* May 13, 1802 ; *d.* April 24, 1804.

vii.   **PHILIP THOMAS,** *b.* June 26, 1803.

viii.   **CAROLINE,** *b.* January 4, 1807.

ix.   **JOHN P.,** *b.* February 25, 1809 ; *d.* August 20, 1819.

x.   **JAMES,** *b.* October 6, 1811.

xi.   **ISAAC,** *b.* September 9, 1813.

xii.   **WILLIAM,** *b.* May 20, 1815.

SAMUEL, eldest son of **Philip** and **Patience (Hopkins) Snowden,** *b.* January 13, 1794 ; *m.,* January 18, 1822, **MARY RICHARDSON.** Issue :

i.   **JOHN THOMAS,** *b.* December 21, 1822 ; *m.,* November 16, 1847, **MARIA L. SCHWRAR.** Issue :

i.   ERNEST, *b.* in August, 1848 ; *d.* in November, 1849.
ii.   SAMUEL GEORGE, *b.* June 27, 1850 ; *m.,* December 26, 1877, **MRS. MELINDA W. HOLMES.**
iii.   WILTON, *b.* June 5, 1852.
iv.   MARY R., *b.* in March, 1855.
v.   EVERETT, *b.* in December, 1856.
vi.   CLARA, *b.* in July, 1858.
vii. JOHN THOMAS, *b.* in November, 1860 ; *d. i.*
viii. PHILIP LEE, *b.* in January, 1863.
ix.   HOWELL, *b.* in July, 1865.
x.   MARIE LOUISE, *b.* in May, 1869.

ii.   **MARCELLUS P.,** *b.* June 16, 1824.
iii.   **RICHARD HOPKINS,** *b.* November 19, 1827 ; *m.,* January 18, 1853. **MARTHA SELLS** and *d.* December 15, 1877. Issue :

> i.   WILBUR LEE, *b.* December 7, 1854 ; *m.,* March 16, 1875, **MARY REILLY.** Issue :
>
> > i.   Francis Reilly, *b.* October 4, 1876.
> > ii. Mattie Sells, *b.* June 26, 1877 ; *d.* August 19, 1878.
>
> ii. ANNIE RICHARDSON, *b.* May 25, 1856 ; *m.,* April 4, 1877, **CHARLES M. LANAHAN.** Issue (surname LANAHAN) :
>
> > Mary Sells, *b.* June 4, 1878.
>
> iii. KATE, *b.* December 27, 1857.
> iv. v. HARRIS and LOUIS, *b.* September 16, 1860.
> vi. RICHARD HOPKINS, *b.* May 8, 1864.
> vii. RAY COOPER, *b.* July 16, 1870.

iv.   **PHILIP M.,** *b.* June 14, 1831 ; prominent politician of Baltimore, and, in 1879, Sheriff of the city. He *m.,* November 18, 1851, **SALLIE E. KNIGHTON.** Issue :

> i.   FLORENCE MAY, *b.* October 22, 1856.
> ii. ELLA, *b.* in October, 1859.

v.   **SAMUEL,** *b.* October 13, 1833, Attorney-at-Law in Baltimore ; *m.,* May 14, 1863, **S. EMMA HOFF,** and *d.* November 9, 1894. Issue :

> i.   CORINNE ADELINE, *b.* in March, 1864.
> ii. MARY IDA, *b.* in June, 1865.
> iii. SAMUEL GUY, *b.* in September, 1868.
> iv. MARGARET ELIZABETH, *b.* in August, 1875.

RICHARD, third son of **Philip** and **Patience (Hopkins) Snowden,** *b.* March 19, 1800 ; *m.,* June 17, 1829, **MARY,** *dau.* of **Isaac** and **Letitia West,** of Sandy Spring. Issue :

i.   SARAH AMANDA, *b.* December 11, 1829.
ii.   ELLEN JANE, *b.* August 19, 1831.
iii. HENRY ALLEN, *b.* August 9, 1833.
iv. CHARLES EDWARD, *b.* October 19, 1836.

SAMUEL, third son of **Samuel** and **Elizabeth (Thomas) Snowden,** *b.* in 1766 ; *m.,* December 1, 1796, **ELIZABETH,** *dau.* of **John Cowman** (*q. v.*), and *d.* May 26, 1823. Issue :

i. ii.   **SAMUEL** and **ELIZABETH**, twins, *b.* October 27, 1797; Samuel *d.* June 29, 1798.
iii.   **JOHN**, *b.* January 25, 1799; *d.* September 19, 1826.
iv.   **SAMUEL**, *b.* September 13, 1800; *d. s. p.*
v.   **RICHARD**, *b.* July 26, 1802; *d.* March 26, 1813.
vi.   **MARY**, *b.* March 2, 1804; *m.* **THOMAS TYSON** (*q. v.*).
vii.   **MARTHA**, *b.* June 28, 1810; *d.* September 1, 1836.
viii. ix.   **REBECCA** and **JOSEPH**, twins, *b.* December 17, 1814.

JOHN, youngest son of **Richard** and **Elizabeth (Thomas) Snowden**, inherited "Birmingham Manor;" *m.*, at the age of forty, **RACHEL**, *dau.* of **Richard Hopkins** (*q. v.*). Issue:

i.   **RICHARD PHILIP**, *d. u.*
ii.   **ANNA MARIA**, *b.* in 1787; *m.* **JOSEPH R. HOPKINS** and *d.* March 27, 1864.
iii.   **GERARD HOPKINS**, *b.* April 27, 1788; *m.*, and had an only son, **JOHN**, *b.* November 11, 1827; *d.* July 7, 1828.
iv.   **JOHN T.**, *d. u.*, January 13, 1813.
v.   **MARGARET**, *m.* —— **HOPKINS**.
vi.   **REZIN HAMMOND**, *b.* September 8, 1796, *of whom presently.*
vii.   **RACHEL**, *m.* **JUDGE JOHN S. TYSON** (*q. v.*).

REZIN HAMMOND, youngest son of **John** and **Rachel (Hopkins) Snowden**, *b.* September 8, 1796; inherited "Birmingham Manor;" *m.*, November 24, 1829, **MARGARET**, *dau.* of **John McFadon**, who *d.* July 30, 1858; and her husband *d.* July 23, 1866. Issue:

i.   **JOHN**, *b.* November 24, 1830, *of whom presently.*
ii.   **WILLIAM**, *b.* April 1, 1833 (*q. v.*).
iii.   **RICHARD PHILIP**, *b.* November 13, 1834; *d.* November 23, 1863.
iv.   **ANTOINETTE**, *b.* November 2, 1836.
v.   **JULIUS**, *b.* May 16, 1838; *d.* at Upperville, Va., December 11, 1855.
vi.   **HARRY WILSON**, *b.* April 12, 1841; *m.*, September 7, 1865, **SOPHIA**, *dau.* of **Rev. T. B. Sargeant**. Issue:

    ACHSAH, *b.* March 25, 1869; *d.* March 29, 1869.

vii.   **MARIA LOUISA**, *b.* June 9, 1843; *m.*, June 30, 1869, **PROFESSOR ALFRED M. MAYER**, the distinguished scientist. Issue:

  i.   **BRANTZ**, *b.* June 1, 1870; *d.* December 22, 1874.
  ii.   **JOSEPH HENRY**, *b.* January 12, 1872.

JOHN, eldest son of **Rezin H.** and **Margaret (McFadon) Snowden**, *b.* November 24, 1830; resided at "Snowden Hall," Prince Georges Co., Md.; *m.*, June 16, 1857, **SARAH E.**, *dau.* of **Basil Hopkins**, and *d.* August 16, 1872. Issue:

i.   **MARGARET**, *b.* May 21, 1858.
ii. **JOHN**, *b.* January 17, 1860.
iii. **ELIZABETH HOPKINS**, *b.* May 8, 1861 ; *d.* December 25, 1894.
iv. **BASIL HOPKINS**, *b.* January 14, 1863.
v.   **HARRY FENWICK**, *b.* August 30, 1865 ; *d.* December 6, 1865.
vi. **HERBERT**, *b.* July 3, 1868.
vii. **SARAH ENGLISH**, *b.* June 28, 1870 ; *d.* September 1, 1870.
viii. **VIRGINIA HOPKINS**, *b.* November 20, 1871 ; *d.* July 8, 1872.

WILLIAM, second son of **Rezin H.** and **Margaret (McFadon) Snowden**, *b.* April 1, 1833 ; inherited " Birmingham Manor," and resided there. He *m.*, April 29, 1857, **ADELAIDE**, *dau.* of **Dr. Gustavus Warfield** (*q. v.*).   Issue :

i.   **REZIN HAMMOND**, *b.* May 31, 1858 ; *d.* November 9, 1863.
ii. **MARY THOMAS**, *b.* June 27, 1860 ; *d.* November 10, 1863.
iii. **GUSTAVUS WARFIELD**, *b.* March 4, 1862 ; *d.* May 3, 1870.
iv. **JULIUS**, *b.* October 23, 1863.
v.   **WILLIAM**, *b.* April 18, 1866 ; *d.* August 3, 1866.
vi. **LOUISA VICTORIA**, *b.* March 13, 1868 ; *m.*, April 29, 1895, **GEORGE CROSBY DE LANNOY**.
vii. **MARIA ANTOINETTE**, *b.* June 3, 1870.
viii. **ADELAIDE WARFIELD**, *b.* June 24, 1872 ; *m.*, December 12, 1894, **GEORGE ADDISON COOKE HODGES**.
ix. **SOPHIE CARROLL**, *b.* February 24, 1875.
x.   **EUGENIA**, *b.* August 24, 1877 ; *d.* January 13, 1881.

Authorities : Friends' Records and family papers, through Mrs. Edward Snowden and others.

STABLER

WILLIAM STABLER, *b.* in 1767; *m.,* June 4, 1789, **DEBO-RAH PLEASANTS,** and *d.* January 24, 1806. Issue:

i. **THOMAS PLEASANTS,** *b.* November 5, 1791, *of whom presently.*
ii. **EDWARD,** *b.* September 26, 1794 (*q. v.*).
iii. **JAMES P.,** *b.* September 14, 1796 (*q. v*).
iv. **CALEB BENTLEY,** *b.* January 24, 1799 (*q. v.*).
v. **WILLIAM HENRY,** *b.* April 13, 1802; *m.* **ELIZA,** second *dau.* of **William** and **Martha (Patrick) Thomas** (*q. v.*), who *d.* 1884; her husband *d.* 1883. Issue:

    i. **MARTHA,** *b.* February 9, 1826; *m.* **THOMAS MOORE REESE** (*q. v.*).
    ii. **JOSEPH,** *b.* January 24, 1827.
    iii. **HENRIETTA,** *b.* January 27, 1829; *m.* **NICHOLAS SNOWDEN** (*q. v.*).
    iv. **LUCY,** *b.* September 11, 1830.
    v. **WILLIAM,** *b.* March 16, 1832.
    vi. **ELLEN,** *b.* February 16, 1834.

THOMAS PLEASANTS, eldest son of **William** and **Deborah Stabler,** *b.* November 5, 1791; *m.,* June 2, 1813, **ELIZA-BETH P.,** youngest child of **Gerard** and **Margaret (Thomas) Brooke** (*q. v.*). Issue:

i. **BROOKE,** *b.* April 25, 1814.
ii. **SARAH,** *b.* January 31, 1816; *m.* **AUGUSTUS JORDAN,** of Norfolk, Va. Issue (surname JORDAN):

    i. **THOMAS,** *d. y.*
    ii. **MARCUS.**
    iii. **ELIZABETH.**

iii. **GEORGE,** *b.* May 18, 1818; *m.,* November 22, 1843, **MARY W.,** *dau.* of **Phineas** and **Rachel Paxson**; both deceased. Issue:

    i. **ELIZA W.,** *b.* September 17, 1847; *d.* before 1878.
    ii. **WILLIAM,** *b.* August 20, 1849; *d.* before 1878.

iv. **JOHN,** *b.* April 13, 1820; *m.,* May 8, 1851, **ALICE ANN,** *dau.* of **Joseph E. Bentley.** Issue:

    i. **FLORENCE,** *b.* June 24, 1852.
    ii. **ALICE EVELYN,** *b.* August 14, 1854.

   iii.   **CORA,** *b.* October 6, 1856.
   iv.   **ANNA B.,** *b.* February 24, 1859.
   v.   **FANNIE,** *b.* October 15, 1860.
   vi.   **ELIZA BROOKE,** *b.* May 15, 1863.
   vii.   **JOHN,** Jr., *b.* November 15, 1865.
   viii.   **ALICE BENTLEY,** *b.* January 8, 1868.

v.   **DEBORAH,** *b.* April 7, 1822.

vi.   **JAMES,** *b.* May 30, 1827 ; *m.*, February 28, 1865, **PHEBE A. RUS-SELL,** of Frederick Co., Md.

vii.   **HOWARD,** *b.* August 5, 1829 ; *m.*, November 25, 1858, **ESTHER G.,** *dau.* of **James** and **Esther G. Moore,** and *d.* July 18, 1876. Issue :

   i.   **MILTON,** *b.* August 21, 1859.
   ii.   **CLARA,** *b.* November 1, 1861.
   iii.   **LEONARD,** *b.* August 17, 1863.
   iv.   **AUGUSTUS,** *b.* September 18, 1865.
   v.   **LOUIS H.,** *b.* May 18, 1868.
   vi.   **LILIAN,** *b.* August 26, 1872.

viii.   **WILLIAM,** *b.* July 11, 1831 ; *d.* November 19, 1832.

ix.   **WILLIAM HENRY,** *b.* May 6, 1833.

x.   **DEBORAH,** *b.* June 27, 1836 ; *m.*, November 22, 1864, **SAMUEL M. RUSSELL,** of Burt Creek, Frederick Co., Md. Issue (surname RUSSELL) :

   i.   **ELLEN,** *b.* September 30, 1867.
   ii.   **ELIZA,** *b.* December 5, 1869.
   iii.   **RACHEL,** *b.* June 17, 1874.

xi.   **THOMAS P.,** Jr., *b.* August 30, 1840.

EDWARD, second son of **William** and **Deborah Stabler,** *b.* September 26, 1794 ; *m.*, December 23, 1823, **ANN ROBINSON,** third *dau.* of **Bernard** and **Sarah Gilpin** (*q. v.*), and *d.* September 3, 1883 ; his wife *d.* May 3, 1882. Issue :

i.   **MARGARET,** *b.* November 19, 1824 ; *m.*, May 7, 1846, at her father's residence, **JAMES S.,** son of **James S.** and **Amelia Hallowell,** of Pennsylvania. Issue (surname HALLOWELL) :

   i.   **EDWARD STABLER,** *b.* November 26, 1847 ; *d.* March 18, 1866.
   ii.   **ANNIE STABLER,** *b.* August 1, 1849 ; *m.* **WILLIAM C. RIGGS.** Issue (surname RIGGS) :

           Florence and Margaret.

   iii.   **ALICE,** *b.* December 15, 1851.
   iv.   **JAMES BYRD,** *b.* September 23, 1854.
   v.   **FLORENCE,** *b.* June 23, 1861.
   vi.   **JULIA,** *b.* August 5, 1859 ; *d.* in childhood.
   vii.   **JULIA,** second, *b.* March 29, 1863.

ii.   **ALBAN GILPIN,** *b.* May 9, 1826 ; *m.*, April 30, 1861, **JULIA DULANEY BENNETT,** of Virginia.

iii.   **CATHERINE,** *b.* January 20, 1828.

iv.   **SAMUEL JORDAN,** *b.* May 12, 1830 ; *m.*, November 27, 1861, **ALICE FRONK.** Issue :

i.   LUCY A., *b.* August 23, 1862 ; *d. y.*
ii.   HENRY FLEASANTS, *b.* May 13, 1864.
iii.   KATE, *b.* December 13, 1867.
iv.   MARGUERITE, *b.* November 29, 1870.

v.   PHILIP THOMAS, *b.* September 21, 1831 ; *m.*, November 10, 1870, CORNELIA NICHOLS, of Virginia. Issue :

    i.   VIRGINIA McPHERSON, *b.* November 29, 1871.
    ii.   MAURICE JANNEY, *b.* March 12, 1880.
    iii. iv.   BERTHA and JULIA, twins, *b.* April 26th ; *d.* August 2, 1882.

vi.   BERNARD GILPIN, *b.* February 2, 1834.
vii.   EDWARD, Jr., *b.* March 16, 1836 ; *m.*, November 15, 1865, ELIZA BUTLER, of Columbus, O. Issue :

    i.   EMILY BUTLER, *b.* November 7, 1868.
    ii.   LOUISE, *b.* October 15, 1870 ; *d.* May 17, 1878.
    iii.   HELEN, *b.* April 25, 1874 ; *d.* January 12, 1876.
    iv.   EDWARD ALFORD, *b.* September 11, 1878.
    v.   RAYMOND PLEASANTS, *b.* December 23, 1881.

viii.   LOUIS C., *b.* January 30, 1838 ; *m.* EFFIE LEE WRIGHT, of Missouri. Issue :

    i.   GILPIN LOUIS, *b.* November 25, 1884.
    ii.   KATIE LEE, *b.* February 19, 1889.
    iii.   ETHEL MARK, *b.* October 31, 1890.

ix.   JORDAN, *b.* January 16, 1840 ; *m.*, first, February 14, 1877, CAROLINE E. SEMPLE, of Philadelphia, who *d.* April 11, 1886. Issue :

    i.   EDITH CAROLINE, *b.* May 31, 1878.
    ii.   FLORENCE, *b.* March 16, 1880.
    iii.   JORDAN HERBERT, *b.* October 16, 1885.

He *m.*, second, March 21, 1894, MRS. ELLEN (WALKER) STEARNS, *dau.* of Rev. Horace Dean Walker, deceased, of New York City.

x.   ARTHUR, *b.* December 25, 1842 ; *m.*, April 6, 1871, ANNA McFARLAND.

JAMES PLEASANTS, third son of **William** and **Deborah Stabler**, *b.* September 14, 1796 ; *m.*, first, October 13, 1816, **ELIZABETH**, *dau.* of **Bernard** and **Sarah (Thomas) Gilpin** (*q. v.*), who *d.* February 16, 1823. Issue :

i.   PLEASANTS, *b.* August 4, 1817.
ii.   JOSEPH, *b.* November 14, 1818 ; *d. i.*
iii.   JOSEPH, second, *b.* June 30, 1820.
iv.   DEBORAH, *b.* November 12, 1821 ; *d.* March 25, 1822.
v.   ANN, *b.* January 26, 1823 ; *d.* in November, 1827.

JAMES P. STABLER *m.*, second, January 13, 1830, **SARAH B.**, *dau.* of **Isaac** and **Hannah Briggs** (*q. v.*), and *d.* February 13, 1840. Further issue :

vi. **FRANCES**, *b.* March 31, 1831 ; *d.* April 6, 1836.
vii. **ELIZABETH G.**, *b.* May 18, 1834.
viii. **FRANCIS D.**, *b.* April 9, 1837.
ix. **JAMES P., Jr.**, *b.* June 12, 1839 ; *m.*, December 1, 1870, **ALICE**, *dau.* of **George** and **Eliza Brooke** (*q. v.*). Issue :

    i. **JESSIE BROOKE**, *b.* June 16, 1872.
    ii. **HAROLD BROOKE**, *b.* March 26, 1875.
    iii. **NORA**, *b.* May 15, 1878.

CALEB BENTLEY, fourth son of **William** and **Deborah Stabler**, *b.* January 24, 1799 ; *m.*, August 17, 1825, **ANN**, *dau.* of **Thomas** and **Mary (Brooke) Moore** (*q. v.*). Issue :

i. **CHARLES**, *b.* October 28, 1826 ; *m.*, June 16, 1853, at Mr. Samuel Ellicott's residence, **SARAH E.**, *dau.* of **Mahlon** and **Elizabeth Kirk.**
ii. **MARY M.**, *b.* June 11, 1828 ; *m.*, May 9, 1848, **WARWICK P. MILLER.** Issue (surname MILLER) :

    i. **ANNIE**, *b.* May 4, 1849.
    ii. **FREDERICK**, *b.* July 9, 1850.
    iii. **ROBERT H.**, *b.* August 29, 1851.
    iv. **CORNELIA**, *b.* December 17, 1854.
    v. **ISABEL**, *b.* September 11, 1856.
    vi. **CALEB STABLER**, *b.* February 21, 1859.
    vii. **WARWICK P., Jr.**, *b.* October 28, 1860.
    viii. **BERTHA**, *b.* February 14, 1863.
    ix. **MARY JANET**, *b.* November 18, 1865.

iii. **ROBERT MOORE**, *b.* March 15, 1830 ; *m.* **HANNAH B. TAILOR.** Issue :

    i. **CAROLINE T.**, *b.* October 5, 1860.
    ii. **CLARKSON T.**, *b.* March 2, 1862.
    iii. **ALBERT**, *b.* August 30, 1863.
    iv. **MARY M.**, *b.* February 5, 1865.
    v. **ALICE T.**, *b.* October 24, 1866.
    vi. **EMMA T.**, *b.* September 18, 1868.
    vii. **LYDIA B.**, *b.* August 19, 1870.
    viii. **FLORENCE**, *b.* November 23, 1873.

iv. **FREDERICK**, *b.* December 19, 1831 ; *m.* **MARTHA R. BROOKE** (*q. v.*). Issue :

    i. **TARLTON BROOKE**, *b.* March 26, 1868 ; *m.* **REBECCA T.**, *dau.* of **William W.** and **Mary E. (Thomas) Moore** (*q. v.*). Issue :
        Frederic and **Richard Hallett.**

    ii.   **ROSE MILLER,** *b.* May 18, 1869.
    iii.   **CALEB,** *b.* June 14, 1872.

v.   **WARWICK,** *b.* November 29, 1833.
vi.   **ASA M.,** *b.* July 2, 1837 ; *m.* **ALBINA OSBORN.** Issue :

    i.   **NEWTON,** *b.* January 10, 1868.
    ii.   **MORTIMER,** *b.* June 10, 1869.
    iii. **LLEWELLYN,** *b.* August 20, 1872.
    iv. **CAROLINE MILLER,** *b.* March 23, 1874.

vii.   **DEBORAH B.,** *b.* May 3, 1843.

Authorities : Friends' Records and family papers, through Miss Ellen Stabler, Edward Stabler, Jr.,
and others.

STANARD, OF VIRGINIA

WILLIAM STANARD, *b.* February 16, 1682 ; *m.*, first, in 1709, **ANN**, *dau.* of **George Hazlewood**.   Issue :

> **ANN**, *m.* **ROBERT BEVERLEY.**

He *m.*, second, in 1717, **ELIZA BEVERLEY**, and *d.* December 3, 1732, having had, with other issue, a son, **BEVERLEY**, *of whom presently.*

BEVERLEY, son of **William** and **Eliza (Beverley) Stanard**, *b.* February 24, 1721 ; *m.* **ELIZABETH BEVERLEY**, *dau.* of **Larkin** and **Mary (Beverley) Chew** (*q. v.*) (who afterward *m.*, second, **MORDECAI BUCKNER**), and *d.* in 1765. Issue :

i.   **WILLIAM**, of " Roxbury," and Stanardsville, Spottsylvania Co., appointed Justice of the County, 1787 ; High Sheriff, 1802-4 ; was a member of the House of Delegates ; *m.* **ELIZABETH**, *dau.* of **Colonel Edward Carter**, of " Blenheim," Albemarle, and *d.* October, 1807.

ii.   **LARKIN**, *of whom presently.*

iii.   **BEVERLEY**, *d. u.*

iv.   A *dau.*, *m.* —— **MONTAGU**, of Essex Co., Va.

LARKIN, second son of **Beverley** and **Elizabeth Beverley (Chew) Stanard**, was of " Stanfield," Spottsylvania Co., Va., a captain in the Continental forces, and member of the Virginia House of Delegates, 1798–1804.   He *m.* **ELIZABETH**, only *dau.* of **Robert** and **Molly (Parrot) Chew** (*q. v.*).   Issue :

i.   **BEVERLEY CHEW**, *b.* 1779 ; resided in Chesterfield Co., Va.; was a Justice, member of the Virginia House of Delegates, 1805-1812, Captain and Adjutant First Virginia Regiment, War of 1812; *m.* **MARY BOLLING**, *dau.* of **Judge William Fleming**, of the Court of Appeals, and *d.* July 11, 1823.

ii.   **ROBERT**, *b.* August 1, 1781 ; member of the House of Delegates, 1810-17, Speaker in 1815 ; removed to Richmond in 1816 ; United States District Attorney, 1821-31, Judge of the Court of Appeals ; *m.* **LOUISA**, *dau.* of **Adam Craig**, and *d.* May 14, 1846.

iii.   **MARY PARROTT,** *m.* **EDMUND FOSTER.**

iv.   **JOHN,** was Ensign Second United States Infantry, 1807, Captain Twenty-sixth Infantry, 1812, promoted Colonel ; retired, being crippled in a duel with Dr. Bronaugh. He *m.* **CAROLINE MATILDA,** *dau.* of **John** and **Ann (Fox) Chew** (*q. v.*), and *d.* September 23, 1833.

v.   **THOMAS,** removed to Mississippi and *m.* —— **PENNY,** of Louisiana.

vi.   **HUGH,** *m.* **MRS. ANN SIMPSON.**

vii.   **ELIZABETH,** *m.* **Dr. WOOLDRIDGE.**

viii.   **KITTY,** *m.* **CHRISTOPHER BRANCH,** and *d.* in 1822.

ix.   **LAVINIA,** *d. u.*

x.   **CAROLINE MATILDA CHEW,** *m.* **EATON STANARD.**

xi.   **COLUMBIA,** *m.* —— **PRATT.**

xii.   **LUCY ANN,** *d. i.*

Authorities : Family papers and articles in the William and Mary College Quarterly, 1894.

SULLIVAN, OF MOORESTOWN, N. J.

ROBERT W., son of **Dennis** and **Margaret Sullivan,** *b.* June 1, 1824; *m.,* May, 1853, **MARCELLA,** *dau.* of **Edward** and **Lydia (Gilpin) Thomas** (*q. v.*), and *d.* February 9, 1892; his wife *d.* May 20, 1893. Issue:

i.   **MARY EMMA,** *m.* **JOHN KING,** in Maryland. Issue (surname KING):

     WILLIAM, LAWRENCE, and **CHARLES.**

ii.   **JOSEPH THOMAS,** removed to Moorestown, N. J., and is Treasurer of the Moorestown Electric Company. He *m.* there **SARAH C. ROGERS.** Issue:

     MARSHALL PHILLIPS, HELEN, ALICE R., and **MABEL CRETH.**

iii.   **ANNIE ELIZABETH.**

iv.   **FLORENCE MATILDA,** *m.,* in Maryland, **SAMUEL B. WETH-ERALD.** Issue (surname WETHERALD):

     HARRY, HELEN S., DOROTHY, JOSEPH STANLEY, and **ROBERT PARKER.**

v.   **FRANK BRINTON,** *d.* aged sixteen.

vi.   **ROBERT MILTON,** *m.,* in New Jersey, **KATHERINE TURNER.** Issue:

     ELTON and **FLORENCE LOUISA.**

vii.   **IDA PHILLIPS.**

Authority : Family papers, through Joseph T. Sullivan, of Moorestown, N. J.

TALBOT

RICHARD TALBOT, of Anne Arundel Co., Md., *m.* **ELIZA-BETH,** *dau.* of **Major Richard Ewen** (who afterward *m.* **William Richardson** (*q. v.*), and *d.* in 1663. Will proved April 21, 1663. Liber I, 180. Issue:

i.   **RICHARD,** inherited "Poplar Knowle."
ii.   **EDWARD,** *of whom presently.*
iii.   **ELIZABETH,** *m.*, first, **BENJAMIN LAWRENCE** (*q. v.*); *m.*, second, **RICHARD GALLOWAY,** Sr. (*q. v.*).
iv.   **JOHN,** *m.*, before September 27, 1690, **SARAH,** *dau.* of John and Sarah (Thomas) **Mears** (*q. v.*), and *d.* June, 1707. Issue:

     i.   **ELIZA.**
     ii.   **RICHARD.**
     iii.   **DANIEL.**

EDWARD, second son of **Richard** and **Elizabeth (Ewen) Talbot,** *b.* November 6, 1658; was a prominent member of the Society of Friends at West River and its vicinity. He *m.* **MRS. ELIZABETH (THOMAS) COALE,** widow of **William Coale** (*q. v.*), and *d.* 1692–93. (Will proved January 6, 1692–93. Liber H, folio 13.) His widow *d.* 1725. Issue:

i.   **RICHARD,** *b.* February 6, 1680–81; *d.* November 26, 1681.
ii   **EDWARD,** *b.* December 3, 1682.
iii.   **ELIZABETH,** *m.* —— **MACINTOSH.**
iv.   **JOHN,** *m.*, first, 1705 (they passed West River meeting the first time July 25, 1705), **ELIZABETH,** *dau.* of **Samuel Galloway,** Jr. (*q. v.*); *m.*, second, **MARY WATERS.** In 1725 he had issue:

     i.   **CASSANDRA,** *m.*, April 23, 1730, **SAMUEL WALLIS.**
     ii.   **ELIZABETH.**
     iii.   **LUCEY.**

Authorities: West River Quaker Records and Wills at Annapolis, Md.

TILGHMAN

DR. RICHARD TILGHMAN, *b.* September 3, 1626, came to Maryland in 1661, settled at "the Hermitage," on Chester River, and *d.* January 7, 1675. By his wife, **MARY FOXLEY,** he left issue :

i.   **MARIA,** *b.* 1655 ; *m.* **MATTHEW WARD.**
ii.   **RICHARD,** *b.* February 23, 1672 ; *m.,* January 7, 1700, **ANNA MARIA,** *dau.* of **Philemon Lloyd,** and *d.* January 23, 1738. Issue. with others :

     i.   RICHARD, of "the Hermitage," Judge of the Provincial Court. *m.* SUSANNA FRISBY, and *d.* September 29, 1768, leaving an eldest son, Richard, *m.* Elizabeth, *dau.* of Colonel Edward and Elizabeth (Chew) Tilghman (*q. v.*), and had a son, Richard Edward.

     ii.   EDWARD, *b.* July 3, 1713, *of whom presently.*

COLONEL EDWARD, younger son of **Richard** and **Anna M. (Lloyd) Tilghman,** *b.* July 3, 1713, was a member of the Stamp Act Congress of 1765, and one of the committee which drew up the remonstrance presented to Parliament. He *m.,* first, **ANN,** *dau.* of **Major William Turbutt.** Issue :

i.   **ANNA MARIA,** *m.* **BENNET CHEW** (*q. v.*).

COLONEL TILGHMAN *m.,* second, in 1749, **ELIZABETH,** third *dau.* of **Samuel** and **Mary Chew** (*q. v.*). Further issue:

ii.   **RICHARD.**
iii.   **EDWARD,** *b.* February 11, 1750–51, *of whom presently.*
iv.   **BENJAMIN.**
v.   **ELIZABETH,** *m.* **RICHARD TILGHMAN** (*q. v.*).

vi.   **ANNA MARIA,** *m.,* first, **CHARLES GOLDSBOROUGH,** of Horne's Point, Dorchester Co., Md., who *d.* shortly afterward from an injury received while on a ducking party.

     MRS. ANNA MÁRIA GOLDSBOROUGH *m.,* second, **RT. REV. ROBERT SMITH,** first Protestant Episcopal Bishop of South Carolina. Issue (surname SMITH) :

      ROBERT and WILLIAM.

COLONEL EDWARD TILGHMAN *m.,* third, in 1759, **JULI-ANNA CARROLL,** and *d.* October 9, 1785. Further issue :

vii.   **MATTHEW.**
viii.   **BENJAMIN.**
ix.   **MARY.**
x.   **SUSANNA.**

EDWARD, second son of **Colonel Edward** and **Elizabeth (Chew) Tilghman,** *b.* February 11, 1750–51, was an eminent lawyer of Philadelphia, *m.,* May 26, 1774, **ELIZABETH,** *dau.* of **Chief Justice Benjamin Chew** (*q. v.*), and *d.* November 1, 1815. Issue :

i.   **EDWARD,** *b.* February 27, 1779 ; *m.* **REBECCA WALN.** Issue :

    i.   **EDWARD.**
    ii.   **ANN REBECCA,** *d. u.* June 28, 1828.
    iii.   **ELIZABETH.**
    iv.   **ANN.**
    v.   **JANE,** *m.,* May 11, 1808, **WILLIAM POYNTELL JOHNSON.**
    vi.   **REBECCA,** *d. u.* June 11, 1887.

ii.   **BENJAMIN,** *b.* January 1, 1785 ; *m.* **ANNA MARIA McMUR-TRIE.** Issue :

    i.   **ANNA MARIA.**
    ii   **EDWARD.**
    iii.   **WILLIAM M.,** *m.* **KATHERINE INGERSOLL.**
    iv.   **BENJAMIN CHEW.**
    v.   **RICHARD A.,** *m.* **SUSAN TOLAND.**
    vi.   **EMILY,** *d. u.* June 3, 1830.

iii. **ELIZABETH,** *m.,* January 24, 1804, **WILLIAM COOKE.**
iv. **MARY ANNA,** *m.* **WILLIAM RAWLE.** Issue (surname RAWLE) :

    i.   **WILLIAM HENRY,** *m.,* first, **MARY BINNEY,** *dau.* of Judge John Cadwalader and his wife, **Mary,** *dau.* of Horace Binney. She *d.* May 26, 1861. Issue :

       i.   **Mary,** *m.* **Frederick Rhinelander Jones.**
       ii. **Edith.**

     MR. RAWLE *m.,* second, **EMILY,** *dau.* of General Thomas Cadwalader and his wife, **Maria C.,** *dau.* of Nicholas and Hester (Kortright) Gouverneur.

ii. **ELIZABETH TILGHMAN, *m.* CHARLES WALLACE BROOKE,** of Philadelphia. Issue :

    i. **Elizabeth Tilghman.**
    ii. **William Rawle,** had his name changed to **William Brooke Rawle** and *m.* **Elizabeth Norris Pepper.**
    iii. **Charlotte.**
    iv. **Charles Wallace,** *d. y.*

Authorities : Colonel Hanson's " Old Kent," Keith's " Provincial Councillors," and family papers, through Judge H. H. Goldsborough and W. B. Rawle, Esq.

TYSON, OF MARYLAND

RENIER or **RYNER TYSON** was a Mennonite and sailed
from Crefeld, Germany, on the Concord, arriving at Philadelphia,
October 6, 1683. He is named in Penn's Patent of August 12,
1689, as one of the original incorporators of Germantown. He
afterward removed to Abington, Philadelphia Co., and March 1,
1700–1701 bought 250 acres of land of John Colley. He *m.*
MARY ——. Issue (order uncertain) :

i.   **MATTHIAS,** *of whom presently.*
ii.   **JOHN,** *m.,* October 31, 1720, **PRISCILLA NAILER.**
iii. **PETER.**
iv. **ABRAHAM,** *m.,* October 30, 1721, **MARY HALLOWELL.**
v.   **DERRICK.**
vi. **HENRY.**
vii. **ISAAC,** *m.,* April 24, 1727, **SARAH JENKINS.** Issue :

       LYDIA, *m.,* May 9, 1765, **JACOB COFFIN.**

viii. **ELIZA.**
ix. **SARAH,** *m.,* August 27, 1722, **JOHN KIRK.**

MATTHIAS, eldest son of **Ryner** and **Mary Tyson,** *m.,* March
29, 1708, **MARY POTTS.** Issue :

i.   **RYNER.**
ii. † **ISAAC,** *of whom presently.*
iii. **JESSE.**

531

iv.   **ELIZABETH.**

v.   **MARGARET,** *m.,* October 23, 1729, **WILLIAM,** son of **Thomas Hallowell.**

ISAAC, second son of **Matthias** and **Mary (Potts) Tyson,** *m.,* May 26, 1748, **ESTHER,** *dau.* of **Isaac Shoemaker,** who *d.* September 8, 1796 ; her husband *d.* before her.   Issue :

i.   **ENEAS.**

ii.   **ELISHA,** *of whom presently.*

iii. **DOROTHY.**

iv.   **TACY,** *m.,* November 24, 1780, **JOHN MITCHELL.**

v.   **ELIZABETH.**

vi.   **JACOB,** *m.* **ANN ——.**   Issue :

    i.   **SARAH,** *b.* July 17, 1796.

    ii.   **GEORGE,** *b.* June 6, 1798.

    iii. **ANN,** *b.* November 8, 1800.

    iv.   **JONATHAN,** *b.* September 9, 1802.

    v.   **WILLIAM AMOS,** *b.* June 12, 1805.

vii. **SARAH,** *m.* **ISRAEL KNIGHT** (*q. v.*).

viii. **GEORGE.**

ix.   **JESSE** (*q. v.*).

x.   **NATHANIEL,** *m.,* 1801, **MARY RANDALL,** and *d.* March 15, 1819. Issue :

    i.   **MARIA,** *m.* **DR. GEORGE S. GIBSON.**

    ii.   **ELEANOR,** *m.* **THOMAS IRWIN, Jr.,** of Alexandria, Va.

ELISHA, second son of **Isaac** and **Esther (Shoemaker) Tyson,** *b.* February 18, 1749–50 ; lived, first, at Jericho, at the Little Falls of the Gunpowder River, in Baltimore Co., Md., where he had a mill ; afterward removed to Baltimore, and became an extensive merchant miller there.   He built a mill on Jones's Falls, near what is now Druid Hill Park.   He was a most highly respected and prominent citizen, full of public spirit and philanthropy, aiding in many ways the development and good order of the city.   He was convinced that negro slavery was wrong and ought to be abolished by law, and aided in every way he legally could those wrongfully held.   He was in no sense a man of one idea, but full of wisdom and courage and conduct in every-day life. Large and majestic in person, with more than ordinary personal strength, and as resolute as conscientious, there is no doubt that he wielded the sword of the spirit with a very strong arm of the flesh.   He is said "to have possessed wonderful acuteness' of understanding, quickness of perception, readiness of reply, and dauntless courage." He was always a member of the Society of Friends. He *m.*, first, November 5, 1776, **MARY**, *dau.* of **William** and **Hannah Amos**, who *d.* in 1811 ; *m.*, second, October 22, 1814, **MARGARET COWMAN**, who *d. s. p.* January 29, 1853. He *d.* February 16, 1824. Issue, by his first wife :

i.   **ISAAC**, *b.* October 10, 1777, *of whom presently.*
ii.   **ESTHER**, *b.* February 23, 1779 ; *d.* in childhood.
iii.   **LUCRETIA**, *b.* January 9, 1780 ; *m.* **JOHN W. WILSON.** Issue (surname WILSON) :

    i.   ELISHA T., *b.* March 14, 1801 ; *d.* September 1, 1804.
    ii.   ISAAC, *b.* July 2, 1802.
    iii. WILLIAM, *b.* April 9, 1805.

iv.   **WILLIAM**, *b.* October 2, 1782 ; *m.* **ELIZABETH**, *dau.* of **Jonathan** and **Sarah Ellicott** (*q. v.*). Issue :

    i.   SARAH E., *b.* September 10, 1804 ; *m.*, December 25, 1835, LLOYD NORRIS, and *d.* August 19, 1867.
    ii.   JONATHAN E., *b.* May 4, 1806 ; *m.*, in 1835, MARIA P. TERREL, and *d.* September 28, 1866.
    iii. WILLIAM A., *b.* November 4, 1807 ; *m.*, April 16, 1840, MARY J. ALLEN.
    iv. SAMUEL E., *b.* November 16, 1809 ; *m.*, September 13, 1848, RACHEL LUKENS.
    v.   MARY A., *b.* September 19, 1811, Principal of the Alnwick Female Seminary, near Contee's Station, Prince Georges Co., Md.
    vi. ELIZABETH E., *b.* February 12, 1813.
    vii. JANE S., *b.* February 23, 1814 ; *d.* May 20, 1815.
    viii. FRANCES E., *b.* August 20, 1815 ; *m.*, in 1859, ROBERT A. PARISH, Sen.
    ix. JANE S., *b.* July 1, 1817 ; *d.* January 30, 1878.
    x.   EDWARD N., *b.* December 23, 1818 ; *m.*, October 3, 1847, ISABELLA HARKNESS.
    xi. CHARLES S., *b.* April 22, 1820.
    xii. MARTHA E., *b.* June 2, 1822.
    xiii. NATHANIEL E., *b.* September 6, 1823 ; *d.* October 10, 1823.
    xiv. LETITIA E., *b.* February 16, 1825.

v.   **MARY**, *b.* September 4, 1785 ; *m.* **ENOCH CLAPP.**
vi.   **NATHAN**, *b.* November 4, 1787 (*q. v.*).
vii. **JAMES**, *b.* March 4, 1790 ; *d. y.*
viii. **SARAH**, *b.* August 19, 1791 ; *d. y.*
ix.   **ELISHA**, *b.* January 28, 1796 ; *m.* **SARAH S. MORRIS.**
x.   **DEBORAH DARBY**, *b.* March 12, 1798 ; *d.* May 12, 1801.

ISAAC, eldest son of **Elisha** and **Mary (Amos) Tyson**, *b.* October 10, 1777, at Jericho, in Harford Co., Md. ; *m.*, first, November 8, 1797, at Sandy Spring Meeting House, in Montgomery Co., Md., **ELIZABETH**, *dau.* of **Evan** and **Rachel (Hopkins) Thomas** (*q. v.*), who *d.* May 12, 1812. Issue :

i.   **PHILIP THOMAS**, *b.* June 23, 1799 ; Geologist of the State of Maryland ; *m.*, January 8, 1824, **REBECCA WEBSTER** ; both *d.*

ii. **DEBORAH**, *b.* May 12, 1801 ; *m.*, November 15, 1825, **CHARLES ELLIS**, of Philadelphia, and *d.* May 9, 1828.   Issue :

    i.   EVAN T., *b.* August 10, 1826 ; *m.* MARTHA SHEWELL, who *d.* January 1, 1895.   Issue :
        Charles, Evan, and Shewell.

    ii. DEBORAH T., *b.* February 19, 1828.

    CHARLES ELLIS, *m.*, second, **MARY**, *dau.* of **Luke** and **Ann Morris** (*q. v.*), and *d.*   Issue by her :

    iii. NANCY M., *m.* WILLIAM M. ELLICOTT, Jr. (*q. v.*).

iii. **MARY I.**, *b.* August 8, 1803.

iv. **EVAN THOMAS**, *b.* November 8, 1805 ; *d.* March 31, 1826.

v.   **RACHEL THOMAS**, *b.* November 9, 1807 ; *m.*, October 14, 1835, **JOHN JACKSON**, of Philadelphia, who *d.* April 14, 1855.   Issue (surname JACKSON) :

    i.   HENRIETTA, *m.* ERNEST TURNER.   Issue : Warner.
    ii. WARNER.
    iii. LYDIA.

vi. **HENRIETTA THOMAS**, *b.* November 12, 1809 ; *m.*, June 7, 1838, **JOHN SAURIN NORRIS**, and *d.* February 27, 1871.   Issue :

    i.   ISAAC TYSON.
    ii. JOHN OLNEY.
    iii. MARY, *m.* GEORGE PERRY, who has since *d.*, leaving one child, Henrietta.
    iv. HENRIETTA.

ISAAC TYSON *m.*, second, June 8, 1815, **PATIENCE MARSHALL**, and *d.*, January 30, 1864, without further issue.

NATHAN, third son of **Elisha** and **Mary (Amos) Tyson**, *b.* November 4, 1787 ; *m.*, September 27, 1815, **MARTHA**, *dau.* of **George** and **Elizabeth (Brooke) Ellicott**, and *d.* January 6, 1867.   His wife *d.* March 5, 1873.   Issue :

i.   **JAMES ELLICOTT**, *b.* August 21, 1816 ; *m.*, first, September 23, 1847, **HARRIET S.**, *dau.* of **John** and **Frances (Helm) Jolliffe**, who *d.*   Issue :

    i.   FRANCIS JOLLIFFE, *b.* June 17, 1848 ; *d. u.* July 27, 1878.
    ii. LILLY, *b.* April 21, 1852 ; *m.*, October 2, 1879, GASTON MANLEY.   Issue (surname MANLEY) :
        i.   Elizabeth Brooke, *b.* June 11, 1881.
        ii. Martha Ellicott Tyson, *b.* February 4, 1883.
    iii. MARTHA, *b.* October 25, 1854 ; *d.* July 15, 1866.

    JAMES E. TYSON *m.*, second, in 1867, **FRANCES E. WILLIAMS**, who *d. s. p.* in July, 1893.

ii. **ELIZABETH BROOKE**, *b.* March 30, 1818 ; *m.*, May 25, 1843, **JOHN MARSH SMITH**, who *d.* July 29, 1890.   Issue (surname SMITH) :

i. GILBERT TYSON, *b.* April 30, 1846; *m.,* first, December 4, 1872, CHARLOTTE
    WATSON, since deceased. Issue:
    Gilbert Tyson, Jr., *b.* September 28, 1873.
    He *m.,* second, EMMA WATSON.

ii. THOMAS MARSH, *b.* January 28, 1848; *m.,* February 13, 1877, HELEN PARRY.
    Issue:
    Helen R., *b.* April 11, 1878; *d.* April 14, 1883.

iii. MARTHA TYSON, *b.* June 28, 1852; *m.* SAMUEL, son of Joseph J., and Eliza-
    beth (Schofield) Hopkins (*q. v.*).

iv. JANE GAMBRILL, *b.* March 8, 1864.

iii. HENRY, *b.* November 18, 1820, *of whom presently.*

iv. ISABELLA, *b.* March 17, 1823.

v. ANNE, *b.* February 26, 1825; *m.,* June 11, 1861, WILLIAM KIRK,
    and *d.* August 27, 1884; her husband *d.* in July, 1879.

vi. MARY, *b.* August 11, 1826; *d.* the same year.

vii. FREDERICK, *b.* April 17, 1828; *m.,* October 29, 1872, FLORENCE
    McINTYRE. Issue:

    MALCOLM VAN VECHTEN, *b.* August 21, 1873.

viii. ROBERT, *b.* March 25, 1830; *m.,* first, June 4, 1863, JANE GAM-
    BRILL, who *d. s. p.* in 1864; *m.,* second, November 25, 1869,
    SARAH R. SMITH.

ix. EVAN, *b.* August 27, 1831; *d.* May 6, 1832.

x. LUCY, *b.* March 20, 1833; *m.,* February 1, 1872, as his second wife,
    HENRY MAYNADIER FITZHUGH (*q. v.*).

xi. NATHAN, *b.* June 24, 1834; *d.* March 27, 1835.

xii. NATHAN, *b.* June 27, 1836; *d.* March 9, 1837.

HENRY, second son of **Nathan** and **Martha (Ellicott) Tyson**, *b.*
November 18, 1820; *m.,* May 13, 1847, MARY GILLING-
HAM, and *d.* September 1, 1877; his wife *d.* in December,
1891. Issue:

i. HANNAH, *b.* March 3, 1848; *m.,* February 11, 1873, ALEXANDER
    HAGUE, son of **Henry** and **Mary Jane (Hague) Simmonds**, of
    England. Issue (surname SIMMONDS):

    i.   HENRY TYSON, *b.* November 23, 1873; *d.* April 8, 1874.
    ii. ALGERNON, *b.* November 10, 1874.
    iii. MARY ELEANOR, *b.* November 15, 1876.
    iv. HENRY, *b.* May 27, 1879.
    v.   MARGARET TYSON, *b.* January 8, 1881.
    vi. HANNAH MELVILLE, *b.* December 26, 1882.
    vii. WINIFRED, *b.* February 5, 1888.
    viii. ALEXANDER ELLICOTT, *b.* November 30, 1889.

ii. LAURA, *b.* October 9, 1849; *d.* October 27, 1850.

iii. ALICE, *b.* August 3, 1851.

iv. MARGARET GITTINGS, *b.* March 11, 1850; *m.,* July 20, 1886,
    ROBERT ROWLAND, son of **William W.** and **Mary E.**
    (Thomas) Moore (*q. v.*).

v.　　**ESTELLE TYSON,** *b.* April 24, 1861 ; *m.,* October 4, 1884, JO-
　　　　SEPH TOWNSEND, son of Joseph Townsend and Anna
　　　　(Leggett) Moore.　Issue (surname MOORE) :

　　　i.　　**ANNA LEGGETT,** *b.* July 31, 1886 ; *d.* September 21, 1887.
　　　ii.　　**MARY GILLINGHAM,** *b.* March 18, 1888.
　　　iii.　　**THOMAS LEGGETT,** *b.* August 25, 1890 ; *d.* July 16, 1891.
　　　iv.　　**ESTELLE TYSON,** *b.* August 25, 1890.
　　　v.　　**BEATRIX TYSON,** *b.* June 19, 1893.

vi.　　**MARY BEATRIX,** *b.* January 28, 1865.
vii.　　**MARTHA ELLICOTT,** *b.* November 19, 1867 ; *m.,* October 4, 1892,
　　　　ROBERT, son of James W. and Jane (Stevenson) Marshall,
　　　　of Virginia.　Issue :

　　　A son, HENRY TYSON, *b.* July 22, 1893.

JESSE, sixth son of Isaac and Esther (Shoemaker) Tyson, *m.,*
first, April 1, 1790, **MARGARET,** *dau.* of John and Elizabeth Hopkins (*q. v.*), who *d.* June 20, 1804.　He *m.,* second,
May 22, 1806, **SARAH,** *dau.* of Henry and Ann Ridgely,
who *d. s. p. ;* and third, **ELIZABETH,** *dau.* of Joshua and
Catherine (Warner) Howell, of Philadelphia, who also *d.s.p.*
Issue, by his first wife :

i.　　**ELIZABETH,** *b.* March 22, 1791 ; *m.,* in 1811, DR. WILLIAM
　　　　WINDER HANDY.　Issue (surname HANDY) :

　　　i.　　**DR. JESSE TYSON,** *b.* in 1814 ; *m.* SARAH COX.
　　　ii.　　**JANE WINDER,** *b.* in 1816 ; *m.* GEORGE R. JUSTICE.　Issue :
　　　　　　George and William.
　　　iii.　　**MARGARET,** *b.* in 1819 ; *m.* SAMUEL J. REEVES, and has had two sons and
　　　　　　four daughters.
　　　iv.　　**HENRY,** *b.* in 1821 ; *m.,* as her second husband, **MAGGIE JENKS,** and had two
　　　　　　children.
　　　v.　　**ELIZABETH,** *b.* in 1823 ; *d. u.*
　　　vi.　　**WILLIAM,** *b.* in 1825 ; *d. u.*
　　　vii.　　**CHARLES,** *b.* in 1827 ; *m.,* as her first husband, **MAGGIE JENKS,** and *d.,* leaving
　　　　　　one child.

ii.　　**ISAAC,** *b.* October 1, 1792 ; *m.* HANNAH ANN WOOD.　Issue :

　　　i.　　**RICHARD WOOD,** *m.,* first, a *dau.* of Dennis A. Smith, of Baltimore.　Issue :
　　　　　i.　　Margaret, *m.* Eugene Ellicott (*q. v.*).
　　　　　ii.　　Annie, *m.* William, son of Captain F. W. Willson.
　　　　　RICHARD W. TYSON *m.,* second, SOPHIA, *dau.* of Hon. Benjamin Chew
　　　　　Howard (*q. v.*), and *d.*　Issue :
　　　　　iii.　　Benjamin and iv. Sophia.

　　　ii.　　**JESSE,** *m .,* January 26, 1888, EDITH, *dau.* of Henry Van Dyke and Ann (Da-
　　　　　vis) Johns, of Baltimore, Md.
　　　iii.　　**JAMES WOOD,** *m.* ELIZABETH, *dau.* of Mordecai Dawson, of Philadel-
　　　　　phia.　Issue :

     i.   Elizabeth, *m.* Harry Lee.
     ii.   Hannah, *m.* Columbus O'Donnell Lee.
     iii.   Mordecai.
     iv.   Letitia.
     v.   Jane.
     And others.

iv.   ISAAC, Jr., *m.* FANNIE, *dau.* of Stephen Thornton, and *d.*   Issue :

     i.   Minnie.
     ii.   Fannie, *m.* Jacob Lindley (*q. v.*).
     iii.   Jesse.

v.   HANNAH ANN, *m.* DR. J. CHESTON MORRIS (*q. v.*).

iii.   THOMAS, *b.* June 1, 1794 ; *m.*, first, October 19, 1825, MARY, *dau.* of George and Elizabeth Ellicott (*q. v.*) ; *m.*, second, in 1836, her sister, ANNA B. ELLICOTT ; and third, MARY, *dau.* of Samuel and Elizabeth (Cowman) Snowden (*q. v.*), and *d. s. p.*

iv.   ESTHER, *b.* March 22, 1796 ; *d.* August 19, 1797.

v.   JUDGE JOHN SHOEMAKER, *b.* November 7, 1797 ; *m.* RACHEL, *dau.* of John and Rachel Snowden (*q. v.*), and *d.*   Issue :

     i.   CORNELIA.
     ii.   ANNA M.
     iii.   JOHN SNOWDEN, *m.* MARY, *dau.* of Levi F. Roberts and *d.* 1894.
     iv.   IDA.

vi.   MARGARET, *b.* July 4, 1802 ; *m.* JOHN JANNEY.   Issue :

     JOSEPH.

vii.   ANNA, *b.* May 10, 1804 ; *m.* JOSEPH ELDRIDGE.

Authorities : Friends' Records, Baltimore and Philadelphia ; Fox, Ellicott, and Evans families, and Mrs. H. M. Fitzhugh.

VERDON, FURNIVAL, MINORS

HUBERT WALTER, living in 1156, had a son, **HERVEY,** *m.* **MATILDA,** *dau.* and *co-h.* of **Theobald de Valoines,** Lord of Parham, Suffolk. Issue:

i. **THEOBALD,** *of whom presently.*
ii. **HUBERT,** Archbishop of Canterbury, Chief Justiciar of England, etc., the celebrated minister of Richard I. ; *d.* July 12, 1205.
iii. **ROGER.**
iv. **HAMO.**

THEOBALD, eldest son and heir of **Hervey Walter,** joined the expedition against Ireland under the King ; was appointed Chief Butler in 1177 ; held the Baronies of Upper and Lower Ormonde ; *m.* **MAUD,** *dau.* of **Robert le Vavasour,** son of **William le Vavasour,** Justiciary of England, living 1166–1189, and grandson of **Mauger le Vavasour,** of Domesday Book. Issue :

i. **THEOBALD,** assumed the name of **LE BOTILER,** in 1221, and *m.,* first **JOAN,** sister and *co-h.* of **Geoffrey de Marreis.** Issue :

    i. **THEOBALD,** ancestor of the Dukes and Marquises of Ormonde.

    THEOBALD LE BOTILER *m.,* second, in 1250, **ROHESE,** only *dau.* and heiress of **Nicholas de Verdon,**[1] descended from **Bertram de Verdon,** of Newbold Verdon, and Farnham Royal, Leicestershire,

---

[1] He was apparently nephew and heir of William, *d. s. p.* 1199, Son of Bertram, Seneschal of Ireland, 1185, a Justice in Eyre, and Sheriff of Leicestershire and Warwick, 1170–1185 ; *d.* 1192 ; son of Norman and grandson of Bertram de Verdon, of Domesday.

a Baron by tenure in Domesday. **THEOBALD LE BOTILER,**
d. July 19, 1230. Further issue :

ii.   **JOHN,** *of whom presently.*

ii.   **MAUD,** *m.* **GEOFFREY DE PRENDERGAST.**

JOHN, only son of **Theobald le Botiler** and **Rohese de Verdon,**
became his mother's heir in 1247, assumed the name of **DE
VERDON,** *m.* **MARGARET,** *dau.* of **Gilbert de Lacy,** Lord
of Trym (*q. v.*), and *d.* 1274. Issue :

i.   **JOHN,** an adventurer in the expedition against Ireland ; slain there in 1278.
ii.   **THEOBALD,** the first Baron by writ, summoned to Parliament from December 29, 1399, to October 8, 1314 ;
m., first **MAUD,** *dau.* of **Edmund
Mortimer,** Lord of Wigmore (*q. v.*) ;
m., second, **ELIZABETH,** *dau.* and
co-h. of **Gilbert de Clare,** Earl of
Gloucester, and *d.* 1316. Issue, an
eldest *dau.* by his first wife, **JOANE**
(*d.* 1334) ; *m.*, first, **WILLIAM DE
MONTAGU ;** *m.*, second, **THOMAS,
LORD FURNIVAL** [1] (*b.* 1302, *d.* 1339),
son of **Thomas** and **Elizabeth** (de Mont-
fort) **Furnival,** descended from **Gerard,**
son of **Gerard de Furnival,** by
Maud, *dau.* and heiress of **William
de Lovetot,** [2] Lord of Hallamshire.

DE VERDON ARMS

THOMAS and **JOAN FURNIVAL** had issue (surname FURNIVAL) :

i.   Thomas, *b.* 1331 ; *d. s. p.* 1366.
ii.   William, *d.* 1383. Issue :
          Joan, *m.* Thomas Nevil, of Westmoreland.
iii.   Gerard, had a *dau.* and *co-h., m.* Sir John Eynsford. Knt. Issue : Eliza-
          beth, *m.*, first, Piers Mylbourne ; *m.*, second, Sir John Baskerville
          (*q. v.*).
iv.   Sir John, had a *dau., m.* Richard Minors,[3] of Treago. Issue (surname
          MINORS) :
          Roger, *of whom presently.*

[1] Arms : *Ar.*, a chevron between six mascles, *gu.*
[2] Descended from William de Lovetot, who founded Worksop Priory, Notts, *temp.* Henry I.
Arms : *Ar.*, a lion rampant *per fesse, gu.*, and *sa.*
[3] Son of Sir Roger, *m.* Joan. *dau.* of Sir John Bostock, Knt., of Cheshire, and grandson of John de
Mynors, Constable of S. Briavels Castle and the Forest of Dene, under Edward II.

ROGER, son of **Richard** and **Margaret (Furnival) Minors**, *m.* **MARGARET**, *dau.* and heiress of **John de la Hay**, of Wallington. Issue:

> **PHILIP**, *m.* **ALLICE**, *dau.* of **William ap Jenkin ap Yerworth**, and had **PAGANUS**, *m. dau.* of **John a Brett.** Issue:
>
> > Jenkin, *of whom presently.*

JENKIN, son of **Paganus Minors**, *m.* **EVA**, *dau.* of **Philip Michell**, of Cornwall. Issue:

> **RICHARD MINORS**, of Treago, in the Parish of S. Weonard's, Herefordshire; Sheriff, 1500; *m.* **JOANE**, *dau.* of **William ap Thomas ap Llewellyn ap Howell Glylough.** Issue:
>
> i.   **SIR ROGER**, *d. s. p.*
> ii. **THOMAS**, ancestor of the **Mynors** of Treago; extinct in the male line, 1765.
> iii. **ALICE**, *m.* **WILLIAM SCUDAMORE** (*q. v.*).

Authorities: F. P. Barnard, "Strongbow's Conquest of Ireland," *pp.* 108, 111, 135; Sir T. C. Banks, "Baronage of England," I., 121, 445; II., 220-224. 566-568; Courthope and Nicolas, "Historic Peerage," *pp.* 206, 488; and R. Cooke's "Visitation of Herefordshire," edited by Rev. F. W. Weaver (1886).

MINORS ARMS

WALKER

THOMAS WALKER, of the town of Leeds, in England, came to
New York about the year 1790 and settled at West Farms ; the
family seat being now incorporated in New York City limits.
He had two sons :

i.   **THOMAS E.,** *of whom presently.*
ii.   **JOHN J.,** *m.* **RACHEL,** *dau.* of Philip E. and Elizabeth Thomas
       (*q. v.*), and *d.,* leaving an only son, **EVAN PHILIP.**

THOMAS E., son of **Thomas Walker,** was a merchant of New
York City ; *m.,* in 1826, **ANN,** *dau.* of **Philip E.** and **Elizabeth Thomas** (*q. v.*).   Issue :

i.   **PHILIP EVAN THOMAS,** Attorney-at-Law, *b.* in 1828 ; *d.* in 1854.
ii.   **ALBERT,** *b.* in 1829 ; *d. i.*
iii.   **ELIZABETH ANN,** *b.* in 1830 ; *m.,* in 1859, **DAVID TWEEDIE,**
       of Glasgow, Scotland.   Issue :

    i.   **THOMAS E. W.,** *b.* in 1860.
    ii.   **ANNE,** *b.* in 1862.
    iii.   **M. STANLEY,** *b.* in 1864.
    iv.   **MARY,** *b.* in 1869.

iv.   **THOMAS GEORGE,** *b.* in 1832 ; a merchant by profession ; *m.,* first, in
       October, 1860, **LUCY BOWMAN HOLBROOK,** a descendant
       of **Nathaniel Bowman,** who came from England about 1630, and
       was one of the original settlers of Watertown, Mass.   She *d.* in 1871.
       Issue :

    i.   **HOLBROOK,** *b.* in 1861 ; *d.* in March, 1862.
    ii.   **ARTHUR LUCIAN,** *b.* in 1863, Manager of the Baltimore Electric Refining Com-
        pany ; *m.,* in 1890, **ANNIE LAURIE McNAIR.**
    iii.   **MARION,** *b.* in 1866.
    iv.   **LOUIS BOWMAN,** *b.* in 1869; *m.,* in 1894, **ELIZABETH CHENEY
        WHEELER.** Issue :

        Margrett Louise, *b.* 1895.

       After the death of his first wife, **THOMAS G. WALKER** *m.,* second, in
       April, 1873, her cousin, **LOUISE JONES BOWMAN** (who *d.*
       December, 1890), and *d.* in February, 1891.   Issue :

    v.   **LUCY**, *b.* in 1874 ; *d.* in 1878.
    vi.   **EDITH**, *b.* in 1878.
    vii.   **IRENE**, *b.* in 1880.
    viii.   **ALICE**, *b.* in 1882 ; *d. i.*
    ix.   **BERTHA LOUISE**, *b.* December, 1883.

v.   **WILLIAM GEORGE**, *b.* in 1834 ; *d. i.*

vi.   **WILLIAM THOMAS**, *b.* in 1836 ; *d. i.*

vii.   **GEORGE EDMONDSON**, *b.* in 1837 ; an Attorney-at-Law ; *m.*, in 1866, **JANET E.**, *dau.* of the Hon. **James W. White**, one of the Justices of the Superior Court of New York City, and his wife, **Rhoda E. Waterman**, a granddaughter of **General Joshua Whitney**, the founder of Binghamton, N. Y. Issue :

    i.   **LLEWELLYN JOHN**, *b.* February 18, 1867.
    ii.   **GERALD GRIFFIN**, *b.* in 1869.
    iii.   **KATHRIN ANN**, *b.* in 1870.
    iv.   **CECIL THOMAS**, *b.* in 1872.
    v.   **RHODA JANET**, *b.* March 16, 1877.

viii.   **LEWIN WETHERED**, *b.* in 1839 ; *m.*, in 1876, **SOPHIE LIE-BENAU.**

ix.   **HARRIET**, *b.* in 1842 ; *d. i.*

x.   A son, *b.* in 1846, *d. unnamed.*

Authority : Family papers, through Messrs. Thomas G. and Arthur L. Walker.

WARFIELD

In December, 1650, land was surveyed in Middle Neck Hundred, S. Ann's Parish, near the site of Annapolis, for **RICHARD** and **ALEXANDER WARFIELD**. Richard's will was proved February 11, 1703, naming his children **JOHN, RICHARD, ALEXANDER, BENJAMIN, RACHEL,** and **ELINOR.**

> **ALEXANDER,** the third son, *m.*, December 3, 1723, **DINAH,** *dau.* of **Robert Davidge.** Issue :
>
> i.   **JOSHUA,** *b.* October 27, 1724.
> ii. **AZEL,** *b.* April 23, 1726, *of whom presently.*
> And eleven other children.

AZEL, second son of **Alexander** and **Dinah (Davidge) Warfield,** *b.* April 23, 1726 ; was *m.*, February 26, 1751, by Rev. Alexander Malcom, of Queen Caroline Parish, to **SARAH,** *dau.* of **Captain Charles** and **Catherine (Baldwin) Griffith** (*b.* August 30, 1730 ; *d.* December 23, 1765). Issue :

i.   **CHARLES ALEXANDER,** *b.* December 14, 1751, *of whom presently.*
ii. **DINAH.**
iii. **CATHERINE,** *b.* April 7, 1757.
iv. **WALTER.**
v.   **ANNE.**
vi. **ZACHARIAH.**

CHARLES ALEXANDER, eldest son of **Azel** and **Sarah (Griffith)-Warfield,** *b.* December 14, 1751, at Bushy Park, in the upper part of Anne Arundel (now Howard) Co., where he resided until his death.

He was graduated at the University of Pennsylvania, and was one of the founders of the Medical School of the University of Maryland. He had a very large practice, extending over several of the counties. In early life he was a prominent member of the Whig Club, and on hearing of the arrival of the Peggy Stewart, at Annapolis, loaded with tea, went with the Club to that town, determined to destroy the vessel and its cargo. Samuel Chase, the signer of the Constitution, who had been employed by Mr. Anthony Stewart, the owner of the vessel, as his lawyer, met them opposite the State House, and attempted to divert them from their purpose. Finding that his speech was having some effect upon the mob, Dr. Warfield interrupted him, pronouncing it submission and cowardice in the Club to hesitate, and called on them to follow him to the vessel. It is said that Mr. Stewart was compelled to kindle the torch which Dr. Warfield carried, and to set fire to his vessel by threats of hanging him if he refused. This act had an extensive influence in deciding the course Maryland took in the Revolution.

DR. WARFIELD *m.*, November 21, 1771, **ELIZA**, *dau.* of **Major Henry** and **Anne (Dorsey) Ridgely**, *b.* September 25, 1752 ; *d.* September 8, 1808 ; her husband *d.* January 29, 1813. Issue :

i.   **ANNA**, who *m.* **SAMUEL THOMAS** (*q. v.*).
ii.   **HENRY RIDGELY**, *b.* September 14, 1774 ; *d. u.* at Frederick, Md., in March, 1839.
iii. **HARRIET**, *d. i.*
iv.   **DR. PEREGRINE**, *b.* February 8, 1779 ; *m.*, May 13, 1806, **HARRIET SAPPINGTON**, and *d. s. p.* July 24, 1856. His wife *d.* July 27th of the same year.
v.   **ELIZA**, *m.* **RICHARD SNOWDEN**, of " Oakland " (*q. v.*).
vi.   **DR. GUSTAVUS**, *of whom presently.*
vii. **CHARLES ALEXANDER**, *b.* November 1, 1787 ; *m.*, February 25, 1812, **ELIZA HARRIS**, and *d.* July 25, 1868. Issue :

    i.   **SALLIE**, *b.* November 30, 1812 ; *d.* at Sykesville, Md., April 12, 1817.
    ii.   **CHARLES ALEXANDER**, *b.* February 18, 1815, killed in the Confederate States Army during the civil war.
    iii. **EDWARD HARRIS**, *b.* November 10, 1817, since *d.*
    iv.   **PEREGRINE**, *b.* in 1819, since *d.*
    v.   **HENRY**, *b.* in 1821, since *d.*

viii. **LOUISA VICTORIA**, *b.* May 4, 1790 ; *m.* her brother-in-law, **RICHARD SNOWDEN**, of " Oakland " (*q. v.*).

DR. GUSTAVUS, sixth child of **Dr. Charles Alexander** and **Eliza (Ridgely) Warfield**, was *b.* March 31, 1784 ; *m.*, October 27, 1810, at " Whitby Hall," to **MARY**, *dau.* of **Evan W.** and **Martha (Gray) Thomas**, by Bishop White, of Pennsylvania. Dr. Gustavus Warfield was an eminent physician, and actively engaged in practice for nearly sixty years. He *d.* August 8, 1866 ; and his widow *d.* January 8, 1884. Issue :

i.   **CHARLES ALEXANDER**, *b.* September 3, 1812, at " Whitby Hall,"
and *d.* there September 21, 1823.

ii.   **MARTHA ANN**, *b.* August 6, 1814, at " Bushy Park ; " *m.* there **DR.
WILLIAM G. KNOWLES** (*q. v.*).

iii.   **ELIZABETH RIDGELY**, *b.* July 9, 1816, at " Bushy Park ; " *m.*,
RICHARD NICHOLAS, son of **Richard Snowden**, of Oakland (*q. v.*).

iv.   **MARY THOMAS**, *b.* June 30, 1818, at " Bushy Park ; " *m.* **EDWARD
SNOWDEN** (*q. v.*).

v.   **EMMA WARFIELD**, *b.* April 19, 1820, at " Longwood Cottage," after
Dr. Warfield's house was burnt ; *m.*, June 11, 1846, at " Longwood,"
REV. DR. THOMAS JAMES SHEPHERD, Pastor of the
First Presbyterian Church, Philadelphia, for twenty-five years.

vi.   **LOUISA VICTORIA**, *b.* June 27, 1822, at " Longwood," which was rebuilt
in 1821, and resided there with her mother.

vii.   **DR. EVAN WILLIAM**, *b.* May 25, 1825, *of whom presently.*

viii.   **GUSTAVUS**, *b.* March 16, 1827 ; *d.* July 19, 1828.

ix.   **EUGENIA GRAY**, *b.* November 27, 1828 ; *m.* **DR. WILLIAM
HENRY STINSON**, of Baltimore, who *d.* at " Falling Water,"
Baltimore Co., December 19, 1864. Issue (surname STINSON) :

    i.   **MARY WARFIELD**, *b.* January 3, 1860 ; *m.*, June 10, 1884, **DR. AUGUSTUS
RIGGS.** Issue (surname RIGGS) :
        i.   **Augustus**, *b.* August 1, 1885.
        ii.   **William Stinson**, *b.* February 8, 1888.
    ii.   **WILLIAM HENRY**, *b.* January 19, 1862 ; *m.*, December 7, 1887, **ESTELLE
TREGO ROANE.** Issue :
        i.   **Helen**, *b.* February 20, 1889.
        ii.   **Mary Warfield**, *b.* March 4, 1890.
    iii.   **ISABELLA**, *b.* January 26, 1864 ; *m.*, January 13, 1886, **DR. WILLIAM PAGE
McINTOSH.** Issue (surname McINTOSH) :
        i.   **William Page**, *b.* March 2, 1887.
        ii.   **Eugenia**, *b.* July 13, 1888.
        iii.   **Isabella**, *b.* March, 1890.
        iv.   **Mary Estelle**, *b.* April 3, 1892.

x.   **ISABELLA**, *b.* February 21, 1832 ; *m.*, May 17, 1853, **CHARLES
DORSEY**, eldest son of **Charles D.** and **Ruth Hammond (Griffith) Warfield.** Issue :

    i.   **CHARLES ALEXANDER**, *b.* April 27, 1854.
    ii.   **GUSTAVUS**, *b.* December 13, 1855.
    iii.   **MARY EMMA**, *b.* September 27, 1857.
    iv.   **HARRY RIDGELY**, *b.* September 12, 1859 ; *d.* May 19, 1865.
    v.   **EUGENIA GRAY**, *b.* August 4, 1861 ; *d.* September 30, 1864.
    vi.   **PEREGRINE WARFIELD**, *b.* January 16, 1864.
    vii.   **HARRY RIDGELY**, *b.* November 8, 1869.
    viii.   **ARTHUR**, *b.* October 3, 1871.

xi.   **ADELAIDE**, *b.* April 13, 1835 ; *m.*, April 29, 1857, **WILLIAM**, son of
Rezin H. Snowden, of " Birmingham " (*q. v.*).

xii.   **GUSTAVUS**, *b.* January 8, 1838 ; *d.* January 10, 1838.

DR. EVAN WILLIAM, eldest surviving son of **Dr. Gustavus** and **Mary (Thomas) Warfield**, *b.* May 25, 1825, at "Longwood," Howard Co.; *m.*, first, November 9, 1848, **SALLIE ANN**, *dau.* of **Charles D.** and **Ruth H. Warfield.**   Issue:

i.   **GUSTAVUS WILLIAM**, *b.* November 24, 1849; *m.* **ELLA GERTRUDE**, *dau.* of **H. K. Hoffman.** Issue:

   HENRY HOFFMAN, LUCILE, SARAH, ELLA GERTRUDE, GUSTAVUS, and EVAN SHEPHERD.

ii.   **OLIVIA GRIFFITH**, *b.* January 14, 1852; *d.* August 21, 1852.
iii. **LOUISA VICTORIA**, *b.* May 9, 1853; *m.*, October 27, 1874, **CHARLES A. HOOK.** Issue (surname HOOK):

   i.   EMMA WARFIELD, *b.* June 6, 1876; *d.* July 3, 1876.
   ii.   EVAN WARFIELD, *b.* February 23, 1877.
   iii. CHARLES A.
   iv.   MARTIN.
   v.   KENLY.
   vi.   GUSTAVUS.
   vii. MARIAN.
   viii. LOUISA VICTORIA.

iv.   **MARY THOMAS**, *b.* June 13, 1855; *m.*, November 17, 1886, **THOMAS B. COCKEY.** Issue:

   i.   EVA, *b.* October 22, 1887.
   ii.   SARAH WARFIELD, *b.* February 22, 1889.
   iii. EMMA SHEPHERD, *b.* June 11, 1891.

v.   **CHARLES DORSEY**, *b.* February 24, 1858; *d.* June 30, 1858.
vi.   **EVAN WILLIAM**, *b.* April 12, 1859; *m.*, June 16, 1891, **LILLY HINES.**
vii. **CHARLES DORSEY**, *b.* December 29, 1860; *m.*, November 17, 1886, **MARY**, *dau.* of **Nicholas** and **Henrietta (Stabler) Snowden** (*q. v.*). Issue:

   i.   AMABEL, *b.* September 8, 1887.
   ii.   CLARA, *b.* September 3, 1889.
   iii. EDWARD SNOWDEN, *b.* April 16, 1892.

viii. **CLARA**, *b.* September 3, 1863; *d.* January 17, 1867.

DR. EVAN W. WARFIELD *m.*, second, June 30, 1890, at Richmond, Va., **JULIA GILMER ANTHONY.**   Further issue:

ix.   **WILLIAM ANTHONY**, *b.* October 23, 1891.

Authorities : Family papers, through Mrs. Edward Snowden and Mrs. W. G. Knowles, Griffith Genealogy, and Maryland Land Records.

WETHERED

SAMUEL WETHERED, a wealthy London merchant, descended from **James Wethered,** of Ashlyns, in Hertfordshire, living about 1400 ; *m.* **DOLLY,** *dau.* of **Sir William** and **Susanna Lewin,** and investing in the South Sea Bubble lost all his fortune, and *d.* from mortification at his failure in 1719. In 1720 his widow removed to America, settling first at Jamaica Plains, Mass. Her son Richard going to Maryland, wrote, saying, " the climate was far more genial, and the people much more like their friends in England," and she removed to Maryland, and *d.* there, leaving, with other issue (for whom see L. B. Thomas's Genealogical Notes, 1877, *pp.* 158, 159), a fourth son, **RICHARD,** who *m.* **ISABELLA,** *dau.* of **Colonel William** and **Isabella (Pearce) Blay,** of Blay's Range, Kent Co., Md. Issue :

i. **WILLIAM,** removed to Virginia ; *m.* —— **HURT. Issue :**

    Peregrine, *m.* —— Turpin and had a son Turpin.

ii. **JOHN,** *d.* in childhood.
iii. **SAMUEL.**
iv. **JOHN,** *of whom presently.*

JOHN, youngest son of **Richard** and **Isabella (Blay) Wethered,** *m.* **MARY,** *dau.* of **Judge J. Sykes,** of Delaware. Issue :

i. **PEREGRINE,** *m.* **HANNAH MEDFORD**, and *d.* 1857. Issue :

    i.   JOHN LATHAM, *m.*, January 16, 1862, CHARLOTTE, *dau.* of George Spencer.

    ii.   MARY ELIZABETH, *m.* WILLIAM JANVIER, who *d.* April 26, 1876.

ii.   **SAMUEL**, *m.* **ELIZA**, *dau.* of **Colonel George Yeates**, of Kent Co., Md. Issue :

    i.   JOHN D.
    ii.   GEORGE YEATES.
    iii.   MATILDA.
    iv.   LEWINA.
    v.   ELIZABETH.
    vi.   SARAH.
    vii. SAMUEL.

iii.   **LEWIN**, *of whom presently.*

iv.   **MARY.**

v.   **SARAH ISABELLA.**

vi.   **ANN CATHERINE**, *m.* **ROBERT C. LUDLOW**, U. S. N. Issue :

    i.   BAINBRIDGE, in the United States Navy.
    ii.   AUGUSTUS, *m.* AUGUSTA CROOK and *d.* Issue :

        i.   Mary Clare, *m.* Samuel G. B. Cook, of Baltimore.
        ii.   Sarah Wethered, *m.* Tatlow Jackson.
        iii.   Charlotte Sellman, *m.* J. Seth Hopkins, of Baltimore, Md.
        iv.   Kate, *m.* Alonzo Lilly, Jr., of Baltimore. and *d.*
        v.   Rose, her twin sister, *m.* Alonzo Lilly, Jr., as his second wife.

        MRS. LUDLOW *m.*, second, **HANS P. MOWINCKEL**, of Baltimore, Md., since *d.* Further issue (surname MOWINCKEL) :

        vi.   Augusta.
        vii. Nettie, *m.* Edmund J. Whelan.

    iii.   MARY WETHERED, *m.*, October 5, 1837, HON. JAMES CARROLL, of Baltimore. Issue :

        i.   Achsah Ridgely.
        ii.   Sarah Wethered.
        iii.   James, *d. i.*
        iv.   Mary Ludlow.
        v.   Sophia Gough.
        vi.   Harry Dorsey Gough, *d.*
        vii. Catherine Ludlow.

    iv.   CATHERINE.

vii.   **CATHERINE MATILDA**, *m.* **GEORGE JEFFRIES**, who changed his name to **JAFFREY**. Issue :

    i.   MATILDA, *d.* in 1850.
    ii.   MARY, *m.* CAPTAIN H. FIELD, United States Army.

viii. **HARRIET**, *m.* **ADMIRAL WILLIAM B. SHUBRICK**, U. S. N. Issue :

    i.   MARY W. B.
    ii.   HARRIET, *d.* in 1830.

ix.   **CAROLINE.**

LEWIN, third son of **John** and **Mary (Sykes) Wethered,** *b.* February 17, 1787, *m.* **ELIZABETH,** *dau.* of **Elias** and **Mary (Thomas) Ellicott** (*q. v.*). Issue :

i.   **PEREGRINE,** *b.* August 10, 1806 ; *m.* **LOUISA MARIA,** *dau.* of **Lambert** and **Alethea (Ireland) Wickes,** and *d.* December 18, 1845. Issue :

       i.   **ANN ELIZABETH,** *b.* March 21, 1829 ; *m.*, June 2, 1857, **WILLIAM NICOLS EARLE WICKES.** Issue :

           i.   **Louisa Maria.**
           ii.   **William N. E.,** *d. i.*
           iii.   **Lewin Wethered.**

       ii.   **LEWIN,** *b.* March 5, 1834.
       iii.   **CHARLES WETHERED,** *b.* January 10, 1836 ; *d.* December 25, 1850.

ii.   **CHARLES ELIAS,** *b.* November 7, 1807 ; *m.*, in 1836, **ISABELLA BATHURST.** Issue :

       Charles, *b.* in 1837 ; *d.* December 25, 1850.

iii.   **JOHN,** *b.* May 8, 1809 ; with his brothers established a woollen mill at Wetheredsville, Baltimore Co., and afterward organized the Ashland Manufacturing Company. He was a member of Congress ; *m.*, in 1835, **MARY,** *dau.* of **Philip E. Thomas** (*q. v.*). In 1844 Professor Samuel F. B. Morse perfected his invention of the Electric Telegraph, and a line of wire was laid between Washington and Baltimore. Mr. Wethered was then in Congress, and present when Morse, announcing that the circuit was completed, and the line ready for messages, asked "Who shall have the honour of sending the first message?" Some one suggested the President (Tyler). Cries of "No! no!" showed his unpopularity ; and the Professor, smiling, repeated, "Well, then, gentlemen, who shall it be?" A gentleman said, "Mrs. Dolly Madison, President Madison's widow." This met the approval of all present, and Mrs. Madison was sent for. When she came she asked, "What is it you wish me to do, gentlemen?" Some one replied, "To send a message to Baltimore, and get a reply in a few minutes." After expressing her disbelief and wonder at this statement, Mrs. Madison selected Mrs. Wethered as her friend in Baltimore, and sent as the message, the following words : " Message from Mrs. Madison. She sends her love to Mrs. Wethered." This was preserved by the latter as the *first* ever sent by telegraph.[1] **MR. WETHERED** *d. s. p.*, February, 1888.

iv.   **SAMUEL,** *b.* February 22, 1811 ; *d. u.*, June 17, 1878.

v.   **MARY LEWIN,** *b.* December 2, 1812 ; *m.* **WILLIAM G. THOMAS** (*q. v.*).

vi.   **ANN POULTNEY,** *b.* November 26, 1814 ; *m.*, in August, 1846, **HENRY CARVILL.** Issue (surname CARVILL) :

       i.   **MARY,** *d.* in December, 1849.
       ii.   **JOHN,** *d.* in 1859.

---

[1] This narrative was taken down from the lips of the Hon. John Wethered, in 1877, his wife concurring in it, and the actual telegraphic slips being shown to the author. (The first *private* message.)

vii.   **LEWIN,** *b.* May 8, 1819 ; *d.* March 11, 1826.
viii. **ELIZABETH,** *b.* February 2, 1822 ; *m.*, August 15, 1848, **HON. DANIEL MOREAU BARRINGER,** of North Carolina, who was United States Minister at the Court of Spain from June 18, 1849, to September 4, 1853 ; *d.* September 1, 1873. Issue (surname BARRINGER) :

    i.   **LEWIN WETHERED,** *b.* at Madrid, Spain, March 30, 1850; *m.*, February 10, 1874, **MARY C. MILES.** Issue :

        i.   **Mary C.,** *b.* December 11, 1874.
        ii.   **Lewin W.,** *b.* February 15, 1876.
        iii. **Edmund,** *b.* March 16, 1878.

    ii.   **ELIZABETH B.,** *b.* March 24, 1851.
    iii. **PAUL MOREAU,** *b.* October 13, 1858.
    iv.   **DAVID MOREAU,** *b.* May 25, 1860.
    v.   **SAMUEL W.,** *b.* November 28, 1861.

ix.   **JAMES SYKES,** was a California pioneer, and member of its first Legislature ; *m.*, in San Francisco, Cal., August 21, 1860, **MARY J.,** *dau.* of the poet **Samuel Woodworth,** author of " The Old Oaken Bucket " and other well-known poems. Issue :

    i.   **LEWINA,** *b.* April 29, 1861.
    ii.   **CAROLINE,** *b.* August 9, 1862.
    iii. **MARY,** *b.* August 31, 1864.
    iv.   **WOODWORTH,** *b.* August 9, 1866.

Authorities : Family papers, through the late Hon. John Wethered, and Colonel Hanson's Old Kent.

WILCOCKS AND INGERSOLL

ALEXANDER, son of **John** and **Elizabeth (Wooddrop) Wilcocks,** *b.* 1741 ; graduated in law at Philadelphia, and March 4, 1774, was a Justice for Philadelphia Co. ; October, 1775, was a Member of the Committee of Safety, and was Recorder of the city of Philadelphia for a number of years after the Revolution. He *m.*, May 18, 1768, **MARY,** eldest *dau.* of **Chief-Justice Benjamin** and **Mary (Galloway) Chew** (*q. v.*), who *d.* August 22, 1794. Her husband *d.* July 22, 1801. Issue :

i.   **JOHN,** *b.* December 25, 1769 ; *d. y.*
ii.   **MARY,** *b.* October 5, 1771 ; *d. y.*
iii. **ELIZABETH,** *b.* July 9, 1773 ; *d. y.*
iv. **ELIZABETH,** *b.* August 27, 1774 ; *d. u.*, March 11, 1864.
v.   **BENJAMIN CHEW,** *b.* December 13, 1776 ; *m.*, October 10, 1842, **MARY,** *dau.* of **William** and **Mary (Wilcocks) Waln,** and *d.* December 1, 1845. Issue :

    i.   MARY WALN, *m.* ALEXANDER DALLAS CAMPBELL.
    ii. HELEN JULIA, *m.* CHANDLER ROBBINS, and *d. s. p.* in 1868.

vi. **ANN,** *b.* November 13, 1781 ; *m.*, September 22, 1813, **JOSEPH REED INGERSOLL,** a prominent lawyer of Philadelphia ; *b.* June 14, 1786 ; Member of Congress, 1835-37, 1842-49 ; United States Minister to England, August 21, 1852 ; President of the American Philosophical Society, of the Philadelphia Academy of Fine Arts, and the Historical Society of Pennsylvania ; *d.* February 20, 1868, without surviving issue ; his wife *d.* May 28, 1831.
vii. **MARY,** *b.* January 2, 1784, *of whom presently.*
viii. **SAMUEL,** *b.* March 1, 1786 ; *m.* **HARRIET,** *dau.* of **Gabriel** and **Margaret (Izard) Manigault,** of South Carolina, and *d.* March 22, 1824. Issue :

    i.   ALEXANDER, *d.* November 10, 1880.
    ii. MARY M., *m.* KIRK B. WELLS.
    iii. CHARLOTTE M., *m.* HARRY McCALL, and *d.* May 21, 1875.

MARY, youngest *dau.* of **Alexander** and **Mary (Chew) Wilcocks,** *b.* January 2, 1784 ; *m.*, October 18, 1804, **CHARLES**

JARED INGERSOLL, son of **Jared Ingersoll, LL.D.,** Attorney-General of Pennsylvania ; Member of the Continental Congress, and Judge of the United States District Court, and grandson of **Jared Ingersoll,** Agent of the Colony of Connecticut in London, etc. **CHARLES J. INGERSOLL** was *b.* at Philadelphia, October 3, 1782, was author of "Cheomora," in the *Portfolio,* 1800 ; "Edwy and Elgiva, a Tragedy," 1801 : "Inchiquin, the Jesuit's Letters on American Literature and Politics," 1810, and of a "History of the War of 1812." He was a Member of Congress, 1813–15, 1841–47, serving as Chairman of the Committee on Foreign Affairs. He *d.* May 14, 1862, and his wife *d.* August of the same year. Issue (surname INGERSOLL) :

i.   **CHARLES,** Attorney-at-law ; author of " Fears for Democracy ; " *m.* **SUSAN CATHERINE BROWN,** of Tennessee. Issue :

     i.   FRANCES MARIA, *d.* March 18, 1846.
     ii.   ADÈLE CATHERINE, *m.* JOHN MOYLAN THOMAS, Esq. (*q. v.*).
     iii.   ANN WILCOCKS, *m.* DR. JAMES HOWELL HUTCHINSON, of Philadelphia.
     iv.   ELIZABETH WILCOCKS, *m.* ARTHUR AMORY, of New York.
     v.   KATHERINE MARGARET PRESTON, *m.* DR. FRANCIS FONTAINE MAURY, Professor in Jefferson College, Philadelphia, and both *d.* in 1879.

ii.   **ALEXANDER WILCOCKS.**
iii.   **HARRY,** *m.* **SARAH E. ROBERTS.**
iv.   **JOHN,** *m.,* first, **MARGARETTA SMITH** ; second, **SARAH GRIFFIN,** and *d.* in 1859.
v.   **BENJAMIN WILCOCKS,** *d. u.* in January, 1859.
vi.   **ELIZABETH,** *m.* **SYDNEY GEORGE FISHER,** and *d.* May 27, 1872.
vii.   **EDWARD,** Attorney-at-law. *m.* **ANNA C. WARREN.**
viii.   **ANN WILCOCKS,** *m.* **DR. JOHN FORSYTH,** son of **Dr. Charles D.** and **Mary (Montgomery) Meigs,** and *d.* December 30, 1856. Issue (surname MEIGS) :

     i.   EMILY, *d. y.*
     ii.   REV. HARRY INGERSOLL, Clergyman Protestant Episcopal Church.
     iii.   JOHN FORSYTH, Lieutenant United States Navy ; *m.* JANE PERRY RODGERS.
     iv.   DR. ARTHUR VINCENT, of Philadelphia ; *m.* MARY R., *dau.* of Edward Browning.
     v.   WILLIAM MONTGOMERY.
     vi.   ALEXANDER W.
     vii.   ANN I.
     viii. MARY H., *d. i.*

ix.   **SAMUEL,** *d. i.,* February 23, 1827.

Authorities : Family papers, through the late Samuel Chew, of Germantown, and Keith's Provincial Councillors.

WINDSOR ARMS

WINDSOR AND HUNTERCOMBE

OTHO or **OTHERE**, living *temp.* Edward the Confessor, by some called a Norwegian, by others a scion of the **Gherardini** of Italy, had a son, **WALTER FITZ OTHO**, Castellan of Windsor, and Warden of the forests of Berks. He *m.* **GLADYS**, *dau.* of **Rhiwallon ap Cynfyn**, Prince of North Wales. Issue :

i.   **WILLIAM**, *of whom presently.*
ii.   **ROBERT.**
iii.   **GERALD**, ancestor of the **Fitzgeralds** of Ireland.

WILLIAM, eldest son of **Walter**, called himself **William de Windsor**, and the Empress Maud confirmed to him his father's offices. He *m.* a *dau.* of **Robert Fitz Walter**, Lord of Estaines, in Essex. Issue :

i.   **WILLIAM**, *d.* 1194. Issue :

    i.   **WALTER**, had two daughters :
        i.   **Christian**, *m.* Duncan Lascelles.
        ii.   **Gunnora**, *m.* Ralph de Hodeng, *of whom presently.*

    ii.   **WILLIAM**, ancestor of the Lords Windsor, Viscounts Montjoy, and Earls of Plymouth.

ii.   **HUGH**, seated at West Horsley, in Surrey.

RALPH and **GUNNORA (Windsor) HODENG** had issue :

    SIR HUGH, whose only *dau.* **ALICE** *m.*, as his second wife, **WILLIAM DE HUNTERCOMBE**, *temp.* Henry III. Issue (surname HUNTERCOMBE) :

        Thomas, whose grandson John had a *dau.* and heiress, Agnes, *m.* Philip Scudamore (*q. v.*).

Authorities : Sir T. C. Banks's Baronage, II., 347, 445 ; Dingley's History from Marble, *p.* xili.

553

WINTHROP, FONES, AND FEAKE

ADAM, youngest son of **Adam**[1] and **Agnes (Sharpe) Winthrop**,
b. August 10, 1548, on Grace-Church Street, in the Parish of S.
Peter's, London, was a lawyer, Auditor of Trinity and S. John's
Colleges, Cambridge. He *m.*, December 16, 1574, **ALICE**, *dau.*
of **William Still**, and sister of **Bishop John Still**. She *d.* in
childbed, December 24, 1577, and he *m.*, second, February 20,
1579, **ANNE**, *dau.* of **Henry** and **Agnes Browne**, of Edward-
ston, clothier, and *d.* between March 25 and April 20, 1623.
Issue :

i.   **ANNE**, *b.* January 5 ; *d.* January 20, 1580–81.
ii.   **ANNE**, *b.* January 16, 1585–86, *of whom presently.*
iii.   **JOHN**, *b.* January 12, 1587–88, the first Governor of the Massachusetts Bay
         Colony, *m.*, first, April 16, 1605, **MARY**, *dau.* and heiress of **John**
         Forth, who *d.* June, 1615. Surviving issue :

    i.   **JOHN**, *b.* February 12, 1605-6 ; Governor of Connecticut ; *m.* his cousin, **MARTHA**
            FONES (*q. v.*).
    ii.   **HENRY**, *bapt.* January 20, 1607 ; *m.*, April 25, 1629, his cousin, **ELIZABETH**
            FONES (*q. v.*), and *d.* July 2, 1630.
    iii. **MARY**, *m.*, about 1632, **REV. SAMUEL**, son of Governor Thomas Dudley, and
            d. April 12, 1643.

    GOVERNOR WINTHROP *m.*, second, December 6, 1615, **THOM-
    ASINE**, *dau.* of **William Clopton**, of Castleins, who *d.* in child-

---

[1] He was *b.* October 9, 1498, at Lavenham, in Suffolk ; Master of the Cloth Workers' Company of
London, 1551 ; granted the Manor of Groton in 1544 on payment of £408 18*s.* 3*d.* to the Treasury, and
d. November 9, 1562. Son of Adam and Joane (Burton) Winthrop, of a family anciently seated in
Northumberland.

bed in a year, and he *m.*, third, before April 24, 1618, **MARGA-RET,** *dau.* of **Sir John Tyndal, Knt.,** of Great Maplested, Essex, who *d.* June 16, 1647. Issue surviving :

iv. **STEPHEN,** *b.* March 24, 1618-19 ; Colonel and M.P. under Cromwell ; *d.* 1658.
v. **ADAM,** *b.* April 7, 1620; *d.* 1652.
vi. **DEANE,** *b.* 1623 ; *d.* March 16, 1704-5.
vii. **SAMUEL,** Deputy-Governor of the Island of Antigua, 1668.

GOVERNOR WINTHROP *m.*, fourth, 1648, MARTHA (NOW-ELL), widow of **Thomas Coytmore,** and *d. s. p.* by her surviving, March 26, 1649.

iv. JANE, *bapt.* June 17, 1592; *m.*, January 5, 1612, THOMAS GOST-LING.

v. LUCY, *b.* January 9, 1600-1601 ; *m.*, April 10, 1622, EMANUEL DOWNING.

ANNE, eldest surviving child of **Adam** and **Agnes (Browne) Winthrop,** *b.* January 16, 1585–86 ; *m.*, first, February 25, 1604–1605, **THOMAS FONES,** apothecary, of London, sixth in descent from **William Fownes,**[1] of Saxbie, Esq., who *m.* a *dau.* of **Sir Robert Hyelton, Knt.** Issue (surname FONES) :

i. DOROTHY, *b.* October 24, 1608 ; *d.* December 24, 1608.
ii. ELIZABETH, *b.* January 21, 1609, *of whom presently.*
iii. MARTHA, *m.* February 8, 1631, her cousin, JOHN WINTHROP, Jr. (*q. v.*).

MRS. ANNE (WINTHROP) FONES, *d.* May 16, 1619, and her husband *m.*, second, August 28, 1621, MRS. PRISCILLA SHERMAN (?), *dau.* of Rev. John Burgis, D.D., removed to Ipswich in 1622, and *d.* April 15, 1629 ; his widow *m.*, second, 1630, REV. HENRY PAINTER, of Exeter, afterward a member of the Westminster Assembly of Divines.

ELIZABETH, second *dau.* of **Thomas** and **Anne (Winthrop) Fones,** *b.* January 21, 1609 ; *m.*, first, April 25, 1629, her cousin, HENRY, son of Governor John Winthrop (*q. v.*). He was a planter at Barbadoes in 1627, but came home in 1628, and after his marriage was persuaded by his family not to return there. In 1630 he sailed for New England in the ship Talbot, and was accidentally drowned July 2, 1630, at Salem, the day after his landing. Issue (surname WINTHROP) :

MARTHA JOHANNA, *bapt.* May 9, 1630, at **Groton** ; *m.*, about 1646, THOMAS LYON, of Stamford, Conn.

[1] Arms : *A z.* two eagles displayed, in chief, and a mullet in base *ar. crest.* An oak stump, with a branch on each side, *ppr.*

MRS. ELIZABETH (FONES) WINTHROP, about the middle of August, 1631, with her mother-in-law and family, embarked in the Lion, William Peirce, master, for New England, arriving at Natascot November 2d.   She *m.*, second, before January, 1632, **ROBERT FEAKE** or **FEKE,** who was a Lieutenant in Captain Patrick's Company Massachusetts troops 1632–36, and member of the First General Court of the Massachusetts Bay Colony, 1635–36.   He was seven years insane, and *d.* February 1, 1662–63.   His inventory was only £9 9s. 2d.   His widow is said to have *m.*, third, **WILLIAM HALLETT,** afterward of Long Island.   By a former wife **LIEUTENANT FEAKE** had issue (surname FEAKE):

ROBERT and **JOHN.**

By **ELIZABETH FONES** he had :

HANNAH, *m.* **JOHN BOWNE** (*q. v.*).

Another *dau. m.* **CAPTAIN JOHN UNDERHILL,** the noted Indian fighter.

HENRY FEAKS, of Lynn, Mass., in 1632, who came to Newtown, Long Island, in 1655–56, was probably a brother of Lieutenant Feake, as also **TOBIAS FEAKE,** schout-fiscal, or sheriff, of Flushing, Long Island, under the Dutch, and son of **James Feake,** of London.   He *m.*, between 1644–49, **ANNETJE,** widow of **Captain Daniel Patricke,** and had a son, **JAMES,** and four other children. He *m.*, second, **MARY** ——, another widow.

Authorities: Hon. Robert C. Winthrop's Biography of Governor Winthrop ; Savage's Dictionary, II., 150 ; IV., 608 ; New York Genealogical and Biographical Record, II., 109, 159 ; IV., 26 ; VIII., 91.

ANDERSON,¹ OF BOTETOURT COUNTY, VA.

COLONEL WILLIAM ANDERSON, of "Walnut Hill," Botetourt Co., Va. (son of **Robert** and grandson of **Robert Anderson,** of the Parish of Killagarven, County Donegal, Ireland), was a prominent man in Church and State ; many times Member of the House of Delegates of Virginia, and Ruling Elder in the Presbyterian Church ; was a volunteer at less than sixteen years of age in the American Revolution ; was one of Greene's "picked men" to cover the famous retreat through the Carolinas which resulted so gloriously for the cause of liberty at Yorktown ; was at the Battles of Eutaw, Cowpens, and Guilford Court House. He *m.* **ANN,** second *dau.* of **Francis** and **Grace (Metcalfe) Thomas** (*q. v.*). Issue (surname ANDERSON) :

i.   **JOHN THOMAS,** eminent lawyer ; Ruling Elder of Presbyterian Church ; appointed Visitor to West Point Military Academy, by President Andrew Jackson ; residence "Montjoy," near Buchanan, Botetourt Co., Va. He *m.* **CASSANDRA PATTON,** widow, and *d.* Issue :

     i.   **MARY,** *d. i.*
     ii.   **JOSEPH WASHINGTON,** *b.* 1836 ; graduate of University of Virginia with highest honor in Law ; resided at "Montjoy ;" Chief of Artillery in Civil War ; slain in battle leading on the Infantry at Vicksburg ; *m.* **SUSAN MORRIS,** and *d.* Issue :
         i.   John Francis Thomas, of Richmond, Va.
         ii.   Anna Morris, *m.* Professor Richard T. Ely, the well-known writer on Political Economy, now of Madison University, Wisconsin. Issue : John Thomas Anderson Ely, *b.* 1895.

ii.   **WILLIAM NEELY,** *b.* at "Walnut Hill," *m.* —— **KERR,** of Augusta Co., Va., and *d.* Issue : one son, RUSH, *d. y.*
iii.   **FRANCIS THOMAS,** *b.* at "Walnut Hill," 1808 ; *of whom presently.*
iv.   **MARGARET,** *b.* at "Walnut Hill ; " *d.* aged nineteen years.
v.   **GRACE,** *b.* at "Walnut Hill ; " *d.* aged twenty-seven years.
vi.   **MARY,** *b.* at "Walnut Hill ; " *d.* aged twenty-one years.

¹ The ensuing pedigrees of **Anderson, Blackburn, Crabb, Gillespie, Glasgow, and Junkin,** were received too late for insertion in their alphabetical order and hence are grouped together here.

vii.   KATHARINE ("KITTY"), *b.* at "Walnut Hill;" *m.* ROBERT
         GLASGOW (*q. v.*).
viii.   JOSEPH REID, *b.* at "Walnut Hill," 1813 (*q. v.*).

FRANCIS THOMAS, third son of Colonel William and Ann
(Thomas) Anderson, of "Walnut Hill," *b.* 1808; educated at
Washington College, Va.; admitted to the Bar, 1830; became a
brilliant and able lawyer and orator, and practised his profession
with distinguished success; was repeatedly Member of the House
of Delegates of Virginia; large land owner in Rockbridge, Botetourt, and Bedford Counties, Va.; Ruling Elder of the Presbyterian Church; a leader of the Whig Party of his State; Member
from Virginia, and President of the Electoral College to elect President of the United States in 1860; Judge of the Supreme Court
of Appeals of Virginia 1870–82; many years and until his death
the Rector of Washington and Lee University; a promoter and
fosterer of education in all its branches; devoted throughout
his life to the interests of his people and State; the friend of
the poor, and the defender of the weak and oppressed; a godly
man. On his death the Bar of his State and the Supreme Court
of Appeals of Virginia, honoured his memory by eulogistic resolutions (*vide* Records of that Court, 1887). Resided at "Montrose," near Fincastle, Botetourt Co., Va.; later "Glenwood,"
near present Glenwood Post Office, Rockbridge Co., Va.; later,
Lexington, Va.; *m.* MARY ANN (*b.* 1806; *d.* 1881), *dau.* of
Colonel Andrew Alexander, of "Liberty Hall," near Lexington, Va., and *d.* 1887. Issue:

i.   ANNA AYLETT, *b.* at "Montrose," 1833; *m.* REV. WILLIAM F.
        JUNKIN, D.D., LL.D. (*q. v.*).
ii.   MARY EVELYN, *b.* at "Montrose," 1835; *m.*, 1855, at "Montrose,"
        ALEXANDER, son of James C. Bruce, of "Berry Hill," near
        South Boston, Halifax Co., Va. Issue (surname BRUCE):

    i.   ANNA, *b.* 1856; *d.* 1861.
    ii.   RICHARD, *b.* 1857; *d.* 1861.
    iii. MARY ALEXANDER, *b.* 1859; *m.*, 1884. WILLIAM ARMSTEAD PEN-
          DLETON, of St. Louis; resided at "Penn Gap," near Glenwood Post Office,
          Rockbridge Co., Va.; *d.* 1890. Issue (surname PENDLETON):
          i.   William Armstead, *b.* 1885.
          ii.   Alexander Bruce, *b.* 1887.
          iii. Allan Bruce, *b.* 1888; *d.* 1889.
    iv.   FRANCIS ANDERSON, *b.* at "Berry Hill," 1862; *d.* 1877.
    v.   ALEXANDER, *b.* at "Berry Hill," 1864; *d.* 1877.
    vi.   WALTER COLES, *b.* at "Berry Hill," 1868; Broker, Lynchburg, Va.

vii.   **MALCOLM GRAEME**, *b.* at "Berry Hill," 1869 ; Lawyer, Washington, D. C.
viii.   **ELLEN DOUGLAS**, *b.* at "Berry Hill," 1871.

iii.   **THEODORE**, *d. i.*
iv.   **KATHARINE**, *d. i.*
v.   **FRANCES MARGARET**, *b.* 1836 ; resides at Washington, D. C.
vi.   **JOSEPHINE**, *b.* 1838 ; *m.*, 1867, **WILLIAM BOWYER POIN-DEXTER** ; resides at Glenwood Post-Office, Va. Issue (surname POINDEXTER) :

    i.   **MILES**, *b.* 1868 ; resides at Walla Walla, Wash. ; *m.*, 1892, **ELIZABETH GALE PAGE**. Issue : one son, Gale Aylett, *b.* 1893.
    ii.   **FIELDING LEWIS**, *b.* 1871 ; resides at Glenwood, Va.
    iii. **ERNEST**, *b.* 1872 ; Lawyer, Walla Walla, Wash.
    iv. **WILLIAM A.**, *b.* 1874 ; resides at Glenwood, Va.
    v.   **GEORGE FAUNTLEROY**, *b.* 1876.
    vi. **MARY MACON**, *b.* 1878.

vii.   **WILLIAM ALEXANDER**, *b.* 1840 ; eminent Lawyer, Lexington, Rock-bridge Co., Va. ; *m.*, first, 1871, **ELLEN GRAHAM ANDER-SON** (*q. v.*), who *d. s. p.* 1872 ; *m.*, second, 1875, **MARY LOUISA**, *dau.* of Colonel William B. Blair,[1] U. S. A., and Judith Cornelia (Nichol) Blair.[2] Issue :

    i.   **RUTH FLOYD**.
    ii.   **ANNA AYLETT**.
    iii. **WILLIAM DANDRIDGE ALEXANDER**.
    iv. **JUDITH NICHOL**.
    v.   **ELLEN GRAHAM**.

viii.   **BELLE GRAHAM**, *b.* 1847 ; *m.* **WILLIAM BALLARD BRUCE**, formerly of "Morotock," Charlotte Co., Va. ; now residing at Staunton, Va.

ix.   **FRANCIS THOMAS**, *b.* 1849 ; *m.*, 1872, **ROSA**, *dau.* of Thomas and Nannie Carrington (Clark) Bruce, of "Tarover," near South Boston, Halifax Co., Va. (Nannie C. Clark was *dau.* of William B. and Elvira Clark, *née* Henry, *dau.* of John Henry, son of Patrick Henry, the Revolutionary Patriot, Statesman, and Orator. Issue :

    i.   **ROSA BRUCE**, *b.* 1873.
    ii.   **NANNIE CARRINGTON**, *b.* 1874.
    iii. **MARY AYLETT**, *b.* 1876.
    iv. **FRANK T.**, *b.* 1878.
    v.   **ELIZA WILKINS**, *b.* 1880.
    vi. **THOMAS BRUCE**, *b.* 1882.
    vii. **WILLIAM ANDREW**, *b.* 1884.
    viii. **ISABELLE GRAHAM**, *b.* 1887.
    ix. **DOROTHEA DANDRIDGE**, *b.* 1889 ; *d.* 1889.

JOSEPH REID (General C. S. A.), youngest son of **Colonel William** and **Ann (Thomas) Anderson**, of "Walnut Hill,"

---

[1] Colonel William B. Blair was son of John G. Blair, of Richmond, Va., son of Rev. John D. Blair, of Richmond, Va., son of Rev. John Blair, of Princeton, N. J.
[2] Judith C. Nichol was *dau.* of Henry and Louisa Anna (Ireland) Nichol, of New York City.

b. 1813 ; graduated at West Point Military Academy, second in a class numbering 68 ; Lieutenant U. S. A. in Engineer Corps until 1838 ; founder of Tredegar Iron Works, Richmond, and President of Tredegar Co. until his death ; commissioned Brigadier-General Confederate Government, 1861 ; served with great gallantry in the field, and later, ordered to take personal charge of Tredegar Works, which were impressed by the Confederate Government, and upon which it was almost entirely dependent for ordnance and supplies ; several times member of House of Delegates of Virginia ; President Chamber of Commerce, Richmond, 1874, 1875, 1876, from which he resigned on his election to Presidency of City Council of Richmond, 1876 ; Vestryman of S. Paul's Church from its founding in 1844, and Senior Warden, 1873, until his death ; memorial windows there ; buried with public and military honours, September 9, 1892, in Hollywood Cemetery, Richmond ; *m.*, 1837, **SALLY**, *dau.* of **Dr. Robert Archer**, Surgeon U. S. A., *d.* 1892.   Issue :

i.   **ARCHER** (Colonel C. S. A.), *b.* 1838 ; Lawyer, and President of the Tredegar Iron Works ; *m.*, 1859, at Paris, France, **MARY ANNE**, *dau.* of Hon. **John Y. Mason**, U. S. Minister to the Court of France, 1853 to 1859 ; U. S. Secretary of the Navy, 1844 and 1846.   Issue :

      i.   **JOHN Y. MASON**, *b.* 1860 ; *d.*, 1866.
      ii.   **SARAH ARCHER**, *b.* 1862.
      iii.   **ARCHER**, *b.* 1866.
      iv.   **JOSEPH REID JOHNSTON**, *b.* 1868.
      v.   **MARY MASON**, *b.* 1871.
      vi.   **ST. GEORGE MASON**, *b.* 1873.
      vii.   **KATHLEEN GRAHAM**, *b.* 1876.

ii.   **KATHLEEN**, *b.* 1840 ; *m.* **DAVID S. WATSON, M.D.**, and *d.* 1863. Issue : **GEORGE**, *b.* 1861 ; *d.* 1880.

iii.   **ANNA THOMAS**, *b.* 1842 ; *d.* 1852.
iv.   **WILLIAM GRAHAM**, *b.* 1844 ; *d.* 1846.
v.   **FANNIE ARCHER**, *b.* 1846 ; *m.*, 1865, **EDWIN LAFAYETTE HOBSON** (Colonel C. S. A.), of Greensboro', Ala., now of Richmond, Va.   Issue (surname HOBSON) :

      i.   **JOSEPH REID ANDERSON**, *b.* 1867.
      ii.   **EDWIN LAFAYETTE**, *b.* 1869.
      iii.   **GRAHAM BRUCE**, *b.* 1871 ; *m.*, 1895, **ELIZABETH MACGILL BRIDGES**.
      iv.   **ELLEN GRAHAM ANDERSON**, *b.* 1873.
      v.   **MATTHEW de GRAFFENREIDT**, *b.* 1874.
      vi.   **FRANK ARCHER**, *b.* 1876.
      vii.   **ALFRED MOORE**, *b.* 1878 ; *d.* 1879.
      viii. **ALEXIS CORYDON**, *b.* 1880.

ix. **SALLY ARCHER ANDERSON,** *b.* 1881.
x. **ROBERT ARCHER,** *b.* 1884.
xi. **FANNIE ANDERSON,** *b.* 1886.

vi. **ELLEN GRAHAM,** *b.* 1849 ; *m.,* 1871, **HON. WILLIAM A. AN-
DERSON** (*q. v.*).

vii. **JOSEPH REID,** *b.* 1851 ; *m.,* 1873, **ANNIE W. B. MORRIS.**
Issue :

i. **MORRIS,** *b.* 1874 ; *d.* 1892.
ii. **JULIAN WATSON,** *b.* 1876 ; *d.,* 1882.
iii. **JOSEPH REID,** *b.* 1879.
iv. **CALVERT ALLEN,** *b.* 1881.
v. **GEORGE WATSON,** *b.* 1885 ; *d.* 1886.
vi. **WILLIAM,** *b.* 1887 ; *d.* 1888.

viii. **SALLY ARCHER,** *b.* 1852 ; *d.* 1854.
ix. **MARY BRUCE,** *b.* 1855 ; *m.,* 1875, **THOMAS SEDDON,** son of
Charles Bruce, of "Stanton Hill," Halifax Co., Va. Resides at
"Newmarket," near Milford Post - Office, Va. Issue (surname
BRUCE) :

i. **SALLY ARCHER,** *b.* 1876 ; *m.,* 1896, **REV. ARTHUR BARKSDALE KIN-
SOLVING,** formerly of Halifax Co., Va., now Rector of Christ Church,
Brooklyn, N. Y.
ii. **CHARLES,** *b.* 1877.
iii. **JOSEPH REID ANDERSON,** *b.* 1880.
iv. **THOMAS SEDDON,** *b.* 1883.
v. **KATHLEEN EVELETH,** *b.* 1885.
vi. **REGINALD,** *b.* 1890.

x. **JOHN FRANCIS THOMAS,** *b.* 1858 ; *m.,* 1880, **ELIZABETH
CAMPBELL,** *dau.* of **Dorsey Cullen, M.D.,** of Richmond, Va.
Issue :

i. **SALLY REID,** *b.* 1881.
ii. **DORSEY CULLEN,** *b.* 1883.
iii. **ELLEN GRAHAM,** *b.* 1884 ; *d.* 1894.
iv. **ELIZABETH CULLEN,** *b.* 1886.
v. **JENNIE CULLEN,** *b.* 1893.

xi. **LILY REID,** *b.* 1861 ; *d.* 1865.
xii. **ROBERT EDWARD LEE,** *b.* 1863 ; *d.* 1863.

Authority : Family papers and records, through Francis T. A. Junkin, Esq., of New York City.

BLACKBURN, OF JEFFERSON COUNTY, VA.

DR. RICHARD SCOTT BLACKBURN, of Jefferson Co., Va.; *m.,* November 13, 1833, **SARAH ANN ELEANOR,** youngest *dau.* of **John** and **Eleanor (McGill) Thomas** (*q. v.*), of Montevue, Md. ; *d.* September 3, 1867. Issue (surname BLACKBURN):

i.   **THOMAS,** *b.* September 11, 1834 ; *d. u.* January 15, 1853.

ii.   **ELIZA SINCLAIR,** *b.* September 23, 1836 ; *m.,* April 4, 1866, **CHARLES H. SMITH,** and *d.* February, 1896. Issue (surname SMITH):

    i.   **ELEANOR B.,** *b.* April 23, 1867.
    ii.   **EMILY H.,** *b.* April 4, 1869.
    iii.   **RICHARD SCOTT,** *b.* December 9, 1870.
    iv.   **ANNIE LOUISE,** *b.* November 16, 1872 ; *d. u.* September 29, 1891.
    v.   **ELIZABETH SINCLAIR,** *b.* October 15, 1874.

iii.   **JOHN SINCLAIR,** *b.* October 9, 1838 ; *m.,* June 27, 1871, **SUSAN BEVERLY TAYLOR** (*great-great-granddau.* of **Thomas Jefferson**). Issue (surname SINCLAIR):

    i.   **RICHARD SCOTT,** *b.* April 29, 1875.
    ii.   **JOHN TAYLOR,** *b.* June 7, 1877 ; *d.* September 3, 1878.
    iii.   **CHARLOTTE MONCURE,** *b.* January 14, 1881.

iv.   **CATHERINE THOMAS,** *b.* November 25, 1840 ; *m.,* July 21, 1864, **BUSHROD C. WASHINGTON** ; *d.* September 18, 1876. Issue (surname WASHINGTON):

    i.   **BUSHROD C.,** *b.* December 28, 1865 ; *m.,* October 12, 1887, **EMMA ALLEN.** Issue :

        i.   Catherine C., *b.* August 13, 1888.
        ii.   Emma, *b.* April 22, 1890.
        iii.   Bushrod C., *b.* November 25, 1892.

    ii.   **ELEANOR B.,** *b.* August 15, 1867 ; *m.,* August 26, 1889, **JOHN S. CASTLEMAN,** *d.* October 25, 1894. Issue (surname CASTLEMAN):

        i.   John S., *b.* August 13, 1890.
        ii.   Corbin W., *b.* October 24, 1893.

    iii.   **JANET FAIRLIE,** *b.* December 23, 1868.
    iv.   **CATHERINE B.,** *b.* September 5, 1870.
    v.   **HALLIE LEE,** *b.* December 30, 1871.
    vi.   **RICHARD SCOTT BLACKBURN,** *b.* September 6, 1873.
    vii.   **THOMAS C.,** *b.* February 9, 1875.
    viii. **ANNIE,** *b.* September 1, 1876.

v.   **JANE WORMELEY,** *b.* November 14, 1842 ; *m.,* June 29, 1871, **FRANK BERGER MORAN.** Issue (surname MORAN) :

    i.   **ARABELLA ADAMS,** *b.* March 19, 1872.
    ii. **ELEANOR BERGER,** *b.* February 11, 1875.

vi.   **ELLEN THOMAS,** *b.* October 22, 1844 ; *m.,* November 15, 1874, **THOMAS BLACKBURN WASHINGTON.** Issue (surname WASHINGTON) :

    i.   **REBECCA JANET,** *b.* December 3, 1875.
    ii. **ELEANOR THOMAS,** *b.* April 30, 1878.
    iii. **SADIE WATTS,** *b.* August 13, 1883.

vii.   **SARAH ELIZABETH,** *b.* November 22, 1846 ; *m.,* June 11, 1874, **WILLIAM B. HARRIS,** *s. p.*
viii. **MARY GRACE,** *b.* April 17, 1849 ; *d.* November 25, 1849.
ix.   **MARY WATTS,** *b.* August 22, 1850 ; *unm.*
x.   **RICHARD SCOTT,** *b.* September 13, 1854 ; *d.* January 30, 1856.

Authority : Family papers, through Francis T. A. Junkin, Esq., of New York City.

CRABB AND GILLESPIE

RALPH CRABB was *m.*, May 3, 1787, by the Lutheran Pastor at Frederick, Md., to **MARY**, fifth *dau.* of **Francis** and **Grace (Metcalfe) Thomas** (*q. v.*), Frank, William, and John Thomas being witnesses. Removed to Botetourt Co., Va., where he built a handsome mansion on the Catawba River, afterward sold to General James Breckenridge, when they removed to Tennessee. His wife was a noted beauty even in old age, and equally lovely in character. Issue :

i.   **HENRY,** Chief-Justice of the Court of Appeals, Tennessee, when very young ; *m.* a Mexican, and was killed at Sonora, Mexico.

ii.   **JOHN,** *m.* ——.

iii.   **GEORGE WHITEFIELD,** U. S. Representative from Alabama, 1839–41; *m.* **ELIZABETH,** *dau.* of **Samuel W. Inge,** U. S. Representative from Alabama, 1849–51. Issue :

       MARY GRACE, *m.* **REV. JOHN PRATT.** Issue (surname PRATT): Grace and Herbert.

iv.   **MARY LILEY,** *m.* **CHARLES J. GILLESPIE,** *of whom presently.*

CHARLES JOSEPH GILLESPIE, son of **Rev. James Smiley** and **Fanny (Henderson) Gillespie,**[1] and grandson of **Colonel Daniel Gillespie,** of the Revolutionary Army, *m.* **MARY LILEY,** *dau.* of **Ralph** and **Mary (Thomas) Crabb** (*q. v.*). Issue (surname GILLESPIE) :

i.   **MARY LILEY,** *m.* **WILLIAM WILLIS WILEY WOOD,** of North Carolina (*b.* 1818 ; *d.,* 1882) ; Engineer-in-Chief United States Navy (son of **Newton Wood,** son of **William Wood**). Issue (surname WOOD) :

       i.   **FANNY,** *m.* **CONWAY HILLYER** (*b.* 1848), son of **Commander Henry Nathan Tewksbury Arnold,** U. S. N., Annapolis, 1863 ; Ensign U. S. N., 1868 ; Mas-

---

[1] Fanny Henderson was the first child born of white parents who were married in Kentucky, being *dau.* of Colonel Samuel Henderson and Elizabeth Calloway, the latter being one of the three Calloway girls who were stolen by the Indians and rescued by Colonel Samuel Henderson, as set out in Cooper's novel, "The Last of the Mohicans."

ter, U. S. N., 1870; Lieutenant, 1871; Lieutenant-Commander, 1892. Issue (surname ARNOLD):

    L.   Conway Hillyer, *b.* 1871; graduate of West Point Military Academy, 1895; Lieutenant Fifth Artillery, U. S. A.; *m.*, 1895, Gertrude Harvey, *dau.* of Major Harvey, U. S. A.

    ii.   William Wood, *b.* 1876; Naval Cadet, Annapolis.

ii.   **MARY ELIZA,** *m.* **EUGENE DE FOREST HEALD,** Lieutenant-Commander U. S. N. Issue (surname HEALD):

        Eugene de Forest, *b.* 1875; Student, Johns Hopkins University.

iii.   **WILLIAM WILLIS,** *d. y.*

iv.   **LILEY WEIR,** *m.* **CHARLES ALSTON STONE,** Lieutenant U. S. N. Issue: a *dau.* Mary Francis, *b.* 1880.

v.   **THOMAS NEWTON,** Captain U. S. Marines; *m.* **KATHERINE CORCORAN THOM.** Issue:

        Katherine Thomas Newton, *b.* 1883.

vi.   **CHARLES GILLESPIE,** *d. i.*

vii.   **EMILY GRACE,** *m.* **HENRY FRICK REACH,** Lieutenant U. S. N. Issue (surname REACH):

    i.   Mary Grace, *b.* 1883.

    ii.   Liley, *b.* 1894.

viii.   **FRANCIS GREGORY,** *unm.*

ii.   **FANNY HENDERSON,** *m.* **GENERAL ANTHONY STREET** (C. S. A.), of Mississippi. Issue (surname STREET):

    i.   **MARY,** *d. i.*

    ii.   **SALLY,** *m.* ——.

    iii.   **CHARLES.**

    iv.   **LEILA.**

    v.   **PORTER.**

    vi.   **WALTER,** *d. i.*

    vii.   **JENNIE,** *and four others.*

Authority : Family papers through Francis T. A. Junkin, Esq., of New York City.

GLASGOW, OF ROCKBRIDGE COUNTY, VA.

ROBERT GLASGOW, of "Green Forest," Rockbridge Co., Va., *m.* **KATHARINE THOMAS,** fourth *dau.* and seventh child of **Colonel William** and **Ann (Thomas) Anderson,** who *d.* aged seventy-nine years. Issue (surname GLASGOW):

i.   **MARGARETTA GORDON,** *b.* 1822.
ii.   **JOSEPH REID,** *b.* 1823 ; *d.* 1847.
iii.   **WILLIAM ANDERSON,** *b.* 1825, *of whom presently.*
iv.   **REBEKAH ANDERSON,** *b.* 1827.
v.   **FRANCIS THOMAS,** *b.* 1829 (*q. v.*).
vi.   **JOHN McNUTT,** *b.* 1831 ; *d.* 1837.
vii. **ROBERT ARTHUR,** *slain in battle,* 1862.
viii. **KATHARINE McNUTT,** *b.* 1835 ; *m.,* 1862, **JAMES H. PAXTON** of Rockbridge Co., Va., and had issue (surname PAXTON):

    i.   **ELLENER M.**
    ii.   **ROBERT GLASGOW,** Lieutenant U. S. A.
    iii.   **WILLIAM T.,** of Buena Vista, Va.
    iv.   **JAMES HAYE,** Instructor at University of Virginia, 1896.
    v.   **KATHARINE ANDERSON,** Elizabethtown, Ky.
    vi.   **JOSEPH GORDON,** Student, Central University, Kentucky, 1896.
    vii. **ARCHY HAYS.**

ix.   **MARY JANE,** *b.* 1838 ; *m.,* 1865, **JOHN DUNLOP,** of Maryland, now of Virginia, and *d.* 1890.

WILLIAM ANDERSON, second son of Robert and Katharine Thomas (Anderson) Glasgow, *b.* 1825 ; *m.,* first, 1847, **ELIZABETH M. SPEARS,** who died 1862. Issue :

i.   **JOSEPH ANDERSON,** *b.* 1849 ; *d.* 1849.
ii.   **CHARLES CHRISMAN,** *b.* 1849 ; *d.* 1853.
iii.   **MARGARET ANDERSON,** *m.* **WILLIAM D. ARMSTRONG,** M.D., of Salem, Va. Issue :

    WILLIAM GLASGOW ARMSTRONG.

iv.   **KATE CHRISMAN,** *d.* 1862.
v.   **FRANCIS THOMAS,** *m.* **GRACE ELLEN McPHEETERS** (*q. v.*). Issue :

    i.   **GRACE ELLEN.**
    ii.   **SAMUEL McPHEETERS.**
    iii. **FRANCIS THOMAS.**
    iv. **CHARLES SPEARS.**
    v.   **THOMAS SHANKS.**

vi.   **ROBERT, M.D.**, Lexington, Va., *m.*, first, **KATE McPHEETERS**, who *d.* leaving issue :

    i.   **ROBERT.**
    ii.   **ARTHUR**, *d. i.*

    He *m.*, second, **NANNIE BROWN MORRISON**. Issue :
    iii. **MARY MORRISON.**

vii. **BETTY SPEARS**, *b.* 1859.
viii. **WILLIAM ANDERSON**, *d.* 1862.

WILLIAM A. GLASGOW, *m.*, second, 1864, **GRACE ELLEN SHANKS** (*q. v.*). Issue :

ix.   **WILLIAM ANDERSON**, *b.* 1865 ; Lawyer, Roanoke, Va.
x.   **JOSEPH ANDERSON**, *b.* 1867 ; Lawyer, Staunton, Va.
xi.   **SAMUEL McPHEETERS**, *b.* 1870 ; M.D., Philadelphia, Pa.

FRANCIS THOMAS GLASGOW, third son of **Robert** and **Katharine Thomas (Anderson) Glasgow**, *b.* 1829 ; *m.*, 1853, **ANNE GHOLSON** ; resides in Richmond, Va. Issue :

i.   **EMILY TAYLOR.**
ii.   **ANN G.**, *m.* **FRANK CLARK** ; residence, Norfolk, Va. Issue :
       JOSEPHINE, *b.* 1891.
iii. **JOSEPH REID**, *d.*
iv. **ARTHUR GRAHAM**, settled in London, England.
v.   **SALLY CARY**, *m.* **WALTER McCORMICK**, of Charleston, S. C.
vi. **ELLEN ANDERSON GHOLSON.**
vii. **FRANCIS THOMAS.**
viii. **REBE GORDON.**

COLONEL THOMAS SHANKS, *m.*, May 30, 1825, **GRACE METCALFE**, third *dau.* of **John** and **Eleanor (McGill) Thomas** (*q. v.*), who *d.* July 26, 1833. Issue (surname SHANKS) :

i.   **GRACE ELLEN HANNAH**, *b.* May 12, 1826 ; *m.* **WILLIAM A. GLASGOW** (*q. v.*).
ii.   **ELIZA CRABB**, *b.* September 6, 1826 ; *m.* **REV. SAMUEL McPHEETERS, D.D.**, of St. Louis, Mo. ·Issue (surname MC-PHEETERS) :
       GRACE ELLEN, *m.* **FRANCIS T. GLASGOW** (*q. v.*).
iii. **JOHN THOMAS**, *b.* April 9, 1828.
iv. **DAVID WILLIAM**, *b.* December —, 1830.

Authority : Family papers, through Francis T. A. Junkin, Esq., New York City.

JUNKIN

REV. WILLIAM FINNEY JUNKIN, D.D., LL.D., *b.* 1831,
A.B. 1851, A.M. 1853, Washington College; B.D., Princeton,
1854; Pastor "Falling Spring" Presbyterian Church, Rock-
bridge Co., Va., 1855–68; First Presbyterian Church, Danville,
Ky., 1868–76; Westminster Church, Charleston, S. C., 1876–87;
First Presbyterian Church, Montclair, N. J., 1888, son of
George Junkin, D.D., LL.D., Founder and President of La-
fayette College, Pa., also President Washington College (now
Washington and Lee University) in Virginia, and President Miami
University, O.; grandson of **Joseph Junkin,** Captain, Pennsyl-
vania Line, Revolutionary Army; *great* grandson of **Joseph
Junkin,** who, in 1742, emigrated to Delaware from Ulster, Ire-
land, whither his ancestors, who were Huguenots, had gone
from Scotland, to which place they had previously been driven
by the persecutions in France; *m.,* at "Glenwood," 1855,
ANNA AYLETT, eldest child of **Francis Thomas** and
Mary Ann (Alexander) Anderson (*q. v.*). Issue (surname
JUNKIN):

i.   **MARY EVELYN,** *b.* at "Falling Spring," Rockbridge Co., Va., 1856;
        m., 1876, **LAWRENCE RUST** (*b.* 1851; *d.* 1895), LL.D. (*q. v.*),
        formerly of Loudon Co., Va.; then Professor of Greek, Kenyon Col-
        lege, Gambier, O.; afterward Dean of Kenyon College; Founder and
        Regent Kenyon Military Academy and Harcourt Place Seminary.
        Issue (surname RUST):

        i.   **ANNA AYLETT,** *b.* 1877.
        ii.   **LILY LAWRENCE,** *b.* 1881.
        iii. **REBEKAH,** *b.* 1883; *d.,* 1883.

ii.   **JULIA IRVIN,** *b.* at "Falling Spring," 1859; *m.,* 1884, **LOUIS RAV-
        ENEL,** of Charleston, S. C.; *d.* February 6, 1893. Issue (surname
        RAVENEL):

        JULIA IRVIN, *b.* February 6, 1893.

iii.   **ANNE DANDRIDGE**, *b.* at " Falling Spring," 1860 ; *m.*, 1884, **TRE-ZEVANT WILLIAMS**, of Charleston, S. C., now residing at Washington, D. C. Issue (surname WILLIAMS) :

        EVELYN TREZEVANT, *b.* 1887.

iv.   **FRANCIS THOMAS ANDERSON**, *b.* at " Falling Spring," 1864 ; Lawyer, New York City.

v.   **ELINOR JACKSON**, *b.* at " Falling Spring," 1866 ; *m.*, 1890, **LEWIS BERKELEY COX**, Lawyer, formerly of Washington, D. C., then and now of Portland, Ore. Issue (surname COX) :

    i.   **ISABELLE SPOTTSWOOD**, *b.* 1891 ; *d.*, 1893.
    ii.   **LEWIS BERKELEY**, *b.* 1894.

vi.   **BELLE SPOTTSWOOD**, *b.* in Danville, Ky., 1869 ; *d.* 1887.

vii.   **WILLIAM DANDRIDGE ALEXANDER**, *b.* in Danville, Ky., 1875 ; Law Student, New York City, 1896.

Authority : Family papers, through Francis T. A. Junkin, Esq., of New York City.

APPENDIX I

ARMS OF WALES

PRINCES OF WALES

(In this table the line of descent is from father to son, except where stated otherwise.)

ʼACITUS, a Roman.

ʼADARN BEISRUDD.

ETERNUS (Edeyrn) = GWAWL.

ʹUNEDDA WLEDIG, *d.* 389. "Dux Britanniarum."

ʹINION.

ʹASWALLON LAWHIRN, *d.* 517.

ʹAELGON GWYNEDD, King of North Wales; built Aberconway, Harlech, and Shrewsbury castles; *d.* 560.

ʹHUN, *d.* 586.

ʹELI, *d.* 599.

AGO, killed at battle of Chester, 613.

ʹADVAN, *d.* 616; epitaph extant, "Catamanus Rex, etc."

ʹADWALLON, killed, 635, at battle of Hefenfelth.

ʹADWALADYR, defeated Penda, of Mercia, at battle of Winwaed, 655; *d.* of the plague,
664.

ʹDWAL WRYCH, or "the Roe," *d* 720.

ʹHODRI MALWYNOC, *d.* 754.

ʹYNAN TINDATHWYR, *d.* 818.

ʹSSYLT (only *dau.*) = MERVYN VRYCH,[1] or "the freckled;" King of Man, thus connecting the Roman and Trojan royal lines.

ʹHODRI MAWR = ANGHARAD, *dau.* of Meiric, Prince of South Wales.

---

[1] The 9th in descent from Llywarch Hen; 15th from Coel Goedhebawg (King Cole), of Colchester
whose *dau.* Helena was mother of Constantine the Great); 30th from Beli Mawr, King of Britain, *d.*
ʹ.C. 69; 61st from Dyvnwal Moelmud, *d.* B.C. 401, the great lawgiver, and 81st from Brutus, the
Trojan King of Britain, great grandson of Æneas. See the MS. pedigree of Sir Rhys ap Thomas,
K. G.

ʋ

CADELH, Prince of South Wales, *d.* 907.

HOWEL DDA (the Lawgiver) (Prince of all Wales, *d.* 948) = ELEN, *d.* 943.

OWEN, *d.* 987.

EINEON, killed 982.

TEWDOR MAWR, slain at Llangwm, 993.

RHYS (Prince of South Wales in 1077, *d.* 1093) = GLADYS, *dau.* and heiress of Rhiwalloe ap Cynfyn, Prince of Powys.

GRUFFYD (Prince of South Wales, *d.* 1137) = GWENLLIAN, *dau.* of Griffith ap Cynan, Prince of North Wales.

RHYS [1] (Prince of South Wales, *d.* April 24, 1197) = GWENLLIAN, *dau.* of Madoc ap Meredith, Prince of Powys.

GRIFFITH (Prince of South Wales) = MAHAULT, *dau.* of William de Braose (*q. v.*).

OWEN, Lord of North Cardigan, *d.* January 18, 1235.

MEREDITH (*d.* March, 1265) = ELEN, *dau.* of Maelgwyn Vychan.[2]

OWEN (*m.* 1273; *d.* August 15, 1275) = ANGHARAD, *dau.* of Owen ap Meredith, Lord of Kedewen.

LLEWELLYN (*d* 1309) = ELEN, *dau.* of Sir Robert de Valle, Lord of Trefgarn.

THOMAS (*d.* before August 14, 1343) = ELEN, called by some *dau.* of Philip ap Ivor.

ELEN (*co-h.*) [3] = GRIFFITH VYCHAN.

OWEN GLENDOWER (*q. v.*), Sovereign Prince of Wales in right of his mother.

Authorities: Hon. G. T. O. Bridgeman's Princes of South Wales, 1876; J. Aspin's Universal History, 1820; L'art de verifier des dates, etc.; G. T. Clark's Limbus patrum Morganniæ, 1876; and the return of the Commission sent into Wales by King Henry VII. to search out the pedigrees of Owen Tudor.

[1] Lord Rhys, Chief Justice of South Wales, 1172; built Kidwelly Castle, endowed Strata Florida Abbey, 1164.

[2] He was Lord of Cardigan uch Ayron and *m.* Angharad, *dau.* and eventually heiress of Llewellyn ap Jorwerth, Prince of North Wales by Joan, natural *dau.* of King John.

[3] From her sister Margaret, descends Owen Tudor and the present Royal family of Great Britain.

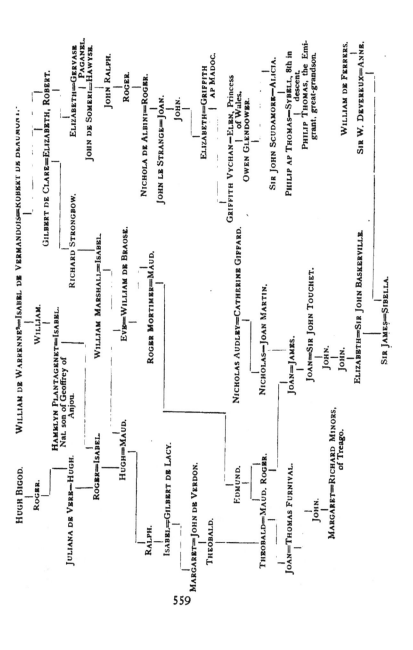

APPENDIX III

AN ECCLESIASTICAL GENEALOGY

The earlier records of consecrations among the Britons and Saxons are not now extant, and the lists of bishops, while sufficiently complete for all historical purposes, do not state the particulars of their consecrations. But covering a thousand years they can be given for England with an accuracy unparalleled elsewhere.

PLEGEMUND, consecrated nineteenth Archbishop of Canterbury by Formosus, Bishop of Rome, in A.D. 890, begins the line.

A.D.

Who consecrated Aethelm,[1] Bishop of Wells....................................... 909
"   "   Wulfhelm,[1] Bishop of Wells................................... 914
"   "   Odo,[1] Bishop of Ramsbury.................................925–927
"   "   Dunstan,[1] Bishop of Worcester................................. 957
"   "   Sigeric,[1] Bishop of Ramsbury................................. 985
"   "   Aelfric,[1] Bishop of Ramsbury................................. 990
"   "   Wulfstan, Bishop of Worcester................................. 1003
"   "   Aethelnoth, Archbishop of Canterbury...........November 13, 1020
"   "   Eadsige,[1] Bishop of S. Martin's............................. 1035
"   "   Stigand,[1] Bishop of Elmham...........................April 3, 1043
"   "   Siward, Bishop of Rochester................................. 1058
"   "   Lanfranc, Archbishop of Canterbury..................August 29, 1070
"   "   Thomas, Archbishop of York................................. 1070
"   "   Anselm, Archbishop of Canterbury................December 4, 1093
"   "   William de Giffard, Bishop of Winchester...........August 11, 1107
"   "   Thomas II., Archbishop of York......................June 27, 1109
"   "   Ralph, Bishop of Orkney......................Between 1109–1114
"   "   William Fitz-Herbert, Archbishop of York.........September 26, 1143
"   "   Hugh de Puisac, Bishop of Durham...............December 20, 1153
"   "   Hubert Fitz-Walter,[1] Bishop of Sarum..............October 22, 1189
"   "   William de S. Mère l'Église, Bishop of London...........May 23, 1199
"   "   Walter de Gray, Bishop of Worcester.................October 5, 1214
"   "   Walter de Kirkham, Bishop of Durham...........December 5, 1249
"   "   Henry, Bishop of Whithern........................February 7, 1255
"   "   John de Halton, Bishop of Carlisle................September 14, 1292
"   "   Roger de Northburgh, Bishop of Lichfield.............June 27, 1322
"   "   Robert Wyville, Bishop of Sarum......................July 15, 1330
"   "   William Edendon, Bishop of Winchester................May 14, 1346
"   "   Simon Sudbury,[1] Bishop of London................March 20, 1362
"   "   Thomas Brentingham, Bishop of Exeter..................May 12, 1370
"   "   Robert Braybrooke, Bishop of London.................January 5, 1382
"   "   Roger Walden, Archbishop of Canterbury..............February 3, 1398

[1] Afterward Archbishop of Canterbury.

560

JOHN THOMAS, D.C.L.
BISHOP OF ROCHESTER, 1774-1793

A.D.

Who consecrated	Henry Beaufort, Bishop of Lincoln	July 14, 1398
"	"	Thomas Bourchier,[1] Bishop of Worcester	May 15, 1435
"	"	John Morton,[1] Bishop of Ely	January 31, 1479
"	"	Richard Fox, Bishop of Exeter	April 8, 1487
"	"	William Warham,[1] Bishop of London	September 25, 1502
"	"	John Longlands, Bishop of Lincoln	May 5, 1521
"	"	Thomas Cranmer, Archbishop of Canterbury	March 30, 1533
"	"	Hugh Latimer, Bishop of Worcester	September 26, 1535
"	"	Henry Holbeach, Suffragan Bishop of Bristol	March 24, 1538
"	"	Nicholas Ridley, Bishop of Rochester	September 25, 1547
"	"	Miles Coverdale, Bishop of Exeter	August 30, 1551
"	"	Matthew Parker, Archbishop of Canterbury	December 17, 1559
"	"	Edmund Grindal,[1] Bishop of London	December 21, 1559
"	"	John Jewell, Bishop of Salisbury	January 21, 1560
"	"	Edmund Gheast, Bishop of Rochester	March 24, 1560
"	"	Richard Curteis, Bishop of Chichester	May 21, 1570
"	"	John Whitgift,[1] Bishop of Worcester	April 21, 1577
"	"	Richard Bancroft,[1] Bishop of London	May 8, 1597
"	"	Launcelot Andrewes, Bishop of Chichester	November 3, 1605
"	"	George Abbot,[1] Bishop of Lichfield	December 3, 1609
"	"	George Monteigne, Bishop of Lincoln	December 14, 1617
"	"	William Laud,[1] Bishop of S. David's	November 18, 1621
"	"	William Juxon,[1] Bishop of London	October 27, 1633
"	"	Henry King, Bishop of Chichester	February 6, 1642
"	"	Gilbert Sheldon,[1] Bishop of London	October 28, 1660
"	"	John Cosin, Bishop of Durham	December 2, 1660
"	"	Isaac Barrow, Bishop of Sodor and Man	July 5, 1663
"	"	Peter Mews, Bishop of Bath	February 9, 1673
"	"	Gilbert Burnet, Bishop of Salisbury	March 31, 1689
"	"	John Tillotson, Archbishop of Canterbury	May 31, 1691
"	"	Thomas Tenison,[1] Bishop of Lincoln	January 10, 1692
"	"	William Wake, Bishop of Lincoln	October 21, 1705
"	"	Edmund Gibson, Bishop of Lincoln	February 12, 1716
"	"	Nicholas Claggett, Bishop of S. David's	January 23, 1732
"	"	Joseph Butler, Bishop of Bristol	December 3, 1738
"	"	John Thomas, Bishop of Peterborough	October 4, 1747
"	"	Richard Terrick, Bishop of Peterborough	July 3, 1757
"	"	John Thomas, Bishop of Rochester	November 13, 1774
"	"	John Moore,[1] Bishop of Bangor	February 12, 1775
"	"	William White, Bishop of Pennsylvania	February 4, 1787
"	"	Thomas Church Brownell, Bishop of Connecticut	October 27, 1819
"	"	Thomas March Clark, Bishop of Rhode Island	December 6, 1854
Who ordained	Lawrence Buckley Thomas, Priest	May 9, 1883

As more than one bishop took part in each consecration (three at least being required by the canons), I have selected those of special distinction where it was possible to continue the line through them, in a few cases slightly increasing its length in doing this. To illustrate: From Bishop Clark to the English and Scottish consecrators thirty-nine bishops have taken part, but I have taken the shortest possible line.

Principal Authority: Dr. William Stubbs's Registrum Sacrum Anglicanum, Oxford, 1858, and its references.

[1] Afterward Archbishop of Canterbury.

APPENDIX IV

WILLIAM THOMAS, OF CHESTER

THOMAS COATS OF ARMS

SIR RHYS AP THOMAS, K.G.—*Ar.* a chevron *sa.* between three ravens *ppr.* Crest, a raven *ppr.* Mottoes : " *Secret et hardi* " and " *Deus pascit corvos.*" Engraved, p. 1.

S. THOMAS, PRIORY, CANTERBURY.—*Ar.* three Cornish choughs *ppr.*

THOMAS, OF BRANTON, CUMBERLAND, AND BROMLEY, KENT.—*Ar.* a fesse daucettée *sa.* between three Cornish choughs *ppr.* Crest, a demi-leopard rampant *ppr.* holding in both feet a baton erect *or.*

THOMAS, OF BRIGAN.—*Gu.* three chevrons *ar.* Crest, a paschal lamb. Engraved, p. 137.

THOMAS, OF BUSAVERNE, CORNWALL.—Per pale nebulée *ar.* and *as.*

THOMAS, OF CAERMARTHEN (HERBERT).—Per pale *as.* and *gu.*, three lions rampant *ar.* Engraved, p. 77.

THOMAS, OF CHESTER.—*Ar.* a chevron *sa.* between three Cornish choughs *ppr.* Crest, a Cornish chough *ppr.* Engraved at head of this Appendix.

THOMAS, CLERK OF THE EXCHEQUER, 1599.—*Ar.* a fesse *as.* between three wolves' heads erased *sa.*

THOMAS, OF CLIFFORD'S INN, 1609.—*Or* a fesse indented *sa.* between three Cornish choughs *ppr.*

THOMAS, OF CORNWALL.—Per pale crenellée *or* and *as.*

THOMAS, OF COURT HOUSE, GLAMORGANSHIRE.—Arms, a lion rampant holding a laurel branch in the paws. Crest, a demi-lion, as in the arms.

THOMAS, OF DANYGRAIG.—*Sa.* a chevron between three fleur de lis *ar.* Engraved, p. 93.

562

THOMAS, OF ESSEX CO., VA.—See BRIGAN.

THOMAS, OF GLAMORGANSHIRE (VAUGHAN).—*Sa.* three boys' heads couped at the necks *ppr.* crined *or*, enwrapped around the neck by a serpent also *ppr.*

THOMAS, OF HEREFORDSHIRE, 1826.—Per pale *az.* and *gu.*, an oak tree *ppr.* supported on the sinister side by a lion rampant *ar.* Crest, a dragon's head erased *ppr.*

THOMAS, OF HIGHGATE AND ISLINGTON.—Same as Branton. Crest, a Cornish chough, wings expanded *ppr.* Engraved, p. 120.

THOMAS, OF KESGRAVE.—Per fesse daucettée *or* and *sa.*, three Cornish choughs *ppr.* Crest, a Cornish chough *ppr.*

THOMAS, OF LELANT, CURY, AND CHIVERTON, CORNWALL.—*Gu.* a chevron and canton *erm.* Another. Per pale nebulée *ar.* and *az.* Engraved, p. 135.

THOMAS, OF LEWES, SUSSEX, 1628.—*Or* on a cross *sa.* five crescents *ar.* Crest, a tabot sejant (another, passant), spotted *ar.* and *sa.* eared of the last.

THOMAS, OF LLANVIHANGEL.—Same as Brigan.

THOMAS (originally TREHERNE), OF LLETTYMAWR, CAERMARTHENSHIRE.—*Gu.* on a chevron *or* between three herons *ar.* four barrulets *az.* Crest, a heron's head erased, gorged with a chaplet of roses *gu.* Engraved, p. 139.

THOMAS, OF LLYN MADOC, BRECONSHIRE.—*Ar.* on a chevron engrailed *az.* two griffins rencontrant combatant of the field, gorged with two bars *gu.*, on a chief of the second three cinquefoils pierced *or.* Crest, out of a ducal coronet a demi-seahorse saliant.

THOMAS, OF MICHAELSTOWN, GLAMORGAN.—Same as BRIGAN.

THOMAS, OF NORTHAMPTONSHIRE.—*Ar.* on a chevron *gu.* and amulet *or.*

THOMAS, OF PROVENCE, FRANCE.—Quarterly gules and azure, over all a cross flory, the foot fitchée *or.*

THOMAS, OF PWLLYWRACH.—See BRIGAN.

THOMAS, OF S. MARY'S CO., MD.—See SUSSEX.

THOMAS, OF SELLING, KENT.—Confirmed, June 11, 1622. Arms. See BRANTON. Crest, a Cornish chough *ppr.* between two spears erect *or.*

THOMAS, OF SUSSEX.—*Ar.* three lions rampant *gu.*, a chief *az.* Crest, a demi-lion rampant *gu.* Motto: Honesty is the best policy. Engraved, p. 167.

THOMAS, OF TREGOLLS, CORNWALL.—*Ar.* two swords in saltire *ppr.* hilts and pommels *or.*, in chief a bunch of grapes of the second, leaved and stalked as the same. Crest, three arrows, two in saltire and one in pale *ppr.* banded *gu.*

THOMAS, OF UNIVERSITY COLLEGE, OXFORD, May 5, 1673.—*Ar.* three Cornish choughs *ppr.*

THOMAS, OF WENVOE CASTLE, GLAMORGAN.—*Sa.* a chevron and canton *erm.* Crest, a demi-unicorn *erm.*, armed and unguled *or* supporting a shield *sa.* Motto: "*Virtus invicta gloriosa.*" Engraved, p. 175.

THOMAS, OF WEST RIVER, MD.—*Ar.* a chevron lozengy *or* and *sa.* between three crows or ravens close of the last. Crest, on the branch of a tree lying fesseways (at the dexter end some sprigs *vert*) a raven with wings expanded *sa.* Mottoes: "*Deus pascit corvos*" and "*Non volet sine pennis.*" Engraved, p. 27.

THOMAS, OF WILTSHIRE.—*Ar.* on a cross *sa.* five crescents of the field.

THOMAS, OF WROTHAM, KENT, 1574.—Per pale *ar.* and *sa.* a chevron between three Cornish choughs all counterchanged, beaked and legged *gu.* Crest, a Cornish chough *sa.* wings expanded, beaked and legged *gu.* between two spears erect *or* headed *ar.*

THOMAS, *temp.* HENRY VII.—*Ar.* a chevron *sa.* between three Cornish choughs *ppr.*

THOMAS.—*Ar.* a chevron between three birds *sa.* Crest, on a crossalguise *ar.* The foot trunked and middle stem raguled a bird *sa.*

THOMAS.—*Or* a buck trippant *ppr.* Crest, a buck as in the arms.

APPENDIX V

BIOGRAPHICAL NOTICES OF PERSONS OF THE NAME THOMAS, IN ALL
ITS VARIOUS FORMS, INCLUDING CELEBRITIES, OFFICERS OF
THE AMERICAN REVOLUTIONARY ARMY, EARLY EMI-
GRANTS TO THE AMERICAN COLONIES, AND SOME
IN GREAT BRITAIN, POSSIBLE ANCESTORS
OF COLONIAL FAMILIES

The following notices are taken principally from Oettinger's "Manual des Dates,"
etc.; Allibone's "Dictionary of Authors;" Horace Ockerby's "Book of Dignities,"
London, 1890; Smith and Wace's "Dictionary of Christian Biography," 4 vols., London,
1877-1887; F. B. Heitman's "Historical Register of Officers of the Continental Army,"
Washington, 1895; C. C. Saffell's "Records of the Revolutionary War," Baltimore, 1895;
S. G. Drake's "Founders of New England," Boston, 1860; J. C. Hotten's "Emigrants to
America," London, 1874; James Savage's "Genealogical Dictionary of the First Settlers
of New England," 4 vols., Boston, 1860-1862; Publications of the English Record Com-
mission; Publications of the London Harleian Society; Maryland Archives in print and
MSS.; engraved portraits in the author's collection; and the biographical dictionaries.

THE NAME "THOMAS"

Thomas, from the Hebrew, meaning "twin," has its historic beginning with the doubt-
ing Apostle, but does not seem to have been a popular name until a late date. The
saint having a place in the calendar, those born on his day (December 21) were at times
no doubt given the name, but only after it had received additional lustre from its
mediæval bearers, Thomas à Becket, Thomas Aquinas, and Thomas à Kempis, do we
find it at all common. In England at least, from the strange delusion that Becket in his
self-willed quarrel with the king, fought their battle and fell a martyr to their cause
when murdered at his own high altar in Canterbury, the people gave him special rever-
ence, and his shrine was the most frequently visited of all, his name the most popular.
Illustrations of this may be seen in the family of the premier duke of England, which has
seldom lacked a Thomas Howard; or the Thomas Butlers of Ormonde in Ireland, said
to descend from a sister of Becket. How early the name became popular we see in the
fact that Tom was its recognized diminutive when "Piers Plowman" talks of Tomme
Trewe-tonge as a proverbial personage; also in the large stock of words it has contributed to the language, such as "tom-cat," "tom-boy," etc., which seem to show a
certain idea of manliness and virile strength, a masculine character at least, as associated
with the name. "Tomfoolery" is a later derivative, "Jack-fool," or as we have it to-day in
the clown, "Jack-pudding," preceding and still retaining its vogue. The derivatives or
modifications of the name in its use as a surname are very many, as Thomason, Thomson,
Thompson or Tomson, Thomes, Thoms or Toms, Thompkins, Tompkins, Tomkins, and

564

From an old Engraving after Raphael

Tomkinson, Tomlin, Thomlins, and Tomlinson. The use of Thomas as a patronymic I believe is generally a sign of Celtic, ordinarily of Welsh descent. This probably results from the impossibility of combining the *ap* or *ab*, which signifies descent, with Thomas, as is easily done with other Welsh names, as ap Rice becomes Price, or ab Evan becomes Bevan. At the present day Thomas is one of the most common surnames ; Dr. A. R. Thomas in his family history (Philadelphia, 1891), from calculations based on its occurrence in the Directories of New York, Philadelphia, Baltimore, Boston, Chicago, and Washington, estimates that in 1888 there were 134,418 persons of the name in the United States. There will be found an entertaining article on the name in the *Cornhill Magazine*, vol. lxi., p. 628, to which I am indebted for some of this sketch. In Latin the name becomes Thomasius ; in French, Thomas or Thomassin ; in German, Thomae ; in Italian Thomasis, Tomáso, Tommaseo, Tomasini, and Tomitano ; and in Portuguese, Thoma or Thomè.

THOMA, JOAŌ A SANCTO, *b.* 1589, Portuguese Dominican ; *d.* 1644.

THOMA. RUDOLPH, German musician, *b.* 1832.

THOMACELLI or TOMACELLI, Pietro of Naples, Roman Pope in 1389 as Boniface IX., was notorious for his shameless sale of benefices and dispensations, *d.* 1404.

THOMAE, ELIAS, *b.* 1628, Rector of Gymnasium, at Breslau, *d.* 1687.

THOMAE, JOHANNES, German mathematician. *b.* 1840.

THOMAE, JOHANNES, *b.* 1624, professor at Jena, *d.* 1680.

THOMAS, called Didymus, or the Twin, one of the Apostles of Christ, requiring proof of the resurrection of his Master, when that was given, made the supreme acknowledgment of his faith, calling him " My Lord and my God." (S. John xx. 28.) He is said to have carried the light of the Gospel to the Parthians, Medes, and Persians, and even, following an ancient tradition, to the Indians. One account says he was martyred in the city of Calamine and his body carried to Edessa ; another that it was at Meliapur or San Thomé in India, and the Portuguese claim to have his relics at Goa. In art his emblems are the spear of his martyrdom, or a builder's square, in allusion to the legend that he was put to death by the heathen king because he used for the poor the treasure given him to build a palace, building, as he said, " A palace in heaven " for the king.

THOMAS, Patriarch of Constantinople from 607 to 610.

THOMAS, Monothelite Patriarch there in 666, *d.* 668.

THOMAS was Bishop of the East Angles 647–654, the second Saxon promoted under the Normans.

THOMAS, a soldier of an obscure family, became Generalissimo of the Eastern Empire under Leo the Armenian. After the emperor's assassination, in 820, he claimed to be a son of the Empress Irene, and was crowned at Antioch by the Patriarch Job. He failed in his attempt and was put to death by Michael Le Begue in 823.

THOMAS, Bishop of Breslau and author, *d.* 1268.

THOMAS, Bishop of Strengnas and poet, *d.* 1443.

THOMAS, author of a Greek dictionary printed in Rome 1510.

THOMAS, a philosopher of Ravenna, Italy. Portrait engraved 1560.

THOMAS AQUINAS, or of Aquino, called Doctor Angelicus, *b.* at Rocca Secca near Aquino, Italy, in 1225, one of the greatest of the schoolmen. Entered the Dominican order 1243 ; studied under Albertus Magnus at Gologne ; lectured at Paris, Rome, Bologna, and Pisa ; author of " Summa Theologiæ " and other works. Printed first complete in 17 volumes folio, Rome, 1570 ; *d.* near Terracina, March 7, 1274. Canonized by Pope John XXII. July 18, 1335, and his theology practically rules in the Roman Catholic Church.

THOMAS HYBERNICUS, Latin writer between 1556–1567.

THOMAS WALDENSIS, called Netter. Carmelite monk and author, *b.* 1367, *d.* 1430.

THOMAS WALLENSIS, English Dominican author, flourished 1331.

THOMAS À BECKET was son of Gilbert Portreeve of London and his wife Rohesia, whom the legend makes a Saracen. The surname Atte Becket or à Becket, by the beck or stream, is derived from one by his father's house. S. Thomas's Hospital is on the site. This, like most churches of the name in England, is under the invocation of the Archbishop, not of the Apostle, and his shrine at Canterbury was the most popular place of pilgrimage in the kingdom. Chaucer's poem describing a party making the journey is familiar to all students of our literature. Thomas, *b.* 1118, entered the household of Theobald, Archbishop of Canterbury, 1142, and was much favored by him. Took deacon's orders; was Archdeacon of Canterbury 1154; appointed Chancellor 1155; lived magnificently, and discharged vigorously the duties of his office. In the war with Toulouse, 1159, he fought as a knight and seemed to regard himself as a layman and the king's friend. June, 1162, he became Archbishop of Canterbury with the full approval of the king, who expected him to sympathize and aid in his statesmanlike plans for England. Instead he became an ecclesiastic pure and simple, an unflinching and unreasoning supporter of all clerical claims, right or wrong. In the quarrel with the king his object is to put him in the wrong and craftily to embroil him with his many enemies; his conduct is in the last degree exasperating. There is no earnest striving for peace and very little care of the flock over which he was overseer. By some strange misconception he was regarded by the people as their champion against the nobility and a martyr to their cause when, December 29, 1170, the three knights murdered him at the altar of S. Benedict in the north transept of Canterbury Cathedral. Two years after his death he was canonized. King Richard I. instituted an order of Knights of S. Thomas after taking the city of Acre, probably as a branch of the Hospitallers. The garment was white; ensign, a red cross charged with a white escallop shell.

THOMAS À KEMPIS, *b.* in 1379 at Kempen, Holland. Family name Hämerken. In 1406 became an Augustinian monk at Agnetenberg, near Zwölle. Sub-prior 1429, *d.* 1471. Best known as the author of " De Imitatio Christi," The Imitation of Christ. Over six thousand editions are known. A facsimile of a copy written by the author in 1441 was published in London in 1879.

THOMAS DE CANTIMPRÉ, *b.* near Brussels 1201. His father was a soldier under Richard I. of England. He was a Dominican writer and *d.* 1280.

THOMAS DE DOUVRE. See Thomas family of Bayeux.

THOMAS DE THOMASI, astrologer and chemist of Venice, portrait engraved about 1600.

THOMAS DE TREBIANO, *b.* 1539, a Capuchin monk, *d.* 1634 " in the odor of sanctity " at Genoa.

THOMAS DE TRUXILLO, Spanish Dominican author, *d.* before 1591.

THOMAS DE VALENTIA, Spanish Dominican, lived in the sixteenth century.

THOMAS, OF ARGOS, a commander in Henry the Eighth's Scotch war, 1544, of whose courage, prudence, and experience in arms Nicander Nucius speaks, page 90.

THOMAS, OF BEVERLY, author of " Life of S. Margaret," about 1170.

THOMAS, OF BRESLAU, Bishop and author, *d.* 1268.

THOMAS, OF CAPUA, Cardinal in 1212, *d.* at Anagni, August 22, 1243.

THOMAS, OF CELANO, living 1221, author of the hymn " Dies Iræ."

THOMAS, OF EDESSA, living about 550. with Mar Abas translated the works of Theodore of Mopsuestia and the Liturgy still in use by the Nestorians.

THOMAS, OF ELY, Monastic writer in 1107.

THOMAS, OF ELMHAM, English historian, flourished in fifteenth century.

THOMAS, OF ERCILDOUNK, the Rhymer, otherwise Thomas Learmont, flourished 1260-1297. Earliest poet of Scotland.

THOMAS, OF HARKEL, or Harklensis, Bishop of Mabug in first half of seventh century, translated the New Testament into Syriac 616.

THOMAS, SAINT, of Hereford, Chancellor of Oxford, Bishop of Hereford, September 8, 1275. Chancellor of England under Edward I., *d.* August 25, 1282.

THOMAS, OF KENT, English astronomer, 1447.

THOMAS, OF MALDON, in Essex, Carmelite author, *d.* 1404.

THOMAS, OF RAVENNA, Italian philosopher in 1560.

THOMAS, OF STAVESHAW, English Franciscan author, *d.* 1346.

THOMAS, of STRASBOURG, General of the Augustinian Order and author, July 11, 1345, *d.* at Vienna 1357.

THOMAS, OF STRENGNAS, Bishop and poet, *d.* 1443.

THOMAS, OF VILLANOVA (Tomas Garcias), *b.* at Fuenlana in Leon, 1488, confessor to Charles V., Archbishop of Valencia, *d.* there November 8, 1555, canonized 1668 by Pope Alexander VII.

THOMAS, A., Supreme Court reporter of Wyoming, 1879.

THOMAS, ABEL, master of the " Swan," of Lyme, October 3, 1628. Abel, of Southampton, on a voyage to Newfoundland. April 24, 1637, with John Hallett, owner of the " Swan " of Lyme and the " Goose," October 17, 1629. (S. P. D.)

THOMAS, ABEL C., Universalist preacher, *b.* 1807, author of " Hymns of Zion," 1839, *d.* 1880.

THOMAS, ADAM, was a jurat of Villata de Asp'ton, Co. Devon, Anno 3. Edward I., 1274-1275.

THOMAS, ALEXANDER, was of Somerset Co., Md., November, 1678.

EFFIGIES THOMÆ DE KEMPIS
Canonici Regularis S. Augustini ad vivum

From a Rare Old Engraving

THOMAS, ALEXANDER, Lieutenant, from Rhode Island, 1776.

THOMAS, ALEXANDER, enlisted February 26, 1776, in Colonel William Irvine's Pennsylvania regiment.

THOMAS, ALEXANDER, German historical painter, *b.* 1820.

THOMAS, ALEXANDRE GERARD, French historian, *b.* 1818, *d.* 1857.

THOMAS, ANN, of Milbrook, Cornwall, author of poems, 1834.

THOMAS, MRS. ANNA (Willemer), German engraver, *b.* 1782, *d.* 1845.

THOMAS, ANNIE GREGORY, and JULIA, sisters, inventors and teachers of psychophysical culture, New York, 1876.

THOMAS, ANTHONY, of Maryland, had a son, Benedict, *b.* in the District of Columbia in 1789; *m.* Ann Smith, and had Judge William Smith Thomas, *b.* in Georgetown, Scott Co., Ky., April 18, 1821; moved to Missouri; *m.*, January 15, 1846, Eliza J. Hull, and has a son, Braxton H.; resides at Moberly, Carroll Co., Mo. Authority: Biographical Cyclopædia of Missouri, p. 725.

THOMAS, SIR ANTHONY, engineer of the Bedford level, draining the fens of England, *d.* before 1661.

THOMAS, ANTOINE, Chevalier de Maudinet du Plessis, Captain in the French contingent, American Revolution.

THOMAS, ANTOINE LEONARD, French writer, member of the Academy, etc., *b.* in the diocese of Clermont, October 1, 1732, *d.* September 17, 1785, at Chateau of Oulins, near Lyons.

THOMAS, ARNOLD, of Haverford West, was High-Sheriff of Pembrokeshire in 1648.

THOMAS, ARTHUR GORING, English composer, *b.* November 21, 1851, committed suicide March 22, 1892.

THOMAS, ARTUS, Sieur d'Embry, French poet of the sixteenth century.

THOMAS, BEN., author of "The Shooter's Guide," 1809.

THOMAS, BERTHA, English novelist since 1877.

THOMAS, BROWN, Captain of the privateer Wheel of Fortune, October 17, 1653.

THOMAS, CHARLES, DE, general of the troops of Gilbert, Count of Provence, in 1006, *d.* August 13, 1119. Was ancestor of Thomas of Provence, Moréri (1759) X. 157–60.

THOMAS, CHARLES, *b.* in Pennsylvania about 1800. Lieutenant-Colonel in the Mexican War, Major-General in the Civil War; *d.* at Washington, February 1, 1878.

THOMAS, CHARLES LOUIS AMBROISE, *b.* at Metz, August 5, 1811. French musician, composer of "Le Carnaval de Venise," "Mignon," "Hamlet," "Françoise de Ri-

mini," and other operas. Director of the Conservatoire 1871; *d.* February 12, 1896.

THOMAS, CHARLES R., *b.* in Carteret Co., N. C., February 7, 1827; member of Congress, 1871–1874.

THOMAS, REV. CHARLES W., a Georgia Methodist minister in 1860.

THOMAS, CHRISTIAN, was taxed in 1678 as of Talbot Co., Md.

THOMAS, CHRISTIAN GOTTFRIED, German composer, *b.* 1748, *d.* 1806.

THOMAS, CHRISTIAN LOUIS, *b.* 1815. German author, *d.* 1878.

THOMAS, CHRISTIAN LUDWIG, *b.* 1757. German engineer, *d.* 1817.

THOMAS, CHRISTIAN SIGMUND, general senior of the Evangelical Lutheran Church in Great Poland, *b.* 1695, *d.* 1751.

THOMAS, CHRISTOPHER Y., *b.* in Pittsylvania, Va., March 24, 1818; member of the State Senate, Constitutional Convention, and Forty-third Congress.

THOMAS, CLEMENT, *b.* December 31, 1809. French politician and general, murdered at Paris with General Lecompte by the Commune March 18, 1871.

THOMAS, CORBINIAN, German Jesuit, *b.* 1694, *d.* 1767.

THOMAS, CORNELIUS, was a magistrate and Church Warden in Amherst Co., Va., June 1, 1761.

THOMAS, CYRUS, *b.* in Tennessee, 1825. American antiquarian and scientist.

THOMAS, D. EDWARD, Lieutenant, New Jersey Battalion, American Revolution.

THOMAS, D. R., Rector of S. Mary's, Cefn, Wales; author of "History of S. Asaph," 1874.

THOMAS, DADDY, religious enthusiast at Philadelphia. Portrait engraved in 1819.

THOMAS, DAFYDD, Welsh bard, nineteenth century.

THOMAS, DANIEL, Royalist Officer of Quality at Rye, June, 1653, goes to Ireland July 25, 1653. Captain, 1651, Major, 1653.

THOMAS, DANIEL, commissioned Chaplain Eighteenth British Regiment in America, October 8, 1767.

THOMAS, DAVID, was of Llanwrystyd Co., Cardigan, June 19, 1634; fined £200 by Star Chamber, April 18, 1638. (S. P. D.)

THOMAS, DAVID, aged twenty-six, sailed for the "Bormodes" in the Dorsset, John Flower, Master, September 3, 1635.

THOMAS, DAVID, was of Marblehead, Mass., 1648 to 1668.

THOMAS, DAVID, Baptist preacher at Cilfowyr, Wales, 1725–1773.

THOMAS, DAVID, *b.* August 16, 1732, at London Tract, Pennsylvania; leading Baptist preacher in Virginia.

THOMAS, DAVID, son of Thomas Lewis, son of Philip Rytherach, was *bu.* at Newtown, Chester Co., Penn., in 1734, aged sixty-four.

THOMAS, DAVID, a miller in Baltimore Co., Md., August 31, 1769—December 6, 1771.

THOMAS, DAVID, *b.* 1776, *d.* 1859. American engineer and florist.

THOMAS, DAVID, First Lieutenant, from Massachusetts, 1776.

THOMAS, DAVID, enlisted April 17, 1776, in Captain Persifor Frazer's Company of Wayne's Battalion, Pennsylvania Troops.

THOMAS, DAVID, *b.* 1813, an Independent minister, editor of "The Homilist," author of "Problemata Mundi, Commentaries," etc. Memorials of, by his son H. Arnold Thomas, 1876.

THOMAS, DAVID (Dewi, hefin), Welsh poet; published "Blodauhefin," with a portrait, Llanbedr, 1883.

THOMAS, DAVID RICHARD, Welsh antiquary; editor "Archæologia Cambrensis," etc.; graduated in 1856.

THOMAS, DAVIE, aged twenty, sailed for Barbadoes in the Expedition, Peter Blackler, Master, November 20, 1635.

THOMAS, DOROTHY PATRICIA, *dau.* of Richard, *b.* at Haverford West in 1777, *m.*, 1797, William Edwards, Second Lord Kensington, *d.* December 29, 1843.

THOMAS, EDITH MATILDA, *b.* August 12, 1854, at Chatham, Medina Co., O. American poetess; author of "A New Year's Masque," and other poems, 1885; "The Round Year," 1886; "Lyrics and Sonnets," 1887, etc.

THOMAS, EDMÉ, *b.* at Dijon, France, February 9, 1591; son of Jacques and Jean (Chasot) Thomas; was an antiquary and historian, *d.* October 28, 1660.

THOMAS, EDMUND, of Molton, Co. Glamorgan, distrained for tithes £7.0.0 in 1656. (Besse's "Sufferings of Quakers," i. 737.)

THOMAS, EDMUND DISNEY, Brevet-Captain New Jersey, 1783.

THOMAS, EDWARD, of S. John Zachary and KATHERINE SHERRINGTON, of S. Leonard, Shoreditch, licensed to marry January 1, 1577–78.

THOMAS, EDWARD, Warden of Free School, Wolverly, Co. Worcester, June 18, 1635. Edward opposed collection of ship-money in Co. Merioneth. March 10, 1636. Edward, of St. Albans, to be arrested for inciting a mutiny, June 1, 1649. (S. P. D.)

THOMAS, EDWARD, printer at Green Arbour Court, London, in 1657.

THOMAS, EDWARD, was in Maryland in September, 1681.

THOMAS, EDWARD, was American agent of Joseph Thompson, of London, merchant, 1685.

THOMAS, EDWARD, of Pwllywrach, Glamorgan, was Deputy-Sheriff in 1696. David was Sheriff in 1777, and William of Llanblethian, probably of this family, in 1771. The present representative is Hubert de Burgh Thomas, Esq., *b.* at Pwllywrach, September 6, 1842, late Captain 18th Glamorgan Rifle Corps; a J. P.; in 1872 one of the co-heirs to the Barony of Burgh. Authority: Nicholas's Annals of Wales, ii. 642.

THOMAS, EDWARD, of Pembroke, Mass., had Nathaniel, *bapt.* November 11, 1750; Joseph, *bapt.* April 8, 1753; Sarah, *bapt.* February 8, 1755.

THOMAS, EDWARD, a private in Captain Samuel Lapsley's Company, Colonel Nathaniel Gist's Virginia Regiment, 1777.

THOMAS, EDWARD, Lieutenant, New York Militia, 1781.

THOMAS, EDWARD, *b.* 1813. Orientalist and author of books on East Indian coins and antiquities, *d.* 1886.

THOMAS, EDWARD D., Lieutenant of New Jersey, a Revolutionary half-pay officer.

THOMAS, EDWIN, was of Barbados and Virginia in 1665.

THOMAS, EDWIN, Surgeon Sixteenth British Regiment, in America, commissioned May 14, 1768.

THOMAS, ELIJAH, enlisted March 1, 1780, in Colonel John Gibson's Detachment in the Western Department.

THOMAS, ELINOR, wife of Ellison, Esq., of Hereford, *bu.* at S. Dunstan's in the West, London, September 11, 1616.

THOMAS, ELISHA, son of Thomas David Rees, of Rhydwilim, Wales, *b.* 1674, a Baptist preacher, emigrated with fifteen others to Welsh Tract, Pennsylvania, and *d.* November 7, 1730.

THOMAS, MRS. ELIZABETH, *bu.* at S. Peter's, Cornhill, London, May 6, 1582, aged thirty, possibly was Elisabeth Cox; *m.* —— Thomas, September 1, 1566, at S. Antholin's, London.

THOMAS, ELIZABETH, called "Corinna." English writer, *b.* 1675, *d.* February 21, 1730.

THOMAS, ELIZABETH, of Tidenham, Gloucester, poetess, 1847.

THOMAS, ERNST DIERNEGOTT, German singer, *b.* 1792, *d.* 1824.

THOMAS, EVAN, Merchant Tayller, had servants *bu.* in S. Mary Aldermary, London, between 1578 and 1585, and was *bu.* March 18, 1588; another Evan *bu.* there August 19, 1680.

ANTOINE THOMAS

De l'Académie Françoise

Né à Clermont en Auvergne

From an Engraving by Cochin

THOMAS, EVAN, Deputy Searcher of the Custom House under the Collector of Customs at Ipswich, Sandwich, Chichester, and Southampton in February, 1591.

THOMAS, EVAN, in Pembrokeshire, was fined for absence from church, 16—.

THOMAS, EVAN, Vicar of Malmesbury, Wiltshire, England, *bu.* there February 19, 1611.

THOMAS, EVAN, ap Evan, Under-Sheriff of Glamorgan, 1615.

THOMAS, EVAN ap, of Halghton, Co. Flint ; will at Chester, 1622.

THOMAS, EVAN, *b.*, according to his memorial, in Wales, was of Goshen, Chester Co., Pa. ; afterward, June 15, 1730, with his wife, Katherine, was of East Nottingham, Pa. In 1732 he removed, with Alexander Ross, to the Valley of Virginia, at Hopewell Meeting, near the present town of Winchester.

THOMAS, EVAN, JR., son of above, *m.*, before 1741, Albenah, *dau.* of Alexander and Catherine (Chambers) Ross, and left issue, for whom see William Jolliffe's "History of the Jolliffe Family," p. 72, where this family is erroneously connected with that of West River, Md.

THOMAS, EVAN, Private, Company 4, Colonel Alexander Spotswood's Second Virginia Regiment, April 30, 1777.

THOMAS, EVEN, Private in Company 6, Colonel Wm. Heth's Third Virginia Regiment, April 1, 1778.

THOMAS, FELIX, French artist, *b.* 1815.

THOMAS, FOXWELL, Second Lieutenant, Third Massachusetts Infantry, 1776, *d.* September 10, 1829, or January 29, 1829, in Franklin Co., Mass.

THOMAS, FRANCIS, was of Boston, Mass., 1674, *m.* Rebecca, *dau.* of Matthew Lyons, or Iyans, and had John, *b.* 1665.

THOMAS, FRANCIS, and Mary, his wife, widow of Matthias Calman, were of Baltimore Co., Md., in 1769.

THOMAS, FRANCIS, director of the Porcelain Manufactory at Chelsea, England, has a monument in S. Luke's Church there dated 1770.

THOMAS, FRANCIS SHEPPARD, Secretary English Public Record Department and author of a guide to the Records, *b.* 1794, *d.* 1857.

THOMAS, FRANCOIS DE, Seigneur de la Valette in Provence, carried arms with distinction under Louis XIV. ; his son, called Père de la Valette, was Seventh Superior-General of the Fathers of the Oratory in 1733 ; *d.* 1773.

THOMAS, FRANK, a well-to-do surgeon in the north of Ireland ; emigrated to America about 1815, taking with him a number of children and a nephew named Barney

Thomas, *b.* 1795. The latter settled at Thomaston, Me., and *d.* 1852 ; his son Ambrose L., *b.* 1851, is in business as an advertising Agent (Firm, Lord & Thomas) at Chicago, and a *dau. m.* Abner Crossman of the same city.

THOMAS, FREDERICK, German baker, built a brick house on Market Street, Baltimore, Md., on a lot bought August 14, 1757 ; *d.* 1764.

THOMAS, FREDERICK JENNINGS, *b.* 1787, retired Rear-Admiral, English Navy, 1846, *d.* 1855.

THOMAS, FREDERICK WILLIAM, American author, *b.* at Baltimore, 1810.

THOMAS, FRIEDRICH WILHELM, founder of the Philadelphia *Freien Presse*, *b.* 1801, *d.* 1877.

THOMAS, GABRIEL, author of a scarce "Account of Pennsylvania and New Jersey" in 1698.

THOMAS, GABRIEL JULES, French sculptor, *b.* 1821.

THOMAS, GENTIEN, "*Maître des comptes*" in the Chamber of Normandy under King Henri III., was ancestor of the House of Thomas du Fosse (Moréri X., 156-7).

THOMAS, GEORGE, was of Salem, 1668.

THOMAS, GEORGE, Gent., of Marsh Court, in Wincanton, Somersetshire, England, *m.* Katherine ——, and *d.* 1685-86 ; will proved January 30th ; he leaves lands in Stoke Broadhembury, Devon Mendip. Issue : i. George, ii. Morgan, iii. Katherine, iv. Maria, v. Sarah, vi. Frances, vii. Elizabeth, *m.* Thomas Wickham, probably of Westbury, Wilts. She made her will as his widow, with a *dau.*, Elizabeth, wife of Richard Thomas ; proved June 1, 1714. Authority : Their wills.

THOMAS, GEORGE, went to India in a man-of-war in 1781–1782 and served various chiefs in southern India, and by 1787 had found his way into the far northwest to the Court of the Begum Samru at Sardhana, whose service he entered. This he quitted in 1792 for that of Apa Khanda Rao, a Maratha chief, with whom he quarrelled in 1795. He was now a personage of importance in possession of a *jagir* granted by his late chief, and was able to help Begum Samru when in distress. Upon Apa Khanda Rao's suicide, in 1797, Thomas seems to have been on uniformly bad terms with his successors, and spent most of his time in defending his *jagir* from their attacks. In 1798, taking advantage of the troubles of the times, he appears to have given up the lands he held from the Marathas and to have seized the district round Hisar and Hansi, known as Hariana. The latter town he made his capital and established himself as Rajah thereof. His territory comprised two hundred and fifty-three villages, and paid a revenue of about Rs. 300,000. Again, according to his biographer, quoting his own words, "Here," says Mr. Thomas (with that energy and spirited animation which distinguished him throughout the scenes of his extraordinary life), " I established a mint and coined my own rupees, which I made current in my army and country," &c. After establishing himself at Hansi, the rest of Thomas's life, like that of the neighboring chiefs, was one of perpetual war, in his case against the Marathas and the Sikhs, as represented chiefly by the chiefs of Patiala, Nabha, and Jind. In his case, also, it ended in a general combination against him, his flight into British territory, and his death at Berhampore in 1802. He built a fort due east of, and not far from, Delhi, which he named after himself — Georgegarh — but which is now known as Jahazgarh, just as he is known as Jahaz (ship) Sahib, apparently in recollection of his origin.

THOMAS, GEORGE, Quaker philanthropist, *b.* 1791, *d.* 1869.

THOMAS, GEORGE HENRY, *b.* in Southampton Co., Va., July 31, 1816, of a family said to be of Welsh descent, but whose pedigree is not given in any memoir of the General. Graduated at West Point and entered the artillery 1840; served in Florida and the Mexican War; brevetted at Monterey and Buena Vista; 1861, Brigadier-General of Volunteers; January, 1862, won battle of Mill Springs; Major-General in April, commanding the centre at Murfreesboro and Chickamauga; saved the Union Army from rout and earned the sobriquet of "The rock of Chickamauga;" October, 1863, appointed to command the Army of the Cumberland; the next month won the battle of Missionary Ridge; the next year commanded the centre in Sherman's march to Atlanta, and then was sent to oppose Hood in Tennessee. In December, with troops that he had had to reorganize, he won the battle of Nashville, destroying the last considerable Confederate Army of the Southwest. For this he received the thanks of Congress and was appointed Major-General in the regular army. After the war he commanded the military division of the Pacific, and *d.* at San Francisco, March 28, 1870. He was of a nature kindly, gentle, and singularly modest, of unswerving loyalty and sterling integrity, a soldier trained in nearly every arm of the service, he won and held the confidence of all who served under him. One of the noblest characters and best generals of the Civil War. See his life by Van Horne, New York, 1882.

THOMAS, GEORGE HOUSMAN, English painter, *b.* 1824, *d.* 1868.

THOMAS, GEORGE MARTIN, Librarian at Munich, *b.* 1817.

THOMAS, GEORGE SEBASTIAN, German horn-player, *b.* 1788, *d.* 1866.

THOMAS, GILES, was Treasurer of the Duke of Brittany, November 22, 1483.

THOMAS, GRIFFIN, and Elizabeth Rise, widow, of Whitechapel, licensed to marry, May 17, 1566.

THOMAS, GRIFFITH, was in Maryland in November, 1678. Taxed as of Talbot Co. that year.

THOMAS, GUSTAV ADOLPH, German musician, *d.* 1870.

THOMAS, H. J., Canon of Liege Cathedral, author of C. Sermons, printed 1859.

THOMAS, H. S., author of "The Rod in India," published at Mangalore in 1873.

THOMAS, HENRI DE, Marquis de la Gardevill, called on his engraved portrait "father of all the indigent, and zealous without equal for State and King," eighteenth century; probably was of the Provençal family.

THOMAS, HENRY and ELIZABETH, petition for estate of wife's deceased husband, January 16, 1624. State Papers, Colonial, East Indies.

THOMAS, HENRY, of Luxulian, aged fifteen, indentured for three or four years, Sailed in the Robert Bonaventure for New England about 1634.

THOMAS, HENRY, Private in Colonel John Gibson's Detachment in the Western Department, March 1, 1780.

THOMAS, REV. HIRAM W., a Chicago preacher of prominence to-day.

THOMAS, DR. HONORATUS LEIGH, President English College of Surgeons, 1829 and 1838.

THOMAS, HOWELL, Baptist preacher at Llantrisaint, Wales, in 1646.

THOMAS, HUBERT, of Liège, in Flanders, historian and diplomatist in Germany, 1541-1560.

THOMAS, HUGH, *m.* September 2, 1571, Margaret Paynter, at S. Peter's, Cornhill. London.

THOMAS, HUGH, was admitted Freeman at Roxbury, 1651; *d.* May 6, 1683, aged seventy-six, leaving his property in trust for Roxbury schools.

THOMAS, HUGH, was taxed in S Mary's Co., Md., in 1678 and in 1681.

THOMAS, HUGH, author of a history of Wales, published in 1729, and probably an introduction to " British History," n. d.

THOMAS, HUGH, Dean of Ely, England, 1758, *d.* July 11, 1780.

THOMAS, HUGH, Rector of Pengow, Montgomeryshire, Wales, *b.* 1765, *d.* 1827.

THOMAS, HUMPHREY, prisoner in the Tower, February 1, 1654, offers to discover several robbers.

THOMAS, IGNAZ, *b.* 1693, German Jesuit, *d.* 1768.

MAJOR-GENERAL GEORGE H. THOMAS, U. S. A.
From a Negative in the Treasury Department, Washington

THOMAS, ILTID, of Swansea, was Portreeve (or Mayor) 1770 and 1779, Deputy-Sheriff of Glamorganshire 1768, 1773, 1775, and 1778. He was represented in 1872 by Iltid Thomas, of Glanmor, same county.

THOMAS, ISAAC, *b.* 1735, in Virginia, scout and pioneer in the middle West, *d.* 1819 at Sevierville, Tenn., which town he founded.

THOMAS, ISAAC (possibly the same), Representative in Congress from Tennessee, 1815-1817.

THOMAS, ISAAC B., Justice of the Supreme Court of Illinois, *d.* February, 1850, at Chicago.

THOMAS, ISAIAH, Revenue Commissioner for the Parliament at Cork, Ireland, January 26, 1654.

THOMAS, REV. J., author of "Religious Emblems," 1809.

THOMAS, J. P., author of "Universal Jurisprudence," 1829.

THOMAS, JACOB, First Lieutenant, Fourth New York Regiment, 1776.

THOMAS, JACOB, Corporal of Captain Rudolph Bunner's Company, St. Clair and Woods' Pennsylvania Battalion, June 13, 1776, enlisted February 7, 1776.

THOMAS, JAMES, was of Salem, Mass., 1646-1649.

THOMAS, JAMES, had a warrant for two hundred acres of land in Maryland, 1664. Land Office, Liber 7, 86.

THOMAS, JAMES, Captain, was of Philadelphia, Pa., in 1703.

THOMAS, JAMES, in Kent Co., Md., 1710. For his pedigree, see a forthcoming book by Douglas H. Thomas, of Baltimore, Md.

THOMAS, JAMES, was commissioned February 19, 1762, Lieutenant of Forty-fourth British Regiment in America.

THOMAS, JAMES, was private in Captain John Lacey's Company, Wayne's Battalion, Pennsylvania Troops, November 1, 1776.

THOMAS, JAMES, was matross for three years in Colonel John Lamb's New York Regiment of Artillery before January 1, 1777.

THOMAS, JAMES, private, Second Company Colonel Alexander Spotswood's Second Virginia Regiment, March 1, 1771.

THOMAS, JAMES, one of the head carpenters on the Great Eastern. Accumulated a fortune, organized an expedition to the Arctic regions about 1879, *d.* penniless, August, 1894.

THOMAS, JAMES HOUSTON, *b.* in Iredell Co., N. C., September 22, 1808, Attorney-General of North Carolina, 1836-1842, Representative from Tennessee in 1847-1851, again in 1859, presidential elector in 1846.

THOMAS, JAN, *b.* 1610, a Flemish painter and engraver, *d.* after 1662, when the Emperor Leopold appointed him his principal painter.

THOMAS, JASPER, master of post bark between Dublin and Holy Head, January 27, 1652.

THOMAS, JEAN, *b.* at Dijon, France, magistrate and author, *d.* July 1, 1586.

THOMAS, JEAN BAPTISTE, *b.* 1791, French painter, *d.* 1834.

THOMAS, JEFFERY, Bailiff of Exeter, Devonshire, Eng., 1560; sheriff, 1579.

THOMAS, JOB, was a hunter in Cumberland Co., Va., between 1746 and 1753.

THOMAS, JOHANN EHRENFRIED, *b.* 1716, German theologian, *d.* 1754.

THOMAS, JOHANN GEORG, *b.* 1715, German theologian, *d.* 1771.

THOMAS, JOHANN GERHARD CHRISTIAN, *b.* 1785, German statesman, *d.* 1838.

THOMAS, JOHN, John Duboys, and John Morgan, merchants, have license to go into Normandy with two ships, September 28, 1417.

THOMAS, JOHN, Bailiff or Steward of Exeter, Eng., 1459, another, 1503 and 1540.

THOMAS, JOHN, of Collumpton, Devon, *m.* about 1540, Elizabeth Norris, of Plate, at S. James's, Clerkenwell, London.

THOMAS, JOHN, alias John Gryme, and Elen Duckerd, licensed to marry at S. Catherine Cree Church, London, January 25, 1547-1548.

THOMAS, JOHN, son of John, *bu.* May 5, 1563, at S. Dionis Backchurch, London.

THOMAS, JOHN, and Rose Typshawe, widow, of Westminster, licensed to marry, October 27, 1574.

THOMAS, JOHN, Captain of the Marigold, one of Drake's squadron, lost at sea in the Straits of Magellan, September 30, 1577, the vessel drifting and never after heard from.

THOMAS, JOHN, of S. Dunstan West, and Margaret Jones, of S. Mary Aldermanbury, London, licensed to marry, September 20, 1578.

THOMAS, JOHN, master gunner, 1586.

THOMAS, JOHN, of London, gentleman, licensed to marry Margaret Evans, spinster, of Oswestry, Salop, at S. Andrew Wardrobe, London, January 25, 1611-1612.

THOMAS, JOHN, recommended to be a purser, April 14, 1627.

THOMAS, JOHN, of S. Teath, Cornwall, aged twenty-six, sailed for S. Christopher's from Plymouth, in February, 1633.

THOMAS, JOHN, sailed to Barbadoes in the Peter Bonaventure about 1634.

THOMAS, JOHN, aged fourteen, sailed in the Matthew of London, Richard Goodladd, master, to S. Christopher's, May 31, 1635.

THOMAS, JOHN, of Isle of Wight Co., Va., or that section of the State, had a son, John, who removed to North Carolina and *m.* Mollie Edwards, nearly related to the Hon. Wedon Edwards, of Franklin Co., N. C., and had a son, Jordan, *m.* Ann, *dau.* of Gabriel and Sarah (Richmond) Long, and *granddau.* of Colonel Nicholas Long, of Quankey, Halifax Co., N. C., and Rebecca Hill, of Virginia. They had a son, William George, of Wilmington, N. C., living in 1876. Authority: Family papers, through Mr. William G. Thomas.

THOMAS, JOHN, and others, owners of the John and Mary of London, July 3, 1634.

THOMAS, JOHN, purser of the Moon to be purser of the Lion's Fourth Whelp (his petition of September 6th sets forth his services), November 4, 1634.

THOMAS, JOHN, Mayor of Bideford, Co. Devon, February 20, 1636.

THOMAS, JOHN, a minor, October 29, 1639, has the presentation to the Rectory of Llangan, Diocese of Llandoff.

THOMAS, JOHN, Captain in Colonel Philip Jones's Regiment, Parliamentary Army, December 12, 1651.

THOMAS, JOHN, the Navy Commissioners hire of him the Culpepper, 400 tons, March 28, 1653.

THOMAS, JOHN, of York Co., Va., ordered to pay Matthew Page a good sea-bed between 1657-62. Was *d.* in 1665, his estate included 20 swine, 10 shoats, 11 sickles and reap-hooks, and a lot of grain.

THOMAS, JOHN, was of Stratford, Conn., in 1665.

THOMAS, JOHN, son of Jasper of Wellington, Dorset, is named in a will, January 5, 1671.

THOMAS, JOHN, was in Dorchester Co., Md., in 1678.

THOMAS, DR. JOHN, celebrated antiquary, 1688, edited "Dugdale's Warwickshire" in 1730.

THOMAS, JOHN, was of Woodbury, 1690; had John, *bapt.* August 30, 1695, Samuel, September 10, 1690, and Thomas, March 5, 1700-1701.

THOMAS, JOHN, Presbyterian minister, Cilcam, Pembrokeshire, 1692.

THOMAS, JOHN, Major in Maryland, July 18, 1692.

THOMAS, JOHN, was of the sloop Content, belonging to Barbadoes, 1695-1703.

THOMAS, JOHN, *b.* 1695; Bishop-elect of S. Asaph, 1743, but consecrated Bishop of Lincoln, April 1, 1744; Bishop of Salisbury, 1761; *d.* July 19, 1766.

THOMAS, JOHN, *b.* 1696, Rector of S. Benet's and S. Peter's, Paul's Wharf, London, 1733; Bishop of Peterborough, October 4, 1747; of Salisbury, 1757; and of Winchester and Prelate of the Order of the Garter, 1761; *d.* May 1, 1781.

THOMAS, JOHN, "Ye taylor," was in Philadelphia, Pa., in 1703.

THOMAS, JOHN, *b.* 1712, at Carlisle. Prebend of Westminster, Dean, 1769; Bishop of Rochester, 1774; *d.* August 22, 1793.

THOMAS, JOHN, of Ince, Cheshire, wrote "Funebria," 1728.

THOMAS, JOHN, of Upper Harley Street, one of the governors of the Foundling Hospital, London; *b.* 1761, *d.* December 25, 1849; *m.* Ann, *dau.* of Josias Le Marchant of Haye du Puits, Guernsey, who *d.* April 22, 1833, aged sixty-eight.

THOMAS, JOHN, commissioned Chaplain Sixtieth British Regiment in America, August 15, 1764.

THOMAS, JOHN, of Pembroke, Mass., had Deborah, *bapt.* April, 1771, and Sarah, *bapt.* May, 1773.

THOMAS, JOHN, JR., Lieutenant, Third Battalion, Maryland Flying Camp, 1776.

THOMAS, JOHN, JR., Second Lieutenant Fourth Maryland Battalion, 1776.

THOMAS, JOHN, English Lieutenant-General, 1777.

THOMAS, JOHN, private, Company 3, Colonel Daniel Morgan's Virginia Regiment, June 1, 1777, and November 1, 1778.

THOMAS, JOHN, private, Company 4, Colonel William Heth's Third Virginia Regiment, April 1, 1778.

THOMAS, JOHN, surgeon Eighth Massachusetts Regiment, 1783; *d.* October 30, 1819.

THOMAS, JOHN, *b.* at London, April 12, 1805; came to America in 1850, founded the sect of the Christadelphians; *d.* at Jersey City, March 5, 1871.

THOMAS, JOHN, *b.* 1812, English sculptor; *d.* April 9, 1862.

THOMAS, JOHN, first Baptist missionary to Bengal. His life appeared in 1873.

THOMAS, JOHN A., *b.* in New York. Assistant Secretary of State, United States, 1855.

THOMAS, JOHN AUDISON, *b.* in Tennessee, 1811, *d.* at Paris, France, March 26, 1858, American soldier.

THOMAS, JOHN EVAN, Welsh sculptor, *d.* 1873.

THOMAS, JOHN L., JR., *b.* May 20, 1835, at Baltimore, Md.; admitted to the bar, 1856, State's Attorney, 1863; Representative from Maryland, 1865, and to the Philadelphia Loyalists' Convention, 1866; has since *d.*

See Colonel Brantz Mayer's "Mayer Family of Pennsylvania," 1878, for this family, which is of German ancestry.

THOMAS, JOHN P., edited Carolina's tribute to Calhoun, Charleston, 1857.

THOMAS, JOHN R., b. at Newport, Wales, 1830; song writer; author of "'Tis but a Little Faded Flower," etc.

THOMAS, REV. JOHN WESLEY, translated "Dante" into English; b. 1798, d. 1872.

THOMAS, JONAH, of Baltimore, Md., b. January 8, 1761, disowned by Quaker Meeting, November 10, 1796; m. Rebecca —— (who m., 2d, —— Macatee, and was disowned October 8, 1801), and had issue: i. Benjamin, b. September 12, 1790; ii. Rebecca, b. July 13, 1793.

THOMAS, JOSEPH, private, Company 8, Colonel Alexander Spotswood's Second Virginia Regiment, April 1, 1777.

THOMAS, JOSEPH, Captain, Second Continental Artillery from Massachusetts, d. 1804.

THOMAS, JOSEPH, was Captain-Lieutenant in Captain Gersham Mott's Company, Colonel John Lamb's New York Artillery, March 4, 1779.

THOMAS, JOSEPH, enlisted in Colonel John Gibson's Detachment in the Western Department, March 1, 1780.

THOMAS, JOSEPH, of Baltimore; sleighing with a party, the sleigh upset and a dau. of Levi Hollingsworth was drowned in Darby Creek, Pennsylvania, in February, 1788.

THOMAS, JOSEPH, M.D., LL.D., b. 1811, author of a medical dictionary, a gazetteer, and the standard "Dictionary of Biography and Mythology," d. about 1890.

THOMAS, JOSEPH, English surgeon, d. 1843.

THOMAS, JOSEPH, printer and translator at London, between 1838-1841.

THOMAS, JOSEPH M., First Lieutenant, Third New Hampshire, killed September 19, 1777.

THOMAS, JOSHUA, Second Lieutenant, Twenty-third Continental Regiment from Massachusetts, 1776.

THOMAS, JOSHUA, b. at Penycoed, South Wales, Baptist preacher from 1743 at Olchon and Maesyberllan, Wales and Leominster, England; author of the standard "History of the Baptists in Wales," London, 1795; his brother Timothy, in 1743, and his son Timothy were Baptist preachers.

THOMAS, JULIAN, author of "Personal Experiences in the Western Pacific," 1887.

THOMAS, LAMBROOK, Dean of Chichester, 1671.

THOMAS, LEON-BENOIT, b. at Paray le Monial, France, May 29, 1826, Bishop of La Rochelle, Cardinal, 1893, d. March 9, 1894.

THOMAS, LEWIS, Abbot of Kyme some time between 1521-1540. (Lansdowne MSS., 979.)

THOMAS, LEWIS, Bishop Suffragan of Shrewsbury, 1537.

THOMAS, LEWIS, preacher on the Commandments; sermons printed, 1638.

THOMAS, LEWIS, Baptist preacher at Swansea, Wales, 1653, d. 1703. It was said "He seemed to have a forehead made of brass, and his shoes of iron."

THOMAS, LEWIS, lent £15,000 to Sir John Aubrey, of Llanthrithyd, in Glamorganshire, Wales, and d. July 31, 1660.

THOMAS, LEWIS, a Captain of North Carolina troops, entitled to half-pay under the Acts of 1776-1784.

THOMAS, LEWIS, was Lieutenant in Colonel John Gibson's Detachment in the Western Department, 1780-1781.

THOMAS, LEWIS, was Captain-Lieutenant, Seventh Virginia Regiment, in 1781.

THOMAS, LORENZO, b. October 26, 1804, at New Castle, Del., was Chief of Staff to General Winfield Scott in Mexico; Adjutant-General of the United States in the Civil War, and under President Johnson for a short time Acting Secretary of War, d. March 2, 1875.

THOMAS, M. LOUISE (PALMER), b. 1830, wife of Rev. Abel C. Thomas, President of Sorosis and active in all matters that interest women.

THOMAS, MR., Resident from England to Scotland 1525-1526. F. S. Thomas's "Historical Notes," 1069.

THOMAS, MR., a solicitor, was dwelling in Chancery Lane, London, over against the Rolls, February 21, 1632.

THOMAS, MR., of Newbury, petitions the Council of State, October 2, 1652.

THOMAS, MARGARET, was committed to Newgate Prison, Bristol, for bearing testimony in Church in 1656. Another Margaret as a Quaker, 1681.

THOMAS, MARK, Mayor of Rye, December 14, 1638.

THOMAS, MARK, officer of a privateer, July 27, 1653.

THOMAS, MARK, was Captain in a Virginia Regiment, 1777-1781.

THOMAS, MARTIN, m ——, sister of Martin Roberts, of Truro, Cornwall. Issue: John, b. before March 1, 1594.

THOMAS, MARY, of Orange Co., Va., licensed to marry Thomas Barbour, July, 1771, was mother of James Barbour, Governor of Virginia, 1812-1814.

THOMAS, MARY, petitions about an annuity due her by Thomas Payne, a printer, "She and her husband aged and poor," January 20, 1640; may be wife of Edward the printer.

THOMAS, MARY, aged sixty - five, a Quaker in Bristol, Bridewell, England, in 1681.

THOMAS, MARY, a fasting woman in 1780, described in "Granger's Museum," ii. 1146.

THOMAS, MESAC, first Bishop of Goulburn, New South Wales, 1863, *d.* 1892.

THOMAS, MORGAN, husbandman, of Easton, in Gordano, Somerset (?); will proved January 10, 1602-1603.

THOMAS, MORGAN, member of Baptist congregation, Swansea, Glamorganshire, Wales; emigrated to Pennsylvania in 1710.

THOMAS, MOSES, was one of the proprietaries of the Delaware Company and settled in Sullivan Co., N. Y., about 1758. His son Aaron had a son, Joseph, *b.* May, 1761; *m.* Phebe, *dau.* of Bezaleel Tyler (*b.* August, 1769; *d.* March, 1747), and *d.* April, 1831. Their *dau.*, Sarah, *m.* William Conklin, and had a son, George, whose *dau.*, Elila, *m.* James K. Shaw, of New York City.

THOMAS, NAPOLEON, French engraver, about 1840.

THOMAS, NATHAN, *m.* Martha, *dau.* of Major Joel Roundtree, and had a third son, Joel, *b.* at Shelbyville, Ky., May 22, 1831; *m.*, December 11, 1854, Hannah, *dau.* of Baker Guest, and has a *dau.*, Emma Gertrude. ["Biographical Cyclopædia of Missouri," *p.* 345.]

THOMAS, NATHANIEL, aged twenty-three, is transported to Virginia as a servant by Abraham Peirsey, merchant, on the Temperance, in 1621. Neill's "Virginia Carolorum," p. 23.

THOMAS, NATHANIEL, *b.* 1730, English philologist, *d.* 1795.

THOMAS, NED, servant to John Baxter, was Corporal of Captain Richard Bourn's Company against the Indians in Maine, May 12 to July 14, 1725.

THOMAS, NICHOLAS, Chevalier, was Master Falconer to King Charles V., of France, November 28, 1371.

THOMAS, NICHOLAS AP, at S. Dionis Backchurch, London; had a *dau.*, Katherine, *bapt.* August 25, *bu.* September 1, and wife, Elizabeth, *bu.* November 5, all in 1557.

THOMAS, NICHOLAS, of St. Mawes, Co., Cornwall, merchant, reported worth £2,000, February 5, 1639.

THOMAS, NICHOLAS, a matross in Captain Bernard Roman's Pennsylvania Artillery, enlisted May 4, 1776.

THOMAS, REV. OBADIAH, of Hooke, Dorset, proves a will in Somerset, June 7, 1700.

THOMAS, OWEN, *b.* 1691, in Cilmanllwyd Parish, Wales, Baptist preacher, emigrated to Welsh Tract, Pennsylvania, 1707, *d.* 1760; a *dau. m.* David Davis, Baptist preacher at Welsh Tract.

THOMAS, PERCY, English etcher, 1886.

THOMAS, PETER, was of Springtown. Chester Co., Pa., *m.*, April 15, 1686, Sarah Stedman, and *d.* at Willistown, Pa., June 5, 1722. Issue: i. Lydia, *m.*, 1710, John Pyle. ii. Peter, *m.*, 1711, Elizabeth Goodwin. iii Jacob, *m.*, November 6, 1717. Elizabeth Richards. iv. Joseph, *m.*, 1718, Jemima David; an account of his descendants will be found in Futhey and Cope's "History of Chester County," p. 739.

THOMAS, PETER, *b.* 1745, a Welshman, mason by trade, of a ruddy complexion, dark hair, 5 feet 8 inches tall, was Corporal, Company 3, First Pennsylvania Regiment; enlisted, 1777; *d.* May 25, 1782. Regimental Size-roll in American Historical Register August, 1895.

THOMAS, P. F., *b.* 1577, a Capuchin Friar preacher; portrait engraved; *d.* March 9, 1664.

THOMAS, PHILEMON, *b.* 1764, in North Carolina, a soldier in Florida and Louisiana; member of Congress, 1831-1835; *d.* November 18, 1847.

THOMAS, PHILIP, petitions East India Company for wages. His behavior is complained of and he is discharged Company's service, December 17, 1621.

THOMAS, PHILIP, petitions for his half-brother John Stacy's estate, March 26, 1624.

THOMAS, PHILIP, son of Daniel, *bapt.* July 7, 1633, at S. James's Clerkenwell, London.

THOMAS, PHILIP, *m.*, September 3, 1652, Bridget Ashbury at S. James's, Clerkenwell, London.

THOMAS, PHILIP, of Henrico, Va., a tailor in 1678.

THOMAS, PHILIP, Captain - Lieutenant, Third New Hampshire, American Revolution, 1775.

THOMAS, PHILIP, Captain in Tenth Massachusetts Regiment, 1776; retired, 1779.

THOMAS, PHILIP, private in Company 1, Lieutenant-Colonel Francis Marion's South Carolina Regiment, November 1, 1779.

THOMAS, PHILIP RHYS AP, was Mayor of Caermarthen in succession to Sir Griffith Rhys. Nicholas's "Wales," 267.

THOMAS, PHILIP WILLIAM, of Anne Arundel Co., Md., *b.* about 1780 (son of Philip William), *m.*, first, November 9, 1803, Julia Chisholm. Issue: Jane, *m.* William Rawlings; *m.*, second, September 19, 1806. Rebecca, eldest *dau.* of Dr. Wilson Waters surgeon in the army of the Revolution. Issue: i. Mary, *m.* Edwin Watkins. ii. Margaret, *d. u.* iii. Wilson, *d. s. p.* iv. Philip William, *m.* March 15, 1842, Fanny, eldest *dau.* of Judge Nicholas and Julia (Stewart) Brewer, he *d. s. p.* before 1850 at Mineral Point, Wis. v. Elizabeth, *m.* John B. Nichols. vi. William Montgomery, *m.* and *d.* leaving issue.

THOMAS DU FOSSÉ, PIERRE, *b.* at Rouen, 1634; descended from Gentien Thomas, "maitre des comptes" in the Chamber of Normandy under Henri III., chose poverty that he might bestow his fortune in benevolence; wrote lives of the saints; *d.* November 4, 1698.

THOMAS, R., author of the "Glory of America," containing lives and portraits of officers in the War of 1812; printed, 1833.

THOMAS, R. and P., had a mill in Northumberland Co., Va., in 1717.

THOMAS, RALPH, *b.* 1861, bibliographer, author of "Olphar Hamst;" "Handbook to Fictitious Names," etc., *d.* 1880.

THOMAS, RALPH WALDO, *b.* at Dowagiac, Mich., of good family, a noted and very successful trainer of race-horses, 1882-1888.

THOMAS, RAPHE, merchant tailor of S. Mary Aldermary Parish, London; had wife Ales and *dau.* Timothe *bu.* there September 14, 1560; son, Moses, *bu.* September 30, 1569; a servant *bu.* 1576. Was he father of Evan, *bu.* there in 1588?

THOMAS, REGINALD, resigns the Rectory of Cameltone, in Bedfordshire, June 10, 1462.

THOMAS, RICE, gunner of the Tenth Lion's Whelp, June 6, 1632, to be replaced by John Mears, gunner's mate. Rice's petition of May 8, 1633, gives his wife's extreme sickness as reason for his absence when the ship sailed. July 8, 1637, he was released from prison, where he had been two years, for being short nine barrels of gunpowder, which charge he denied. Was restored as gunner of the Tenth Whelp, November 29, 1637.

THOMAS, RICE, of Biston, Co. Monmouth, husbandman, December 3, 1638.

THOMAS, RICE, or RISE, was at Kittery, Me., 1647; at Boston, 1654, then aged thirty-eight.

THOMAS, RICE, was in S. Mary's Co., Md., in 1682.

THOMAS, RICHARD, for forty shillings land in Gosetrowe, Rape of Hastings, England, furnishes one bowman, 1339-1340.

THOMAS, RICHARD, and Agnes Arnold, of Kingston, in Diocese of Winchester, licensed to marry, May 7, 1546.

THOMAS, RICHARD, of Spergerwere, tenant of William Carnsew, May 2, 1569.

THOMAS, RICHARD, aged forty, and Roger, aged twenty-two, sailed for S.

Christopher's on the Matthew of London, Richard Goodladd master, May 31, 1635.

THOMAS, RICHARD, *late* Mayor of Caermarthen, January 20, 1638.

THOMAS, RICHARD, bell-ringer at Whitehall, October 24, 1649.

THOMAS, RICHARD, appointed to the Royal Household, April 13, 1685.

THOMAS, RICHARD AP, of a family said to have been long seated at Whitford Garden, Crossforth, in Flintshire, Wales, bought from William Penn five thousand acres of land in 1681, and came to Philadelphia with his son Richard, in 1683. He *d.* about 1684, his will being dated ninth month, 18, 1683. Richard, his son, was of Lewes, in Sussex Co., Del., in 1693. In 1695 he located land on his father's patent in Great Valley, Chester Co. In 1704 he is styled "of Meirion, carpenter;" in 1711, "of Blockley;" but in that year settled at West Whiteland, Chester Co. He *m.*, by Friends' ceremony, at his own house, January 15, 1712-1713, Grace Atherton, late of Liverpool, England, and *d.* in 1744, leaving issue, whose genealogy may be found in Futhey and Cope's "History of Chester County," *pp.* 740-742.

THOMAS, RICHARD (wife Sarah *d.* 1711), was a London merchant, August, 1711.

THOMAS, RICHARD, *b.* 1745; a Revolutionary soldier; M. C. from Pennsylvania, 1795-1801; *d.* 1832.

THOMAS, RICHARD, of Orange Co., Va.; licensed to marry Mildred Taylor, August 24, 1753.

THOMAS, RICUS, armiger, held lands, woods, and pastures at Hengstrig and at Heuston, Somerset, Anno, 2d Henry IV.

THOMAS, ROBERT, made his will, 1532, Cotton MSS., Vitellius A. xvi. 209, b.

THOMAS ROBERT, *m.*, July 17, 1642, Ailles Mowre, at S. Mary Aldermary, London.

THOMAS, ROBERT, *b.* 1753, English surgeon, *d.* 1835.

THOMAS, ROBERT, was of Orange Co., Va., April 9, 1757.

THOMAS, ROBERT, commissioned, March 2, 1770, Ensign, Twenty-sixth British Regiment in America.

THOMAS, ROBERT, late of Nevis Island; author of "Advice to Inhabitants of Warm Climates," 1790.

THOMAS, ROBERT BAILY, *b.* 1766, editor of "The Farmers' Almanac;" *d.* 1846.

THOMAS, ROBERT HARPER, *b.* in Philadelphia, January, 1834; editor, Mechanicsburg, Pa. Commissioner to New Orleans, 1885, and London, 1887, Expositions.

THOMAS, ROBERT P., Philadelphia, physician and author; *b.* 1821; *d.* 1864.

THOMAS, ROLAND, of Orange Co., Va., licensed to marry Jane Thurston, April 5, 1757.

THOMAS, ROWLAND, Dean of Bangor, 1570.

THOMAS, ROWLAND, of Swansey; *m.*, April 1, 1653, Susanna Saunders, of London, at S. Michael's, Cornhill.

THOMAS, RYCHARD, *bapt.*, June 25, 1547, at S. Michael's, Cornhill, London.

THOMAS, RYCHARD, *m.*, November 3, 1566, Ellyn Moore, at S. Michael's, Cornhill, London.

THOMAS, SALLY, of Orange Co., Va., licensed to marry John Willis, April 27, 1772.

THOMAS, SAMUEL, Captain, Revolutionary pensioner, *d.* in Penobscot Co., Me., February 13, 1823.

THOMAS, SAMUEL, Private, Fifteenth U. S. Infantry, was a prisoner of war at Chatham, Eng., September 9, 1814.

THOMAS, SAMUEL, *b.* in Lawrence Co., Ohio, April 27, 1840, his parents being of Virginia ancestry. Served through the Civil War, winning the commission of Brigadier-General of Volunteers ; settled in New York City ; is engaged in railway management. Several requests for his genealogy remain unanswered.

THOMAS, SAMUEL WRIGHT, Second Lieutenant, Fourth Maryland Battalion, 1776.

THOMAS, SIMON, Presbyterian minister, author of "History of the World" in Welsh, 1724.

THOMAS, S. SEYMOUR, of San Antonio, Tex., American artist, exhibited at Paris, 1892, and Philadelphia, 1893-1894.

THOMAS, SPENCER, author of "Torquay, Past and Present," 1877.

THOMAS, STEPHEN, Master of the ship La Trinité Royale, recovers an annuity of £6 13*s.* 4*d.* in 1417. See Nicolas's "Battle of Agincourt," Appendix 24.

THOMAS, STEPHEN, assessed five pounds of tobacco in S. Mary's Co., Md., November 25, 1642.

THOMAS, STEPHEN, *b.* 1750, at Eyoult, France; emigrated to America in 1764; served at Fort Moultrie and under General Francis Marion; *d.* at Charleston, S. C., June 17, 1839.

THOMAS, STEPHEN, *b.* in 1809. Brigadier-General U. S. A.; Lieutenant-Governor of Vermont, 1867-1868; Pension Agent, 1870-1877.

THOMAS, STEPHEN JONES, of New Hampshire, Second Lieutenant, Eighth Continental Regiment, 1776.

THOMAS, STERLING, *b.* in Kent Co., Md., January, 1790; removed to Baltimore, was a Defender in War of 1812; engaged in trade as a victualler; *d.* 1865, and was succeeded by his sons.

THOMAS, SYBELL, widow, of Chester ; will at Probate Court, Chester, 1634.

THOMAS, T. H., illustrated Sikes's "British Goblins," 1880.

THOMAS, THEODORE, *b.* at Esens, Hanover, Germany, October 11, 1835. His family emigrated to America in 1845. He became leader of an orchestra; his first symphony concerts, 1864-1865; *m.*, June, 1890, —— Fay, of Chicago.

THOMAS, THEODORUS, of Switzerland, emigrated to Pennsylvania; settled at Heidelberg, and a pedigree of his descendants will be found in Dr. William H. Egle's "Pennsylvania Genealogies," *p.* 601 *et seq.*

THOMAS, THOMAS, printer to the University of Cambridge, 1585-1588.

THOMAS, THOMAS, of Haighton, Co. Flint ; will at Chester, 1628.

THOMAS, THOMAS, is to be transported to New England "to be resident upon a plantation there," March 7, 1631.

THOMAS, THOMAS, of S. Martin's-in-the-Fields, London, tailor, bond with two others for £1,000, May 14, 1636.

THOMAS, THOMAS, *b.* 1755, son of Judge Thomas, of Harrison, N. Y., a Colonel, New York Militia, 1776, *d.* May 29, 1824.

THOMAS, THOMAS, was Ensign-Lieutenant, Eleventh Virginia Regiment, 1776.

THOMAS, THOMAS, Ensign, Company 5, Colonel Daniel Morgan's Virginia Regiment, June 1, 1777.

THOMAS, THOMAS, an English coin collector ; his English series alone made twenty days' sale ; portrait engraved about 1840.

THOMAS, TIMOTHY, Baptist preacher at Wrexham, Wales, and Pershore, Worcestershire, England, *b.* 1676, *d.* January 10, 1716. B. Keach, called him "The best preacher in the kingdom."

THOMAS, REV. URIJAH R., minister of Redland Park Chapel, Bristol, England, 1869.

THOMAS, W. H., edited a collection of poems by Cornish authors, 18—.

THOMAS, WALTER, had resigned as Muster-Master of Co. Pembroke, June 14, 1630.

THOMAS, WALTER, was in Maryland September, 1681.

THOMAS, WILLIAM, of Portsmouth, was concerned in a suit about thirteen bales of corn, 8th of S. Michael's Term, Anno 51-52, Henry III. Placitorum abbreviatio, 166.

THOMAS, WILLIAM, had land grants, temp. Henry VIII. ; see Jones's "Index to the Records."

THOMAS, WILLIAM, Gentleman, of Frères Minors, London, and Lamberhurst, Kent ; will proved, 1530, Register 25, Jankyn.

THOMAS, WILLIAM, and Alice More, widow, of the Diocese of Worcester, licensed to marry, March 12, 1545-1546.

THOMAS, WILLIAM, an officer of the Courts of Henry VIII. and Edward VI., clerk of the Privy Council in 1549 ; author of "Principal Rules of Italian Grammar, with a Dictionary," 1548, a very plainspoken "History of Italie," printed at London in 1549, and rigidly suppressed, many copies publicly burnt, a dialogue called the "Pilgrim," and a curious and circumstantial account of the reign of Henry VIII., with six essays written by command of Edward VI., printed from the MS. in 1774. He was executed by hanging and quartering on a charge of treason, May 18, 1554.

THOMAS, WILLIAM, messenger from the Queen's Ambassador at the Emperor's Court, June 17, 1558.

THOMAS, WILLIAM, *m.*, June 30, 1572, Elizabeth Luntlowe, at S. Peter's, Cornhill, London.

THOMAS, WILLIAM, *b.* 1593, a Puritan preacher, Rector of Ubleigh, Somerset, forty years, *d.* 1667.

THOMAS, WILLIAM and JOHANE, children of William, *bapt.*, March 9, 1598, at S. James's, Clerkenwell, London.

THOMAS, WILLIAM, erected the first window in the West Cloister of Worcester Cathedral, probably in the sixteenth century.

THOMAS, WILLIAM, of Abergavenny, Wales, had a *dau.*, Ann, *m.* Robert, fifth son of William Carey, Mayor of Bristol in 1611.

THOMAS, WILLIAM, of Stepney, Middlesex, mariner, and Olive, widow of John Chittlebrough, chandler, were licensed to marry, January 30, 1620-1621.

THOMAS, WILLIAM, of Cwyrt, Carnarvonshire, was High Sheriff of Anglesea, 1625.

THOMAS, WILLIAM, and others own the ship Gift of God, of Newport, also the Francis, September 1, 1629.

THOMAS, WILLIAM, of Molton, in Glamorganshire, Wales, *m.* Mary, sister of Admiral Sir Thomas Button, Knt., and had a son, William, who was Captain of the Ninth Whelp, and served for a number of years under his uncle. In March, 1634, he is defended by the Admiral from the charge that he tortured the gunner of a captured privateer, the S. John, of Dunkirk. Numerous notices of this Captain Thomas may be found in the printed calendars of the English Record Office.

THOMAS, WILLIAM, in a petition, April 16, 1634, states he has been at sea since 1617 ; purser in the Antelope since 1625.

THOMAS, WILLIAM, was purser of the ship Swallow, February 19, 1635.

THOMAS, WILLIAM, aged seventeen, sailed for "the Bormodes" on the Dorset, John Flower, master, September 3, 1635.

THOMAS, WILLIAM, carpenter, values lead at Conway Castle, August 12, 1636.

THOMAS, WILLIAM, husbandman, of Great Comberton, Worcester, aged twentysix, sailed for New England, May, 1637, in the Mary and Anne, of Yarmouth ; was of Newbury, Mass. ; *m.*, March 8, 1666, Susanna, widow of Robert Rogers, and *d. s. p.* by her September 30, 1690 ; she *d.* March 29, 1677.

THOMAS, WILLIAM, was Baptist preacher at Llanfaches, Glamorganshire, Wales, 1638 ; *d.* July 26, 1671.

THOMAS, WILLIAM, was master of the ship Mary, of London, June 23, 1640.

THOMAS, WILLIAM, was Burgess from Surrey Co., Va., in November, 1652.

THOMAS, WILLIAM, was a Justice in Northumberland Co., Va., in 1656.

THOMAS, WILLIAM, of Folkington, Sussex, created Baronet, July 23, 1660, *d. s. p.* November 13, 1705, aged sixty-five.

THOMAS, WILLIAM, clergyman, of Penbryn, Cardigan, June 23, 1660.

THOMAS, WILLIAM, in S. Mary's Co., Md., November, 1681.

THOMAS, WILLIAM, has a warrant for one thousand five hundred acres in Maryland, 1663.

THOMAS, WILLIAM, of Virginia, has a warrant for three hundred acres in Maryland, 1664. Liber 7, 469.

THOMAS, WILLIAM, *m.* Catherine, second *dau.* of Arthur Mansel, of Britton Ferry ; *d.* June 3, 1665, aged fifty-eight, and is *bu.* in S. Mary's, Swansea, Wales.

THOMAS, WILLIAM, of Calvert Co., Md., has a warrant for four hundred and fifty acres in 1668. Liber 12, 332.

THOMAS, WILLIAM, purchased land in Newtown, Pa., in 1698, and left descendants there. Futhey & Cope's "Chester County," *p.* 742.

THOMAS, WILLIAM, *b.* at Llanwenarth, South Wales, in America. 1712; pastor of Baptists at Montgomery, Pa. ; *d.* 1757.

THOMAS, WILLIAM, private in Captain William Canedy's Company, Maine, November, 1724, to November, 1725, against the Indians.

THOMAS, WILLIAM, of Ireland, 5 feet 5 inches tall, dark complexion, brown hair, a laborer, enlisted at Chester in 1777, was a private in the Light Infantry Company, First Pennsylvania Regiment, in 1782.

THOMAS, WILLIAM, October 16, 1778, commanded the Privateer schooner Molly, 10 men, 6 guns, 4 swivels, owned by Archibald Patterson, of Dorchester Co., Md.

THOMAS, WILLIAM, October 25, 1782, commanded schooner Freeman, 21 men, 6 guns, owned by C. Crookshank, of Baltimore, Md.

THOMAS, WILLIAM, surgeon in Cotton's Massachusetts Regiment, American Revolution.

THOMAS, WILLIAM, English Lieutenant-General, 1814; d. 1848.

THOMAS, WILLIAM, an English architect, issued "Designs for Monuments, &c.," 4to, London, 1843.

THOMAS, WILLIAM CAVE, English historical painter, b. 1820.

THOMAS, WILLIAM L., and his son Harvey, founders and editors of the London *Graphic* and of the *Daily Graphic*. The first number of the former issued December 4, 1869.

THOMAS, WILLIAM MEREDITH, English sculptor, b. 1820; d. 1877.

THOMAS, WILLIAM MOY, b. 1828, an English writer.

THOMAS, WILLIAM PENN, son of Aubrey Thomas, merchant of London, and Gulielma Maria, dau. of William Penn, of Worminghurst, Sussex, d. October 27, 1743, aged twenty-two; on his memorial slab in the nave of Stoke Ferry Church, Norfolk, arms *Ar.* a chevron between three birds.

THOMAS, WOODLIEF, was Sergeant of Company 3 of Colonel Alexander Spotswood's Second Virginia Regiment, March 1, 1777.

THOMASI, THOMAS DE, astrologer and chemist of Venice; portrait engraved about 1600.

THOMASIN, of Zirklaria, in Tyrol, wrote "Der Wälsche Gast" in 1215, first great German didactic poem of the Middle Ages.

THOMASIS, GIUSTINIANI DE, Italian writer, 1767-1830.

THOMASIUS, CAROLUS, Italian theologian, 1614-1675.

THOMASIUS, CHRISTIAN, b. January 1, 1655, was Rector of Halle University, the first to lecture in the vernacular in 1687; d. 1728.

THOMASIUS, FRIEDRICH CHRISTIAN, German theologian, 1770-1847.

THOMASIUS, GODEFRIDUS, a physician of Nuremberg in the eighteenth century.

THOMASIUS, GOTTFRIED, German author, 1807-1875.

THOMASIUS, GOTTLOB, German statesman, 1703-1758.

THOMASIUS, JACOB, professor at Leipsic, b. August 25, 1622; d. 1684.

THOMASIUS, JAKOB, German philosopher, Rector of the Thomas-Schule, Leipzig, 1703-1758.

THOMASIUS, JOSEPH MARIA, of the Theatine Order, Cardinal Presbyter; of a noble family of Palermo, Sicily; author of "Opuscula Canonica," Palermo, 1763.

THOMASIUS, MICHEL, b. at Majorca, was living in 1560; Bishop of Lerida, secretary and councillor of Philip II. of Spain, called also Tanaquetius.

THOMASIUS, TRAUGOTT, German statesman, 1709-1775.

THOMASSEN, THEUNIS, has a child bapt. at the Dutch Church, New York, November 25, 1640, and children of Frederic, Gabriel, Hendrick, Jan, Johannes, Jorgiaen, Juriaen, Jurgie, Lawrens, and Urbanus, also appear on the register before 1700.

THOMASSIERE, G. THAUMAS (or THOMAS) DE LA, was author of the "Assizes of Jerusalem and other Ancient Customs," published at Bourges, France, 1690.

THOMASSIN, HENRY SIMON, b. at Paris, 1688; d. 1741; French engraver.

THOMASSIN, LOUIS, b. at Aix, in Provence, August 28, 1619, of an ancient family in church and robe, a theologian; d. Christmas, 1695.

THOMASSIN, PHILIP, b. at Troyes, about 1536; d. after 1613. French engraver at Rome.

THOMASSIN, SIMON, b. at Troyes, 1638 or 1652; d. 1732. French engraver.

THOMÉ DE JESUS, b. in Portugal of an illustrious house; an Augustinian hermit; at fifteen went to Africa with Sebastian of Portugal, and when captured by the Moors refused deliverance that he might console his brethren in captivity; d. four years later, April 17, 1582.

THOMÉ, PIERRE, of the city of Romans, in Dauphiny, France, founded a family there about 1400; Philippe, *Seigneur de Rentilly*, of the family, d. May 26, 1752.

TOMAEUS, LEONICUS, professor of philosophy, Padua; portrait engraved about 1600.

TOMASINI, JAMES PHILIP, b. at Padua, November 17, 1597, d. 1654; son of James Tomasini, of Lucca, and Hippolyte Panizzola, was Bishop of Citta Nuova, in Istria, July 22, 1642, and author of "Elogia," with portraits of famous Paduans, published there, 1630.

TOMASINI, PAUL, son of Marco of Padua, Rector of S. Lawrence, Venice; d. 1576, aged sixty-six.

GODEFRIDUS THOMASIUS, M.D.

From an Old Mezzotint

TOMASIUS, JUGURTHA, of Sens, France, historian; portrait engraved, 1763.

TOMASO AGNELLO, corrupted to Masaniello, a Neapolitan fisherman, leader of an insurrection in 1647; *b.* 1622; *d.* 1647.

TOMASO GUIDI DI SAN GIOVANNI, di- minutive Masaccio, Italian painter; *b.* 1417; *d.* 1443.

TOMITANO, BERNARDINO, physician and philosopher of Padua; *d.* 1576.

TOMMASEO, NICCOLO, edited "Dante" with notes, in three volumes, folio, Milan, 1865.

OTHER THOMAS PEDIGREES EXTANT

English or Welsh ones may be found in W. Berry's "Kent," 416; Berry's "Sussex," 290, 299; Dallaway's "Sussex," II., i. 44, 187; Lewis Dwynn's "Visitations of Wales," i. 47, 58, 60, 125, 159, 192, 201, ii. 133, 151, 190, 271; Gage's "Thingoe Hundred, Suffolk," 359; "The Genealogist," iii. 212; "Harleian Society Publications," ix. 215; Hasted's "Kent," ii. 243, 382; Hoare's "Wiltshire," I., ii. 261; Sir John Maclean's "Trigg Minor," i. 305, ii. 171, 174; S. R. Meyrick's "Cardigan," 160; T. Nicholas's "Country Families of Wales," as per its index; Sir Thomas Phillipps's "Caermarthenshire Pedigrees," 66; "Cardiganshire Pedigrees," 114; "Glamorganshire Pedigrees," 7, 13, 14, 22, 33, 34, 40, 41; "Visitation of Middlesex," 18, 20, 44; "Harleian MSS.," Vol. IV. 412; "Harleian Roll," CC. 9; "Charter Catalogue," V. iii., these last three at the British Museum. American pedigrees or notices of the name (list mainly from Munsell's "Durrie's Index"). "American Ancestry," ii. 125, v. 125, 207, vii. 149, viii. 101; Austin's "Rhode Island Genealogical Dictionary," 198; Baird's "Rye, N. Y.," 492; Bolton's "Westchester County, N. Y.," i. 254, ii. 760; Boyd's "Conesus, N. Y.," 172; Brown's "W. Simsbury, Conn.," 124; Butler's "Farmington, Me.," 583; Caverly's "Pittsford, Ver.," 727; "History of Clermont County, Ohio," 330; Cleveland's "Yates County, N. Y.," 519; Cothren's "Woodbury, Conn.," i. 722, ii. 1561; "Cunnabell Genealogy," 87-89; Davis's "Plymouth, Mass.," 259-262; Dow's "Hampton, N. H.," 993; Eaton's "Warren, Me.," Second Edition, 633; Eaton's "Thomaston, Me.," ii. 425; W. H. Egle's "Lebanon County, Pa.," 254; Egle's "Pennsylvania Genealogies," 601-620; Farrow's "Islesborough, Me.," 284-287; Futhey and Cope's "Chester County, Pa.," ii. 425; Gregg's "Old Cheraw's, So. Ca.," 94; Colonel G. A. Hanson's "Old Kent of Maryland," 130-136; Hines's "Lebanon, Conn.," Address, 171; Holton's "Winslow Memorial," i. 168-178; Jackson "Genealogy," 127; Keyes's "West Boylston, Mass., Register," 36; Lapham's "Rumford, Me.," 407; Lincoln's "Worcester, Mass.," 246; Littell's "Passaic Valley," 412-423; Mitchell's "Bridgewater, Mass.," 313; "Old Kent, Md.," 130-136; Orcutt's "Stratford, Conn."; Orcutt's "Wolcott, Conn.," 563; Paige's "Hardwick, Mass.," 513; Pierce's "Gorham, Me.," 211; Power's "Sangamon County, Ill.," 713; Prime's "Sands Genealogy," 50-53; "Richmond Standard," iii. 44; Roe's "Sketches of Rose, N. Y.," 258; Runnell's "Sanbornton, N. H." ii. 775-778; Savage's "Genealogical Dictionary," iv. 279-283; Rev. P. Slaughter's "S. Mark's Parish, Va.," 148; Smith's "Delaware County, Pa.," 507; Stearn's "Rindge, N. H.," 726; "Strong Genealogy," 786; Thatcher's "Plymouth, Mass.," 90; "Tabular Thomas Pedigree," 1883; "Thomas of Hilltown, Pa.," published 1884; Walworth's "Hyde Genealogy," 29, 110-112, 470-473; "Whitman Genealogy," 21; Whitmore's "Copp's Hill Epitaphs;" Winsor's "Duxbury, Mass.," 325; Wyman's "Charlestown, Mass., Genealogies," ii. 939; Young's "Wayne County, Ind.," 301-304.

APPENDIX VI

WILL OF SIR RHYS AP THOMAS, K.G.

(From the Original.)

" In the name of God. Amen. The thirde day of the moneth of ffebruary In the yere of our lord god a Thousande fyve hundred and xxiiij^{to}. I Sir Rys ap Thomas, Knyght of the order of the garter. hole of mynde and memory notwithstanding being syke in my body. And submyttyng my selfe unto the hands and mercy of the high omn'potent doo ordeyn and constitute my testament in thys forme folowing. ffirste I bequeth my soule unto almighty god, his meke mother mary and to all the blessid company of hevyn. And my body to be buried in the Chauncell of the gray freres of Kermerdyn there as my mother lyeth and whansoever it please god to call my wife out of this transitory lyfe my will is that she be buried by me. Item. I bequeth to the Cathedrall Churche of Sainct David xx^{li}. Item to the ffreres of Kermerden xx^{li}. Item to the Priory of Kermerden vi^{li} xiij^s iiij^d. Item to sainct Peter's Churche at Kermerden a vestment price liij^s iiij^d. Item to sainct Peter's Churche at Kermerden a vestment and a chaleis price v^{li}. Item to sainct Barbara Chapell a vestment price xl^s. Item to sainct Kustyd a vestment price xl^s. Item to sainct Sadorn a vestment price xl^s. Item to our lady of llan ll⁻with a vestment price xl^s. Item to our lady Church of llandivaison by Newton a vestment price xl^s. Item to the freres of Brecknock liij^s iiij^d to bye a vestment before our Savyour Jesus. Item to the ffreres of Hau'ford West a vestment prc. liij^s iiij^d. Item to the freres minors of hau'ford Est a vestment price liij^s iiij^d. Item to the Abbey of Aidbure viij^{li} in money to bye a paire of Organs to honour god w^t in the said Abbey. Item to our lady Chapell at the Bridge ende of Cothy a vestment price xl^s. Item a crosse of silver to be made for the p'ishe Church of Carowe as my wife shall thinke good. Item I will that my wyfe during her lyfe n'turall shall enjoye all my londes in newe Kermerdyn and oulde Kermerdyn w^t the ffraunches of the same which she is seased in, except suche howses as my doughter the lady Kateryn haward hath for th accomplisshement of her Joynto^r. Item more I geve and bequeth to my said wife in money one hundred pounds, oon of the best basyns and ewer, a standinge Cupp gilt w^t all the plate that cam to me from maister John Griffith. Item more to my said wife xij fether bedds with th appurten'nces with ij hangings of silke xij paire of shets xij borde clothes, four doseyn napkyns and xij towells. Item I will that my said Wife enioye the thirde part of all my lordshipps and lands I have during her said lyfe except suche londes as my said doughter the lady haward hath for her joynto^r as is aforesaid. Item I will that all my plate be weyed and valued to the uttermost except suche plate as I have before bequeathed to my wife. And that my sonne Rys Griffith sett owl as moch money as my said plate will draw to. to mary his sister Elizabeth and ouer that to geve w^t her asmoch as he shall thinke good yf she will be ordred by hym. Item I geve and bequeth unto my

Baase sonnes all my Catall as Oxen. **Kyne shepe and Kothiis.** To be devided betwene them as by the ouerseers of this my testament shallbe thought goode trusting that they will consider that those which be (not ?) maried to have more to their porcions than they that be maried and hath somewhat alredy. Item I geve and bequeth unto eu'ery houshold serv'nt of myn their hole wages for oon yere. And will that their horses and harneys remayn w^t them and not to be taken from any of theym. Item I will that fyue poundes in londes be surely founded to the gray freres of Kermerdyn for a Chauntry there to fynde two prests to pray for me and my wife forever. Item I geve and bequeth to the overseers of this my testament to se my will p'fourmed for their payne· an labour xx!!. The Residue of my goodes and catell not bequethed I geve and grannt to my sonne Ris Griffith whom I do ordeyn and constitute to be myn executour through th advice of the right honourable and mighty prince the Duke of Norffolks grace. So as my said sonne may ordeyn and dispouse the same as he shall think goode unto the pleasure of almighty god for the welthe of my soule. Moreover I doo ordeyn and constitute to be overseers of this my will and testament my lord pryour of Kermerdyn, Doctour John Vaughan, Maister lloid Chaunter of sainct David, Maister Stradling, Chauncelo^r of the same. Maister Lewis Griffith, William John ap Thomas, Thomas John's, David Lloid, Lewis Thomas ap John and howell ap Ridderch. Witnesse beinge present att the making herof Doctour David Mathvey, wardeyn of the gray ffreres of Kermerdyn, Maister John Lewis, Tresorer of sainct David, Jem'i (?) Lloid, &c̨. &c̨, with all the overseers aforenamed and many others."

Proved in the Prerogative Court of Canterbury, July 5th, 1525.

APPENDIX VII

WILL OF PHILIP THOMAS, THE EMIGRANT

(From a copy preserved at Lebanon, Md.)

———

Addressed " For Mother Thomas at heer hous on ye Poynt."

———

In ye name of God Amen X I Phillip Thomas of ye County of Annarundell In ye provence of Maryland being weake in body but of sound & perfect memory & being made sensible of ye unccertainty of this mortall Life & ye sertainty of Deat have Thought covenant to will & bequeath of my worldly Istate as folloeth in this my last will & testament. IPS. I Bequeath my soull to my Redeemer & my Body to the dust from whence it came. IPS. I will & bequeath unto my two Sonns Philip Thomas And Sam¹¹ Thomas five hundred acrs of land lying att ye Clefts in Calvert County in ye foresaid Province of Maryland caled Beakely & ye same to bee equallie divid*e*d betwene them or to bee sold by them as my said suns shall think fitt. IPS. I will & bequeath unto my beloved & faithful wife Sarah Thomas all ye poynt of Land called fullers-poynt being one hundred & twenty acars & lying in The County of Annarundell aforesaid to be disposed of or Imployed or sold for ye only use of & behoofe of my wife as shee shall think good. IPS. I give bequeath unto my said wife five hundred acars of Land called ye playns lying in puttapsco River in ye County of Baltemore in ye provin*c*e of Maryland to be disposed Imployed for ye only (*profit*) : (*or*) yous of my sd wife ass shee shall think good during her naturall life & after to bee delivered to my sun Sam¹¹ as his posesion. IPS. I give & bequeath unto my said wife, all my personall Estate, both moveable & immoveable, viz : goods marchandise plate money sarvants chattles Eaither In this province or Else whear except what before two my two suns & what after shall bee mentioned or disposed of by me. IPS. I give & bequeath unto my sun Sam¹¹ Thomas four Cowes or heaifers to bee delivered to him forth withafter my decese & one feather Bead. IPS. I give and bequeath unto my Dafter Martha Thomas four Cows or heaifers to be delivered unto heer forth with after my descease & one feather bead. IPS. I give & bequeath unto my grand Child Mary the Dafter of John Mears five Eues to be delivered to the Sd John Mears forth with after my desease to be kept by him for ye yous of ye said Mary. IPS. I give & bequeath unto my two grandchildren Phillip and Elizabeth ye sun & Dafter of Wm Coale nine eues & one Rame to be delivered unto ye sd Wm Coale forth with after my Deseas for ye yous of ye sd Phillip & Elizabeth. IPS. I give & bequeath unto my wife afore sd ye Rent Rents & Revenues of two houses y^t I have in Bristol During her naturall Life and after to bee sould and the produce thear of to bee equally divided between my five Children viz Phillip Sam¹¹ Sarah Elizabeth and Martha. IPS. I give & bequeath unto ye Coman stock for the Relefe of pore frends Caled quakers four hundred pounds of tobacco to bee payd forth with after my deseas. Ips. I will & declare my trew & loveing wife Sarah Thomas afore sd to bee my (*wh/e*) & sole Executrix of this my Last will & testament. Ips. I will & desieir y^t if itt shuld soe hapen y^t aney difference or contravarsey shuld arise after my desease betwene aney of my children and my wife concarning ye primises aforesd y^t then itt bee broght Before & a Judged of by ye body of frends Comonly Called quakers & what theay shall agree upon in that behalfe is by mee Rattefied & a Lowed of to stand in Law to all Intents & porposes. Ips. I will & declare this to bee my last will & testement hereby Disanuling & making voyd all other wills or Testements by me formerly made In withness whearof I have here unto sett my hand & seal Dated this ninth day of ye seventh month Called September Anno

1674

Singed Sealed & Delivered
   in ye prst of us
JOHN RICKE
MARMUEDUKE NOBLE

PHILLIP THOMAS.

Probated
   July 10th 1675

N. B.—The spelling of this will is due to the copyist, not to the testator, judging from the official record at Annapolis.

APPENDIX VIII

WILLS OF JOHN CHEWE, AND ANN (CHEW) THOMAS

John Chewe the father of the Emigrant made his will as " John Chewe of Bewdley, Co. Worcester. Gent. Whereas there is justly due unto me from my Soveraigne Lord & Master King Charles now King of England and his royal father of ever blessed memory King James late King of this Kingdom deceased the Sum of four hundred and fifty pounds & more for my Salary and fee behind and at this present to me unpaid for his majesty's service and his said late father King James done by me in my Post Master's place in the town of Bewdley which I now serve & hold under his Majesty." He makes bequests as follows :

" To my loving son John Chewe £5. To my daughter Dyna wife of Thomas Berkham 40 s. To my daughter Susan wife of John Leland 40 s. To my daughter Hester wife of Edmond Duncombe 40 s. To my daughter Sarah wife of John Eldridge £5. To John Harman. To Henry Coles my servant ' my white suite of apparell wt. glasse buttons which is now at Bewdley.' To young Thomas Bowyer who used to walk and dress my horses. To my old servant Alice Bowyer. To my dearly beloved daughter-in-lawe Elizabeth Chew the now wife of my beloved son Samuel Chewe whom I much respect for her tender care love & goodness towards me at all times the sum of £5—for a gold ring to wear in remembrance of me. Lastly in respect of the dutiful care and regard wᶜʰ my said son Samuel Chewe now hath & ever hath had of me and my prosperity &c. I bequeath him the rest and residue of my goods &c. and make him Executor."

Witnesses Benjamin Wilson, William Hiett, Thomas Gardon & Thomas Dunn (11 Coventry) Dated April 9. 1636. proved 17. Jany. 1639–40.

The will of Ann (Chew) Thomas was made December 2, 1771. Proved July 21, 1777, recorded Liber E V No. 1, Folio 17. Leaves one hundred pounds to her sons Samuel, Philip, and Richard Thomas, the same to her daughter Elizabeth Snowden, also to her " my silver baking dish, my wearing apparel, my Desk with glass doors & its contents.

" To my son in law William Thomas as a token of affection six silver table spoons marked ₚᵀᶠ. To my grandaughter Henrietta Ogle my diamond ring. To my grandaughter Ann Thomas Pleasants 200 pounds. Their freedom to her maids Hannah and Patt. To my son John Thomas all the residue of her estate."

584

APPENDIX IX

OTHER THOMAS WILLS IN MARYLAND BEFORE 1776

BALTIMORE COUNTY.

DAVID, made May 13, 1720. Names sons David and Henery, *dau.* in law Sarah Ruff, sister Priscilla Freeborn. Liber T. B. No. 5, folio 36.

DAVID, in 1746. Liber D. D. 3, folio 494.

DAVID, proved in 1769; names wife Hannah, son Giles, sister Elizabeth, wife of Benjamin Green. Liber W. D. No. 2, folio 8.

CAROLINE COUNTY.

JOSHUA, in 1775; names son Samuel, brother Samuel and his son Joshua. Liber W. F. No. 1, folio 538.

CHARLES COUNTY.

BENONI, in 1711; names wife Catherine. Liber W. B. No. 5, folio 678.

JOHN, in 1770; names his brother Philip Thomas, and sisters Ann and Purseuma Elinor Jenkins. Liber W. D. No. 3, folio 123.

WILLIAM, in 1773; names his brother Massey Thomas, children George and Elizabeth and undutiful *dau.* Susanna, wife of Matthew Rigg. Liber W. F. No. 1, folio 688.

DORCHESTER COUNTY.

WILLIAM, in 1714; names wife Mary (probably Williams), children William, John, and Mary. Liber W. B. No. 6, folio 180.

WILLIAM, in 1747; names wife Judith, sons John and William, *d.* 1775, leaving a *dau.* Betzey. Liber D. D. No. 6, folio 296, and Liber W. F. No. 1, folio 688.

HENRY, proved in 1770; wife Sarah, *d.* in March, 1773, children Levi, Rosannah, Henry, Billey, Armelia, and Sarah. Liber W. D. No. 3, folio 144.

KENT COUNTY.

WILLIAM, in 1693; sons David, William, and James. Liber H., additional leaves, folio 18.

JAMES, of S. Paul's Parish, in 1733; children Samuel, James, Rebecca, *m.* Nicholas Neale, Rachel, *m.* Benjamin Green, Henry, Joseph, John, and Hannah. Liber C. C. No. 3, folio 863.

SAMUEL, in 1730; wife Mary, sons Edward and William. Liber C. C. No. 3, folio 39.

WILLIAM, in 1738; wife Johanna, children Henry, William, David, *d.* after 1743, leaving a *dau.* Johanna, and Mary. Liber D. D. No. 1, folio 47.

HENRY, his son, in 1743; wife Rebecca, children William, Henry, David, Samuel, and Elizabeth, and brother David. Liber D. D. No. 2, folio 427.

585

WILLIAM, in 1744; wife Sarah, children William and Mary, cousin Richard Gresham. Liber D. D. No. 2, folio 689.

SAMUEL, in 1752; names nephews Henry and Thomas Thomas and James and Thomas, sons of the latter. Liber D. D. No. 7, folio 287.

JAMES, in 1760; children Sarah, Rebecca, and Philip. Thomas Thomas, a witness. Liber D. D. No. 1760, &c., folio 209.

HENRY, in 1760; wife Sarah (her will, 1760), children Mary Wilson, Rachel Strong, Ebenezer and Joseph Eill Thomas, brother Thomas Thomas. Liber D. D. No. 1760, &c., folio 507.

JAMES, proved in 1771; wife Mary, sons William, James, and David. Liber W. D. No. 3, folio 225.

PRINCE GEORGES COUNTY.

DANIEL, Senior, in 1742; wife Anne, *d.* 1746, children William, Daniel, John, Grace Turnely or Fenaly, who had sons, William and Philip, Jr.; Wenefrid Lewis, and Eliza Clancy, and Sarah and Ann, children of deceased *dau.* Ann Berry. Liber D. D. No. 1, folio 505.

QUEEN ANNE'S COUNTY.

WILLIAM, of Kent Island, in 1755; names no relatives. Liber B. T. No. 1, folio 292.

SOMERSET COUNTY.

ROGER, in 1703; names no relatives. Liber T. B. No. 2, folio 264.

S. MARY'S COUNTY.

LUKE, in 1740; names wife Winifred, children Robert, James, and Mary. Liber D. D. No. 1, folio 164.

THOMAS, in 1741; wife Elianor, *dau.* Elizabeth Biggs and her *dau.* Sarah, and Mary Magdalen Elliss and her son Thomas. Liber D. D. No. 1, folio 339.

JAMES, in 1761; names children Robert and Jemima. Liber D. D. No. 1760, &c., folio 198.

JOHN, of S. Inigoes, in 1768; wife Sarah (*d.* 1774), children Philip (eldest), John, and William (youngest) Thomas, Ann, wife of Stephen Milburn, Mary, Sarah, and Elizabeth Thomas. Liber W. D. No. 1, folio 666.

TALBOT COUNTY.

THOMAS, in 1758; names sons Samuel and William; witnesses are John and Joseph Thomas. Liber B. T. No. 2, folio 572.

JAMES, in 1771; names wife Elizabeth, *b.* Manship. Liber W. D. No. 3, folio 291.

NO COUNTY NAMED.

ALEXANDER, proved 1693; names *dau.* Elizabeth and Frances. Liber K., folio 179.

ROBERT, in 1720; names wife Mary, sons James, Luke (see S. Mary's Co.), Henry, and *dau.* Mary Cooke. Liber T. B. No. 5, folio 444.

DAVID, in 1776; names wife Mary, children John, James, Isaac, Owen, Martha, and Rebecca Thomas, and Mary McDaniell. Liber W. F. No. 2, folio 37.

Authorities: Will books at Annapolis, Md.

APPENDIX X

COLONIAL THOMAS GRANTS IN VIRGINIA

By Robert A. Brock

The following describes the mode of acquiring lands in Virginia from the settlement of the Colony until 1776:

The first adventurers who came to Virginia as colonists were, with the exception of a favored few blessed by birth or family influence, practically for a season the servants of the London Company. They were brought hither at the expense of the company, supported by its means, subject to martial law, and bound by contract to obey all of its orders for the term of five years; at the expiration of which they were "*set free*," becoming entitled to one hundred acres of land, termed a dividend, or, as it was usually spelled, "the *divident*" of the planter. This was required to be seeded and planted—by the clearing of a small portion of its area, the planting of a few fruit trees, and the building of a house upon it within the period of three years from the date of the grant, when the first dividend was augmented by the granting of one hundred acres more. But if the first allotted dividend was not planted and seeted within the three years the land was said to be "*diverted*," or lapsed, reverted to the grantor and became subject to reappropriation. The lands of orphans, however, were specially exempted from forfeiture for diversion until three years after their full age.

This was the earliest mode of acquiring lands in Virginia, and such grants are confined to the "old planters," or those who were in the country "*at the last coming of Sir Thomas Gates*," that in August, 1611.

By one of the ordinances adopted by the Virginia Company, which was continued in force by the Crown, after the revocation of the charter, every person removing to Virginia at his own expense with the intention to settle and remain there was entitled to fifty acres of land. The same rule extended also to every member of his family; and a husband was entitled to the same number of acres for his wife and children.

All of these rights were called "*head-rights*," and were assignable. If one returned to England and came again to the colony, it appears from the grants that each coming to the colony was allowed as a head-right. The names of the head-rights are not always given in the grant or appended to it. In some instances the statement is made that settlement has been made with the Auditor or Receiver-General by payment. All of the books of the patents are not the original books. Some of them are copies, in which, although the statement is made that the patent is in consideration of the transporting of persons to the colony, the names of such transports are omitted.

The mode of taking up lands was this: the individual entitled to any dividend or head right made affidavit to such fact, appending a list of the names of those to whom the rights claimed originally attached, who were described as "*transports*." This affidavit was ordinarily submitted to the court of the county in which the applicant was resident, by which it was forwarded to the officer of the Secretary of the Colony, was there examined and verified, and if found regular was recorded; a certificate or warrant was then given to the claimant for the guidance of the surveyor. The survey being made, a copy was returned to the Secretary's office, together with the warrant whereon it had been made. If no objection was urged, a patent was made out in conformity with the survey and warrant, signed by the Governor and recorded in the office of the Secretary. A patent so obtained gave to the grantee a fee simple estate in the land conveyed, upon condition of paying an annual "*quit rent*" of one shilling for every fifty acres, and of planting and seeding thereon within three years from the date of the grant.

Lands were allotted and laid off from a known base of a water-course, in strips or parallelograms, running back, the back lines of the same furnishing in turn a basis for succeeding grants.

Lands were granted later in consideration of the payment of ten shillings per hundred acres and sometimes partly for such consideration and partly for the transportation of persons to the colony, the quit-rent being also required.

The immense tract of the Northern Neck, comprising quite half of the territory of the colony, was granted by Charles II., regardless of any rights or privileges of the colonists, in the twenty-first year of his reign, to Lord Hopton and others, and became by purchase the sole right of Lord Thomas Culpeper, to whom it was repatented. It comprehended the counties of Lancaster, Northumberland, Richmond, Westmoreland, Stafford, King George, Prince William, Fairfax, Loudoun, Fauquier, Culpeper, Madison, Page, Shenandoah, Hardy, Hampshire, Morgan, Berkeley, Jefferson, and Frederick.

Catherine, the daughter of Lord Culpeper, married Thomas, Lord Fairfax, to whom she brought as dower the Northern Neck. Their son, Thomas Fairfax, Sixth Lord, and Baron Cameron, in consequence of continued territorial disputes, petitioned the King in 1733 to order a commission to ascertain the bounds of his patent. Commissioners were appointed severally in behalf of the Crown and Lord Fairfax. These were respectively Wm. Byrd, John Robinson, and John Grymes; and Wm. Beverley, Wm. Fairfax, and Charles Carter.

They made their report December 14, 1736, to the Council for plantation affairs, which body, on the 6th April, 1745, confirmed the report, which was in turn confirmed by the King, who ordered the appointment of Commissioners to run and mark the dividing line. This was done in 1746. The conflicting rights of the Northern Neck patent with those claimed by Jost Hite and others, have been the cause of innumerable lawsuits, which crowded the records of the State courts to a period advanced into the nineteenth century. There was an attempt made by Maryland, in 1832, to extend her boundary line by an infraction of the line of the Northern Neck established in 1746.

An office was established in Virginia by the proprietors for the granting of lands in 1690. Their agents were successively Philip Ludwell, George Brent, Edmund Jenings, Robert Carter, and Thomas Lee. The proprietor, Thomas, Sixth Lord Fairfax, coming to the colony, established his seat at "Greenway Court" in Frederick Co., where he lived in much style to a good old age. He died, unmarried, in 1782, at the age of ninety-two, from grief, it has been stated, at the surrender of Cornwallis and the defeat of the Royal Cause. His principal agents were his kinsmen Col. Wm. Fairfax, Geo. Wm. Fairfax, and Col. Thomas Bryan Martin, who had collectors and surveyors under them in the several counties. George Washington served for several years as a surveyor ere he attained his majority. The provisions under which lands were granted by the proprietor were similar to those under which grants from the crown were issued. The lands were escheated to the State in 1783, and the grants within their limits were signed thereafter by the Governor of the State.

THE COLONIAL SERIES OF GRANTS.

THOMAS, CHRISTIAN, No. 1, p. 637. 200 acres in Accomac Co., east of lands of Captain John Howe ; west of a branch of Cherry-stone Creek ; south of land of Edward Drew.

> Head-rights, March 10, 1638, granted by *Sir John Harvey.*
> Christian Thomas, Senr.,   George Menslye,
> Christian Thomas, Jr.,   John Greenfield

THOMAS, WILLIAM AP, No. 2, p. 139. 335 acres in Elizabeth City Co., east of Broad Creek ; south of land of Thomas Watts ; north of land of Lucy Purifoy ; 100 acres formerly granted Nicholas Hill, November 25, 1637, and purchased of him by Wm. Ap Thomas ; quit-rents to begin on same seven years after April 25, 1637 ; 150 acres assigned by Walter Cade, granted for three transports, and 85 acres for two transports ; quit-rents on 235 acres to begin after June 2, 1648.   *Sir Wm. Berkeley.*
    Walter Cade and his wife, twice,   Wm. Ap Thomas,   Jean Killocke.

THOMAS, JOHN, No. 2, p. 158. 350 acres on the north side of Queen's Creek in York Co. ; west of lands of Joseph Croshaw ; 300 acres formerly granted to John Broach and assigned 17th 8ber, 1649.   *Sir Wm. Berkeley.*
    50 acres for wife Dorothy.

THOMAS, JOHN, No. 2, p. 543. 450 acres in Gloucester Co., November 6, 1651.
                                                    Sir Wm. Berkeley.

Edward Hide,	Grace Musgrove,	John Richards,	Wm. Peale.
Kath. Thomas,	James Thomas,	Geo. Locke,	John Brocas.
Abigail Longdale,			

THOMAS, RICHARD, No. 3, p. 32. 185 acres in Henrico Co., on the north side of Appamattocks River ; north side of Colmcock's Creek, opposite Scurvy Hill, March 24, 1652.   *Sir Richard Bennett.*

Wm. Blackburn,	Margaret Loyd,	Tho. Dyar,	Hen. Mitchell.

THOMAS, WILLIAM, No. 3, p. 20. 100 acres in Lancaster Co., on the north side of Rappahannock River, July 13, 1653.   *Sir Richard Bennett.*
    Wm. Thomas, and his wife.

THOMAS, WILLIAM, No. 3, p. 87. 400 acres in Northumberland Co., on the south side of Wicocomoco River, opposite to the landing of Thomas Luffall, October 19, 1651.
                                                    Sir Richard Bennett.

Mary Boone,	Richard Groves,	Mary Light,	Ann Slaughter,
John Newton,	Thos. Dushell,	Philip Beadle,	Michael Juges.

THOMAS, JOHN, and WM. LITTLEMORE, No. 3, p. 138. 400 acres on the east side of Eastermost River, in Mobjack Bay, beginning at a marked tree on the land of Richard Ripley, December 6, 1652.   *Sir Richard Bennett.*

ffra. Carr,	One Negro,	Chris. Hurd,	Thomas Scott,
John Steward,	Aug. Hart,	Robt. ffletcher,	Thomas, a boy, by
assignment from J. Walker.			

THOMAS, WILLIAM AP, No. 3, p. 146. 700 acres on the north-east side of Mobjack Bay, near land of Thomas Purton, fourteen transports, November 6, 1652.
                                                    Sir Richard Bennett.

Charles Doiyle,	John Barlow,	John Nash,	Joane Middleton,
John Rawlins,	Thos. Bayley,	Wm. Chiddick.	[These names only.]

THOMAS, JOHN, No. 3, p. 300. 174 acres in "Nanzemon" Co., on the east side of Newtowne Haven River, near his own land and land of Mr. Jordan and Thos. Best ; 150 acres formerly granted to Peter Mountague, December 8, 1645, and assigned ; 24 acres one transport, November 19, 1654.   *Sir Richard Bennett.*

Wm. Skeed,	Susan Jacob,	Edwd. Powell,	Mary Watkins.

THOMAS, LAZARUS, No. 3, p. 380. 250 acres in New Kent Co., on east side of Rickohock Creek. near land of Charles Edmonds, October 12, 1655.   *Edward Digges.*
    Five transports. [No names.]

THOMAS, WILLIAM, No. 4, p. 303. 500 acres in Northumberland Co., near land of Henry Smith, orphan ; 250 acres formerly granted Wm. Thomas, July 16, 1656, and renewed and 250 acres added for five transports [no names], March 23, 1657. Assigned to Richard Gibbes and renewed by Sir Wm. Berkeley, October 9, 1662.
                                                  Saml. Matthews.

THOMAS, ROBERT, and WM. MASSIE, No. 4, p. 393. 800 acres in Rappahannock Co., near land of John Weire, formerly granted April 12, 1657 ; sixteen transports [no names], renewed March 24, 1660 ; 500 acres assigned by John Barrow, being due on a patent of 500 acres. Renewed by new rights.   *Sir Wm. Berkeley.*

THOMAS, WM., of Yeocomoco, No. 4, p. 20. 200 acres in Northumberland Co., near lands of John Earle and John Waram ; four transports, October 24, 1655.
                                                    Edward Digges.

John Gibson,	Elizb. Glisson.	Jean Biorket,	Joan, an Irish woman.

THOMAS, ROBERT, and WM. MASSIE, brothers, No. 4, p. 128. 800 acres in Lancaster Co., on the south side of the freshes in Rappahannock River, formerly granted November 20, 1654 ; regranted April 12, 1657 ; renewed December 20, 1662.
                                                    Samuel Matthews.

THOMAS, WILLIAM AP, No. 4, p. 416. 700 acres on the north-east side of Mobjack Bay, formerly granted November 16, 1652, and renewed October 28, 1662.
                                                    Francis Moryson.

THOMAS, DAVID, and RICHARD MACUBINS, No. 4, p. 420. 100 acres in Lancaster Co., formerly granted Kendal Chambly, May 10, 1654; assigned John Henly and by him back to Chambly, and Chambly to Wm. Johnson; by Johnson to Richard Stephens, and by Stephens to David Thomas and Richard Macubins, July 28, 1662.
Francis Moryson.

THOMAS, WILLIAM, Jr., No. 4, p. 630. 100 acres in Lancaster Co., formerly granted to Wm. Thomas, July 13. 1653; February 11, 1663. *Sir Wm. Berkeley.*

THOMAS, WILLIAM, Sr., No. 4, p. 631. 150 acres on the north side of Rappahannock River in Lancaster Co., north of the head of a creek called Powell's Creek. Three transports [no names], July 10, 1663. *Sir Wm. Berkeley.*

THOMAS, MARK, No. 4, p. 528. 350 acres on the south side of Home Harbour Creek, near lands of Mr. Morrison, Mr. Armistead, and Mr. Hall, formerly granted John Bannister, Thos. Foot, and John Bortner, November 25, 1653; assigned to Foot and by him to Mark Thomas, November 20, 1661. *Francis Moryson.*

THOMAS, WM., CAPTAIN PETER ASHTON, and HENRY CORBIN, No. 4, p. 476. 900 acres in Northumberland Co., near lands of John Shropard and Major Hoccady, May 24, 1660. *Sir Wm. Berkeley.*

THOMAS, WILLIAM, Sr., No. 5, p. 335. 250 acres in Northumberland Co., in Yeocomico River Neck, near land of Richard Holding, formerly granted Wm. Bacon, August 28, 1657; May 30, 1663. *Sir Wm. Berkeley.*

THOMAS, WILLIAM, No. 5, p. 502. 680 acres in Northumberland Co., in Yeocomico Creek, King's Neck, formerly granted Richard Thompson, 560 acres April 4, 1649, 120 acres December 15, 1651, and by Richard Thompson devised to Sarah and Elizabeth Thompson heirs, and by Thomas Willoughby and Peter Prisley, who married them [respectively], assigned to Wm. Thomas, October 19, 1645.
Sir Wm. Berkeley.

THOMAS, WILLIAM, and THOS. CHETWOOD, No. 6, p. 133. 176 acres in Northumberland Co., March 7, 1666. *Sir Wm. Berkeley.*

| Rose Parsons, | Robt. Oteodan, | Rich'd Atkins, | Robt. Sarlett. |

THOMAS, JOHN, No. 6, p. 355. 1000 acres on a branch of Potomac ffreshes, beyond the land of Colonel Speake, April 4, 1671. *Sir Wm. Berkeley.*

Thos. Appleton,	Henry Dodd,	Henry Nistor,	John Carner,
Richd. Brewton,	Mary Cole,	John Briggs,	Mary Meriwether,
Mary Brussels,	John Gregory,	Wm. Thurston,	Thos. Dunstone,
Thomas Portris,	Anna Gundweeke,	John Moody,	John Rosse.
Robt. Thorogood,	Thomas Lawrence,	Susan ffradson,	

THOMAS, JOHN, No. 6, p. 358. 1000 acres, at the head of a creek in Potomac ffreshes beside the Doeg's Island, and the land of Colonel Speake, April 4, 1671.
Sir Wm. Berkeley.

John Rainther,	Jeffrey Mosse,	Robt. Lawson,	John Jones,
John Ricks,	Peter Hardyway,	John Thompson,	Mary Jones,
Rebec. Turner,	Wm. Wilson,	Peter Gill,	Thos. Turlya,
Henry Morley,	Wm. Mallory,	James Bray,	Anna Hunt.
Thos. Coghill.	John Pegalin,	Nicholas Caron,	

THOMAS, RICHARD, No. 6, p. 605. 174 acres in "Nanzamond" Co., formerly granted John Thomas, November 19, 1656. *Sir Wm. Berkeley.*

THOMAS RICHARD, JOHN SANDERS, and JONATHAN ROBINSON, No. 7, p. 72. 1650 acres on the south side of King Saile Swamp, in Isle of Wight Co., April 23, 1681.
Sir Wm. Berkeley.

Rand. Hill,	James Gifford,	Peter Stone,	Jn. Perry,	Jno. Bevin,
Richd. Allen,	Wm. Taylor,	Wm. Mansfield,	Mary Curlett,	Wm. Nash,
John Golley,	John Rassor,	John Simons,	An. Horne,	Wm. Nodadye,
Bar. Holland,	Jo. Wigmore.	John Taylor,	Jn. Evins,	Jno. fford,
Jeffrey Pitton,	John Mitchell,	Geof. Davis,	Simon Collier,	Hugh Edwards,
Dan. Plumer,	Ro. Rolph,	Ca. Alden,	Phil Pope,	Ja. Peacock.
Thos. Bleth,	Wm. Nash,			

Sir Henry Chesterley.

THOMAS, EDWARD, No. 7, p. 285. 350 acres on the south side of Rappahannock River, near lands of Jones and Jackman, formerly granted Wm. Price, May 9, 1664, and deserted, April 16, 1683. *Thomas, Lord Culpeper.*

| Thos. Vintner, | Peter Hudson, | Matthew Hixson, | Henry Manley. |
| John Austin, | Sarah Breeden, | Wm. Jolly, | |

THOMAS, ROBERT, of Isle of Wight Co., No. 7, p. 407. 10 acres in Isle of Wight Co., near land of Wm. Cowen and John Murray, in the upper part of the county, October 20, 1684. *Francis, Lord Howard.*

THOMAS, MICHAEL, and JAMES KNIGHT, No. 7, p. 502. 450 acres in the upper parish of Nansemond Co., April 27, 1686 ; nine transports. *Francis, Lord Howard.*
Thos. Conroe, Cock. Cromwell, Wm. Moundor. [No other names.]

THOMAS, EDWARD, No. 8, p. 198. 450 acres in Rappahannock Co. ; 240 acres of the same being part of a patent formerly granted Rice Jones, September 10, 1664 ; 95 acres, a part of a patent to Anthony Jackman, September 21, 1664, and the residue to Edward Thomas ; two transports, Mary Quigley, Ann Harwood, October 20, 1691.
Francis Nicholson.

THOMAS, ROBERT, of Essex Co., No. 8, p. 397. 569½ acres in Essex Co., October 26, 1694. *Sir Edmond Andros.*
Anthony Dolby, Lewis Rice, Wm. Robinson, Geo. Kirkey,
Wm. Reynolds, James Harper, Knight Richeson, Robt. Gregory,
Ann Jeffrey, Alice Child, Mary Clark, Richard Barnette.

THOMAS, EDWARD, No. 9, p. 81. 2750 acres in the ffreshes of Rappahannock River, in Essex Co., formerly granted Arthur Spicer, April 29, 1690 ; now granted Edward Thomas by order of the General Court, October 15, 1696, patent granted October 28, 1697. *Sir Edmond Andros.*
Arthur Spicer, Edward Bray, Arabella Cocke, Patk. Magbie, John Craff.
John Spicer, Tho. Hardage, Catherine ——, Danl. Carroll,
Barth. Darcy, John Compton, M. Marra, Wm. ffarrell,
Mary Ornter, Michael Little, Jn. Waid, Lawrence Barnet & 38 negroes.

THOMAS, ROWLAND, No. 9, p. 464. 100 acres in King and Queen Co. ; granted John Arnold, September 25, 1702, and escheated Wm. Jones, Deputy Escheator ; re-granted R. T. *Francis Nicholson.*

THOMAS, EDWARD, No. 9, p. 669. 2200 acres, late in the possession of John Broach, dec'd ; escheated in York Co., John Lightfoot, Escheator, May 2, 1705.
Francis Nicholson.

THOMAS, ROBERT, Sr., No. 9, p. 691. 966 acres in Essex Co. ; twenty transports, November 2, 1705. *Francis Nicholson.*
Wm. Roe, Rebecca Edmonds, Thos. Webb, Arthur Danale, John ffoster,
Edm. Henley, Peter Levere, Philip Larmour, Richd. Honling, Wm. Jordan,
John Davis, Abm. Little, Geo. Rondye, John Gills, Wm. Dyer.
Edmond Stone, Geo. Tompson, Robt. ffranklyn, Peter Davis,
Elizh. ffulgham.

THOMAS, ROBERT, Sr., No. 9, p. 691. 684 acres lying in Essex Co., on a branch of Ware Creek, called Moll Webb's branch, near Solomon's Garden, and land of Prosser Creighton, Robert Thompson, and Charles Taliaferro, September 2, 1705.
Edward Nott.
David Douglas, James Prescott, Claude Lawson, James Bowers,
Wm. Simpson, Richd. Cooper, Arthur Bowers, Garrett Burne,
Launcelot Gandry, Abm. Lawson, Nichs. Hoskins, Thos. Weaver.
Edward Boxley, Thos. Threshley,

THOMAS, JOSEPH, No. 10, p. 140. 175 acres in the upper parish of Nansemond Co., January 16, 1714. *Alex. Spotswood.*
Joseph Thomas, Michael Thomas,
Elizh. Thomas, and his wife.

THOMAS, WILLIAM, of Prince George parish, Spotsylvania Co., No. 12, p. 474. 331 acres in St. George's parish, Spotsylvania Co., in the ffreshes of Rappahannock River, June 4, 1726, in consideration of the payment of 35 shillings. *Hugh Drysdale.*

THOMAS, DANIEL, of Henrico Co., No. 13, p. 81. 300 acres on the south side of James River, in Henrico Co.; consideration 30 shillings, June 16, 1729. *Robert Carter.*

THOMAS, RICHARD, of King and Queen Co., No. 13, p. 371. 880 acres ; consideration £5 ; on the north side of the forks of the Northward River, in St. George's parish, Spotsylvania Co., September 28, 1728. *Wm. Gooch.*

THOMAS, JOSEPH, and ASHFORD HUGHES, No. 13, p. 408. 400 acres ; consideration 40 shillings ; on the west main fork of Muddy Creek, in Goochland Co., September 27, 1729. *Wm. Gooch.*

THOMAS, PHILIP, No. 13, p. 464. 400 acres ; consideration 40 shillings ; on the north fork of Appomattox River, in Goochland Co., June 30, 1730. *Wm. Gooch.*

THOMAS, JOHN, of S. George's parish, Spotsylvania Co., No. 14, p. 97. 400 acres ; consideration 40 shillings ; on the great fork of Rappahannock River, in S. George's parish, Spotsylvania Co., September 18, 1728. *Wm. Gooch*

THOMAS, JOHN, No. 15, p. 470. 400 acres ; consideration 25 shillings and transporting three persons to the colony ; on the great fork of Rappahannock River, in Orange Co., March 24, 1734 ; Robert Turner, Mary Turner, Perva Turner. *Wm. Gooch.*

THOMAS, JOHN, No. 15, p. 503. 400 acres ; consideration 40 shillings ; in Hanover Co., May 20, 1735. *Wm. Gooch.*

THOMAS, JOHN, No. 15, p. 534. 400 acres; consideration 40 shillings; in Hanover Co.,
June 19, 1735.   *Wm. Gooch.*

THOMAS, NATHANIEL, No. 16, p. 328. 380 acres on the west side of "Opekon," out of
a branch of the same called Red Bud Branch, under "a grant of April 20, 1735, to
Alex. Ross and Morgan Bryan of 1000 acres to each family of seventy families as settlers," November 2, 1735.   *Wm. Gooch.*

THOMAS, EVAN, No. 16, p. 392. 1014 acres on the west side of "Opekon," out of a
branch of the same called Red Bud Branch, under "a grant of April 20, 1735, to Alex.
Ross and Morgan Bryan of 1000 acres to each family of seventy families," November
12, 1735.   *Wm. Gooch.*

THOMAS, DAVID, No. 18, p. 183. 198 acres; consideration 20 shillings; in Amelia Co.,
February 1, 1738.   *Wm Gooch.*

THOMAS, JOHN, No. 18, p. 332. 180 acres; consideration 20 shillings; in Isle of Wight
Co., June 29, 1739.   *Wm. Gooch.*

THOMAS, JOHN, No. 18, p. 490. 400 acres; consideration 40 shillings; in Amelia Co.,
September 22, 1739.   *Wm. Gooch.*

THOMAS, PETER, No. 19, p. 1100. 301 acres; consideration 30 shillings; in Prince
George Co., August 20, 1741.   *Wm. Gooch.*

THOMAS, MICHAEL, Jr., No. 22, p. 285. 200 acres; consideration 20 shillings; in Goochland Co., July 10, 1745.   *Wm. Gooch.*

THOMAS, PHILIP, No. 23, p. 718. 400 acres; consideration 40 shillings; in Goochland
Co., June 16, 1744.   *Wm. Gooch.*

THOMAS, WILLIAM, No. 24, p. 241. 400 acres; consideration 40 shillings; in Amelia
Co., June 5, 1746.   *Wm. Gooch.*

THOMAS, EDWARD, No. 25, p. 129. 168 acres; consideration 20 shillings; in Prince
George Co., July 25, 1746.   *Wm. Gooch.*

THOMAS, EDWARD, No. 26, p. 94. 140 acres; consideration 15 shillings; in Albemarle
Co., August 26, 1747.   *Wm. Gooch.*

THOMAS, HENRY, No. 26, p. 678. 122 acres; consideration 20 shillings; in Albemarle
Co., August 20, 1748.   *Wm. Gooch.*

THOMAS, MICHAEL, Jr., No. 27, p. 24. 400 acres; consideration 40 shillings; in Albemarle Co., December 1, 1748.   *Wm. Gooch.*

THOMAS, JOSEPH, No. 28, p. 188. 200 acres; consideration 20 shillings; in Albemarle
Co., August 20, 1748.   *Wm. Gooch.*

THOMAS, JOHN, No. 28, p. 593. 100 acres; consideration 10 shillings; in Albemarle Co.,
April 1, 1749.   *Wm. Gooch.*

THOMAS, MICHAEL, No. 31, p. 29. 300 acres; consideration 30 shillings; in Albemarle
Co., September 20, 1751.   *Lewis Burwell.*

THOMAS, JOHN, No. 31, p. 334. 1161 acres; consideration 10 shillings; in Essex Co.,
July 3, 1750.   *Robt. Dinwiddie.*

THOMAS, SAMUEL, No. 31, p. 705. 476 acres; consideration 50 shillings; in Amelia Co.,
September 10, 1755.   *Robt. Dinwiddie.*

THOMAS, WILLIAM, No. 31, p. 719. 326 acres; consideration 25 shillings; in Brunswick
Co., September 10, 1755.   *Robt. Dinwiddie.*

THOMAS, WILLIAM, No. 33, p. 760. 400 acres; consideration 40 shillings; in Halifax
Co., March 3, 1760.   *Francis Fauquier.*

THOMAS, THOMAS, and JOHN MORTON, No. 33, p. 765. 340 acres; consideration 35
shillings; in Brunswick Co., May 29, 1760.   *Francis Fauquier.*

THOMAS, WILLIAM, No. 34, p. 92. 350 acres; consideration 35 shillings; in Lunenburg
Co., August 16, 1760.   *Robert Dinwiddie.*

THOMAS, PETER, Jr., No. 34, p. 775. 230 acres; consideration 20 shillings; in Dinwiddie
Co., September 26, 1760.   *Francis Fauquier.*

THOMAS, THOMAS, No. 34, p. 1067. 150 acres; consideration 15 shillings; in Prince
George Co., September 25, 1762.   *Francis Fauquier.*

THOMAS, DANIEL, No. 35, p. 136. 200 acres; consideration 20 shillings; in Albemarle
Co., May 23, 1763.   *Francis Fauquier.*

THOMAS, JESSE, No. 36, p. 1011. 350 acres; consideration 35 shillings; in Buckingham
Co., September 22, 1766.   *Francis Fauquier.*

THOMAS, WILLIAM, No. 38, p. 619. 65 acres; consideration 10 shillings; in Halifax Co.,
April 6, 1769.   *Botetourt.*

THOMAS, CORNELIUS, No. 38. p. 884. 2000 acres; consideration £10; in Albemarle Co.,
May 12, 1770.   *Botetourt.*

THOMAS, CORNELIUS, No. 38. p. 885. 250 acres; consideration 25 shillings; in Albemarle Co., May 12, 1770.   *Botetourt.*

THOMAS, JAMES, No. 39, p. 158. 122 acres; consideration 15 shillings; in Augusta Co.,
March 16, 1771.   *Wm. Nelson, Pres't.*

THOMAS, CORNELIUS, No. 40, p. 774. 180 acres; consideration 20 shillings; on the branches of the Wilderness and Thomas' Mill Creek, in Amherst Co., August 1, 1772. *Dunmore.*

THOMAS, CORNELIUS, No. 41, p. 47. 63 acres; consideration 10 shillings; on the branches of the Otter, in Amherst Co., August 1, 1772. *Dunmore.*

THOMAS, JOHN, No. 41, p. 134. 300 acres; consideration 30 shillings; on Brock's Creek, in Augusta Co., March 1, 1773. *Dunmore.*

THOMAS, REECE, No. 41, p. 171. 433 acres; consideration 20 shillings; in Augusta Co., March 1, 1773. *Dunmore.*

THOMAS, EVAN, No. 41, p. 241. 97 acres; consideration 10 shillings; in Augusta Co., March 1, 1773. *Dunmore.*

THOMAS, CORNELIUS, No. 42, p. 472. 204 acres; consideration 20 shillings; in Amherst Co., June 5, 1773. *Dunmore.*

THOMAS, WILLIAM, No. 42, p. 474. 324 acres; consideration 35 shillings; in Bedford Co., June 15, 1773. *Dunmore.*

THOMAS, WM. ACHILLES FANNING, No. 42, p. 477. 308 acres; consideration 35 shillings; in Halifax Co., June 15, 1773. *Dunmore.*

THOMAS, CHARLES, No. 42, p. 853. 160 acres; consideration 20 shillings; in Pittsylvania Co., December 2, 1774. *Dunmore.*

THE NORTHERN NECK GRANTS.

THOMAS, ZACHARIAH, No. 2, p. 239. 65 acres, in Northumberland Co., near the land of Thomas Hobson, Sr., and John Bearmore, May 27, 1696.

THOMAS, JAMES, No. 3, p. 159. 729 acres, in Richmond Co., September 7, 1707.

THOMAS, JOHN, Sr., No. 4, p. 118. 331 acres, in Northumberland Co., August 7, 1712.

THOMAS, EVAN, and WM. GOING, No. 5, p. 8. 124 acres, in Stafford Co., November 21, 1714.

THOMAS, EVAN, and JOHN TODD, No. 5, p. 212. 1215 acres, in Stafford Co., August 3, 1719.

THOMAS, EVAN, and JOHN TODD, No. 5, p. 47. 236 acres, in Stafford Co., January 23, 1718.

THOMAS, JAMES, B, p. 56. 1725 acres, in Stafford Co., March 28, 1727.

THOMAS, JAMES, B, p. 163. 1450 acres, in Stafford Co., October 23, 1728.

THOMAS, HUMPHREY, B, p. 68. 514 acres, in Richmond Co., April 4, 1727.

THOMAS, JAMES, Jr., of Westmoreland Co., B, p. 163. 1450 acres, in Stafford Co., October 30, 1728.

THOMAS, CATHERINE, B, p. 105. 615 acres, in Stafford Co., January 22, 1721.

THOMAS, JAMES, D, p. 7. 1000 acres, in Prince William Co., August 25, 1731.

THOMAS, JAMES, D, p. 8. 1504 acres, in Prince William Co., August 26, 1731.

THOMAS, JAMES, Jr., D, p. 71. 24 acres, in Westmoreland Co., November 16, 1731.

THOMAS, DANIEL and HUGH, of Westmoreland Co., E, p. 236. 667 acres, in Prince William Co., January 23, 1740.

THOMAS, OWEN, H, p. 88. 400 acres, in Frederick Co., January 8, 1752.

THOMAS, GRIFFITH, H, p. 263. 93 acres, in Frederick Co., March 20, 1753.

THOMAS, GRIFFITH, H, p. 264. 265 acres, in Augusta Co., March 19, 1753.

THOMAS, JOHN, H, p. 280. 460 acres, in Frederick Co., April 26, 1753.

THOMAS, JAMES, H, p. 687. 375 acres, in Augusta Co., September 30, 1756.

THOMAS, EDWARD, K, p. 128. 203 acres, in Frederick Co., May 12, 1760.

THOMAS, EDWARD, K, p. 129. 182 acres, in Frederick Co., May 13, 1760.

THOMAS, NATHANIEL, K, p. 257. 240 acres, in Frederick Co., March 25, 1761.

THOMAS, MORRIS, R, p. 131. 16 acres, in Hampshire Co., March 12, 1779.

THOMAS, MORRIS, R, p. 132. 276 acres, in Hampshire Co., March 13, 1779.

THOMAS, MORRIS, R, p. 133. 86½ acres, in Hampshire Co., March 15, 1779.

THOMAS, BENJAMIN, S, p. 319. 89 acres, in Fauquier Co., November 16, 1787. *Edmund Randolph.*

THOMAS, LUKE W., W, p. 61. 217 acres, in Shenandoah Co., July 11, 1792. *Henry Lee.*

THOMAS, WILLIAM, W, p. 533. 68 acres, in Shenandoah Co., August 10, 1794. *Henry Lee.*

THOMAS, DANIEL and HUGH, of Westmoreland Co., B, p. 214. 300 acres, in Stafford Co., at the head of the branches of Bull Run, called Elk Lick, March 11, 1724.

THOMAS, JOHN, X, p. 262. 272 acres, in Hampshire Co., August 3, 1796. *Robert Brooke.*

THOMAS, JOHN, X, p. 353.   27 acres, in Madison Co., September 21, 1796.
Robert Brooke.

THOMAS, MOSES, X, p. 413.   84 acres, in Hampshire Co., October 2, 1796.
Robert Brooke.

THOMAS, JOHN, X, p. 449.   120 acres, in Shenandoah Co., September 21, 1796.
Robert Brooke.

THOMAS, REUBEN, X, p. 523.   67 acres, in Madison Co., July 25, 1796.
Robert Brooke.

THOMAS, MOSES, X, p. 606.   16 acres, in Hampshire Co., November 13, 1797.
James Wood.

THOMAS, MOSES, Y, p. 39.   50 acres, in Hampshire Co., February 9, 1798.
James Wood.

THOMAS, JASON, Jr., Z, p. 261.   25 acres, in Culpeper Co., October 20, 1802.
James Monroe.

APPENDIX XI

MARRIAGE INTENTIONS OF SAMUEL THOMAS AND MARY HUTCHINS

At a Quarterly Meeting held at the house of Ann Chew the 2 day of 3 Mo. 1688. Sam! Thomas & Mary Huchens laid their Intentions of marriage before this Meeting, this being the second time & those friends that were appointed by the last man's Meeting at the Cliffs doe give account that the parents are willing & for what Thomas Smith did object of anything to the Contrary of their Coming together Richard Harrison & Nathan Smith doe Inform this Meeting that the said Thomas Smith did discharge the said Mary Huchens from any Ingagement whatsoever whereupon this meeting doe leave them to their liberty as to the time of their marriage & doe advise them to follow the advice of Edward Talbott & Solomon Sparrow in that matter according to the good order of truth & upon due Consideration of this Meeting & in a weighty Sence for the honor of God this meeting doe desire & advise all Parents that doe profess the truth of God & All friends' children that for the futor they may be very carefull in their takeing husband or wives & that they do not lett their eyes out after any that doe not profess the truth of God. least they bring dishonor to God. grief to their parents & an exercise to friends that are truly Concerned for God & the honour of his truth.

From the Meeting Records by Kirk Brown, Clerk of Park Avenue Meeting, Baltimore, 1894.

MARRIAGE CERTIFICATE OF SAMUEL THOMAS AND MARY HUTCHINS

Whereas Samuell Thomas of Annarundell County in the Province of Maryland and Mary Hutchins of Calvert County in the County aforesaid (*sic.*) having declaired their Intentions of Marriage two sundry times att several Publich meetings of the People of God called Quakers In the County aforesaid which was admitted on by the said Meetings Now these are to Certifie all people whom it may concerne that for the full determining of the Intentions aforesaid this 15th day of the 3d moneth called May 1688 In an assembly of the people of God aforesaid att the house of Samuell Thomas in Annarundell County The said Samuell Thomas did According to the Example of the holy men of God. Recorded in the scriptures of truth, take Mary Hutchins to be his Wife and in like manner she the said Mary Hutchins did then and there take the said Samuell Thomas to be her husband, Each of them promising to be loving and faithfull one to another as husband and wife so long as they both should live.

595·

And wee who were present att their takeing Each other have hereunto sett our hands as wittnessess unto the same the day and year afforesaid.

Francis Hutchins
Margaret Evans
Job Evans
Margarett Tench
Grace Scrivener
Elizabeth Coale
Sarah Hooker
Elizabeth Smith
Thomas Smith
Philip Cole
Samuell Coale
Sam^ll Lane
Benjamin Scrivener
William Coale Jun.
William Richardson
Elizabeth Richardson
Richard Galloway
Elizabeth Galloway.

Samuell Thomas
Mary Hutchins

William Richardson Jun.
Joseph Heathcote
Mary Knighton
Elizabeth Battee
Joseph Richardson
Joseph Hanslap
Solomon Sparrow
Sophia Richardson
Francis Hanslap.

From West River Marriage Book, folio 19

APPENDIX XII

ADDENDA

Page 38, line 18. Omit "second" after *m.*

Page 43. REV. T. S. THOMAS *m.*, second, April 7, 1896, DR. SUSAN F. PLATT.

Page 45. The author was elected March 17, 1896, Corresponding Member of the Maryland Historical Society.

Page 56. **Warren L. Thomas** was elected, August 31, 1895, Grand Master of the Masonic Knights Templars of the United States.

Page 113, line 13. For "1859," read "1759."

Page 141, line 22. SAMUEL THOMAS had also a *dau.* SUSANNAH, *m.*, first, JAMES TURNER. Issue: JEANNETTE, *m.* GENERAL DAVID THOMAS (*q. v.*). MRS. TURNER *m.*, second, GENERAL JOHN WILLIAMS, and had a great-granddaughter Harriet M. Williams, editor of the Salem Book, 1896.

Page 186, line 6. For "**Whitwon**," read "**Whitman**."

Page 219, line 3. For "Robert," read "Roger."

Page 220, line 20. Add *m.*, 1783, RICHARD THOMAS, Jr. See *p.* 58.

Page 232, line 4. For "HUTCHINS," read "HUTCHIN."

Page 234, last line. Add *m.*, April 9, 1896, COLONEL ALFRED RONALD CONKLING.

Page 256, line 2. This marriage is probably an error. See *pp.* 267 and 350.

Page 258, line 30. "**Philemon Hallam**," add "*m.*, January 6, 1881, **Grace Gilmore Devries**. Issue: Margaret Chew and Grace Devries."

Page 260, lines 25 and 29. Omit LLOYD, and the military commissions, as Captain Samuel Lloyd Chew was probably the second son of Richard Chew, on page 257, line 11.

Page 269. Type sizes of all the issue of JOHN JAMES should be reduced one degree.

Page 269, line 4. Insert i. before "DEBORAH."

597

Page 287, line 29. For "**JANE,**" read "**Junior.**"

Page 336, line 7. For "**Rivid,**" read "**Ririd.**"

Page 346, line 3. For "1562," read "1652."

Page 353, line 2. Omit (*q. v.*). I cannot place "**Rachel Snowden.**"

Page 390, line 15. ANNE was *dau.* of Edward English and Elizabeth, his wife, sister of Henry Williams, alias Cromwell, of Ramsey, Hunts.

Page 472, line 41. For "second son and heir of **Henry,**" read "eldest son and heir of **Walter.**"

Page 479, line 33. For "**BEART,**" read "**BEARD.**"

Page 499, line 4. Brackets should be around **Smith** instead of **Bellanger.**

Page 508, line 5. Omit comma between Henrietta and Maria.

Page 571, line 28. The family were at Collumpton in 1694, when Agnes Thomas executed a deed there.

REFERENCE INDEX

Containing every surname in the pedigrees given, and also such names as appear on more than one page, either by marriage[1] into another family whose genealogy is given, or by transference to another part of the same genealogy. Throughout the book, names have been spelled as in the original records. Certain names and folios are here put in black, to denote that some genealogy may be found at the pages given.

[1] Under each family, females connected by marriage follow in alphabetical order of their maiden names.

[1] Dates following a name usually are of birth, to distinguish the individual.

[1] See page 362, for her parents.

[1] It was her mother who *m.* Richard Johns.

[1] Probably a grandson of Richard Johns. on p. 370.
[2] Not identified ; the marriage is probably an error.

[1] Cannot be identified under Hopkins.

[1] His marriage is probably an error.

THE END.

CPSIA information can be obtained
at www.ICGtesting.com
Printed in the USA
BVHW040854141220
595659BV00023B/365